READING SACRED SCRIPTURE

Reading Sacred Scripture

*Voices from the History
of Biblical Interpretation*

Stephen Westerholm *&* Martin Westerholm

WILLIAM B. EERDMANS PUBLISHING COMPANY
GRAND RAPIDS, MICHIGAN / CAMBRIDGE, U.K.

Published 2016 by
Wm. B. Eerdmans Publishing Co.
2140 Oak Industrial Drive N.E., Grand Rapids, Michigan 49505 /
P.O. Box 163, Cambridge CB3 9PU U.K.

Printed in the United States of America

22 21 20 19 18 17 16   7 6 5 4 3 2 1

Library of Congress Cataloging-in-Publication Data

Westerholm, Stephen, 1949-
Reading sacred scripture: voices from the history of biblical interpretation /
Stephen Westerholm & Martin Westerholm.
pages   cm
Includes bibliographical references and index.
ISBN 978-0-8028-7229-6 (pbk.: alk. paper)
1. Bible — Criticism, interpretation, etc. — History.
I. Title.

BS500.W445   2016
220.6 — dc23
2015034463

www.eerdmans.com

For Paul and Jill
ὑπηρέται τοῦ λόγου

Contents

Preface

Some years ago, in reviewing a book with "an enormous bibliography," the eminent New Testament scholar C. K. Barrett subtly suggested that the author might have been better served by "wrestling with the relatively few books that are really important."[1] His point is surely well taken. We should all be grateful for reference works that introduce dozens, or even hundreds, of figures in the history of biblical interpretation; as need arises, we consult them. The authors of the present work, however, have adopted Barrett's proposed approach, inviting readers to engage seriously in the study of a mere dozen of the more important interpreters of Christian Scripture, from the second century to the twentieth.

No dozen figures, however significant, can adequately represent the history of biblical interpretation or exhaust the approaches that have been taken to reading the sacred text; nor would any two informed readers think the same twelve figures most worthy of consideration. But selections have to be made, and no informed reader will doubt the importance of each of the interpreters treated here. The present project was begun by Stephen, who intended to write on ten figures — until he was told by a colleague that, however selective his undertaking, he could not omit Barth. That made sense, of course; but it also made sense, for one daunted by the prospect of tackling the *Church Dogmatics,* to invite the collaboration of Martin, who at the time was working intensively on Barth. Once on board, Martin agreed to treat Schleiermacher as well; the pairing with Barth is a natural one, given the way the latter used Schleiermacher as a foil for his own theology. But Schleiermacher merits study in his own right as one who profoundly influenced later Protestant thought.

1. Barrett, "Review," 114.

Our project is clearly distinct from the several histories of critical scholarship on the Bible that have little or nothing to say on how the Bible was read prior to the seventeenth (or even the eighteenth) century. That story privileges those who programmatically read the Bible "like any other book."[2] The interpreters here portrayed, though by no means uniform in their approaches, all insist that the Bible is like no other book, and must be read accordingly. That, too, is a story worth telling — indeed, one that, exhaustively told, would encompass many millions of readers more than the other. We stopped at twelve.

It remains only to repeat what Gunilla Westerholm (Stephen's wife, Martin's mother) is wont to say to dinner guests: *Var så goda!* (in the vulgar tongue, roughly, "Dig in!").

2. Cf. Jowett, "Interpretation," 377.

CHAPTER 1

The Voice of Scripture

Among the slogans that set the agenda for much modern study of the Bible, the prescription that it should be read "like any other book" seems to me singularly unhelpful.[1] We do not read *Stiff Upper Lip, Jeeves* or *Have It Your Way, Charlie Brown* the same way we read *Hamlet* or *King Lear*. *Critique of Pure Reason* and *The House at Pooh Corner* are both, I believe, eminently worth reading (though, in the one instance, I am relying on others' assurances), but they call for rather different approaches. *Textbook of Medical Oncology* requires yet another. To cut short a game becoming more fun by the minute, we may well ask: Like *which* other book are we supposed to read the Bible?

To be sure, these and other books *can* all be read the same way if we approach each with a particular question in mind: How frequently does the author split infinitives, dangle participles, or quote Russian proverbs? Or, what do *Romeo and Juliet, Concluding Unscientific Postscript,* and *Pippi Longstocking* tell us about eating habits at the time of their composition? (This game, too, could be fun.) These are, I suppose, legitimate questions — doctoral dissertations have certainly been written on stranger topics — but they seem somewhat limiting. Classic literature — William Shakespeare, Søren Kierkegaard, Astrid Lindgren — has more to offer its readers; those open to experiencing the "more" soon learn that different books make different demands on their readers.

Unless, then, we are reading the Bible merely to carry out our own limiting agendas, the notion that it should be read "like any other book" will be true only in the sense that the Bible, like any other book, calls for a particular kind of reading. Sensitive readers of the Bible, like sensitive

---

1. Jowett, "Interpretation," 377.

readers of any text, will be alert to what is being asked of them, given the nature of the text before them; it is then, of course, up to their discretion whether they will attempt to measure up to those demands. Before we launch into a survey of how Christians have, in fact, read the Bible, it will be worth our while to reflect briefly on the kind of reading called for by the biblical writings themselves, highlighting aspects of the texts that have been obvious enough to sensitive readers over the centuries, though they have largely escaped the attention of academics blithely bent on reading the Bible "like any other book."[2]

The Letters of Paul[3]

Paul's Mission and Mandate

When the apostle Paul wrote his first epistle, scarcely twenty years had passed since the central events of his message — and that of the other "apostles" — had taken place (cf. 1 Cor. 15:3-11).[4] His last letters were com-

---

2. For our purposes here, a brief look at major writings of the NT will carry the weight of the argument, though a few comments will be added about other NT writings and those of the OT. (The designation "Old Testament" presupposes a corresponding New Testament and is, of course, Christian nomenclature. Jews refer rather to the Tanakh, an acrostic designation based on the first letters of the three subdivisions of the text. In a discussion [like this one] of Christian readings of Scripture, "Old Testament" remains appropriate.) Among the questions *not* ignored in recent scholarship is that of the genre of NT writings, particularly the Gospels and Acts (see the fine treatment in Aune, *Environment*). Though the determination of genre is of importance for knowing how a text is meant to be read, it is not the focus here. What is said below does not hinge, e.g., on the extent to which the Gospels correspond to Greco-Roman biographies.

3. Some relationship to Paul may be assumed of each of the NT letters bearing his name, though differences among them (in vocabulary, argumentation, historical context, etc.) suggest that that relationship was not always the same. Scholarly explanations vary from the involvement of coauthors in certain epistles (see, e.g., Bruce, *Thessalonians,* xxxii; and note Gamble, *Books,* 99), to differing roles assigned to (different) secretaries in the composition of the epistles (cf. Richards, *Secretary*), to the composition of certain epistles by disciples of Paul, adapting his message to altered conditions (a common position on Ephesians and the Pastoral Epistles, also adopted by some for Colossians and 2 Thessalonians). For purposes of this survey, the Pauline corpus may be treated as one segment of the NT writings: each of its letters invokes Paul's authority and — what is crucial in a historical survey — each has been read as possessing it.

4. Paul's first extant epistle is generally thought to be 1 Thessalonians; some argue that Galatians was written even earlier, perhaps in the late 40s of the first century A.D.

2

posed little more than a decade later. At that point, the gospel he brought to Gentiles was not only "good news," but fresh.

Its backdrop, to be sure, was bleak: no early Christian writer portrays in more dismal terms than Paul's the human condition, or that of the wider creation, apart from Christ.[5] But Paul's depictions of a desperate plight merely set the stage for news of its stunning transformation: though human wickedness abundantly warrants the outpouring of God's wrath, the Son of God brings deliverance to all who trust in him (1 Thess. 1:10; 5:1-11); though the whole world is culpable before God, God has intervened to put things right, and to declare sinners righteous, through the redemption he has provided in Christ Jesus (Rom. 3:19-24). "God demonstrates his love for us in that, while we were still sinners, Christ died for us. . . . When we were enemies, we were reconciled to God by the death of his Son" (Rom. 5:8, 10).

Clearly, for Paul, the transformation of the human condition required, and was brought about by, divine intervention:

> [T]here is a new creation; the old has passed away; look, the new has come into being! All this is from God, who reconciled us to himself through Christ, and gave us the ministry of reconciliation; that is, in Christ God was reconciling the world to himself, not counting their trespasses against them; and he has committed to us the message of reconciliation. (2 Cor. 5:17-19)

Yet, as the same quotation makes clear, divine intervention extended beyond the recent work of Christ (through whom God "reconcile[d] the world to himself") to include the commissioning of Paul (and the other apostles) to convey to the world the "message of reconciliation." Consciousness of a divine commission and a concomitant sense of accountability mark all of Paul's letters and undoubtedly lent conviction to his spoken message as well.

> As we have been approved by God to be entrusted with the gospel, so we speak, not pleasing people, but pleasing God who tests our hearts. (1 Thess. 2:4)

> If I proclaim the gospel, it is nothing I can boast about; for I am under an obligation, and woe to me if I do not proclaim the gospel! (1 Cor. 9:16; see also Rom. 1:5, 14-15; 1 Cor. 4:1-5; 15:15; 2 Cor. 2:17; 4:1; Gal. 1:1-12)

5. I have argued that Paul's "anthropology" was more "pessimistic" than the norm in Judaism in S. Westerholm, "Pessimism"; cf. also Shuster, "Sin."

That Paul's message carried conviction is apparent from the communities of believers that arose wherever he went. To believers in Rome he wrote of the success that attended his mission "from Jerusalem and as far around as Illyricum [in northwestern Greece]" (Rom. 15:19). Not surprisingly, he attributed the success of his mission to the work of Christ within him and the "power" of God's Spirit (Rom. 15:18-19; cf. 1 Cor. 2:4-5; 15:10; 2 Cor. 12:9-10). More specifically, Paul believed that God himself was active whenever he proclaimed the gospel (cf. 1 Cor. 3:6), using the apostle's words to address the hearts of Paul's listeners with his own divine appeal. As a result, Paul's (human) words served as the vehicle for the word of God.

> We serve as Christ's ambassadors, as God makes his appeal through us. . . . As we work together with him, we urge you not to receive the grace of God in vain. (2 Cor. 5:20; 6:1)

> When you received the word of God that you heard from us, you accepted it not as the word of human beings but as what it truly is, the word of God. (1 Thess. 2:13)

Paul makes the same point when he indicates that, in his proclamation of the gospel, people heard the "call" of God; those who responded in faith ("believers") were thus "called ones."

> God called you through our proclamation of the gospel for this purpose: that the glory of our Lord Jesus Christ might be yours. (2 Thess. 2:14)

> God is faithful; by him you were called into the fellowship of his Son, Jesus Christ our Lord. (1 Cor. 1:9)

> To those who are the called, both Jews and Greeks, Christ is the power of God and the wisdom of God. (1 Cor. 1:24; see also Rom. 8:30; 9:24; 1 Cor. 1:26; 7:17-24; Gal. 1:6; 5:8)

To the gospel message itself, Paul attributes power — the "power of God" — that is effective in bringing "salvation" to those in whom it elicits faith. He speaks in similar terms of "the word of God" (1 Cor. 14:36; 2 Cor. 2:17; 4:2), or "the word of the Lord" (1 Thess. 1:8; 2 Thess. 3:1), or simply "the word" (Gal. 6:6; Phil. 1:14; 1 Thess. 1:6) — all understood as equivalents of "the [proclaimed] gospel": it was an active force that, once released, accomplished God's purposes (see Isa. 55:11):[6]

> The gospel . . . is the power of God for salvation to everyone who believes, to the Jew first and also to the Greek. (Rom. 1:16)

> To us who are being saved [the message about the cross] is the power of God. (1 Cor. 1:18)

> When you received the word of God that you heard from us, you accepted it not as the word of human beings but as what it truly is, the word of God, *which is also at work in you who believe.* (1 Thess. 2:13; cf. 1:5)

> The word of truth, the gospel . . . came to you; and among you, as indeed in all the world, it has been bearing fruit and increasing from the day you heard and came to know the grace of God in truth. (Col. 1:5-6)

Paul's Correspondence

While in Ephesus, Paul could claim that his spirit was present in Corinth (1 Cor. 5:3); but something more concrete was needed if Paul was to communicate with the Corinthians — so he sent them a letter. By this time, it had in fact become a habit: the apostle regularly dispatched delegates and letters to established communities when he himself was compelled to be elsewhere. Paul's letters, though "occasional" in the sense that they dealt with specific issues in particular communities, were not *casual* communications.[7] Rather, they were the words of an apostle in his role as an apostle, "urging in the Lord Jesus" (1 Thess. 4:1); delivering instructions "through the Lord Jesus" (4:2); declaring "the will of God" (4:3); insisting that those who disregarded what he wrote disregarded not him but God (4:8; cf. 1 Cor. 14:37). Paul believed that his divine commission extended beyond the proclamation of the gospel to include caring for "all the churches" (2 Cor. 11:28; cf. 10:8; 13:10), a care that he exercised "in the presence of God" (i.e., with a sense of accountability to God [2 Cor. 2:17]) no less by letter than by personal visit: he was the same person, communicating the

---

6. Cf. the "living and active" word of God of Heb. 4:12; see also James 1:21; 1 Pet. 1:23-25.
7. Cf. Gamble, *Books*, 95.

same message — either way (2 Cor. 10:11; 1 Thess. 4:6, 11; 2 Thess. 2:15). Everything he did as an apostle, including the writing of his epistles (Rom. 12:3; 15:15), was carried out "by the grace of God" (1 Cor. 15:10); the words he used were "taught by the Spirit [of God]" (1 Cor. 2:13). Even when recording his mere "opinion" on matters that permitted flexibility, Paul was conscious both of his responsibility to be faithful in his service of Christ and of "having the Spirit of God" (1 Cor. 7:25, 40).

Paul's letters were read aloud in the churches to which they were sent — and undoubtedly *reread* and studied, since no reader for whom a communication from the apostle was important has ever felt that a single reading sufficed. First Thessalonians 5:27 conveys unmistakably both the seriousness with which Paul took his letter-writing and his expectation that his churches would treat them with equal seriousness: "I adjure you by the Lord that this letter be read to all the brothers [and sisters]."

Paul also anticipated a limited circulation of his letters: Romans would have been read in various house churches in Rome; Galatians was written to all "the churches" of a wider geographical area (Gal. 1:2); and Colossae and Laodicea were to exchange apostolic communications (Col. 4:16).[8] Not all who heard Paul's letters (particularly in Corinth and Galatia) will have been happy with their content.[9] But as a general rule, we may assume that the letters were acknowledged by their first readers to be what they purported to be: authoritative communications from an apostle commissioned by God, conveying a divine message to God's people.

Nor should the point of the epistles be restricted to the message they communicated. Typically, they begin and end by invoking God's "grace [and peace]" on the assemblies to which they were read, and with an invitation to join Paul in thanksgiving to God for sundry blessings. Those who sympathetically engaged with the words being read were thus inevitably drawn into an act of divine worship.[10] A message received (as it was meant to be received) as from God was intended to elicit an appropriate response to God.

---

8. Cf. Gamble, *Books,* 97; Hartman, "Letters." Noting that Paul includes in the addressees of 1 Corinthians "all those who in every place call on the name of our Lord Jesus Christ, both their Lord and ours," Hartman observes: "Although the matters he dealt with in 1 Corinthians were 'occasional' and particular, Paul discussed them in such a way that the letter could serve as an apostolic message to other churches as well" (144).

9. Isolated opposition to Paul among certain Jewish followers of Jesus who insisted on the observance of Mosaic laws continued for centuries (see the Pseudo-Clementine literature of the fourth century) — without affecting the way Paul was read and regarded by most Christians.

10. Cf. Heil, "Believers," 90-91.

The Gospel of Mark[11]

The Subtext of the Gospel

The Gospel of Mark is commonly taken to be the first of the New Testament Gospels to be written. Near its beginning we encounter the following familiar narrative:

> As Jesus passed along the Sea of Galilee, he saw Simon and Andrew, Simon's brother, casting a net into the sea — for they were fishermen. And Jesus said to them, "Follow me and I will make you fishers of people." And immediately they left their nets and followed him. He went on a little farther and saw James son of Zebedee and his brother John; they were in their boat mending their nets. Immediately he called them; and they left their father Zebedee in the boat with the hired men, and followed him. (Mark 1:16-20)

As elsewhere in Mark, the narrative is readily accessible. Neither vocabulary nor syntax is complex. References to fishermen, boats, and nets require no explanatory annotations. If modern readers do require clarifications at other points in the Gospel, the need is created, not — as, for example, with T. S. Eliot's *The Waste Land* — by difficulties inherent in the text itself, but merely by the distance between Mark's world and our own. Readers in other times and places have not required the same notes. Even without explanations, most readers in most times and places have had little difficulty grasping the thrust of the story.

And yet, the narrative baffles. How could the simple words "Follow me and I will make you fishers of people" move fishermen to abandon their families, possessions, and livelihood and commit themselves to following an apparent stranger? At the very least, readers have often supposed that Mark's laconic narrative has failed to mention some previous contact that Peter and Andrew (and James and John) had had with Jesus. Even so, we may well wonder what kind of favorable impression would warrant so radical a response.

If we turn our attention away from what motivated the fishermen and

---

11. Throughout the discussion that follows, I use the traditional names of the evangelists without entering the debate (which is, in the end, inconclusive anyway) about their identity. In the sections on Mark and Matthew in this chapter, I draw extensively on my article "Hearing."

instead ask why the evangelist reports the incidents as he does, we must say at once that he betrays no interest in providing insight into the psychology, character, or life stories of Peter, Andrew, James, or John. What any or all of them were thinking calls for no comment, and even what they were doing is noted only to provide content to what they abandoned. Precisely the same pattern, in terms equally laconic, is repeated a little later:

> As [Jesus] was walking along, he saw Levi son of Alphaeus sitting at the tax station. He said to him, "Follow me." And he got up and followed him. (Mark 2:14)

Mark, we might say, is concerned to convey, not what is peculiar to each of these incidents, but what *typically* occurs — or *should* occur — when people encounter the demands of Jesus. Given his concern, we may surmise that, in Mark's mind, such encounters are by no means confined to the past. He anticipates that his readers will have parallel experiences; indeed, he may well write in the expectation that his narrative will provoke them. Circumstances vary, but Mark has minimal interest in circumstances. What matters is that Jesus' demands meet with instant and absolute obedience.

If Jesus' initial demands on his followers, as cited above, strike us as extreme, Mark might well reply, "You haven't seen anything yet!" Later, Jesus will require of his disciples that they "deny" themselves, "take up [their] cross and follow [him]," adding the paradoxical warning that if they would save their lives, they will lose them; only if they lose their lives *for his sake and the gospel's* will they save them (8:34-35). Mark's readers, like Jesus' disciples, are thus given due warning. Jesus' own path leads to his crucifixion; those who follow him are promised nothing better (cf. 10:38). Again, Mark wants his readers to take note, though he does not want them to be deterred.

Mark does not spell out the logic behind these demands; still, it has been grasped without being articulated by readers over the centuries. Indeed, to spell it out is, in a sense, to diminish its impact. Nonetheless, a simple, three-point summary is possible.

1. People have an absolute duty toward God.[12] Because God is God, and because we are utterly dependent on God, our ultimate duty — transcending all other duties — is to God. This, for Mark and his implied readers, is self-evident: "Hear, O Israel: the Lord our God, the Lord is one. And you shall love the Lord your God with your whole heart, your whole

---

12. I borrow the expression from Kierkegaard's *Fear and Trembling*.

soul, your whole mind, and all your strength" (Mark 12:29-30, citing Deut. 6:4-5).

2. Our absolute duty toward God is encountered in the demands of Jesus. Again, duty does not need to be articulated to be felt; only the sense that the overriding duty to God was at stake can justify Jesus' demands in Mark's Gospel — and Mark's conviction that they should be met with instant and absolute obedience. Without pausing here to examine other narratives, we may fairly say that the whole of Mark's Gospel — its account of John the Baptist and of Jesus' baptism, of Jesus' healings and exorcisms, of his forgiving of sins and authoritative teaching, of his transfiguration, of his purposeful advance to an ordained death and resurrection — *everything* in the Gospel serves to enforce the point that those who witness the actions of Jesus and hear his words are thereby confronted with, and asked to respond to, the call of God on their lives.

3. Given that our absolute duty toward God is encountered in the demands of Jesus, the *right* thing to do and, in the end — whatever suffering may be involved in the interim — the *blessed* thing to do, is to give one's allegiance to Jesus.

This is the evident subtext of Mark's Gospel. In effect, the Gospel was written to confront later readers with the same choices as confronted the contemporaries of Jesus. Christian readers, sensing the point, have attempted — with varying degrees of success — to comply with Mark's agenda. Others reject it outright. But only, I suppose, academics preoccupied with the "Synoptic Problem" or Mark's redactional techniques, his narrative world or the social setting of his community, can have read the Gospel while oblivious to the demands it makes of its readers.

The Text of the Gospel

Yet Mark's call for a faithful following of Jesus remains a *sub*text of the Gospel: at no point does the evangelist interrupt his narrative of the past with an appeal to readers to order their lives by its implications. He tells a story, convinced that the mere telling of the story will bear the freight of his agenda.

That he designates his story "the gospel [or "good news"] of Jesus Christ" (1:1) is the most overt indication of his thinking. Though his text marked an important stage in the process by which "gospel" came to mean "a written account of the life and teaching of Jesus," in Mark's own day the term *euangelion* denoted (as it does in Paul's letters) the message of the early church (1 Cor. 15:1-11; Gal. 1:11, etc.). Mark also uses the term for the basic proclamation of Jesus (Mark 1:14). Behind both usages is the understanding that the coming of Jesus marked the fulfillment of promises made by the prophets in Scripture:[13]

> How fair upon the mountains are the feet of the one who *brings good news,*
> who proclaims peace,
> who *brings good news* of good,
> who proclaims salvation,
> who says to Zion, "Your God reigns." (Isa. 52:7; cf. 40:9; 61:1)

Mark may well have been the first to use the term "Gospel" for a consecutive account of the story of Jesus. Such an account cannot, of course, have been the content of the "gospel" that Jesus himself proclaimed, nor was it identical with the message of the early church. But Mark believed that the essence of each was the same: in the person of Jesus, God had launched a project for the inauguration of the promised new age and the salvation of human beings. In the proclamation of Jesus and that of the early church, though not by the evangelist of Mark's Gospel, the obvious implication was made explicit: it is incumbent on human beings to respond by believing in, and getting on board with, the divine initiative (Mark 1:14-15; Acts 2:38-41, etc.).

In Mark, as in other early Christian writings (including the letters of Paul), "the word" functions as an equivalent of "the gospel" (compare Mark 1:14 with 2:2; 4:33). No more than other early Christians will Mark have understood "the word" (or "the gospel") as inert material serving merely to inform its listeners: when *the* word, or the *gospel,* is spoken,[14] God is at work, "calling" hearers into his kingdom (see Heb. 3:1; 1 Pet. 1:15; 2:9; Jude 1). Note, for example, how, in the explanation given to the parable of the sower, "the word" is said to bear or not to bear "fruit" in the lives of its hearers, depending on their responses to it (4:14-20). But if Mark (like

---

13. Cf. Dunn, "Gospel," 139-40.

14. In Greek, the word "word" *(logos)* is related to the verb "to speak" and is generally used of the *spoken* word, or speech: note, e.g., the combination "word[s]" and "deed[s]," referring to what one says and does (Luke 24:19; Acts 7:22, etc.), and "word" and "letter" (2 Thess. 2:2, 15) to cover both oral and written communications. References to "the word of the Lord" (or, simply, "the word") are thus implicitly references to the *proclaimed* gospel message, the *kerygma.* Even where "the word of God" is used of an OT text (e.g., Mark 7:13; John 10:35), the reference is to a word spoken by God recorded in Scripture.

other early Christians) believed that God was at work whenever the gospel was proclaimed orally, he undoubtedly expected that the gospel, when he *wrote* it, would similarly prove a vehicle of "the [living and active] word of the Lord."[15] To return to the narrative with which we began: in cutting to its core the story of Jesus calling his disciples, Mark clearly intended those who read his account to hear, through his words, their own "call" to obedient faith: "What I [Jesus] say to you [the disciples], I say to all" (13:37). The words "Give careful heed to what you hear" are meant for Mark's audience no less than for that of Jesus (4:24; cf. 4:3, 9, 23).

In short, Mark wrote his Gospel — just as early Christians proclaimed the gospel — in the confidence that God would address his readers through his words. In receptive hearts, those words would bear fruit.

The Gospel of Matthew

Like Mark, Matthew tells a story of the past — the crucial, unsubstitutable story on which the church was founded — conscious throughout of the distance of that past, and at no point interrupting his narrative to exhort or appeal directly to his readers in the present.[16] Even the Sermon on the Mount (Matt. 5–7), for all its pressing importance for every follower of Jesus, is introduced as words spoken at a particular place and time to a particular group of people; and it ends by noting their response, and where Jesus went once he finished addressing them.[17] No less than Mark, however, Matthew expects that, at least at many points,[18] his readers will see parallels to their own lives and sense the need to respond appropriately. The call of Jesus' disciples is related in Matthew (4:18-22; 9:9) very

15. Against the notion of Kelber, *Gospel,* that the medium of writing necessarily conveys a very different message from that of "orality," see Halverson, "Gospel"; see also Gamble, *Books,* 28-32; Gerhardsson, "Secret"; Schwartz, "Origins."

16. Note, e.g., the awareness of how conditions have changed since the time of Jesus in 9:14-15; 28:19 (cf. 10:5-6; 15:24).

17. Cf. Gerhardsson, *Origins,* 67, commenting on the Synoptic Gospels as a group: "The mystery of Jesus is not presented here in the framework of proclamation, teaching, or admonition. We find here that a number of independent words and narratives have been brought together to form an account of a bygone period in the history of salvation. The fact that there is an *edifying intention* in the evangelists' presentation in no way belies this assertion."

18. But *not* all; much is told, purely and simply, because it had become a fixed part of the unsubstitutable story: from John the Baptizer, clothed with camel's hair and preparing the way of the Lord (Matt. 3:1-12), to the woman whose costly ointment prepared Jesus for his burial (26:6-13).

much as in Mark, and doubtless with the same expectation: readers are to "hear" their own "call" to follow Jesus.[19] In the many petitioners who bring their needs to Jesus and find relief, hearers are to see parallels in their own lives.[20] Moreover, as Günther Bornkamm famously demonstrated years ago, Matthew's readers are meant to identify with the disciples who follow Jesus into a boat, discover themselves in the midst of a storm, react with a fear that overwhelms their faith, but find the power of Jesus more than adequate to bring them to safety.[21] In referring to the disciples' dullness and weakness, and yet their experience of Jesus' patience and forgiveness, Matthew prompts his readers to personal reminiscence, ruefulness, and gratitude. In short, at numerous points the narratives of the Gospel are meant to be heard on more than one level: as stories of the past in which hearers in the present can recognize something of their own experience.[22] On the other hand, the Gospel of Matthew does seem to be a more learned, "bookish" composition than its Markan source — with a broader agenda. More specifically, from its very first verse, the Gospel appears designed to serve as a continuation of, and fitting climax to, the scriptures of Israel.[23] And by the Gospel's end, it is clear that the evangelist intended his work to serve as a handy but authoritative guide to Jesus' life and teaching for converts ("disciples"), Gentiles as well as Jews, throughout the world (28:19-20).

The former agenda is obvious both from the sweeping claim that Jesus "fulfilled" the "law and the prophets" (5:17) and from the many texts in which particular moments in Jesus' life or aspects of his ministry are said to have "fulfilled" particular Old Testament texts (see 1:22-23; 2:15, 17-18, 23; 4:14-16; 8:17, etc.). But the point is made in subtler ways as well. The Gospel begins with words borrowed from (the Greek translation of) Genesis 2:4; 5:1, implying that the story that follows represents both a new beginning and the culmination of the sacred history begun in (the old book of) Genesis.[24] Note, too, how Matthew's genealogy of Jesus (1:2-16) is structured in such a way as to convey the point that Jesus' birth — like the call of

19. Note, too, 8:19-22, where the demands of discipleship are put to particular inquirers, but with so little interest in the latter that their response is left unstated.

20. Cf. Luz, *Matthew*, 17.

21. Bornkamm, "Stilling," on Matt. 8:23-27.

22. Cf. Luz, *Matthew*, 11.

23. This is a common observation; see, e.g., Smith, "Gospels," 7-8.

24. Greek *biblos geneseōs*, translated by NRSV: "an account of the genealogy." But the term rendered "genealogy" (Greek *genesis*) is ambiguous: it may also mean "birth" (as in 1:18) or even "history." In fact, the echo of Gen. 2:4; 5:1 may well be more important to the evangelist than the precise denotation of the term.

Abraham, the reign of David, and the deportation to Babylon — marked a crucial turn in the history of God's people (1:17). Indeed, much in the story of Jesus, as Matthew portrays it, recalls the Old Testament story of Moses, or even of Israel itself as a nation.[25] In short, Matthew has adopted a biblical style, patterned a number of his narratives on Old Testament models, and indicated in ways both subtle and direct that the story he tells represents the fulfillment of "the law and the prophets." He will hardly have thought his Gospel of lesser status or importance than those earlier writings.

Perhaps the clearest statement of Matthew's intentions comes at the end of the Gospel. The risen Jesus addresses his worshiping but perplexed disciples in these terms:

> To me has been given all authority in heaven and on earth. Go, then, make disciples of all nations, baptizing them in the name of the Father and of the Son and of the Holy Spirit, and teaching them to observe everything I have commanded you. And lo, I am with you always, to the end of the age. (28:18-20)

Wherever later disciples are made, they are to be taught all that Jesus commanded their predecessors to do. In the obvious question concerning where, decades later, those commands could reliably be found, Matthew has seen his mandate. As elsewhere, here, too, he keeps within the constraints of a narrative of the past: when Jesus demands that all his commandments be passed on, Matthew does not add, in parentheses, "Cf. the five extended discourses and numerous other logia recorded earlier in this book." But he might as well have. Ulrich Luz puts it this way:

> Proto-canonical tendencies are apparent at the end of Matthew's Gospel. With the mission command . . . [28:20a], Matthew can actually be said to "canonize" his own book. It contains — especially in the discourses of Jesus spoken into the present — everything the messengers of Jesus need for their missionary proclamation.[26]

---

25. Compare, e.g., Matt. 2:16 with Exod. 1:22; Matt. 2:20 with Exod. 4:19; Matt. 4:2 with Deut. 9:9, 18; Matt. 5:1 with Exod. 19:16–20:21. Note also Jesus' forced sojourn in Egypt (2:13-15; cf. Ps. 105:16-23); Matthew's application to Christ of the prophetic text: "Out of Egypt I called my son" (2:15; cf. Hosea 11:1); his citing a prophetic lament over past devastations in Israel to characterize the grief that followed Herod's massacre of Bethlehem's children (2:17-18; cf. Jer. 31:15); and the numerous echoes, in the temptation narrative (4:1-11), of Israel's experience in the wilderness (treated in Gerhardsson, *Testing*).

26. Luz, *Studies*, 337.

Matthew has provided an authoritative record of Jesus' teachings — to be read, taught, and obeyed. Essentially, then, he intended his writing to serve the role of Scripture in Christian communities, those already founded and those yet to be established among "all nations."[27]

The teachings of Jesus form the backbone of the Gospel of Matthew. Yet even these ever-relevant instructional texts here find their place *within* the broader story of the Gospel. The Gospel of Matthew is, in the first place, a telling of the story of Jesus that *includes* his teachings; in the end, the uniqueness of the Teacher takes priority over the substance of his teaching. As much as we need to know *what* he taught, we need to understand, at a still more basic level, why he is and must be the only Teacher.[28] Matthew takes on himself the task for his readers that, within his narrative, the transfiguration plays for the disciples: eliciting or enhancing their faith in the beloved Son as the necessary first stage to commending his commands to their obedience (Matt. 17:5). Beyond, then, the practical purpose of conveying the Lord's instructions, Matthew, like Mark, has written an authoritative account of the church's foundational story intended to be an instrument for evoking faith in, allegiance and obedience to, and worship of the Teacher among all who hear his words.

The Gospel of Luke

Luke, too, had a story to tell — and access to an audience less likely to be reached by the other evangelists. In the prologue to his Gospel (1:1-4; cf. also Acts 1:1), Luke dedicates the work to a certain Theophilus, following a format — with its implicit request for help in circulating the dedicated work — that was common in literary compositions of the period.[29] These verses feature prose as polished as anything we encounter in the New Testament. Briefly, we seem in a Greco-Roman literary world, far removed from that of Matthew and Mark.

But with the fifth verse of his first chapter, Luke clearly and deliberately adopts for his narrative the language of sacred Scripture (i.e., of the Greek Old Testament):[30] regardless of audience, no other idiom would do

27. Hengel (*Gospels*, 77) notes that Matthew's intention to provide material for catechetical and ethical instruction in the "whole church" contradicts the "widespread view" that he wrote "only for his communities in Southern Syria and Palestine."

28. Byrskog, *Teacher;* cf. Gerhardsson, *Origins,* 47-49.

29. Cf. Gamble, *Books,* 84, 101-2.

30. On Luke's "Septuagintal" style, see Fitzmyer, *Luke* 1.113-25. The inference from

for his story of how God had "visited"[31] his people.[32] A sense of wonder pervades Luke's account — in Acts as in the Gospel — as it moves from one extraordinary disclosure of God's presence and power to another. Zechariah is "terrified" (1:12; cf. 1:29-30), then struck dumb, as the angel Gabriel foretells the birth of his son John, who is to prepare the way of the Lord. When, at the naming of the child, Zechariah's "mouth was opened and his tongue loosed, . . . fear came over all" who heard of it (1:64-65). Shepherds, too, were terrified by the appearance of the Lord's angel, in a display of divine "glory," announcing the birth of the Savior (2:9-12). When the shepherds later told others what the Lord had made known to them, "all who heard it were amazed" (2:18; cf. 2:33). Repeatedly, we are told of the wonder that greeted Jesus' words (2:47; 4:22, 32). His miracles, too, brought a sense of God's presence — and a sense, at times, that this was more than mortals could endure.

> Amazement came over them all and they kept saying to each other, "What kind of word is this? For with authority and power he gives orders to the unclean spirits, and they go away!" (4:36)

> They were all beside themselves with amazement; they glorified God and were filled with awe, saying, "Today we have seen things wonderful beyond belief!" (5:26)

> The dead man sat up and began to speak. . . . Fear took hold of all of them; and they glorified God, saying, "A great prophet has arisen among us!" and "God has visited his people!" (7:15-16)

> [Jesus] woke up and rebuked the wind and the rough water; they ceased, and there was a great calm. . . . Terrified and amazed, [the disciples] said

---

Luke's adoption of this style and from the fulfillment motif within his Gospel that Luke saw his writings as a continuation of (OT) Scripture is made by a number of scholars. See the literature cited in Smith, "Gospels," 9 n. 18.

31. The term itself is taken over from the Greek Old Testament (e.g., Gen. 21:1; 50:24; Exod. 3:16; 4:31; 13:19). It refers here to a patently divine intervention to bring help or blessing to those in need (cf. Luke 1:68, 78; 7:16; 19:44).

32. That is, Israel (cf. Luke 1:68). For Luke, as for other early Christians, the series of events that make up the gospel represents the culmination of the OT scriptures and of all that God promised within them (cf. 1:1 ["accomplished/fulfilled"], 54-55, 69-70, 72-73; 4:21; 10:23-24; 18:31; 24:25, 27, 44); particular OT texts are cited as finding, in the events of Luke's narrative, their fulfillment (Luke 3:4-6; 4:18-21; 7:27; 20:17-19; 22:37).

to one another, "Who in the world is this, that he gives orders even to the winds and the water, and they obey him?" (8:24-25; cf. 5:8-9)

They found the man from whom the demons had gone sitting at the feet of Jesus, clothed and in his right mind. And they were frightened. . . . Then all the people of the surrounding country of the Gerasenes asked Jesus to go away from them; for they were in the grip of a great fear. (8:35, 37; see also 8:56; 9:43; 11:14; 13:17)

The appearance of the resurrected Jesus, too, "startled and terrified" his disciples (24:37), though here the terror gave way to incredulous joy — and worship (24:41, 51-53).

The story Luke wants to tell is thus how God has demonstrably acted, in the lifetime and experience of people he knew, for the salvation of human beings (cf. 1:68-69, 77; 2:11, 30; 3:6, etc.): these were "things fulfilled *among us*" (1:1). Such news by its very nature invites, if not demands, telling: though Luke never uses the noun "gospel" in his Gospel, the related verb ("proclaim good news") appears frequently, with a variety of subjects: angels (1:19; 2:10), John the Baptist (3:18; cf. 16:16), Jesus himself (4:18, 43; 8:1; 20:1), and his disciples (9:6). The good news to be shared is at times a specific incident within the broader narrative of the divine "visitation" (1:19; 2:10); at other times it represents the thrust of the narrative as a whole (4:18; 7:22; 9:6; 20:1). Among the latter we may include texts that speak of "proclaiming the good news of the kingdom of God" (4:43; 8:1; 16:16).[33] Luke thus sees himself as one of a series of "evangelists," using his gifts as a writer to spread the good news announced first by the angels, then by the Lord himself, then by those who heard him.

The Gospel-writer makes clear that, though he was not among the latter, he was in close contact with those who were, deriving his narrative from "eyewitnesses and servants of the word" (Luke 1:2). That his sources were "eyewitnesses" was an important assurance, for readers ancient as well as modern, of the reliable nature of his account (cf. 1:4; 24:48; Acts 1:8, 21-22; 2:32; 10:39).[34] But these eyewitnesses were also

---

33. The salvation of human beings is to be found only within the sphere of God's rule. The activity of Jesus marks the inauguration of that rule (cf. Luke 11:20) and the opportunity, by one's response, to ensure "entrance" into it (cf. 10:9, 11; 18:17); but the consummation of the kingdom remains in the future (11:2; 19:11; 22:16). The "kingdom of God" serves to designate the content of the early church's message in Acts as well (8:12; 19:8; 20:25; 28:23, 31).

34. Cf. Byrskog, *Story*, 48-91.

"servants of the word."[35] We have already encountered similar usages of "the word" — without further qualification — meaning "the gospel" as proclaimed by both Jesus and the early church. As elsewhere, so in Luke's writings, "the word" is used interchangeably with "the word of God" (Luke 5:1; 8:11; 11:28) or "the word of the Lord" (Acts 8:25; 13:49). Thus, when Luke identifies his sources as "eyewitnesses and servants of the word," he indicates that his narrative preserves and transmits what was simultaneously the firsthand testimony of Jesus' disciples *and* the "word of God." His Gospel is intended to be a medium for communicating "good news" from God.[36]

Throughout Luke's narrative, the announcement of God's good news — whether by angels sent from God, by commissioned but otherwise ordinary human beings, or by the Son of God himself — provokes a crisis among those who hear it. At times it meets with an initial disbelief that later gives way to faith (1:20; 24:11; cf. 24:25); at other times the rejection of the message is decisive, leading to exclusion from God's kingdom (10:10-12; 11:31-32; 14:15-24). A response of faith is said to be blessed and to bring salvation (1:45; 8:12; cf. 5:20; 7:50, etc.). Like these earlier announcements of the good news, Luke's Gospel invites faith on the part of its readers and hearers; as in the Gospels of Matthew and Mark, however, the invitation is left implicit. At no point do the Synoptic evangelists directly call their readers to obedient faith, though each assumes that the divine source of their good news will use their account to do so.[37]

The Gospel of John

The Gospel of John tells the story of the mission of God's Son, bringing light and salvation to a world in darkness.

The Son of God is first introduced in John's Gospel as the Logos, existing in the beginning with God and as God, the very Word by which God

---

35. On the most likely interpretation of the verse, see Fitzmyer, *Luke,* 1.294.

36. No less than other early Christians, Luke believed that the words of the OT are those of God (or the Holy Spirit; cf. Acts 1:16; 4:25; 28:25). But he, too, typically reserves references to "the word" (or "word of God," "word of the Lord") for its latest incarnation, the message of the gospel (e.g., Luke 5:1; 8:11; Acts 4:31; 6:7).

37. Note, however, Luke 12:41-48, where (as in Mark 13:37) it is clear that Jesus' words are directed to a wider audience than the disciples present when they were spoken. The same is, of course, true — though not explicit — of much of what Jesus says throughout the Gospel.

spoke and the worlds came into being (John 1:1-3; cf. Ps. 33:6).[38] As Logos, the Son of God is not only Creator of the cosmos but also the one in whom its good order consists and by whom it is sustained, the source of all life, light, and understanding (1:4-5, 9). But the Word is also inherently the conveyer of divine revelation: having shared intimacy and glory with the Father before the world was created, the Word/Son "became flesh" (1:14) to make God known (1:18; 17:5, 26).

Appearances to the contrary notwithstanding, the Son's mission was successful (17:4; 19:30). The words he spoke and the works he performed were those given him by the Father (5:36; 8:26; 12:49-50; 14:24; 17:8). Everything he did brought pleasure and glory to the Father and light to the world (7:18; 8:29; 17:4; 9:5). That the world did not embrace him — indeed, that it hated him — was only to be expected, given the world's preference for darkness over light as a cover for its evil (3:19-20; 7:7; 15:18-25). Though he came to bring salvation, the practical effect of his coming for those who rejected him and would not receive his words was self-condemnation and judgment (3:17-21; 12:48).

That Jesus, the Son of God, was "lifted up" and crucified represented, not the triumph of the evil world, but his triumph over the world and the accomplishment of his mission (12:31-33; 16:33). His life was not taken from him against his will, but he laid it down of his own accord: greater love could not be shown than when he, "the lamb of God," gave his life to "take away the sin of the world" (1:29; cf. 10:17-18; 15:13). If, through unbelief, the sins of many were retained (8:24; 9:41; 15:22-24), nonetheless there were those given to the Son by the Father who did believe, and to whom he brought light, life, and salvation (8:12; 10:27-29; 17:2).

Why *should* all have responded to the mysterious mission of the Son of God with faith? And, in fact, how did some believe? Faith was to be based on testimony given, from various sources, about who he was and of the divine origin of his mission: to believe the testimony was thus to believe in Jesus as the Christ, the Son of God. John the Baptist was explicitly "sent from God" to "give testimony concerning the light, in order that, through him, all might believe" (1:6-7). His testimony brought Jesus his first disciples (1:35-37; cf. 10:40-42). The Samaritan woman with whom Jesus conversed at Jacob's well gave testimony of what she had learned to those she knew, "many" of whom believed (4:39; see also 12:17). The mighty works that Jesus performed were

---

38. Perhaps because "the Word" designates God's Son in the Prologue, the Gospel of John (unlike the Synoptics, Paul, etc.) does not use "the word" without further definition to refer to the fundamental message of Jesus or the early church.

"signs" pointing to, or giving "testimony" to, the divine source of his mission; they, too, should have evoked faith (5:36; 10:25, 37-38; 14:11; cf. 12:37).[39]

And Scripture gives testimony to Christ — though, like the other sources of testimony, it gains more attention than faith. Even John the Baptist was, for a time, a popular sensation (5:35), and the miracles of Jesus certainly drew crowds (6:2, 26). Similarly, Jesus' contemporaries certainly attended to Scripture, "searching" it diligently (5:39). They read of Jacob's ladder reaching from earth to heaven, but without asking where, outside Jacob's dream, such a ladder might be found, thus missing this adumbration of Christ in Scripture (cf. 1:51). They read of the bronze serpent "lifted up" by Moses in the wilderness, bringing life to all who turned to it in faith; but they failed to see in the ancient story a pointer to the Son of Man, "lifted up so that everyone who believes in him may have eternal life" (3:14-15). They read of the manna from heaven that for a time sustained the lives of Israelites in the wilderness without recognizing its testimony to the true "bread" come from heaven that, by its very nature, imparts eternal life to all who eat it (6:31-58). In the end, what is most important about Moses and the prophets is that they wrote about Christ (1:45; 5:46; 12:16, 41): he is the "righteous" speaker in the Psalms (2:17; 15:25; cf. 19:24), the subject of Isaiah's report to which people gave no credence (12:38). In short, thinking to find life in the words of Scripture, Jesus' hearers refused to look *beyond* the sacred page to the subject of Scripture's testimony: "[The scriptures] testify concerning me; and you are not willing to come to me in order that you may have life" (5:39-40).

The Father, too, gives testimony to the Son (5:32, 37-38; 8:18). In a sense, of course, the testimony of John, of Jesus' works and words, and of Scripture all have God as their ultimate source: John appeared as a "man sent from God . . . to give testimony" (1:6-7); the Son of God spoke and acted according to the Father's commission; Scripture was itself "given" by God (cf. 1:17). But Jesus distinguishes the testimony of the Father from these other sources of testimony (5:31-40) and speaks of it in ways that suggest that, unlike them, it is not encountered externally or perceived by the senses (5:37); rather, it appeals to hearts that are open to the word of God (5:38; cf. 7:17; 1 John 5:9-10). We are reminded elsewhere that "no one

---

39. Through his words as well, Jesus gives testimony — to himself (8:12-18; cf. 3:32; 18:37). The principle that testimony to oneself cannot be true (5:31) would apply to Jesus only if his testimony *originated* with himself rather than being words given him by the Father (5:32; 8:13-18). In any case, the principle, though true of the self-testimony of human beings with limited knowledge, cannot apply to the one come from heaven, fully conscious of his divine mission (8:13-14).

can come to [Christ] unless the Father draws him" (6:44): the "testimony" of the Father thus appears to be another way of speaking of the Father's "drawing" — imperceptibly to the senses, but powerfully in the heart — people to faith in Christ. It remains true, of course, that the other sources of testimony provide the external stimuli by which people come to believe (1:7; 4:39; 19:35); but they serve that end effectively only when they are lent persuasive power by the "drawing of the Father"; only, that is, when their testimony is taken up into and becomes the testimony of the Father himself. Those in whom God's word finds no place never "hear" the testimony of the Father to the Son, whether in the words of John, Scripture, or the works of Christ (5:37-38; 8:37, 47). But where God's word finds a home, the testimony is received (3:33; 8:47; 18:37; 1 John 2:14, 24).[40]

And what about the Gospel of John itself? It, too, is a "testimony" written so that its readers may come to faith in Jesus as the Christ, the Son of God (19:35; 20:30-31; 21:24). Its witness is "true," in part because the evangelist writes about what he has himself experienced (1:14; 15:27; 19:35; 21:24), but also in part because he writes guided by the "Spirit of truth," sent by the Father and the Son to bear witness to Christ (15:26-27; 16:14) and to remind Christ's followers of all that Christ had spoken to them (14:26).[41] What is more, John's Gospel reproduces and thus preserves the testimony of John the Baptist, of the Samaritan woman, of the mighty works and words of Jesus: through the Gospel these witnesses continue to "speak" to people of other times and places.[42] Like them, the Gospel of John will prove effective in evoking faith as the Father makes its testimony his own and "draws" readers to the Son (cf. 17:20).

40. The same point is made differently when Jesus develops the metaphor of the good shepherd in John 10. Those who are not his "sheep" do not "hear" his voice (cf. 8:43; 10:26); but his sheep do so — they will hear no other — and they follow him (10:3-5, 8, 16, 27; cf. 5:25). They belong to the Son because they are given him by the Father (10:29).

41. That the evangelist believes his testimony to be true does not, of course, mean that his intention or approach was that of a nineteenth-century German historian (à la Ranke) or of a prosecuting attorney who will allow no "interpretation," nothing but "the facts." Most biblical scholars would agree that John exercises greater freedom than do the Synoptic evangelists in recasting traditional material to convey the essential "truth" about Christ; some would add that the task of distinguishing core from interpretive recasting is difficult where it is not impossible. Once we have said that, however, we should resist the temptation to discount any historical intention on the evangelist's part or any value in his testimony for historical reconstruction. In addition to the earlier, magisterial work of Dodd *(Tradition),* see Anderson, Just, and Thatcher, *History;* Blomberg, *Reliability.*

42. See, e.g., 1:15: "John bears witness [present tense] concerning him"; 1:19: "This is [present tense] the testimony of John."

Nor is the work of John's Gospel complete when faith in the Son is first evoked. Those who believe in Christ are to "remain" ("abide") in him, which means (at least in part) that Christ's words — as recorded in the Gospel — are to "abide" in them (15:7; cf. 8:31, 51; 1 John 2:24). Their faith is thus to be sustained and nourished by reflection on the Gospel. The word of Christ (again, as found in the Gospel) will "cleanse" (15:3) and "sanctify" (17:17; cf. v. 14) them. As they meditate on the Gospel, they will themselves experience the peace Jesus left his disciples (14:27), the joy with which they were to be filled (15:11), the reality of Christ's love (13:1); they will know themselves commanded to love and serve others as Christ has loved and served them (13:14, 34); and they will receive the dominical blessing pronounced specifically for their benefit (20:29). To contemporaries within hearing distance, Christ spoke "the words of eternal life" (6:68). John wrote his Gospel to mediate those words — and their power — to all who hear or read its message.

Did John, then, intend to write Scripture? The question may fairly be put; but, to be meaningful, it should probably be reworded: Did John, *in effect,* mean to write Scripture?[43] "Scripture," for John and his contemporaries, meant "Moses and the prophets" (cf. 1:45), that is, sacred books from the (distant) past. Of course, John does think that the words of Scripture and of his Gospel form a united testimony to Christ (note the parallels in 2:22; 5:47); indeed, he uses a formula familiar from New Testament citations of (Old Testament) Scripture in quoting words of Jesus cited earlier in the Gospel (18:9; cf. 17:12; see also 18:32 and 12:32-33). But "Scripture" no doubt forms a distinct category in his mind. Still, it seems apparent that he intended his Gospel to serve the same functions as does Scripture: to be read and spoken of when believers assemble, to be the subject of their meditation and study, to strengthen their faith, to be the means of their communion with God (cf. 14:23; 15:7; 1 John 1:3; 2:24). Furthermore, as noted above, he implicitly attributes to the Spirit a role in the Gospel's composition (14:26; 15:26-27). John might not have put it thus, but he was, in effect, writing Scripture.

. . . and Elsewhere

Broadly speaking, we may say that the New Testament documents were all written in the conviction that God was at work in the person of Jesus Christ

---

43. Cf. Moloney, "Scripture"; Scholtissek, "Beobachtungen"; Smith, "Gospels," 12-13.

for the salvation of human beings, and with the intention of evoking or enhancing faith in Christ and providing encouragement and guidance for believers. Such a statement could no doubt be refined, and further points of commonality found. But this is adequate for our purposes.

In producing a written version of "the gospel of Jesus Christ," Mark intended his text to serve the same function, and to carry the same force, as the oral proclamation of the gospel: to be the instrument by which God would "call" hearers to obedient faith. The same vision underlies John's (rather different) Gospel. It was no doubt shared by Matthew and Luke as well, though the former gives much greater emphasis to the instruction of disciples (an element also found, though less prominently, in Mark), and Luke appears bent on addressing the claims of faith to a more educated audience in a form that they would recognize and respect. Uniquely, Luke extends his narrative to include the inspiring, edifying story of God's continued activity in the early church.

The remaining documents in the New Testament (including the Revelation of John) are all letters directed to communities of believers, intended to encourage and guide them to live as they ought. Each speaks with authority: compliance with their directives is the right thing to do and will result in God-pleasing behavior; failure to comply will bring judgment. John of Patmos writes to convey the "revelation of Jesus Christ" given to him in words and visions.[44] Attentive readers will "hear" — in what they read — "what the Spirit is saying to the churches" (2:7, 11, etc.). Letters naming James, Peter, and Jude as their authors come with the authority of these leading figures in the first generation of the church, each a "servant" of the heavenly Lord with close ties to the earthly Jesus (James 1:1; 1 Pet. 5:1; Jude 1); 1 John, too, is written by one who has "seen and heard" first-hand the "word of life" (1:1-3). No similar claim is advanced in the letter to the Hebrews (note Heb. 2:3), though the author nonetheless assumes that

44. Cf. 1:3: "Blessed is the one who reads and those who hear the words of the prophecy and who keep the things written in it." Gamble (*Books,* 104) remarks: "The text is to be read aloud to the gathered community, and the text that is read aloud is identical with the prophecy that is heard. . . . The prophecy and the book are one and the same." Note also 22:7, 9, 18-19. In the letters to the seven churches (Rev. 2-3), John indicates that the very words he writes were given him by revelation. No other NT writer makes the same claim, though Paul clearly believes he exercises his role and authority as a divinely commissioned apostle when he writes his letters, and Luke and John explicitly (Matthew and Mark implicitly) claim to provide reliable accounts of what God has done in Jesus Christ (Luke 1:1-4; John 19:35; 21:24). That the Spirit's guidance (spoken of in John 14:26; 15:26; 1 Cor. 2:13; 7:40) extends to the writing of the texts in which these references are made seems a natural inference. NT writers routinely treat OT texts as divine speech.

God will address his readers through his appeal — and for that reason, one refuses the appeal at one's peril (12:25).

In essence, then, the New Testament documents were written by people who believed that the God who spoke through the prophets of old has now "spoken" in the person of his Son (Heb. 1:1-2); but they also believed that their writings — as faithful accounts of what God has done through his Son (the four Gospels) or in the earliest days of the church (Acts), and as faithful statements of what is entailed in following Jesus (the letters) — were vehicles by which the word of God, uniquely and climactically spoken through Jesus Christ, could now address those who never encountered him in the flesh.

The Old Testament

And what about the Old Testament? It may, of course, be read for what it can tell us about Ancient Near Eastern history or the nature of Israelite religion. But these are modern preoccupations, and purely academic: however legitimate they are in themselves, they are remote from the human concerns of the texts and, indeed, frivolous by comparison.[45] To read the Old Testament *merely* for such ends is to neglect its call to live responsibly before God. Most obviously, the Psalms summon every human being ("kings of the earth and all peoples, . . . young men, maidens too, old men and children") to join in all creation's praise of the Lord (Ps. 148); and they call on all who suffer — from frailty, sickness, slander, or foe — to see their own experience through the eyes of the psalmist, and to make of his words their prayers. The book of Proverbs is equally universal in its appeal: every reader is invited to play the role of a "son" admonished (through the text) by his "father" to take up the pursuit of wisdom, beginning with "the fear of the Lord" (Prov. 4:1; 5:1; 1:7).

"The word of the Lord came" to prophets (Jer. 2:1; 7:1, etc.), who duly delivered it to their contemporaries; yet those who later recorded what the prophets had spoken did so because they believed that the divine word, once spoken, was not spent but had abiding significance. Not only could God's word not "fall to the ground" (cf. 1 Sam. 3:19); it would freshly address new generations. Like a stone that skips over water rather than making a single splash, it would find, in varying degrees of completeness, multiple applications and forms of fulfillment.

45. Cf. the remarks of Søren Kierkegaard in the preface to his *Sickness unto Death*.

And so the texts were read, already by later writers of Scripture themselves.[46] Daniel 9 looks forward to a new fulfillment of Jeremiah 29:10, different from what is celebrated in Ezra 1:1-4.[47] The New Testament writers repeatedly see Jesus (or the community of his followers) as fulfilling prophetic texts whose original referent was another; at times at least (Matt. 2:16, 18 seem to be clear examples), they must have been aware that this was what they were doing, believing simply that the words of the prophets had found fresh significance in their day. The writer of the book of Revelation, in pronouncing the fall of a metaphoric "Babylon," did so in terms drawn from prophecies denouncing the historical city (cf. Rev. 18:2 and Isa. 21:9; Rev. 18:3 and Jer. 51:7; Rev. 18:4 and Jer. 51:45, etc.).

The "word of the Lord" was thus seen, not simply as divinely given knowledge-before-the-fact of some future event, but as a divine force that, once spoken by the prophet, was "released" into the world where it might *shape* any number of events: as the word of God, it remained living and active and could not fail to have effect. In some cases, its immediate effect seemed obvious: the Israel denounced by Amos did not long survive his castigations; Jeremiah lived to see his pronouncements of Jerusalem's doom proved true. Yet even oracles that found no obvious — or only limited — fulfillment in the circumstances first addressed were not expunged from the record: faith simply awaited their outworking in the future. In God's way and God's time, God's word would accomplish the purpose for which it had been spoken (cf. Isa. 55:10-11; Hab. 2:3). The unfaithfulness of David's descendants meant that their kingdom was *not* "made sure forever" before the Lord; God's promise (2 Sam. 7:12-16) would nonetheless find fulfillment in the future (Jer. 23:1-6, following 22:1-30). Babylon fell, as Jeremiah said it would (Jer. 50–51). Still, its initial fall by no means corresponded to the devastation portrayed by the prophet; only in multiple events, occurring over several centuries, could Babylon's prophesied doom

---

46. Similarly, the Old Greek translator of Isaiah frequently saw the prophetic text as addressing events in his own day, and rendered it accordingly (see Seeligmann, *Version,* 4, 76-91). And the people of the Dead Sea Scrolls famously saw the raison d'être of their community in a contemporized reading of Isa. 40:3 (1QS VIII.14; the same verse is seen in the NT as speaking of John the Baptist [Matt. 3:3, etc.])!

47. The wording of Dan. 9:24 suggests that Jer. 29:10, understood (see Dan. 9:2) as prophesying the "end of the desolation of Jerusalem" in seventy years, could only partially be fulfilled by the events of Ezra 1:1-4; after all, further desolation would await the city. Not for "seventy *weeks*" would Jerusalem's iniquity be fully atoned for and righteousness prevail. The (much debated) meaning of the "seventy weeks" need not concern us here; the point is that Jeremiah's reference to "seventy" is being freshly applied to a time when his words would find further — and fuller — fulfillment. Cf. Baldwin, *Daniel,* 162-63.

be deemed complete.[48] And even then, Jeremiah's words continued to be read (as in Rev. 18) as an indictment of whatever empires or rulers opposed God's purposes. When exiles returned to Judea from fallen Babylon, as Isaiah 40–55 said they would, the struggles they faced on their arrival bore little resemblance to the glorious future portrayed in those chapters.[49] Skeptics noted the discrepancy and remained unimpressed.[50] The faithful concluded that responsibility for the blockage of further blessing must lie in human, not divine, failure (Isa. 59:1-15); and they clung to the hope, against all hope, that God would yet accomplish what his prophet had spoken (62:1, 6-9; 63:15–64:12).[51] Typically, the New Testament writers believed that much that was written in these chapters had found fulfillment in their day (e.g., 2 Cor. 6:2 [Isa. 49:8]; 1 Pet. 1:24-25 [Isa. 40:6-8]); even for them, however, parts of Isaiah's text remained a hope for the future (e.g., Phil. 2:9-11 [Isa. 45:23]; Rev. 7:16 [Isa. 49:10]). "The grass withers, the flowers falls, but the word of the Lord abides forever" (1 Pet. 1:24; cf. Isa. 40:7-8).

And what about the Old Testament narratives? Though recounting the past, their "voice," too, resists confinement to the past: their charac-

48. This was noted, e.g., by John Calvin, *Com. Jer.,* on 50:3; 51:25, 44. Calvin is wont to point to multiple *partial* fulfillments of OT prophecies where no single event matched the prophets' words; see Chapter 9 below.

49. To be sure, the language of passages such as Isa. 40:3-5; 41:14-16; 54:11-12; 55:12-13, even when first spoken, can hardly have been intended for literal fulfillment; nonetheless, such passages will necessarily have evoked expectations of prosperity among the returning exiles that went unfulfilled. A similar issue confronts us with Haggai's announcement that messianic blessings would flow once his listeners devoted their energy to rebuilding the temple (Hag. 2; cf. Zech. 8:9-13).

50. Their voices can still be heard behind the prophetic responses, e.g., in Isa. 50:1-2; 56:1; 59:1-15.

51. The pattern repeated itself when the early Christians pointed to OT texts that they believed had been fulfilled by Jesus the Messiah. As others were quick to observe, the isolated texts cited by Christians repeatedly occurred in contexts containing other aspects that Jesus clearly had *not* fulfilled (not, at least, in any literal sense; note, e.g., that Isa. 7:14 is followed by 7:15-16; 9:6 is preceded by 9:4-5 and followed by 9:7; 11:1-2 is followed by 11:3-9; Mic. 5:2 is followed by 5:4; Zech. 9:9 is followed by 9:10). Thus, those who were not inclined to believe saw no reason in these "messianic prophecies" to change their minds. Marcion's very literalistic reading of OT prophecies kept him, too, from seeing Jesus as fulfilling them (Harnack, *Marcion,* 58-59). The early church followed the interpretive model summarized above, seeing the prophecies fulfilled in more than one way and time. Parts of the prophetic texts had been fulfilled at Jesus' *first* coming; other parts were deemed to require "spiritual" interpretation (i.e., material blessings are spoken of where spiritual blessings are meant); still other parts awaited fulfillment at Jesus' *second* coming.

ters, long dead, still speak (see Heb. 11:4). Instinctively, we sense that the very essence of these stories is missed by those who would domesticate them, whether historians occupied only with establishing what really happened *in the past;* or tunnel-visioned apologists, concerned only to prove that what really happened *in the past* was precisely what the texts say happened; or moralists, determined to discover *from the past* "three lessons we may learn" for the present.[52] As the point of Jesus' parables was realized only by those blessed with the imagination and spiritual insight to see, *through* the stories, what was true about themselves, so, too, the message of the Old Testament narratives is heard only by those with the imagination and spiritual insight to see, beyond the details of an ancient story, how they impinge on their own lives and frame the world in which they live. Scholars[53] may or may not be correct in thinking that the patriarchal narratives as we know them were shaped in part by the intention to address the analogous situation of the exiles; but they undoubtedly capture an important aspect of these texts (cf. Isa. 51:1-3).[54] The competent reader of Genesis senses at once that Abraham is not *just* Abraham but his "seed" as well. In his experience — holding on to promises that in his lifetime will never be more than partially fulfilled; intermittently trusting and despairing of the promises as they seem increasingly impossible to be realized; tempted by lesser and closer goals within his realm of achievement; but ultimately faithful, because (it may seem) he has no choice but to believe — they perceive their own. Paul read the text in the spirit in which it was written, seeing Abraham as the "father" of all who believe (Rom. 4:11-12; Gal. 3:7), his story as theirs (Rom. 4:18-24). The author of Hebrews was an equally sensitive reader (Heb. 11:8-19). The wilderness generation as depicted in Exodus through Deuteronomy was certainly meant to be seen as a warning for all who live between the beginning and the end of their redemption, in danger of falling short of their goal because more immediate desires crave fulfillment, circumstances conspire to undermine faith, and unbelief demands proof on its own terms before it will capitulate. The psalmist surely captures the thrust of the narratives when he calls on those "today" who "hear God's voice" not to "harden their hearts" or tempt God's patience lest

---

52. Cf. Sternberg, *Poetics*, 37-38, where the author substantiates the claim that "the whole idea of didacticism is alien, if not antipathetic, to the spirit of Israelite storytelling."

53. E.g., Rendtorff, *Introduction*, 137; van Seters, *Abraham*, 311.

54. That is, God's people in exile, like their patriarchal forebears, had no land to call their own; they could only cling to divine promises while they lived among strangers.

they share the fate of those who perished in the desert (Ps. 95:7-11; cf. 1 Cor. 10:1-13; Heb. 3:7–4:11).[55]

In short, the Old Testament no less than the New summons readers to a life lived before God. Of course, the way a book "asks" to be read does not secure its own reading. The proclaimed gospel of Jesus Christ met with all possible responses; so have its written accounts in the Gospels. The message of Paul, as delivered in person, carried conviction for some listeners but not others; equally diverse has been the reception of his letters. And so with all of Scripture. At the beginning of this chapter, reflection on the dictum that the Bible should be read "like any other book" prompted the observation that different books call for different kinds of reading; this in turn led to the realization that the writings of the New Testament and the Old are characterized by an implicit claim to convey the call of God to their readers, whose absolute duty it is to respond with obedient faith. That being the case, the actual force of the requirement to read the Bible "like any other book" is to deny — at the outset, and as a matter of principle — the Bible a reading in tune with its peculiar nature, to close one's ears to its call, and to preclude for oneself the possibility of experiencing the transformative impact that the biblical texts have always had within communities of faith.[56]

To be sure, such a preclusion is not deemed lamentable by all; indeed, the history of biblical interpretation is often told as the story of the process by which the study of the Bible has come to escape the "biases of faith." A millennium and a half of scriptural interpretation is routinely passed over without regret, since the type of reading championed in such accounts is indeed a modern phenomenon.[57] The resulting story is certainly one worth

---

55. The openness of OT stories to the future finds further expression in their repeated retellings, often with differences in emphasis or detail introduced because of their appropriateness for new situations. Note, e.g., the diverse depictions of the Israel that departed from Egypt found in Jer. 2:1-3 and Ezek. 20:6-17. The retelling of stories from Samuel-Kings in the books of Chronicles offers many examples. Compare, e.g., the account of Joash's coronation in 2 Kings 11:1-16 with that of 2 Chron. 22:10–23:15: the latter shows a concern for the sanctity of the temple area that is conspicuously absent in 2 Kings, but characteristic of the period in which Chronicles was written (cf. Williamson, *1 and 2 Chronicles*, 314-18). On the historical genre of biblical narrative and what it entails, see the reflections of Sternberg, *Poetics*, 23-35.

56. See the ironic observation of Levenson (*Criticism*, 93) that, with the prescription that the Bible should be read "like any other book," "an assumption external to both Judaism and Christianity was put forth as the regulative principle for reading their respective foundational literatures."

57. See Kümmel, *History*, 13: "It is impossible to speak of a scientific view of the New Testament until the New Testament became the object of investigation as an independent

telling, and there is no doubt that scholars who, as a matter of principle, have refused to see anything special about the Bible have noted aspects of its text otherwise overlooked, and have asked questions that have led to insights now shared by all interpreters. The focus of this present study, however, is on how the Christian Bible has been read and understood by influential interpreters sympathetic to its implicit claim to represent and convey the word of God. That story, too, merits recounting: we cannot tell the history of Christianity and of Christian spirituality while ignoring how Christians have read the Bible. It is also at least possible that readings of Scripture in tune with its intended purpose have produced valuable insights for all who would understand its texts.

---

body of literature with historical interest, as a collection of writings that could be considered apart from the Old Testament and without dogmatic or creedal bias. Since such a view began to prevail only during the course of the eighteenth century, earlier discussion of the New Testament can only be referred to as the prehistory of New Testament scholarship. . . . It is improper to speak of scientific study of the New Testament or of a historical approach to primitive Christianity prior to the Enlightenment."

CHAPTER 2

Before the Christian Bible

The earliest followers of Jesus revered the same Bible as other Jews did, though they read it differently: "the law and the prophets" required a fresh look now that the story they introduced had culminated unexpectedly in the death and resurrection of Jesus. The resultant "good news" — the "word" God *now* was speaking — was proclaimed by Jesus' apostles, but not recorded for several decades. By the end of the first century, however, most, if not all, of the writings later included in the New Testament were being circulated individually among Christian communities (letters of Paul appear to have been assembled already).[1] But it would take another century or so before collections of such writings began to be seen as forming

---

1. The remarkable extent to which, from the very beginning, communities of believers in diverse locations maintained contact with each other — through personal travel, the sending of letters, and the sharing of important texts — has often been noted. See Williams, "Orthodoxy," 11: "The Christianity of the New Testament documents and of the broadly non-gnostic churches of the second century presents us with an enormous amount of evidence for what can sometimes seem like an almost obsessional mutual interest and interchange." See also Bauckham, "Gospels," 30-44; Gamble, *Books,* 142; and Harnack, *Mission,* 369-80. Two distinctive features common to the earliest Christian manuscripts — the marked preference for the codex over the scroll, and the use of *nomina sacra* (i.e., contracted or abbreviated forms, with supralinear horizontal lines at the point of shortening, for "God," "Lord," "Jesus," and "Christ," etc.) — supply material evidence of the ties maintained between the various "assemblies of Christ" and their common sense of identity. See Hengel, *Gospels,* 118-22; Hurtado, *Artifacts,* 43-134. Close contact between various communities of believers and a common sense of identity is apparent also in the development of what Graham Stanton calls "'in-house' language patterns" (*Gospel,* 49-52, 61). The convictions and experiences shared by "all those who call on the name of our Lord Jesus Christ in every place" (1 Cor. 1:2) found expression in the way, with each other, believers used ordinary words in distinctive ways. Note, e.g., the following common terms, each of which, without further definition, bore special significance among believers: "gospel," "word," "believers" (as well as "faith" and "the faith"), "call" (or "calling," "the called"), and "assembly."

an entity (a "New Testament") comparable to the "Old Testament," the two together constituting Christian Scripture.[2] That stage is apparent in the writings of Irenaeus, who can sum up the content of Scripture in expressions like "the writings of the evangelists and the apostles ... with the law and the prophets" (*A.H.* 1.3.6). Before we look specifically at *how* Irenaeus read Scripture, we should say something about the process by which a New Testament came into being, as well as about how, by the time of Irenaeus, the "Old Testament" — once the only Bible the Christians knew — had become a subject of serious contention.

The New Testament in the Making

Toward the end of the second century A.D., Irenaeus, bishop of Lyons (in modern France), could claim that in his youth he had been taught by a man who in *his* youth had been taught by men who in *their* youth had been taught by Jesus (Eusebius, *E.H.* 5.20). The claim is not at all implausible. An older man at the end of the second century, Irenaeus would have been born in the 130s or early 140s. As a young man, he had known Polycarp, bishop of Smyrna in western Asia (modern Turkey); indeed, like many of advanced age, Irenaeus tells us that he has clearer memories of listening to Polycarp in his youth than he has of more recent events. Polycarp died in about 155 at the age of 86. As a young man in the closing decades of the first century, he was certainly in a position to know (as he claims to have known) some who in *their* youth had followed Jesus.

The substance of Irenaeus's claim is thus plausible enough, and the significance he attributes to it understandable. But what Irenaeus says he learned about Jesus through this oral chain of tradition does not inspire confidence[3] and may serve to illustrate why, in the last third of the first century, as the generation that had known Jesus was dying off, it became important to record traditions about him in (what would become) our New Testament Gospels.

---

2. "By the close of the second century, however, we can see the outline of what may be described as the nucleus of the New Testament. Although the fringes of the emerging canon remained unsettled for generations, a high degree of unanimity concerning the greater part of the New Testament was attained among the very diverse and scattered congregations of believers not only throughout the Mediterranean world but also over an area extending from Britain to Mesopotamia" (Metzger, *Canon*, 75).

3. Most notoriously, Irenaeus claims to have learned from those who heard John and other followers of Jesus that the Lord reached old age before dying (*A.H.* 2.22.5).

On the most commonly adopted understanding of the relationship between the Synoptic Gospels, the Gospel of Mark was the first to be written (around the year A.D. 70). Immediate recognition of its value is apparent from its adoption by Matthew and Luke as the core of their own Gospel narratives. That the latter evangelists (again, on the most common understanding) each took over Mark's narrative without knowing the other's work suggests their distance from each other — thus also suggesting a wide circulation of Mark.[4] Since very little is found in Mark that is not also present in one or both of the later Gospels, and since both Matthew and Luke contain much additional material, it is not surprising that, after their publication, Mark's Gospel was deemed less useful; in fact, it is seldom cited in the second century. The importance accorded Mark by Matthew and Luke, on the one hand, and the fact that Mark's place among the church's Gospels was never in doubt even after its substance had been reproduced in later Gospels, on the other, may well be due to the belief that Mark preserves the memories of Peter (Eusebius, *E.H.* 2.15; 3.39).[5]

Matthew's well-organized Gospel was a success from the start, and was clearly the most widely used of all the Gospels in the second century.[6] The early history of Luke's Gospel is more difficult to trace. Written for a more targeted audience (Luke 1:1-4; cf. Acts 1:1), it may not at first have circulated within the broader Christian community to the same extent as the Gospel of Matthew.[7] Nonetheless, its place among the church's Gospels and its traditional association with the apostle Paul[8] were sufficiently established by the time of Marcion (ca. 140) for the latter to regard it as the only authentic Gospel (since, in Marcion's view, Paul was the only authentic apostle) and for the wider church not to have been tempted by Marcion's misuse of the Gospel to reject it.[9]

The early reception of Matthew, Mark, and Luke may have depended in part on the belief that these Gospels preserve the testimony of particular apostles; but a further, essential factor was surely that they were immediately recognized to be handy collections of traditions that had long been fa-

---

4. See Gamble, *Books,* 102.

5. The traditional relationship between Peter and the Gospel of Mark is defended by Bauckham, *Eyewitnesses,* 124-27, 155-82; Hengel, *Peter,* 36-48.

6. See Köhler, *Rezeption.*

7. See Campenhausen, *Formation,* 128.

8. See Muratorian Fragment 3-6; Irenaeus, *A.H.* 3.1.1; 3.14.1; Tertullian, *Against Marcion* 4.2; 4.5.

9. Marcion recognized the Gospel of Luke to the exclusion of the other Gospels, and he removed from its text parts that did not accord with his views (cf. Irenaeus, *A.H.* 1.27.2).

miliar within Christian communities.[10] Had the Jesus of these Gospels not been the Jesus people knew, even claims of apostolic origins are not likely to have secured their acceptance. As the Johannine Jesus puts it, "My sheep hear my voice"; "they will not follow a stranger . . . for they do not know the voice of strangers" (John 10:27, 5). Naturally, treasured traditions in oral circulation did not cease to be repeated the moment written Gospels appeared. As a result, when sayings of Jesus are quoted in early second-century literature, it is often impossible to be sure whether the quotation is taken from one of our written Gospels or from the oral tradition; either way, the same Lord was the speaker. In time, believers naturally became increasingly dependent on the written Gospels as sources for the words and deeds of Jesus. But, as a general rule, the authority associated with traditions of Jesus was still perceived to derive, not from the sacredness of the texts that contained them, but from the Lord to whom the texts bore witness and whose voice they served to convey.[11]

The Gospel of John is in many ways very different from the Synoptics; but the suggestion that it was regarded with suspicion in the early church on that (or some other) account appears to be unfounded: the Gospel was known and used by Christians of varying stripes throughout the second century.[12]

The task of tracing the process by which our Gospels came to be recognized as Scripture has, in much recent literature, lost urgency, inasmuch as it appears now to be little more than a question of definition. As we have seen, the Gospels were intended at the time of their writing to be authoritative accounts of the words and deeds of Jesus, and to serve as the medium by which God would address readers with the demands of discipleship. At least Matthew and Mark may have been intended for liturgical use as well.[13] These are characteristics commonly attributed to Scripture. On the other hand, given that the term "Scripture" suggested to ancient readers a sacred writing from the distant past,[14] and, moreover, that the term was already in use to designate a (more or less fixed) body of writings, it naturally took time before the term was extended to our Gospels. The adoption of the

---

10. What Arnaldo Momigliano (*Essays*, 195) wrote of the Hebrew historians can also be said of the evangelists: "The Biblical historian . . . only gave an authoritative version of what everybody was supposed to know."

11. See Barton, *Writings*, 79-91.

12. See Charles E. Hill, "Gospel," which updates his earlier *Corpus*, with extensive bibliography.

13. See Hartman, "Gottesdienst."

14. Barton, *Writings*, 65, 67-68.

terminology did nothing to enhance their long-acknowledged authority. It would take still longer (not until the fourth century) before a need was felt to draw up lists specifying precisely which books belonged to "canonical" Scripture. The latter development, too, had zero impact on the high esteem in which the Gospels were already held.[15]

Irenaeus is dogmatic in declaring that the church has four — and only four — authoritative Gospels. Others may not have been as explicit, but the substance of the claim probably did not originate with Irenaeus: a four-fold gospel is acknowledged in roughly contemporary literature from a wide variety of geographical locations.[16] Precisely how much earlier the notion can be traced is a matter of ongoing debate. Since each of the four New Testament Gospels was individually regarded, from the first half of the second century, as an authoritative source of the stories and sayings of Jesus, and since no other Gospel writing was ever a serious candidate for adoption by the wider Christian community,[17] it was only a matter of

15. The preceding discussion attempts to briefly summarize the complicated issues that are dealt with more adequately, e.g., in Barton, *Writings.*

16. Cf. Charles E. Hill, *Gospels,* 44-51; Piper, "Four," 269-72; Stanton, *Gospel,* 63-91; Verheyden, "Dispute," 513-20. On a second-century date for the Muratorian Canon (a clear witness to the "fourfold gospel"), see Verheyden, "Dispute"; see also Stanton, *Gospel,* 68-71. It is also worth noting that collections of the four canonical Gospels in a single codex are found from the early third century (Stanton, *Gospel,* 71-75). Finally, it is probably significant that no other Gospel is ever combined with any of the four canonical Gospels in a single codex (Elliott, "Codex," 107).

17. Throughout the second century (and later), natural curiosity inevitably produced a market for texts that would tell more about Jesus, and more than a few undertook to meet the demand. This is not the place to trace the reception of noncanonical Gospels. Some were intended to satisfy curiosity by filling in gaps left by the narratives of the four Gospels (e.g., the *Infancy Gospel of Thomas,* the *Protevangelium of James,* and the later *Gospel of Nicodemus*). They may never have been intended to do more than provide edifying entertainment (see Schneemelcher, "Introduction," 55-56). In any case, their usage in our period never rivaled that of the Gospels whose accounts they supplemented. At the other extreme are Gospels (e.g., *Gospel of Mary, Gospel of Judas,* the Coptic *Gospel of Thomas*) that emerged from communities that were rivals to the mainstream church (which they indirectly critique), purporting to contain superior and esoteric revelations. The Jesus portrayed in such Gospels (traditionally labeled "gnostic") differs widely from the Jesus of the mainstream church: his mission no longer bears a positive relationship to anything in the Jewish scriptures or even to the deity there revealed. He brings salvation by imparting (to the spiritually elite) knowledge of the divine spark that they (but only they) possess, and of how it may be delivered from imprisonment in the material body and returned to the divine realm from which it came. Duly sanitized and strategically reduced, in popular literature, to an exotic spirituality with a vaguely defined message of self-realization, these "gnostic" texts have attracted many (see the ironic comments of Perkins, *Introduction,* 254-55, 292-93; see also Pearson, *Gnosticism,*

time before the four were recognized as a closed group. The exact point at which that closure was first proposed is not, in the end, very important.

Whatever rough edges the apostle Paul's personality may have had were worn smooth by the end of the first century, when he was remembered simply as "the blessed apostle" (*1 Clement* 47.1; cf. 5.7), "the blessed and glorious Paul" (Polycarp, *To the Philippians* 3.2; see also Ignatius, *To the Ephesians* 12.2). Already Ignatius, at the beginning of the second century, can look back on the days of the apostles as a bygone era, and on the authority of the apostles as far surpassing anything to be found in the church of his day (*To the Trallians* 3.3; *To the Romans* 4.3). That a collection of ten letters of Paul was in circulation by that time seems clear (precisely when the Pastoral Epistles were added is not known),[18] itself an indication that their significance was seen to extend beyond their original audience.[19] Unlike the Jesus tradition, quotations of Paul were inevitably drawn from written sources, reflecting the acknowledged authority of his letters throughout the second century.[20]

The early church seems never to have reflected on the canonicity of the four Gospels or the letters of Paul.[21] Their authority was simply assumed

---

333-41); but their adoption by the wider Christian community in antiquity was never — and in the nature of things could not have been — an issue for serious discussion. See Gamble, *Books*, 127: "That not many heterodox texts survived into later periods or did so haphazardly is often taken as evidence that they were systematically repressed by an emerging orthodoxy.... From a bibliographic point of view it is far more likely that heterodox texts failed to survive because the limited circulation they enjoyed did not generate enough copies to establish a textual tradition that would sustain their transmission over time."

18. See Gamble, "Research," 282-87; Stuhlhofer, *Gebrauch*, 105, 111; Zuntz, *Text*, 279. How the process began is uncertain. Some have envisioned a devotee of the apostle visiting various Pauline communities to assemble whatever writings of Paul still survived; it is more likely, however, that the collection was put together by someone in Paul's immediate circle, using originals of the letters that were retained by the apostle at the time of their composition (Gamble, *Books*, 100-101). For a summary of various proposals about the initial collection and circulation of Pauline letters, see Porter, "Canon."

19. It is perhaps worth recalling the similar development that took place with the OT prophets: their words, though initially directed to particular people in particular situations, were collected and recorded in the conviction that the God who once spoke through the prophets to their contemporaries would continue to speak through their words to later generations.

20. Gamble (*Canon*, 43-46) effectively counters the suggestion that the heretical use of Paul's letters brought them for a time into disrepute within the mainstream church.

21. Gamble, *Books*, 216; Stuhlhofer, *Gebrauch*, 70. Cf. Barton, *Writings*, 59: "No other reason for accepting books as canonical or scriptural ever approaches in importance the argument that they have always been so accepted. And, as we have seen, apart from the

by all who adhered to the mainstream church; indeed, to a large extent, acceptance of their authority can serve to define these communities. Judging by actual usage,[22] we may add 1 Peter and 1 John as other texts that were especially treasured in Christian communities of the second century.[23] Other writings — both some that in the end were accepted as parts of the New Testament (e.g., Hebrews, Revelation) and others that were not *(1 Clement, Shepherd of Hermas)* — were known and accepted in some communities but not in others.[24] But in no case did their actual usage rival that of the New Testament's essential core. That no need for clear boundaries of Scripture was felt before the fourth century is likely due to the fact that what was most important was not in question.[25]

Already in the second century, a concern to transmit these texts accurately was in evidence in Alexandria;[26] elsewhere, however, the needs of Christian communities were largely met by nonprofessional scribes drawn from their own members. While the importance that was ascribed to the substance of the texts is apparent in their efforts, the pragmatic demands on their work apparently were not felt to require, and were not met with,

---

very fringes of the canon, both Old and New Testaments were already in this sense 'ancient landmarks' by the mid-second century."

22. The Acts of the Apostles may have been equally accepted, though it was little used. Stuhlhofer (*Gebrauch,* 48-49, 119) compares the historical books of the Old Testament, whose status as Scripture was never in question, though they proved less useful and were thus less cited in later literature than other parts of Scripture. Even by writers with whom — and in periods in which — Acts unquestionably found acceptance, it is cited much less frequently than the Gospels or Paul. Cf. Barton, *Writings,* 23-24.

23. Gamble notes, as points of agreement by "all" scholars in the field, "that (1) by the end of the second century the four gospels, the letters of Paul, and 1 Peter and 1 John had acquired very broad use and high authority in almost all regions of early Christianity, (2) that the status and use of other writings continued to be variable through the third and well into the fourth century, and (3) that lists that strictly delimit the scope of authoritative writings clearly belong mainly, perhaps exclusively, to the fourth and fifth centuries." Stuhlhofer finds the history of the Christian Bible to be characterized by "a remarkable stability and constancy — it is a history without revolutions." To be sure, the status of certain books was a matter of discussion; precise boundaries were drawn somewhat differently by different churches. Essentially, however, "the same books were used with the same intensity from the beginning on. All the books used intensively are part of our New Testament, and make up the largest part of our New Testament." Gamble, "Research," 271; Stuhlhofer, *Gebrauch,* 69.

24. E.g., broadly speaking, in the early period the book of Revelation found more acceptance in the West than in the East, the epistle to the Hebrews more acceptance in the East than in the West.

25. Stuhlhofer, *Gebrauch,* 55.

26. Cf. Fee, "Myth"; see also Metzger and Ehrman, *Text,* 277-78.

the same concern for precision.[27] By the end of the second century, most of the New Testament texts had been translated into Latin, Syriac, and perhaps Coptic; translation into other languages would follow.[28] As most Christians of the period encountered the Old Testament in Greek translations of varying quality, so many now read and treasured the New Testament in translations[29] that left ample room for improvement.[30] Clearly, the import and power of the texts were not perceived to be dependent on their being encountered either in their exact wording or even in their original language:[31] the word of God was not so bound.

The Old Testament before Irenaeus

Before turning to the controversies surrounding the Old Testament in the second century, we should look briefly at its appearance and interpretation in the first.

What Did It Look Like?

The average baseball fan talks eagerly and often about the stars of the team, can name with little difficulty others in the starting line-up, but may be hard pressed to name the long reliever who has not pitched in three weeks, or the utility infielder.[32] Jews at the turn of the era had a similar awareness of their scriptures; so (as we have seen) did Christians at the end of the second century. The core books of Scripture figured largely in their thoughts; they could name without difficulty a number of other books deemed to be

27. "In a time when the majority of people were illiterate and when Christianity periodically underwent severe persecution, there were probably few professionally trained scribes in the service of the church. . . . Scribes in the first two centuries . . . were more interested in making the message of the sacred text clear than in transmitting errorless [manuscripts]" (Fee, "Criticism," 9). (On p. 7, however, Fee notes that the text-type derived from Alexandria was "the product of a carefully preserved transmission.") Gamble (*Books*, 74), too, suggests "a greater interest in making these texts available than in the strict accuracy of their transcription."

28. Metzger and Ehrman, *Text,* 94-115.

29. Indeed, almost from the beginning the (Aramaic) words of Jesus were encountered in Greek translation by most of his followers.

30. Cf. Augustine, *Teaching Christianity* 2.11.16.

31. As, e.g., is the case in Islamic tradition with the Arabic wording of the Qur'an.

32. The movie buff's familiarity with actors in a favorite film would also have illustrated my point; but baseball remains a superior mirror on life.

Scripture; still other books of uncertain (or not agreed on) status remained on the fringes.[33]

Two thousand years ago there was no debate among Jews about nearly all of the books in the Jewish Bible (the *Tanakh*) today,[34] though — to judge by actual usage — some played a more significant role than others. Whether books on the fringes (such as Ecclesiastes and Song of Songs) were the subject of debates then is a subject of debate among scholars today.[35] Conversely, certain Jewish writings *not* in the canon today (*Jubilees,* the *Temple Scroll* from Qumran, and *1 Enoch* among them) purport to be the product of divine revelation. In the thinking of some Jews, such texts appear to have played as central a role as the universally acknowledged writings. The New Testament can probably be seen as fairly reflecting what Scripture meant for most Jews of the day: by far the most references are to the "bestsellers" (the Psalms, Isaiah, the Pentateuch — especially Genesis and Deuteronomy); fewer references are found to other books included in what was later called the Old Testament. One explicit quotation is taken from *1 Enoch,*[36] and a number of possible allusions are found to books of the Apocrypha and other noncanonical literature.

Most of the Jewish scriptures were written in Hebrew, a few chapters in Aramaic (a closely related language). The traditional form of the Hebrew text today is referred to as the Masoretic Text (MT). Its direct ancestor became the standard form of the text among Jews by the second century of our era, and has been transmitted with extraordinary fidelity ever since. Indeed, already in pre-Christian times an earlier form of this traditional text was being transmitted with great care: it may well have been the text preferred in temple circles.[37] To this day, it is the only Hebrew text we have for the entire Old Testament.

33. Some scholars believe that precise limits of the Jewish scriptures were already fixed in the time of Jesus; more commonly, it is thought that there was clarity regarding the core, ambiguity about the boundaries. Cf. Collins, "Scriptures"; Lim, *Formation.*

34. These are the same books (though not in the same order) as those found in the Protestant OT. The Catholic OT includes books and parts of books not found in the Jewish Bible but preserved (in some cases, actually written) in Greek, rather than Hebrew (or Aramaic): Tobit, Judith, Wisdom of Solomon, Ecclesiasticus, Baruch, 1 and 2 Maccabees, and additions to Esther and Daniel. The status of these "apocryphal" or "deuterocanonical" books was a matter of discussion already in the early church.

35. Cf. Barton, *Writings,* 108-21.

36. See Jude 14-15. Second Peter, while taking over much of the substance of Jude's epistle, pointedly omits this reference, perhaps reflecting doubts about (or a rejection of?) the status of *1 Enoch* as Scripture.

37. Cf. Tov, *Criticism,* 30, 36-37.

Prior to the second century A.D., however, Hebrew texts of Scripture were circulated in a variety of forms. This is apparent from the biblical manuscripts discovered among the Dead Sea Scrolls, some dating back to as early as the mid-third century B.C.,[38] as well as from the version of the Pentateuch preserved by the Samaritan community.[39] For our purposes, however, the most important evidence is found in the Old Greek translations (dating from the mid-third to the first century B.C., and commonly designated "Septuagint") of the various books of the Old Testament: these, after all, were the source of (most, if not all) New Testament quotations of the Old; and it was in this form (or in translations into still other languages, based on the Greek) that most Christians of the early period encountered Old Testament Scripture.

The name "Septuagint" misleadingly suggests that we are dealing with a uniform translation. Not only were different parts translated at different times, but they were rendered with wildly different levels of skill and standards of literalness.[40] Generally speaking, Old Greek Genesis admirably renders the Hebrew text into intelligible Greek,[41] while the Greek renderings of Job and Proverbs are, at their best, free paraphrases of the originals. The translation of Isaiah tends to be paraphrastic as well, and additionally suffers from the translator's limited grasp of Hebrew, a deficiency he at times masks by finding something appropriate of his own to say when he fails to understand the Hebrew.[42] Conversely, Greek Jeremiah is marked by literalness; so, too, the Greek Psalms.[43] Of course, each of these translations was based on a Hebrew text current at the time of translation. Often it

---

38. Over 40 percent of the biblical manuscripts found at Qumran show an early form of the text tradition now known as MT; these include an important Isaiah scroll (1QIsa^b), noted for its close proximity to MT. (Another, virtually complete Isaiah scroll [1QIsa^a] shows greater differences.) Five percent represent a text closest to that used by the Old Greek translators; these include Hebrew manuscripts (4QJer^{b,d}) showing the shorter version of Jeremiah found in the Old Greek. Eleven percent of the Torah texts more closely resemble the Samaritan Pentateuch. Other biblical manuscripts are nonaligned. For the figures, see Tov, *Criticism*, 108.

39. See Tov, *Criticism*, 74-93.

40. For the different values underlying different translation styles in the Septuagint and other translations in antiquity, see Brock, "Translating."

41. So Wevers, "Reflections," 58. Wevers goes on to offer helpful comments on the distinct attitude toward the translator's task taken by the translators of each book of the Old Greek Pentateuch (58-59).

42. Ottley, *Isaiah*, 49-50; Seeligmann, *Version*, 56-58.

43. See the introductions to the individual books of the Septuagint in Pietersma and Wright, *Translation*.

is clear that that text differed from the Hebrew Old Testament as we know it (MT), at times quite extensively. The book of Jeremiah, for example, only took on its present shape over a protracted period of time; it appears to have been translated into Greek at an earlier stage of the process than that reflected in the MT (which is longer than the Greek version by approximately one-sixth).[44]

To complicate matters still further, the Old Greek translations themselves were subject to revision. The prime witness here is a Greek text of the Minor Prophets discovered in a Judean cave, dating from the mid-first century B.C., and representing a revised form of the Old Greek translation of those books.[45] The revision was clearly motivated by a concern to bring the translation closer to the Hebrew text — and the Hebrew text toward which the translation is revised is an earlier form of what would become the MT. Apparently, already in pre-Christian times, some Jews were disturbed by the freedom exercised by the Septuagint translators;[46] and for some Jews at least, the text that would later be adopted as the MT was already regarded as the standard to which other texts should conform.

Most Jews in the time of Jesus no doubt used whatever texts of their sacred scriptures lay to hand — with little if any awareness that other forms existed.[47] This certainly appears to be the case with the New Testament authors. Writing in Greek, they naturally quoted existing translations of the scriptures into Greek, even where these departed considerably from the Hebrew.[48] Quotations closer to the Hebrew than to the

44. Emanuel Tov believes that there is sufficient evidence, based primarily on differences between the Old Greek and/or biblical manuscripts from Qumran, on the one hand, and MT, on the other, to speak of different editions of a number of books or sections of books in the Hebrew scriptures. See Tov, *Criticism*, 283-326. Cf. Ulrich, *Origins*, 11: "There were multiple editions of the biblical books in antiquity — one form of which survives in each of the books of the MT collection, while other forms may or may not have had the good fortune to survive in the S[amaritan] P[entateuch], the LXX [Septuagint], at Qumran, or elsewhere."

45. The nature and significance of the scroll were the subject of the groundbreaking work of Dominique Barthélemy, *Les Devanciers d'Aquila*.

46. The process would continue through other revisions (or "recensions") of the Greek text credited to Aquila, Symmachus, and Theodotion. On these works, see Jobes and Silva, *Introduction*, 37-42.

47. See Tov, "Significance," 299: "[The Qumranites] apparently paid no special attention to textual differences such as those described here." See also Lim, *Formation*, 127.

48. Of many examples, note Matt. 21:16 (Ps. 8:2); Mark 7:6-7 (Isa. 29:13); Acts 15:16-18 (Amos 9:11-12); 1 Cor. 2:16 (Isa. 40:13); Heb. 1:6 (Deut. 32:43); Heb. 10:37-38 (Hab. 2:3-4); cf. Acts 7:14 (Gen. 46:27; Exod. 1:5). Philo (*Life of Moses* 2.37, 40) justified his usage of the Septuagint rather than the Hebrew by claiming inspiration for the translators. When Jews

Old Greek[49] may reflect the author's familiarity with the Hebrew text. But we must now also reckon with the strong possibility that the author was simply using a Greek text that had been revised to bring it closer to the Hebrew.[50] At no point does any New Testament author betray an awareness of (still less, anxiety over) the diversity of forms in which the scriptures were being circulated, or of differences in the Greek text they cited from the Hebrew original: mercifully, the voice of the living God was not tied to a particular version of Scripture.[51]

How Was It Read?

Like their contemporary non-Christian Jews, the early Christians saw the scriptures as spoken in the past by God through human mediators, and at the same time as texts through which God continued to speak. The former conviction is occasionally spelled out (e.g., Rom. 1:2; Heb. 1:1; 1 Pet. 1:11); more frequently, we encounter it in the formulas with which quotations from Scripture are introduced.[52] At times, both divine origin and human mediator are mentioned (e.g., "the word spoken by the Lord through the prophet" [Matt. 1:22; 2:15; cf. Acts 28:25]); but nothing different is meant when either the human mediator ("spoken by [or 'through'] the prophet" [Matt. 2:17; 3:3; 4:14, etc.]) or the divine speaker alone is named (2 Cor. 6:16; Heb. 3:7; 10:15). Though, as we saw in Chapter 1, the New Testament writers generally reserve references to "the word" (or "word of the Lord,"

---

contested Septuagint readings used by Christians, the early church defended the Septuagint on various grounds, including its purported inspiration. Cf. Müller, *Bible,* 68-97; see also Hengel, *Septuagint.*

49. E.g., Matt. 2:15 (Hos. 11:1); Matt. 12:18-21 (Isa. 42:1-4); Acts 13:47 (Isa. 49:6); Rom. 11:35 (Job 41:11); 1 Cor. 3:19 (Job 5:13).

50. See Menken, *Bible,* 282: "Matthew had a revised LXX text for Isaiah, Jeremiah, the Minor Prophets, and the Psalms, and an unrevised LXX text for Deuteronomy"; see also 280: "There are no indications that it was Matthew who translated the Hebrew or revised the LXX." For the use of revised LXX texts by Paul, see Koch, *Schrift,* 57-81. The use of such texts is particularly likely where the wording of the New Testament quotation is also found in one of the revisions of the Septuagint text known to us from antiquity (Aquila, Symmachus, and Theodotion), and may reflect a precursor to their work. So, e.g., Matt. 21:5 (Zech. 9:9); John 19:37 (Zech. 12:10); 1 Cor. 15:54 (Isa. 25:8). Cf. Harl, "Septante," 277.

51. The nature of the Old Testament text cited by individual New Testament authors, and their method and purpose in citing it, have been the subject of many scholarly monographs. See Beale and Carson, *Commentary;* see also Carson and Williamson, *Scripture.*

52. Parallels between the introductory formulas used for scriptural quotations in the Qumran materials and those in the New Testament are shown by Fitzmyer, "Use," 7-16.

"word of God") for the message of the Christian gospel, occasionally it is used for divine speech in the Old Testament as well (cf. Matt. 15:6, referring to the quotations of Exod. 20:12 and 21:17 in v. 4; Heb. 4:12, apparently referring back to the quotation from Ps. 95 in 3:7-11): such a divine word, like that of the gospel, is necessarily "living and active" (Heb. 4:12; cf. 1 Pet. 1:23-25), addressing its hearers "today" (Heb. 3:7).

Christian and non-Christian Jews alike regarded the scriptures as the words of God; yet their understanding of what God was saying differed markedly. Readers of a novel surprised by the ending may well want to look back at earlier chapters for missed clues of what was coming. Similarly, the unanticipated events of the first Easter forced Jesus' followers to go back to Scripture in search of overlooked clues of what God must have intended all along. Not surprisingly, the clues they turned up proved unconvincing to Jews not engaged in the search.

Something similar went on in a slightly earlier period among the people who produced the Dead Sea Scrolls. Convinced that they were living in the "last days" of prophecy, they found in Scripture references to themselves (cryptic at best and lost on others, but clear to those whose eyes had been opened), their leaders, and their times.[53] Still, though the contemporizing interpretations of the early Christians and the covenanters of Qumran were not shared by outsiders, the conviction underlying such interpretations — that the texts of Scripture are relevant in every age — was shared by all religious Jews.[54] So, too, the belief that no detail of the sacred text can lack significance.[55]

That the early Christians interpreted many Old Testament passages as prophecies of Christ and his church goes without saying; but these were by no means the only texts of contemporary relevance. Patterns discerned in

---

53. Most obviously (though by no means exclusively) in the commentaries *(pesharim)* on Habakkuk, Nahum, and Psalm 37. See VanderKam, *Scrolls,* 43-51; Wendel, *Interpretation,* 55-78. VanderKam and Wendel both note that the interpreters, like the texts they interpreted, were believed to be inspired.

54. See Barton, *Writings,* 137-39; cf. Kugel, *Guide,* 15.

55. Cf. Gal. 3:16. Barton (*Writings,* 142) notes: "The text meant more than any naïve reader would think. This comes out especially in a tendency to atomize the text, to read meaning into elements that to us seem sub-semantic: inflections and other bound forms, unusual spellings, even letters and the shapes of letters." Such exegesis, justified by the claim that no part of Scripture can be trivial, and characteristic both of much rabbinic material and of the allegorical interpretations of Origen and his heirs, has from of old been met with the commonsense objection: "Torah speaks in the language of people [= You're reading way too much into it]" (so R. Ishmael ben Elisha, of the exegesis of Rabbi Akiba ben Joseph; cf. Moore, *Judaism,* 87-89).

Scripture's accounts of God's people were seen to be repeated and at the same time transcended in Christ's and Christian experience.[56] Matthew tells of Jesus' birth and infancy in ways that deliberately recall Scripture's stories of Moses; but Jesus is greater than Moses.[57] The temptation of God's Son in the wilderness repeats a number of features of the story of Israel, "God's son" (Exod. 4:22-23), in the wilderness; but *this* Son of God, when tempted, proves faithful.[58] The feeding of the five thousand and the spiritual sustenance Jesus offers were prefigured in God's provision of manna to feed his people; but only the "bread" that Jesus gives "endures for eternal life" (John 6:27). The rejection Christ experienced, and ultimately his execution, fit all too well the pattern long established as the fate of God's messengers (Mark 12:1-12; Acts 7:52; 1 Thess. 2:14-15). As Jonah emerged from seeming death in the belly of the whale, so Christ emerged from death itself (Matt. 12:40). The role assigned to, and imperfectly fulfilled by, the Aaronic priests found perfect fulfillment in Christ, the great high priest (Heb. 4:14; 5:1-10; 7:1-28).

The early Christians were convinced that the scriptures of Israel were only correctly understood when Christ was seen at their center. Conversely, Christ himself was understood in the light of Israel's scriptures. Jesus' conception of his own mission was undoubtedly shaped by Scripture, and his disciples were no disciples if they were not, in some measure, brought to share the same conception.[59] That Jesus' crucifixion represented the fulfillment rather than the frustration of his divine commission was ensured but not explained by his resurrection: the mysterious purpose of God in "handing Jesus over" to such a death was discerned through a fresh appreciation of Isaiah 53. The present status and activity of the risen Christ were illuminated by one of the New Testament's favorite texts, Psalm 110:1 (e.g., Acts 2:34-36). Every scriptural text that the early Christians interpreted as foreshadowing Christ contributed at the same time to their understanding

---

56. Cf. Goppelt, *Typos*. Again, the Christian practice had its precedents. In prophetic literature, Judah's release from captivity in Babylon was described in terms that echoed the deliverance from Egypt (Isa. 11:15-16; 43:16-21; 51:9-11; Jer. 16:14-15); the idealized reign of David established the pattern for what the messianic age would be like (Isa. 11:1-5; Jer. 23:5; Ezek. 34:23-24).

57. See Brown, *Birth*, 112-16; Allison, *Moses*.

58. See Gerhardsson, *Testing*.

59. Cf. Allison, *History*, 78-82; Chilton and Evans, "Scriptures." Indeed, it is likely that events such as the "triumphal" entry into Jerusalem and the cleansing of the temple were deliberately undertaken by Jesus in order to fulfill Scripture. Cf. Sanders, *Jesus*, 254; Davies and Allison, *Matthew*, 3.113-14, 136-37.

of his mission. He was the second Adam, the prototype of a new humanity (1 Cor. 15:45-49), whose obedience overturned the consequences of the first Adam's transgression (Rom. 5:12-19). He was the prophet like Moses, to whose voice all must give heed (Acts 3:22-23), and so on. Most significantly, when the early Christians saw Christ in Old Testament references to the "word" (Ps. 33:6) or the "wisdom" (Prov. 3:19) with which God created the cosmos (John 1:1-3; Col. 1:16), and when they applied to Christ Old Testament references to the Lord God himself (e.g., John 12:41 [cf. Isa. 6:1]; Rom. 10:13 [Joel 2:32]; Phil. 2:10-11 [cf. Isa. 45:23]; Heb. 1:10-12 [Ps. 102:25-27]), we may be sure that Scripture was informing their Christology as much as Christology was dictating their reading of Scripture. Scripture was an irreplaceable witness to Christ; it was irreplaceable, too, as the framework within which Christ was understood.

Still, the early Christian conviction that Scripture is ultimately about Christ leaves unexplained the relationship between Christ and the center of Scripture for non-Christian Jews: the Torah[60] given by God to Moses. Non-Christian Jews had their own parties, with different interpretations of Torah's statutes and contested views of who were Torah's authoritative interpreters. But they were united in their devotion to Torah: "according to the law," one was a Pharisee (Phil. 3:5), or a Sadducee, or perhaps an Essene. If, in one sense, the earliest followers of Jesus constituted yet another first-century Jewish sect — they, too, claimed to be the true interpreters and legitimate inheritors of God's promises to Israel in Scripture — it must be added that what separated them from other Jewish sects was not their own distinctive approach to the law of Moses (indeed, on that subject there were issues that remained to be resolved within their own communities) but faith in Jesus as Israel's Messiah and the world's Savior.

How were the early Christians to read what, for their contemporaries — if not for themselves — was the core of the Scripture that they, too, revered?[61] To deny that the law had been given by God would have been an easy solution: as we shall see, it was in fact proposed by some in the second century. But Torah's importance in Scripture, and Scripture's importance to the early Christians, made such a proposal unthinkable to the first believers in Christ. Yet for all but the most conservative of their

---

60. In Second Temple Jewish literature, the term is used in different ways, one of which (and the one in view here) is to designate the sum of commandments and prohibitions given by God to Israel at Sinai. See S. Westerholm, "Meaning."

61. Trypho no doubt speaks for many Jews when he wonders how Christians can "expect to obtain some good thing from God" when they "do not obey His commandments" (Justin Martyr, *Dialogue with Trypho* 10).

number,[62] the redemption wrought by Christ and the new age introduced by his resurrection made it unthinkable that the law — whose divine origins they did not question — should continue to play the same role as it had before.

The apostle Paul focused on the *soteriological* aspects of the law. The law promised life to those who kept its commandments (Lev. 18:5, quoted in Rom. 10:5; Gal. 3:12; cf. Rom. 7:10); on judgment day, the "doers of the law" would be found righteous (Rom. 2:13). The principle was clear, but had it proved possible for human beings to be righteous in this way, Christ would not have needed to die (Gal. 2:21; cf. 3:21). And when Scripture declared that "no one living is found righteous before [God]" (Ps. 143:2), that assessment must include those who strive for righteousness by keeping the law (Rom. 3:20; Gal. 2:16). Thus, though the law's commands are "holy, just, and good" (Rom. 7:12), and though a manifestation of God's glory accompanied its revelation (2 Cor. 3:7, 9), the practical effect of its giving was to exacerbate the rebelliousness of the human heart (Rom. 7:7-11) and activate the law's curse on all who transgress it (Gal. 3:10). The divine order introduced by the law proved to be an order of condemnation and death (2 Cor. 3:7, 9; Rom. 7:10).

The law, divinely given, retained a limited place in God's plan. It served to reveal the character and pervasiveness of human sin (Rom. 3:20; 7:7, 13), but its validity was meant all along to be temporary (Gal. 3:19, 23-25; cf. 2 Cor. 3:11). From the law and its curse, Christ has set believers free (Gal. 3:13; 4:5; cf. Rom. 7:6; Gal. 2:19); righteousness is theirs, not by the terms of the law (which they did not meet), but as a gift granted by God to those who believe (Rom. 3:21-22; 5:17; Phil. 3:9).[63] Now they live, not under law, but under grace (Rom. 6:14-15). And even though the moral requirements of the old order overlap with those of the new, and though the love that flows through believers as the gift of God's Spirit in effect fulfills the righteousness aimed at by the law (Rom. 13:8-10; Gal. 5:14, 22-23), Paul generally expresses the ethics of Christian living in terms of Christian principles (e.g., 1 Cor. 6:12-20; Gal. 5:16-24) rather than by citing the corresponding demands of a former dispensation.[64]

The epistle to the Hebrews focuses on the *cultic* aspects of Torah: its

62. Cf. Acts 15:1, 5. Paul's Galatian opponents were among them (Gal. 4:21), and he feared that their representatives might trouble believers in Philippi (Phil. 3:2). For the later period, see Skarsaune, "Ebionites."

63. That God was right in granting righteousness to sinners required, however, Christ's atonement of their sins (Rom. 3:25-26).

64. Cf. S. Westerholm, *Perspectives*, 408-49.

priesthood, sanctuary, and sacrifices. The planned obsolescence of these elements is signaled within Scripture itself (7:11; cf. 8:13); lacking the capacity to cope with the reality of human sin (7:11, 18-19; 9:6-10; 10:1-4, 11), they have been displaced by the perfect high priesthood of Christ, his once-for-all sacrifice for sin, and his subsequent entry into the heavenly sanctuary and the very presence of God (7:26-28; 9:13-14, 24-26; 10:12-14). None of this is meant to suggest, however, that the cult of the Mosaic order had not been divinely ordained (through angelic mediation; cf. Heb. 2:2; 9:19-20). Unable itself to bring sinful human beings into communion with God, its rites nonetheless served to draw attention to their dilemma (10:3) and provided a foreshadowing — a kind of interpretive framework, we might say — of the redemption to be effected through Christ (10:1; cf. 9:9).

The Gospel of Matthew focuses on the *moral* aspects of Mosaic law. The compassion and forgiveness that Jesus extends to "sinners" must not be misconstrued, as though his demands for righteousness are less than those of Moses. This appears to be the thrust of Matthew 5:17-20 rather than an insistence on literal observance of every statute in Torah, including those of ritual purity, tithing, and the like.[65] Indeed, in Matthew 5:31-42 and 19:3-9, Jesus declares that provisions of Mosaic law are inadequate as a statement of God's will, presumably in each case because they represented concessions made to human sinfulness; and though much of Matthew's Gospel consists of instructions given by Jesus to his disciples, he never tells them to observe Sabbath laws, tithe, or maintain ritual purity.[66] Naturally, Jesus does not condemn "scribes and Pharisees" for observing such laws; but he lampoons their scrupulousness in external matters and neglect of matters more important (Matt. 23:23-26); and he suggests that, in the end, purity of heart alone is decisive (5:8; 15:11, 17-20; 23:26). The essence of the whole law is found in the commandments to love God and neighbor (22:37-40; cf. 7:12). In short, though the Matthean Jesus subtracts not a whit from the demands of righteousness made in Mosaic law, the contours of the righteousness God requires are defined by the teaching of Christ: the invitation to take up his yoke (Matt. 11:28-30) transforms as it adopts language traditionally used of the Torah.[67]

---

65. Note both what is denied in Matt. 5:17 and what is insisted on in v. 20. Is the point of 7:17-23 any different?

66. Followers of Jesus are in effect told to pay the temple tax *for strategic reasons* (i.e., "not to give offense"; Matt. 17:24-27); but they are explicitly said to be under no obligation to do so. For strategic reasons ("that I might win those under the law") Paul, too, lived as a Jew among Jews, though insisting on his freedom from any such obligation (1 Cor. 9:19-23).

67. See Acts 15:10; Gal. 5:1; *m. Avot* 3:5. Cf. Davies and Allison, *Matthew*, 2.289-90 (on

One other early Christian reading of the law of Moses is worth mentioning here, this time from outside the New Testament.[68] An anonymous writing traditionally known as the *Epistle of Barnabas* and dating from the end of the first or beginning of the second century insists that, in observing Torah's laws literally, Israel had missed their true significance. Like the author of the epistle to the Hebrews, the author goes on to interpret various aspects of Israel's cultic law as designed to foreshadow Christ, their true meaning being "plain to us" though "obscure" to Jews (*Barn.* 8:7). True circumcision is spiritual, not physical (*Barn.* 9:4-5; cf. Phil. 3:2-3); references to Sabbath rest are meant to point toward the day when God will make all things new; the temple in which God dwells is not a building (a heathenish conception) but the people of God (*Barn.* 16:1-10; cf. 1 Cor. 3:16; Eph. 2:19-22). As for the food laws, Israel was misled by the "desire of the flesh" into thinking that they referred to real food, thus missing their spiritual (i.e., allegorical) sense (*Barn.* 10.9).[69] As an example of the latter, he cites an ever-wise principle: "Don't associate with people who are like pigs" (*Barn.* 10.3).

The conviction that Christians are not only in possession of the true interpretation of Scripture but (as the true "children of Abraham" [Gal. 3:7, 29]) also the rightful inheritors of its promises to Israel seems to be common to all the early Christians.[70] Furthermore, designations once given to God's covenant people of old are routinely appropriated for the people of the "new covenant" (e.g., 1 Pet. 2:9).[71] But Paul at least insists that, inasmuch as the promises God made to the patriarchs are irrevocable, Israel's present unbelief will one day give way to faith (Rom. 11:23), and

---

Matt. 11:29): "Jewish teachers commonly spoke of the yoke of the Torah. . . . The identification of Jesus with Torah makes Jesus the full revelation of God and of his will for man." Cf. Deines, "Righteousness" (an updated summary of his *Gerechtigkeit*), with ample references to other literature.

68. For a concise general treatment of various understandings of the Mosaic law in the New Testament, see S. Westerholm, "Law."

69. The *Letter of Aristeas* 142-69 had already explained the purpose of the food laws in terms of their allegorical significance; and Philo interpreted such laws — as he interpreted other aspects of the Pentateuch — allegorically. In neither of these cases, however, was the interpretation intended to do away with the literal observance of the laws. Paul himself puts forward an allegorical interpretation of one provision of the law in 1 Cor. 9:9-10. This and other Pauline ventures into allegory (1 Cor. 10:4; Gal. 4:21-31; cf. Eph. 5:31-32) would of course be cited by Origen in support of his approach to Scripture.

70. E.g., Rom. 9:25, 26 (Hos. 2:23; 1:10; cf. 1 Pet. 2:10); Rom. 10:20 (Isa. 65:1); Gal. 4:27 (Isa. 54:1). Wendel (*Interpretation*) documents the point with reference to the writings of Luke and Justin Martyr.

71. The term itself is, of course, taken from Scripture (Jer. 31:31-34; cf. 1 Cor. 11:25; 2 Cor. 3:6; Heb. 8:8-13).

God will redeem his (now partly hardened) people Israel (Rom. 11:25-32). Matthew, too — and presumably for the same reason — holds out hope for the ultimate salvation, through their now rejected Messiah, of the Jewish people (Matt. 23:37-39).

On a practical level, the Old Testament provided the early Christians (and their Jewish contemporaries) both with examples of proper (and improper) behavior and with words of exhortation, encouragement, and warning: Scripture is "profitable for teaching, for reproof, for correction, and for training in righteousness" (2 Tim. 3:16). To multiply references would only labor the obvious; but Hebrews 11 draws on the Old Testament for a chain of positive examples; 1 Corinthians 10:1-12 supplies a negative counterpart; 1 Peter 3:10-12 uses Psalm 34 to admonish; Matthew 24:37-39 uses the days of Noah to warn; and Hebrews 12:5-6 finds encouragement for those experiencing hard times in the words of Proverbs 3:11-12.

One other aspect of Jewish readings of Torah merits attention. Meditation on Torah "day and night" is enjoined in Scripture itself (Josh. 1:8; Ps. 1:2). Psalm 119 speaks of "learning" God's commandments (v. 7), of "treasuring" them (11), "meditating on" them (15), "delighting in" them (16), "longing for" them (20), "clinging to" them (31), "hoping in" them (43), even "loving" them (47). To seek and delight in God's commandments is to seek and delight in God (119:2, 10, 12, etc.). The people of the Dead Sea Scrolls took turns at appointed hours, so that, within the community as a whole, Torah was studied continuously "day and night" (1QS VI, 6-8). The most famous tractate of the Mishnah *(Avot)* claims that human beings were created for the study of Torah (2.8). Where ten people — or five, three, even two — gather and occupy themselves with Torah, God's presence rests upon them. Indeed, it rests on single individuals when they study God's law (3.6). And where people discuss God's law at the meal table, "it is as if they had eaten from the table of God" (3.3).

The counterpart to this devotion to Torah in early Christian communities is found in reverence for "the word of Christ," a "word" that included both words that Christ had spoken and the message of his salvation. That word was to "reside" in them "richly," and to serve as the substance of mutual teaching and admonishment (Col. 3:16). The Johannine Jesus calls on his disciples to "abide in [him]," as a branch "abides" in the vine (John 15:4, 5); and part of what it means for believers to "abide" in Christ is to have Christ's words "abiding" in them (15:7), the subject of their meditation as well as the object of their obedience. In this respect, too, Christ took the place among early Christians that was occupied by Torah among their contemporary non-Christian Jews.

Second-Century Challenges

The only Bible Jesus and his disciples knew was the Jewish scriptures. Jesus defined his mission by its words. His followers found in Scripture the key to understanding Christ, in Christ the key to understanding Scripture. Astonishingly, in the second century, there were those claiming allegiance to Jesus who insisted that he represented the antithesis rather than the fulfillment of Scripture, and that in his mission he opposed, and was opposed by, the God of Scripture. Modern scholars, wary of the value judgment implied in talk of "heretics," should have no hesitation applying it here. These, if any, were the real thing: so willful, bold, and creative[72] in their departures from the message of Jesus and his apostles that, had they prevailed, the church would have lost connection in all but name to the Jesus it claimed as its redeemer.[73]

We may be brief, since theirs is not our story; some account is necessary, however, since our story proper begins with Irenaeus, and his greatest work was composed to refute them. For our purposes, it will suffice to speak of Marcion, on the one hand, and various claimants (here grouped together) of revealed *gnosis* (knowledge), on the other. Both regarded the Creator God revealed in the Old Testament as an inferior deity; with some simplification, we may say that Marcion did so on moral grounds, the claimants of *gnosis* on metaphysical.

Marcion grew up in the church in Sinope, a port on the southern shores of the Black Sea. Around 140, he came to Rome, and was attached to the local church before being excommunicated for his heretical views in 144. He was able, nonetheless, to win many converts to his position; in the late second century (he himself died around 160), Marcionites represented a serious threat to the mainstream church. However dramatic his departure from the message of Jesus, we must concede both that he derived his position from his reading of Scripture, and that many — to this day — read Scripture similarly.

---

72. Adolf von Harnack begins his classic treatment of Marcion with the words, "The man to whom the following pages are devoted was the founder of a religion" (*Marcion*, 1).

73. Cf. Minns, *Irenaeus*, 17: "If we can speak of a 'Great Church' at all, this is at least partly because polemical theologians like Irenaeus identified certain views as incompatible with Christian truth and declared those who persisted in holding them to be beyond Christian fellowship. Often, this was a thoroughly sensible line to take. There seems, even now, little point in worshiping the Creator of all material things as good, all-powerful, provident and beneficent, alongside someone who despises this creator as an ignorant and vindictive tyrant whose power is relative and limited."

It seemed to Marcion that the God he encountered in the Old Testament is a God of wrath, whereas the God of Jesus is one of love; the God of the Old Testament enforces strict justice, whereas the Father of Jesus shows mercy; the God of the Old Testament promotes violence and war, whereas the God of the Savior brings peace. Marcion pressed the logic of this reading to its conclusion: the Old Testament and the New speak of different deities; the mission of Jesus on behalf of the (hitherto unknown) heavenly Father was to bring deliverance from the law and the power of the Old Testament's creator deity.

Marcion found support for his views in the letters of Paul. Noting, in the opening chapters of Galatians, Paul's insistence that he had received his gospel directly from Christ and not from human beings, and that he was opposed by false apostles (indeed, by Peter himself [Gal. 2:11-14; cf. 2 Cor. 11:13]), Marcion concluded that Paul was Christ's only true apostle, while others remained blindly in the service of the creator. That — as Marcion claimed — Christ brought deliverance from the latter's law was similarly based on a misconstrual of Galatians. Moreover, since Paul was the only true apostle, it followed that only his epistles and the Gospel of Luke (identified as Paul's Gospel) were authoritative. This convenient dismissal of other writings that contradicted Marcion's views was matched by an elimination of inconvenient passages in Luke and the Pauline epistles themselves on the grounds that they must have been introduced by false apostles.

The *gnosis*-claiming dismissers of the Old Testament's God whom Irenaeus opposed were motivated in large part by their contempt for the physical body and the material world, both of which they saw as imprisoning the divine spark possessed by those predestined for salvation.[74] The Creator of the material cosmos — the Demiurge — can only have been an inferior divinity, a distant emanation from the transcendent deity; creation itself was a tragic mistake. Christ, cast in the role of redeemer, (1) must have been sent from the unfallen, heavenly realm to deliver the elect from their cosmic prison; (2) could not have taken on an ordinary physical body, since his nature would not have allowed that; and (3) must have redeemed the elect by imparting to them knowledge *(gnosis)* of their true condition, and of the means to escape their captivity and return to the heavenly realm from which they came and to which they belonged.

74. The view that the visible, changeable world is inferior to an invisible world of eternal forms was widespread enough in the Greco-Roman world to give resonance and credibility to a gnostic-type view of redemption. Cf. Pearson, *Gnosticism*, 16: "Gnostic dualism is hardly conceivable without Platonist dualism. Gnostic dualism can be seen as a reinterpretation of traditional Platonist dualism."

There is, of course, much more to their schemes, and there are distinctions to be drawn between various *gnosis*-claiming groups; these need not concern us here. It is important to note, however, that they found support for their views in highly idiosyncratic interpretations of Scripture (see the discussion of Irenaeus's responses in Chapter 3 below) as well as in claims to be in possession of secret revelations given by Jesus to particular disciples and passed on by the latter to *gnosis*-gifted teachers.

Both Marcion and the claimants of *gnosis* cited Scripture in support of their positions. Irenaeus, in opposing what he saw as false interpretations of Scripture, was forced to spell out principles of its proper interpretation, making him a logical starting point for our survey of Christian readers of Scripture.

CHAPTER 3

Irenaeus

The earliest followers of Jesus knew no other scriptures than those of Second Temple Judaism; what set them apart was their faith in "the word" of Christ's gospel. In the beginning, that "word" was exclusively a spoken word, a medium eminently suited to the message: in the proclaimed word of the gospel, God — through his ambassadors — addressed people with an offer of salvation and a call to faith. When, in time, circumstances demanded that the church's testimony to Christ be written,[1] the resulting writings were still understood as vehicles of divine communication: they were read aloud as such (alongside the Old Testament scriptures) in meetings of believers.

Well into the second century the early Christians continued to distinguish "Scripture" from "the word." With few exceptions, quotations from "Scripture" meant Old Testament citations; "the word" (or "word of the Lord," or "word of God"), when not a title for Christ ("the Word"), meant some aspect of the message about Christ, indifferently drawn from

---

1. Irenaeus gives the following account (*A.H.* 3.1.1): "We have learned from none others the plan of our salvation, than from those through whom the Gospel has come down to us, which they did at one time proclaim in public, and at a later time, by the will of God, handed down to us in the Scriptures, to be the ground and pillar of our faith. For, after our Lord rose from the dead, [the apostles] were invested with power from on high when the Holy Spirit came down [upon them], were filled from all [His gifts], and had perfect knowledge; they departed to the ends of the earth, preaching the glad tidings. . . . Matthew also issued a written Gospel among the Hebrews in their own dialect, while Peter and Paul were preaching at Rome, and laying the foundations of the Church. After their departure, Mark, the disciple and interpreter of Peter, did also hand down to us in writing what had been preached by Peter. Luke also, the companion of Paul, recorded in a book the Gospel preached by him. Afterwards, John, the disciple of the Lord, who also had leaned upon his breast, did himself publish a Gospel during his residence at Ephesus in Asia."

oral tradition or a written source. As time went on, memories of what the Lord had said and done were increasingly shaped by written accounts recognized as reliable. Dependence on authoritative texts from the days of the apostles can only have increased when wildly different portrayals of Jesus began to proliferate. By the end of the second century, the origins of the four Gospels and the Pauline epistles were sufficiently remote in time, and their recognition as authoritative sufficiently self-evident, that the terminology "Scripture" seemed as appropriate for them as for the writings of the Old Testament. Irenaeus had (in effect) a Christian Bible, with "New Testament" writings to balance the Old.

To be sure, when Irenaeus speaks of the "old testament" and the "new," he appears to be referring to covenants rather than to bodies of writings (e.g., *A.H.* 4.9.1; 4.28.1; 4.32.2). On the other hand, he does use the term "Scripture" for the Gospels[2] and epistles as well as for the law and the prophets (e.g., *A.H.* 1.3.6; 3.12.12). And though he does not clearly define the boundaries of Scripture, the central elements are those of the Christian Bible today.[3] The writing of all its parts was prompted by the Spirit of God (see, e.g., *A.H.* 3.7.2 [Paul]; 3.10.3 [David]; 3.21.4 [the prophets]; 5.30.4 [John, author of Revelation]), and hence "perfect" throughout (*A.H.* 2.28.2). As Adam and Eve were invited to eat from "every tree of the garden" (Gen. 2:16), so the Spirit of God invites the church to eat "from every Scripture of the Lord" (*A.H.* 5.20.2).

Irenaeus wrote no commentaries on Scripture or handbooks on its interpretation. His importance for our purposes is twofold: (1) called upon to defend the *Old* Testament as a revelation of the same God whose Word was Jesus Christ, Irenaeus did much to show how the Bible of the Jews can be read as *Christian* Scripture; and (2) called upon to refute the idiosyncratic readings of Scripture by which teachers of heresy supported

---

2. In a famous passage, Irenaeus finds it, in the very nature of things, both appropriate and necessary that there should be four, and only four, authoritative Gospels (*A.H.* 3.11.8): "The Word . . . has given us the Gospel under four aspects, but bound together by one Spirit." He then points out the distinctive aspect of Christ emphasized in each Gospel: in John, his "glorious generation from the Father"; in Luke, his "priestly character"; in Matthew, his true humanity; in Mark, the prophetic character of the gospel. Cf. Resch, "Fittingness," 77-78.

3. In the case of the Old Testament, Irenaeus makes occasional reference to apocryphal/deuterocanonical books, and his accounts of Old Testament stories occasionally include noncanonical traditions (e.g., *A.H.* 4.16.2; *Dem.* 24). He makes much of the four canonical Gospels, Acts, the Pauline epistles (including the Pastorals), 1 John, and Revelation; the odd reference to 1 Peter, 2 John, and the Shepherd of Hermas; apparent citations of Hebrews, James, and 2 Peter, though without naming his source; no apparent reference to 3 John or Jude.

their views, Irenaeus defined principles of interpretation that have proved important for its reading ever since. After a brief summary of the little we know about his life, I will address these topics in turn.

Life

As noted in the preceding chapter, Irenaeus (his dates are, roughly, A.D. 130-200) grew up in western Asia Minor (modern Turkey), where as a young man he had known Polycarp, bishop of Smyrna, who, in turn, had known John and other disciples of Jesus. (This spiritual genealogy was important to Irenaeus [cf. *A.H.* 3.3.4; Eusebius, *E.H.* 5.20].) When and how Irenaeus went from Asia Minor in the East to Gaul (modern France) in the West is not known; but he is named as the bearer of a letter from the Gallic churches of Vienne and Lyons to Rome (Eusebius, *E.H.* 5.4) around the time when horrendous persecutions broke out against those churches (A.D. 177).[4] Any temptation to reduce his later writings against heretics to unwarranted assertions of ecclesiastical power should be tempered with the realization that, in replacing the martyred bishop of Lyons, Irenaeus took on a position more akin to that of beleaguered church leaders in many Middle Eastern countries today than to that of officeholders in the post-Constantinian church: his effective "powers" were limited to those of persuasion.[5] A much-traveled man — a veritable "representative Christian" of the late second century[6] — he knew the churches of Rome in addition to those of Asia Minor and Gaul. Eusebius (*E.H.* 5.24) preserves a letter he wrote to the bishop of Rome (190), rebuking him for the lack of tolerance he showed toward Asian Christians who wanted to preserve their own customs for observing Easter. The late tradition that he himself died a martyr's death is by no means implausible, though it probably owes

---

4. Substantial parts of a letter describing the persecution and the stories of individual martyrs are preserved in Eusebius, *E.H.* 5.1-2. That Irenaeus himself drafted the letter is a plausible, though not demonstrable, suggestion.

5. Minns notes that Irenaeus never in fact calls himself a bishop, and that it is unclear "whether he exercised this office alone, or as a member of a college of elders and overseers" (*Irenaeus,* 2).

6. So Bingham, "Irenaeus," 139; cf. Grant, *Irenaeus,* 1: "In his own person he united the major traditions of Christendom from Asia Minor, Syria, Rome, and Gaul, although his acquaintance with Palestine, Greece, and Egypt was minimal. We cannot say that he represents the whole of second-century Christianity, but he does represent the majority views outside Alexandria."

more to the sense that that was what happened to faithful church leaders of his day than to an actual recollection of his fate.

Irenaeus was a prolific author, but his only works to survive (apart from a few fragments of other writings) are the massive *Against Heresies,*[7] in five books, written and circulated in several installments while Eleutherus was bishop in Rome (175-189), and the somewhat later *Demonstration of the Apostolic Preaching.* The former is primarily known from a Latin translation, supplemented by an Armenian version; the latter is known only from its translation into Armenian. In antiquity as in the modern world, Irenaeus was famous as the author of *Against Heresies.*

The Old Testament as Christian Scripture

Like most Christians of all ages, Irenaeus did not read the Old Testament in its original language.[8] Unlike many Christians today, who regret their inability to do so, Irenaeus was unapologetic. More credulous than some early church fathers, he accepted at face value enhanced versions of the legend related in the *Letter of Aristeas* by which it was not just the Pentateuch but the entire Old Testament that had been translated into Greek at the behest of Ptolemy in Egypt.[9] Moreover, each of the seventy translators was now said to have worked independently of the others and to have translated the entire Old Testament; and, *mirabile dictu,* the independently produced translations turned out to be identical in every detail (*A.H.* 3.21.2). If we grant the premises, the conclusion that a notable miracle had occurred is, indeed, incontrovertible. Irenaeus felt justified in claiming that the Old Testament in Greek was no less the product of divine inspiration than the original texts in Hebrew (*A.H.* 3.21.2, 4). More prosaically — but perhaps more persuasively — he cites as a further argument for accepting the translation that it was used by the apostles themselves (*A.H.* 3.21.3).

As we have seen, no conviction was more determinative of early Christian reading of the Old Testament scriptures than the belief that Christ had fulfilled them: the claim (which has its origins in Jesus' own

---

7. Or *Refutation and Overthrow of Knowledge Falsely So Called* (the title given in Eusebius, *E.H.* 5.7).

8. This did not, however, prevent him (nor has it prevented others) from an unfortunate suggestion as to what a text in Scripture *really* meant in the original language: in *Dem.* 43, he proposes that the Hebrew of Gen. 1:1 is to be translated: "A Son in the beginning God established then heaven and earth."

9. Cf. Hengel, *Septuagint,* 25-56.

self-understanding) seems fundamental to Christian faith. But, as we shall see, Christians from antiquity to the present day have differed widely in the degree to which they have been prepared to see particular Old Testament texts as prophecies of Christ. Irenaeus must be reckoned among the more expansive.[10] Though he gives many examples, there is nothing original in his doing so, and we may be content here with a few illustrations and observations on these and other ways in which he is merely representative of early Christian approaches to the Old Testament, before addressing two of his more distinctive contributions.

It is doubtful whether any New Testament reference to a prophecy fulfilled by Christ or his church is omitted from the wide-ranging lists supplied by Irenaeus. But the category (in Irenaeus as already in Justin) appears to have expanded exponentially under the belief that the true point of a scriptural text is often concealed beneath its surface meaning.[11] Irenaeus himself says as much about the texts he sees as prophetic:

> The treasure hid in the Scriptures is Christ, since He was pointed out by means of types and parables. Hence His human nature could not be understood, prior to the consummation of those things which had been predicted, that is, the advent of Christ. . . . Jeremiah also says, "In the last days they shall understand these things" [Jer. 23:20]. For every prophecy, before its fulfilment, is to men [full of] enigmas and ambiguities. But when the time has arrived, and the prediction has come to pass, then the prophecies have a clear and certain exposition. And for this reason, indeed, when at this present time the law is read to the Jews, it is like a fable; for they do not possess the explanation of all things pertaining to the advent of the Son of God, which took place in human nature; but when it is read by the Christians, it is a treasure, hid indeed in a field, but brought to light by the cross of Christ. (*A.H.* 4.26.1)

Thus, in addition to the standard Old Testament texts that Christians have always viewed as messianic, we find texts such as Isa. 57:1-2 (in its incarnation in the Septuagint) given novel interpretations:

10. He was hardly, however, more expansive than Justin Martyr; Irenaeus appears to have drawn on the latter's *Dialogue with Trypho*.

11. The belief was, of course, shared by non-Christian Jews and characterizes much Jewish exegesis as well. Cf. Kugel, *As It Was*, 18: "The first assumption that all ancient interpreters seem to share is that the Bible is a fundamentally cryptic document. That is, all interpreters are fond of maintaining that although Scripture may appear to be saying X, what it really means is Y."

Lo, how the just perisheth, and no man layeth it to heart; and just men are taken away, and no man understandeth; for the just man is taken away from before the face of iniquity. His burial shall be peace, He hath been taken away from the midst. And who else is "the just man" to perfection, but the Son of God . . . ? But in saying: *His burial shall be peace,* he tells how He died for the sake of our salvation — for "in peace" means, in that of salvation — and that by His death, those who were before mutually hostile and opposed, believing with one accord in Him, will have peace with one another, made well-disposed and friendly because of common faith in Him; as also happens. But the words: *He hath been taken away from the midst* refer to His resurrection from the dead — for He was no more seen as one dead, after His burial. (*Dem.* 72)

Daniel's stone "cut out without hands" (Dan. 2:34) has become a prophecy of the virgin birth: "[Christ's] coming into the world was not by the operation of human hands . . . that is, Joseph taking no part with regard to it, but Mary alone co-operating with the pre-arranged plan" (*A.H.* 3.21.7). Isaiah (65:2) speaks of God's compassionate but rejected appeals for the loyalty of his people by saying: "I held out my hands all day long to a rebellious people"; Irenaeus takes the outstretched hands, with their compassionate appeal, to be those of Christ on the cross (*Dem.* 79; cf. *A.H.* 4.33.12). In the warning of Deuteronomy 28:66 ("And thy life shall be hanging before thine eyes, and thou shalt fear night and day, neither shalt thou trust thy life" — a punishment to be imposed should God's people disobey his commands), the reference to "life . . . hanging" was all Irenaeus needed to see another reference to the crucifixion.[12] The psalmist expresses his supreme trust in God when, in the midst of trouble, he gives himself to sleep, assured that, sustained by God, he will rise again (Ps. 3:5); for Irenaeus, he is prophesying Christ's resurrection (*Dem.* 73). In short, the Old Testament is all about Christ.[13]

Already in the New Testament, narratives and institutions from the

---

12. *Dem.* 79; cf. *A.H.* 4.10.2. The same interpretation is found in Tertullian, Cyprian, and other church fathers.

13. The reminder of Barton (*Writings,* 70-71) is very much in order: "To a modern reader the force of the argument from prophecy may seem greatly diminished by the fact that it often requires the alleged 'prophecies' to be read in a far from natural sense. . . . Once one grants that holy texts are liable to contain hidden and mysterious meanings, there is no reason why the interpretations given by Paul or the evangelists [or Justin or Irenaeus] should not be the right ones. Thus the argument from prophecy, ramshackle as it may look to us, was quite capable of being a serious form of argument in the ancient context."

Old Testament were construed as "types," real enough in their own time, but gaining their full and intended significance when understood as foreshadowing some aspect of Christ's mission or the life of the church (so, e.g., the Passover lamb [1 Cor. 5:7-8]; the rites of the Day of Atonement [Heb. 9:7-14, 24-28]; the Levitical priesthood [Heb. 7:5-28]).[14] This category, too, expands exponentially with Justin and Irenaeus. Only a few of the juicier examples can be cited here. Moses took to wife "an Ethiopian woman, whom he thus made an Israelitish one"; in so doing, he showed by anticipation that Gentiles would become part of the people of God (*A.H.* 4.20.12, alluding to Num. 12:1). Jacob received as his wages "various coloured sheep" (Gen. 30:37-43); similarly, "the wages of Christ are human beings, who from various and diverse nations come together into one cohort of faith" (*A.H.* 4.21.3). The dew that fell first on Gideon's fleece but not on the earth around it, then on the earth around it but not on the fleece (Judg. 6:36-40), represents the Holy Spirit: before Christ's coming, it fell on Israel but not the Gentiles; after Christ's appearing, it has been given to Gentiles but not Jews (*A.H.* 3.17.3).

> As [God] patiently suffered Jonah to be swallowed by the whale, not that he should be swallowed up and perish altogether, but that, having been cast out again, he might be the more subject to God, and might glorify Him the more . . . so also, from the beginning, did God permit man to be swallowed up by the great whale, who was the author of transgression, not that he should perish altogether when so engulphed; but . . . that man, receiving an unhoped-for salvation from God, might rise from the dead, and glorify God. (*A.H.* 3.20.1)

Like other early Christian readers of the Old Testament, Irenaeus occasionally gives allegorical interpretations to Old Testament texts whose relevance for Christian readers was not otherwise apparent ("for with God there is nothing without purpose or due signification" [*A.H.* 4.21.3]). As in the *Letter of Aristeas,* laws permitting the eating of "clean" but not "unclean" animals are construed as speaking of people whom one should, or should not, emulate (*A.H.* 5.8.4). Though at one time eager to preserve Isaiah 11:6 ("the wolf shall dwell with the lamb") as a prophecy of Christ's

14. Irenaeus himself supplies us with a quasi-definition: "For a type and emblem is, no doubt, sometimes diverse from the truth [signified] as to matter and substance; but it ought, as to the general form and features, to maintain a likeness [to what is typified], and in this way to shadow forth by means of things present those which are yet to come" (*A.H.* 2.23.1; cf. 2.20.4).

future kingdom (*A.H.* 5.33.4), Irenaeus later adopted the allegorical interpretation that saw its present fulfillment in the uniting, within the church, of peoples once hostile to each other (*Dem.* 61).

Finally, a christological reading of the Old Testament is apparent in Irenaeus, as in other early Christian writers (though not Augustine), when texts in which God is said to have appeared to human beings are interpreted as manifestations of God's "Word" or "Son."[15] Behind such interpretations lies the conviction that, since "no one has ever seen God [i.e., the Father]," it is necessarily the Son who reveals him (John 1:18; cf. Matt. 11:27), a principle operative supremely in the incarnation but in earlier manifestations of the deity as well (*Dem.* 45; *A.H.* 4.6.6; 4.10.1).[16] Thus it was the Son who walked and talked with Adam in the Garden of Eden (*Dem.* 12), discussed the fate of Sodom and Gomorrah with Abraham (*Dem.* 44), appeared to Jacob in a dream (*Dem.* 45), to Moses in the burning bush (*Dem.* 46), and so on. Moreover, it was the Son (or Word) of God who gave Moses and the prophets their message (*A.H.* 4.2.3; 4.7.2; cf. *Dem.* 5).

In all that has been said up to this point, Irenaeus is merely representative of early Christian readings of the Old Testament. If, in particular cases, his christological construal of the texts seems overly optimistic, from a Christian perspective he clearly got the "big picture" right: the God of the Old Testament *is* the God of Jesus Christ. And he used its pages (and the history it recounts) to prepare for Christ's coming.[17] In two respects, however, Irenaeus's approach to the Old Testament is distinctive.

1. Like his predecessors, Irenaeus believed that God intended Old Testament prophecies and types to provide confirmation of the truth of Christian faith.[18] But though arguments from fulfilled prophecy were first

---

15. Cf. Farkasfalvy, "Theology," 324.

16. Augustine, however, insisted that, inasmuch as the Son of God is fully divine, he must be as inaccessible to human sight as the Father (or the Spirit); no person of the divine Trinity can be perceived as they are in themselves, but only as they adopt a created medium (e.g., a human form or voice) to appear to, or communicate with, human beings. Any or all of the three persons of the Trinity may thus have been the subject of an Old Testament theophany. See book 2 of Augustine's *The Trinity*.

17. Irenaeus notes that Philip had no great difficulty bringing the Ethiopian eunuch to faith inasmuch as the latter had already been instructed by the prophets (*A.H.* 4.23.2, referring to Acts 8:26-39). Conversely, Paul necessarily "worked harder" than all those apostles whose mission field was the Jews (1 Cor. 15:10), since the Gentiles whom he evangelized lacked such instruction (*A.H.* 4.24.1).

18. Cf. *Dem.* 42: "That all these things would come to pass was foretold by the Spirit of God through the prophets, that those who served God in truth might believe firmly in them; for what was quite impossible to our nature, and therefore like to be little believed in

advanced in disputations with non-Christian Jews, who accepted the prophetic texts as sacred but denied their Christian interpretations, Irenaeus's argument from prophecy was primarily directed against Marcion and gnostics who, for different reasons, denied any positive connection between the mission of the Savior and the Old Testament scriptures. Against such people, Irenaeus argued that scriptures speaking of Christ and preparing for his coming must themselves be the revelation of the same God who sent the Savior.[19]

But Irenaeus goes beyond the proof from prophecy in showing continuity between the Old Testament and the New. Marcion had simplistically distinguished the God of the Old Testament, a God of law and strict judgment, from the Father of Christ, a God of mercy and love. Irenaeus remarks that, for God to be God, he cannot be just but not good, or good but not just; he must of necessity be both.[20] Irenaeus goes on to account for apparent differences between the Testaments by developing the idea (suggested by Gal. 3:23-25; 4:1-7) that humankind, when first created, was necessarily in a state of infancy.[21] As parents deal with children in different ways depending on their degree of maturity, so God necessarily dealt with human beings differently at different stages in their history, though always with the ultimate goal of bringing them into communion with himself: God "prepares man for His friendship" (*A.H.* 4.16.3).

That notion is strategically important to Irenaeus in that it enables him to show (against Marcion and the claimants of *gnosis*) how the same God can have imposed laws and regulations in the Old Testament that

---

by men, God caused to be announced in advance by the prophets, that from the prediction made long beforehand, when at last the event took place just as had been foretold, we might know that it was God, who had revealed to us in advance our redemption." See also *Dem.* 86; Farkasfalvy, "Theology," 320-24.

19. Cf. *A.H.* 4.10.1; 4.11.1. Some scholars believe that Justin's real (though not ostensible) purpose was the same in his *Dialogue with Trypho.* Cf. Barton, *Writings,* 72; Campenhausen, *Formation,* 88-91.

20. See *A.H.* 3.25.3: "Marcion, therefore, himself, by dividing God into two, maintaining one to be good and the other judicial, does in fact, on both sides, put an end to deity. For he that is the judicial one, if he be not good, is not God, because he from whom goodness is absent is not God at all; and again, he who is good, if he has no judicial power, suffers the same [loss] as the former, by being deprived of his character of deity." See also *A.H.* 4.28.1; 4.29.1.

21. Cf. *Dem.* 12: Though man was created "lord of the earth," he was "a little one; for he was a child and had need to grow so as to come to his full perfection. . . . But the man was a little one, and his discretion still undeveloped, wherefore also he was easily misled by the deceiver."

he did away with in the New (*A.H.* 3.12.11). But beyond its argumentative value, the idea that humanity, under divine tutelage, passed through various stages of development is in fact fundamental to his whole understanding of salvation history. Adam and Eve were created in "the innocence of childhood" (*Dem.* 14); the command to "increase and multiply" (Gen. 1:28) imposed on them the duty to grow in maturity as well as in numbers (*A.H.* 4.11.1; cf. 4.38.3). "Unaccustomed to, and unexercised in, perfect discipline," they could only learn by experience that obedience to God preserves life, while disobedience deprives them of it (*A.H.* 4.38.1; 4.39.1). It was natural, then, for God to deal with them as infants who were not ready for strong food (*A.H.* 4.38.1). Later, when "mankind had forgotten and fallen away and rebelled against God, He brought them into subjection through the Law, that they might learn that they had a Lord who was author and maker, who grants the breath of life; and to Him we must return homage by day and by night" (*Dem.* 8). The commands of the Decalogue are, indeed, such as should be practiced by human beings of any time and place (*A.H.* 4.13.1; 4.15.1). God, who has implanted them in human hearts (*A.H.* 4.15.1; 4.16.3), reiterated them for Israel. When Israel nonetheless turned to idolatry and expressed a desire to return to slavery in Egypt, God dealt with them appropriately — slaves as they were (*A.H.* 4.14.2) — by imposing further laws on them (*A.H.* 4.15.1). Moreover, they were required to offer God sacrifices and offerings of which he had no need, in order that they might learn to serve him. "For, as much as God is in want of nothing, so much does man stand in need of fellowship with God. For this is the glory of man, to continue and remain permanently in God's service" (*A.H.* 4.14.1).

The covenant God made with Israel, therefore, "was not given without reason, or to no purpose, or in an accidental sort of manner"; rather, "it subdued those to whom it was given to the service of God, for their benefit (for God needs no service from men), and exhibited a type of heavenly things, inasmuch as man was not yet able to see the things of God through means of immediate vision; and foreshadowed the images of those things which [now actually] exist in the Church, in order that our faith might be firmly established" (*A.H.* 4.32.2; cf. 4.14.3). It was, however, always God's purpose, when the right time (the "fullness of time") had come, to set free those bound by the laws of slavery in order that they might serve God freely, with lives transformed by faith.

> For the law, since it was laid down for those in bondage, used to instruct the soul by means of those corporeal objects that were of an external

nature, drawing it, as by a bond, to obey its commandments, that man might learn to serve God. But the Word set free the soul, and taught that through it the body should be willingly purified. Which having been accomplished, it followed as of course, that the bonds of slavery should be removed, to which man had now become accustomed, and that he should follow God without fetters. (*A.H.* 4.13.2)

Therefore also we have no need of the law as pedagogue. Behold, we speak with the Father and stand face to face with Him, become infants in malice, and made strong in all justice and propriety. For no more shall the law say: *Thou shalt not commit adultery,* to him who has not even conceived the desire of another's wife; or *thou shalt not kill,* to him who has put away from himself all anger and enmity; *thou shall not covet thy neighbour's field, or his ox, or his ass,* to those who make no account whatever of earthly things, but heap up profit in heaven. Nor *an eye for an eye and a tooth for a tooth,* to him who counts no man his enemy, but all his neighbours, and therefore cannot even put forth his hand to revenge. (*Dem.* 96)[22]

2. In Romans 5:14, Paul spoke of Adam as a "type" of Christ, and went on to insist that the effect of Christ's obedience was to offset (and more than offset) the disobedience of Adam. Irenaeus picked up the suggestion and ran with it: the unity of Old Testament and New is demonstrated by showing that the redemption accomplished by Christ corresponds point by point, but in a positive way, to each detail in the story of humanity's fall; only thus, according to Irenaeus's way of thinking, could it overcome the negative effects of the latter.[23] As was the case with Irenaeus's perceptions of fulfilled prophecy, we may say that the "big picture" Irenaeus presents (that Christ, as human, counters the effect of human sin) is essential to

---

22. In this paragraph, Irenaeus simply assumes that Christ's followers live up to his commands in the Sermon on the Mount.

23. The principle that only by a human's obedience could human sin be overcome was crucial to Irenaeus's argument, against the gnostics, in favor of Christ's real incarnation (*Dem.* 31; *A.H.* 3.18.7; 3.19.1). It lies behind his most famous words: "Our Lord Jesus Christ, who did, through his transcendent love, become what we are, that He might bring us to be even what He is Himself" (*A.H.* 5, preface). That Christ must have experienced *all* that humans experience in order to provide full redemption motivated Irenaeus's insistence that Christ, too, must have lived to, and died in, old age (*A.H.* 2.22.4-6). Christian tradition (perhaps taking into account its incongruity with the facts) has not shared Irenaeus's sense of the latter necessity.

Christian faith. But not all will find each point of correspondence he saw between Christ's "recapitulation"[24] and Adam's story convincing.

> From this earth, then, while it was still virgin [i.e., no rain had fallen upon it], God took dust and fashioned the man, the beginning of humanity. So the Lord, summing up afresh this man, reproduced the scheme of his incarnation, being born of a virgin by the Will and Wisdom of God, that He too might copy the incarnation of Adam. (*Dem.* 32; cf. *A.H.* 3.21.10)

> And just as it was through a virgin who disobeyed that man was stricken and fell and died, so too it was through the Virgin, who obeyed the word of God, that man resuscitated by life received life. (*Dem.* 33; cf. *A.H.* 3.22.4)

> And the sin that was wrought through the tree was undone by the obedience of the tree, obedience to God whereby the Son of man was nailed to the tree, destroying the knowledge of evil, and bringing in and conferring the knowledge of good; and evil is disobedience to God, as obedience to God is good. . . . So by the obedience, whereby [Christ] obeyed unto death, hanging on the tree, He undid the old disobedience wrought in the tree. (*Dem.* 34; cf. *A.H.* 5.16.3)

Principles for Interpreting Scripture

As early followers of Jesus searched the (Old Testament) scriptures for prophecies fulfilled by Christ, *gnosis*-claiming heretics searched early Christian (and Old Testament) writings for texts that they could construe as supporting their positions. Again, theirs is not our story, so a few examples must suffice.

In one gnostic scheme (*A.H.* 1.1.1–1.2.3), the "fullness" of divinity began with Depth (Bythos), the transcendent, eternal, incomprehensible divine principle. Depth and his consort Thought (Ennoia) produced two emanations or "aeons," Mind and Truth; together these four divine powers at the top of the hierarchy of divine beings formed a tetrad. Mind and Truth

---

24. See *A.H.* 3.21.10. Irenaeus's use of the term is commonly connected to its use in ancient writers on rhetoric (e.g., Grant, *Irenaeus,* 47; O'Keefe and Reno, *Vision,* 38-39); Eph. 1:10 supplied him with a more immediate and obvious warrant. Cf. Minns, *Irenaeus,* 108.

produced two further emanations, Word and Life, who in turn produced Man and Church. At this point we have an *ogdoad* of eight divine powers. From Word and Life then came ten other powers (a decad); from Man and Church, twelve others (a duodecad), making a total of thirty aeons, the "fullness" of deity. The twelfth (and lowest) aeon of the duodecad was Sophia, or Wisdom, whose uncontrolled passion led to the creation of matter, evil, and suffering (the details need not detain us).

It was typical of the exegesis of those who proposed such a scheme to see in every mention of the number thirty in Scripture a concealed reference to the thirty aeons of the divine "fullness" (e.g., that the Savior was about thirty years of age when he began his public activities [Luke 3:23]; or that, in Jesus' parable of the vineyard workers [Matt. 20:1-16], some worked from the first hour, some from the third, others the sixth, the ninth, and the eleventh — the numbers totaling thirty [*A.H.* 1.1.3])! Likewise, every mention of the number eight (e.g., the number of those saved in Noah's ark [*A.H.* 1.18.3; cf. 1 Pet. 3:20]) was thought to allude to the ogdoad of divine powers at the top of the divine hierarchy; references to twelve (e.g., the twelve apostles [*A.H.* 2.21.1]) point to the duodecad, or perhaps to Sophia, the twelfth aeon in the lowest grouping within the divine hierarchy (thus, e.g., the number of years in which a woman who came to Jesus for healing had suffered from a hemorrhage [*A.H.* 1.3.3; cf. Mark 5:25]). As for the tetrad, were there not four rows of precious stones on the robe of the high priest (*A.H.* 1.18.2; cf. Exod. 28:17)?

Irenaeus has no difficulty demonstrating the arbitrary nature of such interpretations; and he does so with some wit (*A.H.* 2.20-24).[25] His work takes on greater significance, however, when he attempts to articulate basic principles of interpretation that they violate. Three of those principles call for our attention here.

1. In order to understand any part of Scripture, one must have a grasp of its overall message: to use the term Irenaeus borrowed from the rhetoricians, one must be familiar with Scripture's "hypothesis," the gist or thrust of its argument as a whole.[26] In what has proved his most memorable illustration (*A.H.* 1.8.1), Irenaeus speaks of a beautiful picture of a king formed as a mosaic by a skillful artist using precious jewels; he then compares the heretics' use of Scripture to someone who would remove the jewels from

---

25. *A.H.* 2.24.3: "[The truth is that] every number occurs with the utmost variety in the Scriptures, so that, should any one desire it, he might form not only an Ogdoad, and a Decad, and a Duodecad, but any sort or number from the Scriptures, and then maintain that this was a type of the system of error devised by himself."

26. Cf. Grant, *Irenaeus,* 47-49; O'Keefe and Reno, *Vision,* 34-37.

the artist's work, reassemble them into a poorly executed picture of a dog or fox, then claim that the picture is the same because it is made up of the same jewels. Similarly, the heretics take individual texts of Scripture out of their original context and reassemble them into a quite different picture, one based on a gnostic "hypothesis" — a basic understanding of creation and redemption that is alien to the "hypothesis" of Scripture. In a second illustration (*A.H.* 1.9.4), Irenaeus himself takes individual verses from the epics of Homer and reassembles them in such a way that they become a lament about Hercules rather than an epic tale of Achilles or Odysseus. Familiar words can be used to create a novel story.

Where, then, is the true hypothesis of Scripture to be found? What is the grand story that Scripture as a whole is meant to convey, in accordance with which its individual parts must be understood? Irenaeus finds it in the "rule of the truth" (*A.H.* 1.9.4; 1.22.1),[27] a forerunner of what we know as the Apostles' Creed.[28] Passed on to the church (Irenaeus believed) by the apostles and their disciples (*A.H.* 1.10.1), its content is naturally in harmony with their writings as well.[29] *Conformity with the rule of faith is thus an essential component of any correct interpretation.*

2. By giving obscure texts in Scripture interpretations that supported their teaching, the heretics (in Irenaeus's view) merely distracted attention from the many plain texts that flatly contradict it. *Interpretation of Scripture must begin with what is plainly stated;* if interpretation of ambiguous texts is

---

27. Young (*Exegesis*, 18) rightly notes, however, that "all along creed-like statements and confessions must in practice have provided the hermeneutical key to public reading of Scripture before Irenaeus articulated this."

28. Cf. O'Keefe and Reno, *Vision*, 119-21. Irenaeus's "rule of the truth" has no fixed wording, but the following statement indicates its basic substance: "[The Church believes] in one God, the Father Almighty, Maker of heaven, and earth, and the sea, and all things that are in them; and in one Christ Jesus, the Son of God, who became incarnate for our salvation; and in the Holy Spirit, who proclaimed through the prophets the dispensations of God, and the advents, and the birth from a virgin, and the passion, and the resurrection from the dead, and the ascension into heaven in the flesh of the beloved Christ Jesus, our Lord, and His [future] manifestation from heaven in the glory of the Father 'to gather all things in one' [Eph. 1:10], and to raise up anew all flesh of the whole human race, in order that to Christ Jesus, our Lord, and God, and Saviour, and King, according to the will of the invisible Father, 'every knee should bow, of things in heaven, and things in earth, and things under the earth, and that every tongue should confess' to Him [Phil. 2:10-11], and that He should execute just judgment towards all" (*A.H.* 1.10.1).

29. See *A.H.* 3.5.1: "Since, therefore, the tradition from the apostles does thus exist in the Church, and is permanent among us, let us revert to the Scriptural proof by those apostles who did also write the Gospel, in which they recorded the doctrine regarding God."

to be ventured at all (see point 3 below), the results must harmonize with what Scripture says clearly elsewhere (cf. *A.H.* 2.10.1).

> A sound mind, and one which does not expose its possessor to danger, and is devoted to piety and the love of truth, will eagerly meditate upon those things which God has placed within the power of mankind, and has subjected to our knowledge, and will make advancement in [acquaintance with] them, rendering the knowledge of them easy to him by means of daily study. These things are such as fall [plainly] under our observation, and are clearly and unambiguously in express terms set forth in the Sacred Scriptures. (*A.H.* 2.27.1)

> But since parables admit of many interpretations, what lover of truth will not acknowledge, that for [the heretics] to assert God is to be searched out from these, while they desert what is certain, indubitable, and true, is the part of men who eagerly throw themselves into danger, and act as if destitute of reason? And is not such a course of conduct not to build one's house upon a rock which is firm, strong, and placed in an open position, but upon the shifting sand? (*A.H.* 2.27.3)

3. *That much in Scripture is beyond our understanding, or that much into which curiosity might inquire is not addressed in Scripture, is only to be expected, and calls for modesty in interpretation rather than presumptuous speculation.*

Since God does nothing without a purpose, Irenaeus is certain that no detail in Scripture or, for that matter, arrangement within creation lacks significance (*A.H.* 2.25.1; 2.26.3; 4.21.3); but human beings are infinitely inferior to God, and it is no wonder that the Scriptures, "spoken by the Word of God and His Spirit," contain mysteries beyond our understanding (*A.H.* 2.28.2) — just as much in the realm of creation transcends our comprehension.[30]

> If, therefore, even with respect to creation, there are some things [the knowledge of] which belongs only to God, and others which come within the range of our own knowledge, what ground is there for complaint, if, in regard to those things which we investigate in the Scriptures (which are throughout spiritual), we are able by the grace of God to explain some of them, while we must leave others in the hands of

---

30. See Resch, "Fittingness," 77.

God, and that not only in the present world, but also in that which is to come, so that God should forever teach, and man should forever learn the things taught him by God? . . . If, therefore . . . we leave some questions in the hands of God, we shall both preserve our faith uninjured, and shall continue without danger; and all Scripture, which has been given to us by God, shall be found by us perfectly consistent; and the parables shall harmonize with those passages which are perfectly plain; and those statements the meaning of which is clear, shall serve to explain the parables; and through the many diversified utterances [of Scripture] there shall be heard one harmonious melody in us, praising in hymns that God who created all things. (*A.H.* 2.28.3)

Much that we have seen in this chapter will, of course, be found in later writers as well. But Irenaeus merits our attention as among the first to wrestle with the issues of a Christian interpretation of Scripture. We turn now to Origen, in whose work the study of Scripture takes on an entirely new degree of sophistication.

CHAPTER 4

Origen

If it is at the time of Irenaeus that we can first speak of a distinctively *Christian* Bible, it is with Origen, a half century later (ca. 185-254), that we see the beginnings of Christian biblical scholarship. It had, of course, long been the practice of Christian preachers and teachers to cite Scripture for homiletic or apologetic purposes. With Origen, however, the study of Scripture became important for its own sake. He preached and composed commentaries on nearly every book of the Bible.[1] His pastoral concerns are certainly evident throughout, but so, too, is his careful scholarship. He notes the different readings he has come across in various biblical manuscripts,[2] as well as differences between the Old Testament text in Hebrew and that of its Greek translation. He comments on unusual words he has encountered in the texts, and on details of geography or chronology. His discussion of the historical background of Paul's letter to the Romans corresponds, to a remarkable extent, with what would be found in any modern commentary (*Com. Rom.,* preface; see also 10.18.3). Moreover, drawing on his extraordinary familiarity with the biblical text, his commentaries are marked by frequent and impressive word studies, in which he discusses

1. For details, see McGuckin, "Works."
2. One should not, of course, expect Origen to use the criteria developed by modern textual critics to adjudicate between variant readings. At times he is content to find homiletic significance in each of the variant readings (*Hom. Num.* 18.4.1; *Hom. Jer.* 14.3.1); at other times, one reading commends itself as better suiting his sense of what the text ought to say (*Hom. Num.* 9.6.1; *Com. John* 6.206-7); and sometimes ordinary plausibility decides the issue (*Com. John* 6.204-5, 208-11). In any case, his awareness of the extent of variation in biblical manuscripts is remarkable. See *Com. John* 6.212-15. Fee ("Text") notes that Origen generally worked with the New Testament text in use in the community in which he resided (Alexandria, then Caesarea).

different occurrences of the same term in all parts of Scripture.[3] He took the trouble to learn enough Hebrew[4] to make his way through the Old Testament text in its original language,[5] and he consulted Jewish interpreters where he found the text baffling (*Hom. Num.* 13.5.1; *Com. Matt.* 11.9). He gratefully acknowledged and passed on information or interpretations that he had gathered from others (*Hom. Gen.* 2.1.1; *Hom. Exod.* 5.5; *Hom. Jer.* 11.3.2; 20.3.1). And we have yet to mention his most stupendous achievement, the production of the *Hexapla:* for study purposes,[6] in side-by-side columns, he reproduced the entire text of the Old Testament in Hebrew, its Greek transliteration,[7] and the Greek versions of Aquila, Symmachus, the Septuagint, and Theodotion. For parts of the Old Testament (notably the Psalms), he included other Greek versions as well.[8] In addition to all this,

3. Repeatedly, he shows himself capable of citing — exhaustively or nearly so — every occurrence of a particular word in Scripture; he then modestly adds that, at the moment, he cannot think of other occurrences (*Com. Cant.* 3.15; cf. *Hom. Luke* 6.7). If the belief underlying many of these studies is that Scripture generally uses words in the same sense wherever they occur, he knows that this is not always the case (*Hom. Ezek.* 11.3.2); and he can (as in his discussions of "law" in Romans; see *Com. Rom.* 3.6.1; 3.7.5) carefully distinguish the various senses before deciding which, in a particular context, is most appropriate.

4. How much Hebrew he actually knew remains a matter of debate; see Ulrich, "Text," 20-24.

5. Origen uses the term "Passover" to illustrate the importance of knowing Hebrew. The Hebrew term is said to mean "passage"; Christians who (mis)interpret the term to mean "suffering" on the basis of its form in Greek would be ridiculed by Jews (*Pasch.* 1-2). Though he is at times critical of inaccuracies in the Septuagint translation (*Hom. Jer.* 16.10.1; *Com. John* 6.40, 212), Origen nonetheless used it as the basis of his Old Testament commentaries and homilies, not because he believed the translation inspired (he never repeats the claims to that effect made by Irenaeus) but simply because it was the version used in Christian churches — and thus the version used by Providence for their edification (*Ep. Afr.* 4). In any case, one should not "remove the ancient landmarks" (*Ep. Afr.* 5). Elsewhere he cites the same consideration for refusing to admit apocryphal writings rejected by "our fathers" (*Com. Cant.,* prologue 4) while accepting such works as (Greek) Tobit, Judith, and the expansions of Daniel, though acknowledging that the latter were not recognized by Jews (*Ep. Afr.* 13; cf. Eusebius, *E.H.* 6.25, where Eusebius quotes Origen's [more restrictive] list of the books recognized by Hebrew tradition). Cf. Daniélou, *Origen,* 137.

6. Work on the *Hexapla* naturally provided the basis for Origen's observations, in commentaries and homilies, on differences between the Hebrew and Greek texts; it also allowed him to carry on informed discussions with Jews, who were wont to point out discrepancies between readings used by the church and those in the Hebrew text as they knew it (*Ep. Afr.* 5).

7. I.e., its Hebrew pronunciation in Greek letters.

8. As noted in Chapter 2 above, the term "Septuagint" (abbreviated "LXX") is commonly used for the first, or original, translations of the books of the Old Testament into Greek, produced over an extended period of time. The versions of Aquila, Symmachus, and Theodotion represent later reworkings of these translations, generally bringing them closer

Origen was the first Christian to address in a sustained way the issue of *how* Scripture is to be interpreted: the fourth book of his *On First Principles* is a kind of introduction to biblical hermeneutics, apparently the first such text to have been written. In short, Origen devoted his life to the study of Scripture, and he can fairly be regarded as both the first and the greatest Christian biblical scholar of the ancient world.[9]

But Origen is also the first great exemplar of Christian scriptural piety, and in this regard he has never been surpassed. To be sure, the New Testament authors, the apostolic fathers, the apologists of the mid-second century, and Irenaeus (among others) at its close — all esteemed Scripture (as they knew it) highly. They were quick to draw on Scripture to defend the faith or edify believers, and they could fault opponents for not knowing, not obeying, or misconstruing the sacred texts. But in the substantial body of Christian literature before Origen, it is remarkable how seldom we encounter explicit injunctions to study Scripture, or see indications that scriptural reading and meditation were deemed essential to Christian living.[10] That is, *before* Origen: for no one in the history of the Christian church has treasured Scripture more deeply, meditated on its every word more profoundly, or commended its importance for the Christian life more earnestly than he.[11] Scripture was the center of Origen's devotional and

---

to the current Hebrew text. Origen's *Hexapla* was far too massive a work to be reproduced, and later perished.

9. After noting that almost all the individual characteristics of Origen's exegesis have parallels in the work of earlier interpreters, Simonetti (*Interpretation,* 39) summarizes Origen's contribution in these words:

> Compared to his predecessors, Origen organized and systematized these more or less traditional features, using an incomparably superior knowledge of the actual biblical text, a far greater depth of exegetical reflection, and an unprecedented critical intelligence sharpened by debate with the Gnostics. He not only widened and deepened all that he received, but he ordered it, for the first time on precise methodological criteria, into a total synthesis which would in many ways remain definitive. In short, Origen made biblical hermeneutics into a real science, and, in that sense, he conditioned decisively all subsequent patristic exegesis.

10. We need to remember that the majority of Christians in the period were illiterate: in addressing congregations, Origen typically commends closer attention to the *public* reading and exposition of Scripture. Harnack (*Reading,* 32-47) finds little direct, though much indirect, evidence for the private use of Scripture among Christians in the period before Irenaeus. Cf. also Gamble, *Books,* 231-32. Direct evidence becomes abundant from roughly the beginning of the third century (Harnack, *Reading,* 48-89). But the centrality of Scripture in Origen's thought, works, and life towers above anything found in his predecessors.

11. See Peter W. Martens, *Origen.* Note particularly the counsel Origen gives in his "Letter to Gregory" (*Philoc.* 13).

spiritual life, as well as the object of his best intellectual endeavors; the extent to which this is true is in both respects without precedent in the earlier Christian church.

One further preliminary note is in order. The creeds and doctrinal statements of the Christian church(es) took shape over many years as church leaders struggled to arrive at formulations that did justice to both the manifold testimony of Scripture and the practice and experience of believing communities. Inevitably, first attempts at formulation captured important aspects of what Christians believed but proved inadequate or misleading in other regards. As a result, theologians of earlier periods, when viewed by those schooled on more mature creedal statements, appeared deficient in their theology. Origen was himself the greatest victim of this process of history. No one was more eager than he to be faithful to the tradition of the church[12] or to condemn heresy in all its forms (*Hom. Luke* 16.6). For love of Christ and the church of Christ, he endured, in his later years, excruciating torture that likely cost him his life. But his was a restless, fertile, venturesome mind, exposed to many streams of thought, and given to speculation about a host of questions that were both beyond the horizons of ordinary believers and unresolved by the theologians of his day.[13] As a result, his writings, when judged by the mature formulations of a later day, were deemed unorthodox, condemned — and consequently destroyed. Most of the massive corpus of his work was lost,[14] and much of what survives exists today only in Latin translations of disputed reliability. It is only in relatively recent times that a renewed study of his work has led to the restoration of his reputation as one of the greatest theologians and spiritual writers of the early Christian church.

In one significant respect, however, later condemnations of Origen

---

12. I.e., "the Great Church" (*Cels.* 5.59), that "of the multitude" (*Cels.* 5.61). Clearly there was for Origen (and even for the second-century pagan Celsus, from whom he borrowed these expressions), as for Irenaeus, a mainstream, normative church known throughout the world, and distinct from heretical groups (Origen's usual suspects — Marcion, Basilides, and Valentinus [*Hom. Num.* 12.2.1; *Hom. Jer.* 17.2.1] — were also those of Irenaeus).

13. E.g., the origin and preexistence of souls and the fall of angels. Origen's attempts to define the nature of Christ's divine Sonship, and relationships among the members of the Trinity, were also deemed inadequate in the light of later orthodoxy.

14. Martens declares him "one of the most prolific authors . . . of all antiquity," and notes Jerome's remark: "Who of us can read everything he wrote?" (*Origen*, 1-2). "Origen's method of composition, dictating to stenographers and revising little while relying on his elephantine memory for most details, enabled him to achieve this astonishing output" (Trigg, *Origen*, 245). Given its imposing extent, the loss of great quantities of Origen's work is not, for the modern student, an unmixed disaster.

had no apparent impact on his legacy. His influence on the Christian reading of Scripture throughout the premodern period exceeded that of all
other early church theologians.[15] Though widely criticized and largely
abandoned in much of the modern era, his approach to Scripture has of
late found a number of advocates and is once again the subject of lively
debate.[16] Origen will always be of interest to students of the early church;
but contemporary fascination with his interpretation of Scripture is by no
means confined to historians.

Life

Origen was raised in Alexandria by a Christian father, who taught him
the scriptures from his childhood.[17] He also received a standard Hellenistic education; his familiarity with the various philosophical schools
(particularly the Platonists) is readily apparent in his writings.[18] When
his father died a martyr's death in A.D. 202, the family estate was confis-
cated. A sympathetic woman of wealth provided the means for Origen to
complete his education, after which he supported his family by teaching
Greek literature. Around the same time, Origen began providing instruction for catechumens in the basics of the faith. The persecutions continued,
and within the space of a few years, seven of his own students had been
martyred. Origen exposed himself to danger by associating with them to
the last, but he escaped execution himself — perhaps because only Roman
citizens were targeted.

By the time the persecution was over, he "was the most revered spiritual guide in the city."[19] He abandoned his secular teaching and devoted
himself to a rigorously ascetic lifestyle and the intense study of Scripture.
Through his writings and travels, he gained a considerable reputation out-

15. See Smalley, *Study,* 14: "To write a history of Origenist influence on the west would
be tantamount to writing a history of western exegesis."

16. Most influential has been de Lubac's *History;* it remains the place to begin a serious
study of Origen's hermeneutics. For a more recent (and spirited) defense of the allegorical
reading of Scripture, see Wilken, "Defense."

17. The primary source for the life of Origen is Eusebius's *E.H.,* book 6. For recent
accounts, see the "Introduction" (by Ronald Heine) to Origen's *Homilies on Genesis and
Exodus;* McGuckin, "Life."

18. The notion that Origen was himself a Platonist is, however, effectively challenged
by Edwards, *Origen.*

19. Williams, "Origen," 133.

side Alexandria, though he was not on the best of terms with his local bishop. On a journey through Caesarea, he accepted ordination as a priest. That procedural irregularity, combined with other factors, led Demetrius, bishop of Alexandria, to see that he was condemned by a synod of Egyptian bishops. In the early 230s, Origen moved to Caesarea and remained there for the rest of his life, devoting himself to the study and exposition of Scripture.

When Decius became emperor in 249, he launched an empire-wide persecution of Christians, directed particularly at church leaders. Origen was imprisoned and dreadfully tortured, though his torturers kept him alive in the hope that he would deny the faith. He survived the ordeal, but his health was broken and he died shortly thereafter.

The Divine Scripture

Origen routinely defines "Scripture" more closely as "divine" or "holy."[20] Its sacredness is attributed to its inspiration by God's Spirit (*Hom. Num.* 26.3.2; *Hom. Ezek.* 2.2.2-3; *Philoc.* 2.4),[21] but can also be said to result from

---

20. Writing in the early years of the third century, Origen speaks repeatedly of "the divine Scripture(s)" or "the holy Scripture(s)" as a (seemingly) defined body of texts (cf. "the scriptures accepted in the churches of God" [*Cels.* 6.21]; "the scriptures which we believe to be genuine and divine" [*Cels.* 6.23]). In addition to the books of the Hebrew Bible, Origen frequently cites Sirach and Wisdom of Solomon, less frequently the Epistle of Jeremiah, Baruch, Tobit, Judith, 1 and 2 Maccabees, and the Greek expansions of the book of Daniel. Cf. Heine, *Origen*, 68-69. Origen's New Testament includes without question nearly every book in that part of the Bible today (cf. *Hom. Josh.* 7.1); he did, however, note that the authorship of 2 Pet. was in dispute, and that the short letters of 2 and 3 John were not accepted by all (*Com. John* 5.3). When he occasionally refers to works that would later be excluded from the canon, he typically notes their disputed status (e.g., *Cels.* 5.54; *Com. John* 2.188; 13.104; 20.91). Observing that others pride themselves on their knowledge of noncanonical Gospels, Origen can say, "We approve of nothing but what the Church approves of, namely only four canonical Gospels" (*Hom. Luke* 1.2). At one point he offers, as his personal opinion, that the *Shepherd of Hermas* was written by a contemporary of Paul and divinely inspired (*Com. Rom.* 10.31.1); that it should be accepted as Scripture was, however, dubious (*Hom. Num.* 8.1.5). Cf. Heine, *Origen*, 82. Origen was clear that Scripture was no longer being written in his own day, since apostles were no longer being sent (*Hom. Luke* 28.6). No third testament was to be added to the Old and New that God has given us. The two we have more than meet our needs, and "God did not want us to know everything in the present life" (*Hom. Lev.* 5.9.3).

21. This explains how the writers of Scripture could not only foretell the future but also relate what happened in the past in their absence (e.g., the baptism of Jesus), or even before they were born (e.g., creation itself) (*Hom. Num.* 26.3.2; *Cels.* 1.44).

its being "spoken" by God's Son (*Hom. Lev.* 4.1.1). After all, the "word of the Lord" that came to, and lived in, the Old Testament prophets[22] can be none other than the Word who was with God, and was God, "in the beginning" (so John 1:1; cf. *Hom. Jer.* 9.1.1-2). As for the New Testament, the words of the Savior are to be heard not only in the Gospels, but also in the writings of his apostles, as Paul indicates when he writes, "You desire proof that Christ is speaking in me" (2 Cor. 13:3; so *F.P.* 1.1; cf. *Com. Rom.* 2.6.1). Indeed, the words of Scripture, like the human flesh of the Savior, are merely the external clothing of the eternal Word, bringing that Word within the realm of human experience. The vision of many people, to be sure, is confined to what meets their (physical) eyes: the human being Jesus and a book like any other. But those with "spiritual" eyes and ears perceive, beneath the outer "clothing," the divinity within (*Hom. Lev.* 1.1.1). The modern reader may often wonder whether, by "the Word (of God)," Origen means the divine person or the written word. Origen himself may not have seen a question.

Origen is wont to apply Paul's expression "treasure in clay jars" (2 Cor. 4:7) to Scripture: the "splendour of its teachings" is often "concealed under a poor and humble style" (*F.P.* 4.1.7; cf. *Com. John* 4.2). Critics may mock the latter, finding it fit only for "the vulgar and illiterate." For his part, Origen sees it rather as a token of God's concern for all humankind, on the one hand (*Cels.* 1.27; 6.1-2), and proof that Scripture[23] derives its power from God, not human rhetoric, on the other (*F.P.* 4.1.7; *Com. John* 1.48; 4.2-3).

Scripture — the word of God — is divine in its living power as well as in

---

22. Origen took some interest in the mode of prophetic revelation. Since it is at times apparent that prophets chose whether to speak or keep silent, it follows that "it is not the case, as some people surmise, that the prophets were out of their minds and spoke by the Spirit's compulsion" (*Hom. Ezek.* 6.1.1); rather, they were in full possession of their senses (*Cels.* 7.3-4). But the ears with which they heard the divine message, and the eyes with which they perceived visions, were spiritual in nature; they were no more the physical ears and eyes of human beings than it is with the latter that we "see" and "hear" when we dream (*Cels.* 1.48; cf. *Hom. Gen.* 3.1.2). For Origen, it is self-evident that the prophets (including Moses) understood the full spiritual significance of the words they spoke (*Com. Num.* 5.1.3; *Com. Rom.* 10.43.4).

23. Origen contrasts Scripture's appeal to the "mass of the common people" with the "fine utterances" of "Plato and the wise men of the Greeks," who "cared only for those supposed to be the better classes, while they have despised the multitudes of men" (*Cels.* 7.60). Paul's stylistic deficiencies are the subject of frequent comments (e.g., *Com. Rom.* 1.9.6; 4.5.7; 4.9.1; 7.18.2). At times, Origen is content to attribute them simply to Paul's "lack of [rhetorical] training" (*Com. Rom.* 6.3.2, alluding to 2 Cor. 11:6; cf. *Com. Eph.*, on Eph. 3:1-3); at other times, he sees a divine purpose in the apparent defects (*Com. Rom.* 2.6.1; 5.1.2-7).

its inspired origins: indeed, its divine power gives evidence of its divine origin and character.[24] By its divine power, the word "conquers" its readers, persuading them of its truth (*Cels.* 1.18; 1.62; 2.15) and transforming their lives from licentiousness to virtue (*Cels.* 3.39; 3.68). The reading of Scripture provides nourishment by which the spirit grows (*Hom. Lev.* 9.7.6; *Hom. Num.* 27.1.2). Meditating on Scripture renews the mind, deepens the understanding, and develops wisdom (*Com. Rom.* 9.1.12). Indeed, when received with "faith and devotion," the word of God meets the believer's every need: "If you are afflicted, it consoles you. . . . If you rejoice in your future hope, it heaps up joys for you. . . . If you are angry, it calms you. . . . If you are in pain, it heals you. . . . The manna of the word of God imparts into your mouth whatever taste you wish" (*Hom. Exod.* 7.8; cf. *Com. Rom.* 9.3.12). If Origen here attributes to the written texts of Scripture blessings usually associated with God himself, it is because he believes that God is encountered in the proper reading of his word, and that, through Scripture, God communicates his blessings.[25]

Moreover, Scripture meets every need of *every* believer, whatever his or her capacity or level of maturity (*Hom. Jer.* 18.4.1; *Cels.* 4.18). Not that all parts of Scripture are equally suited to all who read them: some parts, like "strong meat," are meant for the mature, while other parts, like milk and vegetables, nourish infants and the young so that each may grow to a greater stage of maturity (*Hom. Num.* 27.1.2-5; *Com. Rom.* 2.14.14; 9.36.1; cf. 1 Cor. 3:1-2; Heb. 5:12-14; 1 Pet. 2:2).

Given Scripture's divine character,[26] certain consequences followed

---

24. "He who approaches the prophetic words with care and attention will feel from his very reading a trace of their divine inspiration and will be convinced by his own feelings that the words which are believed by us to be from God are not the compositions of men" (*F.P.* 4.1.6).

25. That the Word of God speaks effectively through the words of Scripture "is an integral part of Origen's doctrine of the Logos" (Torjesen, *Procedure,* 135-38, citing *Hom. Jer.* Fragment II.1: "And it should be no surprise if every word spoken by the prophets produces an effect commensurate with the word. In fact, I think that every marvelous word recorded in the words of God produces an effect and that there is not a single jot or tittle written in the Scripture which does not produce an effect of its own on those who know how to be helped by the power of the Scripture").

26. Origen makes many general statements about the divinity and sacredness of Scripture. Occasionally, however, confronted by particulars of the text, he offers qualifying statements. Paul's writings are deemed throughout to be "wise and trustworthy and most beneficial" (*Com. John* 1.15). But Origen finds within them evidence that the apostle wrote his different letters at different stages of his own maturity (*Com. Rom.,* preface 3-6); and, though elsewhere speaking of Paul's writings as divine and inspired Scripture, he can — in light of statements like "I speak, and not the Lord" (1 Cor. 7:12) — raise the question whether one

for Origen. "Everything that Scripture records is true" (*Hom. Luke* 17.5): the axiom naturally follows from Scripture's divine inspiration, but in an apologetic context, Origen thinks it also worthwhile to point out, for example, the honesty of the Gospel writers that is evident both in their recording of incidents that brought discredit on church leaders (Peter's denial of Christ; the flight of Christ's disciples at his arrest [*Cels.* 2.15; cf. 1.63]) and in their willingness to suffer persecution for their convictions (*Cels.* 2.10; 3.23). Their "good conscience" is, he believes, apparent in what they wrote (*Cels.* 3.24; 3.39): "No one of the evangelists errs or lies" (*Comm. John* 6.171).

Confidence in the truth of Scripture did not blind Origen to aspects of the texts that, in some people's minds, call such an assurance into question. Much that needs to be said on the matter will be discussed below when we look at the limitations Origen sees in the literal sense of Scripture. The following observations also did not, to his mind, undermine the fundamental truth of the divine texts.

1. No conviction was more central to Origen's thought than that of God's incorporeality: that "God is Spirit" (John 4:24) means, for Origen, that God has no body. References in Scripture to God's eyes, ears, hands, arm, and the like disturbed him more than they do most readers; so, on other grounds, did references to divine emotions (*Hom. Num.* 23.2.6), or to divine warnings issued in apparent ignorance of how those warned would respond, or to God's changing his mind in response to human actions. In each case, Origen believes, God is adapting the language of Scripture to human capacities to understand, as adults do when speaking to children (*Hom. Jer.* 18.6.4; *Cels.* 4.71): he can even say that God "pretends" (*Hom. Jer.* 18.6.5)! *We* know what it is to change our mind; so Scripture speaks as though God does the same. *We* know what it means to be the objects of another's anger; so God speaks of the pain we experience as a result of our sin as the effect of God's wrath (*Hom. Gen.* 3.1.2; *Hom. Judg.* 2.4; *Hom. Jer.*

---

should not distinguish them from the more direct revelation implied by the prophetic "thus says the Lord," and whether Paul would even have included his own writings in the claim that "all scripture is inspired of God" (*Com. John* 1.15-16, referring to 2 Tim. 3:16). Similarly, he at least wonders whether unfulfilled prophecies (Nineveh would be destroyed within forty days, Jonah 3:4; God would send death on Israel for three days as punishment for David's sin, 2 Reigns 24:11-16 LXX [English versions, 2 Sam. 24:11-16]) may have been spoken by prophets themselves (here Jonah and Gad) apart from divine prompting; in these cases, however, he prefers to see the incidents as reflecting God's incomprehensible goodness in revoking or reducing announced judgments (*Hom. Num.* 16.4.1-6, citing also Jer. 18:7-10). For Origen's understanding of inspiration, see Nardoni, "Concept."

18.6.5-7; 20.1.1–20.3.5). In such cases, the truth of Scripture is necessarily conditioned by the capacity of human beings to receive it.

2. No one was more aware than Origen of the differences between Old Testament texts as quoted in the New Testament and the same texts as they appeared in Hebrew and Septuagint manuscripts (*Com. John* 10.162; *Com. Rom.* 5.8.7); indeed, he often itemizes the differences (*Com. Rom.* 8.8.4; 10.8.4). He notes where a single New Testament quotation combines different Old Testament texts (e.g., *Com. Rom.* 7.19.7), and even where Paul uses a text from Hosea to make quite a different point from that of the prophet (though expressing the same underlying principle [*Com. Rom.* 7.18.7, referring to Rom. 9:25-26]). These are freedoms that apostolic authority could allow itself (*Com. Rom.* 8.8.4; 8.12.5); as a rule, moreover, where the words are changed, the sense is not (*Com. Rom.* 10.8.4). Assessing the evidence, Origen concludes:

> In almost all passages the Apostle [Paul] adheres to the edition of the seventy translators [= the Septuagint], except when, perchance, they seem less necessary to him than the argument he is pursuing, or when he wants to make use of not so much the words of the translators as the sense of the Scripture, brought forth with his own expression. (*Com. Rom.* 10.8.5)

3. Origen was aware, as are modern biblical scholars, that the headings of a number of psalms do not correspond to their actual content (*Com. Rom.* 2.14.22).

4. Origen deemed it incredible that the sins and weaknesses confessed by such saints as David, Daniel, and Paul were really their own. "It is customary in the Holy Scriptures for saints to take on the *personae* of sinners. . . . Thus it is fitting for us, when we read the things said by the saints . . . to interpret and understand that in themselves they are describing our passions and sins; and the reason they weep is in order that we might be invited to shed tears by their weeping" (*Com. Rom.* 6.9.12).

Given that all Scripture is true, it follows that no passage within Scripture can contradict any other. Origen sees it as the task of all who would interpret Scripture faithfully to show how texts that appear contradictory are in fact in harmony with each other (*Com. John* 6.127; *Com. Rom.* 3.7.4; 3.9.3). In so doing, the interpreters act in the role of the "peacemakers" whom Christ pronounced "blessed" (Matt. 5:9), demonstrating

> that what to the eyes of others seems like disagreement in the Scriptures is not really so, and [proving] that harmony and concord exist. . . . For

as the different strings of the psaltery or the lyre, each of which gives forth a note of its own seemingly unlike that of any other, are thought by an unmusical man who does not understand the theory of harmony to be discordant, because of the difference in the notes: so they who have not ears to detect the harmony of God in the sacred Scriptures suppose that the Old Testament is not in harmony with the New, or the Prophets with the Law, or the Gospels with one another, or an Apostle with the Gospel, or with himself, or with the other Apostles. But if a reader comes who has been instructed in God's music . . . he knows that the whole Scripture is the one perfect, harmonious instrument of God, blending the different notes, for those who wish to learn, into one song of salvation. (*Philoc.* 6.1-2)

Though Origen believed that the truth and harmony of Scripture at times lay only at the spiritual level, he could also expend considerable effort to show, for example, how the dimensions and construction of Noah's ark, understood literally, were well suited to the task of preserving from the flood both humans and "the diverse kinds of animals" (*Hom. Gen.* 2.1.1-2); and he occasionally proposed harmonizations at the literal level for apparent discrepancies among the Gospels (e.g., *Com. John* 6.171-72; *Cels.* 5.56).

Not only are the divinely inspired scriptures necessarily both true and coherent; they are also beneficial for their readers. Paul says as much in words Origen never tires of repeating: "All scripture is inspired by God and is useful for teaching, for reproof, for correction, and for training in righteousness" (2 Tim. 3:16). The usefulness of a divine text extends to its every detail: if God commanded that no Israelite man celebrating the prescribed feasts should "appear before [him] empty" (Exod. 23:15), and if Christ warned that mortals would be judged for "every careless word" (Matt. 12:36), then surely the divine author of Scripture holds himself to an even higher standard: "Not even one dot" of the sacred text is "empty of the wisdom of God" (*Hom. Jer.* 28.2.3; *Com. Rom.* 2.6.1; 5.1.22; *Philoc.* 10.1). A single word in Scripture, like a seed that is planted, may seem "small and insignificant," but "if it find a skillful and diligent farmer, as it begins to be cultivated and handled with spiritual skill, it grows into a tree and puts forth branches and foliage" (*Hom. Exod.* 1.1). To adopt a different metaphor:

> The saint is a sort of spiritual herbalist, who culls from the sacred Scriptures every jot and every common letter, discovers the value of what is written and its use, and finds that there is nothing in the Scriptures

77

superfluous. . . . If you are [not] a scriptural botanist . . . blame yourself and not the sacred Scriptures when you fail to find the point of what is written. (*Philoc.* 10.2)

Not a word in Scripture, then, is to be passed over quickly (*Hom. Num.* 11.7.3). The apparent redundancy of Genesis 24:16 in saying both that Rebekah was a "virgin" *and* that "no man had known [her]" in fact makes the point that she was holy both in body *and* spirit (*Hom. Gen.* 10.4). When God says, "I have received the Levites from the midst of the sons of Israel" (Num. 3:12), the words "the midst of" seem unnecessary. A careful search for other uses of the same expression in Scripture reveals its significance: to *stand* "in the midst" is never to turn aside to the right or to the left, that is, to be sinless. This can only be affirmed of Christ (according to John the Baptist, Christ "stands *in the midst of* you" [John 1:26]). The righteous (who, admittedly, are not sinless) may nonetheless be said to "*dwell* [not 'stand'] in the midst" (so 2 Kings 4:13), and it is from their number that the Levites were chosen (*Hom. Num.* 3.2.3).

The reading of Scripture brings benefits even where it is not understood. Pronouncing its discourses or even its names serves to banish the powers of evil and bring deliverance from their snares. As Paul could pray with his spirit though his understanding was unfruitful (1 Cor. 14:14), so our spiritual "powers"[27] can be nourished and refreshed even by words we do not understand. The benefits of medicine are real though not always immediately discernible; we should expect no less of divine Scripture. "Believe that your soul is profited by the mere reading, even though your understanding does not receive the fruit of profiting by these passages. Our inner nature is charmed; its better elements are nourished, the worse weakened, and brought to naught" (*Philoc.* 12.1-2).

Among the benefits enjoyed by those who devote themselves to the divine Scriptures is that of fellowship with God.[28] For when the Lord Jesus sees us occupied with Scripture, he comes to us, feeds us, and brings the

27. The English translation of the *Philocalia* speaks of human "faculties"; but here (and with "better elements" in the quotation in the text) Origen may mean angelic powers to whom the well-being of the believer is entrusted. "Worse elements" would then refer to malevolent powers. See the note of Harl, in *Philocalie*, 396-97.

28. Cf. de Lubac, *History*, 346-47: "Scripture is not a document handed over to the historian or the thinker, even to the believing historian or thinker. It is a word, which is to say, the start of a dialogue. It is addressed to someone from whom it awaits a response. More precisely, it is God who offers himself through it, and it awaits more than a response: a return movement."

Father to the banquet: "Truly I say to you that the Father and I shall come and shall make our abode and dine with that person" (*Hom. Josh.* 20.1, referring to John 14:23).

Inspired Scripture, then, is true, harmonious, and profitable. It is also surely inevitable that the mysteries of a divine text will frequently transcend human understanding. Only with the aid of the Spirit of God who inspired the texts — if at all, in this life — can their mysteries be grasped.[29]

> The further we progress in reading, the greater grows the accumulation of mysteries for us. And just as if someone should embark on the sea borne by a small boat, as long as he is near land he has little fear. But, when he has advanced little by little into the deep and has begun either to be lifted on high by the swelling waves or brought down to the depths by the same gaping waves then truly great fear and terror permeate his mind because he has entrusted a small craft to such immense waves. So also we seem to have suffered, who, small in merits and slight in ability, dare to enter so vast a sea of mysteries. But if by your prayers the Lord should see fit to give us a favorable breeze of his Holy Spirit, we shall enter the port of salvation with a favorable passage of the word. (*Hom. Gen.* 9.1)

Confronted by the mysteries of divine Scripture, Origen asks with the apostle Paul, "Who is sufficient for these things?" (*Hom. Gen.* 13.1, referring to 2 Cor. 2:16). Frequently he confesses his own inability to penetrate them (*Hom. Exod.* 4.2; *Hom. Num.* 1.3.5; *Hom. Ezek.* 13.3.1); the acknowledgment, admittedly, seldom keeps him from trying.

The presence of mysteries in the divine text is hardly accidental: as we have seen, the struggle to understand them is one of the divinely appointed means for bringing believers to maturity (*Hom. Num.* 27.1.7; *Cels.* 3.45). Thus, texts incomprehensible at one stage in one's life may not be so at another (*Hom. Josh.* 20.1). What we must not do, then, is avoid texts we find difficult and declare them useless.[30] Those who avoid difficult passages are

---

29. Origen anticipates that some mysteries in Scripture will become clear only in the life to come (*Hom. Josh.* 20.1).

30. Martens rightly speaks of Origen's emphasis on the need for faith in the usefulness of all Scripture when the interpreter encounters perplexing texts: "For Origen, the circumstance in which faith ornamented the exegetical life was invariably the same: interpreters, himself included, were confounded by exegetical aporia and needed to exercise trust in God that the passages in question carried an edifying sense, even if it was far from evident what this message actually was. This trust buoyed the interpretive enterprise" (*Origen*, 180-81).

likely to end up abandoning the study of Scripture altogether, so pervasive are its mysteries (*Hom. Num.* 27.1.6). Such passages should rather move us to give God glory because, just as he has seen fit to supply different animals with different types of food, so he provides in Scripture nourishment to suit the capacity of every reader (*Hom. Num.* 27.1.5). And if there are mysteries in God's word that transcend *all* human understanding, the same can be said of God's work in creation (*Philoc.* 2.5).

The Interpretation of Scripture

Scripture is divine, and as such it must be true, unified in its witness, profitable, yet mysterious. It is Origen's view, however, that it shows none of these characteristics consistently at the literal level.

Literally construed, Origen insists, Scripture is not always *true*. Of the many examples he gives, a number, it must be said, are problems only in his own mind. At times, Origen appears to reject the "literal" truth of a text simply because he fails to recognize an obvious metaphor. We really do not need Origen to tell us that "circumcision of the heart" is physically impossible; he not only tells us, but prosaically explains *why* (*Hom. Gen.* 3.4; cf. *Com. Rom.* 2.9.2). In a no less needless, labored, though unintentionally humorous way, he dismisses a literal understanding of the text "How beautiful are the feet of those who preach good news!" (*Com. Rom.* 8.5.5, referring to Isa. 52:7). More than once, Origen's own hopelessly literal reading of a text provides the grounds on which he dismisses its literal interpretation. When, in the book of Joshua, we are told that Joshua circumcised the sons of Israel "a second time" (Josh. 5:2), the obvious point is that the same operation that was carried out on the generation that left Egypt was repeated on their sons when they entered the promised land. Origen, however, cites the physical impossibility of circumcising anyone twice as a reason for rejecting a literal interpretation of the text (*Hom. Josh.* 5.5; *Com. Rom.* 2.13.26). When he takes the despair of Ecclesiastes — "I praised the dead more than the living" (Eccles. 4:2) — to imply (when read literally) that the Egyptians who drowned in the Red Sea were to be praised more than the Israelites who were miraculously delivered (*Hom. Num.* 7.3.3), he only proves himself incapable of reading Ecclesiastes.

Unlike modern critics, Origen never questions the presence of the miraculous in scriptural narratives. But there are stories where nothing miraculous is suggested in the text that nonetheless strike Origen as implausible — again, at the literal level. Are we really to believe that Abraham, whose body was said to be "dead" when he begat Isaac at a hundred years old, begat a number of sons from his new wife, Cetura, when he was 137 (*Hom. Gen.* 11.1)? More curiously, Origen finds improbable a number of innocent-seeming details in the stories of Jesus cleansing the temple (*Com. John* 10.143-51) and triumphantly entering Jerusalem (*Com. John* 10.159-66).

Origen claims, moreover, that many prophecies must be said to have gone unfulfilled — that is, if literal fulfillment is required. Ezekiel's words notwithstanding, Egypt had never been " 'laid waste forty years' so that 'no foot of man' [was] found there" (*F.P.* 4.3.9, referring to Ezek. 29:11-12). More crucially, Origen found that non-Christian Jews expected more tangible results from the coming of Messiah than anything Christians could point to as the outcome of Christ's ministry: captives had not been released, nor were the instruments of war done away with, nor the city of God built — though these and other messianic blessings were called for by (a literal reading of) the prophets (*F.P.* 4.2.1; cf. *Com. John* 10.161, 163; *Com. Rom.* 8.8.10).[31]

Taken literally, Scripture's promises, no less than its prophecies, have often gone unfulfilled. In spite of the assurance given in Exodus 15:26, Origen dismisses as palpably false the notion that none of the diseases that afflicted the Egyptians will strike those who obey God's commands: the example of Job seems sufficient refutation (*Hom. Exod.* 7.2). When Celsus ridicules the Old Testament writings because of their promises of earthly success, Origen responds:

> [Celsus] has fallen into a very vulgar error concerning the meaning of the Bible. He thinks that in the law and the prophets there is no deeper doctrine beyond that of the literal meaning of the words. He fails to notice that the Word would not have promised material wealth to those who live upright lives, since that would be obviously unconvincing: very righteous people have manifestly lived in extreme poverty. In fact, the prophets, who received the divine Spirit because of their purity of life, "went about in sheepskins, in goatskins, being destitute, afflicted, evil entreated, wandering in deserts and mountains and caves and the holes of the earth." As the Psalmist said, "Many are the afflictions of the righteous." (*Cels.* 7.18, referring to Heb. 11:37-38; Ps. 34:19; cf. *Hom. Lev.* 16.5.4; *Com. Eph.*, on Eph. 1:3)

31. See Martens, *Origen*, 143-45.

These latter observations, at least, are hardly peculiar to Origen. Nor is he alone in thinking that a nonliteral understanding is required of the "days" of Genesis 1, given that the sun and moon were not created until the fourth "day" (*F.P.* 4.3.1); of the description of the "prince of Tyre" as "created in the midst of the cherubim" and present "in the paradise of God" (*Hom. Ezek.* 13.1.2, referring to Ezek. 28:13-14); of the statement that the period between David and the exile was occupied by fourteen generations (here three generations have been omitted [compare Matt. 1:8-9 with 1 Chron. 3:11-12] to construct a meaningful pattern) (*Com. Rom.* 1.5.5, referring to Matt. 1:17); of the "mountain" to which Satan took Jesus, from which he purportedly could see all the kingdoms of the world (*F.P.* 4.3.1, referring to Matt. 4:8). Of none of these statements, Origen believes, can literal truth be affirmed.

Nor does he find Scripture, literally understood, always *unified in its witness.* The issue arises particularly when one compares parallel accounts in the Gospels. Though occasionally proposing harmonizations, Origen was often content to let apparent discrepancies stand as evidence that the text is not to be read literally. If, as the Synoptic Gospels relate, Jesus' baptism was followed ("immediately," according to Mark 1:12-13) by forty days of fasting in the wilderness and temptation by Satan, it is noteworthy that John's Gospel not only fails to mention the temptation, but that its chronology ("the next day" after Jesus' baptism, "the next day" after that, "on the third day" [John 1:35, 43; 2:1]) apparently excludes it (*Com. John* 10.10). John the Baptist is said to have been arrested "about the time of Jesus' temptation" in Matthew (Matt. 4:1-12); but he is active "for a long time" in the Gospel of John (*Com. John* 10.35). Events that, in the Synoptics, are said to have taken place on a single trip to Jerusalem (e.g., the triumphal entry and the cleansing of the temple), are divided up, in John, between two trips separated from each other by a host of other deeds and travels (*Com. John* 10.129). "On the basis of numerous other passages also, if someone should examine the Gospels carefully to check the disagreement so far as the historical [i.e., literal] sense is concerned . . . he would grow dizzy" (*Com. John* 10.14).

Not only does Scripture — at the literal level, as Origen construes it — often fail to be true or consistent; read at that level, much in Scripture seems unprofitable. Origen makes the point frequently by asking what benefit the reader could possibly derive from some detail in the biblical narrative:

> We ought not believe that it was of greatest concern to the Holy Spirit to write in the books of the Law where Abraham was standing. For what

does it help me who have come to hear what the Holy Spirit teaches the human race, if I hear that "Abraham was standing under a tree"? (*Hom. Gen.* 4.3, referring to Gen. 18:8)

Do we think that it is the Holy Spirit's intention to write stories and to narrate how a child was weaned and a feast was made, how he played and did other childish things? (*Hom. Gen.* 7.1, referring to Gen. 21)

Are we to believe that the Holy Spirit, who dictated these things to be written, composed these things for the sole purpose of informing us who was numbered among the people at that time, and who remained outside of the number? Just what progress will come from this to those who are eager to be instructed by the sacred volumes? For what profit is there in having learned this? Or what is conferred to the soul's salvation, if one knows that a certain part of the people was numbered in the desert, but a part was left unnumbered? (*Hom. Num.* 1.1.2, referring to Num. 1:1-54)

When people hear these things, it is likely they say, "What is this to me? What does it contribute to me if I know that those who were living in Ai were conquered?" (*Hom. Josh.* 8.2)

Someone might say, "Evangelist, how does this narrative help me? How does it help me to know that the first census of the entire world was made under Caesar Augustus?" (*Hom. Luke* 11.6, referring to Luke 2:1-2)

In a pointed passage in a homily on Numbers (26.3.3), Origen reminds his readers that Abraham, in Jesus' parable, directed the rich man's brothers to heed "Moses and the prophets" if they would avoid the torments of Gehenna (Luke 16:28-31). Listing various stages in the story by which the tribes of Reuben, Gad, and the half-tribe of Manasseh received their inheritance on the east side of the Jordan River (Num. 32), Origen imagines a reader asking, "How will it help me escape Gehenna if I read [of these events]?"

Then there is the problem of the presence of Mosaic laws in Christian Scripture. Certain commandments, to be sure, even the believer should observe: parents should be honored; murder, adultery, and stealing are to be avoided (*F.P.* 4.3.4; cf. *Hom. Num.* 11.1.2). Reading such commands raises no issues, even at the literal level. But how is the man who has neither land nor daughters to profit by reading laws prescribing the inheritance of daughters (*Hom. Num.* 22.1.2)? Or how is the believer, eager to "learn about things that pertain to salvation," to read with profit rather than annoyance the commandments about "sacrifices of rams and goats and calves" (*Hom. Num.* 24.1.2)? If such texts are to be read only at their literal level, Origen believes,

> I, myself, a man of the Church, living under the faith of Christ and placed in the midst of the Church, am compelled by the authority of the divine precept to sacrifice calves and lambs and to offer fine wheat flour with incense and oil. (*Hom. Lev.* 1.1.2)

Is that not to live as a Jew (cf. *Cels.* 5.60)?[32]

Indeed, Origen believes that *some* parts of Scripture, when read at the literal level, are positively dangerous. The Song of Songs is the most obvious entrant in that category.

> If any man who lives only after the flesh should approach it, to such a one the reading of this Scripture will be the occasion of no small hazard and danger. For he . . . will twist the whole manner of his hearing of it away from the inner spiritual man and on to the outward and carnal; and he will be turned away from the spirit to the flesh, and will foster carnal desires in himself, and it will seem to be the Divine Scriptures that are thus urging and egging him on to fleshly lust. (*Com. Cant.,* prologue 1)

But the Song of Songs is not alone. Origen cannot bring himself to believe that "such a great patriarch" as Abraham "not only lied to king Abimelech, but also surrendered his wife's chastity to him." In any case he can see nothing edifying in (a literal understanding of) the story (*Hom. Gen.* 6.3, referring to Gen. 20). The same applies to the story of David's "extraordinary" crime against Uriah, opening the king to "the charge not only of licentiousness, but also of savagery and inhumanity" (*Philoc.* 1.29).

And yet, as Origen constantly reminds us, "All scripture *is* profitable" (2 Tim. 3:16; see *Hom. Judg.* 5.1); it was written "for our sakes" (Rom. 4:23-24 [*Com. Rom.* 4.7.9]) and "for our instruction" (Rom. 15:4; 1 Cor. 10:11). The conclusion, for Origen, is obvious: these (apparently *un*profitable) scriptures cannot be meant to be read literally. Neither the truth that God means to convey through Scripture nor its divine power to transform lives requires the literal truth of all its statements.[33] Indeed, as we shall see, Ori-

---

32. Cf. Martens, *Origen,* 140-43.
33. Cf. M. W. Holmes, "Inerrancy."

gen believes that *inaccuracies* have been deliberately placed in Scripture in order to direct readers to a truer grasp of its nature and import.

It is axiomatic for Origen that everything in the word of God must be "worthy of God" (see *Hom. Num.* 24.3.2; *Hom. Josh.* 8.1; *Hom. Luke* 9.1). When he finds nothing but banality in the literal interpretation of a text, he can only assume that, beneath its trivial surface meaning, the text conceals mysteries that are "worthy of God" — the more trite the literal sense, the deeper the mystery.

> We should pray the Father of the Word during each individual reading "when Moses is read" [2 Cor. 3:15], that he might fulfill even in us that which is written in the Psalms: "Open my eyes and I will consider the wondrous things of your Law" [Ps. 119:18]. For unless he himself opens our eyes, how shall we be able to see these great mysteries . . . which are pictured now in terms of wells, now in marriages, now in births, now even in barrenness? (*Hom. Gen.* 12.1)

> In this way I think that an interpretation worthy of the laws of the Holy Spirit may be taught in regard to what is read. For what benefit is there in my knowing the location in the desert which is said to be, for example, where the sons of Israel camped as they were passing through? (*Hom. Num.* 27.6.1)

> If these words are not to be spiritually understood, are they not mere tales? If they conceal no hidden mystery, are they not unworthy of God? (*Hom. Cant.* 1.2)

It follows that the lists of sites at which the Israelites stopped on their way to the Promised Land (*Hom. Num.* 27.1.7; 27.4.2, referring to Num. 33), or the lists of cities assigned to each tribe by Joshua (*Hom. Josh.* 23.4), or the list of precious stones with which the king of Tyre was adorned (*Hom. Ezek.* 13.3.1, referring to Ezek. 28:13) must contain very great mysteries indeed.

Thus, the word of God, understood literally, is not, in Origen's mind, consistently true, harmonious, useful, or even worthy of its divine author. In a divinely inspired text, this cannot be accidental. To be sure, Origen insists that much of Scripture *can* be read profitably at a literal level, and the needs of infants in the faith are addressed when they do so.[34] However,

---

34. "That it is possible to derive benefit from the first [i.e., literal], and to this extent

had the surface meaning of the text been problem free, "we should be unaware that there was anything beyond the obvious meaning for us to understand in the scriptures. Consequently, the Word of God has arranged for certain stumbling blocks, as it were, and hindrances and impossibilities to be inserted in the midst of the law and the history" to impel readers to a *spiritual* (or allegorical) understanding of the text (*F.P.* 4.2.9). Such a spiritual sense, Origen believes, is in fact present in every text of Scripture,[35] whereas a literal sense that is both true and edifying is only found in *most* texts (*F.P.* 4.3.5).[36] Where both are present,[37] the Spirit of God has marvelously arranged things in such a way that wondrous secrets, of benefit to the spiritually mature, are concealed beneath an "outer covering" (i.e., the literal narrative) that itself is "capable of improving the multitude in so far as they receive it" (*F.P.* 4.2.8).[38] But it is the spiritual truth that is, in the end, most essential, and where the writers of Scripture could only convey spiritual truth by means of a minor "material falsehood," Origen says that, for his part, he will not condemn them.[39]

---

helpful meaning, is witnessed by the multitudes of sincere and simple believers" (*F.P.* 4.2.6). "Yet there are very many things in these [writings] that are spoken openly and simply enough to edify the hearer of limited intelligence" (*Hom. Num.* 27.1.6). This Origen clearly takes to be a good thing, however faint the praise.

35. This claim notwithstanding, Origen finds the literal level of some texts "sufficiently complete and perfect" that pursuit of a spiritual understanding seems unnecessary (see *Hom. Num.* 22.2.1 — where he nonetheless embarks on the latter pursuit). The opening verses of John's Gospel and much of the epistle to the Romans are interpreted without recourse to allegory. More surprisingly, perhaps, Origen interprets the temptation of Abraham in Gen. 22 in an almost Kierkegaardian way — largely at the literal level (*Hom. Gen.* 8).

36. "The passages which are historically true are far more numerous than those which are composed with purely spiritual meanings" (*F.P.* 4.3.8).

37. In his discussion of the proper interpretation of Scripture in *On First Principles,* Origen in fact speaks of two *or three* levels at which Scripture can be interpreted, the latter number corresponding to the body, soul, and spirit possessed by human beings (*F.P.* 4.2.4-5). In his commentaries and writings, in addition to a literal interpretation and a spiritual one (by which some mystery of the Christian faith is disclosed), he occasionally speaks of another level of interpretation where the disciplines of the moral life are commonly the focus (e.g., *Hom. Gen.* 2.6; *Hom. Num.* 9.7.3). He is generally content, however, to speak simply of the literal or historical level, on the one hand, and the spiritual, mystical, or allegorical level, on the other, with the latter receiving greater attention. For discussion of the "three levels" of Scripture interpretation, see Lauro, *Soul;* see also Torjesen, *Procedure.*

38. Consistent with this principle, Origen's commentaries frequently note first how we can "be edified by the text of the historical narrative" (*Hom. Num.* 20.1.5) before moving on to a "spiritual" (or "mystical" or "allegorical") reading.

39. "I do not condemn . . . the fact that [the Gospel writers] have also made some minor changes in what happened so far as history is concerned, with a view to the usefulness of the

From what has been said up to this point, the resort to allegorical interpretation might appear a case of making virtue of necessity, a spouting of pretentious claims to conceal deficiencies in a treasured text. Such may well have been the origins of the method among devotees of Homer,[40] but in Origen's day, it was seen by many as both a characteristic and a requirement of an inspired, hallowed text that profound mysteries should underlie its surface meaning.[41] Origen argued vigorously for the suitedness of Christian scripture to allegorical interpretation against a critic who would allow it only for pagan texts (*Cels.* 4.48-51, 87).[42] There is, he believed, even more to be said for the allegorical interpretation of Scripture than its capacity to make Scripture true, harmonious, profitable, and worthy of God throughout.

After all, the correct way to interpret Scripture must be derived from Scripture itself; and texts from both Testaments commend its allegorical reading. The foremost instructor in this area is the apostle Paul (*Hom. Exod.* 5.1). Jews may have interpreted the scriptural account of Israel's exodus from Egypt in a literal way. But

> what the Jews supposed to be a crossing of the sea, Paul calls a baptism; what they supposed to be a cloud, Paul asserts is the Holy Spirit. . . . And again, the manna which the Jews supposed to be food for the stomach and the satiation of the appetite, Paul calls "spiritual food." . . . Then again Paul declares plainly of the rock which followed them, "the rock was Christ." (*Hom. Exod.* 5.1, referring throughout to 1 Cor. 10)

Paul interprets allegorically the command "You shalt not muzzle an ox while it is treading out the grain" (*Cels.* 4.49, citing 1 Cor. 9:9-10; also

---

mystical object of [those matters]. Consequently, they have related what happened at this time as though at another time, and they have composed what is reported in this manner with a certain degree of distortion. For their intention was to speak the truth spiritually and materially at the same time where that was possible but, where it was not possible in both ways, to prefer the spiritual to the material. The spiritual truth is often preserved in the material falsehood, so to speak" (*Com. John* 10.19-20). The language is certainly striking. But is Origen really saying more than others who allow that Luke reworked the order of Jesus' last two temptations (Luke 4:1-13; cf. Matt. 4:1-11) to make a theological point; or more than the often advanced claim that, whereas, according to the Synoptic Gospels, Jesus was crucified the day after the Passover lamb had been slaughtered and eaten (see Luke 22:15), John makes a theological point by having Jesus ("our Passover lamb") crucified at the same time as the lambs were being sacrificed in the temple (cf. John 18:28; 1 Cor. 5:7)?

40. Cf. Dawson, *Readers;* Lamberton, *Homer.*
41. Cf. Barton, *Holy Writings,* 141-42.
42. Cf. Lamberton, *Homer,* 81.

F.P. 4.2.6), as well as the declaration in Genesis that a husband and wife "become one flesh" (*Cels.* 4.49, citing Eph. 5:31-32). Abraham's sons Isaac and Ishmael, together with their mothers, are interpreted allegorically in Galatians (4:21-31; see *F.P.* 4.2.6). More fundamentally, the significance of the whole system of cultic worship ordained in the Old Testament lay, not in the literal understanding and observance of these texts, but in the realities to which they pointed. In Colossians, Paul "briefly epitomis[es] the meaning of the entire system of the law" by saying that its provisions are "a shadow of the things to come" (*F.P.* 4.2.6, citing Col. 2:16-17; cf. *Hom. Lev.* 3.5.1). The Old Testament tabernacle is declared in Hebrews to be "a copy and shadow of the heavenly things" (*F.P.* 4.2.6, citing Heb. 8:5). And it is Paul who tells us that "the law is spiritual [i.e., it has a spiritual dimension, and requires spiritual interpretation]" (*Hom. Gen.* 6.1, referring to Rom. 7:14) and that "the letter [i.e., the Old Testament in its literal understanding] kills," whereas "the spirit [i.e., the spiritual understanding of Scripture] gives life" (*Hom. Lev.* 7.5.5, referring to 2 Cor. 3:6).

To read the Old Testament spiritually rather than literally is, in effect, to read it in a Christian rather than Jewish way (*Hom. Gen.* 6.1). But these are not simply alternative ways of construing the text, akin to Hamlet's varied and fanciful proposals of what Polonius's cloud resembled. As the words of God, Scripture is rather like the mysterious discourse of a man dropping hints about his future plans. Perhaps no one "catches" the hints at the time; but later, once the plans have been carried out, at least some hearers come to understand what the speaker was saying all along. To read the Old Testament simply at face value is to *misread* the Old Testament, to fail to grasp the nature of its divinely given hints. Those who read the Old Testament spiritually grasp the text's deeper (and intended) meaning. Its laws, sacrifices, and institutions were historical realities, to be sure; but to read of them merely as such is to miss their true nature as anticipations of, preembodiments of, and pointers to Christ and realities he brings (*Hom. Lev.* 3.5.1). Any number of Old Testament saints — though, to be sure, historical figures — were at the same time "types" of Christ: aspects of their lives anticipated, preembodied, and pointed to Christ (*Hom. Gen.* 14.1). Again, to read their stories simply at a literal level is to fail to grasp what they were really all about. And the messianic prophecies, though cast in material terms because spiritual realities can only be expressed in terms drawn from their material analogies, are rightly understood as finding (spiritual) fulfillment in Christ (*Com. Rom.* 8.8.10).[43] Origen sums up

43. Along the same lines, Origen rejected a literal reading of the book of Revelation. In

the point memorably by saying that, for those aware of its forward-looking, spiritual dimension, the so-called Old Testament is itself properly a "New" Testament.

> The law becomes an "Old Testament" only for those who want to understand it in a fleshly [i.e., literal] way; and for them it has necessarily become old and aged, because it cannot maintain its strength. But for us, who understand and explain it spiritually and according to the gospel-meaning, it is always new. Indeed, both are "New Testaments" for us, not by the age of time but by the newness of understanding. (*Hom. Num.* 9.4.2)

Clearly, however, it was only with the coming of Christ that the true and spiritual significance of the Old Testament became evident — and the Old Testament became New.[44] Origen believed that the Old Testament writers themselves were aware of the mysteries, the spiritual dimension, present in their words;[45] but only occasionally did they intimate that there was more to what they wrote than meets the eye (*Com. Cant.* 2.8). The prayer "Open my eyes, so that I may behold wondrous things out of your law" (Ps. 119:18) is one such intimation; and when Asaph introduces what appears to be a straightforward review of Israelite history in Psalm 78 by saying that he will speak "parables" and "dark sayings," he, too, implies that untold mysteries underlie the Old Testament narratives (*Cels.* 2.6; 4.49-50). But "as long as my Lord had not come, the law was closed, the prophetic words were closed, the reading of the Old Testament was veiled" (*Hom. Ezek.* 14.2.3). With "the coming of God our Savior," however, "truth descended from heaven . . . and the shadow and copies have fallen. . . . With the truth present, 'the type and shadow' have ceased" (*Hom. Josh.* 17.1).

---

the process, according to de Lubac, he "destroyed the millenarian error, which was at that time still powerful" (*History,* 117), thus achieving "one of the greatest" of "those victories that have ensured the purity of the faith" (43-44). De Lubac's enthusiasm notwithstanding, the game in which he claims victory for Origen had not at the time advanced beyond the second or third inning.

44. "A sign was given at His Passion that the things which were concealed in secrets and mysteries were now to be brought into the light and come to manifestation. For the veil of the Temple, by which the hidden and secret parts of the Holies were curtained off, was rent from the top to the bottom, thus openly declaring to all men that that which had been formerly concealed within could now be seen" (*Com. Cant.* 2.8).

45. Origen normally expresses himself confidently on the issue (e.g., *Hom. Num.* 5.1.3; *Com. John* 6.15, 22); but at least once he leaves the question open (*Com. John* 13.314-19).

Not only was Christ the fulfillment of Old Testament Scripture, the reality to which it pointed, the subject of its spiritual dimension; it was also Christ who revealed to his disciples that Scripture is rightly read as written about him. To this day, if we are to understand Scripture, Jesus must be our teacher.

> Just as . . . our Lord and Savior put his physical hand on the eyes of the blind man and restored his sight which he had lost, so also he put his spiritual hands on the eyes of the Law, which had been blinded by the corporeal understanding of the Scribes and Pharisees, and he restored sight to them, that to those to whom the Lord has opened the Scriptures spiritual vision and understanding might appear in the Law. And would that the Lord Jesus might "put his hands on" our eyes too. (*Hom. Gen.* 15.7)

> We [must] ask that Jesus come and make clear to us and teach us now what is written here. (*Hom. Jer.* 19.10; cf. *Hom. Exod.* 12.4)

Seeing Joshua, who led Israel into the Promised Land, as a type of Jesus (the names, in Greek, are identical), Origen discovers profound truth in Joshua 8:34-35 [LXX 9:2e-f]: "Jesus [i.e., Joshua] read all the words of the Law, blessings and curses, according to all that was written in the book of the Law; and there was no word out of all that Moses commanded that Jesus did not read in the presence of the whole church of the sons of Israel." For Origen, this means that, if we have rightly (i.e., spiritually) understood the law, it is Jesus who has "read" it to us. "For we who are of the catholic Church do not reject the Law of Moses, but we accept it if Jesus reads it to us. For thus we shall be able to understand the Law correctly, if Jesus reads it to us, so that when he reads we may grasp his mind and understanding" (*Hom. Josh.* 9.8).

By now it should be clear that, however common outright dismissals of Origen and his "allegorical method" may be, much that he included under the category has always been the stock-in-trade of Christian preachers. Later writers (as we shall see) divided what he spoke of as the "allegorical" or "mystical" or "spiritual" level of the text into two or three categories. For Origen, the terms were catchall expressions for whatever goes beyond a rigidly literal, bare-facts reading of the text. Reading the text "allegorically" included translating obvious metaphors into plain speech, seeing Old Testament sacrifices as foreshadowing Christ, and seeing various aspects of the lives of Old Testament saints as ("types") prefiguring Christ.[46] It also included the standard Christian procedure (suggested already by 1 Cor. 10 and Heb. 3 and 4) of seeing pictures of the beginning, middle, and end of the Christian life in stories of the Israelites' redemption from slavery, their departure from Egypt and deliverance at the Red Sea, the daily provisions and divine guidance they experienced through years of wilderness wanderings, the battles they fought, and their final entrance into the Promised Land (*Hom. Num.* 7.5.3-5; 27.2.1-4).

Special note should be made of Origen's treatment of Israel's wars. He, like many modern readers, found a literal reading of these narratives troublesome. But Origen had a ready answer: read the stories "spiritually" — that is, as pictures of the believer's struggles with sin. Again, his basic approach is no different from that of countless preachers (including some for whom the term "allegory" would be anathema).

> Within us, indeed, are all those breeds of vices that continually and incessantly attack the soul. Within us are the Canaanites; within us are the Perizzites; here are the Jebusites. In what way must we exert ourselves, how vigilant must we be or for how long must we persevere, so that when all these breeds of vices have been forced to flee, "our land may rest from wars" [Josh. 11:23] at last? (*Hom. Josh.* 1.7)

> You will read in the Holy Scriptures about the battles of the just ones, about the slaughter and carnage of murderers, and that the saints spare none of their deeply rooted enemies. . . . You should understand the wars of the just by the method I set forth above, that these wars are waged by them against sin. But how will the just ones endure if they reserve even a little bit of sin? Therefore, this is said of them: "They did not leave behind even one, who might be saved or might escape" [Josh 8:22]. (*Hom. Josh.* 8.7)

> When that Israel that is according to the flesh read these same Scriptures before the coming of our Lord Jesus Christ, they understood nothing in them except wars and the shedding of blood. . . . But after the presence of my Lord Jesus Christ poured the peaceful light of knowledge into

46. Some modern authors are careful to distinguish typology (good) from allegory (bad): whereas the former attaches additional significance to a text that is also meaningful at a literal level, allegory ignores or dismisses the literal sense as mere code-language for spiritual realities. The terminological distinction is, however, a modern creation; and both typology and allegory, so defined, are found in abundance in Origen's works. For a summary and assessment of the debate, see Martens, "Revisiting."

human hearts, since, according to the Apostle, he himself is "our peace" [Eph. 2:14], he teaches us peace from this very reading of wars. For peace is returned to the soul if its own enemies — sins and vices — are expelled from it. And therefore, according to the teaching of our Lord Jesus Christ, when we indeed read these things, we also equip ourselves and are roused for battle, but against those enemies that "proceed from the heart" [Matt. 15:19]. (*Hom. Josh.* 14.1)

Origen applies the same "spiritual" approach to the wish expressed in Psalm 137 that someone would "dash" the "little ones" of Babylon against a rock.

> Blessed is the one who seizes . . . the little ones of Babylon, which are understood to be nothing else but these "evil thoughts" that confound and disturb our heart. For this is what Babylon means. While these thoughts are still small and are just beginning, they must be seized and dashed against the "rock" who is "Christ" [1 Cor. 10:4], and, by his order they must be slain, so that nothing in us "may remain to draw breath" [Josh. 11:14]. (*Hom. Josh.* 15.3, referring to Ps. 137:8-9)

Up to this point, we have considered a number of examples of Origen's "allegorical" interpretations whose substance few Christian readers would oppose. But, of course, Origen goes much further. Convinced that Scripture is inspired in its every detail, and that, therefore, every part of Scripture must not only be true (at some level) but profitable as well, Origen set about the imposing task of finding edification in every detail of every text. And, granted a massive measure of good will, he found it. However arbitrary his interpretations may appear, it must be remembered that Origen's intention was merely to discover the spiritual meaning (the depth dimension) that he believed was inherent in the text itself. The task of the interpreter, he believed, was to find the "conceptual bridge" that linked the words of the text with the spiritual reality to which they (intentionally, though mysteriously) pointed, thus showing the intrinsic relationship between them.[47] A few examples of his procedure follow, with parenthetical comments on their typical features.

According to Numbers 12, Moses married an Ethiopian woman; for

---

47. Cf. Dawson, *Figural Reading,* 53-54, 72. Note that Origen dismissed attempted allegorical readings where he could see too little correspondence between the terms of the text and their purported spiritual interpretation. Cf. Martens, "Revisiting," 303, 310-11.

this, he was criticized by Miriam. As a result, Miriam became leprous for a time, but, in response to Moses' intercession, she was healed and received back into the Israelite camp.[48] Moses, of course, represents the law, but understood in a spiritual rather than a fleshly way: that is, the circumcision it prescribes is really that of the heart; its Sabbaths are a rest from sinning; its sacrifices, those of praise; and so on. When spiritually understood, the law (Moses) is embraced even by Gentiles (the Ethiopian woman), but criticized by Miriam (the synagogue), who then suffers leprosy (soul un-cleanness) and is banished from the "camp" (the church of God). The end of her leprosy will come "when the fullness of the Gentiles has entered in" and "all Israel will be saved": then "the leprosy will cease from the countenance of Miriam; for she will receive the beauty of the faith and she will accept the splendor of the knowledge of Christ" (*Hom. Num.* 6.4.1-2; 7.1.2, referring to Rom. 11:25-26). And Moses' intercession? "Perhaps this was what he discussed in his conversation with the Lord Jesus Christ, when he was transfigured on the mountain. Perhaps he asked him that all Israel be saved, once 'the fullness of the Gentiles has entered'" (*Hom. Num.* 7.4.1, referring to Matt. 17:3). (Note the tentativeness of the latter proposal; it is typical of many of Origen's "spiritual interpretations" that they are proposed with some hesitation — Origen will confess that he is dealing with great mysteries — and frequently accompanied by expressions of his willingness to entertain alternative suggestions from others, and to adopt them should they prove superior.[49])

When the Lord said to Moses in the wilderness, "Gather the people together [at the well] and I will give them water to drink" (Num. 21:16), the command, at the literal level, seems superfluous — surely people do not need divine instruction to gather at a well to drink. "Thus, the low value of the letter sends us back to the treasure of the spiritual interpretation" (*Hom. Num.* 12.1.1-2). Again, Moses represents the law (Origen believes the same symbols generally have the same referent throughout Scripture); the well stands for Jesus Christ (Origen arrives at this interpretation, as is his wont, only after collecting a number of passages in Scripture referring to wells, and concluding that the Son of God is their common referent). That Moses summons people to the well means, then, that the law summons us to faith in Christ — an interpretation for which (as again is his wont) Ori-

---

48. From the surface meaning of the text, Origen draws the evident moral lesson that we are not to speak evil of our neighbor, then moves on to the "mystical" understanding summarized above (*Hom. Num.* 7.1.1).

49. See de Lubac, *History*, 369-74.

gen finds confirmation in another text of Scripture: Christ himself declared that "Moses wrote about me" (*Hom. Num.* 12.1.8, referring to John 5:46).

In a famous homily (*Hom. Num.* 27, based on Num. 33:1-49), Origen suggests that each of the forty-two places at which the Israelites stayed on their way to the Promised Land represents a stage in the life of the Christian. The number is (of course) not accidental:[50] as "the coming of our Lord Jesus Christ into this world is traced through forty-two generations" (thus Matt. 1:17), so the reverse journey taken by Christians, from the world to the Father, is comprised of forty-two stages (27.3.1). The pillar of fire and the cloud that led the Israelites represent the Son of God and the Holy Spirit, "just as the prophet says in another place, 'The Lord himself was leading them'" (27.5.1). The particulars Origen finds in the passage about each stage of the Christian life are based on current understandings of the names of the places where the Israelites stayed. "Buthan" is taken to mean "valley," and thus represents the adversity with which virtue is inevitably tested (27.9.2). "Iroth" is said to mean "village," not "city," for progress begins with small things before coming to greater (27.9.3). "Elim," where there were twelve springs of water and seventy palm trees, means "rams": "Rams are the leaders of flocks. Who, then, are the leaders of Christ's flock if not the apostles, who are also the twelve springs? But since our Lord and Savior chose not only those twelve but also seventy others, for that reason there are not only twelve springs recorded, but also there are seventy palm trees" (27.11.1, referring to Luke 10:1). And so on. However arbitrary this procedure may seem to us,[51] Origen (we may say) was acting on the basis of the best science of his day.[52] And when he was unable to discover the meaning (and hence spiritual significance) of a name, he confessed as much and refused to say more than that, doubtless, this name, too, must refer to a stage in the life of the believer (27.12.11).

When the Israelites took possession of the Promised Land, the two

---

50. Numbers, for Origen, are never accidental or insignificant; they tend to retain the same significance wherever they occur in Scripture: "five" points to the number of senses (and hence to purely sensory perception), "fifty" speaks of forgiveness and pardon (cf. the year of Jubilee, and Luke 7:41-42 [*Hom. Num.* 5.2.2]), etc.

51. Origen himself was sensitive on this point: "Now possibly this kind of exposition, which relies on the meaning of Hebrew terms, may seem contrived and violently forced to those who do not know the conventions of that language" (*Hom. Num.* 27.13.1). In fact, the interpretation of names based on their presumed meaning was a crucial element in much of Origen's spiritual exegesis, allowing him to find significance in what might otherwise seem to be pointless lists of names wherever they occur in Scripture.

52. See Martens, *Origen*, 54-55.

tribes of Reuben and Gad and half the tribe of Manasseh assisted the other tribes in the conquest, but chose to live themselves on the east side of Jordan rather than in the promised inheritance. For Origen, those remaining outside the Promised Land (the two and a half tribes) represent the people of Israel, living under the law, whereas the land is possessed by Christians, who inherit it through faith and grace (the nine and a half tribes). Yet, as in Numbers 32, the latter are assisted by the former:

> Consider how those who were justified by the Law before the coming of Jesus Christ my Lord come to my aid as I struggle today in the trials of this life and strive against enemies. . . . Consider how Isaiah furnishes me aid when he illumines me with the words of his text. Consider Jeremiah coming to our aid, well-girded and unencumbered, putting to flight the most violent enemies, the gloom of my heart, with the javelins of his volume. . . . Hosea leads twelve squadrons of a prophetic band [i.e., the twelve Minor Prophets], and all advance with "their loins girded with truth," which they proclaim to aid their brothers so that, instructed by their writings, we may not be ignorant of devilish designs. (*Hom. Josh.* 3.1)

Very ingenious, we may say — but why precisely two and a half tribes? Why is the third tribe left incomplete? Perhaps, we are told, because "those prior ones" — the saints of Israel — had only an inkling of the *three* persons of the Trinity: they fell short of fully grasping it (*Hom. Josh.* 3.2). Here, at least, Origen does not interpret "spiritually" the words of one text by invoking the use of the same words in another. Where that recourse fails, proper interpretation is still steered (as with Irenaeus) by the faith of the church.[53]

The text of Jeremiah 17:11, as Origen read it, is as follows: "The partridge cried out; she has gathered what she did not lay, making her riches not with judgment. In the midst of her days, they will leave her behind; at her end she will be a fool."[54] To the crucial task of interpreting Scripture,

---

53. Cf. Martens, *Origen,* 127-31.

54. It is worth noting that, in spite of Origen's remarkable familiarity with variant readings and the errors found in biblical manuscripts, and in spite of his awareness that the Greek Old Testament text often mistranslates the Hebrew, it never (to my knowledge) occurs to him that a text might be unintelligible because of errors introduced in the process of its transmission or translation. Instead, he labors mightily to find both sense and edification in texts like that above. Origen is often criticized for the atomistic way he interprets texts. In his defense, we may at least say that such an approach, in addition to being typical of much biblical interpretation in his day, was, in a number of instances (particularly in the

Origen believed that one must bring all the resources at one's disposal. That meant, where the Bible speaks of particular animals, acquiring whatever information one could (from books, of course!) about those animals' habits. Of the partridge: "It is said that the animal is most malicious and wily and unscrupulous, and wants to deceive hunters" (*Hom. Jer.* 17.1.1). On the basis of that information, Origen proceeded (predictably enough) to see the partridge as representing the devil, who "cried out" (through the voice of heretics) in order to "gather what she does not lay" (i.e., the believers deceived and gathered by the devil are not the devil's creatures [*Hom. Jer.* 17.2.1]) — and so on.

The Song of Songs, for Origen (and for a host of Christian interpreters in his wake) speaks of the love between the bridegroom (Christ) and his bride (either the church as a whole or the individual believer). When the bride cries out, "Let him kiss me with the kisses of his mouth" (1:2), it is the church speaking: no longer content with the "kisses" of Moses and the prophets, she desires that the bridegroom himself would come and embrace her. "The Bridegroom's Father listens to the Bride and sends His Son" (*Hom. Cant.* 1.2). As Origen notes, in the Song of Songs, the bride frequently finds delight in the appearance of her groom only to have the groom suddenly vanish. "And that is something nobody can understand who has not suffered it himself. God is my witness that I have often perceived the Bridegroom drawing near me and being most intensely present with me; then suddenly He has withdrawn and I could not find Him, though I sought to do so. I long, therefore, for Him to come again, and sometimes He does so" (*Hom. Cant.* 1.7).

Origen did not confine his spiritual interpretations to Old Testament texts. When the five thousand whom Jesus fed were told to sit on the grass (Matt. 14:19), a worthy interpretation must be sought for the otherwise pointless recording of so insignificant a detail. Isaiah's "all flesh is grass" (Isa. 40:6) provides the clue: Those who would partake of the blessings of Jesus must (spiritually) "sit on the grass," that is, subjugate the flesh (*Com. Matt.* 11.3). In very much the same vein, when Jesus instructs his disciples to go to "the other side" of the lake, the spiritual point being made is that they are "to pass beyond things seen and material, as temporal, and to go on to things unseen and eternal" (*Com. Matt.* 11.5). And what are the two

---

Old Testament prophets), necessitated by the state of the text of his day: where a sentence yields no sense, significance can still be derived from its individual words. It should also be noted that Origen was certainly capable of following the thread of an argument (as in Paul's letter to the Romans), or the progression of a narrative (e.g., in Genesis, Joshua, or the Gospels), when edification was served by his doing so.

shoes of Jesus, whose latchet not even John the Baptist was fit to unloose (John 1:27)? Perhaps his incarnation is the one shoe, his descent into Hades the other (*Com. John* 6.174).

To the modern reader, such examples — and they could easily be multiplied many times — are simply bizarre as interpretations of the text. Still, it should be said that Origen's interpretations generally follow certain patterns, even rules: that is, there is a certain method to the apparent madness. Most importantly, for Origen, Scripture interprets Scripture: truth proposed (perhaps optimistically) as the meaning of one passage is found (unequivocally) in another. For that reason, however far-fetched Origen's interpretation of a particular text may seem, the Christian reader at least will seldom object to its content. And even where Origen seems simply to have prayed for guidance, then gathered the thoughts that the words of the text prompted in his mind, such thoughts are patently the product of a mind profoundly shaped by Scripture, and inspired by intense love for the Savior. Even those who dismiss his hermeneutics have often found devotional value in reading his homilies and commentaries.

The Interpreter of Scripture

We do not give all who speak to us the same type or degree of attention. We attend differently to the words of a child than to those of an adult, and differently to those of one adult than to those of another. But no mortal merits the attention we should devote to the words of Scripture, spoken as they are by the Spirit of God (*Hom. Num.* 26.3.1-2).

> Surely this is also why the Lord was saying, "Search the Scriptures!" [John 5:39] since he knew that these things are opened not by those who fleetingly listen to or read [the Scriptures] while occupied with other business, but by those who with an upright and sincere heart search more deeply into the Holy Scriptures, by constant effort and uninterrupted nightly vigils. . . . If anyone seeks in this way, he will find. (*Com. Rom.* 7.17.4; cf. *Hom. Gen.* 10.2; *Cels.* 6.7)

> If any of us is anxiously concerned about food and drink and devotes all his concern to secular affairs, but who assigns to God one hour or two out of the whole day, and comes to the church for prayer, or who listens to the word of God in passing, but who devotes his chief interest to anxious concern for the world and for his own belly — such a man does

not fulfill the command that says that a man should "advance according to his own order" [Num. 2:1-2], or that says, "Let all things be done according to order" [1 Cor. 14:40]. For the "order" [*ordo*] appointed by Christ is "to seek first the kingdom of God and his justice" [Matt. 6:33], and to believe that God adds these things to us in the second place. (*Hom. Num.* 2.1.3)

Origen frequently interrupted his homilies to express his exasperation at his congregation's inattention to the reading and exposition of Scripture (*Hom. Gen.* 10.1; *Hom. Exod.* 12.2; 13.3).

In counseling his former student Gregory, Origen notes that the study of philosophy, geometry, and astronomy can all be of benefit for the interpreter of Scripture. Just as the Israelites, by "spoiling" the Egyptians when departing from their land, acquired materials useful for the construction of the tabernacle, so the believer can make good use of pagan education. On the other hand, there are great dangers in sojourning too long in the land of Egypt. "Do you, then, my lord and my son, chiefly give heed to the reading of the Divine Scriptures; do give heed. For we need great attention when we read the Divine writings, that we may not speak or form notions about them rashly" (*Philoc.* 13.4).

Diligence by itself, however, is not enough. Though the physical eyes of human beings are sufficient to read the letter of Scripture (as they were to see the flesh of the Savior), spiritual faculties are required to perceive the divinity within (cf. *Dial.* 17).

Our Lord Jesus knows that there are other ears, besides those fleshly ones, that are required for the hearing of his words and the hearing of the law. Why, then, even in the Gospel, after he taught what was fitting about different things, does he add and say, "Whoever has ears to hear, let him hear" [Matt. 13:9]? Certainly, if he had spoken concerning fleshly ears, that would seem to be superfluous; for no one had gathered to hear his words who did not have ears. But because he knew the words that were said had to be received in the inner ears of a person, that is, in the understanding of the heart . . . he demanded ears from his hearers. (*Hom. Josh.* 9.9)

The same divine Spirit who inspired the writers of Scripture must illuminate the understanding of its readers. Spiritual perception, moreover, is obstructed by sin. Purity, then, must be added to spiritual perception as necessary for anyone who would interpret Scripture aright; and both are necessarily divine gifts. Hence the most essential requirement for the proper reading of Scripture is prayer.[55]

> It is not proper that a soul that is not holy should receive the holy words; but when he has purified himself from every filth of the flesh and bad habits, then having become "a holy place," he will receive the [spiritual] food of that "bread which descended from heaven" [John 6:41]. (*Hom. Lev.* 13.5.5; cf. *Com. Rom.* 8.8.13)

> The Holy Spirit himself must be entreated by us to remove every cloud and all darkness which obscures the vision of our hearts hardened with the stains of sin in order that we may be able to behold the spiritual and wonderful knowledge of his law, according to him who said, "Take the veil from my eyes and I shall observe the wonders of your Law" [Ps. 119:18]. (*Hom. Lev.* 1.1.4)

> To know these things clearly, that is, the things that are present and the things that are being indicated in these narratives . . . belongs to the same Holy Spirit who inspired these things to be written, and to our Lord Jesus Christ, who said of Moses, "For he wrote about me" [John 5:46], and to the almighty God, whose ancient plan for the human race is not openly indicated, but veiled in the letters. But let us pray from the heart to the Word of God, who is his only-begotten and who "reveals the Father to whom he wills" [Matt. 11:27], that he may deign to reveal these things even to us. (*Hom. Num.* 26.3.5)

On one level, the desired result of the proper reading of Scripture is for the interpreter to arrive, under the guidance of the divine Spirit, at its true, intended, spiritual meaning. But that is not all. The proper reading of Scripture is also the means by which believers mature in their faith. As we have seen, divine Scripture addresses the needs of all believers, whatever their capacities or degrees of maturity. In the very process by which immature readers begin with — and derive moral wisdom from — the "letter" of the text, then gradually develop a yearning to grasp its deeper, more spiritual dimensions, and at length grow in their understanding of these truths, believers are weaned from their attachment to the visible, transitory, earthly realm and come to fix their minds and their devotion on what is invisible, eternal, and heavenly. The progression corresponds,

---

55. Cf. Martens, *Origen,* 161-91.

in Origen's mind, to the sequence in which the works of Solomon appear in Scripture.[56] The prayerful reader of Proverbs "receive[s] the word of wisdom and the word of knowledge through the Holy Spirit," and is made "a partaker of that Wisdom who said: *I stretched out my words and ye did not hear* [Prov. 1:24]." Reading Ecclesiastes, he comes to realize

> that all visible and corporeal things are fleeting and brittle; and surely once the seeker after wisdom has grasped that these things are so, he is bound to spurn and despise them; renouncing the world bag and baggage, if I may put it in that way, he will surely reach out for the things unseen and eternal which, with spiritual meaning verily but under certain secret metaphors of love, are taught in the Song of Songs.

The reading of the Song of Songs (and the spiritual reading of Scripture in general) "instills into the soul the love of things divine and heavenly." Under the figure of the bride and bridegroom, it "teaches us that communion with God must be attained by the paths of charity and love."

> If, then, a man has completed his course in the first subject, as taught in Proverbs, by amending his behavior and keeping the commandments, and thereafter, having seen how empty is the world and realized the brittleness of transitory things, has come to renounce the world and all that is therein, he will follow on from that point to contemplate and to desire *the things that are not seen, and that are eternal* [2 Cor. 4:18]. To attain to these, however, we need God's mercy; so that, having beheld the beauty of the Word of God, we may be kindled with a saving love for Him, and He Himself may deign to love the soul, whose longing for Himself He has perceived.

---

56. Quotations in what follows are taken from *Cant. Com.*, prologue 3; see also Torjesen, "Theory."

CHAPTER 5

Chrysostom

Like Origen, Chrysostom heard the voice of God in the words of Scripture; strange that what he heard should be so different.

If Origen was the early church's first and greatest biblical scholar, John Chrysostom was its foremost preacher. The name by which he is universally known — "Chrysostom" means "Golden Mouth" — reflects his reputation, both ancient and modern. The elegance of his sermons has been deemed comparable to that of Demosthenes;[1] their interpretive riches (particularly when he treats the Pauline epistles) are mined and cited even in the most recent commentators.[2] Origen's exegetical approach set the course that the Western church would largely follow for a thousand years and more; but Chrysostom's work was also well known in the West, while, to this day, no one is held in higher esteem in the Eastern churches: "Even today John Chrysostom enjoys the love and veneration of all denominations."[3] In short, if early church leaders of the stature of Origen and Chrysostom took opposing approaches to Scripture, then, it must be said, the Christian church, from its very beginnings, has had its "battles of the Bible."

---

1. Kelly, *Golden Mouth,* 7: "If a junior contemporary like Isidore of Pelusion (d. ca. 435), himself a highly polished writer, could wax lyrical on the music of [Chrysostom's] prose, modern connoisseurs of Greek literature have united in acclaiming him 'an almost pure Atticist,' the only prose author of his epoch who can stand comparison with Demosthenes."

2. Kelly, *Golden Mouth,* 94: Chrysostom's "sermon-commentaries . . . form the most impressive, and also most readable, collection of patristic expositions of scripture." *The Oxford Dictionary of the Christian Church* pronounces him flatly "the greatest of Christian expositors" (345).

3. Campenhausen, *Fathers,* 144.

Life

Roughly a century after Origen's death, John (honored from the fifth century onward with the name Chrysostom) was born in Antioch.[4] Though his father died shortly after his birth, his mother took steps to see that he enjoyed a good education. Among his teachers was Libanos, a renowned orator, who must have cultivated Chrysostom's own flair for elegant prose and eloquent public speaking. (Theodore [ca. 350-428], later bishop of Mopsuestia, was a fellow student of Libanos.) Though raised as a Christian, John was first baptized in 368, after which he served as a kind of bishop's aide for three years while studying — again with Theodore — under Diodore, later bishop of Tarsus (d. ca. 390); from Diodore, he and Theodore derived their basic approach to the interpretation of Scripture. John was then appointed an official reader of the church; but rather than allow himself to be ordained as a priest (a task for which he deemed himself unworthy), he withdrew for six years to the mountains around Antioch and adopted a rigorously ascetic lifestyle. Forced by ill health to return to the city, he resumed his position as a reader (378) before becoming a deacon (380), then a priest (386). He quickly gained a reputation as an outstanding preacher. In 398, against his will, he was made bishop of Constantinople. There his forthright condemnation of evil as he perceived it brought him powerful enemies, and he was ultimately banished from the city. Subjected to a brutal forced march in severe weather conditions, he died in 407.

The Nature of Scripture

In the beginning there was no Scripture; if we lived as we should, we would not need Scripture today.[5] God spoke directly to Noah, Abraham, Job, and Moses — but their lives were pure (*Hom. Gen.* 2.4; *Hom. Matt.* 1.1).[6] Divine

---

4. Kelly (*Golden Mouth,* 4), noting that dates between 344 and 354 have been proposed, gives the probable year as 349.

5. Our primary focus in this chapter is on Chrysostom's homilies on Genesis, Isaiah, and other isolated Old Testament texts; Matthew, John, Acts, and all the Pauline epistles (including Hebrews, but apart from Galatians, on which a "commentary" is extant); also on (what are referred to as) commentaries on Job, certain Psalms, Proverbs, Ecclesiastes, a few chapters in Isaiah, and Galatians. The latter, as now extant, lack the trappings of sermons; whether they ever represented the substance of preached sermons is not clear. For issues related to the dating and provenance of the sermons, see Mayer, *Homilies.*

6. To facilitate locating references used in this chapter, I have included the volume

instruction, moreover, was accessible, not through books read only by the literate, but through creation, whose wonders are evident to all — and are wondrously portrayed by Chrysostom (*Hom. Statues* 9-12). Beyond even that, God planted within human beings an instinctive awareness of what they should and should not do (*Hom. John* 14 [FC 33.136]; *Hom. Statues* 12.9). Job required no teaching from Moses to be virtuous (*Com. Job,* prologue). It was only after human beings had distanced themselves from God and fallen into sin that God, desiring to reestablish friendship, resorted to an inferior but now necessary form of communication: he sent "letters." The first letters (i.e., the books of Genesis through Deuteronomy) were delivered by Moses (*Hom. Gen.* 2.4).

Oracles known from the pagan world were, Chrysostom believed, delivered through those possessed by demons, who "cripple[d] their mind and cloud[ed] their reasoning"; as a result, the seers themselves had not a clue of what they uttered (*Com. Ps.,* on 45:1).[7] The Holy Spirit, in contrast, communicated his messages to the understanding of Scripture's writers, who then meditated on them before passing them on to others (*Com. Ps.,* on 49:3-4). Chrysostom often speaks of how the "wisdom" of Scripture's (human) authors is apparent in what they wrote. Closely identifying the writers with their writings, he insists that those who read Scripture enjoy living communion with — and even hear the voices of — those authors: they actually "have Moses and the prophets" with them through their writings (*Hom. Ps.,* on 146:1 [*O.T.H.* 3.116]). Jesus declared that David, in the Psalms, "calls him Lord" (Matt. 22:43-44, citing Ps. 110:1); Chrysostom claims that the present tense "calls" serves "to bring out that [David] is still present and speaks through his writings" (*Hom. Ps.,* on 146:1 [*O.T.H.* 3.117]). Those who sailed with Paul to Rome would have avoided shipwreck had they obeyed his warning (Acts 27:9-10, 21-22); through his writings, Paul accompanies us, too, on our journey through life, and it is no less incumbent on us to heed his words (*Hom. Acts* 53 [NPNF 11.318]). Chrysostom himself, it seems, knew no greater joy than that of "conversing" with Paul:

---

and page number from the Fathers of the Church series (FC) and the first series of the Nicene and Post-Nicene Fathers (NPNF), where (but only where) the homily from which the quotation is taken is not divided into sections; these include the Homilies on John, Acts, Romans, Colossians, and 1 Thessalonians. Volume and page number are also given for quotations from the three volumes of *Old Testament Homilies.*

7. Because I cite Hill's translation of Chrysostom's work on the Psalms, I follow his practice of retaining the numbering of the Psalms found in the standard English translations rather than that of the Septuagint.

Gladly do I enjoy the spiritual trumpet [i.e., Paul], and get roused and warmed with desire at recognizing the voice so dear to me, and seem to fancy him all but present to my sight, and behold him conversing with me. But I grieve and am pained, that all people do not know this man, as much as they ought to know him. . . . And this comes not of incapacity, but of their own not having the wish to be continually conversing with this blessed man. (*Hom. Rom.,* Prologue)

Where did Priscilla gain the wisdom to teach Apollos? No doubt from having Paul as a guest in her home for two years (Acts 18:2-3, 26). But we, too, can "have Paul" — and Peter and John, and the "whole choir" of prophets and apostles — by making their books our constant companions (*Hom. Rom.* 30 [NPNF 11.551]).

This striking claim notwithstanding, Chrysostom repeatedly — and instinctively — qualifies statements of what a Moses or a Matthew had to say by adding that the real speaker is divine,[8] and that "we" are those whom God would teach: "Let us see if we can learn what it is today, too, the blessed Moses wants to teach us — or rather the Holy Spirit through his tongue" (*Hom. Gen.* 7.7). It was the Spirit who spoke through David in the Psalms (*Hom. Acts* 3 [NPNF 11.18]).[9] As for Isaiah, the "mouth" indeed was his, but the words came from God above (*Hom. Matt.* 5.2). If Luke emphasized his reliance on eyewitnesses rather than on the Holy Spirit, it was only because the former claim would be deemed more credible by unbelievers; but he, too, partook of the Spirit (*Hom. Acts* 1 [NPNF 11.3]). Paul had no need to introduce his words by saying, "Thus saith the Lord," for Christ spoke from within him; in any case, an apostle says nothing of himself but only "speaks the things of Him who sent him" (*Hom. 1 Thess.* 8 [NPNF 13.355]).

---

8. Chrysostom thinks that the psalmist's use (according to the Septuagint) of the term "belch" to denote the mode of his speaking can apply to all the inspired authors: their writings, after all, were the product of divine impulse, not human effort, and in Chrysostom's own, somewhat limited experience of humankind, "we do not belch when we choose to" (*Com. Ps.,* on 45:1).

9. Chrysostom treats David as the author of the whole Psalter. Nonetheless, he does recognize that the historical circumstances presupposed in certain psalms were those of later times, including those of the Babylonian exile and even (he proposes) the Maccabean revolt. In these cases, inspiration allowed the author to speak, not in his own person, but in that of one living at those times (e.g., *Com. Ps.,* on 44:1; cf. *Hom. 1 Cor.* 33.5). This understanding of the Psalms is shared by other "Antiochene" interpreters (on the term "Antiochene," see the discussion below). Cf. Wiles, "Theodore," 497-501.

O! the wisdom of the Apostle! or rather, not the wisdom of Paul, but the grace of the Spirit is the thing to wonder at. For surely he uttered not these things of his own mind, nor in that way did he find his wisdom. . . . But it was from the working of God. (*Hom. Heb.* 1.3; cf. *Hom. Heb.* 10.1)[10]

Chrysostom's own love of Scripture is unmistakable; equally apparent is the failure of his congregation to match his devotion. He knows, and has an answer for, all their excuses. Are some too poor to have their own copies of Scripture?[11] But even the poor find means to acquire tools to earn their physical livelihood, and for their spiritual well-being Scripture is no less essential. Besides, they could start by paying better attention to the public readings of Scripture in church (*Hom. John* 11 [FC 33.105]; cf. *Hom. John* 58 [FC 41.115]). Do others claim that, since they are not monks but ordinary people, they are too busy with family and work to have time left over for Scripture? But those daily wounded by the world are in most need of Scripture's remedy (*Hom. Matt.* 2.10; cf. *Hom. Gen.* 21.20). Have they forgotten that "not on bread alone does man live . . . but on every word coming from the mouth of God" (*Hom. Gen.* 21.22, citing Deut. 8:3)?

Do still others neglect Scripture because it is difficult to understand and reading it seems a waste of time? They should learn from the Ethiopian eunuch: even while riding in a chariot, he pored over the words of a prophet that he could not understand — until "the loving Lord, seeing

---

10. Though Chrysostom often speaks generally of the inspiration of the biblical authors, Robert C. Hill suggests that he may not have considered the authors of the Old Testament wisdom literature and historical books "to be the recipients of the charism of divine inspiration to the same extent as the prophets [including Moses] and psalmists" ("Introduction," 1-2; cf. Hill, *Reading,* 32; also Garrett, *Analysis,* 181). Chrysostom does frequently comment on the (merely) human wisdom and common sense underlying particular verses in Proverbs and Ecclesiastes, and notes their limited truth (e.g., *Com. Prov.,* on 9:8; on 10:4; on 11:24, 30; *Com. Eccl.,* prologue; on 1:2; on 3:21). Observing that Chrysostom seldom cites the Apocrypha (apart from Sirach, spoken of merely as "another wise man"), and that there are no extant homilies or commentaries on any of these books, Garrett suggests that he may have had some hesitancy about their authority (*Analysis,* 181-82). Cf. Baur, *Chrysostom,* 1.317, who also notes that, "among his eleven thousand citations from the New Testament the following are missing: the Apocalypse, the second Epistle of Peter, the second and third Epistles of John, and the Epistle of [Jude]." But in general, "Antiochene commentators do not debate the contents of the canon of the Old Testament on which they are commenting" (Hill, *Reading,* 20).

11. On the other hand, Chrysostom is not impressed, either, by those who desire to impress others by having copies of Scripture in their homes that they never read (*Com. John* 32 [FC 33.319]).

his desire, . . . sent him a mentor" (*Hom. Gen.* 35.3-6, referring to Acts 8:26-39). If we show a similar zeal, the Lord himself will "come from on high to enlighten our minds, shed light on our thinking, bring to our attention what had slipped our notice, and act as our instructor in what we have no knowledge of" (*Hom. Gen.* 35.2). Have some abandoned the study of Scripture because there are so many different interpretations that they never know what to believe? They do not give up so easily when buying a cloak. Besides, they became Christians because they recognized that the gospel was true and its rivals were not; they exercised similar judgment in rejecting the teaching of the heretics. Clearly, then, they are not as bereft of discernment as they suppose (*Hom. Acts* 33 [NPNF 11.211]). In any case, God will make the truth clear to those who truly seek him.

> We have, you see, a loving Lord, and when he sees us anxious to learn and demonstrating a keen appetite for understanding the divine sayings . . . he immediately enlightens our thinking, bestows illumination from himself, and in his inventive wisdom he implants in our soul the whole of his trustworthy instruction. . . . In the phrase "those who hunger and thirst after righteousness," [Jesus] taught his listeners the great degree of enthusiasm with which they ought to proceed to the study of the spiritual sayings. (*Hom. Gen.* 24.2, referring to Matt. 5:6)

> It often happens that what we could not discover today in our reading we all of a sudden come across the next day in returning to the task as the loving God in unseen fashion sheds light on our mind. (*Hom. Gen.* 35.6; cf. *Hom. Gen.* 9.2)

If Chrysostom finds the perennial excuses for neglecting Scripture exasperating, a sanctified but stronger word must be found for his response to the perennial — and trivial (or even sinful) — pursuits to which his congregants give greater attention. How can they have no time for Scripture when time is never lacking for gossip in the marketplace (cf. *Com. Ps.,* on 6:2)? Christians unable to recite a single psalm know all the words of the devil's songs (*Hom. Matt.* 2.9). Christians ignorant of the names and number of the books of the Bible are experts when asked about the horses and charioteers at the racetracks or entertainers in the city (*Hom. John* 32 [FC 33.320]; 58 [FC 41.117]). When Scripture is read in church, the least inconvenience prevents their attendance; the most inclement weather does not keep them from the races. People who yawn when God addresses them through the reading of Scripture can give undivided attention for half a day to actors in the theater (*Hom. John* 58 [FC 41.116]). To give brief attention to Scripture, then fill one's mind with worldly matters, is like allowing a bandage just applied to a wound to fall off, exposing the sore to all manner of aggravation (*Hom. John* 84 [FC 41.426]).

It seems clear to Chrysostom that those who neglect Scripture have no grasp of the price they pay for their indifference: the good they forfeit, and the harm they incur. He at least does everything in his power to inform them. Scripture is the remedy for all our needs; its neglect, the cause of all our ills.

> Great is the profit to be derived from the sacred Scriptures and their assistance is sufficient for every need. . . . The divine words, indeed, are a treasury containing every sort of remedy, so that, whether one needs to put down senseless pride, or to quench the fire of concupiscence, or to trample on the love of riches, or to despise pain, or to cultivate cheerfulness and acquire patience — in them one may find in abundance the means to do so. (*Hom. John* 37 [FC 33.359]; cf. *Hom. Gen.* 29.4)

> From this it is that our countless evils have arisen — from ignorance of the Scriptures; from this it is that the plague of heresies has broken out; from this that there are negligent lives; from this labors without advantage. For as men deprived of this daylight would not walk aright, so they that look not to the gleaming of the Holy Scriptures must needs be frequently and constantly sinning, in that they are walking in the worst darkness. (*Hom. Rom.*, Prologue; cf. *Hom. Heb.* 8.9-10)

> Hearken, I entreat you, all ye that are careful for this life, and procure books that will be medicines for the soul. If ye will not any other, yet get you at least the New Testament, the Apostolic Epistles, the Acts, the Gospels, for your constant teachers. If grief befall thee, dive into them as into a chest of medicines; take thence comfort of thy trouble, be it loss, or death, or bereavement of relations; or rather dive not into them merely, but take them wholly to thee; keep them in thy mind. This is the cause of all evils: the not knowing the Scriptures. We go into battle without arms, and how ought we to come off safe? (*Hom. Col.* 9 [NPNF 13.300-301])

From Scripture we learn both correct doctrine and the right way to live (*Hom. John* 53 [FC 41.61]). It arms us to resist the heretics (*Hom. John* 40

[FC 33.412]), "overcome with ease troublesome passions and escape the devil's wiles" (*Hom. Gen.* 14.22; cf. *Hom. John* 32 [FC 33.320]). Naturally, there is much to be learned from Scripture's instructions and admonitions, but no less from its stories and psalms (*Hom. Acts* 29 [NPNF 11.186-87]). To say with the psalmist "Blessed the man who fears the Lord" is to realize that it is not the wealthy, the well-positioned, the handsome, or the healthy who merit emulation, but those with sound values and reverence for God (*Hom. Ps.,* on Ps. 42 [*O.T.H.* 3.84]). To read stories of the righteous is to perceive our frailties by comparison (*Hom. Matt.* 4.16) and to be invited to imitate their virtues (*Hom. Gen.* 11.12; 28.2; 29.1). That even the sins of the righteous are recorded in Scripture should keep pious readers from overconfidence; conversely, accounts of the radical conversion of the wicked should prevent sinners from despairing (*Hom. Gen.* 29.1). Nor is Chrysostom insensitive to the effect Scripture — and particularly its psalms and its stories — has on the will and desires of its readers; there is more here than instruction for the mind. To meditate on the Psalms is to kindle one's desire for God, to inflame one's soul, to fill it with "great goodness and love" (*Com. Ps.,* on 141:1). To nourish oneself on the story of David sparing the life of his enemy Saul is to immunize oneself against passion (*Hom. David* 1 [*O.T.H.* 1.24-25]). Those who read of Jesus' birth "at once scorn all the things of this life."

> If you are wealthy, you will not rejoice in your wealth, because you have heard that she who was the wife of a carpenter and born of a humble family became Mother of your Lord. Moreover, if you are poor, you will not be ashamed of your poverty, because you have learned that the Creator of the world was not ashamed of a very poor dwelling. (*Hom. John* 53 [FC 41.62-63])

> [Through reading Scripture], the soul too is given wings and becomes elevated, glowing with the light of the Sun of Justice, freed at that time from the harm of evil thoughts and enjoying great peace and tranquility. What bodily nourishment is for the maintenance of our strength, reading is for the soul. You see, its nourishment is spiritual, and it both invigorates the mind and makes the soul strong, better attuned and wiser . . . rendering its wings light and transferring it to heaven itself, so to say. (*Hom. Gen.* 29.4)

Scripture thus delights as well as instructs the faithful; indeed, it instructs while it delights.

Delectable indeed are the meadow, and the garden, but far more delectable the study of the divine writings. For there indeed are flowers which fade, but here are thoughts which abide in full bloom; there is the breeze of the zephyr, but here the breath of the Spirit; . . . there is the sound of cicadae, but here the melody of the prophets; there is the pleasure which comes from sight, but here the profit which comes from study. The garden is confined to one place, but the Scriptures are in all parts of the world; the garden is subject to the necessities of the seasons, but the Scriptures are rich in foliage, and laden with fruit alike in winter and in summer. Let us then give diligence to the study of the Scriptures; for if thou doest this the Scripture will expel thy despondency, and engender pleasure, extirpate vice, and make virtue take root; and in the tumult of life it will save thee from suffering like those who are tossed by troubled waves. The sea rages but thou sailest on with calm weather; for thou hast the study of the Scriptures for thy pilot; for this is the cable which the trials of life do not break asunder. (*Hom. Eutropius* 2.1)

In short,

it is not possible for one who perseveringly attunes himself to the words of God to remain fixed in his present weakness; he will of necessity acquire wings and fly aloft to the heavenly abode itself and become possessed of an infinite treasure-trove of blessings. (*Hom. John* 1 [FC 33.12])

The Interpretation of Scripture

Like Origen, Chrysostom believed that God's purpose in revealing Scripture was to bring human beings to salvation (*Hom. Gen.* 14.5; 17.3). But Chrysostom's rather different understanding of how God achieves that end means that he has a different view of how Scripture is to be interpreted.

Origen believed that God addresses human beings at various stages of spiritual maturity through the distinct levels at which Scripture can be read. The surface meaning of the text is designed to meet the needs of the most immature; as readers progress in their level of maturity, they are equipped to perceive, and to be guided by, what Scripture conveys at its deeper levels, made accessible through spiritual interpretation. For Origen, a mark of the divinity of Scripture is precisely this capacity to communicate truth at more than one level of meaning; its profoundest truths lie hidden beneath the surface of the text. Scripture itself signals, through *un*truths appearing intermittently at its literal level, that its most significant truths are to be sought elsewhere. The search for "spiritual" truth beyond the plain meaning of the biblical text is characteristic of what has come to be called the "Alexandrian" school of interpretation.

For Chrysostom (and other "Antiochene" interpreters), the plain meaning of the biblical text, as understood and intended by its (human) authors, is the medium of divine revelation and should be the focus of interpretation.[12] Pursuing the meaning of the author through a contextual, historical interpretation, the more rigorous Antiochenes found themselves denying many of the traditional christological or Trinitarian readings of Old Testament texts.[13] Such, they believed, were beyond the horizons of the Old Testament authors.[14] In any case, closer attention to the context from which such texts were lifted showed that their authors were not thinking in these terms.[15] Still, the Antiochenes did not deny that the Old

12. The primary representatives of this school of interpretation are the aforementioned Diodore of Tarsus; his pupils Theodore of Mopsuestia and John Chrysostom; and Theodoret of Cyrus (ca. 393–ca. 460). Recent scholarship, noting the considerable differences among interpreters traditionally identified as Antiochene, is less inclined to speak of a "school." Among other recent trends, we may note the claim that differences between the Alexandrian and Antiochene interpreters, and particularly the proximity of the latter to modern (historical-critical) biblical scholarship, have been greatly exaggerated; and that the Antiochene approach to Scripture is rooted in the methods and virtues promoted by a rhetorical education in antiquity; that of the Alexandrians, in those espoused within the philosophical tradition. It lies outside my purpose to explore these observations here. Readers should consult, in particular, the classic work of Francis Young, *Exegesis*.

13. Hill, *Reading*, 170-72.

14. Cf. Wiles, "Theodore," 503-4.

15. Diodore, e.g., allows that there are "similarities" between certain verses in Ps. 22 and what happened to Christ; but noting parts of the psalm of which this cannot be said, he concludes that "it is not applicable to the Lord" (Diodore, *Commentary*, 69-74). Quasten, speaking of Theodore, formulates the underlying principle: "He rejects the Messianic interpretations proposed by the allegorical school of Alexandria which violate his sound principle that each Psalm must be treated as a literary whole and that a verse cannot be divorced from its context. He refuses to admit any change of person, time or situation in the same Psalm" (*Patrology*, 3.404-5). As a result, Theodore recognizes only Psalms 2, 8, 45, and (apparently, though his commentary is not extant here) 110 as, strictly speaking, predictions of Christ, though he, too, allows that in other psalms (e.g., Pss. 22 and 69) the situation spoken of by the psalmist, while not that of Christ, may have analogies in his life. Similarly, Theodore denies that a number of prophetic texts traditionally regarded as messianic are in fact predictions of Christ, believing them to have a more immediate referent; he allows, however, that their words may nonetheless function as a kind of type,

Testament narratives contain a number of "types" that foreshadow the life and work of Christ. Since the typological significance does not emerge from a surface reading of the texts, and since the term "allegorical" was taboo, Antiochenes spoke of the *theōria,* or spiritual "insight," by which such significance was perceived.[16] The term is in fact used wherever the Antiochenes find significance in a text that goes beyond its surface sense, though (nota bene) rooted in the latter[17] and in no way compromising its truth or significance.

> For the Antiochenes, the narrative logic, the plain meaning, the "earthly" reality of the text read in a straightforward way, was the vehicle or "ikon" of deeper meanings of a moral and dogmatic kind. What was needed was "insight."[18]

---

anticipating the fuller reality of Christ's work; indeed, the hyperbolic language of such passages (he cites explicitly Ps. 16:10) shows that, whatever their initially intended referent, their true fulfillment is achieved in Christ. Cf. Theodore, *Com. Twelve Prophets,* on Joel 2:28-32; on Mic. 5:2; on Zech. 9:9. For a similar principle in Chrysostom, see *Hom. Matt.* 8.5 (referring to Hos. 11:1; Matt. 2:15): "And if the Jews should raise a question touching the prophecy, and say that the words, 'Out of Egypt have I called my son,' were uttered concerning themselves; we would tell them, This is a law of prophecy, that in many cases much that is spoken of one set of persons is fulfilled in another. . . . Both the people and the patriarch, going down [to Egypt], and coming up thence, were together completing the type of *His* return." Cf. *Com. Isa.,* on 2:1-4.

16. See Diodore's *Commentary on the Psalms,* preface 7 (reproduced in Froehlich, *Interpretation,* 82-86, here 85). The Antiochenes criticized the allegorists for their readiness to dispense with the surface sense of the text altogether: allegorical interpretation (they claim) maintains that while the text says one thing, it means another, so that "Adam is not Adam, paradise is not paradise, the serpent is not the serpent"; moreover, by lifting these terms from their place in the biblical narrative and effectively reducing their significance to their purported "spiritual" sense, the allegorists lose sight of their true place in Scripture's grand story of redemption (so Theodore, commenting on Gal. 4:22-31, reproduced in Froehlich, *Interpretation,* 95-103, here 97). Diodore also discusses the difference between *theōria* and allegory in his "Preface to the Commentary on Psalm 118" (reproduced in Froehlich, *Interpretation,* 87-94). For the continuing significance of *theōria* in Orthodox hermeneutics, see Breck, *Power,* 93-113.

17. I.e., there is some recognizable correspondence between what is said at the plain level of the text and the higher meaning attributed to it.

18. Young, *Exegesis,* 211. The term "ikon" is meant to convey the need (as the Antiochenes saw it) for some resemblance between the text and its deeper meaning. It is contrasted with the merely symbolic use of words in Alexandrian allegory, where the words, taken by themselves (in a way that destroys the coherence of the biblical narrative), are mere tokens or symbols standing for something else, with which they bear no obvious resemblance. See Young, *Exegesis,* 161-85, 210-11.

Though far and away the most influential, Chrysostom was neither the most doctrinaire nor the most militant of the Antiochenes.[19] He rarely points out the errors of the allegorists,[20] and at times can refer to their readings without implying any condemnation (e.g., *Com. Ps.*, on 116:13; *Hom. Matt.* 52.1; *Hom. John* 85 [FC 41.431]). Indeed, particularly in the Psalms, he frequently proposes a "spiritual" interpretation of his own, whereby some aspect of the reality of Christ and his church is disclosed; but such readings are always proposed alongside a treatment of the plain sense of the text and (he insists) "without doing violence to" the latter (e.g., *Com. Ps.*, on 8:5; on 44:1; on 46:8-9; on 48:2; on 50:1).[21] While hardly expansive in his christological (or Trinitarian) readings of the Old Testament,[22] he was at least less rigorous than others of his school.[23] Where, for example, the christological reading of a particular verse required that it be given a different referent from that of neighboring verses, the more rigorous Antiochenes saw the resulting incoherence as reason to reject the interpretation. Chrysostom proposed that, in the divine purpose, neighboring verses could well have different referents, thus deliberately concealing pointers to Christ until their fulfillment made clear their true significance.[24] To the objection why

19. For that reason, Theodore of Mopsuestia is considered the better subject in histories of biblical interpretation.

20. But cf. *Com. Isa.*, on 5:7: "This is everywhere a rule in Scripture: when it wants to allegorize, it tells the interpretation of the allegory, so that the passage will not be interpreted superficially or be met by the undisciplined desire of those who enjoy allegorization to wander about and be carried in every direction." The examples Chrysostom gives of allegories identified as such in Scripture are Prov. 5:15-19; Isa. 5:1-7; 8:7-8; Ezek. 17. See also *Hom. Gen.* 13.13, 15; *Com. Isa.*, on 1:22.

21. Cf. *Com. Job,* on 40:15: "We ought firstly to give attention to the factual sense, and then, if there is some benefit for the listener, not neglect the spiritual sense as well." See also *Hom. Gen.* 13.13, where Chrysostom similarly insists that literal, earthly truth is not to be denied in the search for heavenly truth.

22. E.g., he did not interpret Gen. 3:15 christologically (*Hom. Gen.* 17.27-29) or identify Wisdom in Prov. 8 with the Son (*Com. Prov.*, on 8:22-27). Garrett (*Analysis*, 226) notes that he did not treat Isa. 4:2-6 or 8:8-10 as eschatological and messianic.

23. E.g., he sees Father and Son in the "let us" of Gen. 1:26 (*Hom. Gen.* 8.8; cf. 14.16); a hymn to the Trinity in the *Trisagion* of Isa. 6:3 (*Com. Isa.*, on 6:3); Christ in Ps. 118:22-27a, though acknowledging at 27b that the text has returned from "inspired [prophetic] commentary" to "historical narrative" (*Com. Ps.*, on 118:22-27); Christ in Isa. 7:14-16, though acknowledging that these verses interrupt words pertaining directly to Ahaz (*Com. Isa.*, on 7:14-16).

24. Cf. *Com. Ps.*, on Ps. 109. In a direct counter to the position of Diodore and Theodore, he writes: "To whom does the psalm refer? Some things are in reference to Judas, the Spirit [prophesying] through David, the remainder about others. Again, you see, this is the manner of inspired composition. Often you will find it so composed that the opening refers

prophets would even bother making a prediction if its true nature went unnoticed by those who heard it, Chrysostom replied:

> So that when [Christ] did come they might have teachers of their own number to prompt them, and they might realize that what was happening was no novelty nor was the plan recently formed, and instead that this had been proclaimed ahead of time from on high even a long time before — a fact of no little significance for winning them over to faith. (*Hom. Obscurity* 2 [*O.T.H.* 3.29])[25]

Chrysostom, of course, shared the openness of other Antiochenes — indeed, of all the early Christians — to the typological interpretation of the Old Testament.[26]

These qualifications notwithstanding, in his interpretation of the overwhelming majority of biblical texts, Chrysostom showed his Antiochene allegiance by devoting attention primarily if not exclusively to the surface

---

to one person and the remainder to another." After his comments on 109:4, he continues: "Having described the fate of Judas, how he condemned himself, how he passed the sentence of death on himself, how he hanged himself, how his apostleship passed to another, the psalmist then returns to his former theme. This too, you see, is characteristic of inspired composition, to interrupt the thread in the middle and insert some story, then after telling that in full, go back to the former theme." See also *Com. Isa.,* on 2:5: "Having finished his prophecy about the Church, he again returns to history, which occupies him in the following verses. This was [the prophets'] custom . . . that they may conceal the prophecy by the form of what follows"(cf. *Com. Ps.,* on 118:22; *Com. Isa.,* on 7:16). Chrysostom also notes (approvingly) that the New Testament writers sometimes interpreted Old Testament texts in a different, deeper sense than that intended by the Old Testament writers themselves (*Com. Ps.,* on 116:10, citing 2 Cor. 4:13; *Hom. 2 Cor.* 19.2, on 9:7, citing Prov. 22:8a [LXX]; cf. *Hom. Heb.* 4.2, citing Ps. 8:4-5).

25. On a similar note, Chrysostom grants that the merely temporary validity of the Mosaic law was kept obscure in the Old Testament, since otherwise Israel would have scorned it from the beginning (*Hom. Obscurity* 1 [*O.T.H.* 3.22, 24]).

26. For examples, see *Hom. Gen.* 35.16; 47.14; 61.10-11; *Hom. John* 14 (FC 33.138-39); 26 (FC 33.255-56); 27 (FC 33.262-63); 36 (FC 33.352-53). As Chrysostom puts it, faith in things otherwise unbelievable (e.g., Christ's virgin birth and resurrection) was divinely facilitated by their partial anticipation in Old Testament types (e.g., the miraculous childbearing of barren women; Jonah's emergence from the whale) (*Hom. Gen* 49.7; *Hom. 1 Cor.* 7.8; cf. *Hom. Matt.* 2.4; 43.2). The types, Chrysostom insists, were only partial anticipations of what would come: sufficiently like to be a type, but sufficiently unlike to be a shadow of the truth rather than its actual realization (*Com. Ps.,* on 110:4; *Hom. John* 14 [FC 33.133]). Conceding that what the Old Testament texts say applies in the first place to the types, Chrysostom declares that the texts are first "fulfilled" (i.e., gain their true significance) when what they point to comes true (*Hom. John* 85 [FC 41.436]).

level or plain meaning of the text.[27] His homilies often read as little more than paraphrases of a passage in Scripture: clarifying obscurities, to be sure; filling out the flow of an argument where its transitions seem abrupt;[28] proposing motives for the actions in a narrative where these are not apparent;[29] pointing out dogmatic implications where he found them; and (even more assiduously) underscoring the moral behavior exemplified in a narrative or commended in a discourse, often with references to other illustrations in Scripture of the same virtue.[30]

By focusing on the plain, surface meaning of the biblical text,

27. Like most Christians in most ages, Chrysostom read and interpreted the Old Testament in translation, in this case that of the Septuagint in the form that was current in fourth-century Antioch (cf. Hill, *Reading,* 47-61; Fernández Marcos, *Septuagint,* 223-28; Jobes and Silva, *Introduction,* 53-55, 281-83): though aware of the difficulties introduced by translations (*Hom. Obscurity* 2 [*O.T.H.* 3.29]), he nonetheless treated the Greek text as Scripture — even in books (like Proverbs and Job) where it differs markedly from the original. He knew no Hebrew: occasional references in his sermons to what the Hebrew text allegedly says were based on hearsay — and frequently mistaken. Though never attributing divine inspiration to the translators, he recognized their work as providentially ordained in that it made Scripture accessible to a worldwide readership (*Hom. Gen.* 4.9; *Hom. Obscurity* 2 [*O.T.H.* 3.29-30]).

28. E.g., *Hom. John* 27 (FC 33.261): "'But what connection,' you say, 'has this with the preceding?' A very close connection and one entirely in harmony with [Jesus'] foregoing words"; *Hom. John* 49 (FC 41.17): "'Now how does this follow from what precedes it,' you will say, 'or what connection has it with what [Jesus] had just said?'"; *Hom. John* 72 (FC 41.268): "Yet, what logical sequence is there between this statement and the words that precede it?" Chrysostom knows very well that in order to understand a particular statement in Scripture, one must grasp its place in the train of thought: "It is not sufficient to say, after all, that it is written in the Scriptures, nor by lifting the words out of context mangle the limbs of the body of the divinely inspired Scriptures, and by leaving them naked and bereft of their inter-connection arrogantly abuse them." "One should not carelessly cite the verses of Scripture, removing them from their context, separating them from related material, isolating the words from the assistance given by what follows and what precedes" (*Hom. Jer.* 10.23 [*O.T.H.* 2.9-10, 13]).

29. Chrysostom's omniscience in this regard is often astounding, extending, e.g., even to the motive of the Spirit in descending on Jesus at his baptism (so the crowds would not think that the heavenly voice identifying the beloved Son referred to John the Baptizer [*Hom. Matt.* 12.2, referring to Matt. 3:13-17]); and that of the demon who identified Paul and Silas as servants of the Most High God (hoping he would be left in peace if he preached the same things as they [*Hom. Acts* 35 (NPNF 11.221), referring to Acts 16:16-18])! If you have wondered why, after Judas's death, only two candidates were considered to fill the role of a twelfth apostle, Chrysostom has the answer: to head off the disappointment that would inevitably have been felt by those who lost the lottery (*Hom. Acts* 3 [NPNF 11.21], referring to Acts 1:23-26).

30. Cf. Young, *Exegesis,* 248-57.

Chrysostom avoided some of the questions provoked by Alexandrian exegesis — though inevitably raising issues of a different sort. The distinctive emphases and implications of his approach to Scripture merit further reflection.

1. The plain, surface meaning of the biblical text is, for Chrysostom, the medium of divine revelation. But it also represents what the original human authors intended to say to their contemporaries. Neither their meaning nor the divine revelation can be understood unless close attention is paid to the historical conditions under which the authors of Scripture wrote. In this awareness lies the greatest strength of Chrysostom's exegesis.

It follows that Scripture cannot be read as though it were an encyclopedia, containing timeless truths to be read the same way by anyone, anywhere, at any time.[31] On the contrary, nothing is more typical of Chrysostom than the insistence that this or that statement in Scripture, read "barely" — that is, at face value, without consideration of who is speaking, and to whom, under what circumstances, and to what purpose — is misleading, contradictory of other texts in Scripture, or simply untrue.

> We need much watchfulness, or, rather, God's grace in abundance, lest we go no further than the bare words. It is in this way that the heretics go astray, because they seek to know neither the point of view of the speaker nor the attitude of his hearers. Accordingly, if we do not add this information and other items as well, such as times and places and opinion of the listeners, many ridiculous conclusions will follow. (*Hom. John* 40 [FC 33.404])

> This expression [in Scripture] nakedly considered may easily prove a snare and offence to many hearers. But if the cause of it is subjoined, all will applaud and admire the speaker. . . . For it is not the right course to weigh the mere words, nor examine the language by itself, as many errors will be the consequence, but to attend to the intention of the writer. (*Com. Gal.,* on 1:17)

---

31. See, e.g., *Hom. 1 Cor.* 34.9-10 (after noting that a text in Proverbs is not universally true): " 'Doth then the Scripture speak falsely?' God forbid! But they do foolishly, who neglect to examine with due exactness all things written. . . . Let us also add the solution, having first mentioned the speaker, and when it was spoken, and to whom. For not alike to all doth God speak, as neither do we deal alike with children and men."

It is a mark of divine "considerateness"[32] that God addresses people where they are, with the measure of truth that they are capable of receiving or that will render them amenable to the reception of further truth. The most appropriate way to address people of one time and place will mislead readers in a different context, should they read it as absolute truth.

(a) These considerations did not, in Chrysostom's view, affect Scripture at its factual level. As we have seen, Origen found tensions and impossibilities in Scripture at its surface level, deliberately introduced (he believed) to provoke readers to pursue other, more profound levels of meaning: minor *untruths* point to loftier truth. Chrysostom, content with the plain meaning of the text, has no obvious reason for thinking God would do anything other than keep his facts straight. Where Origen sees improbabilities and falsehood, Chrysostom has an explanation to rescue Scripture's truth; where Origen sees tensions, Chrysostom finds ways to harmonize. A talking serpent in the Garden of Eden? Of course, serpents do not speak; but nothing prevents Satan from using a serpent as a mouthpiece (*Hom. Gen.* 16.4). A wife for Cain? He must have married his sister, an (unmentioned) daughter of Adam and Eve (*Hom. Gen.* 20.3). Does Mark 2:26 identify Abiathar as high priest at a time when, according to 1 Samuel, the priest was Ahimelech, Abiathar's father (1 Sam. 21:1-6; 22:20)? Then Ahimelech had two names, one of which was the same as his son's (*Hom. Matt.* 39.1).

As for tensions between the several Gospel accounts of Jesus' ministry, Chrysostom can see how a divine purpose might be at work here, and so is prepared — at least in principle — to allow that there may be minor discrepancies (in matters of time or place) between the Gospels: after all, differences in trivial matters confirm the independence of the evangelists' witness, and thus serve to establish the value of their united testimony on issues more substantial (*Hom. Matt.,* prologue, 5-6).[33] Such is the theory.

---

32. The Greek term *synkatabasis,* a crucial term in Chrysostom's understanding of Scripture, is commonly rendered "condescension." Robert Hill, who has translated much of Chrysostom's work on the Old Testament, thinks the English word has patronizing connotations foreign to the Greek; he insists on the rendering "considerateness." See Hill, *Reading,* 36-37.

33. Cf. the words of (Chrysostom's friend) Theodore of Mopsuestia (who was, in fact, more inclined than Chrysostom to see discrepancies between the Gospel accounts):

This is the tradition of the four Evangelists about the resurrection. I do not know what those who want to censure their words as inconsistent exactly mean. If the opinion of them all about the resurrection had not been the same, if they had not written that it was the same day when it happened, or if they had not unanimously said that it was the women who first came to the tomb in order to honor the dead, perhaps such a vain

In practice, however, Chrysostom seems ready to harmonize every apparent contradiction (cf. *Marcionites* 3-4). If the call of Peter and Andrew as described in Matthew 4:18-20 differs from that in John's account (1:40-42), then John tells of an initial, Matthew of a second summons (*Hom. Matt.* 14.3). Similarly, the temple was cleansed both early (John 2:13-16) and late (Matt. 21:12-13) in Jesus' ministry (*Hom. Matt.* 67.1; *Hom. John* 23 [FC 33.225]). Mark and Luke, who speak of one demoniac being healed where Matthew refers to two, have merely singled out for special attention the fiercer of the pair (*Hom. Matt.* 28.2, referring to Matt. 8:28; Mark 5:2; Luke 8:27). If Jesus' last supper with his disciples was a Passover meal in Matthew (Matt. 26:17-29) but preceded the Passover in John (13:1; cf. 18:28), then perhaps Christ ate the Passover a day early, or other Jews did so a day late (*Hom. Matt.* 84.2; *Hom. John* 83 [FC 41.409-10]). Matthew says Peter denied Christ three times before the cock crowed (Matt 26:74-75), whereas in Mark the denials precede the *second* crowing of the cock (Mark 14:72). Both are right, since Mark counts as a second crowing the repeated cries that made up Matthew's single crowing (*Hom. Matt.* 85.2). Examples could be multiplied, but the point is clear: at the factual level, Chrysostom is convinced, Scripture is true.

> and foolish reproof would be tolerable. But since in all these details [the Evangelists] demonstrate perfect harmony — they all declare the resurrection, and indicate the same day and assert that the women came first to the tomb — I really do not know why they want to argue about minor details. In my opinion, nothing else is needed to confirm the truth of their words than the fact that in the necessary details they demonstrate overwhelming harmony. In the small details, and in those things which they considered not to be important from their human point of view, it can be found that their words are not unanimous with regard to moments and hours. If they had really wanted to deceive, they would have had the same consistency in all their words. Nothing, in fact, prevented those who wanted to deceive from agreeing among themselves, so that they might maintain perfect agreement in their narratives. But since they wanted to relate the facts, and each of them wrote on his own, it is inevitable that there would be some difference in minor details. And there are any number of reasons why this happened to them: first of all because not all of them were among the disciples who lived with our Lord; Luke and Mark were not in the group of those who always accompanied him; second, not even the others were present for those events that happened toward the end since they ran away in the turmoil of those [dramatic] events. Therefore also in those details where the slanderers find discrepancies, I find perfect consistency. (Theodore of Mopsuestia, *Com. John*, on 20:1)

Chrysostom similarly notes that John gives "a more accurate account than the others did" of what took place when he himself was present (*Hom. John* 83 [FC 41.404]). Clearly, the inspiration of the Spirit was not thought to have eliminated the distinctive contributions that each evangelist was in a position to make.

Don't worry, dearly beloved, don't think Sacred Scripture ever contradicts itself, learn instead the truth of what it says, hold fast what it teaches in truth, and close your ears to those who speak against it. (*Hom. Gen.* 4.8)

(b) On the other hand, since truth coldly conveyed can be uninviting, and since God uses Scripture to lead readers further on the path to salvation, a certain tolerance must be allowed for purposeful creativity in narration and effective rhetoric in speech. Satan did not really enter God's presence with the angels and discuss Job with God. But what would be the appeal of the simple statement that "the devil schemed against Job with God's permission"? However true, such a sentence is dull — and God is not indifferent to the art of persuasion (*Com. Job,* on 1:6). Nor did a wicked spirit ever propose to God that he could deceive Ahab through lying prophets; the story is told in this way to engage simple listeners (*Com. Job,* on 1:6, referring to 1 Kings 22:19-23). God did not really want Jeremiah to stop praying for his compatriots; but telling him to do so would serve to terrify them into appropriate action. For the same reason, God had Jonah pronounce Nineveh's pending doom without giving them any grounds for hope (*Hom. Rom.* 14 [NPNF 11.448], referring to Jer. 11:14; Jon. 3:4). At times even Jesus, like a parent with a child, puts off his disciples' further inquiry by suggesting (what, for Chrysostom, *cannot* be true) that he does not know the answer himself (*Hom. Matt.* 77.1, referring to Matt. 24:36; *Hom. Acts* 2 [NPNF 11.11-12], referring to Acts 1:6-7).[34]

The art of persuasion is abundantly evident in the letters of Paul:[35] the apostle "lets slip no mode of persuasion" (*Hom. 2 Cor.* 17.1). Chrysostom sees nothing inappropriate, for example, in Paul's attempts to capture the good will of his readers by expressing more confidence than he actually feels in their spiritual maturity (*Hom. David* 2 [*O.T.H.* 1.32]; *Hom. 1 Cor.* 2.5 ["although the praises be not very close to the truth"]; 38.2); the apostle exaggerates his praise to save, not flatter, his readers (*Hom. 1 Cor.* 26.2). In Romans 14, he effectively but surreptitiously instructs the weak by appearing to rebuke the strong (*Hom. Rom.* 25 [NPNF 11.522]). When Paul informs the Romans of the collection for the saints in Jerusalem, his real

34. Cf. *Hom. Acts* 2 (NPNF 11.12): "Just as when we see a child crying, and pertinaciously wishing to get something from us that is not expedient for him, we hide the thing, and show him our empty hands, and say, 'See, we have it not': the like has Christ here done with the Apostles."

35. Cf. Mitchell, "Rhetoric"; Thurén, "Critic." Paul's rhetoric, though effective, was not, in Chrysostom's view, the product of a rhetorical education. See Mitchell, *Trumpet,* 241-45.

goal is to move them, too, to give to the poor (*Com. Gal.*, on 2:15). Most famously, Chrysostom (like Origen, and later Jerome) believed that the dispute in Antioch between Paul and Peter was not a genuine disagreement, but play-acting, planned in the hope that opponents, who would have been outraged had Paul attacked their position directly, would give way when they saw Peter meekly yield to Paul's point (*Com. Gal.*, on 2:11-13).[36]

(c) As we have seen, Origen proved singularly obtuse in his reading of biblical metaphors, declaring the untruth of their surface meaning a reason for resorting to allegorical interpretation. Chrysostom, on the other hand, grasped that the *sense* of a metaphorical text is that conveyed by the metaphor, not that of a woodenly literal understanding of its *words*. Interpreting Psalm 47:5 ("God has gone up with shouting") as a reference to Christ's ascension, Chrysostom notes that the latter actually "happened in silence, with only eleven disciples present. Do you see that you must not take the expressions superficially at face value but recognize the meaning conveyed by them? . . . *with shouting,* that is to say, that he went up with victory, having conquered death, overthrown sin, subdued the demons, expelled error, changed everything for the better" (*Com. Ps.*, on 47:5). One other delightful example may be cited. According to Psalm 114, when the Israelites escaped from Egypt, "the mountains skipped like rams, the hills like lambs" (114:4). Chrysostom observes:

> The inspired author, in his wish to present in exaggerated fashion [the Israelites'] satisfaction and the greatness of the marvels, introduces also inanimate things themselves as though dancing and bounding, which happens with people overjoyed. . . . Just as, therefore, another author says in times of calamity that even vineyard and wine grieved — not that the vineyard was grieving (after all, how would a vineyard grieve?), but in his desire to bring out the extraordinary degree of dejection he speaks in hyperbolic fashion as though inanimate creatures themselves were all but affected, just so in this case he presents creation sharing the satisfaction so as to show the degree of joy. (*Com. Ps.*, on 114:4)

(d) Like Origen, Chrysostom is exercised by the way Scripture speaks as though God has body parts (the eye, ear, arm of the Lord, etc.), outbursts of anger, moments of ignorance, and the like. Chrysostom, too, believes that God, for the sake of human salvation, accommodates himself

---

36. For a helpful discussion of this interpretation, and of (what Chrysostom would have seen as) its exegetical warrant, see Heath, "Rhetoric," 385-94.

to human understanding.[37] God uses "terms that we have grown up with" to teach us "truths that are above us" (*Com. Ps.*, on 8:3).

> When you hear of anger and rage in God's case, do not get the idea of anything typical of human beings; the words, you see, arise from considerateness. The divine nature, after all, is free of all these passions. On the contrary, he speaks this way so as to make an impression on the minds of more materialistic people. For in our case, too, when we converse with foreigners, we use their language; if we speak with children, we babble away with them, and even if we are extremely gifted, we show considerateness for their underdeveloped state. . . . God likewise, wanting to make an impression on materialistic people, made use of such words. For in so speaking, you see, his concern was not for his own glory but for the benefit of his listeners. (*Com. Ps.*, on 6:1; cf. *Com Ps.*, on 7:12-13)

> We must not stop short at the words ["Who is like the Lord our God, dwelling on the heights"], but go on to the meaning. I mean, how can he dwell in the heavens who fills heaven and earth . . . ? Well, since those words of his were addressed to the Jews, that fact determined the words he used for the time being while he gradually raised the level of their thinking, uplifted their attitude, and gently refined it. . . . His anxiety, you see, is not to ensure for the time being that what he says is in keeping with the respect due to God, but that it can be grasped by them. For this very reason he leads them upwards, and yet instead of remaining at the level of lowly realities, he opens up other still more elevated senses. (*Com. Ps.*, on 113:5)

(e) The Old Testament cultic worship — with its temple, sacrifices, purifications, festival days, and the like — has all been done away with, and was in any case derived from pagan practices. Why, then, did God institute it and "endure" for a time to be served in this way? Because God, with the goal of the salvation of the world in mind, deals with people in ways familiar and dear to them. He allowed the Israelites to adopt the familiar practices by which the nations of their day served their "gods"

---

37. The difficulty of even speaking about God nonmetaphorically is demonstrated in *Com. Ps.*, on 47:3; for the inadequacy of any human language to speak rightly about God, see *Com. Ps.*, on 8:3. Chrysostom can, of course, find additional reasons for particular anthropomorphisms: when God, e.g., is said to "come down" to see what human beings are doing in the land of Shinar (Gen. 11:5), or how egregious are the sins of Sodom and Gomorrah (Gen. 18:21), part of the reason is to teach us never to condemn others on hearsay evidence without checking into the matter ourselves (*Hom. Gen.* 30.10; 42.12).

(Chrysostom regarded them as demons), amending them only slightly, "that he might draw them off by degrees from their customs, and lead them towards the highest wisdom" (*Hom. Matt.* 6.4; cf. *Hom. Gen.* 27.6; *Com. Isa.,* on 1:12). Thus, by assigning ritual laws to an early stage in a progressive divine revelation, Chrysostom has no need of allegorical interpretation to give them significance. The same notion of progressive revelation allows Chrysostom to approve actions contravening Mosaic law if done before the law was given, and actions forbidden in the New Testament, if done before Christ's coming (e.g., *Hom. Gen.* 56.12; *Com. Job,* on 42:8; *Hom. Rom.* 13 [NPNF 11.431]; *Hom. 1 Cor.* 26.7; 33.5).[38] And he notes that the material blessings promised those who obey God's commands in the Old Testament were designed for those "less mature" (*Com. Ps.,* on 127:3-4); in the New Testament, the blessings promised are spiritual (*Com. Ps.,* on 115:14).

(f) Similarly, Chrysostom is prepared to allow that certain sentiments expressed by the psalmists — both those requesting vengeance on their enemies and those suggesting divine aloofness in times of need — were appropriate in their day but out of keeping with New Testament teaching.[39] At the same time, he is wont to excuse the inspired writers, suggesting that they gave voice, not to their own thoughts, but to those of the oppressed; or not to their settled convictions, but to their current emotional state (e.g., *Com. Ps.,* on 10:1-4; on 137:8-9; cf. *Com. Job,* on 3:3, 20-23).

(g) More serious issues are raised by texts whose surface meaning conveys something less than the full truth about the triune God[40] — and for that reason were cited as proof-texts by opponents of Chrysostom's Nicene orthodoxy.[41] Chrysostom repeatedly found the explanation to lie

---

38. Conversely, Chrysostom deems it remarkable whenever he finds evidence among Old Testament worthies of the kind of virtue he believes first to be required in the New Testament. See *Hom. Gen.* 52.24-25; *Hom. David* 1 (*O.T.H.* 1.10-11), 3 (*O.T.H.* 1.43-44); *Com. Job,* prologue.

39. Cf. *Hom. 1 Cor.* 33.5, commenting on Ps. 139:21-22: "At that time not the ungodliness only, but also the ungodly themselves they were commanded to hate, in order that their friendship might not prove an occasion of transgression unto them. . . . But now because he hath brought us to a more entire self-command and set us on high above that mischief, he bids us rather admit and soothe them. . . . We must not hate, but pity."

40. Cf. Young, *Exegesis,* 207: "The difference between ancient and modern exegesis lies in the massive shift in what is found to be problematic. We have had problems about historical coherence; they had problems about doctrinal coherence."

41. Cf. *Com. Gal.,* on 1:1: "Taking [a verse in Scripture] by itself and insisting on what is of a less exalted nature, and expressed in less exalted terms, either on account of the Son's humanity, or in honor of the Father, or for some other temporary purpose, they outrage, I will not say the Scriptures, but themselves."

in divine considerateness: the goal of Scripture, and of the words of Jesus that it records, was to benefit listeners by addressing them with the degree of truth that they were prepared to understand or receive, not to speak of God in a way commensurate with his divine nature. The Old Testament's insistence on monotheism was designed to combat temptations to worship other gods; clear teaching about God's three-in-oneness, and the divinity of the only begotten Son, could come later (*Com. Ps.,* on 110:1-4). If Jesus is said to have been commissioned by his Father (though he came of his own volition [*Hom. John* 80 (FC 41.372)]); to pray to his Father (in appearance only, since he too was God [*Hom. Matt.* 82.3; *Hom. John* 42 (FC 33.430); 83 (FC 41.400)]); to refer to God as Creator (though he himself made all things [*Hom. Matt.* 16.2]); to be ignorant of the time of his return (though, as God, he knew all things [*Hom. Matt.* 77.1-2]); to ask in prayer if deliverance from the cross were possible, suggesting both ignorance and a reluctance to face crucifixion (though he knew all things, and had, throughout his life, expressed his readiness to endure the cross [*Marcionites* 1-2]); to submit his will to that of his Father (though their wills were really one and the same [*Hom. John* 39 (FC 33.397-98)]); to be able to summon legions of angels to his aid (though, as God, he hardly needed angelic assistance [*Hom. Matt.* 84.1]), and so on — all this is to convey, not the whole truth about himself, but the (limited) truth that he (whom some thought a blasphemer) was not a rival of God (*Hom. John* 24 [FC 33.235]; 64 [FC 41.195]), or to provide instruction, or a model, for his disciples to follow.

Out of a considerateness that took into account what people were, or were not, ready to receive, Christ refrained from speaking of his own Godhead (*Hom. Matt.* 16.2; *Hom. John* 3 [FC 33.35]); John the Baptist said no more than that Christ "has been set above me because He was before me" (*Hom. John* 13 [FC 33.124], referring to John 1:30); Peter spoke of God "exalting" Christ (*Hom. Acts* 13 [NPNF 11.82], referring to Acts 5:30-31); and Paul, addressing the Athenians, spoke of him simply as a man (*Hom. John* 3 [FC 33.35]; *Hom. Acts* 1 [NPNF 11.2], referring to Acts 17:31): "gently and by degrees" God leads people on to higher truths (*Hom. Acts* 1 [NPNF 11.2]). A proper understanding of Christ's nature, and that of the triune God, only emerges from a grasp of the testimony of Scripture as a whole: to base one's understanding on individual texts while disregarding their intended function in a particular historical context (the exegetical sin of proof-texting) is to misunderstand the nature of divine revelation.[42]

---

42. Chrysostom frequently notes that some texts emphasize Christ's incarnate (human)

The upshot of all this is that, for Chrysostom, the writings of Scripture (and the discourses they contain) were intended *in the first place* for the benefit of their original audience — and fashioned accordingly. (The exceptions are certain prophetic texts, whose full significance only became clear upon their fulfillment.) They remain, of course, sacred Scripture for believers of all ages, of abiding significance because the God whose ways are revealed in Scripture's narratives, admonitions, and prophecies remains the same in every age. A right reading of Scripture, then, leads believers to see how what was said in the past can apply to their own analogous circumstances.[43] Indeed, through what Scripture tells of God's goodness and call in the past, God opens the hearts of hearers and readers in the present to a fresh experience of that same goodness and call. But, in interpreting Scripture, believers must bear in mind, and make allowances for, the limited understanding of those for whom its texts were first written (or to whom its words were first spoken). If they fail to do so, and read all texts in Scripture as timeless truth, they will frequently be led astray. The contrast with Origen is both remarkable and telling. For Origen, all of Scripture seems intended primarily for the benefit of mature Christians. To be sure, its surface level generally made sense and conveyed a point to those for whom it was first composed; but the deeper truths found in all parts of Scripture are perceptible only to the mature.

2. Chrysostom shares Origen's conviction that every detail of a text inspired by the Holy Spirit must bear significance. His claims in this regard, like those of Origen, extend to every word, every syllable, even every jot of the sacred text (*Hom. Gen.* 18.17; *Hom. John* 36 [FC 33.351]). But whereas Origen had no difficulty finding edification in a "spiritual" interpretation that, for example, attributed significance to purported etymologies of names and the mysteries he associated with numbers, it is not clear that Chrysostom's more sober exegesis can deliver on its promise. While telling us that lists of names in Scripture cannot be passed over quickly without loss (*Hom. Gen.* 21.1), Chrysostom fails to provide much insight into the edification to be derived from their careful study: the examples he gives are of names (like Abraham) whose significance is already explicit in Scripture; others, typically, he passes over in silence (*Hom. Rom.* 31 [NPNF 11.553];

---

nature, others his pure (divine) nature (e.g., *Hom. John* 3 [FC 33.34]; 39 [FC 33.389-90]; 48 [FC 41.4]). Neither category, then, should be considered apart from the other.

43. Cf. *Hom. Matt.* 15.2: "Let us hearken with strict attention unto what is said. For though [the Sermon on the Mount] was spoken unto them, it was written for the sake also of all men afterwards. . . . He is discoursing not with them only, but also, through them, with all the world."

cf. *Hom. Gen.* 21.9). While insisting that much can be learned from the list of those in Rome to whom Paul sends greetings, Chrysostom makes homiletic hay only of Paul's sundry comments about the people he names; where nothing but the name is given, nothing edifying emerges (*Hom. Rom.* 31). As for the significance of the names in Matthew's genealogy of Jesus, Chrysostom (rather unhelpfully) says he lacks time to explore the subject (*Hom. Matt.* 4.3). To his credit, Chrysostom avoids the kind of atomistic exegesis (finding significance in the words of a sentence while ignoring their place in the sentence itself) for which Origen has been criticized; consistently, the significance he finds, even in the individual words of Scripture, depends on the meaning of the sentence in which they stand. But we should concede that claims for the importance of every syllable of Scripture find more warrant in the work of Origen.

3. On a similar note, Origen was wont to draw attention to seemingly unnecessary details in narrative texts: since nothing in Scripture *can* be superfluous, the intended point of such details must lie in their "spiritual" interpretation. Chrysostom similarly insists on Scripture's "precision" *(akribeia),* its care in reporting every detail; but by dismissing allegorical interpretations, he limits the significance he can find in the details of a narrative to their contribution to a fuller understanding of the story itself.[44] It is, for Chrysostom, a mark of Scripture's precision that it reports no detail without purpose, but even informs us of Isaac's age (he was forty) when he married Rebekah (Gen. 25:20). That way we learn "the greatness of Isaac's patience" when we realize "the number of years he passed without children" (*Hom. Gen.* 49.3). Because of its precision, Scripture does not simply say that Rachel, after meeting Jacob at the well, "went off and reported the happenings"; rather, it says that "she ran." The point of the precision? To show her "great exuberance" (*Hom. Gen.* 55.5, referring to Gen. 29:12). Most readers of Origen, I suspect, attribute to the fertility of his own imagination the mysteries he finds in seemingly innocent details of a narrative; most readers will dismiss as trite the "mysteries" uncovered by Chrysostom's *akribeia,* and will be inclined to advise both Origen and Chrysostom (to quote again the slogan of Rabbi Ishmael) that "Scripture speaks in the language of people"; in other words, don't look for significance where none is to be found (i.e., in *every* detail of the biblical text).

4. Chrysostom's careful exposition of biblical narratives in their his-

---

44. He rightly notes, however, that not every detail in Jesus' parables is significant; interpretation should focus on the point for which the parable is told (*Hom. Matt.* 47.1; 64.3).

torical context, when combined with his normal refusal to probe beneath the surface for deeper significance, means that he avoids (what seem to many) the fanciful interpretations of the Alexandrians. On the other hand, where Scripture (it seems to many) positively *invites* an openness to meaning beyond the literal (especially true of John's Gospel), Chrysostom can be resolutely insensitive. Many think John the Evangelist means to convey something of the superiority of the new dispensation to the old by emphasizing that the water Jesus turned into wine came from jars used for Jewish rites of purification (John 2:6); Chrysostom suspects that John mentioned the purpose of the jars only to rule out any suspicion that they already contained wine to which Jesus merely added water (*Hom. John* 22 [FC 33.215]). When Jesus says that now, and in a coming hour, the dead will hear his voice and live (John 5:25), we are surely to think, not only of the physical raising of Lazarus, but also of how Christ's words bring life to the spiritually dead (cf. John 6:63); Chrysostom sees only the reference to Lazarus (*Hom. John* 39 [FC 33.391-95]). More egregious still, in the pregnant words "and it was night," which follow the statement that Judas went out to betray Jesus (John 13:30), Chrysostom sees nothing more than Judas's eagerness to get on with his treachery: he refused to be delayed even though it was dark outside (*Hom. John* 72 [FC 41.273]).

5. Many readers regard Origen's "spiritual interpretations" as fanciful, imposed on the text by his own creative imagination. But since that imagination itself was profoundly shaped by Scripture, readers find his commentaries devotionally rich, even where exegetically problematic. And to all it is obvious that, by way of spiritual interpretation, he read the Old Testament as a profoundly Christian text.

Chrysostom's reading of the Old Testament, by focusing almost exclusively on its literal, historical meaning, may be said to eliminate both the excesses and the riches of Alexandrian exegesis. Certainly he reads texts more christologically than do the more rigorous Antiochenes. Otherwise, however — and this applies to vast stretches of his Old Testament homilies — what he finds in the text are stories of the past, with examples of virtues to be emulated and vices to be shunned. The homiletical thrust of many sermons thus amounts to little more than moralistic platitudes: be self-controlled like Joseph, humble like Moses, and the like. Perhaps we should not be surprised that the text, when read on a single level, turns out to be disappointingly flat. Chrysostom can repeat the early Christian claim that, though the text of the Old Testament comes from the Jews, it is Christians who possess its true meaning (*Hom. Gen.* 8.6); but there is little that is distinctively Christian (comparatively speaking, at least) when he expounds its texts.

And, we should add, even the most sober interpreters tend to find what they are looking for in Scripture. Reading the Old Testament as an anthology illustrating heroic virtue, Chrysostom discovers virtue in the most unexpected places. Noah had three sons when he was 500 years old — and no more, though he lived to be 950; an admirable display, declares Chrysostom, of passion restrained (*Hom. Gen.* 24.4). Did Abraham lie about his wife and endanger his marriage to save his skin? "Don't, however, dearly beloved, rashly condemn the good man; rather, gain from this a particular insight into his great sagacity and courage — yes, his courage in nobly withstanding and overcoming turmoil of mind to the extent of planning such stratagems" (*Hom. Gen.* 32.13). Sarah's lies on the same subject were a mark of true affection, nobility, and caring for her husband's welfare; the entire episode thus illustrates the harmony of "true wedlock" (*Hom. Gen.* 45.8-9). Equally commendable (for the affection and excellent planning it displayed), and divinely blessed, was the deception Rebekah devised for Jacob to play on his father, at the expense of her firstborn son (*Hom. Gen.* 53.5-10, referring to Gen. 27:5-17). The conclusion is surely unavoidable: fanciful readings of Scripture are by no means the preserve of allegorists.

6. Nearly half of Chrysostom's extant homilies are devoted to explicating the Pauline epistles; here he is at his exegetical best.[45] Himself a master of the Greek language, he is able to capture the natural sense of Paul's writings while being sensitive to their nuances. A rhetorician himself, he grasps the thrust of Paul's arguments while avoiding the overinterpretation of individual statements. To this day, Chrysostom remains a worthy dialogue partner in the interpretation of Paul.

The Interpreter of Scripture

Listening for the voice of God as they read Scripture, Origen and Chrysostom hear very different things; but they are very much in agreement on what it takes to hear them. That Scripture cannot be understood, nor its benefits enjoyed, apart from the grace and illumination of God is obvious to them both. The encounter with God can, however, be prepared for, by prayer, banishing from one's life all that is sinful, and giving undivided attention to the "letters" God has sent us.

---

45. Baur, *Chrysostom*, 1.290.

We must be guided by grace from above and accept the enlightenment of the Holy Spirit, and only then approach the divine sayings. That is to say, Sacred Scripture does not call into play human wisdom for the understanding of its writings, but the revelation of the Spirit, so that we may learn the true meaning of its contents and draw from it a great benefit. (*Hom. Gen.* 21.1)

Let no desire of wealth disturb us, or love of fame, or despotism of anger, or the importunate crowd of the other passions. Indeed, unless the hearing is purified of them, it cannot perceive, as it ought, the sublimity of what is said, nor can it grasp, as it must, the awesome and ineffable character of these mysteries, and all the other virtues contained in these divine utterances. (*Hom. John* 1 [FC 33.8])

For the understanding of Paul's words there is needed also a pure life. . . . For as a stomach which is infirm could not take in wholesome food [which it finds] hard of digestion, so a soul which is become tumid and heated, unstrung and relaxed, could not receive the word of the Spirit. (*Hom. Acts* 55 [NPNF 11.327])

We need much care, dearly beloved, much vigilance, so as to be able to plumb the depths of sacred Scripture. It is not possible to discover its meaning merely incidentally, or while we are asleep, but we have need of careful scrutiny, and of earnest prayer as well, that we may be able to penetrate a little the sanctuary of the sacred mysteries. (*Hom. John* 21 [FC 33.202])

We do not afford to the laws of God so great stillness, even as the spectators in the theatres to the emperor's letters, keeping silence for them. For there, when these letters are being read, deputies at once, and governors, and senate, and people, stand all upright, with quietness hearkening to the words. And if amid that most profound silence any one should suddenly leap up and cry out, he suffers the utmost punishment, as having been insolent to the emperor. But here, when the letters from heaven are being read, great is the confusion on all sides. And yet both He who sent the letters is much greater than this our king, and the assembly more venerable: for not men only, but angels too are in it; and these triumphs, of which the letters bear us the good tidings, are much more [awesome] than those on earth. (*Hom. Matt.* 19.12)

Every word of Scripture must be carefully heeded; at the same time we must quiet our curiosity about what God has chosen *not* to reveal.

"In the year that King Uzziah died," the text says, "I saw the Lord seated on a lofty and exalted throne." How he saw I do not know: while the fact that he saw he mentioned, on the way he saw he kept silence; what he said I accept, into what he left unsaid I do not pry; what has been revealed I grasp, I do not busy myself with what remains concealed — the reason for its being concealed, after all. The explanation of the Scriptures is a golden robe, the warp of gold, the woof of gold; I do not attach to it a border of spiders' webs, conscious as I am of the limitations of my own reasonings. (*Hom. Isa.* 6 [*O.T.H.* 2.105]; cf. *Hom. Matt.* 4.5-6)

Finally, Scripture is not simply to be read, but meditated upon and allowed to fill our thoughts and nourish our souls.

Take up the refrains [of Ps. 42] and make careful note of them as though they were pearls, meditate on them constantly at home and recite them all to your friends and your wives. (*Hom. Ps.,* on Ps. 42 [*O.T.H.* 3.85]; cf. *Hom. John* 15 [FC 33.141]).

You see, as the body has need of material nourishment, likewise, too, the soul needs daily reminders and spiritual nourishment so that it may be strengthened and thus able to resist the rebellion of the flesh and the constant battle waged within us to reduce our soul to servitude if we are disposed to drop our guard even for a short space of time. Hence the inspired author David called that person blessed who gave time to the law of the Lord day and night [Ps. 1:2], and blessed Moses in his instruction of the Jewish people taught them in these words: "When you have eaten and drunk, and taken your fill, give your mind to the Lord your God" [cf. Deut. 8:10-14]. . . . Again in another place this same author says: "Whether sleeping or rising be mindful of the Lord your God" [cf. Deut. 6:7]. Do you see how it never becomes us to drive this awareness from our soul, but rather to have it engraven on our conscience . . . and never neglect our spiritual nourishment. (*Hom. Gen.* 10.20)

CHAPTER 6

Augustine

With good reason we began our study with Irenaeus: he was the finest theologian of the period when a distinctively Christian Bible first emerged. A look at Origen was inevitable: the early church's foremost biblical scholar, he marked out the path that Christian scriptural interpretation would largely take for more than a millennium. Chrysostom merited our attention as the most illustrious representative of a rival school of interpretation and the greatest preacher of the early church. At this point, even more inevitably than with any of our preceding studies, we turn to Augustine, if for no other reason than that he was . . . Augustine.

For starters, Augustine was the greatest theologian of the early church — some would say, in the history of the church.[1] And he wrote *the* book on how Scripture is to be interpreted: his *Teaching Christianity* remains the most influential work ever written on the subject. By the standards it sets, he himself was not a great biblical scholar. Though he acknowledged the importance of knowing Hebrew and Greek,[2] he neither learned the former[3] nor mastered the latter.[4] On the whole, he was content to read and expound Scripture as he encountered it in (very inadequate) Latin translations. The massive corpus of Augustine's writings includes only one complete academic (as opposed to homiletical) commentary on a book of the Bible, written when he was still young in the faith *(Commentary on Galatians).*[5] He followed Origen in interpreting much of Scripture allegor-

---

1. Or at least "the most influential Christian theologian after St. Paul" (Rist, "Augustine," 3).
2. *Teaching Christianity* 2.16.
3. See *Letters* 101.4.
4. See *Trin.* 3.1.
5. Bright ("Augustine," 79) notes that "issues engage [Augustine] rather than minutiae of exegesis. . . . This propensity to be galvanized by the profound questions of human exis-

ically; but whereas Origen's "spiritual" readings were often original and always learned, Augustine's, when they are not derivative, often seem more impressionistic than rigorous. Even those who think Origen's exertions misdirected concede the industry; it was not unusual for him to consult every scriptural use of a term before deciding on its allegorical significance. Augustine was more likely to allow an allegorical interpretation wherever his fertile mind discovered some point of resemblance between the literal sense of a word in the text and a spiritual lesson he wished to impart. These, it must be said, are significant failings in an interpreter of Scripture.

They are more than offset, however, by the riches of Augustine's expositions on the book of Psalms and his homilies on John's Gospel. Moreover, he labored repeatedly and mightily (and profoundly, if not soundly) over the interpretation of the opening chapters of Genesis.[6] He has long been thought to have grasped the radical nature of Pauline theology in a way unmatched by anyone before him.[7] In addition to these particulars, he had a powerful sense of the drama of Scripture as a whole — indeed, through the lens of Scripture, of the drama of *history* as a whole — and succeeded in conveying it in one of the most foundational works in Western literature, *The City of God*. Finally, to his dismay in his own day and only increasingly in the centuries that followed, whatever he wrote (on Scripture or any other subject) was treated by many readers *as* Bible — simply because he was Augustine.[8]

Life

Augustine (354-430) was born in Thagaste, a town in North Africa (in modern Algeria), a century after Origen's death. (He was thus a contemporary

---

tence tends, paradoxically, to make the specific genre of the scriptural commentary alien to the maturing of his genius as a scriptural commentator."

6. That Augustine was bent on finding neo-Platonic truth in Moses accounts for the adverbs used in this sentence.

7. Luther certainly thought so; many have agreed; some still do. On the development of Augustine's own understanding of Paul, see Babcock, "Interpretation"; see also Bright, "Augustine."

8. "In the holy writings we learn how to judge, in our own writings we are quite ready to be judged. . . . Let us treat scripture like scripture, like God speaking. . . . If anybody reads my book, let him pass judgment on me. If I have said something reasonable, let him follow, not me, but reason itself; if I've proved it by the clearest divine testimony, let him follow, not me, but the divine scripture. . . . I get angrier with that kind of fan who takes my book as being canonical, than with the man who finds fault in my book with things that are not in fact at fault" (*Sermons* 162C.15).

of Chrysostom.) He learned of the Christian faith from his devout mother, Monica, but was not taught Scripture. A good education, first in the nearby town of Madaura, then at Carthage, was ensured by the sacrificial support of his father (who did not become a Christian until shortly before his death) and a wealthy benefactor. Augustine then taught for a while in Carthage before moving on to Rome (383); in 384, he was appointed professor of rhetoric in Milan.

A reading of Cicero had persuaded him, in his late teens, that the path to happiness lay in the pursuit of wisdom. A brief foray into Scripture at this point sufficed to convince him that wisdom would have to be sought elsewhere, however, and he turned to Manicheism, a dualistic movement that claimed to represent Christianity in its authentic form and rejected the Old Testament. In time, better acquaintance with Manichean teachers disabused him of their pretensions, and the sermons of Ambrose, the bishop of Milan, convinced him that the Old Testament made sense, when intelligently (i.e., allegorically) interpreted. Converted to Christianity in 386,[9] Augustine was baptized in 387, and he returned to Africa the following year. Life in a small ascetic community allowed him to begin a serious study of Scripture, but in 391 he was pressed into service as a priest in the coastal city of Hippo. His gifts did not go unrecognized, and a few years later he was consecrated bishop.

In Augustine's earliest Christian writings, devoted to philosophical issues, Scripture played little role; its interpretation is central, however, to his later work. His famous *Confessions* appeared in 397; he began work on *The Trinity* in 399, was frequently interrupted, and did not complete it until 419. In response to pagan criticism of the Christian church occasioned by the fall of Rome in 410, he wrote *The City of God* (413-427). He began writing *Teaching Christianity* at about the time he wrote *The Confessions,* but then (for unknown reasons) his work on the former was interrupted and only completed about the time that he finished *The City of God.* Augustine was, of course, occupied throughout these years with the pressures of his office and the theological controversies of his day. Therein lie other tales than ours.

Vandals (a Germanic tribal people) invaded North Africa in 429, and some of Augustine's last letters dealt with the issue whether Christian clergy should remain with their people and fulfill their pastoral responsibilities or flee to prevent the elimination of church leadership. (He concluded that some should do the one, some the other, the issue being determined

---

9. He tells this famous story in book 8 of his *Confessions.*

by lot.) When he died on August 29, 430, Hippo was a besieged but not yet fallen city.

Approaching Scripture

Augustine came to have a great passion for Scripture, but it was hardly a case of love at first sight. Not that his devotion, once come by, was less real for being acquired:

> Let your scriptures be my chaste delight. . . . Let me hear the voice of praise, and drink from you, and contemplate the wonders of your law [i.e., Scripture] from the beginning when you made heaven and earth [i.e., from Genesis] to that everlasting reign when we shall be with you in your holy city [i.e., to Revelation]. Have mercy upon me, Lord, and hearken to my longing; for I do not think it arises from this earth. . . . That law is what stirs my longing. See, Father, have regard to me and see and bless my longing, and let it be pleasing in your merciful eyes that I find grace before you, so that the inner meaning of your words may be opened to me as I knock at their door. (*Conf.* 11.3-4)

> How amazing is the profundity of your words! We are confronted with a superficial meaning that offers easy access to the unlettered; yet how amazing their profundity, O my God, how amazingly deep they are! To look into that depth makes me shudder, but it is the shudder of awe, the trembling of love. (*Conf.* 12.17)

Yet his feelings at one time had been very different:

> I turned my attention to the holy scriptures to find out what they were like. . . . When I studied the Bible and compared it with Cicero's dignified prose, it seemed to me unworthy. My swollen pride recoiled from its style and my intellect failed to penetrate to its inner meaning. Scripture is a reality that grows along with little children, but I disdained to be a little child and in my high and mighty arrogance regarded myself as grown up. (*Conf.* 3.9)

Not only did the younger Augustine find the style of Scripture beneath the contempt of a trained rhetorician; as a devotee of the Manichees, he had for a time shared that sect's delight in pointing out contradictions and absurdities in the Old Testament. Even later, as a Christian, he conceded that it is the easiest thing in the world to find flaws in Scripture, if one makes no effort to understand what it is really saying (*Gen.* 1.2; *Sermons* 50.13). Augustine's frequent warnings against those keen on criticizing Scripture clearly grew out of his own experience.[10]

As a lad I wanted to tackle the divine scriptures with the techniques of clever disputation before bringing to them the spirit of earnest inquiry. In this way I was shutting the door of my Lord against myself by my misplaced attitude; I should have been knocking at it for it to be opened, but instead I was adding my weight to keep it shut. I was presuming to seek in my pride what can only be found by humility. (*Sermons* 51.6)

In earlier days it had seemed to me that [Paul's] teaching was self-contradictory, and in conflict with the witness of the law and the prophets, but now as these problems melted away your chaste words presented a single face to me, and I learned to rejoice with reverence. (*Conf.* 7.27)

Augustine's change of heart began when he heard Ambrose, the bishop of Milan, give reasonable interpretations to passages he had once deemed ridiculous (*Conf.* 5.23-24). More generally, however, he notes that the path to wisdom, when one encounters a text that seems nonsensical, can start with the simple acknowledgment that the writers of the Bible were not, after all, idiots, and with the humility to admit that there must be more than meets the eye to a book that has commanded the attention and devotion of so many people.[11] There is, after all, an immense difference

10. Cf. *Sermons* 2.2: "[Some] would sooner find fault with what they don't understand than seek to understand it. They are not humble seekers but conceited quibblers." *Gen.* 1.5: "Being keener on casting slurs on the divine scriptures than on getting to know them, they fail to understand even the most obvious things." *Gen.* 2.3: "If the Manichees were willing to discuss the hidden meaning of these words in a spirit of reverent inquiry rather than of captious fault-finding, then they would of course not be Manichees, but as they asked it would be given them, and as they sought they would find, as they knocked it would be opened up to them. The fact is, you see, people who have a genuine religious interest in learning put far more questions about this text than these irreligious wretches; but the difference between them is that the former seek in order to find, while the latter are at no pains at all to do anything except not to find what they are seeking." The latter remark is significant. Augustine himself, as a believer, put more questions to Scripture than any critic. But the spirit in which questions are put makes all the difference. Cf. *Letters* 102.38.

11. "Anything in the scriptures that sounds absurd, sounds quite unnecessary, is under

between saying "I want to know why this (apparently absurd) text says what it says" and dismissing it as unbelievable (see *Tract. John* 8.7). The former response leaves the door open to better understanding; the latter peremptorily closes it.

> The psalm indicates to you what you must do if you have difficulty in understanding, for it goes on to say, *The Lord welcomes the meek.* Suppose you do not understand some passage, or understand only a little of it, or at any rate cannot master it: hold God's scripture in honor, respect God's word even when it is not clear to you, maintain a reverent attitude while you wait for understanding to come. Do not be over-bold and find fault with the obscurity of scripture or even allege that it is self-contradictory. There is no contradiction here. Some obscurity there may be, not in order that insight may be denied you, but so that your mind may be stretched until you can receive it. When some text seems dark to you, be sure that the physician has made it so; he is inviting you to knock. . . . As you persevere in knocking you will be stretched; as you are stretched, your capacity will be enlarged; as your capacity grows, you will receive what comes to you as gift. (*Exp. Ps.* 146.12; cf. *Letters* 137.15; *Tract. John* 45.7)

Is this to embrace blind faith and abandon reason? That, in fact, is what the Manichees accused orthodox believers of doing, and Augustine was initially impressed by their own claims to follow reason alone. Closer examination, however, proved their pretensions to be fatuous, and Augustine came to realize the necessity of combining reason with faith. We could not live in this world, after all, if we did not accept the testimony of others on all manner of things that we cannot verify for ourselves; it is only reasonable, then, that we should credit the witness of the church, its leaders and people worldwide, and give Scripture a respectful hearing.[12] That modicum of faith (we might simply call it "good will") paves the way to better understanding, which in turn leads to an increase in faith, which then brings greater understanding, and so on.

---

lock and key, not, however, locked up and empty. . . . Say to yourself, '. . . Moses, who wrote this, was a man of at least average intelligence.' Add, because it is not without reason that these writings have become known to the whole world, and are held in honor throughout the whole world in the religion of the faithful: 'He wouldn't say [what seems absurd] without a reason; it must be because there's something there, I don't know what, that beggars human thought, but is somehow or other locked up. It isn't just empty' " (*Sermons* 341.22; cf. *Faustus* 3.2).

12. *Conf.* 6.7-8; cf. *City of God* 11.3.

Without some understanding no one can believe in God: but the faith whereby we begin to believe in him has a healing effect, so that we come to understand more. . . . How can anyone believe a preacher of the faith unless he or she at least understands the language that is spoken, not to mention all else? . . . We must conclude that our understanding develops to grasp more firmly the truths we have believed and that our faith grows to believe more firmly what we have begun to understand. By its very act of understanding the mind develops and thus penetrates the truths of faith more deeply. This process occurs not through our natural powers but by the help and gracious gift of God. . . . The person who in this psalm begs God, *Give me understanding, that I may learn your commandments,* is not wholly devoid of understanding. . . . It is a mark of no slight understanding to know whom we should ask for understanding. (*Exp. Ps.* 118.18.3)

In fact, any knowledge we have is ours only by divine enlightenment. We have eyes, but we only see what is illuminated for our eyes by an external light; we have minds, but we only grasp what is illuminated for our minds by the divine source of all understanding (*Tract. John* 35.3). The Word of God that both *is* God and was *with* God in the beginning is the "true light that enlightens everyone who comes into the world" (John 1:1-2, 9). When human teachers speak what is true and we accept it as truth, we may think they have taught us; if, however, they speak what is obviously untrue, we do not believe it (*Teacher* 12.40). Ultimately, then, human teachers can only serve as prompters of what we learn (*Teacher* 14.45); our real and only teacher must be within ourselves.

Don't think that a person learns anything from a human being. We can offer a suggestion by the sound of our voice, but if he who teaches isn't within, our voice is of no avail. . . . He who teaches, then, is the inner teacher: Christ teaches; his inbreathing teaches. Where his inbreathing and his anointing don't exist, words sound to no avail. (*Hom. 1 John* 3.13, commenting on 1 John 2:27; cf. *Conf.* 11.10)[13]

13. In the prologue to his *Teaching Christianity,* Augustine criticizes people who have no use for those who offer guidance in interpreting Scripture, thinking divine illumination is all they need for the purpose. He notes that God normally uses human beings to teach other human beings: the Ethiopian eunuch learned how to read Isaiah from Philip; Cornelius was told to get instruction from Peter; and Paul himself was brought into the church by Ananias (Acts 8–10). The point remains that, without the conviction brought about by the divine Teacher within the hearts of the eunuch, Cornelius, and Paul, the words of a Philip, Peter, or Ananias would have been fruitless.

In the end, then, it is the divine Teacher within us who brings conviction of Scripture's truth.

> Let me listen, so that I may understand how you made heaven and earth in the beginning. Moses wrote that statement; he wrote it and went away . . . so he is not here face to face with me now. If he were, I would take hold of him and ask him and in your name implore him to open these mysteries to me. . . . But how would I know whether he spoke the truth? If I were to ascertain that too, could it be on his assertion? No; undoubtedly within myself, in that inner habitation of my thought, the truth that is neither Hebrew nor Greek nor Latin nor any vernacular would speak to me without bodily organ of mouth or tongue, and without any clatter of syllables would tell me, "He is speaking the truth"; and then with instant certainty I would say to that man who served you [i.e., Moses], "What you say is true." (*Conf.* 11.5)

Understanding of Scripture is blocked by pride,[14] and by an unwillingness to obey the truth[15] or be led by Scripture to God.[16] But the divine teacher within grants understanding to those who seek it humbly and with their whole heart: "he who, unasked, offered his word, when asked, offers understanding" (*Tract. John* 22.1).

> All the men of that kingdom shall be taught of God, they will not hear from men. And if they hear from men, still what they understand is

---

14. See *Faustus* 16.14: "This proud and arrogant presumption either closes the eye of the heart so that it does not see at all or distorts it so that it sees incorrectly."

15. See *Exp. Ps.* 119.9: "I want you to hear how true these words are, brothers and sisters. You can test the truth of what you are singing [i.e., the words of a biblical psalm] only if you are beginning to act in harmony with your song. However much I say about this, in whatever way I explain it, whatever words I use, the truth will not penetrate anyone's heart unless he or she has already begun to practice it. Begin to act on it, and then see for yourselves what we are telling you." *Sermons* 85.4: "Many people don't want to understand what they don't want to do." *Sermons* 156.1: "Sometimes people's minds are so twisted, that they are afraid of understanding, in case they should be obliged to carry out what they have understood." Augustine was again speaking from experience; cf. *Conf.* 8.11-12.

16. See *Exp. Ps.* 118.1.2: "Some people . . . search the Lord's testimonies, but their purpose in doing so is to appear learned, rather than to be just. . . . To examine God's testimonies without loving what they reveal, without wanting to be led by them to God — that is not true study." *Hom. 1 John* 4.1: "Although many hear, what is said isn't persuasive to everyone but only to those to whom God speaks within. But he speaks within to those who make room for him."

given within, it gleams within, it is revealed within. What do men who proclaim from without do? What am I now doing when I speak? I bring the noise of words to your ears. Unless he who is within should reveal, what do I say, or what do I speak?

The planter of a tree is outside; its creator is inside. He who plants and he who waters work from the outside; we are doing this. But "neither he who plants is anything, nor he who waters, but God who gives the growth" [1 Cor. 3:7]. That is, "they all shall be taught of God" [John 6:45]. (*Tract. John* 26.7; cf. *Sermons* 152.1; 153.1)

The better they understand Scripture, the more it resonates with, and is confirmed by, their own experience.

This psalm reminds us of the mercies of God that we have known in our own lives, and its accord with our experience makes it all the more delightful. It would be strange if anyone who had not personally learned the truth of what the psalm proclaims were able to perceive its sweetness. (*Exp. Ps.* 106.1)

Like No Other Book

Not all that Augustine wrote has survived, but his extant writings are estimated to contain five million words. He would not have expended the effort had he not thought the endeavor worthwhile: "Room should be left for this sort of writing, and future generations should not be deprived of the highly salutary labor of the pen and the tongue in dealing with and weighing difficult questions" (*Faustus* 11.5). Nonetheless, he insists that a sharp distinction be made between the canonical scriptures[17] and all other

17. Unlike (his older contemporary) Jerome, Augustine accepted the broader Old Testament canon, including works not accepted by Jews as Scripture, but widely used in Christian churches. Both a list, and church usage as the criterion for what it includes, are given in *Teaching Christianity* 2.12-13. Though aware that the Septuagint (Greek) translation of the Old Testament differed in many places from the Hebrew, he insisted on its equal authority (*Agreement* 2.128; *Teaching Christianity* 2.22). He was willing neither to commit to nor to abandon legendary accounts of its miraculous origin (*Teaching Christianity* 2.22; cf. *City of God* 18.42-43). In any case, the translators were experts; and that their translation (like the original Hebrew text) had been divinely inspired (*Exp. Ps.* 135.3; *City of God* 15.23) followed from its adoption by the apostles (*City of God* 15.14): "It can well be the case that [the Seventy] translated the Hebrew in such a way as the Holy Spirit, who was guiding them and gave them all one mouth, judged would be most suitable for the Gentiles" (*Teaching*

writings — including (particularly!) his own (cf. *Letters* 82.24; 93.35-36; 147.4). In the former, God speaks to us with unequaled power.

> The Lord has thundered at us through the prophet Isaiah. (*Sermons* 42.1)

> What [the rich young ruler] heard, we have heard too. The gospel is the mouth of Christ. He is seated in heaven, but he hasn't stopped speaking on earth. Don't let's be deaf, because he's the one who's shouting at us. (*Sermons* 85.1)

> Everything we have heard in the scriptures, brothers, is the voice of God saying, "Watch out!" . . . Repent at the voice of scripture, for at the voice of the [divine] judge when he is here you will repent in vain. (*Sermons* 22.3)

> We know no other books with the like power to lay pride low and so surely to silence the obstinate contender who tries to thwart your reconciling work by defending his sins. Nowhere else, Lord, indeed nowhere else do I know such chaste words, words with such efficacy to persuade me to confession, to gentle my neck beneath your kindly yoke and invite me to worship you without thought of reward. (*Conf.* 13.17)

> This reading will be like oil on a flame: if there is anything that may be nursed in [the reader], it is nursed, and grows, and lasts. Similarly, there are those for whom it must be like a flame to kindling: if once it didn't catch fire, now, having been touched by these words, it catches fire. For in some what is there is being nursed, while in others a fire breaks out if one is lacking, so that we may all rejoice in one charity. *(Prologue to Hom. 1 John)*

> These books [i.e., Scripture] sing in harmony with each other in alternating voices, and by their harmonious chant, as if by a heavenly trumpet, they rouse us from the torpor of mortal life and stretch us toward the reward of our lofty calling. (*Faustus* 13.18)

What is found in other writings must be subjected to judgment — and accepted only when it is confirmed by Scripture or reason (*Sermons* 162C.15;

Christianity 2.22). Like Origen, Augustine did, however, find profound spiritual truths hidden in the purported etymology of *Hebrew* names.

Letters 147.4). But Scripture, by its very nature, *cannot* err: where it appears to do so, either the manuscript is defective, or the translation is incorrect, or the passage has been misunderstood (*Letters* 82.3). Scripture "has been set on high, as if on a kind of throne, and every believing and pious intellect should be obedient to it" (*Faustus* 11.5).

Like all the authors we have considered to this point, Augustine believed that God speaks today through writings he inspired long ago.[18] When Psalm 121:1 talks of "lifting" eyes to the "mountains" from whence "help" comes, it is figuratively directing our attention to the writings of those "lofty souls" who have given us Scripture. But the psalmist immediately adds, "My help is from the Lord": it is not, then, in the "mountains" (the writers of Scripture) that we are to place our trust, but in the God who gave them what they (in Scripture) have passed on to us (*Tract. John* 1.6-7).

Augustine does not deny that the inspired authors themselves played an active role in what they wrote. He notes, for example, that the evangelists conducted their own research before composing their Gospels (*Agreement* 1.1; *Faustus* 7.2), and that much of what they recorded was based on their own memories (memories, to be sure, appropriately brought to their minds by the Holy Spirit [*Agreement* 2.44, 51-52, etc.]). Still, in the end, God is responsible for the words of the text.[19] Two cases where divine inspiration might seem dubious serve, for Augustine, precisely as illustrations of why the texts must originate with God.

Augustine accepted the traditional attribution of Proverbs, Ecclesiastes, and the Song of Songs to Solomon.[20] But could so immoral a man as Solomon possibly have served as a medium of divine revelation? Augustine responds by reversing the direction of the question: Only if we assumed

18. E.g., *Adimantus* 3.3: "Everything both in the Old and in the New Testament was written and entrusted to us by the one Holy Spirit." *Exp. Ps.* 33.2.1: "Let us listen to what the Holy Spirit has said through the mouth of the holy prophet in the rest of the psalm." *Hom. 1 John* 9.5 (reflecting on an apparent contradiction between 1 John and the Psalms): "Let us question both utterances of God. There is one Spirit even if there are two codexes, even if there are two mouths, even if there are two tongues. For the latter was said by John and the former was said by David, but don't think that the Spirit is something else. If one breath blows into two pipes, can't one Spirit fill two hearts and set two tongues in motion? But if two pipes harmonize when they are filled with one spirit — that is, with one breath — can two tongues be disharmonious when they are filled with the Spirit of God?" Cf. *Sermons* 82.8.

19. Cf. *Exp. Ps.* 56.13: "All the preceding verses were spoken by the Lord — and by the prophet, of course, but only because the Lord was speaking in him."

20. While still embracing the authority of Wisdom and Ecclesiasticus, Augustine noted that scholars doubted Solomon's authorship of these books (*City of God* 17.20). "Higher criticism," it appears, is not entirely the preserve of the modern period.

Solomon spoke in his own name would we be compelled to eliminate his writings from the scriptural record; since, however, he was no more than a channel for divine revelation, "God's mercy and the action of God's Spirit worked with sovereign wisdom in this matter, so that whatever good advice was given through Solomon should be attributed to God" (*Exp. Ps.* 126.2).

Matthew 27:9 attributes to Jeremiah a quotation actually taken from Zechariah. Augustine was aware that certain manuscripts of Matthew lacked the name "Jeremiah," but he refused to eliminate the problem by adopting their reading, recognizing (with modern students of the text) that the more difficult reading is undoubtedly the more original.[21] Here, surely, many would say, Matthew proves himself human: he makes an understandable mistake about the source of his quotation. Others would put it somewhat differently: Matthew was divinely *permitted* to err in a matter of no significance to the point of the text; the human element in the inspired text has thus been allowed to shine through. For Augustine, however, simple mistakes are inconceivable in sacred Scripture. The tack he takes is that of Origen: inaccuracies (at one level) have been introduced into Scripture *deliberately* (the God who inspired the text cannot have been mistaken) so that the reader's attention will be directed to a higher truth (here, that Jeremiah, Zechariah, and the other prophets of Scripture all spoke through the same divine Spirit, so that the ascription of words to a particular prophet was a matter of indifference). What is of interest in this context, however, is Augustine's further claim that Matthew, having written "Jeremiah," must certainly have been made aware that the quotation actually came from Zechariah. Why, then, did he not correct his own text? Because, of course, it was not "his own text": he dared not alter what he knew he had written under the direction of the Holy Spirit, who must have had a purpose in prompting him to write "Jeremiah" (*Agreement* 3.30).[22]

---

21. "Most copies include the name of Jeremiah, and those who study the Gospels most carefully in Greek declare that it is found in the more ancient Greek copies. Moreover, there would have been no reason to add this name and thereby make the copy misleading. But there would have been a reason to remove it from so many copies; bold ignorance would have led to this when faced with the problem of why this testimony is not found in Jeremiah" (*Agreement* 3.29). The text-critical principle of *lectio difficilior* is also at work in *Exp. Ps.* 104.20.

22. After the protracted discussion summarized above, Augustine adds "another reason" why the name of Jeremiah was not just allowed but "commanded" by the authority of the Holy Spirit "to be put here instead of Zechariah." The buying of a field, not mentioned in Zechariah, *is* found in Jeremiah (Jer. 32), though it is Zechariah, not Jeremiah, who mentions the thirty silver pieces. Matthew's reader, not finding in the book of Jeremiah the quotation attributed to that prophet, but finding the reference to the purchase of a field, will be led to

The preceding example in particular illustrates the point that the thinking of Augustine (and of Irenaeus, Origen, and Chrysostom) did not move from a demonstration that Scripture contained no errors to the belief that it must be divinely inspired; rather, unshakably convinced on other grounds that it was divinely inspired, they found ways to explain how apparent mistakes or contradictions in Scripture could be understood differently. Augustine was as insistent as any that Scripture is without error, and true in all it says.[23] But in practice he means (as we have just seen above), not that every text in Scripture is literally true, but that truth is conveyed (at *some* level, not always the literal) by every text in Scripture. At the same time, in dealing with problematic passages, he is perhaps more tolerant than some of diversity in Scripture and more expansive than some in his understanding of Scripture's truth. Consider the following:

1. Like Origen and Chrysostom, Augustine believed that Scripture's message is accommodated to the capacity of even the most unlearned people to receive it (*Questions* 52; *Simplician* 2.2). The principle, Augustine insists, extends far beyond the obvious cases: it is easy, for example, to see that accommodation to human ways of thinking is at work when Scripture speaks of God "repenting" (i.e., changing his mind). Such texts should lead us to realize, however, that even where things we deem worthy of God — mercy, for example — are attributed to him, the words cannot mean what we take them to mean when we use them of human beings.[24] "No words are adequate to [God's] ineffable majesty . . . for which a respectful silence is more appropriate than any human word" (*Adimantus* 11; cf. *Gen.* 1.14). Still, the compromised truth of accommodated language gives human beings a starting point for thinking about God. If it causes some people to think of God in human terms, "such people are still children with their carnal outlook, but while their weakness is cradled in scripture's humble mode of discourse as though in their mother's arms, their faith is being built up for salvation" (*Conf.* 12.37; cf. *Exp. Ps.* 8.8).

---

see that Jesus fulfills the words of both Jeremiah *and* Zechariah (*Agreement* 3.31). One way or another, then, truth was conveyed precisely by (what, at the literal level, was admittedly) an inaccuracy in the text.

23. E.g., *Sermons* 1.4: "All the divine writings are at peace and consistent with each other." *Sermons* 82.9: "Holy scripture is never and nowhere at war with itself. It is all absolutely true; each point is true." *Letters* 82.3: "None of [the canonical] authors erred in writing anything."

24. "They say that mercy is so called because it makes the heart miserable over the misery of someone else who is suffering. . . . Let them deny that God is merciful for fear that he be thought to have a heart full of misery" (*Adimantus* 11; cf. *Answer to Enemy* 1.40).

Augustine sees the same principle at work in the creation account of Genesis 1.[25] If Scripture there speaks (misleadingly, though for sound pedagogical reasons) of "days" of creation,[26] and of separate divine speech-acts by which individual items of creation were brought into being,[27] the point is "to suggest sublime things to lowly people in a lowly manner" (*Unfin. Gen.* 3.8).[28]

2. Origen believed that Scripture at times directs the reader to some spiritual truth by stating what, on a literal level, is false. Augustine is much less inclined than is Origen to resort to such an explanation, but (as just illustrated, where he sees Jeremiah credited with a quotation from Zechariah) there are instances where he does so.[29]

In recording Jesus' genealogy, Matthew lists forty men (not including Christ himself). Great significance is, of course, to be found in the number forty (*Agreement* 2.8-10).[30] But Matthew actually distinguishes three periods, each of fourteen generations, suggesting that the number of generations from Abraham to Christ should have been forty-two. That Christ is included in the forty-two but not the forty reduces the anomaly to one. That Jechoniah is counted twice, at the end of one grouping and the beginning of the next, resolves the issue. The distortion in the presentation

25. Curiously, in the examples that follow (and many others), what we would consider *nonliteral* readings of the text are proposed in Augustine's *The Literal Meaning of Genesis*. They are "literal" for Augustine because they are not allegorical (e.g., the "firmament" of Gen. 1:6 is not here read as a code word standing for "Scripture"); the language, though necessarily accommodated to human weakness (and thus not to be taken literally, in our sense of the word), is concerned with what really happened; it is not code language for truths of a quite different nature.

26. "How could there be days before there was time, if time started with the courses of the lights of heaven, which are said to have been made on the fourth day?" (*Unfin. Gen.* 3.8).

27. "God did not in fact say, 'Let this or that creature be made' every single time that the phrase is repeated in the book" (*Lit. Gen.* 2.6.13).

28. See *Lit. Gen.* 4.33.52: "What need was there for the six days to be recounted so distinctly and methodically? It was for the sake of those who cannot arrive at an understanding of the text, 'he created all things together simultaneously' [Sir. 18:1], unless scripture accompanies them more slowly, step by step, to the goal to which it is leading them." See also *Unfin. Gen.* 5.19.

29. "Why would the Holy Spirit include apparently absurd statements about visible things, unless because our very inability to make sense of it literally may drive us to seek a spiritual meaning?" (*Exp. Ps.* 103.1.18): Origen's point exactly.

30. Significant, too, is the number of those included when Luke records Jesus' genealogy (seventy-seven, "which signifies the complete remission and removal of all sins" [*Agreement* 2.12-13, cf. Matt. 18:22]): again like Origen, Augustine discerns spiritual significance in the numbers of Scripture. For an extended justification of the practice, see *Trin.* 4.10.

of the genealogy is introduced to make a significant point "in figures": by appearing in, and thus connecting, two distinct groupings, the name Jechoniah represents a kind of "cornerstone" in the genealogy; similarly, Christ, in "passing" from the circumcised to the uncircumcised, "became the corner-stone to all who believe in him, whether on one side or the other" (*Agreement* 2.10; also *Sermons* 51.12-15).

According to John's Gospel, Jesus was crucified sometime after the "sixth hour" of the day (i.e., noon; cf. John 19:14); Mark (15:25) says he was crucified at the "third hour" (i.e., 9:00 A.M.). Augustine is not one to downplay the problem: "Show me how the Lord could have been crucified at both the sixth hour and the third. For we must admit that John's narrative puts it at the sixth hour, while Mark reports it was at the third" (*Agreement* 3.43). But this is Scripture, so there must be a solution. Tentatively, Augustine proposes that since, when Mark wrote his Gospel, everyone knew the time of Jesus' crucifixion, his apparent error would have deceived no one. It served rather to convey a subtle point: those who really crucified Jesus were not those who obeyed their orders by nailing him to a cross (at the sixth hour), but those who (at the third hour) demanded his execution. Until someone comes up with a better way of showing that both evangelists tell the truth, this explanation, Augustine believes, will serve the purpose (*Agreement* 3.42-43).

Augustine regarded the headings to individual psalms as an integral part of the text (see *Exp. Ps.* 53.1; 58.1); this brought further examples of literal *un*truths conveying spiritual truth. The heading to Psalm 33 (our Psalm 34) speaks of David feigning madness "in the presence of Abimelech"; according to 1 Samuel 21:10-15, he did so rather to confound Achish, king of Gath. "The episode was recalled, yet the name was altered, and there must be some reason for this" (*Exp. Ps.* 33.1.2): reason is found in a spiritual lesson derived from the etymology of the name "Abimelech." Similarly, Augustine's text of the heading of Psalm 51 (our Psalm 52) read "Abimelech," where, if historical accuracy were desired, it should have said "Ahimelech." Again, the etymology of the name "Abimelech" provides Augustine with a mystical interpretation, and thus an explanation "why, when the prophetic spirit wished to assign a title to our present psalm, the name chosen was not Ahimelech but Abimelech" (*Exp. Ps.* 51.5). Though the heading of Psalm 71 (our Psalm 72) refers the text to Solomon, what follows surpasses anything that can be said of *that* son of David; "Solomon" is here used figuratively to indicate Christ (*Exp. Ps.* 71.1).[31]

31. Cf. *Exp. Ps.* 77.26: "Scripture commonly proceeds like this in reporting the oracles

3. Normally, however, Augustine found ways to harmonize, even at the literal level, texts that appear to contradict each other; indeed, he devoted an extended treatise to showing that the New Testament Gospels, in their various accounts of Jesus' words and deeds, have no substantial disagreements. Much of the fare he provides is common to the menu of all Gospel harmonizations: similar accounts with differing details may in fact reflect distinct events (*Agreement* 2.69, 77, 105, etc.); similar sayings with significant differences may have been spoken on distinct occasions (2.77, 106, 119, etc.); and so on. Augustine goes to considerable lengths to show how the very different birth and infancy stories in Matthew and Luke can be united into a harmonious, consecutive narrative (2.14-17); he does the same with the passion and resurrection accounts of all four Gospels (*Agreement,* book 3).

On the other hand, the harmony Augustine finds in the Gospels is not wooden, nor the standard of truth more restrictive than what we allow in everyday speech.[32] He repeatedly emphasizes that we should not be disturbed by the different order in which events are related in the Gospels: the evangelists recorded incidents as they came to their minds (prompted by the Holy Spirit), not necessarily in the order in which they occurred (*Agreement* 2.44, 51-52, 90, etc.). And, provided the point of the story or the saying is the same, some latitude must be allowed the evangelists in their reporting (cf. 2.27-29). Thus, if Matthew (8:5-6) says that a centurion himself came to Jesus, and Luke (7:2-3) says he sent messengers to convey his request, Matthew is simply telling the same story in fewer words (*Faustus* 33.7; *Agreement* 2.49).[33] Again, Matthew (9:18) abbreviates when he has Jairus approach Jesus directly with the message that his daughter has died. The other Synoptic Gospels (Mark 5:22-23, 35; Luke 8:41-42, 49) relate the incident more fully: Jairus told Jesus that his daughter was sick,

---

of the prophets. It makes some assertion for which no ground can be found in the actual event which is apparently being reported; indeed, the facts appear to be at variance with the statement. From this we are meant to conclude that what seems to be said is not the real message; we must be aware of another meaning. Take as an example the prediction that *He will rule from sea to sea, from the river to the ends of the earth* (Ps. 71:8 [English versions, 72:8]). This was manifestly not verified in the reign of Solomon, of which the psalm was ostensibly speaking. It was, in fact, speaking of Christ the Lord." Cf. also *Exp. Ps.* 113.1.1.

32. "When we read, do we forget how we are accustomed to speak? Or was God's scripture going to speak with us in another manner than what we are accustomed to?" (*Faustus* 33.7).

33. Augustine cannot, however, resist adding that the centurion, in his faith, was "approaching Christ" in a more real (though not literal) sense than did those who went to Christ merely to convey the centurion's message (*Faustus* 33.8; *Agreement* 2.50).

and was only later informed of her death (*Agreement* 2.66). Nor should we see a problem if the evangelists altered the words of Jesus, or of another speaker, in order to convey their point more clearly. The heavenly voice at Jesus' baptism says, "You are my beloved Son" in Mark (1:11) and Luke (3:22), but "This is my beloved Son" in Matthew (3:17); the latter version represents a paraphrase of the former, avoiding any suggestion that Jesus himself needed to be informed of his divine Sonship (*Agreement* 2.31). According to Matthew (9:13) and Mark (2:17), Jesus responded to his critics by saying that he had not come "to call the righteous, but sinners." Luke (5:32) repeats the saying, but appropriately adds the clarification "to repentance" (*Agreement* 2.61). The supernatural events that followed Jesus' death evoked from a centurion the cry "Truly this was the Son of God" (according to Matthew [27:54] and Mark [15:39]). Luke (23:47) paraphrases, "Truly this was a righteous man," conveying the essence of what the centurion would have meant in speaking of Jesus as God's Son: "Perhaps the centurion did not understand that he was the Only Begotten, equal to the Father, but he called him the Son of God because he believed him to be a righteous man, as many other righteous men are called sons of God" (*Agreement* 3.57). "Perhaps" indeed! Doubtless it pained the author of *The Trinity* to concede that a Roman centurion, at the time of Jesus' crucifixion, may not have fully grasped Nicene truth. But he, too, could be realistic.

4. Augustine was greatly exercised by the question whether telling a lie was ever the right thing to do. Chrysostom certainly made a place (in his own life, as well as in his writings) for the useful lie — when the motive that inspired the lie was good (*Priesthood* 1.6-8). Augustine believed that lying was always wrong and thus, of course, that Scripture never lies.[34] His compunctions on the issue led to a famous series of exchanges with Jerome, who (like Origen and Chrysostom) could not believe that Peter and Paul really disagreed with each other in Antioch (as reported in Gal. 2:11-14). According to the latter view, they must have feigned a disagreement so that proponents of the position that Peter *appeared* to take would yield when they saw Peter openly accede to Paul. All indications (as we shall see) are that Augustine could have entertained the notion that the apostles acted out a scene to convey a message; but he

---

34. He did, however, allow that the midwives who lied to Pharaoh to preserve Israelite children (Exod. 1:18-19), and Rahab, who lied to those seeking the Israelite spies (Josh. 2:4-6), merit praise. Though it is better never to lie, those who have not yet reached that stage of moral maturity are headed in the right direction when they restrict their lies to those that benefit others (*Lying* 5.7; *Against Lying* 15–16.33; cf. *Questions* 53.1).

could not accept that Paul (in sacred Scripture) misreported the event as an example of Peter's "hypocrisy" (Gal. 2:13). If such "lying" is ever allowed in Scripture, interpreters will feel free to see truth spoken wherever Scripture agrees with their own views, but untruth wherever it differs (*Letters* 28.3; 40.3).

Augustine's firm stance against all deceit, however, led him into a good deal of casuistry in points of detail. Though he grants, certainly in theory and occasionally in practice, that Scripture's saints may have acted wrongly (*Letters* 82.5; cf. *Faustus* 22.60-65; *Teaching Christianity* 3.33), at times he goes to astonishing lengths to demonstrate that what seem to be lies spoken by the righteous were in fact figurative ways of communicating truth — and thus that no wrong was committed.[35] Beginning with the observation that simple metaphors convey truth through literal *un*truths,[36] Augustine sees the same principle at work when Jacob covered himself with goatskins and told his father he was Esau (Gen. 27). The goatskins represented sins, and Jacob's taking them upon himself represented Christ carrying the sins of others. When Jacob claimed to be his older brother Esau, we are to think of the church, which (like a younger brother) "took away the elder brother's [i.e., Israel's] primacy and transferred what was his brother's to himself. . . . When the things signified are true, at least in some past, present, or future sense, without doubt it is a true signification and not a lie" (*Against Lying* 10.24; cf. *Sermons* 4.13-30).[37]

The unique case of the presence, in human flesh, of the eternal Son of God poses a veritable gamut of problems for the interpreter of Scripture. Augustine believes that Christ had full knowledge at all times of what he would do, of the state of affairs around him, and of his eternal relationship with the Father. He is challenged, then, by the need to explain how Christ could at times act in ways seemingly pointless (e.g., looking for figs in the wrong season and cursing a tree that did not have them [Mark 11:13-14]), or

---

35. Abraham's craven "She is my sister" (Gen. 12:19; 20:2) does not even come into question, since Sarah was, in a sense, his sister (Gen. 20:12), and "concealing the truth [that she was also his wife] is not the same as putting forth a lie" (*Against Lying* 10.23; cf. *City of God* 16.19).

36. Indeed, Aesop's fables (and even Jesus' parables) must be considered lies if we ignore what they are intended to convey, allowing only literal truth (*Against Lying* 13.28).

37. Similarly, convinced of the allegorical significance of Samson's deeds, Augustine regarded him rather as a prophet than an immoral person (*Sermons* 364); and Elisha was conveying a prophetic message when he called on she-bears to devour those who ridiculed him (*Exp. Ps.* 46.2; 83.2).

as though about to do one thing (e.g., leave the disciples who were on their way to Emmaus) before doing another (sitting down for a meal with them [Luke 24:28-29]); or as though in need of information (e.g., "Where have you laid [Lazarus's corpse]?" [John 11:34]). Moreover, how could Christ speak as though he were inferior to the Father (repeatedly)? In each case, Augustine believes, truth is communicated — though at a different level from that of appearances.[38]

The Old Testament and the New

From the examples just given, it will be clear that Augustine, like Origen, believed that Scripture at times uses literal *untruths* in order to convey truth at another level.[39] For Augustine, however, such occasions are rare. And whereas, in Origen's view, the literal level of the text was designed to meet the needs of immature believers, while greater mysteries are conveyed allegorically to the mature, Augustine insists that the needs of *all* readers are addressed at Scripture's literal level. The few texts that demand — and the many texts that permit — allegorical interpretation do so merely to present the same truths in a more varied, attractive, and stimulating way (*Letters* 55.21; cf. *Teaching Christianity* 2.7-8).[40]

---

38. Apparently pointless deeds may convey truth figuratively: e.g., cursing a fig tree with leaves but no fruit symbolizes the judgment that awaits those whose words are not matched by deeds (*Sermons* 89.1, 3-4; cf. 77.7); staying with the Emmaus-bound followers after pretending to leave them speaks symbolically of Christ's continued presence with his disciples even after he ascended into heaven (*Against Lying* 13.28; cf. *Sermons* 89.7). Spiritual truth also underlies questions that appear to imply ignorance on Jesus' part: that Jesus asked where dead Lazarus had been laid anticipates the judgment ("I do not know you!" [Matt. 7:23]) he will one day pronounce on the lost (*Tract. John* 49.20; cf. *Sermons* 77.7); explicit statements of Jesus' ignorance (Matt. 24:36) mean merely that he is not about to disclose to his listeners what he does in fact know (*Questions* 60; *Trin.* 1.23; *Exp. Ps.* 6.1; 36.1.1). Augustine applies a simple rule to texts speaking of Christ's relationship with his Father: where the Son is said to be equal to the Father, his divinity is the subject; where he is said to be inferior, the text reflects either Christ's human nature (*Questions* 69.1; *Sermons* 341.17; *Tract. John* 36.2; *Trin.* 1.14) or his eternal derivation from the Father ("what the Son himself is he owes to the Father . . . [including] his equality" [*Creed* 9.18; cf. *Trin.* 2.4]).

39. In such cases, the simple criterion at work is that any text that is absurd at the literal level must be interpreted allegorically. Cf. *Lit. Gen.* 11.2; *City of God* 17.3.

40. Cf. also *Letters* 137.18: "[Scripture] not only feeds [readers] with the evident truth but also exercises them with the hidden truth, though it has the same truth in clear matters as in hidden ones. But so that obvious truths do not become boring, the same truths are again desired as concealed, and as desired are in a sense refreshed, and as refreshed they are

Nearly every Old Testament text can be read as literally true.[41] To *confine* their truth to their allegorical point is, for Augustine, to "build" the latter "on air": normally, at least, truth signified (though spiritual) requires a true signifier (though carnal).[42] On the other hand, in order to discover the full significance of the Old Testament, one must penetrate beneath the surface meaning of the text.[43] God did not intend Scripture to merely convey "bare historical events" (*City of God* 15.27).[44] Augustine thus combines

---

taught with sweetness. By these, evil minds are salutarily corrected, little minds are fed, and great minds are delighted." See also *Sermons* 45.3. In general, God nourishes readers with what is obvious, exercises them with what is obscure (*Questions* 53.2). Students of Scripture may thus begin with what Scripture says plainly and use it as a basis for understanding more obscure passages (*Teaching Christianity* 2.14; cf. *Faustus* 12.7; *Sermons* 46.35).

41. At one stage in his life, Augustine found that Ambrose's allegorical interpretations of the Old Testament gave the latter a credibility he felt it otherwise lacked. His own *On Genesis: A Refutation of the Manichees* represents an early work with the same agenda. Augustine grew increasingly to appreciate the importance of the literal sense of the text, however, and later works on Genesis (*Unfinished Literal Commentary on Genesis; The Literal Meaning of Genesis;* books 11–13 of the *Confessions*), while in no way renouncing the allegorical approach, represent his efforts to show that the text permitted "literal" interpretation as well; cf. *Lit. Gen.* 8.5 and n. 25 above.

42. See *Sermons* 8.2: "Let us observe, brothers, that things which actually happened in the flesh are to be understood in a spiritual way. For we do not imagine that these things were only talked and written about without actually happening; rather we believe that they happened as we read that they happened, and yet we know through the apostle's teaching that the actual events were shadows of things to come. So we are of the opinion that the things which happened must be examined for their spiritual meaning, but we cannot deny that they happened. So please let none of you say, 'It is certainly written that water was turned into blood in one of the plagues of Egypt, but it is a story with a meaning; it couldn't really have happened.' If you say this, you are seeking the will of God in such a way as to do an injury to the power of God. . . . We must begin by laying the foundation of the solid reality of the events, and then go on to inquire into their figurative meaning, or else if we take away the foundation it will look as if we are determined to build on air." See also *Sermons* 2.7-8; *Lit. Gen.* 8; *City of God* 13.21.

43. Most, but not all, of the Old Testament yields meaning beyond the literal level (see *Teaching Christianity* 3.32). Augustine allows, however, that, in a continuous narrative, parts of what is said serve only to tie the story together; they carry no added significance of their own. He compares a plow: only the blade does the work for which the plow is designed, though the plow needs more than a blade to be usable (*City of God* 16.2)!

44. The Old Testament, read at its surface level and apart from its reference to Christ, is tasteless as water. "What was water becomes wine" — when Christ is seen in Scripture. Note too, however, that Christ did not simply create wine for the wedding in Cana, as though having no use for water; he turned water into wine, showing "that the ancient Scripture comes from him too. . . . This Scripture, too, is indeed from the Lord; but it has no taste if Christ should not be understood in it" (*Tract. John* 9.3-5).

Antiochene insistence on historical reality with Alexandrian emphasis on "spiritual" interpretation.

> Just as people are badly mistaken when they think that the events re-
> corded in writings of this kind signify nothing more than the mere event
> itself, so people are far too rash when they insist that everything re-
> corded there carries allegorical significance. . . . I do not condemn those
> who have been able to devise a spiritual meaning for each historical
> event recorded there, just so long as, first of all, they preserve the truth
> of the history itself. (*City of God* 17.3)

1. The *stories* of the Old Testament often represent spiritual realities experienced by Christians. Here, to be sure, Augustine is saying nothing we have not heard before.

> The people, according to the old testament, are liberated from Egypt;
> the people, according to the new testament, are liberated from the devil.
> The Egyptian persecutors and Pharaoh pursue the Jews as they make
> their exodus from Egypt; the Christian people are pursued by their own
> sins and by the devil, the high chief of sins. Just as the Egyptians pursue
> the Jews as far as the sea, so Christians are pursued by their sins as far
> as baptism. Observe, brothers, and see; through the sea the Jews are
> liberated, in the sea the Egyptians are overwhelmed. Through baptism
> Christians are liberated and quit of their sins, while their sins are de-
> stroyed. Those ones come out after the Red Sea and journey through
> the desert; so too Christians after baptism are not yet in the promised
> land, but live in hope. . . . They were given manna in the desert, just as
> we are given the sweetness of the scriptures to help us endure this desert
> of human life. . . . [These things] were performed for them but they were
> figures for us, because they were performed for them materially but they
> had a spiritual meaning for us. (*Sermons* 4.9-10)

Like Origen, Augustine cites Pauline precedent to support the "spiritual" reading of such texts.[45] Naturally, Augustine followed the New Testament

45. Cf. *Lying* 15.26, referring to 1 Cor. 10 and Gal. 4; *Faustus* 12.37; *Lit. Gen.* 1.1. The early Augustine followed Ambrose (*Conf.* 6.6; the ultimate source is, of course, Origen) in citing 2 Cor. 3:6 as providing programmatic justification for the allegorical interpretation of Scripture: "the letter [i.e., a literal understanding of the text] kills, but the spirit [i.e., spiri- tual, or allegorical, interpretation] gives life." Cf. *Teaching Christianity* 3.9. In later work he continued to allow this as one way of reading Paul's text, but he recognized that the apostle

and earlier interpreters in seeing the person and work of Christ prefigured in many Old Testament narratives (see, e.g., *Faustus* 12). If a single example of a ubiquitous phenomenon must suffice, let it be this one:

> Consider Elisha in a great and profound mystery, a real prophet, fore-telling by his actions, not only by his words. The son of his hostess had died. What could the dead boy have represented but Adam? The holy prophet was told about it — he prophetically prefigured the Lord Jesus Christ. He sent his servant with his staff and said to him, *Go, go, place it on the dead body.* Off he went, like an obedient servant.... He placed the staff on the dead body, it didn't rise up. *For if a law had been given that could bring to life, justice would altogether come from laws* (Gal. 3:21). So the law couldn't bring to life.
>
> The adult himself came to the child.... He shrank his limbs to a child's proportions, as though emptying himself to take the form of a servant [see Phil. 2:7]. So he shrank his limbs to a child's proportions, he fitted himself as a little one to the little one, in order to fashion the body of our lowliness into the likeness of the body of his glory [cf. Phil. 3:21]. Thus in this figure of Christ prophetically enacted the dead was raised up, standing for the godless being justified [see Rom. 4:5]. (*Sermons* 26.11)

Unique to Augustine, however, is the depiction of the whole story of human history as the tale of two "cities":

> Two loves, then, have made two cities. Love of self, even to the point of contempt for God, made the earthly city, and love of God, even to the point of contempt for self, made the heavenly city. Thus the former glories in itself, and the latter glories in the Lord.... In the former the lust for domination dominates both its princes and the nations that it subjugates; in the latter both leaders and followers serve one another in love, the leaders by their counsel, the followers by their obedience. (*City of God* 14.28)

Since the story starts when "the first two human beings began to have children" (*City of God* 15.1), Augustine can tell the story of the Old Testament as the significant beginnings of the ongoing drama of the "two cities" (*City of God* 15–18; cf. *Instruct. Beg.* 31–44; *Lit. Gen.* 11.20).

---

was actually saying something quite different: life under the law leads to death, that under the Spirit brings life (*Spirit and Letter* 4.6–5.8; *Revisions* 1.14[13].1).

2. The *laws* of the Old Testament include both commands that "regulate life" (such as "You shall not covet")[46] and others that served to foreshadow aspects of Christ's work and the lives of his followers (*Faustus* 6.2;
10.2; *Spirit and Letter* 14.23):[47] the sacrificial laws, for example, prefigured
Christ's self-sacrifice for sin (*Faustus* 18.6), whereas laws forbidding the
consumption of certain ("unclean") foods signified forms of behavior that
have no place in the lives of believers (*Adimantus* 14.3; 15.1; *Faustus* 6.7).
Literal observance of these latter laws lost its intended significance when
Christ came — and that to which they pointed became reality (*Faustus*
19.11, 13; *Spirit and Letter* 14.23). To continue to observe them now is thus,
in effect, to deny their fulfillment (*Faustus* 19.8); it is to attend to the *sign*
while failing to see what it *signified*.[48] The *spiritual* significance of such rites
remains, to be sure, and gives believers reason to reflect on them still: "It
is not the Old Testament that is taken away with Christ, but the veil over
it" (*Advan. Believing* 3.9).[49]

> We would be sacrilegious and wicked if we thought that we should
> throw away those same books. For they were written for our sake so

46. Augustine came to follow Paul in believing that these laws can only begin to be
fulfilled by those (i.e., believers) to whom the Spirit of God has been given; in others, they
serve to reveal and accentuate their captivity to sin — and need of the saving grace of Christ.
Cf. *Spirit and Letter* 19.34; *Tract. John* 3.14.

47. It is also worth noting that Augustine sees some Old Testament laws as appropriate
for human beings at an early stage of their moral development, though inappropriate later:
"Because at first carnal human beings burned to avenge themselves as if the injury about
which they complained were greater than it was, it was set down for them, as the first step
toward leniency, that the pain inflicted by the avenger should in no way exceed the amount
of the injury received. For in that way someone who had first learned not to go beyond the
injury he received might be able at some point to forgive it" (*Adimantus* 8; cf. *Faustus* 19.25).
Furthermore, the same underlying moral principles can, in certain cases, find different expression in different societies. E.g., the patriarchs were permitted multiple wives because
the world at that time was in need of inhabitants; but the principle remained that relations
with these wives were not to be marked by "fleshly concupiscence" (*Conf.* 3.13; *Faustus* 22.47;
Teaching Christianity 3.20, 27).

48. Augustine allowed, however, that it was appropriate for Jewish Christians to continue observing these laws for a time even after Christ came, as one honors the corpse of
a dead parent. They were not, after all, pagan superstitions that must simply be discarded,
but laws commanded by God (though for a limited time and purpose); respect was due to
them for that reason. See *Faustus* 19.17; *Letters* 82.15-16; *Sermons* 162C.6.

49. Augustine notes that, when the Old Testament calls rites "eternal" that are no
longer to be observed (e.g., Exod. 28:43; Lev. 16:34), the point is that what they *signified*
has not come to an end (*Orosius* 5.6).

that we might know and faithfully and firmly hold that those realities, which have now been revealed to us and proclaimed in full clarity, were foretold by those symbols so long before. . . . That scripture then served as a commandment but is now a testimony. (*Faustus* 6.9; cf. *Sermons* 149.4-5)

3. The *promises* made in the Old Testament generally pertained to temporal, material goods. Such promises served a purpose at the time: it is important that people realize that even earthly goods come from God (*Exp. Ps.* 34.1.7; *Letters* 140.5); but their real significance is only seen when they are understood as pointing to the spiritual blessings promised in the New Testament (*Faustus* 4.2; *Spirit and Letter* 21.36).[50] Indeed, in such promises, spiritual truth is at times concealed beneath literal *untruth*.

The rich have been in need and have gone hungry, but those who seek the Lord will not be deprived of any good thing (Ps. 33:11 [English versions, 34:10]). If you take this literally, it will look like a fallacy, for you see around you plenty of rich, unjust people who die amid their riches. . . . Clearly, the psalm cannot be interpreted in that way. "How am I to understand it, then?" It refers to the good things of the spirit. (*Exp. Ps.* 33.2.14-15)

I was young once, and now I have grown old, and never have I seen a just person destitute, or a child of righteous parents begging for bread [Ps 36:25 (English versions, 37:25)]. . . . [If we look in the sacred scriptures, we find] the just man Abraham in straitened circumstances and forced by the hunger he faced in his own country to travel abroad. . . . [Paul] says, *I have experienced hunger and thirst, endured cold and exposure* (2 Cor. 11:27). . . . [An observer might well say to himself,] "Why should I exert myself in good works? Why break my bread to the hungry, or clothe the naked, or bring the homeless into my house, putting my faith in scripture's declaration, *Never have I seen a just person destitute, or a child*

50. Similarly, "the patriarchs and prophets waged wars for their kingdoms in order to show that the will of God also gives such victories; the apostles and martyrs were slain without resistance in order to teach that it is a better victory to suffer death for faith in the truth. . . . The ministers of the Old Testament, who also foretold the New Testament, served God by killing sinners; the ministers of the New Testament, who also explained the Old Testament, served God by dying at the hands of sinners. Yet both served the one God, who taught during different but appropriate ages that temporal goods were to be sought from him and should be held in scorn for his sake and that temporal difficulties can be imposed by him and ought to be endured for his sake" (*Faustus* 22.76, 79).

of righteous parents begging for bread, when all the while I see so many people who live good lives going hungry?" . . . If you understand what this bread is, you will understand what is meant. The bread is the word of God, which is never absent from a righteous person's mouth. (*Exp. Ps.* 36.3.1-5; cf. also 33.2.22, 24; 36.3.9)

4. Most memorably, perhaps, Augustine reads *the Psalms,* too, as Christian scripture. Unlike the Antiochenes, Augustine betrays almost no interest in the historical setting in which various psalms were composed. The subject of the Psalms that interests Augustine is Christ, sometimes as the one spoken of (e.g., *Exp. Ps.* 18.1.1; 19.1; 20.1), but, more frequently, as himself the speaker (*Exp. Ps.* 131.2).[51] The latter understanding, of course, accounts for words expressed in the first person and traditionally thought to speak of Christ, particularly of his sufferings (e.g., Ps. 22:1; 31:5; cf. *Exp. Ps.* 30.2.11). But Augustine found a way to attribute to Christ even words that, because they refer to the psalmist's sinfulness and infirmities, were thought by the Antiochenes to exclude christological interpretation. In such cases, Christ speaks, not in his own person, but in that of his body, the church.

> He who deigned to assume the form of a slave, and within that form to clothe us with himself, he who did not disdain to take us up into himself, did not disdain either to transfigure us into himself, and to speak in our words, so that we in our turn might speak in his. . . . Christ is speaking. He is going to say certain things in this psalm that we might think inappropriate to Christ, to the excellent dignity of our Head, and especially to the Word who was God with God in the beginning. Some of the things said here may not even seem suitable for him in the form of a servant . . . ; and yet it is Christ who is speaking, because in the members of Christ there is Christ. (*Exp. Ps.* 30.2.3-4)

> *I have sinned against you.* But surely Christ cannot say this? . . . Not as from himself; but as from his members he could, for the voice of his members is his voice, just as the voice of our Head is our voice. (*Exp. Ps.* 40.6)

> The Church is hungry, Christ's body is hungry. This person who is spread worldwide, whose head is on high and whose limbs are here below — this whole person is hungry. We should hear his voice, her voice, in all

51. Cf. *Exp. Ps.* 96.2; 98.1.

the psalms, jubilating or groaning, rejoicing in hope or sighing with love in fulfillment; we should hear it as something already well known to us, a voice most familiar because it is our own. There is no need to make heavy weather over indicating who the speaker is. Only let each of us be within Christ's body, and we shall be the speaker here. (*Exp. Ps.* 42.1)

Believers can and should identify themselves with what Christ says, making the praises and prayers, the laments and thanksgivings, of the Psalms their own.

If the psalm is praying, pray yourselves; if it is groaning, you groan too; if it is happy, rejoice; if it is crying out in hope, you hope as well; if it expresses fear, be afraid. Everything written here is like a mirror held up to us. (*Exp. Ps.* 30.4.1)

Whatever pressure the saints may endure, let them turn their thoughts to this psalm and recognize themselves in it; let those who suffer what is described here make the words the expression of their own prayer. (*Exp. Ps.* 55.4)

Psalms that begin with groans and end with thanksgiving are meant to lead believers from the one to the other.

The psalm grieves with you, and asks questions with you, but not because it does not know. Rather does it ask with you the question to which it knows the answer, so that in it you may find what you did not know. Anyone who wants to console someone else acts like this: unless he grieves with the other, he cannot lift him up. First of all he grieves with him, and then he strengthens him with a consoling word. . . . So too the psalm, and indeed the Spirit of God, though knowing everything, ask questions with you, as though putting your own thoughts into words. . . . Look how the psalm corrects itself now, and allow yourself to be corrected along with it. It was to that end that the psalm adopted your complaint. What did you say? *How long will sinners gloat, O Lord, how long?* The psalm took on your words, so now you take on the words of the psalm. And what does the psalm say? *The Lord has become a refuge for me.* (*Exp. Ps.* 93.9, 27)

Difficulties are, of course, raised by words spoken by the psalmists that are inappropriate even on the lips of Christ's followers: the most obvious example is the imprecatory psalms. Elsewhere, Augustine can justify, as appropriate at the time, behavior reported in the Old Testament that falls short of New Testament standards; but so bent is he on reading the Psalms as Christian Scripture that he generally ignores such considerations, focusing entirely on ways of understanding the texts that render them appropriate for believers. Thus the psalmist is not actually calling down evil on the heads of his enemies, but merely foretelling what will inevitably befall them ("[the psalmists] knew to whom evil had to come and to whom good; and they prophesied it, as though they were demanding what they foresaw" [*Sermons* 56.3; cf. *Exp. Ps.* 34.1.8; 51.8, etc.]); what appears to be a curse upon sinners is in fact a prayer that their *sins* will be destroyed, so that they will no longer *be* sinners (*Exp. Ps.* 78.13-14); the "little ones" of Babylon who are to be dashed against the stones are evil desires newly born, which must be shattered before they have a chance to become habits (*Exp. Ps.* 136.21); the psalmist's "perfect hatred" of sinners is "perfect" because it is targeted exclusively at "everything in [sinners] that makes them sinful," while being at the same time combined with a love for the sinners themselves as God's creatures (*Exp. Ps.* 138.28).

Augustine thus reads the stories, laws, promises, and psalms of the Old Testament as Christian Scripture. So, of course, did Chrysostom, but in a very different way: Chrysostom focused on what he saw as the literal, historical meaning of the Old Testament, with the result that little that is *distinctively* Christian emerges from his treatment of many texts. Augustine finds Christian meaning everywhere; and, on the whole, he assumes that the writers and righteous people of the Old Testament were themselves in full and conscious possession of Christian truth,[52] concealing it only because others were not ready for it. Augustine's Old Testament contains all that the New Testament contains, though in a veiled form. His New Testament advances beyond his Old only in revealing its secrets.

Readers of the Old Testament must penetrate beneath the surface of the text in order to understand it as Christian Scripture; not so, of course, with the New. But Augustine follows Origen in seeing allegorical significance in the accounts of Jesus' deeds. "The deeds of the Lord are not only deeds but also signs. If, therefore, they are signs, besides the fact that they are wonders, they assuredly signify something" (*Tract. John* 49.2). In Augustine (as in Origen), they are subjected to full-fledged allegorical interpretation. An example or two must suffice.

---

52. He is sure, e.g., that Jacob, pretending to be Esau, and Isaac, pretending to be deceived, were both cognizant of the christological truths they were symbolically enacting. See *Sermons* 4.20-21, 23.

On his way to healing the daughter of the ruler of the synagogue (who represents the Jewish people), Jesus is approached by a woman with a hemorrhage (who represents the Gentiles, suffering from extravagant self-indulgence). Jesus' garment represents his apostles (since they stick to him closely); the hem, or least part, of the garment represents Paul, the last of the apostles, but also (suitably for this story) the apostle to the Gentiles. "And the Church of the Gentiles, like the woman who touched the hem, was suffering from a bloody flux; she touched and was restored to health. Let us too touch, that is, let us believe, so that we too can be restored to health" (*Sermons* 63A.2-3).

What, you may wonder, could be plainer? Well, perhaps this. The Gospels tell of three people whom Jesus raised from the dead: one (Jairus's daughter) inside a house; one (the son of the widow of Nain) in a public place; and one (Lazarus) who had been dead four days, and buried in a tomb sealed by a heavy stone. Surely sinners (to whom Jesus brings life) of three types are represented: those who sin inwardly, those who sin outwardly, and those whose sin has become an established habit (*Sermons* 98.5-6).

In Augustine's treatment of New Testament texts, there is, at times, a similar loss of historical perspective to what we found in his readings of the Old Testament (here the same weakness is shared by Chrystosom — and patristic literature in general). Not only are the Old Testament authors taken to be fully aware of New Testament truth; the writers of the New Testament are taken to be in full and conscious possession of the truth as formulated in early Christian creeds. Admittedly, believers even today affirm that the language of Scripture *demands* something like the later creedal formulations. The question of how Christ can be God and man arises from an attentive reading of Scripture itself; so, too, how Father, Son, and Spirit can all be spoken of as God — though God is one. But a Christian who is aware of the course of history must recognize that the early church only gradually arrived at formulas that it believed did justice to the manifold testimony of Scripture. To this *kind* of historical development, Augustine is blithely insensitive. The New Testament writers, he believed, fully shared his dogmatic convictions, though at times challenging readers to discover them beneath the obscure language they employ.[53]

---

53. Unlike Chrysostom, for whom, e.g., the words of Christ in Scripture at times fall short of the full truth about his divine nature out of "considerateness" for what his hearers were prepared to receive, Augustine cannot allow that those words are ever anything other than fully true — though they may, of course, be obscure.

The Interpretative Task

Augustine shows real, if limited, interest in penetrating to the text of Scripture as originally written and making it the basis of interpretation. In theory, he acknowledges that the original languages should be consulted (*Teaching Christianity* 2.16).[54] He himself knew no Hebrew, however, and he struggled with Greek. As a second best, he advises consulting a variety of translations, with preference given to those that render the text more literally (*Teaching Christianity* 2.19). Aware of variations in the text as preserved in different manuscripts, Augustine recommends examining several (*Teaching Christianity* 2.21-22; cf. *Faustus* 11.2). The evidence of Augustine's own writings indicates that he did, on occasion, follow his own advice in these matters; more commonly, he operated (in effect) on the principle that the God who inspired the sacred scriptures is able to speak, and does speak, to readers even through imperfectly preserved and translated texts.[55]

Sometimes it is not problems related to translation that keep us from understanding Scripture, but ignorance of what Scripture is speaking about. Assuming that Scripture refers to specific plants, animals, rocks, and the like with a view to peculiarities of the mentioned types, Augustine (like Origen) concludes that our ability to grasp Scripture's point will depend on our familiarity with those peculiarities (*Teaching Christianity* 2.24).[56] Similarly, knowledge of various academic disciplines can aid our understanding of related passages in Scripture: a classical education (minus, of course, its associated pagan superstitions) can thus serve a useful purpose even for the believer.[57] In the end, however, though truth is not to be despised wherever it is found, all we really need to know is contained in Scripture.

54. We have seen, however, that he regards the Septuagint as an authoritative text of the Old Testament.

55. "So far as [Augustine] is concerned, one form is as good as another for the purpose of preaching" (Bonner, "Augustine," 540). Note, e.g., how Augustine can discuss without apparent perturbation or attempted resolution discrepancies between readings in Hebrew Old Testament manuscripts and those found in Greek and Latin versions (*City of God* 15.10-11, 13; 16.10).

56. Here Augustine does repeatedly follow his own advice, drawing on his familiarity with the (real or alleged) behavior of animals mentioned in the texts (e.g., *Exp. Ps.* 41.2-4; 101.1.7-8; 102.9).

57. In *Exp. Ps.* 10.3-4, Augustine, taking his cue from a reference in the psalm to a darkening of the moon, mentions two different theories about the light of the moon, and several ways in which the moon's light can be "darkened," and he draws spiritual lessons from each.

But the supply of gold, silver and fine raiment which [the Israelites] took with them from Egypt was much less, in comparison with the riches which they acquired later on in Jerusalem, which was most evident in the reign of King Solomon; to the same extent all the knowledge derived from the books of the heathen, which is indeed useful, becomes little enough if it is compared with the knowledge of the divine scriptures. For whatever you learn outside them is there condemned if it is harmful, while if it is useful, it is also to be found there. And when you have found there everything of use that you can learn elsewhere, you will also find there in much greater abundance things that you cannot find anywhere else at all, things that can only be learned in the marvelous heights and equally marvelous lowliness and humility of those scriptures. (*Teaching Christianity* 2.63)

But what are we to do when a passage in Scripture seems to permit more than one interpretation? Readers should confirm that each proposal in fact suits a proper construction of the text and the progression of thought in the context; above all, a valid interpretation must be in agreement with the rule of faith, as defined by unambiguous passages of Scripture and the teaching of the Christian church. For an understanding of the literal meaning of any given text, these tests should suffice to eliminate all but one interpretation. If they do not, multiple interpretations should be allowed (*Teaching Christianity* 3.2.8).

Sensible of the inexhaustible treasures contained in Scripture,[58] Augustine was characteristically open to the possibility of multiple interpretations — particularly, of course, where allegorical readings were involved.[59] And he struggled to restrain his impatience with those who insisted that theirs alone was correct (*Conf.* 12.17, 34).[60] To be sure, the

---

58. Augustine found himself overwhelmed by the mysteries of the opening chapters of Genesis; he was particularly disturbed by those who insisted on the sole rightness of their own interpretations here (cf. *Unfin. Gen.* 9.30; *Lit. Gen.* 2.38). Positively harmful to the Christian faith were those who maintained interpretations contradicted by the clear results of scientific study, thus provoking nonbelievers knowledgeable about science to ridicule Christian Scripture (*Lit. Gen.* 1.39).

59. Augustine does note, however, that only those figurative meanings should be attributed to a text that are stated plainly in other parts of Scripture (*Teaching Christianity* 3.39).

60. Augustine himself would never make such claims; cf. *Exp. Ps.* 74.12: "I think that [the cup of pure wine of Ps. 75:8] symbolizes the law. . . . Some other person may produce a better interpretation, for the obscurity of the scriptures is such that a passage scarcely ever yields a single meaning only. But whatever interpretation emerges, it must conform to the

goal of interpretation is to arrive at the meaning intended by the author (see *Sermons* 7.3). But where more than one interpretation fits the wording of a text and the progression of its thought, and none is opposed to the rule of faith, then there is no reason to exclude any. Augustine is inclined to believe that the (inspired) human authors themselves were aware of all the possible interpretations; and even if *they* were not, the Holy Spirit undoubtedly was. If, then, the Spirit of God allowed the text to be worded in such a way as to admit a plurality of interpretations, Augustine saw no reason to reject any of them (*Conf.* 12.36, 42-43; *Teaching Christianity* 3.38).

Broadly speaking, there need be no doubt about the intention of the divine author who inspired Scripture. Christ declared that the message of "the law and the prophets" can be summed up in the commandments to love God and our neighbor (Matt. 22:37-40). That principle surely applies to all of Scripture (*Instruct. Beg.* 8).[61] It follows that any interpretation of Scripture that does not promote such love *must* be a misinterpretation (*Teaching Christianity* 1.40);[62] and if the literal sense of any text does not lend itself to promoting such love, the truth of that text is necessarily figurative (*Instruct. Beg.* 50).[63]

Augustine can also speak of Scripture as a medicine prepared by God; its whole purpose then becomes to provide healing for ailments brought about by sin.

---

rule of faith. Let us not be jealous of those with more powerful minds than our own, nor despair because we are so small. I am expounding to you, beloved ones, whatever seems right to us, but I do not want to close your ears against others, who may perhaps have better things to say." *Sermons* 5.7: "But what does [the text] mean — I'm speaking as far as the Lord suggests to me, without prejudice to a better understanding — what does this mean?" *Sermons* 51.35: "No doubt other truths can be extracted from these hidden treasures of the mysteries of God, by minds more thorough going and worthier than mine. . . . If any of you is eager for more, you must knock at the door of the one from whom I too have received what I have been able to grasp and to express."

61. Should a preacher want to speak about love, then, he has chosen the one topic for which there is no need to search for a text that treats it; any page of Scripture will serve the purpose (*Sermons* 350A.1). The centrality of love to Augustine's understanding of Scripture and its interpretation is emphasized in Margerie, *Augustine*.

62. Cf. *Conf.* 12.35; *Teaching Christianity* 3.14. In the latter text (and elsewhere; cf. 1.44), Augustine alludes to 1 Tim. 1:5 as likewise defining the purpose of Scripture (i.e., to promote "love" that comes from a "pure heart, good conscience, and sincere faith") — thus also providing a criterion by which to discern its true interpretation. Cf. *Conf.* 12.27.

63. If, e.g., cruel words or deeds are attributed to God or his saints in Scripture, the reader should see in the text a summons to destroy sinful desires (*Teaching Christianity* 3.17).

Our Lord and God takes care of and heals every ailment of the soul, and so he produced many medicines from the holy scriptures (which you could call the shelves of his pharmacy or drugstore). (*Sermons* 32.1)

Every illness of the soul finds its medicine in the scriptures, so any of us who are suffering from the malady that prompts us to think like this in our hearts will do well to drink a draught from this psalm. . . . Take your medicine. Drink it. The Lord himself, about whom you are complaining, has mixed the dose for you. Just consent to take this potion; it will do you a lot of good. (*Exp. Ps.* 36.1.3)

[God's] word has been preached and put into writing exclusively for our healing and salvation. (*Hom. 1 John* 5.2)

Or Scripture can be said to serve the dual purpose of governing how we live on earth and enabling us to attain the life of the age to come (*Faustus* 22.26). It follows that we misread Scripture when we seek in it what it is not intended to provide, or study it for purposes other than those for which it was prepared.

Many people, you see, have many arguments about these points [i.e., the nature of the "sky" spoken of in Gen. 1], which our authors [of Scripture] with greater good sense passed over as not holding out the promise of any benefit to those wishing to learn about the blessed life, and, what is worse, as taking up much precious time that should be spent on more salutary matters. What concern is it of mine, after all, whether the sky encloses the earth like a globe on every side, with the earth held level as the diameter of the total mass of the world, or whether it covers on one side from above, like a lid? . . . It must be stated very briefly that our authors knew about the shape of the sky, whatever may be the truth of the matter. But the Spirit of God who was speaking through them did not wish to teach people about such things which would contribute nothing to their salvation. (*Lit. Gen.* 2.20)[64]

To examine God's testimonies without loving what they reveal, without wanting to be led by them to God — that is not true study. . . . The Spirit is speaking here, and he knows that many engage in careful study of

---

64. Galileo found occasion to cite this text in his famous "Letter to the Grand Duchess Christina."

the scriptures with some object other than that for which it is recommended. . . . They do not aspire to be wise for the glory of God; they only want to appear wise in order to be glorified by other people. Is this not a hatred of wisdom? (*Exp. Ps.* 118.1.2)

If there is one final word of counsel Augustine would give to those who interpret Scripture, perhaps it is this:

Above all, don't forget this: not to be unduly troubled when you don't yet understand the holy scriptures; when you do understand them, not to get a swollen head. Instead, respectfully put to one side anything you don't understand, and anything you do understand hold firmly to in a spirit of love. (*Sermons* 51.35)

CHAPTER 7

Aquinas

Thomas Aquinas was born nearly eight hundred years after the death of Augustine. If the intervening centuries must be passed over here, it is not without loss or regret. Brief reference to Gregory, Bede, and Bernard[1] should suffice to show that Scripture continued to challenge the minds and nourish the spirits of attentive readers.

In Gregory's day (ca. 540-604), the once great city of Rome was wasted by invasion, famine, and plague; not without reason was he convinced that the end of the world was near. Yet alongside heroic efforts to address the needs of his people, he produced a massive commentary on Job and homilies on Ezekiel and the Gospels whose spiritual interpretations were profoundly influential for centuries to come. The patron saint of the preacher pursuing an edifying tangent,[2] he is also the source of as memorable a formulation as any of Scripture's suitedness to its every reader:

1. These and other interpreters of Scripture from the period are discussed in Reventlow, *History,* vol. 2. See also the classic work by Smalley, *Study;* Evans, *Language;* Hauser and Watson, *History,* vol. 2; and McKim, *Dictionary.*

2. "Whosoever is speaking concerning God, must be careful to search out thoroughly whatsoever furnishes moral instruction to his hearers; and should account that to be the right method of ordering his discourse, if, when opportunity for edification requires it, he turn aside for a useful purpose from what he had begun to speak of; for he that treats of sacred writ should follow the way of a river, for if a river, as it flows along its channel, meets with open valleys on its side, into these it immediately turns the course of its current, and when they are copiously supplied, presently it pours itself back into its bed. Thus unquestionably, thus should it be with every one that treats of the Divine Word, that if, in discussing any subject, he chance to find at hand any occasion of seasonable edification, he should, as it were, force the streams of discourse towards the adjacent valley, and, when he has poured forth enough upon its level of instruction, fall back into the channel of discourse which he had proposed to himself" (Gregory, *Job,* [Introductory] Epistle, 2).

For as the word of God, by the mysteries which it contains [i.e., those uncovered by "spiritual" interpretation] exercises the understanding of the wise, so usually by what presents itself on the outside [i.e., the surface meaning of the text] it nurses the simpleminded. It presenteth in open day that wherewith the little ones may be fed; it keepeth in secret that whereby men of a loftier range may be held in suspense of admiration. It is, as it were, a kind of river, if I may so liken it, which is both shallow and deep, wherein both the lamb may find a footing, and the elephant float at large. (*Job,* [Introductory] Epistle, 4)

No less remarkable or compelling is the achievement of the Venerable Bede (ca. 673-735), the foremost scholar of his day, though he spent his entire life at the northernmost edge of a declining civilization. Better known today for his *Ecclesiastical History of the English People,* he himself deemed his most important work to be the commentaries he wrote on much of Scripture, including historical books such as Samuel-Kings, Ezra-Nehemiah, and the Acts of the Apostles, which had earlier attracted little attention. Drawing on his familiarity with diverse branches of contemporary learning (including history, chronology, astronomy, mathematics, grammar, and the study of natural phenomena) to illuminate the text, his commentaries also served to transmit to later generations the wisdom of Augustine, Jerome, Ambrose, Gregory, and other patristic interpreters.

As for Bernard of Clairvaux (1090-1153), his famous (eighty-six!) sermons on the Song of Songs represent perhaps the finest expression of the monastic tradition of scriptural meditation, understood (with Origen) as the divinely given means for raising the soul from worldly preoccupations to union with God. Every phrase of the biblical text was at Bernard's command, the result of daily reading and contemplation; and every phrase is understood to have been written to promote the soul's growth in love and progress toward perfection.

Thomas: Life and Commentaries[3]

The main subject of our present chapter moved in a very different world: Thomas Aquinas (ca. 1225-1274), though raised in the Benedictine monas-

3. In what follows, references to Thomas's commentaries supply the chapter and verse on which he was commenting; where the translation used indicates the paragraph number

tery of Monte Cassino, later became one of the first professors of biblical studies at a European university. After joining the Dominican friars in the early 1240s, he spent the last half of the decade studying with Albert the Great in Paris and Cologne. In the early 1250s, he began teaching at the university in Paris himself, becoming in 1256 a *magister in sacra pagina* (we might say a "professor of biblical studies"[4]). He served in that role until 1259, and again from 1268 to 1272; at other times he taught at Dominican houses of study in Italy. His lectures were devoted to Scripture:[5] his surviving commentaries (on Job, Psalms 1–54, Isaiah, Jeremiah, and Lamentations from the Old Testament; Matthew, John,[6] and all the Pauline epistles, including Hebrews, from the New Testament) originated in these lectures. Several are the product of student notes, only some of which were read over and revised by Thomas himself.

The commentaries betray their academic origins. To be sure, Thomas, like Bernard, can praise the sweetness of Scripture and its power to lift the soul from the things of the world to God.[7] Still, there is not a page in his

---

in the Marietti edition of the Latin text, this appears within parentheses after the reference to chapter and verse; where this is not indicated, there is a parenthetical reference to the page number in the translation cited; thus, *Com. Eph.,* on 2:5 (88); but *Com. Matt.,* on 1:21 (p. 49). References to Thomas's *Summa Contra Gentiles (SCG)* give the book, the chapter, and the paragraph. The *Summa Theologica* (or *Summa Theologiae*) has four parts, the second of which is itself divided into two subparts. Each part (or subpart) deals with a series of *questions;* the discussion of each question is, in turn, divided up into different *articles.* Each article is introduced by various objections to the position Thomas ends up articulating, followed by a summary statement ("On the contrary . . .") of that position. Thomas then argues in favor of his position ("I answer . . ."), and concludes with responses to each of the objections listed earlier. Thus, *ST* 1-2.94.3 means the first subpart of the second part of the *Summa Theologica,* question 94, article 3. If such a reference is followed by "ad 3," it refers to Thomas's response to the third objection to his position.

4. In this period, however, "biblical studies" and "theology" were not distinct disciplines; see below.

5. "Although Thomas wrote a dozen commentaries on various works of Aristotle, he never taught Aristotle in the classroom. Likewise, the two great summas, the *Summa contra gentiles* and the *Summa theologiae,* were private works of the study; Thomas never taught them. What Thomas taught in his classroom as a master of theology was Scripture" (Boyle, "Scripture," 94).

6. Thomas's commentaries on Matthew and John drew heavily on what proved to be his most popular work on the Gospels, the *Catena Aurea:* an impressive collection of the interpretations of Latin and even Greek authors, which Thomas deftly arranged into a readable, continuous text. See Torrell, *Aquinas,* 1.136-41.

7. E.g., "the word of Christ cleanses our hearts from earthly affections by inflaming them toward heavenly things. For the word of God by its power moves our hearts, weighed down by earthly things, and sets them on fire" (*Com. John,* on 15:3 [1987]).

commentaries that does not evidence much more of scholastic rigor than of Bernard's contemplative rhapsody.

In Thomas's mind, everything had its proper place:[8] the same (he naturally assumed) was true of the mind of the Holy Spirit and that of his servant Paul.[9] The apostle's fourteen letters (Thomas included Hebrews among them) have, as their single theme, grace. As Thomas read them, each of Paul's epistles takes up different aspects of grace, according to a divine and apostolic master plan. Thus, grace

can be considered in three ways: In one way, as it is in the Head, namely, Christ, and in this regard it is explained in the letter to the Hebrews. In another way, as it is found in the chief members of the Mystical Body, and this is explained in [the Pastoral Epistles]. In a third way, as it is found in the Mystical Body itself, that is, the Church, and this is explained in the letters sent to the gentiles. These last letters are distinguished from one another according to the three ways the grace of Christ can be considered: in one way, as it is in itself, and thus it is set out in the letter to the Romans; in another way, as it exists in the sacraments of grace, which is explained in the two letters to the Corinthians — in the first of these the nature of the sacraments is treated; in the second, the dignity of the minister — and in the letter to the Galatians, in which superfluous sacraments are rejected against certain men who wanted to join old sacraments to the new ones. In a third way, Christ's grace is considered in regard to the unity it produces in the Church. Hence, the Apostle deals first with the establishment of ecclesial unity in Ephesians; second, with its consolidation and progress in the letter to the Philippians; third, of its defense against certain errors in the letter to the Colossians; against existing persecutions in the first letter to the Thessalonians and against persecutions to come, especially in the time of anti-Christ, in the second letter to the Thessalonians. He instructs the prelates of the Church, both spiritual and temporal. He instructs the spiritual prelates of the Church about establishing, preserving, and governing ecclesial unity in the first letter to Timothy, about resistance against persecutors in the second, and about defense against heretics in the letter to Titus. He instructs temporal lords in the

8. "Anyone who is at all familiar with [Thomas's] work knows full well that he simply could not help putting everything in its proper place. Each thing in its own place, a place for each thing" (Gilson, *Reason,* 70).

9. Cf. Pesch, "Professor."

letter to Philemon. And thus the division and order of all the epistles is clear. (*Com. Rom.,* preface [11])

Indeed it is, but Thomas has not yet begun to divide and classify. As he introduces each individual letter, he reminds us of the subject of the letter as a whole, then of the subject of its major sections, the subject of its subsections, its sub-subsections, sub-sub-subsections — all the way down to the subject of words or phrases in individual verses. The following summary, treating Galatians, must serve as a sample of his approach. The letter's two main sections, we are told, are its greeting (1:1-5) and the body of the epistle (1:6–6:18).

The greeting given [1:1-5], it is followed by the epistle message [1:6–6:18], in which the Apostle refutes their error [1:6–4:31]; second, he admonishes them with a view to their correction, at *stand fast* [5:1–6:18; for the moment, however, Thomas is only concerned with the first of these two subsections, 1:6–4:31]. He refutes their error two ways: namely, on the authority of the Gospel teaching [1:6–2:21]; and by reason of the Old Testament, at *O senseless Galatians* [3:1–4:31; for the moment, however, Thomas is only concerned with the first of these two sub-subsections, 1:6–2:21]. He refutes their error by showing the authority of the Gospel teaching. First, by showing their fickleness in lightly dismissing the Gospel teaching [1:6-10]; second, by commending the authority of the Gospel teaching, as he intimates that in view of the precious value of that which they so lightly regard, their error is seen to be so much the greater, at *for I give you to understand* [1:11–2:21; for the moment, however, Thomas is only concerned with the first of these two sub-subsections, 1:6-10]. Regarding the first he does two things. First, he enlarges upon their guilt [Gal. 1:6-7]; second, he inflicts a punishment, at *but though we* [1:8-10; for the moment, however, Thomas is only concerned with the first of these two sub-sub-sub-subsections, 1:6-7]. Concerning the first, he enlarges upon the guilt both of the seduced [1:6-7a] and of those who seduced them, at *only there are some that trouble you* [1:7b; for the moment, however, Thomas is only concerned with the first of these two sub-sub-sub-sub-subsections, 1:6-7a]. As to the first he does three things. First, he enlarges upon the guilt of those who were misled for their fickleness of mind . . . (*Com. Gal.,* on 1:6 [16-17])

There is, we may concede, method to the madness, and a great deal of learning; but madness it remains. By way of compensation, we may note that Thomas's strong sense that each detail has a place in the overall argument removed any temptation to misinterpret a text by disregarding its context: indeed, suitedness to context is frequently cited as a reason for preferring one interpretation over another;[10] and where the connection between one verse and the next is not immediately apparent, Thomas labors to discover it (e.g., *Com. John,* on 3:3 [431]): the principle is sound, though its application is at times oversubtle.

Naturally, Thomas found order not only within the Pauline corpus and its individual writings, but also in Scripture as a whole.[11] Sacred Scripture is intended to lead us to life, and it does so in two ways: *commanding* (i.e., the mandates of the Old Testament) and *helping* (through the gift of grace, treated in the New Testament). Among its *commands,* we may distinguish three kinds: those of a *king,* those of a *herald,* and those of a *father.* God commands as a king, establishing laws in the Pentateuch. These may then be divided into private laws for individuals and families (as in Genesis) and public laws for the Jewish people (Exodus to Deuteronomy; these latter books are then subjected to further subdivision). God urges obedience to the law through his heralds, demonstrating his beneficence (as a motive for obedience) in the books of Joshua through Kings (which are then subjected to further subdivision) and laying down divine edicts in the prophetic literature (which, again, is subdivided). And so on. (The precepts of fathers are to be found in the Wisdom literature.)

From a mind so given to order, one would expect a careful definition of Scripture's literal and "spiritual" senses; Thomas does not disappoint. The literal sense, we are told, is "that which the author intends" (*ST* 1.1.10). To this apparently straightforward statement, we may add — if the reader will permit a pale imitation of Thomas's style — two clarifications and three implications. First, the clarifications.

As we have seen, a true interpretation of Scripture must, for Augustine, both suit the wording of the text and conform to the rule of faith. If more than one reading meets these conditions, more than one should be allowed: the inspired human author might well have had multiple meanings in mind; in any case, it will have been the Holy Spirit's intention, in inspiring a text that permits a plurality of readings, to communicate truth through each. Noting that God is the true author of Scripture, and citing Augustine as his authority, Aquinas makes a similar claim (*ST* 1.1.10; cf.

---

10. See, e.g., *Com. Matt.,* on 12:32 (pp. 440-41); *Com. Gal.,* on 4:11 (223); *Com. Eph.,* on 2:20 (127).

11. Thomas proposes the division in his "Inaugural Sermons."

Power 4.1.8).[12] And nearly every page of his commentaries provides examples of multiple interpretations (linked simply by a telling "or"), with no suggestion that one is to be preferred over another.[13]

The second clarification Thomas insists on has a parallel in Chrysostom. The true sense of a metaphorical text, Chrysostom notes, is that conveyed by the metaphor, not that of a woodenly literal understanding of its wording. Thomas makes a similar point: since a metaphor is *meant* to be understood metaphorically, and since the literal sense of a text is what the author intends, the *literal* sense of a metaphorical text is found in its *metaphorical* interpretation.

> Nor is the figure itself, but that which is figured, the literal sense. When Scripture speaks of God's arm, the literal sense is not that God has such a member, but only what is signified by this member, namely, operative power. (*ST* 1.1.10 ad 3; cf. *Com. Gal.,* on 4:24 [254])[14]

Thomas largely followed Augustine in three *implications* he drew related to the literal sense: (1) arguments should be based solely on the lit-

12. Conformity with the true faith is as important an interpretive principle for Thomas as it was for Augustine. He at times concedes that, in themselves, the words of a text admit an "unsuitable" interpretation — only to exclude such a reading as false, since "truth" (i.e., a true interpretation of a text that is true) cannot be opposed to "truth" (i.e., the truth of the faith, based on the plain teaching of other scriptural texts, which are then cited). See, e.g., *SCG* 3.96.10-13; 4.8.1, 19.

13. More than individual verses may be involved. In his commentary on Rom. 7, Thomas helpfully shows what each verse means if the "I" spoken of is understood as "a man existing in sin" or as "a man in a state of grace" ("Let us continue, therefore, by showing how these words and those that follow can be explained under both interpretations," though here Thomas does go on to say, "although the second explanation is better" [*Com. Rom.,* on 7:14 (558)]). Like many commentators, Thomas is uncertain whether parts of the Prologue to John's Gospel refer to the continuous presence of the Word in the world, or to its incarnate state: he traces both lines of interpretation (*Com. John,* on 1:4 [95]).

14. In *ST* 1.1.9, Thomas argues that it is appropriate for Scripture to use metaphorical language drawn from the material world to convey spiritual truth: since "all our knowledge originates from sense [i.e., from what we perceive with our senses]," it is "natural to man to attain to intellectual truths through sensible objects. . . . It is also befitting Holy Writ, which is proposed to all without distinction of persons, . . . that spiritual truths be expounded by means of figures taken from corporeal things, in order that thereby even the simple who are unable by themselves to grasp intellectual things may be able to understand it." Anthropomorphic language of God is given its traditional explanation: e.g., to speak of God's "repentance" is to adopt "a metaphorical way of speaking, in the sense that God is disposed like one who repents." Similarly, God is "angry in the sense that, by punishing, He produces the same effect as an angry person" (*SCG* 3.96.15; cf. *SCG* 1.91.15-18).

eral sense of a text; (2) "nothing necessary to faith is contained under the spiritual sense which is not elsewhere put forward by the Scripture in its literal sense" (*ST* 1.1.10 ad 1); and (3) since the literal sense of Scripture is what God, its author, intended to say, the literal sense is necessarily true (*ST* 1.1.10 ad 3).

In addition to the literal sense of Scripture, Thomas (following Origen) speaks of one or more "spiritual" senses: inherent in the very nature of an inspired text is its capacity to convey profound mysteries beyond its surface meaning.[15] To this common conviction Thomas brings predictable precision: God has done something still greater than imbue the words of a text with the capacity to bear multiple layers of meaning. As sovereign of the universe, God (uniquely) can see to it that not only the words of a text, but the very phenomena, people, and events to which the texts refer point beyond themselves to deeper truths. Thus, it is not so much that the biblical *narrative* about Joshua has, in addition to its literal meaning (Joshua brings his people into the promised land), a spiritual meaning (Christ brings his people to a heavenly land). The biblical narrative is to be read (literally) of the historical Joshua; it is the historical Joshua himself who foreshadows the work of Christ (cf. *Com. Matt.,* on 1:1 [pp. 2-3]).[16]

> Signification is twofold: one is through words; the other through the things signified by the words. And this is peculiar to Sacred Scripture and no [other] writings, since its author is God in whose power it lies not only to employ words to signify (which man can also do), but things as well. Consequently, in the other sciences handed down by men, in which only words can be employed to signify, the words alone signify. But it is peculiar to Scripture that words and the very things signified by them signify something. Consequently this science can have many senses. For that signification by which the words signify something per-

15. See *Power* 4.1.8: "It is part of the dignity of Holy Writ that under the one literal sense many others are contained." Thomas goes on to point out two consequences of this "dignity": first, the sacred text "adapts itself to man's various intelligence, so that each one marvels to find his thoughts expressed in the words of Holy Writ"; second, Sacred Scripture is "all the more easily defended against unbelievers in that when one finds his own interpretation of Scripture to be false he can fall back upon some other."

16. In another, telling example, Thomas grants that the wars of the Assyrians and Romans are commonly deemed more noteworthy than those of Israel; but the special role given to Israel in the divine purpose means that "the wars and deeds of this people are expounded in the mystical sense," whereas those of the Assyrians and Romans are not (*ST* 1-2.104.2 ad 2).

tains to the literal or historical sense. But the signification whereby the things signified by the words further signify other things pertains to the mystical sense. (*Com. Gal.,* on 4:24 [254]; cf. *Com. Job,* on 1:6 [p. 76])

The multiplicity of these senses does not produce equivocation or any other kind of multiplicity, seeing that these senses are not multiplied because one word signifies several things; but because the things signified by the words can be themselves types of other things. Thus in Holy Writ no confusion results, for all the senses are founded on one — the literal. (*ST* 1.1.10 ad 1)

In programmatic discussions, Thomas goes on to distinguish three types of "spiritual" sense:

The mystical or spiritual sense is divided into three types. First, as when the Apostle says that the old law is the figure of the new law. Hence, insofar as the things of the old law signify things of the new law, it is the allegorical sense. Then, according to Dionysius in the book *On the Heavenly Hierarchy,* the new law is a figure of future glory; accordingly, insofar as things in the new law and in Christ signify things which are in heaven, it is the anagogical sense. . . . Insofar as the things which in the new law were done in Christ and done in things that signify Christ are signs of things we ought to do, it is the moral sense. Examples will clarify each of these. For when I say, *let there be light,* referring literally to corporeal light, it is the literal sense. But if it be taken to mean, *let Christ be born in the Church,* it pertains to the allegorical sense. But if one says, *let there be light,* i.e., *let us be conducted to glory through Christ,* it pertains to the anagogical sense. Finally, if it is said, *let there be light,* i.e., *let us be illumined in mind and inflamed in heart through Christ,* it pertains to the moral sense. (*Com. Gal.,* on 4:24 [254]; cf. *ST* 1.1.10)

Examples of each of these three types can certainly be found in Thomas's commentaries; more frequently, however, he speaks in an undifferentiated way of a single "spiritual" or "mystical" sense of a text, in addition to its "literal" meaning.

It is sometimes claimed that Thomas championed the literal sense of Scripture at the expense of "spiritual" interpretations. That he accords great significance to the former can be affirmed without reservation; but the grounds that are thought to establish a preference for literal interpretations are at times misleading, and the assumed depreciation of "spiritual" readings is, it seems, less true of Thomas than of those who attribute it to him.[17]

A preference for the literal sense of Scripture has been thought to be evident in Thomas's commentary on Job (which is exclusively literal), in the commentaries on Pauline epistles (which are nearly so), and in that on John (which is so in extended sections). But the commentary on Job is a special case: Thomas notes explicitly that "Blessed Pope Gregory has already disclosed to us its mysteries [i.e., its spiritual interpretation] so subtly and clearly that there seems no need to add anything further to them" (*Com. Job,* prologue [p. 69]); it is left to Thomas to expound the literal sense. And given that "the whole intention" of the book of Job (and thus its literal meaning) concerns a topic of great interest to Thomas ("how human affairs are ruled by divine providence" [*Com. Job,* on 1:1 [p. 71]),[18] no conclusions about a *general* disregard of spiritual interpretations should be based on *this* commentary. That Thomas largely (but by no means exclusively)[19] attends to the literal sense of the

---

17. Cf. Smalley, *Gospels,* 265-66.

18. "The affliction of just men" might well seem to call into question "God's providence where human affairs are concerned." The book of Job, Thomas believes, was written to put such questions to rest "through plausible arguments": the troubles of the righteous are in fact "the result of divine mercy" (*Com. Job,* prologue [p. 68]). In Job's case, God's design was that, through his suffering, Job's virtue would be made obvious to all (*Com. Job,* on 1:11 [p. 83]). Thomas proceeds with a remarkable argument to show that Job remained both righteous and *reasonable* throughout the period of his affliction. His sadness at the death of family members was "moderate" and "subject to reason" (on 1:20 [p. 87]); he endured the loss of temporal goods with "great constancy of spirit" (on 2:10 [p. 95]). Inasmuch as human beings have a "sensual nature" as well as reason, it was only natural for Job to feel grief and pain, and there was nothing inappropriate in his expressing such feelings (on 3:3 [p. 101]; on 3:13-15 [p. 107]; on 6:4 [p. 138]); indeed, apart from such pain, there could be no virtue of patience (on 3:1 [p. 99]). Still, Job's reason was not overcome (on 6:7 [p. 139]; on 6:12 [p. 140]). His claims that his sufferings far outweighed any evil he had done were not directed against God, but were meant to refute his friends' mistaken notion that people receive just recompense in this life (on 8:2 [pp. 157-58]). Job himself believed that the due reward of sinners and righteous alike would be apportioned in the life to come (on 3:11 [p. 96]); if he sometimes said the opposite, he was merely giving voice to others' opinions (on 10:21 [p. 192]). To Thomas's credit, it must be allowed that he was attempting to read consistently a book in which Job's belief in the afterlife seemed to be clearly expressed (in 19:25-26, and elsewhere), his righteousness was affirmed (1:1, 8), and his words were explicitly approved (42:7). Statements in the main body of the book are interpreted in light of what is said in the prologue (chaps. 1-2) and epilogue (42:7-17). Whether interpretations content to assign perceived inconsistencies in the book to different sources represent an improvement on Thomas may be debated. Cf. Yocum, "Exposition."

19. E.g., in Gal. 1:15, Paul speaks of being separated from his "mother's womb." Thomas

Pauline epistles and the Johannine discourses should surprise no one: theological profundity is found at the surface of these texts; not even Origen was tempted to dig deeper. As soon as the Fourth Gospel turns to narrative,[20] however, and throughout his commentaries on Matthew[21] and the Psalms,[22] Thomas is as unabashed as any in supplying "spiritual interpretations," including those based on (supposed) etymologies[23] and the deeper significance of numbers.[24] In short, Thomas pays more at-

---

suggests that Paul, in speaking of his "mother," may have meant the synagogue; by her "womb," he may have meant "the college of Pharisees who trained him in Judaism." Or perhaps "his mother is the Church of Christ, and the womb, the college of apostles" (*Com. Gal.,* on 1:15 [41]). The fifteen days Paul spent in Jerusalem (according to Gal. 1:18) are deemed significant as the total of eight ("the number of the New Testament, in which the eighth day of those who will rise is awaited,") plus seven ("the number of the Old Testament, because it celebrates the seventh day"): "And so [Paul] stayed with Peter fifteen days, conversing with him on the mysteries of the Old and New Testament" (*Com. Gal.,* on 1:18 [154]).

20. The strap of the Baptist's sandals mystically represents the "union of [Christ's] divinity and humanity, which neither John nor anyone can unfasten or fully investigate" (*Com. John,* on 1:27 [250], explicitly following Gregory). When John's disciples ask Jesus where he lives, the question is interpreted allegorically ("they asked where Christ was living because our purpose in following him should be that Christ leads us to heaven") and morally (they desired to "learn what qualities men should possess in order to be worthy to have Christ dwell in them") as well as literally (*Com. John,* on 1:38 [290]). Jesus' departure for Galilee "on the following day" can certainly be explained literally, but also mystically: he wanted to "indicate that 'on the following day,' i.e., on the day of grace, that is, the day of the Good News, he would pass from Judea into Galilee, i.e., to save the Gentiles" (*Com. John,* on 1:43 [310]).

21. "Spiritual" interpretations are found from the get-go: the first six names in the genealogy of Matt. 1, interpreted morally, speak of the six things required for justification: Abraham = faith; Isaac = hope; Jacob = charity; Juda = confession; Phares = the destruction of vices; Zara = the beginning of virtues (*Com. Matt.,* on 1:3 [p. 16]). They continue without abatement. Mystically, the gifts of the wise men represent faith, action, and contemplation (*Com. Matt.,* on 2:11 [p. 72]). The fever of Peter's mother-in-law represents the envy of the synagogue (*Com. Matt.,* on 8:14 [p. 326]). The disciples' plucking ears of corn represents "the multiplicity of understanding of the Scriptures, or the conversion of sinners" (*Com. Matt.,* on 12:1 [p. 423]). Thomas may largely be passing on the spiritual interpretations of others; but he shows not the slightest aversion to doing so.

22. Thomas at times interprets individual psalms at three levels: literally (of David), allegorically (of Christ), and morally (of the lot of the righteous). See, e.g., his interpretations of Psalms 3, 10 (English versions, Ps. 11), and 26 (English versions, 27).

23. In interpreting Salem as "peace," Paul "teaches us to use the interpretation of names in preaching" (*Com. Heb.,* on 7:2 [332]). Genealogies are "proposed in the Scriptures as mysteries [revealed through etymologies] or as containing some historical value" (*Com. Tit.,* on 3:9 [99]).

24. See Baglow, *Approach,* 43-45.

tention than some to the literal sense of Scripture; he adds definitional precision; otherwise, he seems quite traditional in his approach to the multiple "senses" of the biblical text.

It is truly said that, in Thomas's day, biblical and theological studies represented one discipline, not two: indeed, Thomas's own commentaries are highly theological, his theology strongly biblical.[25] The point is worth underscoring, but perhaps should be balanced with the observation that his instincts and interests were those of a theologian, not a biblical scholar — at least as we understand the terms today. Tools and concerns peculiar to biblical scholarship are conspicuously absent from Thomas's repertoire.[26] In a day when some were learning Hebrew and Greek, or endeavoring to restore an uncorrupted biblical text, Thomas was content — and only occasionally at that — to pass on what others had said of variant readings or the force of the original language.[27] On the other hand, he lost no opportunity to explore at length any theological topic suggested by the text,[28] to address every conceivable theological question it raises,[29] or to find some ground for refuting heresy.[30] Now and then Thomas, himself a preacher, offers comments on appropriate pastoral lessons to be derived from the text; but even these are few.[31] He reads the text in search of sound doctrine, and lectures to transmit it.

The Necessity of Scripture

Without Scripture, Thomas believes, we cannot find happiness or be the human beings we were meant to be. After all, the happiness for which hu-

---

25. See Valkenberg, *Words*.

26. See Smalley, "Bible," 216-17.

27. See Prügl, "Interpreter," 397-99.

28. See Emery, "Exegesis."

29. These discussions at times resemble those found in the various *Quaestiones disputatae* that Thomas composed; the latter arose out of his task as a *magister* to engage in disputations. See Persson, *Sacra Doctrina*, 8-10; cf. J. Holmes, *"Lectura,"* 90-94.

30. See Smalley, *Gospels*, 262-63. In a wondrous way, a single verse may serve to refute three or even four heresies (e.g., *Com. Rom*, on 9:5 [747]; on 9:11 [758]).

31. E.g., in being content with ears of corn rather than demanding large plates of food, the disciples give us an example of abstinence (*Com. Matt.*, on 12:1 [p. 423]); that the disciples were troubled when they saw Jesus walking on water shows "that when divine assistance is closer at hand, the Lord permits men to be more afflicted, so that then His assistance may be received with more devotion and thanksgiving" (*Com. Matt.*, on 14:26 [p. 524]; cf. *Com. John,* on 6:19 [880]).

man beings were made is found only in knowing God, beholding him as he is in his divine essence.[32] Apart from the revelation contained in Scripture, we cannot know God in this way.

Logically, the happiness of human beings must lie in the most exalted usage of the highest *human* capacity. Though human beings share with other animals their sensual nature, they alone possess reason (or intellect);[33] thus "the ultimate beatitude of man consists in the use of his highest function, which is the operation of the intellect" (*ST* 1.12.1; cf. 1.26.2). Moreover, there can be no more exalted use of the intellect than in knowing its divine source: "Everyone is blessed from this sole fact, that he understands God, in accordance with the saying of Augustine (*Conf.* V. 4): *Blessed is he who knoweth Thee, though he know nought else*" (*ST* 1.26.3). If human beings were *not* destined to behold God in this way (i.e., intellectually; not, of course, with their physical eyes [*ST* 1.12.3]), then either they were not meant to find happiness or they were meant to find it elsewhere, not in God: and faith must deny any such conclusion.[34] And yet (herein lies the rub), "it is impossible for any created intellect to see the essence of God by its own natural power" (*ST* 1.12.4).

To be sure, we *can* know, simply by our natural reason, that God exists.[35] Our very desire for a happiness that can only be found in God suggests his existence — though we often miss the point, mistaking lesser goods as the object of our desire (*ST* 1.2.1 ad 1). In any case, we can deduce

32. Note how Thomas equates "the vision of the divine essence" with knowing God and possessing eternal life in the following quotation: "Life everlasting consists in the vision of the divine essence, according to the words, *This is eternal life, that they may know Thee, the only true God,* etc." (*ST* 1.12.4, citing John 17:3).

33. To possess intellect is to have the capacity to grasp intelligible truth. Human beings grasp such truth by their reason (or rationally), abstracting concepts in their minds from what they perceive with their senses, drawing implications and conclusions from first principles, advancing from inquiry to discovery. Angels, by way of contrast, grasp intelligible truth directly rather than through the processes of reason. Therefore, for human beings — but not angels — "reason and intellect are the same power" (*ST* 1.79.8).

34. So *ST* 1.12.1. Thomas reaches the same conclusion by a different argument: human beings naturally desire to know the cause of any effect they see. In the end, this means that they cannot be truly happy without knowing the *first* cause of all that is. Furthermore, the intellect cannot be said to know an object perfectly unless it understands its essence. Thus, human beings can find "final and perfect happiness" only in the perfect exercise of their highest faculty, beholding "the very Essence of the First Cause" (*ST* 1-2.3.8).

35. We should remember, however, that human beings possess the capacity for "natural reason" only because God endowed them with it, and they exercise that capacity only through his continuous enablement (*ST* 1-2.109.1); therefore, "natural reason" does *not* mean "reason functioning apart from God." Cf. Gilson, *Elements,* 116-17.

from the *effects* we see of God's creation that they must have a *cause* — and we rightly call that cause God (cf. *ST* 1.2.3).[36] Furthermore, natural reason can deduce that God is one.

> There are some truths which the natural reason also is able to reach. Such are that God exists, that He is one, and the like. In fact, such truths about God have been proved demonstratively by the philosophers, guided by the light of the natural reason. (*SCG* 1.3.2)

But though effects must have a cause, they tell us little *about* that cause, particularly when, as with God and his creation, the greatness of the Cause is out of all proportion to the effects it brings into being.

> From effects not proportionate to the cause no perfect knowledge of that cause can be obtained. Yet from every effect the existence of the cause can be clearly demonstrated, and so we can demonstrate the existence of God from His effects; though from them we cannot perfectly know God as He is in his essence. (*ST* 1.2.2 ad 3)

Moreover, such knowledge as human beings acquire necessarily begins with their perception of sensible objects; and even of these objects our knowledge is often very limited.[37] How much further must we fall short of knowing the nature of One beyond all sensory perception?[38] On

---

36. And some *have* made that deduction. As Gilson notes (*Elements*, 15), Thomas had in Aristotle a witness to how far, apart from Christian revelation, philosophy could proceed on the path to truth.

37. "Our manner of knowing is so weak that no philosopher could perfectly investigate the nature of even one little fly. We even read that a certain philosopher spent thirty years in solitude in order to know the nature of a bee. If, therefore, our intellect is so weak, it is foolish to be willing to believe concerning God only that which man can know by himself alone" (*Creed*, prologue; cf. *SCG* 1.3.5).

38. "The human intellect is not able to reach a comprehension of the divine substance through its natural power. For, according to its manner of knowing in the present life, the intellect depends on the sense for the origins of knowledge; and so those things that do not fall under the senses cannot be grasped by the human intellect except in so far as the knowledge of them is gathered from sensible things. Now, sensible things cannot lead the human intellect to the point of seeing in them the nature of the divine substance; for sensible things are effects that fall short of the power of their cause. Yet, beginning with sensible things, our intellect is led to the point of knowing about God that He exists, and other such characteristics that must be attributed to the First Principle. There are, consequently, some intelligible truths about God that are open to the human reason; but there are others that absolutely surpass its power" (*SCG* 1.3.3; cf. 4.1.1).

their own, finite minds can have no grasp of an infinite being (*Com. John,* on 1:18 [213]). More specifically, though natural reason may come to know that God is one, it cannot, on its own, know God as triune, nor can natural reason deduce the incarnation of the Son (*SCG* 1.3.2; 4.27.1; *ST* 1.32.1).[39] And yet the happiness for which we were made depends on our knowing God as God is. If we are to find such happiness — and in it, our salvation — God must impart to us knowledge of himself by means other than natural reason.

It was necessary for man's salvation that there should be a knowledge revealed by God, besides philosophical science built up by human reason. Firstly, indeed, because man is directed to God, as to an end that surpasses the grasp of his reason: *The eye hath not seen, O God, besides Thee, what things Thou hast prepared for them that wait for Thee* (Isa. lxiv.4). But the end must first be known by men who are to direct their thoughts and actions to the end. Hence it was necessary for the salvation of man that certain truths which exceed human reason should be made known to him by divine revelation. (*ST* 1.1.1)

Man's perfect Happiness . . . consists in the vision of the Divine Essence. Now the vision of God's Essence surpasses the nature not only of man, but also of every creature. . . . Every knowledge that is according to the mode of created substance, falls short of the vision of the Divine Essence, which infinitely surpasses all created substance. Consequently neither man, nor any creature, can attain final Happiness by his natural powers. (*ST* 1-2.5.5)[40]

And so God, of his goodness, has granted us the knowledge we need through divine revelation: the mind of the recipient of revelation was "elevated" supernaturally by an "interior and intelligible light" so that it grasped "things that the understanding cannot reach by its natural light."[41] The grant-

---

39. At best, we can show, e.g., that "it was not out of harmony with the divine goodness for God to become man" (*SCG* 4.54.10).

40. It is noteworthy that Thomas demonstrates humanity's need of divine revelation by speaking of the limitations of human nature *as created,* and without reference to the effects of sin. Thomas believes that the latter effects are much more apparent in the human will and desire for good than in the knowledge of truth (*ST* 1-2.109.2 ad 3). Cf. Persson, *Sacra Doctrina,* 34-35.

41. As we shall see, the content of revelation was not in fact *confined* to matters beyond the reach of natural reason: e.g., in the case of Solomon, inspiration meant that his under-

ing of this inner light was at times accompanied by the hearing of a spoken message or the seeing of visions, dreams, or even a hand writing on a wall. Such "external or internal aids," however, were not of themselves sufficient to convey "knowledge of divine things." Pharaoh, for one, could not interpret his dreams, nor could Belshazzar decipher the message written on his wall (*SCG* 3.154.4; *ST* 2-2.173.2); the inner illumination granted to Joseph and Daniel was needed. Additionally, the recipients of revelation needed the "grace of speech" to communicate to others what they had received (*SCG* 3.154.7). Credibility was given to their message through the miracles they were enabled to perform and through the fulfillment of what they foretold about the future (*SCG* 3.154.8-9). And, crucially, since the instruction given through revelation was to benefit more than one generation, "it was necessary that the things revealed to them . . . be written down for the instruction of men to come" (*SCG* 3.154.19; cf. *Com. John,* on 1:8 [119]).

In a real sense, then, the author of Scripture is God (*ST* 1.1.10); prophets did not speak of themselves, "but God was speaking in them" (*Com. Heb.,* on 1:1 [17]). "The Holy Spirit moves the mind of a prophet as a principal agent moves its instrument" (*Com. Heb.,* on 11:32 [631]). The role of the prophet, though merely instrumental, is nonetheless not to be discounted: unlike those possessed by the devil, prophets were moved by the Holy Spirit while retaining possession of their reason (*Com. Matt.,* on 10:20 [p. 378]).[42] Still, their minds retained their human limitations; even true prophets did not know all that the Holy Spirit meant by the things they saw, or spoke, or did (*ST* 2-2.173.4).[43]

Whatever is contained in Scripture has been divinely revealed: this commonality is the formal feature that makes the study of its diverse contents a single "science" (*ST* 1.1.3).[44] Precisely because its contents are di-

---

standing was so enlightened that he was able to make "more certain judgments than the rest of us about human actions and the nature of things, which we perceive naturally" (*Truth* 12.12). Cf. Baglow, *Approach,* 33; Persson, *Sacra Doctrina,* 22-25.

42. Note, e.g., the combination of divine and human agency implied in what Thomas writes about the Fourth Gospel: "How could John the Evangelist after forty years have remembered all the sayings of Christ he wrote in his gospel unless the Holy Spirit had brought them to his mind?" (*Com. John,* on 14:26 [1960]).

43. Nor, of course, did prophets have special knowledge beyond what they received by revelation. Thomas notes that Paul was ignorant about what awaited him, and "Isaac the great prophet was deceived in Jacob" (*Com. Phlm.,* on 22 [p. 29]).

44. "In the language of Augustine, *scientia* [science] signified a mode of knowing, and therefore a doctrine, both certain and true. In the language of Thomas Aquinas (and this is the mark of the century on his doctrine) *scientia* fully preserved this Augustinian meaning, but it added another one: the Aristotelian meaning of the word as pointing out a body of

vinely revealed, they are true with a certitude surpassing that of all other sciences, dependent as the latter are on fallible human reason. It follows that, whenever any other science contradicts this one, it is the other science that must be wrong (*ST* 1.1.6 ad 2; *Com. John,* on 4:42 [662]). For all its diversity, Scripture does have a single primary subject — God. Creatures are spoken of as well, but secondarily, and only in their relationship to God (*ST* 1.1.3 ad 1). Since the subject matter of sacred science transcends reason, whereas other sciences take up things "within reason's grasp," it is clear that, in "the higher worth of its subject matter" as well as in its certitude, this science surpasses all others (*ST* 1.1.5).[45]

Divine revelation speaks primarily about God, and in doing so discloses truths that lie beyond the capacity of natural reason to discover; but it also includes other truths about God that are essential to salvation, even though these truths *are* accessible to reason and have, in fact, been found by (some) philosophers.[46] After all, salvation is not to be the preserve of those with the time and capacity to devote themselves to philosophy. Moreover, whatever truth philosophers may discover is inevitably mixed with error. "Therefore, in order that the salvation of men might be brought

---

conclusions deduced from principles" (Gilson, *Elements,* 30). "Sacred doctrine" is thus a "science" in that, beginning with principles established by revelation, it proceeds rationally to draw out their implications. That sacred doctrine thus employs human arguments is, for Thomas, both a demonstration of the principle that "grace [here divine revelation] does not destroy nature [here human reason], but perfects it" *and* an example of what Paul meant when he spoke of "bringing into captivity every understanding unto the obedience of Christ" (2 Cor. 10:5); suitably, then, "natural reason . . . minister[s] to faith" (*ST* 1.1.8 ad 2). Cf. Persson, *Sacra Doctrina,* 75.

45. To these superiorities of sacred doctrine as a speculative science (i.e., a science concerned with discovering truth), Thomas adds its superiority as a practical science (i.e., one concerned with directing human activity): the good to which it directs is that of eternal bliss (*ST* 1.1.5). On the speculative and practical intellects, see *ST* 1.79.11; 1-2.90.1 ad 2. I will discuss the "practical" side of sacred doctrine below.

46. As noted above, the purpose of revelation is to make known truths essential to salvation. These include "the Trinity of Persons in Almighty God, the mystery of Christ's Incarnation, and the like." Scripture, of course, contains much else (e.g., "that Abraham had two sons, that a dead man rose again at the touch of Eliseus' bones, and the like"), but the "much else" is all intended to point toward, and underscore ("manifest"), "the Divine majesty or the Incarnation of Christ" (*ST* 2-2.1.6 ad 1). See also *Truth* 12.2: "All those things the knowledge of which can be useful for salvation are the matter of prophecy, whether they are past, or future, or even eternal, or necessary, or contingent. But those things which cannot pertain to salvation are outside the matter of prophecy. . . . Moreover, I say necessary for salvation, whether they are necessary for instruction in the faith or for the formation of morals."

about more fitly and more surely, it was necessary that they should be taught divine truths by divine inspiration" (*ST* 1.1.1; cf. *SCG* 1.4).

Whatever is disclosed through revelation is to be accepted by faith.[47] Thomas is aware that there are those who despise appeals to authority, urging rather that we should accept only what has been demonstrated by reason. Like Augustine, he dismisses this pretension as utterly unrealistic: we could not live if we did not accept, simply on the testimony of others, much that we believe (*Creed,* prologue). Besides, whatever weakness may be perceived in appeals to human authority can scarcely apply where (as with revelation) the authority is divine (*ST* 1.1.8 ad 2).

The problem remains: on what grounds are we to believe that it is divine authority that lies behind Scripture and the faith of which it speaks? Thomas responds to this question with considerations both external and internal, though he acknowledges that only the latter are decisive. The external considerations he cites are, in part (as we have seen), the miracles performed by true prophets, and the fulfillment of prophecies they made (*SCG* 3.154.8-9). If more contemporary evidence is required, Thomas points to the "wonderful conversion of the world to the Christian faith" (the effects of which still seemed apparent in Thomas's day), a conversion that took place apart from the force of arms or the promises of carnal pleasures, "and (what is most wonderful of all) in the midst of the tyranny of persecutors."

> In this faith there are truths preached that surpass every human intellect; the pleasures of the flesh are curbed; it is taught that the things of the world should be spurned. Now, for the minds of mortal men to assent to these things is the greatest of miracles, just as it is a manifest work of divine inspiration that, spurning visible things, men should seek only what is invisible. (*SCG* 1.6.1, 3; cf. *Creed,* prologue)

In the end, however, Thomas concedes that no external evidence on its own can elicit faith.

> As regards . . . man's assent to the things which are of faith, we may observe a twofold cause, one of external inducement, such as seeing a

---

47. Unless, of course, we have come to know it through rational demonstration: by its very nature, rational demonstration precludes faith. Thus, revealed truths inaccessible to reason must simply be believed by all; revealed truths accessible to reason must be *believed* only by those who (because otherwise occupied!) have not come to know them through rational demonstration. See *ST* 2-2.1.5.

miracle, or being persuaded by someone to embrace the faith: neither of which is a sufficient cause, since of those who see the same miracle, or who hear the same sermon, some believe, and some do not. Hence we must assert another internal cause, which moves man inwardly to assent to matters of faith. . . . Since man, by assenting to matters of faith, is raised above his nature, this must needs accrue to him from some supernatural principle moving him inwardly; and this is God. Therefore faith, as regards the assent which is the chief act of faith, is from God moving man inwardly by grace. (*ST* 2-2.6.1; cf. *Com. Rom.*, on 10:16 [842])

Thus, considerations external and internal combine to show that those who believe the truths of faith do so neither foolishly nor lightly (*SCG* 1.6.1; *ST* 2-2.2.9 ad 3). On the other hand, it is a mistake to attempt a rational demonstration of such truths. Reason may appropriately be used to remove objections brought against the faith,[48] or to show that the truths of faith are not impossible (*ST* 2-2.1.5 ad 2; 2-2.2.10 ad 2). After all, "truth that the human reason is naturally endowed to know cannot be opposed to the truth of the Christian faith" (*SCG* 1.7.1). But to attempt a rational demonstration of truths known only through revelation is to detract from the dignity of the faith, reducing its mysteries to such stuff as our minds can master; moreover, it exposes the faith to ridicule through inevitably weak and fallacious argumentation — and thus confirms opponents of the faith in their error (*ST* 1.32.1; *SCG* 1.9.2).[49]

The Authority and Truth of Scripture

The revealed character of the canonical scriptures gives them an incontrovertible authority not possessed by any other "doctors of the Church." As a result, "our faith rests upon the revelation made to the apostles and prophets, who wrote the canonical books," and on that revelation alone — thus declares Thomas, citing Augustine to the same effect (*ST* 1.1.8 ad 2). "Only the canonical scriptures are the standard of faith" (*Com. John*, on

---

48. "Since faith rests upon infallible truth, and since the contrary of a truth can never be demonstrated, it is clear that the arguments brought against faith cannot be demonstrated, but are difficulties that can be answered" (*ST* 1.1.8; cf. *SCG* 1.9.2).

49. "Thomas had gained [from Aristotle] a clear notion of what it meant to philosophize, and this knowledge deprived him of the simple answers to which, before him, theologians had often resorted" (Gilson, *Elements,* 15).

21:24 [2656]).[50] It follows that "we ought not to say about God anything which is not found in Holy Scripture either explicitly or implicitly" (*ST* 1.36.2 ad 1; cf. *Com. Gal.,* on 1:8 [27]).[51]

Since divine knowledge is without error, the same must be said of the revelation from God that prophets receive and transmit (*ST* 2-2.171.6). Thomas makes the point repeatedly of Scripture: "It is unlawful to say that anything false is contained in Sacred Scripture" (*Com. Gal.,* on 2:14 [88];[52] cf. *Com. Titus,* on 3:9 [99]). In our study of Chrysostom, we noted that he (and Theodore of Mopsuestia) allowed that there were differences in detail between the various Gospels; such differences, they claimed, served to underscore the independence of the accounts and thus the truth of their major agreements. Not even for the virtue such interpreters found in necessity is Thomas prepared to concede their point:

> The Greeks [= Antiochene interpreters] respond to this that the other Evangelists did not report this truly; and so John, who wrote the last of the Gospels, corrected them. But it is heresy to say that there is anything false not only in the Gospels but anywhere in the canonical scriptures. Consequently, we have to say that all the Evangelists state the same thing and do not disagree. (*Com. John,* on 13:1 [1730])

It follows that any interpretation of a text by which Scripture appears to say something false is a false interpretation.

> As, however, this theory can be shown to be false by solid reasons, it cannot be held to be the sense of Holy Scripture. (*ST* 1.68.3)

50. To declare, with the Manicheans, that Christ did not assume a real body is to say that Scripture lies in saying "the Word became flesh" (John 1:14); "but, if even in a moderate way the authority of Scripture be decried, there will no longer be anything fixed in our faith, which depends on sacred Scripture" (*SCG* 4.29.2).

51. We *may* speak of what is only implicitly found in Holy Scripture. We may, e.g., properly speak of the "procession" of the Holy Spirit from the Son because the "sense" of this claim is in fact found in Scripture even if it is not "verbally expressed" (*ST* 1.36.2 ad 1). Cf. also *ST* 1.29.3 ad 1: "Although the word *person* is not found applied to God in Scripture, either in the Old or New Testament; nevertheless what the word signifies is found to be affirmed of God in many places of Scripture. . . . If we could speak of God only in the very terms themselves of Scripture, it would follow that no one could speak about God in any but the original language of the Old or New Testament. The urgency of confuting heretics made it necessary to find new words to express the ancient faith about God. Nor is such a kind of novelty to be shunned; since it is by no means profane, for it does not lead us astray from the sense of Scripture."

52. In this quotation, Thomas is summarizing the view of Augustine; but he immediately adds his agreement.

This explanation we consider to be defective in that it ascribes to the Scriptures statements that are proved evidently to be false. (*Power* 4.1 ad 5)

So axiomatic for Thomas is Scripture's freedom from error that he can (as we have seen) maintain both that any claim opposed to Scripture must, for that very reason, be wrong (*ST* 1.1.6 ad 2) *and* that, if a claim we know to be true seems opposed to Scripture, we must abandon our interpretation of Scripture as erroneous.[53] This may seem like a case of "Heads I win, tails you lose" reasoning — and such it would be if Thomas were attempting to *establish* Scripture's inerrancy on the basis of textual phenomena. But he is not. Rather, *starting* with a conviction of Scripture's inerrancy (which he takes to be indisputable on other grounds), he interprets the textual phenomena accordingly.[54]

It fell to his task as a *magister* to do so. Theological questions raised by the text were not the only ones to be addressed; any suggestion of tension between one text of Scripture and another must also be resolved.[55] Of course, no *magister,* taking on the task, was left to his own resources — least of all Thomas, whose familiarity with the work of earlier interpreters was remarkable. Particularly in the case of apparent contradictions between the Gospels, he repeatedly cites solutions proposed by Augustine; they are, largely, the standard fare of Gospel harmonizations, and need not be illustrated here.[56] A few observations about Thomas's procedure in dealing with problematic texts must suffice.

53. "Since Holy Scripture can be explained in a multiplicity of senses, one should adhere to a particular explanation, only in such measure as to be ready to abandon it, if it be proved with certainty to be false; lest Holy Scripture be exposed to the ridicule of unbelievers, and obstacles be placed to their believing" (*ST* 1.68.1)

54. Thomas "was willing to reinterpret a passage when it seemed to assert something he knew could not be true on logical, historical, or scientific grounds. [His] basic principle was: 'nothing false can ever underlie the literal sense of Scripture' [*ST* 1.1.10 ad 3). So when Scripture appears to be claiming something clearly untrue, its divine author must intend a meaning other than the apparent one that can be true. The interpreter's responsibility is to find that meaning" (Healy, "Introduction," 17).

55. Chrysostom's homilies often seem driven by a similar agenda. One suspects that Thomas sensed the same urgency; in any case, expectations of a *magister* did not allow him to avoid such issues.

56. E.g., no contradiction is to be seen when Jesus' words are reported differently in different Gospels, provided that the point being made is the same; apparent differences in chronology may be the result of evangelists' recording of events, not in the order in which they took place, but in the order in which the writers recalled them; what may appear to be the same event with different details in different Gospels may in fact be different events, etc.

1. Origen's standard procedure, of resolving texts that were problematic at the literal level by resorting to spiritual interpretations, is found in Thomas as well (though less frequently, to be sure), at times in addition to possible literal solutions (e.g., *Com. Matt.,* on 1:8 [pp. 24-26]; on 3:11 [pp. 99-100]), but at times on its own. According to Matthew 10:10, for example, the disciples were not to carry a staff; according to Mark 6:8, they were: "What Matthew says here, he says literally, that they ought not to carry a staff: but what Mark says, is understood mystically, namely, that they may not carry temporal things, but they have the right of receiving from others" (*Com. Matt.,* on 10:10 [p. 369]).[57] Augustine is followed in his solution to the timing of Christ's crucifixion, by which only one of the Gospel versions is said to preserve the "history."

> It ought to be said that Matthew recounts the history, in that Christ was crucified at the sixth hour, and that He died at the ninth hour. . . . Why, therefore, does Mark say that it was at the third hour? It ought to be said that He was crucified at the third hour by the tongues of the Jews, but at the sixth hour He was crucified by the hands of the soldiers. (*Com. Matt.,* on 27:45 [p. 936]; cf. *Com. John,* on 19:14 [2405])

2. When Paul (or, for that matter, Christ himself) appears to contravene Christ's instructions in the Sermon on the Mount, Thomas (again like Augustine) insists that their actions point rather to the way those instructions are to be understood.

> But since, as Augustine says, it is the same to say *for God is my witness* [as Paul does in Rom. 1:9] and *I swear by God,* the Apostle seems to be acting against the Lord's command: *I say to you, do not swear at all* (Matt. 5:34); *above all, my brethren, do not swear* (James 5:12). However, as Augustine also says, the meaning of Sacred Scripture is gathered from the actions of the saints. For it is the same Spirit who inspired the Sacred Scriptures . . . [2 Pet. 1:21 is cited] and who moves holy men to

---

57. That the truth of the Markan text is found at the "mystical" level seems to contradict Thomas's thesis that nothing false is found in the *literal* sense of Scripture. The problem is resolved if we remember that the literal sense of the text is, for Thomas, what the author intended — even if the intended sense is *not* that of the surface meaning of the text, but one that would normally be designated "spiritual" or "mystical." At times Thomas is careful to insist on that distinction. At other times (as in the example above), he can speak simply of the "mystical" sense of a text without spelling out that in this case the "mystical" sense *is* (in his terminology) the "literal" sense.

act . . . [Rom. 8:14 is cited]. Consequently, if Paul is found to swear, it shows that the Lord's word and that of the apostle James are not to be understood as indicating that an oath is absolutely unlawful, but that men should strive as far as possible not to use oaths as though they were something good and desirable of their very nature. And this on account of the danger involved in frequent swearing, namely, the possibility of perjury due to a slip of the tongue. . . . Also because it seems contrary to the reverence we owe God for one to call God as witness without necessity. . . . Yet an oath is sometimes necessary to lend credence to a speaker, which in turn often benefits the hearer. Consequently, the Apostle makes an oath for the benefit of his hearer, for whom it was beneficial to believe, as though not seeking what was useful to himself but to the majority, namely, their salvation. (*Com. Rom.*, on 1:9 [80-81]; cf. *Com. Matt.*, on 5:34 [p. 203])

Similarly, when the Lord told his disciples, "But if one strike thee on thy right cheek, turn to him also the other," the words "ought to be understood from the deeds of the holy men." Since neither Jesus himself (John 18:23) nor Paul (Acts 23:3) carried out this command literally, it should be understood as speaking only of what the mind should be prepared to do (*Com. Matt.*, on 5:39 [pp. 209-10]; cf. *Com. John*, on 18:23 [2321]).[58]

3. Thomas delighted in resolutions of problematic texts that used the kind of distinction dear to the heart of a scholastic theologian.

There have been philosophers, the Stoics, who said that those who are wise are not troubled this way or by such passions [as, according to John 13:21, Christ felt]. . . . Note that one can be troubled in two ways. Sometimes it comes from the flesh, which means that one is troubled because of some apprehension by the senses, but independently of the judgment of reason. Yet sometimes this can remain within the limits of reason and not cloud one's reason. . . . The second way of being troubled is to have it come from one's reason, that is, when one is troubled in the sensory appetite because of a judgment of reason and from deliberation. This was the way Christ was troubled. And so the Evangelist is careful to say that *he was troubled in spirit*, that is, the sensory appetite of Christ

---

58. See also *Com. John*, on 6:27 (896): "Certain monks misunderstood our Lord's saying, Do not work for the food that perishes, and claimed that spiritual men should not perform physical work. But that interpretation is false because Paul, who was most spiritual, worked with his hands."

was troubled because of a judgment of his reason. . . . For in Christ all things arose from the deliberation of reason, even in his sensory appetite. (*Com. John*, on 13:21 [1797])

Texts like 1 Timothy 2:4 and 2 Peter 3:9 seemed to contradict Thomas's (very Augustinian) understanding of predestination with their suggestion that God "wills" the salvation of all. But, of course, God "wills" and God "wills": one must distinguish between his "signified will" (i.e., what is indicated by statements of his "will" to save all, meaning that "he offers to all the precepts, counsels and remedies required for salvation") and "the will of his good pleasure," by which, in fact, only some are saved (*Com. 1 Tim.*, on 2:4 [62]). If Christ is said to be the "propitiation for the sins of the whole world" (1 John 2:2), this is true "for all in a sufficient way" (i.e., "the price of his blood is sufficient for the salvation of all"), though not "in an efficacious way" (i.e., effectively, it is true only of some; see *Com. 1 Tim.*, on 2:5 [64]).

4. Where precision is not required to convey Scripture's point, precision need not be expected. According to Matthew 10:29, two sparrows were sold for a penny; Luke 12:6 says five were sold for two. Thomas is content to say, "There is not a great difference" (*Com. Matt.*, on 10:29 [p. 386]). If Paul speaks of 430 years (Gal. 3:17) where Genesis 15:13 speaks of 400, complicated harmonizations may be proposed; but perhaps we should simply say that Scripture "was not concerned with minutiae" (*Com. Gal.*, on 3:17 [160]). Scripture must, moreover, be allowed to use hyperbole without being accused of falsehood.[59]

5. At times, Scripture narrates things as taking place in a way that, understood literally, could not have happened. In such cases, Thomas believes either that the narrative itself contains clues that it is not to be understood literally, or that theological considerations derived from elsewhere in Scripture compel the same conclusion. Genesis 18 is cited as an example of the former kind of narrative: as the story progresses, it becomes clear that the three "men" of 18:2 were not men after all (*SCG* 4.29.5). Theological considerations shape Thomas's interpretation of the first chapters in the book of Job. Since other parts of Scripture seem to speak of Job as a real person, Thomas is not prepared to follow those who suggest that the book of Job is merely a parable (*Com. Job*, prologue [pp. 68-69]). But since only the blessed angels enjoy the vision of God, the statement that "the sons of

---

59. E.g., *Com. John*, on 21:25 (2659); *Com. Heb.*, on 11:32 (628). Thomas also allows Scripture its "custom" of saying "all" when "some" is meant, and using the plural number for the singular (*Com. Phil.*, on 2:21 [91]; *Com. Heb.*, on 11:37 [648]).

God had come to stand in the presence of the Lord," with Satan among them, can only mean that "whatever they do is subject to divine inspection and examination"; and when Scripture says they did so "on a certain day," the phrase follows a pattern in Scripture (evident also in Gen. 1) by which "things which are beyond time" are spoken of as though within it, inasmuch as it is within time that their effects take place (*Com. Job,* on 1:6 [p. 77]).

6. Chrysostom made frequent use of the notion of divine "considerateness" (or "condescension") to explain problematic texts in Scripture. Thomas does so only occasionally: in speaking of a firmament dividing waters below and above it (Gen. 1:6), "Moses was speaking to ignorant people"; "out of condescension to their weakness he put before them only such things as are apparent to sense" (*ST* 1.68.3). If Genesis says God fixed the stars in the firmament (1:17), Moses again "describes what is obvious to sense, out of condescension to popular ignorance" (*ST* 1.70.1 ad 3). When Scripture states that God spoke to Moses "face to face,"

> this is to be understood as expressing the opinion of the people, who thought that Moses was speaking with God mouth to mouth, when [in fact] God spoke and appeared to him, by means of a subordinate creature, i.e., an angel and a cloud. (*ST* 1-2.98.3 ad 2)

And if Matthew 21:19 suggests that Jesus approached a fig tree expecting to find fruit, it merely indicates what the disciples thought he was doing (*Com. Matt.,* on 21:19 [p. 693]).

7. As noted above, Thomas shows little interest in discovering where the Latin text he used might differ from that of the original languages, or where the text may have become corrupted through scribal error; he appears to operate rather on the principle that the word of God may be found in the text in front of him, regardless of such considerations, and even in variant versions of the same text.[60] He is, however, aware (as was Origen) that scribal error was particularly common in the transmission of numbers and genealogies. Bearing that in mind, Thomas underscores the importance of following Paul's counsel not to be troubled overmuch by disputes arising in these matters (*Com. Titus,* on 3:9 [99]; *Com. Matt.,* on 1:12 [p. 31]).

8. The difficulties Scripture poses to its interpreters form an appropriate challenge for those committed to uncovering its mysteries. But since the possibility of taking up that challenge is open to only a few, the Apos-

---

60. See Stump, "Revelation."

tles' Creed — a summary of Scripture faithful to its teaching — serves a useful purpose.[61]

> The truth of faith is contained in Holy Writ, diffusely, under various modes of expression, and sometimes obscurely, so that, in order to gather the truth of faith from Holy Writ, one needs long study and practice, which are unattainable by all those who require to know the truth of faith, many of whom have no time for study, being busy with other affairs. And so it was necessary to gather together a clear summary from the sayings of Holy Writ, to be proposed to the belief of all. (*ST* 2-2.1.9 ad 1)

To sum up: though Thomas was convinced, even apart from any consideration of textual phenomena, that Scripture is true and without error, it is clear from the preceding examples that he did allow textual phenomena to define both the *measure* of truth to be found in Scripture and the *manner* in which it is communicated: the truth of Scripture may be approximate or hyperbolic rather than precise; it may be conveyed metaphorically, or "mystically," rather than through the surface meaning of the text; it may even be couched in language misleading in itself because it is accommodated to the understanding of ordinary people. Such considerations serve to remind us that the *purpose* of divine revelation is to bring human beings to the knowledge and love of God; Scripture's truth must be measured by standards attuned to *that* end. In this regard, we may fairly say that Thomas summed up the accumulated wisdom of a thousand years of Christian scriptural interpretation.

Scripture, then, is authoritative and true, and the revelation it contains is essential for our happiness and salvation. What we *find* in Scripture, in Thomas's account, is the "old law" and the "new."

The Old Law and the New

Thomas "could not help putting everything in its proper place. Each thing in its own place, a place for each thing."[62] Nowhere is this more evident than in what he says about law. Thus, before we take up what Thomas says about the

---

61. On a similar note, Thomas tells us that he wrote his *Summa Theologica* to set forth the substance of the "Sacred Science" as "briefly and clearly" as possible, for the "instruction of beginners" (*ST,* prologue). No irony was intended.

62. Gilson, *Reason,* 70.

twofold "divine law" (i.e., the "old law" and the "new"), even a brief summary requires that we begin by placing that law in the context of other "laws"
of which Thomas speaks: the eternal law, the natural law, and human law.

Clearly, Thomas's natural propensity to put everything in its place
says a good deal about the workings of his mind; but it speaks no less of
his understanding of creation as divinely ordered. God made things for a
reason, and one cannot be said to understand any part of God's creation
unless one grasps *its* place in the whole: the "end" for which it was made
and by which its nature is determined.

Now "law," as Thomas defines the term, is "nothing but a rational plan
of operation" (*SCG* 3.114.5); since God governs the universe by divine reason, his governance may be spoken of as "the eternal law" (*ST* 1-2.91.1).
It is, then, the eternal law that determines the proper end of all things
created and directs them toward it. As builders need direction from an
architect if they are to achieve the end for which they build, and soldiers
need direction from the leader of their army if they are to achieve the end
for which they serve, so creatures need direction from their Creator if they
are to achieve the end for which they were made (*SCG* 3.114.5). Creatures
without reason are moved by divine providence through their natural in-
clinations (*ST* 1-2.93.6).

Rational creatures, however, have choices to make: if they are to pursue the end for which they were made, their choices need to be consistent
with that end. The "end" of human beings (as we have seen) is to find
happiness in knowing God, in beholding the divine essence. This end,
however, is one that, by nature, they lack the capacity to attain.[63] If they
are to know the One toward whom (as their end) they are to direct their
lives, they need revelation of the truth *about* God: "The end must first be
known by men who are to direct their thoughts and actions to the end" (*ST*
1.1.1). But that is not all: if they are to *come to* God, the path they must take
to arrive at that end must also be revealed. Put differently: it is not enough
for people to know Christian doctrine about the God whose beholding is
bliss; they also need to know how to become the kind of people who can
behold him. In Thomas's terms, both their "speculative" intellect or reason (with its quest for the truth about God) and their "practical" intellect

---

63. The incapacity of their nature, as created, to attain the end for which they were created must not be deemed an oversight on the part of their Creator. Human beings *have* been
equipped with a will that can turn to God, from whom the necessary aid can be received.
Similarly, Thomas notes, human beings are not born (as other animals are) with weapons
and clothing, but they are given "reason and hands" so that they can acquire such things for
themselves (*ST* 1-2.5.5 ad 1).

or reason (which directs their actions) are in need of divine revelation.[64] The former necessity was discussed above; here something must be said concerning Thomas's account of the latter.

Truth cannot be opposed to truth. The truth about God revealed by divine revelation cannot contradict such truth as is known by natural reason, but builds upon it: "Grace [here, the grace of divine revelation] does not destroy nature [here, natural human reason], but perfects it" (*ST* 1.1.8 ad 2). This principle applies in the moral realm as well as the speculative: divinely revealed law (the "divine law") builds upon the "natural law." The latter law represents the moral foundation that God has "instilled" in the minds of human beings as part of their nature: "God instilled [the natural law] into man's mind so as to be known by him naturally" (*ST* 1-2.90.4 ad 1); "the law which is written in men's hearts is the natural law" (*ST* 1-2.94.6). Since the "eternal law" means God's governance of the universe, and since God guides human beings through the "natural law," we may say that "the natural law is nothing else than the rational creature's participation of the eternal law" (*ST* 1-2.91.2).

For its part, *speculative* reason begins with first principles (e.g., the law of contradiction) that, though they cannot be demonstrated, are self-evident. Taking these principles as premises, speculative reason then proceeds through argumentation to arrive at other truths, such as that of the existence of God. Similarly, *practical* reason begins with first principles and proceeds to deduce moral truths. The most fundamental principle of the natural law is simply that good (i.e., that which is consistent with the end for which human beings were made) is to be done, and evil avoided. Human beings, moreover, are naturally inclined to preserve their own life; hence, whatever actions appear to preserve life or to oppose what threatens it can be said to fall under natural law. Human beings also have a natural inclination to live in society: natural law will thus include whatever promotes good relationships with others (*ST* 1-2.94.2).

Natural law can be said to include both its first (self-evident) principles and other (secondary) ones that are deduced from the first (*ST* 1-2.94.5). But whereas the first principles of natural law are necessarily true for all human beings, secondary principles may *not* be universally true: there may be, for example, unusual circumstances under which what would normally be the

---

64. See *ST* 1.1.4 ad 2: Since sacred doctrine is chiefly about God, and only secondarily about creatures as they relate to God, it is primarily a speculative rather than practical science. Still, sacred doctrine may be said to include practical science as well, inasmuch as it deals with the human acts by which the "perfect knowledge of God" is achieved.

right thing to do (such as returning goods to their owner) might be harmful, and therefore unreasonable. And whereas the first principles of natural law are known by all, secondary principles are not universally acknowledged: they are, after all, deduced by practical reason from first principles, and such deductions are subject to the variation and fallibility of human judgment that has been perverted by sin (*ST* 1-2.94.4-5; cf. 1-2.98.6).

Finally, we should note that *human* laws are devised for the good ordering of society: they, too, have their basis in the natural law (and thus in the eternal law, of which natural law is a part); these laws are *just* to the extent that they reflect the eternal law (cf. *ST* 1-2.93.3 ad 2).

But just as truths deduced by natural reason are not sufficient to bring true knowledge of God, so neither natural law nor human laws are sufficient to bring human beings to the bliss of divine contemplation. Divinely revealed law is needed.

> If man were ordained to no other end than that which is proportionate to his natural faculty, there would be no need for man to have any further direction of the part of his reason, besides the natural law and human law which is derived from it. But since man is ordained to an end of eternal happiness, which is inproportionate to man's natural faculty, . . . therefore it was necessary that, besides the natural and the human law, man should be directed to his end by a law given by God. (*ST* 1-2.91.4)

> The divine law principally looks to the ordering of man toward God. . . . The divine law primarily directs man to this end: that he may cling to God. (*SCG* 3.115.2-3)

Even within the sphere of its own operation, human practical reason can err in applying the principles of natural law to particular situations: divinely revealed law was thus necessary for the further reason "that man may know without any doubt what he ought to do and what he ought to avoid." Moreover, human laws are restricted in what they can prescribe and enforce: the thoughts of the heart lie outside their competence, and certain lesser evils are inevitably permitted to prevent what is worse. Yet, if human beings are to live in a way consistent with the end for which they were made, and if they are to share in the joys of the eternally blessed, they must break completely with evil. "In order, therefore, that no evil might remain unforbidden and unpunished, it was necessary for the divine law to supervene, whereby all sins are forbidden" (*ST* 1-2.91.4).

"The Divine law is twofold, namely the Old Law and the New Law"

(*ST* 1-2.91.5). Only the new law is sufficient to bring human beings to their desired end; yet its coming was prepared for by the giving of the old, as children must be governed differently than adults (*ST* 1-2.91.5, referring to Gal. 3:24-25). It is, then, with the still imperfect good of the old law that we must begin (cf. *ST* 1-2.98.2 ad 1).[65]

Among its provisions, we may distinguish moral, ceremonial, and judicial precepts.[66] The moral precepts were necessary because God himself is good, and human beings who are not themselves good can enjoy no friendship with him (*ST* 1-2.99.2). The moral precepts of the divine law simply spell out the principles and implications of natural law for the benefit of human beings whose judgment in such matters is fallible and distorted by sin: "As grace presupposes nature, so must the Divine law presuppose the natural law" (*ST* 1-2.99.2 ad 1; cf. 1-2.100.1). Essentially, they are all found in the ten commandments of Exodus 20:1-17: "Other moral precepts added to the decalogue are reducible to the precepts of the decalogue, as so many corollaries" (*ST* 1-2.100.11; cf. 1-2.100.3; *Com. Gal.,* on 5:14 [304]). Their equivalence to the content of the natural law means both that they are applicable to all human beings[67] and that they embody what is right and reasonable for human beings to do. Put differently, it is not the case that they represent the right thing to do *because* they were divinely prescribed; rather, they were divinely prescribed because they *are* the right thing to do. They are "naturally suitable" for human beings, appropriate to human nature; as such, they promote human good (*SCG* 3.129.1-11).

A few examples may be given. Since human sexuality has *its* proper end in the propagation of the species, and since any offspring generated by intercourse needs to be nourished, cared for, educated, and, indeed, corrected over an extended period of time, it is natural and right — and thus in accordance with natural law — for sexual relations to take place within the lasting relationship between a man and a woman that we call matrimony. Conversely, it is wrong and contrary to human good for the sexual act to be performed promiscuously, outside marriage; divine law

65. The old law was *not* given to Adam — not even after he had sinned. Instead, sufficient time was given for the inadequacies of natural reason for combating human ignorance and vice to become apparent (*ST* 1-2.98.6).

66. Thomas sees a reference to each of these categories in Paul's description of the law as "holy and just and good" (Rom. 7:12). "Holy" refers to the ceremonial precepts, "just" to the judicial, and "good" to the moral (*ST* 1-2.99.4).

67. Properly speaking, the old law was given only to the Jewish people. That its moral precepts are nonetheless binding on all human beings thus depends on their being part of the natural law as well (*ST* 1-2.98.5; 1-2.100.11).

prohibits such intercourse (*SCG* 3.122). We may, moreover, say with Aristotle that "man is by nature a social animal," in need of many things beyond what any individual can provide. It follows that the need to live together with other people is inherent in human nature. That being the case, divine law simply builds on natural law when it prohibits murder, adultery, theft, and false testimony (*SCG* 3.128.1, 7).

In addition to its moral precepts, the old law contained ceremonial provisions pertaining to the worship of God and applicable only to the Jewish people to whom that law was given. To be sure, the moral duty to worship God binds all human beings; but the particular rites of worship prescribed by the old law were meant only for the people being prepared for the coming of Christ and the reception of the new law (*ST* 1-2.99.3 ad 2; cf. 1-2.98.5). Unlike the moral precepts of the divine law, the ceremonial ones became the right thing (for Israel) to do only when they were instituted (*ST* 1-2.100.11). The purposes underlying their institution were both long- and short-term. Thomas goes to great lengths to show how various aspects of the saving work of Christ were foreshadowed in Israel's rites of worship.[68] There is, of course, nothing new in this, and we need not linger over the details. It is, however, worth noting that Thomas is careful to point out that these rites, literally understood and observed, also served an immediate purpose at the time they were given:[69]

> Now the end of the ceremonial precepts was twofold: for they were ordained to the Divine worship, for that particular time, and to the fore-

---

68. Though the rites of the old law were not in themselves capable of making sinners righteous, it was nonetheless possible for the Old Testament faithful to be united to Christ, inasmuch as their observance of rites that foreshadowed Christ can be said to express "a sort of profession" of faith in Christ (*ST* 1-2.103.2). Cf. *Com. Heb.,* on 9:9 (431).

69. This insistence, of course, is not unrelated to Thomas's conviction that the literal sense of a text represents the necessary foundation for whatever spiritual truths may be derived from it. Thomas dealt with Old Testament prophecies traditionally read as pointing to Christ in a similar way: generally speaking, these texts had both an immediate reference in the prophets' own day and a further, figurative reference to Christ; the latter is at times signaled by wording in the prophecies that goes far beyond what could be said of anyone but Christ (cf. *SCG* 4.2.3-4; *ST* 1-2.102.2; *Com. Matt.,* on 2:17-18 [pp. 79-81]; *Com. Eph.,* on 5:33 [335]; *Com. Heb.,* on 1:5 [51]). In the case of the Psalms, as we have seen, Thomas can allow a literal reference to David, an allegorical reference to Christ, and a moral reference to the lot of the righteous (so on Psalms 3, 10 [English versions, Ps. 11], and 26 [English versions, Ps. 27]). On the other hand, where the New Testament explicitly indicates that a particular Old Testament text was fulfilled by Christ, Thomas tends to see that fulfillment as the literal meaning of the Old Testament text. See *Com. Matt.,* on 1:23 (p. 53); on 2:15 (p. 77); on 27:46 (p. 937). See Smalley, *Gospels,* 266-68.

shadowing of Christ. . . . Accordingly the reasons for the ceremonial precepts of the Old Law can be taken in two ways. First, in respect of the Divine worship which was to be observed at that particular time: and these reasons are literal: whether they refer to the shunning of idolatry;[70] or recall certain Divine benefits; or remind men of the Divine excellence; or point out the disposition of mind which was then required in those who worshipped God. — Secondly, their reasons can be gathered from the point of view of their being ordained to foreshadow Christ: and thus their reasons are figurative and mystical. (*ST* 1-2.102.2)[71]

In order to direct his mind to God aright, man must recognize that whatever he has is from God as from its first principle, and direct it to God as its last end. This was denoted in the offerings and sacrifices, by the fact that man offered some of his own belongings in honor of God, as though in recognition of his having received them from God. . . . Wherefore in offering up sacrifices man made protestation that God is the first principle of the creation of all things, and their last end, to which all things must be directed. (*ST* 1-2.102.3)

If the moral precepts of the old law can be said to last forever, inasmuch as they represent what is right for human beings to do everywhere and at all times, its ceremonial precepts can be said to last forever only in the sense that the reality to which they pointed is of lasting significance (*ST* 1-2.103.3 ad 1).[72] A few specific observances enjoined by the old law have been replaced by others in the new: circumcision was replaced by baptism, for example, and observance of the Sabbath by that of the Lord's day (*ST* 1-2.103.3 ad 4). But now that Christ has appeared, to continue practicing rites of the old law that were given to *foreshadow* his coming is to act as though he has not yet come, and thus to deny Christian faith by one's deeds (*ST* 1-2.103.4).[73]

70. I.e., part of the point of the many ceremonial precepts was that people burdened by their observation "might have no time for the service of idols" (*ST* 1-2.101.3).

71. Note also *ST* 1-2.101.3; 102.2 ad 1. As we have seen, Chrysostom's focus on the literal sense of Scripture led him to a similar account of the immediate purpose of Israel's ceremonial laws.

72. Cf. *Com. Eph.*, on 2:14 (114): "[Christ] abolished the ceremonial precepts with regard to what they were in themselves, but he fulfilled them with regard to what they prefigured, adding what was symbolized to the symbol."

73. Thomas is explicitly following Augustine here. He also allows, however, with Augustine, that it was appropriate for the earliest Jewish Christians to observe the old rites in

As the ceremonial rites of the old law represented the appropriate expression, for a particular people at a particular time, of humanity's lasting moral duty to worship God, so its judicial precepts represented the appropriate expression, for the same people at the same time, of humanity's lasting moral duty to practice justice toward other human beings (*ST* 1-2.101.1).[74] Given the figurative significance of the ceremonial precepts, it would be wrong to observe them after Christ's coming; such considerations do not apply to the judicial precepts, whose observance is now a matter of indifference. One must not, however, treat them as binding: after all, the old law was intended only to serve as a "pedagogue" until Christ came (*ST* 1-2.104.3, citing Gal. 3:24).

Such are the precepts of the old law, whose purposes we may sum up as follows. The moral precepts served to set forth the path to righteousness and, by so doing, drew attention to humanity's inability to fulfill its moral obligations. The ceremonial precepts served to sanctify the people to whom Christ would come and to foreshadow his coming. The judicial commands ordered Israel's community life according to justice. No less manifold, however, are the old law's imperfections: it could only promise and foreshadow what would become real first with the coming of Christ;[75] it could not convey the ability to fulfill the moral precepts that it rightly imposed;[76] its laws focused on external acts rather than internal

---

the intermediate period between the passion of Christ (when those rites in fact lost their point and binding force) and the spread of the Christian gospel (*ST* 1-2.103.4 and 1). Cf. *SCG* 4.57.3: "More unreasonable still is the error of the Nazarenes and the Ebionites, who used to say that the sacraments of the Law should be observed simultaneously with those of the Gospel. An error of this kind involves a sort of contrariety. For, while they observe the evangelical sacraments, they are professing that the Incarnation and the other mysteries of Christ have already been perfected; but, when they also observe the sacraments of the Law, they are professing that those mysteries are in the future."

74. "The obligation of observing justice is indeed perpetual. But the determination of those things that are just . . . must needs be different, according to the different states of mankind" (*ST* 1-2.104.3 ad 1).

75. "The end of every law is to make men righteous and virtuous. . . . The [Old] Law, however, could not accomplish this: but foreshadowed it by certain ceremonial actions, and promised it in words. . . . Wherefore the New Law is called the law of reality; whereas the Old Law is called the law of shadow or of figure" (*ST* 1-2.107.2); Moses saw God's "back," i.e., "shadows and figures. But the apostles saw his brightness. . . . For Moses and the other prophets saw in an obscure manner and in figures the glory of the Word that was to be manifested to the world at the end of their times" (*Com. John*, on 1:14 [183]).

76. "It behoved man first of all to be left to himself under the state of the Old Law, so that through falling into sin, he might realize his weakness, and acknowledge his need of grace" (*ST* 1-2.106.3; cf. 98.2 ad 3).

thoughts,[77] though the latter are equally integral to virtue; the promises attending observance of its statutes pertained to temporal, earthly rewards rather than eternal, heavenly ones;[78] the motivation to obey those statutes was primarily that of fear and the avoidance of punishment rather than that of love.[79]

Clearly, the imperfections of the old law have been defined as a foil for presenting the perfections of the new. But what *is* the new law?

The New Law is the law of the New Testament. But the law of the New Testament is instilled in our hearts. . . . Now that which is preponderant in the law of the New Testament, and whereon all its efficacy is based, is the grace of the Holy Spirit, which is given through faith in Christ. Consequently the New Law is chiefly the grace itself of the Holy Spirit, which is given to those who believe in Christ. (*ST* 1-2.106.1)[80]

Thomas insists repeatedly that the "chief" and distinguishing element of the new law is "the grace of the Holy Spirit bestowed inwardly": a grace that could not be so granted apart from the work of Christ, since it required that "sin, which is an obstacle to grace, had been cast out of man through the accomplishment of his redemption by Christ" (*ST* 1-2.106.3). Secondary elements of the new law include both the truths of the gospel — which must be believed if the Spirit's grace is to be received — and the commandments that direct human affections and deeds.[81] Observance of

77. "The New Law surpasses the Old Law, since it directs our internal acts" (*ST* 1-2.91.5). Thomas grants that the "substance" of the precepts of the New Testament is found already in the Old; but it was first Christ who drew out "the true sense of the [Old] Law" (*ST* 1-2.107.3 ad 2; 107.2).

78. See *ST* 1-2.91.5: "Man was directly ordained by the Old Law" to a "sensible and earthly good . . . : wherefore, at the very outset of the law, the people were invited to the earthly kingdom of the Chananaeans." By way of contrast, "man is ordained by the New Law" to "an intelligible and heavenly good." See also *ST* 1-2.99.6; *Com. Gal.*, on 1:6 (19).

79. Cf. *ST* 1-2.91.5: "It belongs to the law to induce men to observe its commandments. This the Old Law did by the fear of punishment; but the New Law, by love, which is poured into our hearts by the grace of Christ." See also *ST* 1-2.107.1 ad 2; *SCG* 3.116.7; *Com. Gal.*, on 4:24 (260).

80. Here I have taken the liberty of substituting "Holy Spirit" for the "Holy Ghost" of the translation.

81. For Thomas, the Sermon on the Mount "contains the whole process of forming the life of a Christian" (*ST* 1-2.108.3). It is here, then, that we find the substance of the new law's moral component. To such commandments we may add those concerning the sacraments ("instituted" by Christ himself in order that we may "obtain grace" [*ST* 1-2.108.2]). Together with these commandments that are intended for all we should also mention, as similarly

the latter is not possible in any case apart from "the inward presence of the healing grace of faith" (*ST* 1-2.106.2; 107.1 ad 3): "The New Law is instilled into man, not only by indicating to him what he should do, but also by helping him to accomplish it" (*ST* 1-2.106.1 ad 2).

Yet even those under the new law do not yet enjoy the bliss of seeing God as he is. They have, to be sure, advanced beyond the condition of those under the old law, for whom the prospect of such bliss was only a hope, and the means of attaining it a faith in what was also yet to come. Under the new law, the means of attaining that vision have been made available through Christ; but the beatific vision itself remains a hope for the future. Only for the blessed in heaven is nothing believed in still lacking, nothing hoped for yet to come (*ST* 1-2.103.3).

Receiving the Word

Though Thomas's lectures (on which his commentaries on Scripture were based) and his systematic presentations of the truth about God and humankind naturally focus on what we may *learn* from Scripture, Thomas knew well that a proper response to the word of God involved more than intellectual assimilation of its teaching. Let the last word be his:

> Now, if the Word of God is the Son of God and all the words of God bear a certain likeness of this Word, then we ought to hear the Word of God gladly; for such is a sign that we love God. We ought also to believe the word of God whereby the Word of God dwells in us, who is Christ: "That Christ may dwell by faith in your hearts" (Eph 3:17). . . . Also we should meditate often upon this; for otherwise we will not be benefitted to the extent that such meditation is a great help against sin: "Your words have I hidden in my heart, that I may not sin against You" (Ps 118:11 [English versions, 119:11]). . . . Then also, one should communicate the word of God to others by advising, preaching and inflaming their hearts. . . . Finally, we ought to put the word of God into practice: "Be doers of the word and not hearers only, deceiving yourselves" (James 1:22). (*Creed*, article 2)

---

pertaining to the new law, its "counsels" of poverty (Matt. 19:21), virginity (1 Cor. 7:25), and obedience (Heb. 13:17). Observance of these is not required of all, nor necessary for right living; but it promotes detachment from earthly care and attachment to God (*SCG* 3.130.1-6; *ST* 1-2.108.4).

Thus he says, *and my words abide in you,* in four ways: by your loving them, believing them, meditating on them and accomplishing them: "My son, be attentive to my words," by believing them; "incline your ear to my sayings," by obeying or accomplishing them; "let them not escape from your sight," because you meditate on them; but "keep them within your heart," by loving them (Pr 4:20). "Your words were found and I ate them" (Jer 15:16). Therefore, the words of Christ are in us when we do as he commands and love what he promises. (*Com. John,* on 15:7 [1995])

CHAPTER 8

Luther

At the end of October 1517, Martin Luther, an Augustinian monk, unwittingly launched the Reformation by posting ninety-five theses for debate on a church door in Wittenberg. Some eighteen years later, by that time a married man at his dinner table, Luther began a simple exposition of the Twenty-third Psalm with the following words:

> In this psalm, David, together with every other Christian heart, praises and thanks God for His greatest blessing: namely, for the preaching of His dear Holy Word. (12.147)[1]

The emphasis on God's Word[2] will surprise no one who recalls Luther's famous self-defense at the Diet of Worms in 1521:

> Unless I am convinced by the testimony of the Scriptures or by clear reason (for I do not trust either in the pope or in councils alone, since it is well known that they have often erred and contradicted themselves), I am bound by the Scriptures I have quoted and my conscience is captive to the Word of God. (32.112)

---

1. Most of the citations from Luther in this chapter are taken from the various volumes of *Luther's Works,* and are cited, as here, simply by volume number and page. Other citations are taken from the *Large Catechism (LC)* and from the seven volumes of *Complete Sermons* (*CS;* note that volumes 1-4 each contain two parts: thus, *CS* 3.2.14 refers to Volume 3, Part 2, page 14); see the bibliography for publication details.

2. Throughout this chapter, the practice adopted in *Luther's Works* of capitalizing references to the divine "Word" will be followed. What Luther means by the term and includes within it will be discussed below.

Those whose knowledge of the reformer is thereby exhausted may find it surprising that Luther highlights specifically the *preaching* of God's Word. And that Psalm 23 expresses the thanksgiving of every Christian for such preaching will come as news to millions who have recited "The Lord is my shepherd" since childhood. Luther may be the only person in history who has heard David's "green pastures" and thought "church benches." And by what befuddlement of thought did an otherwise brilliant mind confuse the idyllic "He leads me beside the still waters" with the weekly endurance of a pedestrian homily?

No easy question, this. We begin our search for clues with a brief look at Luther's life.

Life

Martin Luther was born in November 1483 to a Saxon miner who intended him to become a lawyer. Returning from home to his studies at the University of Erfurt in the summer of 1505, he was struck to the ground in a thunderstorm, cried to St. Anne for help, and vowed to become a monk; two weeks later he entered the Augustinian monastery in Erfurt. Scrupulous to a fault, he subjected himself to extreme deprivations while devoting himself to prayer and — famously — to endless confessions of his sins, large and small, to the point where Johann von Staupitz, his spiritual adviser, told him that if he wanted Christ to forgive him, he should go out and do something worth forgiving ("parricide, blasphemy, adultery") "instead of all these trifles."[3]

Hoping that engagement with Scripture would cure Luther's troubled spirit, Staupitz set him on the path to becoming Professor of Bible at the university in Wittenberg (1512).[4] Years later, Luther recalled that his life had indeed been transformed by his wrestling with Scripture — specifically, with the Pauline text, "In [the gospel] the righteousness of God is revealed" (Rom. 1:17). He initially took "the righteousness of God" in this verse to refer to God's punishment of sinners — a righteousness that he, with his "fierce and troubled conscience," could only hate.

> At last, by the mercy of God, meditating day and night, . . . I began to understand that the righteousness of God is that by which the righteous lives by a gift of God, namely by faith. And this is the meaning:

3. Bainton, *Life*, 41.
4. Bainton, *Life*, 45.

the righteousness of God is revealed by the gospel, namely, the passive righteousness[5] with which merciful God justifies us by faith, as it is written, "He who through faith is righteous shall live." Here I felt that I was altogether born again and had entered paradise itself through open gates. . . . And I extolled my sweetest word with a love as great as the hatred with which I had before hated the word "righteousness of God." Thus that place in Paul was for me truly the gate to paradise. (34.336-37)

One path that the church of his day prescribed for dealing with sin was the sale of "indulgences," which would reduce or eliminate time otherwise spent in purgatory. Luther repeatedly preached against the practice, claiming that it led people to believe that they could be rid of their sins without repentance. Responding to the presence of a vendor of indulgences near Wittenberg, Luther invited an academic debate on the subject by posting, in Latin, his famous ninety-five theses on the door of the castle and university church in Wittenberg (1517). Against his own intentions, the theses were translated and circulated; Luther quickly became the talk of all Germany. The sale of indulgences diminished, complaints were brought to the pope, and Luther found himself charged with heresy. One step led to another, and Luther, who had begun with a (by no means unique) criticism of a particular practice, soon found himself insisting that the pope was not above Scripture, attacking other practices of the church of his day,[6] then being excommunicated for his trouble and outlawed as a heretic (1521).

"Kidnapped" (by allies) for his own safety, he lived in disguise for eight months in a castle near Eisenach, where he began work on a translation of the Bible into German. He returned to Wittenberg to subdue violence bred by more radical reformers. In 1525, having abandoned his Augustinian habit a year earlier, he married a former Cistercian nun. By 1531, the "Protestant" movement had spread to the point where a political confederacy was formed, linking princes and cities sympathetic to the cause. Priests were allowed to marry, the liturgy was reformed, services were conducted in German (rather than Latin), the preaching of the Word became central, and worship included the singing of German hymns — a number of which Luther himself composed. By the time of his death in 1546, Luther's in-

---

5. I.e., a righteousness not actively achieved by righteous behavior, but passively received as a gift.

6. E.g., of the seven sacraments practiced in his day, he found warrant in Scripture only for two (baptism and the Eucharist); he denied that observance of the Eucharist involved a repetition of the sacrifice of Christ, and insisted that laity should be allowed to partake of both elements (i.e., the wine as well as the bread) of the Eucharist.

tended correction of the church he knew had effectively led to the creation of a new church, struggling to exist beside the old.

The Word of God

That Scripture occupied a central place in Luther's thinking is clear enough; but any understanding of his view of Scripture must begin with what he says about a broader category: the Word of God.[7] It was, we recall, the preaching of that Word for which Luther's David gave singular thanks in Psalm 23.

As in the Prologue to John's Gospel, Luther uses "the Word" for the Son of God, who was with God, and was God, from all eternity.

> From all eternity [God] has a Word, a speech, a thought, or a conversation with Himself in His divine heart, unknown to angels and men. This is called His Word. From eternity He was within God's paternal heart, and through Him God resolved to create heaven and earth. . . . This Word was with God, yet not as a separate, distinct, God; no, He was the true, eternal God, of one essence with the Father, equal in might and glory. The distinction is that the Father is one Person, and the Son is another Person. . . . The two Persons are distinguished thus: It is the Father who speaks; the other Person, the Son, is spoken. (22.9, 15-16)

But "the Word (of God)" is also used, by Luther as in Scripture, for all that God speaks. What humans speak are "bare words"; by way of contrast, "the words of God are realities," for all that is real was spoken into being, and now subsists, by the Word of God: "We are all words of God" (1.21-22; 22.26).[8] When God speaks, the sun rises and sets, fruit grows, snow falls, kingdoms are scattered (12.32; cf. 14.124). The birth of every child takes place through the continuing effectiveness of the divine word spoken on creation's sixth day: "Be fruitful and multiply" (4.4, referring to Gen. 1:28). Again, in Luther as in the New Testament, the "Word" frequently refers specifically to the gospel message, "a living Word."

> It announces to us the grace of God bestowed gratis and without our merit, and tells us how Christ took our place, rendered satisfaction for

---

7. Cf. Pelikan, *Expositor,* 48-70.
8. "In the case of God to speak is to do, and the word is the deed" (12.33).

our sins, and destroyed them, and that He makes us pious and saves us through His work. (30.3)

That Word, too, "has power"; it is not "preached in vain" (17.170-71). It is, moreover, the efficacy of the Word enjoining baptism (Mark 16:16) and the observance of the Lord's Supper (1 Cor. 11:23-25) that transforms what is otherwise merely water, bread, and wine into mediums of divine grace (22.515; *LC* 82-83, 91-92). "The Word of God cannot be without effect" (4.103).

Normally, God speaks to human beings *through* human beings. Scripture says repeatedly that "the word of the Lord came" to particular prophets, who were then commissioned to deliver the message to their people. Luther believes that such passages reveal the preferred divine *modus operandi,* so that when Scripture states elsewhere that God spoke to a particular individual, we may often[9] assume that the message was delivered through a human intermediary, even where none is mentioned.[10] God's warning to Cain before he murdered Abel was presumably delivered by Adam (1.262, referring to Gen. 4:6-7). Godly Methuselah may well have been the one to pass on to Noah the divine instruction to enter the ark (2.81-82, referring to Gen. 7:1). Noah's son Shem was still alive at the time of Abraham and Isaac:[11] perhaps, then, it was Shem who communicated God's command to Abraham to leave his father's house for a land that God would show him (2.249, referring to Gen. 12:1-3; cf. 2.358), and Shem who informed Rebekah of the two nations in her womb (4.362, referring to Gen. 25:23).

Today, too, God continues to speak his Word through appointed intermediaries. Since God has told children to honor and obey their parents (Exod. 20:12; Eph. 6:1), and citizens to submit to the governing authorities (Rom. 13:1), the words of parents and rulers fulfilling their divine commission are, in fact, the Word of God, and must be responded to as such: "God commands that we should obey our parents and the government, and that we should listen to His Word from them" (4.362; cf. 2.271-72; 5.71).

9. Luther concedes, of course, that God *can* communicate with human beings through an angel or, directly, by the Holy Spirit; but God does so "only in special situations and very rarely" (2.81-83).

10. "I follow the authority of Scripture, which says that God is speaking when either angels or saintly men speak as a result either of the command or of the revelation of God" (3.219). Cf. Pelikan, *Expositor*, 103-5.

11. So Luther deduced, in but one illustration of his great interest in biblical chronology. Cf. Barr, "Chronology."

Ministers are appointed to speak the Word to their congregations; hence, "whenever we hear a pastor or a minister or servant of the church, we are hearing the Word of God" (4.295; cf. 22.528)[12] — provided, to be sure, that they are faithful in repeating and preaching what they have learned from the prophets and apostles (15.275-76; 58.373). But even individual believers may speak the Word of God to a brother or sister in forgiveness, encouragement, or admonition (see Col. 3:16).[13] "There is no difference between the Word when uttered by a schoolboy and when uttered by the Angel Gabriel; they vary only in rhetorical ability" (22.529).

> Often when I was troubled by something, Pomeranus [John Bugenhagen] or Philip [Melanchthon] or even my Katy [Luther's wife] would speak to me, and I was comforted as I realized that God was saying this because a brother was saying it either out of duty or out of love. (54.89)

Through the Word, however mediated, God "makes life out of death, righteousness out of sin, the greatest wealth out of abject poverty. Briefly, it is He who makes all things out of nothing and calls the things which are not as if they were" (20.5, referring to Rom. 4:17). It follows that what God's Word promises, threatens, or achieves makes no sense to normal human thinking; and this, indeed, is by divine design: "God really has this purpose — to declare things that are totally impossible to our mind and reason — and . . . there is nothing less in agreement than His Word and our judgment" (20.4).[14] Moreover, God's very nature is beyond human com-

---

12. Indeed, Luther's penchant for proposing unmentioned human intermediaries as those who delivered God's messages in the Old Testament is, he says, a way of highlighting the importance of the ministry in every age: "It is sure that God does not make a practice of speaking in a miraculous way and by means of special revelations, particularly where there is a lawful ministry that He has established in order to speak with men through it" (2.82-83).

13. "Cast aside everything that you presently feel and depend entirely on listening to the Word that you hear from your brother. . . . Whoever knows that it has been commanded by God that one comfort the other, can comfort himself and say: 'I am bound to believe my brother, because he is obliged to straighten out my perplexities of conscience and heal them by the Word; so I am obedient to God if I hear my brother'" (12.270-71).

14. Luther notes that, among other obstacles to faith, the Word of God often seems to contradict itself. How could the threat of an all-destroying flood in Noah's day be true, when God himself had given human beings the command to rule the earth? How could God command Abraham to sacrifice the very son through whom he had promised to give Abraham descendants? How could the same God who declared Jerusalem his resting place forever threaten the city with destruction (2.98-100; 4.92, 113)? "We know from Holy Scripture and from actual experience that when God's promises and threats are being fulfilled and taking their course, as it were, they seem to be altogether contradictory" (8.199).

prehension: "reason can know nothing at all about the divine substance" (34.227). "That there are three distinct Persons in the one Godhead," and that God became man — these doctrines, revealed by the Word, "neither will nor can appeal to reason" (34.216).[15] In short,

> [w]hoever wants to be a Christian must be intent on silencing the voice of reason. He must look and cleave to nothing but the Word spoken by the mouth of Christ. For the articles of our Christian faith sound ridiculous and nonsensical to reason. (23.99; cf. 12.288)

> By Scripture we are led to believe things that are absurd, impossible, and contrary to our reason. For this is the work of God to humble the proud and exalt the humble, to make something great of the least and vice versa. (16.183)

Admittedly, 1 Peter 3:15 exhorts believers to give an answer to those who inquire about their faith. They are to do so, Luther believes, simply by citing Scripture: the Word, after all, *is* the basis of their faith. Luther has nothing but scorn for the "sophists" who claim that Scripture is "too weak" to defeat the opponents of faith, so that natural reason must be employed for the purpose.[16] On the contrary,

> our faith transcends all reason and is solely a power of God. Therefore if people refuse to believe, you should keep silence; for you have no

---

15. "If reason here disturbs you and questions arise like those of the Turks [i.e., Muslims]: 'Are there, then, two gods?' answer: 'There is only one God, and still there is the Father and the Son.' 'How is this possible?' Respond with humility: 'I do not know.' For God did not wish these things to be discerned with the eyes. He only made it known in the Word and wished it to be believed" (12.49).

16. Appearances notwithstanding (he can even refer to reason as "Dame Jezebel" [*CS* 1.1.309]), Luther acknowledges reason as a gift of God. Indeed, where our relationship with God is not the subject, God has left it to human beings to manage things by their reason (3.322-23; 24.214, 228). "Other sciences and arts on earth" (i.e., those not concerned with spiritual matters) originate with, and are governed by, human reason (*CS* 1.2.293; cf. 16.82; *CS* 6.31). Scripture itself is rightly interpreted by reason that is illuminated by the Holy Spirit. Reason not so illuminated, however, is "under the devil's control" and "harmful" in its response to the Word (54.71). "Prior to faith and a knowledge of God, reason is darkness, but in believers it's an excellent instrument. Just as all gifts and instruments of nature are evil in godless men, so they are good in believers. Faith is now furthered by reason, speech, and eloquence, whereas they were only impediments prior to faith" (54.183). Cf. Althaus, *Theology*, 64-71.

obligation to force them to regard Scripture as God's Book or Word. It is sufficient for you to base your proof on Scripture. (30.107)

But if "the Word is an offense and foolishness" to unredeemed human nature (15.75, referring to Matt. 11:6), we may well ask how human beings can *ever* believe the Word when they hear it. Luther's simple answer is that, without a miracle, they cannot. "The flesh is not able to believe the Word of God" (19.8).

We have taught on the basis of Scripture that we are unable to perform even the slightest works without the Spirit of God. How, then, could we by our own strength perform the greatest work, namely, to believe? . . . God's power must be present and work faith in us. . . . When God creates faith in man, this is as great a work as if He were to create heaven and earth again. (30.14)

The patriarchs lived saintly lives, performed remarkable deeds, and overcame grave dangers. "But it was by far the greatest miracle that they lived in faith in the promises, since it seemed that the promises had vanished completely, and were invalid" (7.307). With Bernard of Clairvaux, Luther believes that no less a miracle than that of the incarnation itself was Mary's faith in its foretelling (5.234). He dismisses at once any suggestion that faith came easily to people in Bible times when God's Word was conveyed to them by an angel or accompanied by miraculous signs.[17]

Whoever does not receive the Word for its own sake, will never receive it for the sake of the preacher, even if all the angels preached it to him. And he who receives it because of the preacher does not believe in the Word, neither in God through the Word, but he believes the preacher and in the preacher. . . . Moreover, all who believed Christ because of his person and his miracles, fell from their faith when he was crucified. So it is in our day and so has it always been. The Word itself, without any regard to persons, must be enough for the heart, it must include and

17. See 5.21. Though true faith is not created by miraculous signs, Luther grants that such signs did accompany the revelation given to Moses and the initial proclamation of the gospel as *confirmation* of the Word (18.107-9; cf. 12.269). "Now that the apostles have preached the Word and have given their writings, and nothing more than what they have written remains to be revealed, no new and special revelation or miracle is needed. . . . Miracles are no longer necessary to confirm this doctrine. For the accompanying signs were given principally . . . to substantiate the new message of the apostles" (24.367-68).

lay hold of man, so that he, as if taken captive, feels how true and right it is. (*CS* 1.1.162-63)

Human faith is, in fact, the work of the Holy Spirit: "In the end, only the Holy Spirit from heaven above can create listeners and pupils who accept this doctrine and believe that the Word is God, that God's Son is the Word, and that the Word became flesh" (22.8). The Word of God that forms the *content* of faith comes to the individual from outside, proclaimed by another or read in Scripture; but conviction of the *truth* of this "external Word" comes from the inward working of the Holy Spirit (23.94; 38.87; 40.146).[18]

> What means does [the Holy Spirit] use and what skill does he employ thus to change the heart and make it new? He employs the proclamation and preaching of the Lord Jesus Christ. . . . But in addition to what is thus preached, something else is needed; for even though I hear the preaching, I do not at once believe. Therefore, God adds the Holy Spirit, who impresses this preaching upon the heart, so that it abides there and lives. (*CS* 2.1.278-79)

> The Word comes first, and with the Word the Spirit breathes upon my heart so that I believe. Then I feel that I have become a different person and I recognize that the Holy Spirit is there. (54.63)

> The Word I receive through the intellect, but to assent to that Word is the work of the Holy Spirit. (17.230)

As we have seen, Luther defines God's Word in a broad way that includes everything from prophetic oracles to the encouragement one believer offers another; but *beyond* the Word, in spiritual matters, he insists that people must not go.[19] He insists that they must not — because, of course, he sees them doing so, in three fatal ways.

1. Though God has chosen to reveal himself to human beings, that revelation inevitably remains partial; much about God must remain *un*revealed and hidden, since the divine essence transcends all human understanding.

---

18. See Althaus, *Theology*, 35-42.

19. "In matters pertaining to salvation we should learn, know, see, hear, and accept nothing but what God has spoken. We should abide by His Word, and neither try to improve on it nor to follow anything else" (22.313).

And "what is above us is none of our concern" (5.44). No one has taken more delight than Luther in pondering God as God has revealed himself in his Word. At the same time, no one has been more conscious than Luther that the revealed God is not God in his fullness, or more emphatic than Luther on the folly and peril of speculating about the hidden God. "You cannot grasp God in Himself, unless perchance you want a consuming fire" (16.55).[20]

But God himself seeks us. Because we cannot look on his "naked majesty," he has "enveloped" himself in forms suited to our perception (16.54; 1.11). If we would find him, we must "put away speculations and attempts at scaling heaven and cling to the Word." The God who is beyond our grasp can only be found where he has placed himself within our reach (17.375-76).[21]

> This is what St. John emphasizes in nearly every word of his Gospel: that one should abandon the sublime, beautiful thoughts with which reason and clever people occupy themselves, seeking God in the divine Majesty apart from Christ. He wants to see God lying in Christ's manger and at His mother's breast or hanging on the cross, whereas they want to climb up into heaven and find out how He sits on His throne and governs the world. . . . If you intend to discover and apprehend what God is and does and intends, then look for it nowhere else but in the place where He has put it. . . . A Christian should know that he is to seek and find God nowhere else but on the Virgin's lap and on the cross, or however and wherever Christ reveals Himself in the Word. (69.67)

> Anyone who wishes to know God must learn to know Him through the Word. (28.169)

In this connection, it is worth noting that Luther betrays minimal anxiety when he encounters anthropomorphic ways of speaking about God in Scripture;[22] indeed, he can declare them "most delightful."[23] For Ori-

---

20. See Steinmetz, *Luther*, 23-31.

21. For Luther's indebtedness to Staupitz on this point, see Oberman, *Luther*, 181-82.

22. "It is superfluous to enter on the subtle question here how God can repent, turn from and regret His anger, since He is unchangeable. Some people are deeply concerned about this; they complicate the matter for themselves unnecessarily" (19.88; cf. 33.71).

23. "Most delightful are the descriptions of this sort, when Scripture speaks about God as if He were a human being and attributes to Him all human qualities, namely, that He converses with us in a friendly manner and about matters similar to those which human beings discuss; that He is glad, is sad, and suffers like a human being" (4.133).

gen (and his legion of followers), a crucial stage in the process of spiritual maturation lay in rising above such references in order to arrive at a purer conception of the God who is spirit. Luther certainly recognizes the anthropomorphisms for what they are (1.173; 2.22, 94; 3.230; 19.8, etc.). But nobody, he suggests, is really deceived by such language,[24] and, in any case, what other way do we have to speak about God (1.14-15)?[25] God can only reveal himself "in some such veil or wrapper"; therefore, when we embrace the "wrapper" (i.e., Scripture's anthropomorphic language of God), we are embracing God as God has chosen to reveal himself (1.14-15; cf. 4.61-62). Nor should another important function of the anthropomorphisms be overlooked: when Scripture speaks about God in human terms, it prepares us to recognize the incarnate God in Christ (4.133).

At times, however, Luther does see fit to clarify scriptural references to divine emotions; his preferred explanation is that Scripture attributes to God the feelings felt by God's servants.[26] He considers this the "simplest" explanation, but its real virtue in his eyes is that readers, so satisfied, will not abandon the (anthropomorphic) language of Scripture and attempt to arrive at a higher understanding of the divine majesty than what God has revealed; they thus avoid "discussions about the absolute power or majesty of God, which are fraught with very great dangers" (2.44-47). Again,

> if we want to walk in safety, let us accept what the Word submits for our reflection and what God Himself wants us to know. Let us pass by other things — things not revealed in the Word. (1.14)

2. As we have seen, Luther placed great emphasis on the role of the Holy Spirit in creating faith in the believer. Luther's unique gift for clear, simple expression is evident when, in *The Small Catechism,* he explains the third article of the creed: "I believe that I cannot by my own understanding or effort believe in Jesus Christ my Lord, or come to him. But the Holy

---

24. "These are matters of grammar and the figurative use of words, which even schoolboys understand" (33.71).

25. "God lowers Himself to the level of our weak comprehension and presents Himself to us in images, in coverings, as it were, in simplicity adapted to a child, that in some measure it may be possible for Him to be known by us" (2.45).

26. "When Moses says that God sees and repents, these actions really occur in the hearts of the men who carry on the ministry of the Word. . . . When the spirit of Noah, of Lamech, and of Methuselah is grieved, God himself is said to be grieved. Thus we should understand this grief to refer to its effect, not to the divine essence" (2.44, 49).

Spirit has called me through the Gospel, enlightened me with his gifts, and sanctified and kept me in true faith." Note well: "the Holy Spirit . . . *through the Gospel*": the (external) Word (= the gospel) and (the inner working of) the Spirit *together* produce faith. The Word provides the content; the Spirit produces the conviction of its truth.

Luther had learned from experience the perils of neglecting the Word in the misbegotten belief that fresh revelations of the Spirit provide all the guidance one needs. Early on in his efforts as a reformer, Luther found himself beset by "fanatics" telling him what he should do on the basis of special revelations they had received. "Had I listened to any of them, it would certainly have been necessary to change the character of my doctrine 30 or 40 times." Instead, he chose to pray that he might be granted "the sure meaning and understanding of Holy Scripture. For if I have the Word, I know that I am proceeding on the right way" (7.119-20). When Christ declares that his words are "spirit and life" (John 6:63), "He binds us solely to His Word." "Christ does not want to give you the right to run to and fro in search of the Spirit, to lose yourself in reverie and say: 'I have this by inspiration of the Holy Spirit.' Actually, it may be the devil who inspired you!" (23.173). When Paul emphasizes that his teaching is "in accordance with the Scriptures" (1 Cor. 15:3),

> he does this in the first place to resist the mad spirits who disdain Scripture and the external message and in place of this seek other secret revelation. And today every place is also teeming with such spirits, confused by the devil, who regard Scripture a dead letter and boast of nothing but the Spirit. . . . The fact of the matter is that, although the letter by itself does not impart life, yet it must be present, and it must be heard or received. And the Holy Spirit must work through this in the heart, and the heart must be preserved in the faith through and in the Word against the devil and every trial. Otherwise, where this is surrendered, Christ and the Spirit will soon be lost. (28.76-77)

> The devil has no better way to conquer us than by leading us away from the Word and to the Spirit. (54.97)

3. Contrary to rumors that have persisted for half a millennium, Luther was not opposed to "good works." He did, to be sure, believe that a person is justified by faith, not works (more on this below[27]); but he also

---

27. See the section on "Law and Gospel" below.

believed that a genuine faith in response to the gospel — that is, a faith that originates in no merely human decision,[28] but in the convicting power of the Holy Spirit — cannot *but* produce good works.

> O it is a living, busy, active, mighty thing, this faith. It is impossible for it not to be doing good works incessantly. It does not ask whether good works are to be done, but before the question is asked, it has already done them, and is constantly doing them. Whoever does not do such works, however, is an unbeliever. (35.370; cf. 2.267)

But Luther believed the "good works" to be done by the believer are those prescribed in Scripture: "There are no good works except those works God has commanded" (44.23). Rightly understood, the ten commandments themselves give us more than enough to keep us busy every moment of the day. We are, for example, commanded to "honor God's name and not take it in vain" (cf. Exod. 20:7). But every moment of the day we are either receiving God's blessings or experiencing adversity. That means that every moment of the day we have the opportunity to obey God's command to honor his name by blessing him or invoking his aid. Even if we had "nothing else to do at all," this would keep us busy (44.39-40).

What, on the other hand, Luther perceived in the church of his day was a penchant for imposing demands not made in Scripture — to no good end.

> The works which are not commanded are the building of churches, beautifying them, making pilgrimages, and all those things of which so much is written in the ecclesiastical regulations. These things have misled and burdened the world, brought it to ruin, troubled consciences, silenced and weakened faith. It is also clear that a man has enough to engage all his strength to keep the commandments of God, and even if he neglects everything else, he can never do all the good works he is commanded to do. Why then does he seek other works which are neither necessary nor commanded, and yet neglect those that are necessary and commanded? (44.113-14)

---

28. "Faith is not the human notion and dream that some people call faith. . . . When they hear the gospel, they get busy and by their own powers create an idea in their heart which says, 'I believe'; they take this then to be a true faith. But, as it is a human figment and idea that never reaches the depths of the heart, nothing comes of it either, and no improvement follows" (35.370).

There is not a single word of God commanding us to call on either angels or saints to intercede for us, and we have no example of it in the Scriptures. . . . Thus the worship of saints shows itself to be nothing but human twaddle, man's own invention apart from the word of God and the Scriptures. Since in the matter of divine worship, however, it is not proper for us to undertake anything without God's command — whoever does so is tempting God — it is therefore neither to be advised nor tolerated that one should call upon the departed saints to intercede for him or teach others to call upon them. (35.198-99)

Here, again, the principle applies: in spiritual matters, we are to be bound by the Word, and by the Word alone.

The Word and Scripture

As we have seen, the Word of God, as Luther understands it, is by no means confined to Scripture. Indeed, Luther frequently finds it natural to add to "the Word" the qualifying "oral" (or "living"). It is in the spoken (or proclaimed) Word that the true nature of the Word is most clearly seen: through his Word, God addresses human beings. Something is lost when that Word is encountered, not in a living voice, but written on a page.[29] Inasmuch as the New Testament is essentially the proclamation of the gospel ("good news"), Luther finds it particularly inappropriate to speak of the New Testament as "scripture."

> [The Gospel] is the voice of one calling, not a piece of writing. (*CS* 1.1.130; cf. *CS* 2.1.183)

> The Gospel, or the New Testament, should really not be written but should be expressed with the living voice which resounds and is heard throughout the world. (30.18; cf. 30.3)

> [The Old Testament] alone bears the name of Holy Scripture. . . . Christ himself did not write anything but only spoke. He called his teaching not Scripture but gospel, meaning good news or a proclamation that is spread not by pen but by word of mouth. (35.123; cf. *CS* 1.1.44)

---

29. A similar point was made by Chrysostom; see Chapter 5 above.

It was the need to preserve the purity of the Word in the face of false teaching that necessitated the writing — contrary to its essence as proclamation — of the New Testament.

> Christ did not write his doctrines himself as Moses did, but he gave them orally, and commanded that they should be published abroad by preaching, and he did not command that they should be written. . . . That there was a necessity of writing books was in itself a great detriment and denotes an infirmity of the human spirit and does not arise out of the nature of the New Testament. For instead of pious preachers there came heretics, false teachers and all kinds of errorists giving the sheep of Christ poison in the place of pasture. Hence in order to rescue at least some of the sheep from the wolves it was necessary to write books [the New Testament] in harmony with the Scriptures [the Old Testament], so that as much as possible the lambs of Christ might be fed. (*CS* 1.1.372)

That said, it is nonetheless in the writings of Scripture (and in speech faithful to their content) that we meet the Word of God today. Luther can speak of "the Word" and "Scripture" interchangeably (e.g., 19.45; 34.227; *CS* 1.2.30). The apostles who delivered the Word in the past are now to be encountered in their writings — certainly not in displays of their relics!

> This is the true relic: that we have not only Paul and his Epistles but also the prophets and apostles, yes, even the Lord Christ Himself in Scripture, where we read and study them. [There] we hear them speak with us. . . . For when I hear a sermon in church, I am hearing Peter and Paul. Indeed, when in my study or chamber I read what they have written and taught, I am hearing them preach and speak with me there again day after day. For they did not teach or preach anything other than exactly what they had also written down. . . . Therefore, let us hold fast to the genuine and true relic, the noble and eternal treasure: the Word of God, which was taught, preached, and written down by the Holy Spirit through the mouth of the prophets and apostles. It is of benefit to body and soul, gives help and comfort in every need. (58.371-74)

Scripture, then, is the Word of God, in part because God speaks to us today through its words. But Scripture is divine in its origins as well: although "written by men," it is "neither of men nor from men but from God" (35.153). Luther repeatedly refers to the Holy Spirit as Scripture's "author" (e.g., 5.275; 7.314): "We attribute to the Holy Spirit all of Holy Scripture"

(15.275). Of course, he does not deny that human beings played an active role in the process. Typical of Luther, for example, is the suggestion that much of Scripture is the product of one scriptural writer's (Spirit-guided) reflection on the words of an earlier writer (especially Moses).

> This is the way that the prophets studied Moses, and the later prophets studied the earlier ones and wrote down their good thoughts, suggested by the Holy Spirit, in a book. (60.300)

> It is certainly evident that the prophets meditated day and night on the writings of Moses and especially on these accounts of the patriarchs, and that they drew wonderful conclusions from them. For the Holy Spirit comes to the aid of their diligence. (3.115)

> Just as all the art of the Greek poets flowed from Homer as from a spring, so also from [Moses] have flowed all the books of the prophets, and, indeed, also the entire New Testament, which is promised therein. And everything good and godly that has been and will be taught in the midst of the people or Church of God originally came from Moses. (60.299; cf. 9.6; 13.75; 23.35)

The human writers of Scripture also drew actively on sources — oral or written — that were available to them. Obadiah borrowed from Jeremiah (18.193), Isaiah from Micah (18.236). Moses himself drew on stories that had been passed down from Adam, Noah, Abraham, and Jacob in composing his narrative: indeed, Abraham may even have written up an account of the period from Adam to his own day (4.308; 6.134).[30] Luther believes that editors, too, had a role in the composition of various books of Holy Scripture.

> [Ecclesiastes] was certainly not written or set down by King Solomon with his own hand. Instead scholars put together what others had heard from Solomon's lips. . . . Certain persons selected by the kings and the people were at that time appointed to fix and arrange this and other books that were handed down by Solomon. . . . In like manner too, the book of the Proverbs of Solomon has been put together by others, with

30. See also 54.40-41: "I think many things had been written before Moses and that Moses took these things and added to them what God commanded him. No doubt he had the story of the creation from the tradition of the fathers." See 54.373. Luther's hesitation (noted above) to attribute much to unmediated divine revelation no doubt contributed to his inclination to see the writers of Scripture as using sources.

the teaching and sayings of some wise men added at the end. The Song of Solomon too has the appearance of a book compiled by others out of things received from the lips of Solomon. (35.263, interpreting Eccles. 12:11; cf. 15.12, 184-85)

Whether this was done by those who collected and wrote down [Isaiah's] prophecies (as is thought to have happened with the Psalter) or whether Isaiah himself arranged them this way as time, occasion, and persons suggested, I do not know. (35.277)

It seems as though Jeremiah did not compose these books himself, but that the parts were taken piecemeal from his utterances and written into a book. For this reason we must not worry about the order or be hindered by the lack of it. (35.280-81)

The result, nonetheless, is Holy Scripture, "a book which turns the wisdom of all other books into foolishness" (34.285). Its treasures are inexhaustible (14.8). A lifetime of a thousand years would not be long enough to understand fully even the Bible's first verse (54.159). Luther admitted that, after twenty-five years of preaching, he still did not understand the text: "He who through faith is righteous shall live" (54.287, referring to Rom. 1:17). Indeed, he doubted whether "Peter, Paul, Moses, and all the saints" ever really grasped "a single word of God." "Here one forever remains a learner" (54.9; cf. 12.305).[31]

[Mary] diligently searched God's Word, just as all those who firmly cling to God's Word do. They keep on searching and studying God's Word, and the longer they do this, the greater becomes their understanding of that Word, and the greater becomes the comfort they find in it. With each passing day their faith becomes more sure. (CS 5.146, referring to Luke 2:19)

Like Augustine and Aquinas before him, Luther insists that Scripture, as the Word of God, has an authority that cannot be accorded any other

---

31. Given that no single reader can ever exhaust a passage in Scripture, it is important to draw on the insights of others: "One falls short in some ways, another in more ways. I see some things that blessed Augustine did not see; on the other hand, I know that others will see many things that I do not see. What recourse do we have but to be of mutual help to one another and to forgive those who fall, since we ourselves have already fallen or are about to fall?" (14.285).

writing. In a good mood, he can speak respectfully of "the opinion of the holy fathers," but only to add, "We dare not give preference to the authority of men over that of Scripture!" (1.122; cf. 4.377-78; *CS* 1.2.81). "In the books of the fathers themselves we should value nothing that is not in agreement with Scripture; it alone should remain the judge and teacher in all books" (3.306). In less generous moments, he finds it difficult to extend his respect beyond Augustine (60.44); but even with Augustine, the boundaries remain.

> Even if Augustine had said so, who gave him the authority that we must believe what he says? What Scripture does he quote to prove this statement? What if he erred here, as we know he frequently did — just as did all the fathers? (35.150).

Bluntly put,

> the fathers do not count with me at all unless you have first proven that they have never erred. That you will do when the ass gets horns and the goat turns into a sheep! And when you have done that, I shall still say that no holy father has the power to command and to make an article of faith or a sacrament that Scripture did not command or make. (39.156)[32]

Given Luther's insistence on the unique authority of Scripture, we might expect him to define clearly which books belong to Holy Scripture, and which do not; in fact, however, things become fuzzy here, for at least two reasons. First, Luther was enough of a historian to know that the subject was debated in the early church. Augustine accepted a broader canon of Old Testament writings (one that included the apocryphal, or deuterocanonical, writings: Ecclesiasticus, Wisdom of Solomon, Tobit, etc.), whereas Jerome, following Jewish boundaries of Scripture, did not. In the early centuries, controversy surrounded the canonicity of several New Testament books as well, including Hebrews, James, Jude, and Revelation. Luther felt believers were free in such instances to make up their own minds; he famously exercised that freedom himself, though he was

---

32. Implicit in this latter quotation is a major difference between Luther, on the one hand, and Augustine and Aquinas, on the other. The three are agreed on the unique authority of Scripture. Only Luther, however, finds grounds to place the words of Scripture in sharp opposition to contemporary church practices and teaching. Cf. Pelikan, *Expositor,* 71-88; Muller, "Interpretation," 14.

not inclined to impose his opinions on others.[33] Second, Luther believed — following texts such as Luke 24:27, 44 and John 5:39, 46 — that the subject matter of all Scripture is Christ (15.268).[34] It followed that the boundaries of Scripture could be defined by the formula "what promotes Christ." Typically, Luther was not averse to expressing the principle in provocative terms:

> All the genuine sacred books agree in this, that all of them preach and inculcate [*treiben*] Christ. And that is the true test by which to judge all books, when we see whether or not they inculcate Christ. For all the Scriptures show us Christ, Romans 3[:21]; and St. Paul will know nothing but Christ, 1 Corinthians 2[:2]. Whatever does not teach Christ is not yet apostolic, even though St. Peter or St. Paul does the teaching. Again, whatever preaches Christ would be apostolic, even if Judas, Annas, Pilate, and Herod were doing it. (35.396)

As a result, the boundaries of Scripture are somewhat fluid in Luther's writings. The books of the Old Testament Apocrypha, he notes, "are not held equal to the Scriptures, but are useful and good to read" (35.232).[35] In writing prefaces to the individual books, however, he seems at times inclined to view at least some of them as Scripture. Judith "is a fine, good, holy, useful book, well worth reading by us Christians. For the words spoken by the persons in it should be understood as though they were uttered in the Holy Spirit by a spiritual, holy poet or prophet" (35.339). First Maccabees may not be in the Hebrew Bible, "yet its words and speech adhere to the same style as the other books of sacred Scripture," and it "would not have been unworthy of a place among them" (35.350). Noting that some in the early church regarded Wisdom of Solomon and Ecclesiasticus (Sirach) as belonging to Scripture, while others did not, Luther simply adds, "Be that as it may" (35.343), and "We shall let it go at that" (35.347); and throughout his writings he quotes Ecclesiasticus (and other books of

---

33. "To state my own opinion about [the epistle of St. James], *though without prejudice to anyone,* I do not regard it as the writing of an apostle" (35.395-96, italics added).

34. Luther paraphrases Jesus' words in John 5:39 as follows: "Study the Scriptures so as to find Me, Me in them. Whoever reads the Scriptures so that he finds Me in them is the true master of the Scriptures. The dust is removed from his eyes, and he will certainly find life in them. But if you do not find Me therein, then truly you have not rightly understood and studied them, and you do not have eternal life" (58.248; cf. *CS* 1.1.150).

35. On the other hand, he deemed Esther more noncanonical than the books of the Apocrypha (33.110)! See H. Bornkamm, *Luther,* 188-89.

the Apocrypha, though none other as frequently) alongside universally acknowledged texts without apparent differentiation. Second Maccabees he finds problematic and rejects;[36] but he adds immediately, "However, the whole thing is left and referred to the pious reader to judge and to decide" (35.353; cf. 32.96-97).

Among New Testament writings, he finds (but "without prejudice") the epistle of James to be "no truly apostolic epistle."[37] It has nothing to say about the chief articles of Christian faith, and it contradicts Paul's teaching on justification (30.12; 35.395-96; 54.424). The content of the epistle of Jude suggests that it comes from "a much later disciple of the apostles"; besides, nearly everything it contains has been borrowed from 2 Peter (30.203; cf. 35.397-98). The status of the epistle to the Hebrews was debated in the early church; its content shows that it cannot have been written by Paul (Heb. 2:3; contrast Gal. 1:11-12); in places (6:4-6; 10:26-27; 12:17) it contradicts the Gospels as well as the letters of Paul. As a result, "we cannot put it on the same level with the apostolic epistles." Nonetheless, it contains much fine material — "gold, silver, precious stones" — so that "we should not be deterred if wood, straw, or hay are perhaps mixed with them" (35.394-95). Luther was content to "leave everyone free to hold his own opinions" about Revelation (35.398); his own opinions varied. At one point he claimed (again, while allowing others to think differently) that it is "neither apostolic nor prophetic" and betrays no evidence that the Holy Spirit had a role in its production (35.398); later, he at least attempted an interpretation of the book that would yield comfort and warning (35.409).

Among the acknowledged books of Scripture, some are more central than others.

> St. John's Gospel and his first epistle, St. Paul's epistles, especially Romans, Galatians, and Ephesians, and St. Peter's first epistle are the books that show you Christ and teach you all that is necessary and salvatory for you to know, even if you were never to see or hear any other book or doctrine. (35.362)

36. "Just as it is proper for [1 Maccabees] to be included among the sacred Scriptures, so it is proper that this second book should be thrown out, even though it contains some good things" (35.353).

37. "I cannot include [James] among the chief books, though I would not thereby prevent anyone from including or extolling him as he pleases, for there are otherwise many good sayings in him" (35.397).

Because the words of Christ are what give life (John 6:63), John's Gospel surpasses Matthew, Mark, and Luke in importance: "John writes very little about the works of Christ, but very much about his preaching, while the other evangelists write much about his works and little about his preaching" (35.362).[38] But "the chief part of the New Testament" and "the purest gospel" is to be found in Paul's letter to the Romans: "It appears that [Paul] wanted in this one epistle to sum up briefly the whole Christian and evangelical doctrine." It would be a good idea for every Christian to know the entire epistle "word for word, by heart" (35.365, 380).

Luther betrays little awareness of, and even less concern about, variations in biblical manuscripts.[39] Only troublemakers (who "seek to disturb the simplicity of the faithful") make an issue of the absence of much of Mark 16, or of the story of the adulteress in John 8, in some manuscripts. He peremptorily cuts off discussion of the matter with a rhetorical question: Are we to "demand that everything be written and read in all the codices"? (60.55). On the other hand, he is very conscious of the frequent errors to be found in various translations of Scripture,[40] and he laments the cavalier way in which the Greek Septuagint at times rendered the original Hebrew: he assigned it no authority.[41] He himself was a serious student of Hebrew (cf. 8.262), and he advised others to take up its study: "A knowledge of it adds remarkably to the ability of explaining the Scriptures" (12.33; cf. 4.154). "Future teachers of religion," in particular, should apply themselves to the study of Hebrew — "unless you want to be taken for dumb cattle and uninstructed rabble who somehow teach the Sunday

38. Elsewhere, Luther gives priority to John's Gospel because it discusses "the chief article [i.e., faith and Christ] thoroughly and powerfully," whereas Matthew, Mark, and Luke emphasize the importance of good works: they are in fact "better than John" on this latter issue. "Of course, it is appropriate that in Christendom both should be preached, yet each in keeping with its nature and value" (21.65; cf. also 23.108-9).

39. He did, however, allow for errors in transmission of the text. See H. Bornkamm, *Luther,* 191-92.

40. "Whoever the translator of this passage was, he ought to be called a lot of names. Not only did he awkwardly confuse the two parts of the verse, but he produces an ungodly meaning" (12.351). Less colorful complaints can be found in 1.204; 2.185; 12.82; 15.16, 330, etc.

41. "It seems that the translators of the Septuagint were too daring or that some rascal falsified their book. For one must not cover up this error. And there are other passages in which they talked idly either out of ignorance or out of dishonesty. Therefore I do not consider them authoritative" (8.88). Elsewhere, Luther notes simply (and, in many cases, quite correctly): "The translators of the Septuagint likewise appear not to have had adequate knowledge to cope with the vastness of the task they had undertaken" (1.263). Note also the mixed review of one verse in the Septuagint: "The sense of the Septuagint is beautiful, but the grammar of the text militates against it" (18.155).

Gospels and the Catechism with the help of books that have appeared in German. We need theological leaders" (12.199).[42]

> Even if this language [Hebrew] were useless otherwise, one should still learn it out of thankfulness. It is a part of religion and divine worship to teach or learn this language through which alone we can learn anything at all of the divine. In it we hear God speak, we hear how the saints call upon God and achieve the mightiest deeds; thus study directed toward learning this language might rightly be called a kind of Mass or divine service. (12.198-99)

Not that the Word of God is necessarily lost in translation: one of Luther's own most labor-intensive,[43] lasting, and remarkable achievements was the translation of the entire Bible into the German "of the mother in the home, the children on the street, the common man in the market-place." A literal rendering of the original would not do.[44] "We must be guided by [the common people's] language, the way they speak, and do our translating accordingly. That way they will understand it and recognize that we are speaking German to them" (35.189).

In the end, Christians (like Augustine!) who have learned no Hebrew but who know that Jesus Christ is the "meaning and import of the Bible" are better equipped to understand the Old Testament than those who know the Hebrew letters and words but lack this understanding. No real

---

42. Greek, of course, is to be learned as well: "It has been my experience that the languages are extraordinarily helpful for a clear understanding of the divine Scriptures. This was also the feeling and opinion of St. Augustine; he held that there should be some people in the church who could use Greek and Hebrew before they deal with the Word, because it was in these two languages that the Holy Spirit wrote the Old and New Testaments" (36.304). On Luther's enthusiastic reception of Erasmus's Greek New Testament, see Oberman, *Luther,* 171, 214.

43. "I have constantly tried, in translating, to produce a pure and clear German, and it has often happened that for two or three or four weeks we have searched and inquired for a single word and sometimes not found it even then. In translating Job, Master Philip [Melanchthon], [Matthew] Aurogallus, and I labored so, that sometimes we scarcely handled three lines in four days" (35.188). As this quotation indicates, the labor was not entirely Luther's own; he was not in the least hesitant about consulting other scholars, or about acknowledging their assistance (cf. also 35.250-51).

44. At times one must "relinquish" the words in order to render the sense (35.213). On the other hand, when it came to crucial texts whose interpretation hinged on the precise wording used, Luther preferred to keep to the original "quite literally" rather than impose his own understanding through a freer rendering (35.194, 216-17). Translating, he came to recognize, is a skill that cannot be reduced to any set of rules (35.193).

harm comes from mistaking the name of a plant in Jonah 4:6; but those who do not know Christ

> cannot know or understand what Moses, the prophets, and the psalms are saying, what true faith is, what the Ten Commandments purport, what tradition and story teach and prove. . . . Scripture must be to them what a letter is to an illiterate. Indeed, he may see the letters, but he is ignorant of their significance. (15.268-69)

Scripture's Clarity and Truth

To Luther's claim that Scripture alone is our authority in spiritual matters, the objection was raised that Scripture is too obscure to provide the guidance needed. Luther responded by making a variety of distinctions and observations.

1. That there is much about God that is necessarily hidden from us does not mean that what God has chosen to reveal is obscure (33.25, 27).

2. That we cannot understand *how* God can be three persons in one deity, or *how* Christ can be both God and man, does not mean that Scripture's statements to that effect are themselves obscure. Scripture simply is not concerned to tell us *how* these things can be, nor do we need to know (33.28).

3. Many individual passages in Scripture are obscure to us because of our imperfect understanding of the language used.[45] Luther notes repeatedly that there are words and idioms in the Hebrew Bible whose meaning no one knows (e.g., 7.157; 15.105; 16.48; 18.81, 345), grammatical usages that we find difficult (16.47), references to customs with which we are unfamiliar (16.237). It is wrong to ascribe obscurity to Scripture when the problem lies rather with its readers. In any case, the subject matter of Scripture remains clear and accessible, even if the meaning of certain words and phrases escapes us (33.25-26).

4. Nor should Scripture be deemed obscure merely because the spiritual blindness of many readers keeps them from seeing truth that is clearly presented (16.243). The problem may also lie with the "indolence" of readers "who will not take the trouble to look at the very clearest truth" (33.27).

---

45. "I do not claim for myself an exact knowledge of the Hebrew language. Nor do I think that anyone today or anyone at the time of the apostles mastered it perfectly. It is sufficient for us to study it and to make progress as we do so, since we can never reach the stage of perfection that would enable us to speak and judge in the same way Samuel, David, and Isaiah spoke" (8.262; cf. 30.23; 33.25).

Nor should we overlook "the malice of Satan" as a factor in human failure to understand God's words (33.99).

5. Like Augustine, Luther believed that Scripture is "clear enough in respect to what is necessary for salvation," even though it deliberately includes certain obscure passages in order to challenge more "inquiring minds." There is something here for everyone: "Let everyone search for his portion in the most abundant and universal Word of God" (32.217).

6. What Scripture puts obscurely in some texts is clearly expressed in others (33.26). Readers troubled by the obscure should simply "set [it] aside" and "cling to the clear" (32.217).[46]

7. To those who claim that "Scripture is so obscure that we cannot understand it without the interpretation of the holy fathers," it should be pointed out that the writings of the fathers are by no means plainer than Scripture (39.163-64). Moreover, the fathers themselves substantiate their claims by quoting Scripture; they would hardly have done so if they had not considered the Scriptures clear and reliable (32.11).

8. "If Scripture is obscure, or ambiguous, what point was there in God's giving it to us?" And why, then, would Paul have pronounced all Scripture "profitable" (2 Tim. 3:16)? Or why did Christ tell his listeners to "search the Scriptures" in order to find witness to him (John 5:39)? And what are we to make of all the passages in the Psalms (especially Ps. 119) that praise God's Word as a clear light for our paths (33.92-94)?

In short, "it ought above all to be settled and established among Christians that the Holy Scriptures are a spiritual light far brighter than the sun itself, especially in things that are necessary for salvation" (33.91).

And, as the Word of God, Scripture is necessarily true. Stated thus baldly, the point seems self-evident; for Luther, however, it is anything but trivial, and over the course of a life of faith, it often appears false.

The truthfulness of the Word of God is crucial because our eternal salvation depends on it. Where so much is at stake, we cannot rely on the words of "Augustine or another holy father"; after all, they are only human. "Who will be surety and guarantee that they speak the truth? Who will rely upon it and die by it?" (*CS* 1.2.81). "As little as one can come to the knowledge of God and the truth and to the right faith without the Word of God, just so little can one find comfort and peace of conscience without it" (12.164).

But for Luther, the essence of the Christian life consists of the need

---

46. See 20:108: "Those statements which have been uttered very simply without any figurative language and obscure words interpret those which are uttered with figurative and metaphorical language."

to trust the truthfulness of God's Word under circumstances where such faith is severely tested; for God "kills" before he "makes alive," and "brings down to hell" before he "raises up."[47]

> God's faithfulness and truth always must first become a great lie before it becomes truth. . . . God cannot be God unless He first becomes a devil. We cannot go to heaven unless we first to go hell. We cannot become God's children until we first become children of the devil. . . . But this is not the whole story. The last word is: "His faithfulness and truth endure forever." (14.31-32)[48]

In the lectures on Genesis from Luther's later years, he focuses attention again and again on how Moses illustrates the perennial trials of the life of faith.[49] God's people are constantly called on to exercise faith in the truthfulness of God's promises in the most unpromising of circumstances. Noah, in response to the Word of God — itself unbelievable — lived at odds with his entire generation: "Apart from his own children and his godly grandfather, [Noah] did not find one human being in the entire world who approved either of his religious views or of his life" (2.87). What vindication he found in the coming of the flood was offset by new causes for despair: "It was no joke or laughing matter for them to live shut up in the ark for so long, to see the endless masses of rain, to be tossed about by the waves, and to drift" (2.105). When Scripture then says that "the Lord

---

47. So 1 Sam. 2:6, a verse to which Luther makes constant reference. Drawing on another favorite verse (Isa. 28:21), however, Luther will say that when God "kills" and "brings down to hell," he is performing his "alien work" (i.e., something foreign to his nature, though required by human sinfulness); it is God's "proper" work "to raise up" and "make alive" (13.135; 16.233-35).

48. See 7.103: "When God works, He turns His face away at first and seems to be the devil, not God." There is, of course, method to this apparent madness. God "vexes us" (and so takes on the appearance of the devil, while at the same time making his promised blessings appear a lie) in order to humble us and to "clean out" the sin that clings to our nature (8.5). "This is the way the Holy Spirit operates. First, He humbles. Then He lifts up and brings back saved those He has humbled and condemned or hurled down into hell" (20.12-13).

49. "Genesis, therefore, is made up almost entirely of illustrations of faith and unbelief, and of the fruits that faith and unbelief bear" (35.237). Luther notes repeatedly that "the most saintly fathers and mothers [i.e., those whose stories are told in Genesis] underwent the same experiences we are wont to undergo" (4.189-90; cf. 2.53; 4.194). Convinced that human nature is always the same ("the world is always the same" [1.351] and "the same old Adam is present in all of us" [15.21; cf. 14.290; 15.192]), Luther constantly finds counterparts to his own experience in the words of Scripture (e.g., 16.8, 172; 17.298), and he even uses his own experience to fill in gaps in the scriptural narrative (e.g., 2.57, 219; 18.79).

remembered Noah," the words must not be passed over quickly as a mere point of grammar, a figure of speech: "A grammarian does not understand what it means to live in such a manner as to feel that God has forgotten you."[50] "I would despair under such great misfortunes unless the Lord gave me the same spirit that Noah had. Noah is an illustrious and grand example of faith" (2.87).

Or consider the example of Joseph. As the son of Jacob, he had God's promise of blessing. But it was Joseph's experience that God hid himself "under the form of the worst devil" (7.175). Luther uses bold but by no means empty metaphors in saying that "the very saintly and good Joseph was crucified, died, was buried, and descended into hell" before finally being "restored to life" (7.129). Stories like these show us what true worship of God really means. "The worship of the fathers is a waiting. . . . If you want to serve God, you must believe things that are invisible, hope for things that are delayed, and love God — even if He shows Himself unfriendly and opposed to you — and thus persevere until the end" (4.322, 324).

> All the works of God are in conflict with His promise, which nevertheless remains completely true and unshaken. . . . The marvelous counsels of God in governing His saints must be learned, and the hearts of the godly must become accustomed to them. When you have a promise of God, it will happen that the more you are loved by God, the more you will have it hidden, delayed, and turned into its opposite. (4.326)

As we have seen, Christians today encounter God's Word in Scripture. For Christians, then, faith in the truthfulness of God's Word, as exemplified by the saints of Genesis, means clinging — in spite of appearances — to the promises God gives his people in Scripture, convinced of the reliability of God's Word.

> Where this Word enters the heart in true faith, it fashions the heart like unto itself, it makes it firm, certain, and assured. It becomes buoyed up, rigid, and adamant over against all temptation, devil, death, and

---

50. The quotation continues: "The most perfect saints are those who understand these matters and who in faith can bear with a God who is, so to speak, forgetful. For this reason the psalms and the entire Bible are full of such laments in which men call upon God to arise, to open His eyes, to hear, and to awake. . . . This expression should not be passed over as a mere matter of grammar. . . . But one must take into consideration the state of mind and the indescribable groaning of the heart when, in the very feeling of despair, a spark of faith still remains and overcomes the flesh" (2.104-5).

whatever its name may be, that it defiantly and haughtily despises and mocks everything that inclines toward doubt, despair, anger, and wrath; for it knows that God's Word cannot lie to it. (15.272)

But Luther also says that "Scripture does not lie" in contexts where he means that its stories really happened, and its statements are factually correct (cf. 2.232-33). Curiously, he can allow that stories in the Apocrypha may not be historical — and that they are none the worse for that. He is very much taken by the view that Judith is "a beautiful religious fiction [*Gedicht*] by a holy and ingenious man who wanted to sketch and depict therein the fortunes of the whole Jewish people and the victory God always miraculously granted them over all their enemies." It is "a fine, good, holy, useful book, well worth reading by us Christians" (35.338-39). Even if the stories of Tobit are "made up," it too remains "a very beautiful, wholesome, and useful fiction or drama by a gifted poet" (35.345). "It is the work of a fine Hebrew author who deals not with trivial but important issues, and whose writing and concerns are extraordinarily Christian" (35.347). In support of the usefulness of such pious fiction, Luther cites the parables of Jesus and the visions of Daniel and Revelation (35.338).

Still, Luther apparently sees no place for unmarked pious but fictional narratives in the canonical Scriptures. If it could be proved "that the events in Judith really happened, it . . . should properly be in the Bible" — but, implicitly, not otherwise (35.337). Conversely, Luther can say that he would find certain narratives in the canonical Scriptures unbelievable — were it not that they are contained in the Bible (1.123; 19.16, 68). The realism with which he reads (for example) the stories of Noah and Jonah is striking.

> I myself believe that the manure was thrown out, perhaps through the window. Since there were so many animals in the ark for more than a year, it was necessary to get rid of the manure. (2.67)

> Is it not a miracle that these eight human beings [Noah and his family] did not die of grief and fear? We are indeed devoid of feeling if we can read this account with dry eyes. (2.97)

> It must have been a horrifying sight to poor, lost, and dying Jonah when the whale opened its mouth wide and he beheld sharp teeth that stood upright all around like pointed pillars or beams and he peered down the wide cellar entrance to the belly. Is that being comforted in the hour of death? . . . How strange his abode must have been among the intestines

and the huge ribs! . . . Who can really comprehend how a man can survive three days and three nights within a fish, in the middle of the sea,
all alone, without light and without food, and in the end return to dry
land again? (19.67-68)

If the Garden of Eden is not now to be found on earth, it must be
because it was destroyed in the flood (1.89-91).[51] Cain married a sister not
mentioned in Genesis; "I fully believe that during the first thirty years
the marriage of our first parents was very prolific" (1.281-82; cf. 1.306).
Sarah, though in her eighth decade, was so eye-catchingly beautiful that
her husband feared for his life among strangers. "That generation must
have been more vigorous and of a far stronger constitution than is the
case today" — and, besides, they were "aided by a mild climate" (3.322-23,
referring to Gen. 20). If we follow the chronological indications given in
Genesis (and Luther scrupulously does), "Judah was only twelve when he
married" and "his three sons were born during the next two years": again,
"we must conclude that at that time nature was far stronger and far more
robust, both in males and in females, than it is now" (7.9). Luther proposes
various explanations of how language differences between the wise men
and Mary and Joseph could have been overcome (*CS* 1.1.364).

These texts surely suggest that Luther takes statements in the Bible
at face value as factually correct. On balance, this appears to be his settled conviction, and at least part of what he means when he says that "the
Holy Spirit neither lies nor errs nor doubts" (37.279), or that the Holy
Spirit "must not fight against Himself [i.e., contradict himself in Scripture]"
(28.261; cf. 15.313; 26.295). Admittedly, Luther's forthright spontaneity
keeps the evidence from being one-sided.

That he finds statements in the epistle to the Hebrews and the epistle of James contradictory of claims in the letters of Paul means little in
this context, since, as we have seen, Luther treats neither of the former
epistles as on a level with the canonical Scriptures. Further complicat-
ing the issue, though eminently worth bearing in mind in this context, is
Luther's strong sense that some things in Scripture are more important
than others, and his relative indifference toward the latter.[52] Luther is not

51. Part of Luther's agenda at this point is to insist on a historical rather than allegorical
reading of Gen. 1–3; see the discussion of Scripture's "historical sense" below.

52. "The purpose of the whole Scripture is this: to teach, reprove, correct, and train in
righteousness" (15.194, referring to 2 Tim. 3:16-17). Luther has nothing but scorn for those
who make a pretentious display of scriptural erudition on peripheral matters (such as the
details of Moses' tabernacle and the priestly garments) while they dismiss as commonplace

a compulsive harmonizer, as Chrysostom and Augustine at times appear to have been.[53]

> There is no reason for us to bother ourselves with these and similar difficulties.[54] After all, the life and sum of our faith do not lie in them. Those people who labor over nonessential matters of this sort are more than mad. (20.125)

> This question, to be sure, and others like it do not bother me greatly, because they do not serve any great purpose. . . .[55] Whoever likes idle strife, let him go on questioning; he will find that he is doing more questioning than answering. (20.321-22)

> No one will go to heaven or hell on account of whether he thinks that all three [of Peter's] denials occurred in the house of Caiaphas. . . . We do not care to investigate such clever questions and subtle opinions and speculations in detail. In this passage, we should attend above all to the great, boundless comfort afforded to sinners. (69.184-85; see also 69.198-99)

> These are problems and will remain problems.[56] I shall not venture to settle them. Nor are they essential. It is only that there are so many sharp

---

the essentials of the faith ("through Christ we are redeemed and saved from sin and death," "God's law is to be kept," "cross and affliction must be borne, etc.") (20.156).

53. Luther does of course wrestle with texts on more important matters that seem in tension with each other. He does not dismiss, e.g., the question how psalms that speak of hatred toward evildoers can be reconciled with Christ's command to love our enemies. He concludes that people may be hated only with respect to their false teaching (in that regard, "I must hate them or I must hate God, who commands and wills that men should cling to his word alone"); with regard to their persons, however, "I should be at their service" and "love them" (12.194; cf. 14.244-45, 257-58).

54. The issue is the attribution, in Matt. 27:9, to Jeremiah of a quotation not found in that book. In the sentences immediately preceding the quotation above, Luther (like Augustine) asserts that Matthew would have dismissed any suggestion that he should alter what he had written: "There undoubtedly were with Matthew saintly and learned men, filled with the Spirit, who advised him that the Scripture which he cited was in Zechariah, not in Jeremiah. Admonished by their advice, he could have corrected that slight error, had he wished or had he thought it important. But there is no reason for us to bother ourselves with these and similar difficulties. . . ."

55. The issue, here again, is the attribution of the quotation in Matt. 27:9 to Jeremiah.

56. Luther here is speaking of the difference between the dating of the cleansing of the temple in John's Gospel (early in Jesus' ministry) and that in Matthew (just before the crucifixion).

and shrewd people who are fond of bringing up all sorts of subtle questions and demanding definite and precise answers. But if we understand Scripture properly and have the genuine articles of our faith — that Jesus Christ, God's Son, suffered and died for us — then our inability to answer all such questions will be of little consequence. (22.218)

Yet Luther, at times, *does* harmonize, and when he does so, he betrays the same instincts and presuppositions we encounter in the more determined scriptural problem-solvers. Witness the following examples.

According to the narrative of Genesis 29 and 30, Jacob had eleven sons and one daughter during the seven years in which he worked for Laban as compensation for Laban's daughter Rachel. (Laban had already given Jacob, after an initial seven years of service, his older daughter, Leah.) During those seven years, Leah bore him four sons; sufficient time must be allowed for that. *Then* Rachel's maid Bilhah bore Jacob sons five and six. *Then* Leah's maid Zilpah bore him sons seven and eight. Leah *then* bore him sons nine and ten as well as a daughter. *Then* (if we follow the sequence of the narrative) Rachel bore him Joseph. Luther sees the problem ("the question arises how Jacob could beget twelve children in seven years," during the last three of which "eight must have been born . . . which is impossible" [5.337]), and solves it by suggesting that Scripture sometimes tells things out of order: four of Joseph's brothers were in fact born at a later time, during the six years in which Jacob was serving Laban for cattle. Furthermore, and again in spite of the sequence in the Genesis narrative, Joseph himself must have the seventh, not the eleventh, of Jacob's sons to be born. If we thus take into account the recognized and permissible procedure by which events are told out of sequence, the truthfulness of the scriptural narrative is preserved (5.338-40).

According to Numbers 18:21, all tithes were to be given to the Levites; according to Deuteronomy 14:22-27, the Israelites were to take their own tithes up to Jerusalem and consume them there. Many modern scholars attribute such differences in Pentateuchal law to the use of sources from different periods. Rabbinic Judaism accounted for this particular difference by labeling the tithe of Numbers 18 the "first tithe," that of Deuteronomy 14 "the second." Luther proposes another solution. The tithes were to be given to the Levites, as indicated in Numbers. In Deuteronomy 14, Moses is so focused on identifying the *place* where the tithes are to be consumed that he leaves unclear *who* is to do the eating (9.124-25).[57]

---

57. Other examples of harmonization can be found in 1.357-58; 2.239; 22.218-19; 30.121-

On the other hand, at times Luther appears to despair of the possibility of harmonization: "If anyone is able to harmonize these seventy-five years with the age of Terah, who lived two hundred and five years, I shall acknowledge him as a master" (2.277, referring to Gen. 11:32; 12:4; cf. 11:26). In any case, Luther's understanding of the truthfulness of Scripture is broad enough to accommodate such observations as the following.

1. In interpreting Genesis 1, we must bear in mind (as Augustine had already pointed out) that Moses was writing for "uneducated men" (1.19; cf. 1.43).[58]

2. The Greek Old Testament often mistranslates the Hebrew original, and at times the New Testament quotes the mistranslated Greek (19.110, 123; cf. 16.97). In Acts 7:14, Stephen actually repeats an incorrect number given in the Septuagint (8.88).

3. In other ways, too, Moses and Stephen (in Acts 7) contradict each other (2.277). Moses is the accurate historian; Stephen "certainly derived his knowledge of this story from Moses alone. But when we relate something incidentally, it often happens that we do not pay such close attention to all details" (2.278).

4. In general, when the New Testament quotes the Old, it often reproduces the substance — but not the wording — of the original (19.167; 20.125, 148-49, 321-22; CS 1.1.29).

5. Scripture must be allowed its approximations. If one text says 400 years (Gen. 15:13), another 430 (Gal. 3:17), this is close enough. We do the same thing (3.35).

6. "When one often reads [in the Bible] that great numbers of people were slain — for example, eighty thousand — I believe that hardly one thousand were actually killed. . . . Whoever strikes the king strikes everything he possesses. So if the king of France should be defeated with ten thousand of his men, it is said that eighty thousand were defeated because

---

22; CS 1.1.353. A particularly striking example is cited by Barr, "Chronology," 55-56, who pointedly notes a common criticism of modern biblical scholarship: "It is over-devoted to historical reconstructions, which by their nature are hypothetical and speculative. Scholars do not explain the text but the [conjectured] events that lay behind it." Barr says that that applies equally to Luther (66). It remains the case, however, that the occasions when Luther succumbs to the temptation of the harmonizer — to save the veracity of the biblical text by rewriting it — are relatively rare.

58. Astronomers use technical terms. "By way of contrast the Holy Spirit and Holy Scripture know nothing about those designations and call the entire area above us 'heaven.' Nor should an astronomer find fault with this; let each of the two speak in his own terminology" (1.47-48).

he has that many in his power, etc. Otherwise I can't reconcile the numbers" (54.452).[59]

7. Luther believes that the events recorded in Job really took place, but they formed the basic plot on which a writer (perhaps Solomon; in any case, a great theologian), fashioning speeches (that captured the thoughts, though not the words, of Job) and adding characters and circumstances, "paint[ed] a picture of patience" (54.79-80).

That Luther betrays no great zeal for harmonizing texts in apparent tension with each other is no doubt partly because Scripture's truth was not in dispute in his day. Nor (as we have seen) did he think it of any importance to resolve issues like the location(s) in which Peter denied Jesus.[60] He had, as we say, bigger fish to fry.

Interpreting Scripture: The Historical Sense

All of these issues could have been avoided had Luther simply adopted Origen's motto: "When in trouble, allegorize!" After all the bad things Luther had said about Origen, that option may simply not have been open; but one should not underestimate the real differences in their understanding of Scripture. In a nutshell, Scripture's divine character was evident to Origen in its capacity to convey truth at multiple levels; it was evident to Luther in the effective power of its words, understood (necessarily) in their simple, straightforward sense.[61]

> The Word of the Holy Spirit is a sharp arrow, that is, blessed and successful and effective. The Word is not indolent, but accomplishes many great things. It raises the sorrowful, guides the perplexed, calls back and refutes the erring. It provides innumerable other fruits, and is an altogether omnipotent thing. (12.229, referring to Ps. 45:5)

59. Cf. Luther's creative interpretation of Jonah 3:3 (the claim that Nineveh was a city "three days' journey in breadth" is taken to mean that it would take three days to walk through all its neighborhoods step by step "with a leisurely gait such as one usually adopts when strolling on a street"!), in light of his recognition that a city of 120,000 (Jonah 4:11) cannot have been all *that* big (19.22, 84).

60. In noting Luther's lack of concern over such details, we may add that, unlike Origen, he was not inclined to seek profound truth behind every name, number, or word of Scripture's text. His concern was with the "big picture."

61. Muller, "Interpretation," 8-14, notes the measure of continuity between Luther's (and the Reformation's) focus on the literal meaning of the text and similar emphases in some medieval exegetes.

The Christian reader should make it his first task to seek out the literal sense, as they call it. For it alone is the whole substance of faith and Christian theology; it alone holds its ground in trouble and trial, conquers the gates of hell (Matt. 16:18) together with sin and death, and triumphs for the praise and glory of God. (9.24)

First of all the historical sense must be sought. It gives us correct and solid instruction; it fights, defends, conquers, and builds. (5.347; cf. 6.125)

Scripture can only have such force when its meaning is clear; and only the literal sense of Scripture is "simple, pertinent, and sure" (3.27).[62] The "sure and true meaning . . . cannot be any other than that of the letter and the text, or of the historical account" (3.28). Allegorical interpretation yields many possibilities ("just as many shapes can be formed from a single piece of wax" [3.28]); but since they are largely the product of "human guesswork and opinion," they are too "uncertain" and "unreliable" to serve as the basis for a faith seeking guidance and assurance from God (9.24).[63] "Interpretations of God's Word must be lucid and definite having a firm, sure, and true foundation on which one may confidently rely" (40.190).[64]

Luther can cite Augustine in support of the principle that doctrine can only be based on the literal sense of the text. It is there, then, that interpreters must begin. Once they have established the literal sense, they are free — should they so wish — to indulge in allegorical readings as well, but only to illustrate or embellish points whose truth has already been established

62. Luther often speaks of the "literal" sense, but also of the "simple and sound" sense (2.386), the "historical" sense (1.185, 233), "the grammatical and historical sense" (16.328; cf. 39.181), the "grammatical and proper sense" (36.30), and the "simple, pure, and natural sense of the words that accords with the rules of grammar and the normal use of language as God has created it in man" (33.162). "The Holy Spirit is the simplest writer and adviser in heaven and on earth. That is why his words could have no more than the one simplest meaning which we call the written one, or the literal meaning of the tongue" (39.178).

63. "Those who busy themselves with Holy Writ should take pains to have one definite and simple understanding of Scripture. . . . To hold varying views is nothing else than not knowing. . . . If I have to read a passage of Scripture that is so uncertain and equivocal, I shall prefer to read Vergil and Ovid" (8.209-10).

64. Luther's sense (not shared by most of those who interpreted Scripture allegorically) that the church of his day had gone astray both in its teaching and practice and, consequently, that only the authority of the Bible could be relied on, no doubt contributed to his conviction that the language of Scripture must be clear. Cf. Thompson, *Ground*, 196.

by the literal reading of the text (1.233; 6.125; 9.24-25; 16.136-37).[65] Luther often provided secondary allegorical readings of his own, generally ones that illustrated favorite themes, such as the distinction between law and gospel (2.158-64; 5.88; 9.7, 134-35).[66] And provided they were consonant with the faith, he could be tolerant of the allegorical interpretations of others (2.68), even where they were clearly based on error.[67]

It must be granted, too, that at times Luther in effect adopts Origen's principle: a text whose literal meaning is absurd must be interpreted differently (18.114; 32.168; cf. 33.162). He is, to be sure, far less ready than Origen to concede absurdity at the literal level: for example, God speaking to a serpent in the Garden of Eden does not qualify (1.185). But Luther cannot accept that the Song of Solomon might be a "love song"; instead, it is written in praise of the well-ordered state (15.194-96). Equally incredible, in his mind, is the notion that God would literally command Hosea to marry a prostitute: "Hosea is speaking allegorically" (35.318). Moreover, impossible details in the prophetic promises of Israel's (or Judah's) restoration after the exile are, for Luther, indications that the promises are to be applied to the spiritual kingdom of Christ (15.285; 17.315; 18.113-14, 121, 247-48; 35.288, 290-93, 322; *CS* 3.2.336-37).

Interpreting Scripture: Law and Gospel, Old Testament and New

Read at its literal level, the content of Scripture can be divided into two categories: law and gospel (54.111). Keeping the categories distinct is crucial to reading Scripture aright (54.42; *CS* 1.1.100).

The term "law," in this context, represents everything that God expects of us: "what we are to do and give to God" (35.162). "Gospel" then means what God has given or done for us. It is natural to associate the Old Testament with "law" and the New Testament with "gospel"; there is a measure of truth in the simple equation, though it is not the whole story (35.236-37, 358). The Old Testament is primarily "a book of laws" that spell

---

65. "In the Scriptures, therefore, no allegory, tropology, or analogy is valid unless the same truth is expressly stated historically elsewhere. Otherwise, Scripture would become a mockery" (10.4). Cf. 33.162-63.

66. Less so, however, in his later years. Cf. H. Bornkamm, *Luther*, 94-95.

67. "The fact that because of the word 'crib' [in Isa. 1:3] this passage is applied to the birth of Christ is an error we can put up with, since it does not conflict with the faith; it is a childish mistake and one that flows from piety. 'As for the man who is weak in faith, welcome him' (Rom. 14:1)" (16.9).

out what we are, and what we are not, to do (35.236).[68] It preserves this character through the many stories that exemplify the keeping or breaking of those laws and the consequences that follow (35.236, 358), as well as in prophetic texts where obedience is urged and disobedience threatened with judgment (cf. 30.19). But from its very beginning, the Old Testament contains elements of gospel as well: already in the Garden of Eden, the promise is given of the coming Christ (the "seed of the woman" [Gen. 3:15]) who will bring salvation. That promise becomes more specific in further promises given to the patriarchs and prophets (1.191-94; cf. 2.236-37), and it is through faith in that promise that the Old Testament saints found favor with God (12.363-64). Even the mysteries of the Christian faith — that God is triune, that the coming Christ would be both God and man — are abundantly hinted at in Old Testament texts and were perceived by the faithful (1.59; 3.219; 4.279; 5.74).[69] Thus, the Old Testament, though primarily a "book of laws," certainly contains elements of "gospel" as well.

68. All human beings have an awareness of what is right and wrong; it has been divinely implanted in their hearts, and is referred to as the "natural law." The laws of the Old Testament were given to Israel and, as such, binding only on them. They include laws for the administration of Israel's society (i.e., civic laws) and laws prescribing how Israel was to worship and serve God (i.e., ceremonial laws). The civic laws have no force for any nation but Israel, though other nations might do well, at least in certain respects, to imitate them (26.448; 35.166-67). The ceremonial laws served to keep Israel from the worship of other gods and from thinking they could serve the true God on the terms of their own devising (9.134, 156; 12.361; 35.239; 40.93); but they also served to foreshadow the redemptive work of Christ in ways explained most clearly in the epistle to the Hebrews (12.399; 35.247-48). They were only ever binding on Israel, and have no validity now that Christ (whose work they foreshadowed) has come. In addition to its civic and ceremonial laws, the Old Testament contains moral laws, particularly the Ten Commandments. These represent the perfect expression of the natural law implanted in human hearts (35.168, 172-73). They represent what all human beings are to do (Luther summed up the entire duty of Christians in his expositions of the Ten Commandments; see his *Large Catechism* and *Treaty on Good Works* [44.21-114]) *because* they spell out the universally valid law of nature, not because they are contained in Old Testament law (which was specifically enjoined upon Israel [Exod. 20:2; cf. 35.164-65; 54.52]). Christians are, however, free even from the moral law in the sense that, since their sins are forgiven, it can no longer accuse or condemn them (26.447; 35.244).

69. Luther must be considered among the more expansive discoverers of specifically Christian truth in Old Testament texts. In addition to adopting traditional Christian readings of verses like Gen. 1:26 (where the divine "Let *us* make" is understood to represent the deliberations of the divine trinity [1.57-59; cf. also 2.227-28]) and 3:15 (where the "seed" of the woman is understood as Christ [15.317-18]), he added a number of discoveries of his own to the repertoire, based on his access to the original Hebrew text (an access shared by few Christian readers in the preceding millennium and a half). See esp. 15.265-352. Cf. H. Bornkamm, *Luther*, 96-120; Mattox, "Interpretation," 33-57.

The problem with the law is that we, as sinners, have neither the will nor the ability to carry out the "works" that it commands us to do; and beyond telling us what we *should* do, the law, as such, is powerless (35.242). As a result, the practical effect of the law's telling us what to do is to make us conscious of our sin and liability to divine judgment; this, in fact, is the law's primary purpose.

> Scripture, however, represents man as one who is not only bound, wretched, captive, sick, and dead, but in addition to his other miseries is afflicted, through the agency of Satan his prince, with this misery of blindness, so that he believes himself to be free, happy, unfettered, able, well, and alive. . . . It is Satan's work to prevent men from recognizing their plight and to keep them presuming that they can do everything they are told. But the work of Moses or a lawgiver is the opposite of this, namely, to make man's plight plain to him by means of the law and thus to break and confound him by self-knowledge, so as to prepare him for grace and send him to Christ that he may be saved. (33.130-31)

> This presumption of righteousness is a huge and a horrible monster. To break and crush it, God needs a large and powerful hammer, that is, the Law, which is the hammer of death, the thunder of hell, and the lightning of divine wrath. (26.310)

Whereas "law" stands for what God requires us to do (though we have not done it), "gospel" proclaims what God — in Christ — has done for us, and his offer of forgiveness and grace, apart from any works of our own. If the law "serves no other purpose than to create a thirst and to frighten the heart," the gospel "satisfies the thirst, makes us cheerful, and revives and consoles the conscience" (23.272). Inasmuch as the proclamation of this grace represents the essence of the New Testament, we may speak of the New Testament as "gospel" or a "book of grace," in the same way that the Old Testament is (primarily) a "book of laws" (35.236-37, 358).[70]

To be sure, as there was both gospel and law in the Old Testament, so there is law as well as gospel in the New. Believers, though righteous in God's sight, still live in a "flesh" that is constantly beset by temptation and never free from sin — though God, for Christ's sake, does not count

---

70. Of course, the truth about the divine Trinity and the dual nature of the Savior, obscurely hinted at in the Old Testament, is openly proclaimed in the New as well (1.59, 223; 2.228; 15.287).

their sins against them: "Sin is always present, and the godly feel it. But it is ignored and hidden in the sight of God, because Christ the Mediator stands between" (26.133). Throughout their earthly lives, then, believers need the discipline and warnings of the law.

> Now in the New Testament there are also given, along with the teaching about grace, many other teachings that are laws and commandments for the control of the flesh — since in this life the Spirit is not perfected and grace alone cannot rule. (35.236-37)

When, however, the conscience of the believer is troubled by the law, then the law must recede so that grace alone prevails (26.349-51). Here is the bridal chamber for the believing bride and the divine groom: law, with its demands and threats, must not be allowed to intrude (26.120).

Since the author of both law and gospel is God, both need to be heard. By means of law and gospel, the Word of God performs its twofold work of "killing" and "making alive." But the two must be "kept apart." There is a time for "killing" the flesh through the law, and a time for reviving the spirit through the gospel. Complacency and self-righteousness require the former, fear and despair the latter. The one "who masters the art of exact distinction between the Law and the Gospel should be called a real theologian" (23.271; cf. 26.115).

Furthermore, "there is no book in the Bible in which both [law and gospel] are not found. God has always placed side by side both law and promise" (CS 1.1.100). The reader needs to be aware of the presence of both, and must carefully distinguish between them.

> What good will anyone do in a matter of theology or Holy Writ, who has not yet got as far as knowing what the law and what the gospel is, or if he knows, disdains to observe the distinction between them? Such a person is bound to confound everything — heaven and hell, life and death — and he will take no pains to know anything at all about Christ. (33.132)

Interpreting Scripture: The Place of Experience

In a famous passage in the preface to a collection of his German writings, Luther draws on Psalm 119 to spell out three steps essential for anyone who would be a theologian. These are commonly given in their Latin form: *oratio, meditatio, tentatio* (prayer, meditation, and trial [see 34.285]). All three are required for an understanding of Scripture.

Human wisdom or understanding can only despair of ever grasping the wisdom of God. Following David's example in Psalm 119 ("Teach me, Lord, instruct me, lead me, show me"), the student of Scripture should thus kneel "and pray to God with real humility and earnestness, that he through his dear Son may give you his Holy Spirit, who will enlighten you, lead you, and give you understanding" (34.285-86).

Again, following David's example (who "constantly boasts that he will talk, meditate, speak, sing, hear, read, by day and night and always, about nothing except God's Word and commandments"), the budding theologian will meditate on Scripture, "concentrating on it with fear, humility, and diligence," and repeating its words (once or twice will not do) in order to arrive at an understanding of "what the Holy Spirit means" (34.286; 14.7). No one will understand God's words by "skim[ming] over them" (14.7). "Scripture is the stone of offense and rock of scandal for those who are in a hurry" (10.19).

Luther once apologized at the beginning of a lecture on Genesis by saying that he could only speak that day about the "language" of the passage before him; his schedule had not permitted him to meditate on it properly (3.3). Meditation meant for him not only devoting close attention to the words of Scripture, but also drawing together related passages of Scripture to further illuminate the subject (14.296).[71] At first sight, for example, the words "You shall not kill" represent nothing but a straightforward prohibition of murder.

> But pause and observe that it does not say: Your hand shall not kill, but you yourself. Yet who is this "you"? It consists of your soul and body, and in them you also have many powers: hands, tongue, eyes, mind, and will. Therefore when you are prohibited from killing, are you then not also taught that it is wrong to kill with the hand, or with the tongue, or by your desire? For when one of these commits the crime, it is really you. . . . "You shall not kill" will mean that you should not be bitter and angry but agreeable and friendly toward your neighbor. (14.296)

71. Scripture "wants to be interpreted by a comparison of passages from everywhere, and understood under its own direction. The safest of all methods for discerning the meaning of Scripture is to work for it by drawing together and scrutinizing passages" (9.21).

Having come this far, the mind familiar with Scripture will recall other passages that "teach of love, tolerance, friendliness, good will, kindness, and mercy. When you have taken these together, have you not lovingly . . . meditated on the Law of your Lord?" (14.296).

Or consider the words spoken to Rebekah of the twins in her womb: "The elder shall serve the younger" (Gen. 25:23). On the surface, they speak about the future of Jacob and Esau. Meditation, however, finds in these words "the foundations of the entire Christian doctrine," reflecting as they do the overturning of human values.

> Through the birth of these twins God wants to pass sentence in advance on the entire world, yes, even to anticipate and put an end to all righteousness of the flesh. He wants to teach that all wisdom and excellence of the flesh is lost and vain by reason of this one statement: "The elder shall serve the younger." (4.370)

In addition to prayer and meditation, a true understanding of Scripture requires "trial." "As soon as God's Word takes root and grows in you, the devil will harry you, and will make a real doctor of you, and by his assaults will teach you to seek and love God's Word." Beyond simple knowledge and understanding, such trials will lead you "to experience how right, how true, how sweet, how lovely, how mighty, how comforting God's Word is, wisdom beyond all wisdom" (34.286-87).

No one can understand *words* if they know nothing of the *subject* the words are speaking about (4.13; cf. 1.264; 54.476).[72] Although we must be thankful to the rabbis for their efforts in reproducing "a linguistically correct text" of the Old Testament, their ignorance of Christ means they know nothing of the subject matter of their own scriptures (1.269; cf. 1.296; 3.72-73). Nor can the psalmist's words "Out of the depths I cry to Thee, O Lord" (Ps. 130:1) "be understood except by those who have felt and experienced it" (14.189). Speculative theologians who wonder whether Jeremiah sinned in cursing the day he was born have never been in his situation: "Sometimes one has to wake up our Lord God with such words" (54.30). Nor do we really understand what it means to address God as "Our Father who art in heaven" unless we have experienced adversity at his hands (54.9).

> The real mission of the Scriptures is to comfort the suffering, distressed and dying. Then he who has had no experience of suffering or death

---

72. E.g., to one born blind, the words "red," "green," and "yellow" can have no meaning.

cannot at all understand the comfort of the Bible. Not words but experience must be the medium of tasting and finding this comfort. (*CS* 3.2.43-44)

Similarly, even a conviction that the words of Scripture are true is meaningless apart from a grasp of what they mean "for us." One who rightly reads the Psalter will find, whatever the circumstances, that it contains words "that fit his case, that suit him as if they were put there just for his sake" (35.256). The shepherds were not simply told that a Savior was born in Bethlehem; the angel's message began, "Behold, I bring *you* good news.... To *you* is born . . ." (Luke 2:10-11; so *CS* 1.1.143; cf. 30.152; 51.212-16). Christian faith means believing that "Christ is the Saviour not only to Peter and to the saints but also to you" (*CS* 1.1.21).

When you open the book containing the gospels and read or hear how Christ comes here or there, or how someone is brought to him, you should therein perceive the sermon or the gospel through which he is coming to you, or you are being brought to him. For the preaching of the gospel is nothing else than Christ coming to us, or we being brought to him. When you see how he works, however, and how he helps everyone to whom he comes or who is brought to him, then rest assured that faith is accomplishing this in you and that he is offering your soul exactly the same sort of help and favor through the gospel. If you pause here and let him do you good, that is, if you believe that he benefits and helps you, then you really have it. Then Christ is yours, presented to you as a gift. (35.121)

It is not enough only to know the history. One must also go further and possess the power and fruit of the history. That happens when Christ's tomb is regarded not merely with the outward eyes of the body but with the inward eyes of faith: namely, when we believe without any wavering that in Christ's tomb all our sins are covered up and buried. . . . That is the reason why Christ's tomb is so carefully described by the evangelists: namely, so that we may support, fortify, and strengthen our faith in this article so that we are able to comfort ourselves with it amid every sort of temptation and affliction. (69.276-77, commenting on John 19)

It is not enough that God speaks; but it is necessary that He speaks *to you*. (2.271)

Those who sense in Scripture that God is addressing them cannot but be moved in their feelings as well as informed in their faith.[73]

> This is truly to sing psalms, or, as the Scriptures say of David, to strike the harp with the hand. For the light fingers of the harpist are the emotions of the heart moving about in the words of the psalms. Without this the strings do not sound, and the psalm is not sung, because it is not touched. (14.311)

> Although the entire Psalter and all of Holy Scripture are dear to me as my only comfort and source of life, I fell in love with this psalm [118] especially. Therefore I call it my own. (14.45)

> It would not be surprising if a Christian heart that thoroughly pondered and grasped the import of [these texts] would die for joy and again be quickened by joy. (15.294)

And Psalm 23?

God's nature is beyond our understanding. His goodness is known to us, and experienced by us, only as it is revealed through the Word. Therefore it is fair to trace and attribute all God's blessings to the Word. "Accordingly," the psalmist calls the Word of God "a fine, pleasant, green pasture; fresh water; the path to righteousness; a rod; a staff; a table; . . . a cup that is filled to overflowing" (12.148).

If the purity of the Word was to be preserved, it had to be written; we encounter it in Scripture. But the nature of the Word as God's address to human beings is still captured best when it is spoken or preached; and for Luther it is important to honor the ministry of the Word.

> Whenever God's Word is preached properly and purely, it creates as many good things and results as the prophet here gives it names. To those that hear it diligently and seriously — and they are the only ones

---

73. Faith itself, as we have seen, results from the inward working of the Spirit. The faith of one so moved by the Spirit is more than an intellectual conviction: "Faith must spring up and flow from the blood and wounds and death of Christ. If you see in these that God is so kindly disposed toward you that he even gives his own Son for you, then your heart in turn must grow sweet and disposed toward God. And in this way your confidence must grow out of pure good will and love — God's toward you, and yours toward God" (44.38).

whom our Lord acknowledges as His sheep — it is pleasant green grass, a cool draught, by which the sheep of the Lord are satisfied and refreshed. It keeps them in the paths of righteousness and preserves them from suffering misfortune and harm. And it is to them an ever happy life, in which food and drink and all kinds of joy and pleasure abound. (12.148)

In Psalm 23, then, "David, together with every other Christian heart, praises and thanks God for His greatest blessing: namely, for the preaching of His dear Holy Word" (12.147).

CHAPTER 9

Calvin

There is something amiss, is there not, in the Bible's account of godly Jacob's first encounter with his cousin Rachel? According to Genesis 29:11-12, Jacob kissed Rachel, then told her who he was. Now, it is important — nay, crucial — to understand that a kiss then did not mean what a kiss means now. But second, it was surely the case, the Bible's wording notwithstanding, that Jacob told Rachel who he was *before* venturing to embrace her.[1]

If you have ever read Genesis 29 without such concerns arising in your mind, then you are not John Calvin. And still more can be learned from the *real* John Calvin's reflections on these verses: for even the most reverent and sober of Scripture's interpreters — that would be the real John Calvin — there are times when the Bible cannot mean what it says. Furthermore, since the subject has arisen, the observation seems in order that for Calvin more than any other author we examine in this book, KISS can be said to serve as a basic hermeneutical principle: Keep It Simple, Stupid.

Life

John Calvin was born in Noyon, France, on July 10, 1509, a quarter century after the birth of Martin Luther. His father initially intended him for an ecclesiastical career, but then realized that law offered better promise of tangible rewards. Calvin studied the arts in Paris, law in Orleans, then — in

---

1. Thus Calvin, *Com. Gen.,* on 29:4-12. In what follows, quotations from Calvin's Old Testament commentaries are taken from the edition published by the Calvin Translation Society (1844-1856; reprinted 1981); quotations from the New Testament commentaries are taken from the more recent edition (1959-1972) edited by David W. Torrance and Thomas F. Torrance. For details, see the bibliography.

the spirit of the humanism of his day — wrote a commentary on Seneca's *De clementia.* When and where he was first exposed to, and attracted by, the ideas of the Reformation is not known; however, it is thought that he may have helped a personal friend, the rector at the University of Paris, write a provocative address calling on the church to reform. An uproar ensued, and Calvin fled the city in November 1533. Not long afterwards, prudence dictated that he leave France altogether; he arrived in Basel in 1535. There, in March 1536, he published a small handbook of Protestant theology, *The Institutes of the Christian Religion,* to introduce and defend Protestant convictions. A later, much expanded version of the work (1559) represents his magnum opus and ranks with the most significant works ever written in the history of Christian theology.

But any thoughts Calvin may have entertained of a quiet, peaceful life of godly scholarship were, one may fairly say, rudely interrupted on a night in July 1536 as he was passing through Geneva. A local reformer, William Farel, began by "entreating" him to stay and provide leadership in the city. But when he realized that Calvin remained determined to devote himself to private studies, Farel took to stronger language: God, he said, would "curse [Calvin's] retirement, and the tranquility of the studies which [he] sought, if [he] should withdraw and refuse to give assistance, when the necessity was so urgent."[2] Like Luther, Calvin could do no other. He stayed in Geneva.

But Calvin's initial attempts at reform were rebuffed, and in 1538 he found himself an all-too-willing exile from the city. Though eager to return to undisturbed study, he was again "persuaded" to pastor a French congregation in Strasbourg. In 1541, duty called him back to Geneva, where he spent the rest of his life as head pastor and teacher. His reorganization of the Geneva church and city-state, this time more successful, made Geneva a model city for many Protestants. The city also provided a haven for Protestants who were persecuted, while its academy offered theological education to Protestant leaders from all over Europe. Of more immediate significance in this context, Calvin published commentaries (which he had already begun in Strasbourg, but which were largely the product of the Geneva years) on much of the Old Testament and nearly every book of the New Testament;[3] they are hardly less important than the better-known *Institutes.*

John Calvin died, as Galileo and Shakespeare were born, in 1564.

2. Calvin, *Com. Ps.,* preface.

3. The book of Revelation is a notable exception; 2 and 3 John are the others. One can only speculate about why these books were not made the subject of commentaries; see Parker, *N.T. Commentaries,* 75-78.

Knowing God

In modern Psalms scholarship, Psalm 19 is commonly thought to combine two originally independent poems, treating different themes: God's creation in the first (19:1-6), God's law in the second (vv. 7-14). Calvin acknowledges the different themes, but he sees a natural progression from one to the other: the work of God in creation displays God's glory, but knowledge of God is conveyed more clearly by God's word (see *Inst.* 1.6.4).

If Psalm 19:1-6 confines its praise of God's handiwork to the heavens, it is because the heavens represent the "noblest" part of God's creation; their "excellency" is most conspicuous.

> When we behold the heavens, we cannot but be elevated, by the contemplation of them, to Him who is their great Creator; and the beautiful arrangement and wonderful variety which distinguish the courses and station of the heavenly bodies, together with the beauty and splendour which are manifest in them, cannot but furnish us with an evident proof of his providence. (*Com. Ps.,* on 19:1)

In fact, however, something of God's power and wisdom can be seen "even in the minutest plants" and in "the smallest corners of the earth" (*Com. Ps.,* on 19:1). God has so "revealed himself and daily discloses himself in the whole workmanship of the universe" that "men cannot open their eyes without being compelled to see him. . . . There is no spot in the universe wherein you cannot discern at least some sparks of his glory" (*Inst.* 1.5.1). In his summary of the "argument" of Genesis, Calvin notes that God "places the fabric of heaven and earth before our eyes, rendering himself, in a certain manner, manifest in them," in order to "invite us to the knowledge of himself" (*Com. Gen.,* argument). The appropriate response seems self-evident:

> As soon as we acknowledge God to be the supreme Architect, who has erected the beauteous fabric of the universe, our minds must necessarily be ravished with wonder at his infinite goodness, wisdom, and power. (*Com. Ps.,* on 19:1)

That such a response seems appropriate does not, however, mean that it is forthcoming:

> It is doubtless true, that if we were not very dull and stupid, the signatures and proofs of Deity which are to be found on the theatre of the

world, are abundant enough to incite us to acknowledge and reverence God; but as, although surrounded with so clear a light, we are neverthe-less blind, this splendid representation of the glory of God, without the aid of the word, would profit us nothing. (*Com. Ps.*, on 19:7)

Thus, the actual effect of the heavens' testimony to God's glory is only to render inexcusable our failure to acknowledge and give reverence to our maker (*Com. Ps.*, on 19:7; *Com. Rom.*, on 8:20; *Inst.* 1.5.14). If we are to know God, God must address us more directly — as he has done through his word. To this latter revelation, then, David logically turns in the latter half of Psalm 19; we join him there shortly.

But just as sinful human beings turn a blind eye to God's glory in cre-ation all around them, so they make no good use of the "seed of religion," or "awareness of divinity," that God has implanted within their minds (*Inst.* 1.5.1; 1.3.1).

There is, as the eminent pagan [Cicero] says, no nation so barbarous, no people so savage, that they have not a deep-seated conviction that there is a God. . . . Since from the beginning of the world there has been no region, no city, in short, no household, that could do without religion, there lies in this a tacit confession of a sense of deity inscribed in the hearts of all. . . . If, indeed, there were some in the past, and today not a few appear, who deny that God exists, yet willy-nilly they from time to time feel an inkling of what they desire not to believe. (*Inst.* 1.3.1-2)

From true knowledge of God, all have degenerated: some turn to super-stition, others "deliberately and wickedly desert God" (*Inst.* 1.4.1). "In one respect we are indeed unalike, because each one of us privately forges his own particular error; yet we are very much alike in that, one and all, we forsake the one true God for prodigious trifles" (*Inst.* 1.5.11).[4] The upshot, Calvin again concludes, is the need for further revelation: apart from di-vine revelation in Scripture, God *cannot* be properly known. "It is needful

---

4. Cf. *Com. John,* on 3:6: "That some knowledge of God is innate in us, that some dis-tinction between good and evil is engraven on our consciences, that we have the capacity to cope with supporting our present life, that, in short, we excel the brute beasts in so many ways, is excellent in itself, inasmuch as it proceeds from God. But all these things are polluted in us. . . . For the knowledge of God as it now remains in men is nothing but a dreadful foun-tain of idolatry and all superstitions; the judgment of choosing and distinguishing things is partly blind and foolish, partly imperfect and confused; whatever industry we have is wasted on vanity and trifles; and the will itself rushes with raging impetus headlong into evil."

that another and better help be added to direct us aright to the very Creator of the universe. . . . Scripture, gathering up the otherwise confused knowledge of God in our minds, having dispersed our dullness, clearly shows us the true God" (*Inst.* 1.6.1).[5]

The Divine Scriptures

The essence of Scripture may be summed up (as in Ps. 19:7-14) in the term "law."[6] "Law" in this sense of course includes the Ten Commandments, "the rule of living well," given by God to Moses; but it is characteristic of Calvin to use the term to include the entire *covenant*[7] God has made with the church, and the grace and salvation therein offered through Christ.[8] "David, in praising [the law], as he here does [Ps. 19], speaks of the whole doctrine of the law, which includes also the gospel, and, therefore, under the law he comprehends Christ" (*Com. Ps.,* on 19:8; cf. *Com. Isa.,* preface). After all, Christ was the Savior of God's elect in the Old Testament as well as the New, and the object of their hope and faith (*Com. Jer.,* on 31:12); for though the grace of the gospel was not fully revealed until the coming of Christ (*Com. John,* on 1:17), it was known to God's people in Old Testament times through divine promises made to the patriarchs and prophets, as well as through ceremonial aspects of the Mosaic law that foreshadowed Christ's work.[9]

The covenant (or "law") that represents the essence of Scripture was thus divinely revealed already to the patriarchs, and revealed in such a way that they could not doubt its truth: "Firm certainty of doctrine was engraved in their hearts, so that they were convinced and understood that

---

5. A comparison with Aquinas is illuminating. The necessity of Scripture was as evident to Aquinas as it was to Calvin (see Chapter 7 above). But Aquinas found the necessity in the limitations of human nature as created; Calvin emphasizes the blindness caused by sin.

6. Calvin acknowledges that Scripture also uses the term "law" in a more restricted sense; see the discussion below.

7. Calvin typically speaks of a single covenant, operative both before and after Christ's coming; see the discussion below.

8. For Calvin, the church is the people of God in every age.

9. For Luther, the *contrast* between law and gospel was fundamental to an understanding of Scripture. Calvin acknowledges that such a contrast is found in Scripture and (as we shall see) has an explanation for it; but he more typically sees "law" as a simple equivalent of the "word" of God, embracing the entire "doctrine" of Scripture, including, specifically, the gospel (*Com. Isa.,* on 2:3; *Com. Jer.,* on 31:34). It is "law" in this broader sense that he finds the subject of the praises of Ps. 19 (and, of course, Ps. 119).

what they had learned proceeded from God" (*Inst.* 1.6.2). They handed it down to later generations. This same law became the subject of interpretation by the prophets. The apostles in turn spoke of its full realization in Christ; in substance, their message was the same as what was revealed to the patriarchs and Moses.[10] Because human beings easily forget God, fall into error, and fashion new religions of their own, God inspired the authors of Scripture to record the "heavenly doctrine, that it should neither perish through forgetfulness nor vanish through error nor be corrupted by the audacity of men" (*Inst.* 1.6.2-3; cf. *Com. Jer.,* on 36:2). If, then, we would know God aright, we must turn to Scripture.

Though the content of Scripture is the "heavenly doctrine," Calvin was very aware of the role that human beings played in its formulation and preservation. God no doubt instructed Adam about Adam's own origin and that of the creation he enjoyed; since Adam was not dumb, we may be sure that he then began the process of orally transmitting these truths, from one generation to another, until Moses recorded them in the opening chapters of Genesis. The holy patriarchs, too, must have passed on the divine messages they received so that Moses, in the Pentateuch, could preserve them for posterity (*Com. Gen.,* argument; cf. *Inst.* 1.8.3). Someone other than the psalmists themselves — perhaps it was Ezra — collected the various psalms into a single book (*Com. Ps.* 1, introduction). Though the prophets recorded individual oracles as they received and delivered them, the prophetic books as we have them represent collections — not necessarily in chronological order — made by later scribes (*Com. Isa.,* preface; *Com. Jer.,* on 25:1; on 26:1; on 51:64). Furthermore, it is readily apparent that individual prophets had their own style (*Inst.* 1.8.2; *Com. Ezek.,* on 2:3); Solomon wrote differently than David (*Com. James,* introduction); Hebrews does not have the style of Paul (*Com. Heb.,* theme). The style of 2 Peter is so different from that of 1 Peter that, if the former does indeed come from Peter (Calvin is not certain that it does), this can only mean that one of his disciples composed it at Peter's command (*Com. 2 Pet.,* theme).[11] And still we have not exhausted the human component of Scripture. Who

10. "As far as the substance of the Scripture is concerned, nothing has been added [by the New Testament to the Old]. The writings of the apostles contain nothing but a simple and natural explanation of the Law and the prophets along with a clear description of the things expressed in them" (*Com. 2 Tim.,* on 3:17).

11. Calvin does, however, insist that *if* 2 Peter is part of sacred Scripture, then Peter must have been (in some broad sense, since the language is not his) its author: "It would have been a fiction unworthy of a minister of Christ to pretend to another personality" (*Com. 2 Pet.,* theme).

can doubt, after all, that the psalmists recorded their own feelings when they wrote? Indeed, Calvin can even declare inappropriate the very human feelings expressed in certain psalms, in Job, and in Jeremiah (e.g., *Com. Ps.* 39, introduction; on 39:7, 13; on 88:10; cf. *Com. Jer.*, on 20:14; cf. *Com. Jer.*, on 15:18).[12]

None of this means, however, that Scripture is anything other than the inspired word of God, its authors "the instrument[s] of the Holy Spirit for the publication of those things which it was of importance for all men to know" (*Com. Gen.*, argument). That certain books in the Bible are of uncertain authorship is of no concern to Calvin; all we need to know is "that the doctrine herein contained was dictated by the Holy Spirit for our use" (*Com. Josh.*, argument; cf. *Com. James*, theme; *Com. Heb.*, theme; *Com. 2 Pet.*, theme). "The Prophets never uttered a word but as the Spirit guided their tongues" (*Com. Jer.*, on 17:18). "God's Spirit, who appointed the Evangelists as recorders, deliberately controlled their pen, so that all should write in complete agreement, but in different ways. . . . Each of them, without respect to the other, wrote simply and freely what the Spirit dictated" (*Com. Matt.*, on 2:1; cf. *Com. John*, theme). If Hebrews 3:7 introduces a quotation from the Old Testament with the words "as the Holy Spirit says," we should accustom ourselves "to this form of speaking, so that we remember that it is the words of God and not of men which are found in the books of the prophets" (*Com. Heb.*, on 3:7; cf. *Com. Acts*, on 1:16).[13]

Of course, we are not to believe that Scripture has been divinely revealed because Calvin, or any other human being, says so. Nor does Calvin, any more than Luther, think that human arguments are of any use in creating faith in Scripture:

12. Calvin deems it either the task of the commentator in general, or one for which he has been specially gifted, to assign blame where blame is due. The stories of Genesis are famous for leaving unspoken any moral assessment of the deeds it narrates; in his commentary on the book, Calvin consistently makes good the omission (e.g., *Com. Gen.*, on 25:28; on 27:5; on 29:18, 30).

13. Given Calvin's recognition of the human component of Scripture (noted above), he must mean that, *ultimately,* the words of Scripture are the words of God — and are to be read as such — even though differences between the various "instruments" God used to communicate those words are apparent in the communication. For Calvin, God so directed even the psalmists and Jeremiah in recording their (very human, at times inappropriate) feelings that important truths are conveyed in the process: "Let us then learn to check our feelings, that they may not break out thus unreasonably. Let us at the same time know that God's servants, though they may excel in firmness, are yet not wholly divested of their corruptions" (*Com. Jer.*, on 20:18).

They who strive to build up firm faith in Scripture through disputation are doing things backwards.[14] . . . The testimony of the Spirit is more excellent than all reason. For as God alone is a fit witness of himself in his Word, so also the Word will not find acceptance in men's hearts before it is sealed by the inward testimony of the Spirit. The same Spirit, therefore, who has spoken through the mouths of the prophets must penetrate into our hearts to persuade us that they faithfully proclaimed what had been divinely commanded. (*Inst.* 1.7.4)

The only true faith is that which the Spirit of God seals in our hearts. (*Inst.* 1.7.5)

Unless this certainty, higher and stronger than any human judgment, be present, it will be vain to fortify the authority of Scripture by arguments. (*Inst.* 1.8.1)

Those who wish to prove to unbelievers that Scripture is the Word of God are acting foolishly, for only by faith can this be known. (*Inst.* 1.8.13)

In this context, Luther emphasized how foolish God's word must appear to ordinary human thinking. Calvin's primary objection to arguments designed to create faith is that, since Scripture has been given to us in order that we may have "a saving knowledge of God," certainty of its truth is essential to the calmness of our conscience; and such certainty can only come from "the inward persuasion of the Holy Spirit" (*Inst.* 1.8.13). Conviction based on arguments will always be unstable, subject to doubt, and open to quibbles; only "the secret testimony of the Spirit" provides a sufficient foundation for faith (*Inst.* 1.7.4). When Calvin speaks of Scripture as "self-authenticated," he means precisely this: "it is not right to subject it to proof and reasoning. And the certainty it deserves with us,

---

14. "Backwards" because, though arguments are useless for *creating* faith in God's word, they can be useful for *confirming* an existing faith that originated in the "testimony of the Spirit." Among the arguments he lists as serving the latter purpose, Calvin includes the grandeur of Scripture's subject matter and its impact on the reader, the antiquity of Scripture (Calvin believes Moses to be the earliest of all writers), the miracles performed by Moses as attesting his divine mission, and the fulfillment of words spoken by the prophets. He concludes: "Scripture will ultimately suffice for a saving knowledge of God only when its certainty is founded upon the inward persuasion of the Holy Spirit. Indeed, these human testimonies which exist to confirm it will not be vain if, as secondary aids to our feebleness, they follow that chief and highest testimony" (*Inst.* 1.8.1-13).

it attains by the testimony of the Spirit" (*Inst.* 1.7.5). It was, after all, the Spirit who made Moses and the prophets sure that the messages they received were from God in the first place; it is now the Spirit's task to convince *readers* of Scripture of the divine origin of those same messages (*Com. 2 Tim.,* on 3:16).

But if the writing of Scripture was inspired by God's Spirit, and conviction of Scripture's truth is conveyed by that same Spirit, then those who claim that the authority of Scripture depends on the pronouncements of the church are mocking the Holy Spirit. Rather, the church itself is built on the existing foundation of the prophets and apostles (i.e., the writers of Scripture [*Inst.* 1.7.1-2, citing Eph. 2:20]). Apart from faith in the doctrine of the prophets and apostles, the church would not even exist. That the church recognizes and approves the testimony of Scripture by no means implies that Scripture owes its authority to the church (*Inst.* 1.7.2).

God's Spirit must not be so mocked; but nor is God's Spirit to be "honored" at the expense of God's word. Like Luther, Calvin insists that Word and Spirit belong inseparably together. The Spirit does not now abandon the Scripture he authored, or reveal new doctrines that lead believers away from the inspired text. As we have seen, the same Spirit who "dispensed" the Word in the first place now completes his task by illumining and confirming its truth in the hearts of believers.[15] "God does not bestow His Spirit on His people to abolish the use of His Word, but rather to make it bear fruit" (*Com. Luke,* on 24:45). Such, indeed, was the Savior's promise: he would send the Spirit, who would "speak not from himself but would suggest to and instill into [the minds of the disciples] what he had handed on through the Word" (*Inst.* 1.9.1, citing John 16:13). Besides, "it was not a part of the Word that Christ brought, but the last closing Word. . . . If God has now spoken His last Word, it is right to advance thus far, just as we must halt our steps when we arrive at Him" (*Com. Heb.,* on 1:1).[16]

---

15. "Unless the Spirit of wisdom is present, there is little or no profit in having God's Word in our hands, for its meaning will not be certain to us" (*Com. 1 John,* on 4:1).

16. "Although those antichrists are dissimilar in many respects they have a common starting-point: that in the Gospel we are initiated into the true faith, but that the perfection of doctrine must be sought elsewhere, to perfect us completely. . . . By a false claim to the Spirit, the world has been bewitched to leave the simple purity of Christ. For as soon as the Spirit is severed from God's Word the door is open to all sorts of craziness and impostures. Many fanatics have tried a similar method of deception in our own age. The written teaching seems to them to be of the letter. Therefore they were pleased to make up a new theology consisting of revelations" (*Com. John,* on 16:14).

The Divine Lisp

When God speaks to human beings, he must, perforce, keep it simple, "descend[ing] far beneath his loftiness." Like Chrysostom, Calvin believes that readers should be prepared to encounter in Scripture a good deal of divine "accommodation" to human weakness.[17] "As nurses commonly do with infants, God is wont in a measure to 'lisp' in speaking to us" (*Inst.* 1.13.1). "God accommodates Himself to the ordinary way of speaking because of our ignorance, and sometimes even, so to say, stammers" (*Com. John,* on 21:24). In such cases, the divine inspiration of Scripture guarantees not so much the precise truth of what is written as its effectiveness in bringing readers closer to an unexpressed truth that is beyond their capacity to understand.

The most obvious examples of such accommodation — and recognized as such by every author we have considered — are the anthropomorphic ways in which Scripture speaks about God. "Scripture often ascribes to [God] a mouth, ears, eyes, hands, and feet," but "such forms of speaking do not so much express clearly what God is like as accommodate the knowledge of him to our slight capacity" (*Inst.* 1.13.1). "Since the majesty of God, as it really is, cannot be expressed, the Scripture is wont to describe it according to the manner of men" (*Com. Gen.,* on 2:8). Truth is conveyed by such passages, even though the words do not mean quite what they say: Scripture, for example, speaks of God as "affected with grief," though he, in fact,

> remains for ever like himself in his celestial and happy repose: yet, because it could not otherwise be known how great is God's hatred and detestation of sin, therefore the Spirit accommodates himself to our capacity. (*Com. Gen.,* on 6:6)

In short, "God accommodates to our limited capacity every declaration which he makes of himself" (*Com. Rom.,* on 1:19).

Furthermore, Calvin (like Augustine, Aquinas, and Luther) believes we must not look for precision when the Bible speaks of creation and matters of science: Scripture is "the book of the unlearned" (*Com. Gen.,* on 1:6-8); to make its teaching accessible to all without exception, it adopts a "popular" way of speaking, "suited to the lowest apprehension" (*Com. Ps.,* on 148:4). When, then, Scripture speaks of "waters above the heavens," or

17. Chrysostom typically speaks of divine "considerateness," or "condescension."

of the sun and moon as "the two great lights" in the sky (whereas astronomers have proven that there are others much larger), or of the earth as "founded upon the seas," or of a star that led the magi (it was more likely a comet), we miss the very point of these passages if we insist on accepting by faith their statements as scientifically accurate no less than if we dismiss them as products of ignorance (*Com. Gen.*, on 1:6-8, 15-16; *Com. Ps.*, on 24:2; on 148:4; *Com. Jer.*, on 31:37; *Com. Matt.*, on 2:1).[18] The writers of Scripture were theologians, not astronomers; they were more concerned about us than they were about the stars (*Com. Gen.*, on 1:15). The study of astronomy, like that of other sciences, is by no means to be discouraged.[19] But whoever "would learn astronomy, and other recondite arts, let him go elsewhere [than Scripture]" (*Com. Gen.*, on 1:6-8).

> Astronomers investigate with great labour whatever the sagacity of the human mind can comprehend. . . . But because [Moses] was ordained a teacher as well of the unlearned and rude as of the learned, he could not otherwise fulfill his office than by descending to this grosser method of instruction. (*Com. Gen.*, on 1:16)

At times, Calvin finds accommodation in Scripture in places where he thinks its first hearers or readers were not yet ready for the unaccommodated truth; at other times, a fuller statement would have exceeded the capacities of human beings of any age. Among examples of the former category we may perhaps place the promises made to the patriarchs of material blessings and the temporal rewards promised Israel if they obeyed God's law. Calvin believes the actual point of such promises was to educate a primitive people to the point where they could begin to understand the spiritual and eternal blessings God has in store for his people.

> The Lord did not formerly set the hope of the future inheritance plainly before the eyes of the fathers (as he now calls and raises us directly towards heaven), but he led them as by a circuitous route. Thus he appointed the land of Canaan as a mirror and pledge to them of the celestial inheritance. In all his acts of kindness he gave them tokens of his

18. "The assertion of some, that they embrace by faith what they have read concerning the waters above the heavens, notwithstanding their ignorance respecting them, is not in accordance with the design of Moses" (*Com. Gen.*, on 1:6-8).

19. "Astronomy is not only pleasant, but also very useful to be known; it cannot be denied that this art unfolds the admirable wisdom of God" (*Com. Gen.*, on 1:16).

paternal favour, not indeed for the purpose of making them content with present good . . . but that, being aided by such helps, according to the time in which they lived, they might by degrees rise towards heaven. (*Com. Gen.,* on 27:27)

The Lord of old willed that his people direct and elevate their minds to the heavenly heritage; yet, to nourish them better in this hope, he displayed it for them to see and, so to speak, taste, under earthly benefits. But now that the gospel has more plainly and clearly revealed the grace of the future life, the Lord leads our minds to meditate upon it directly, laying aside the lower mode of training that he used with the Israelites. (*Inst.* 2.11.1; cf. *Com. Lev.,* on 26:3; *Com. Joel,* on 3:18)

Moreover, Scripture accommodated itself to the capacities of its first hearers in Old Testament prophecies of blessings to come in the messianic age: "It was a common custom of the prophets to foreshadow the Kingdom of Christ under images appropriate to their own day" (*Com. Acts,* on 2:17). Hence, the prophets speak of material blessings, as was "suitable to their own age," though in fact the blessings of that kingdom will be spiritual (*Com. Hag.,* on 2:6-9). They limit the extent of that kingdom to boundaries with which their readers would be familiar, "the amplitude of the kingdom of Christ not having been, as yet, fully unfolded" (*Com. Ps.,* on 72:8). They speak of the worship of God in that coming day as involving a physical temple and altar, sacrifices, offerings of gold, silver, and frankincense, and the service of priests and Levites. These, after all, were the accouterments of worship with which their contemporaries were familiar (*Com. Acts,* on 2:17; cf. *Com. Joel,* on 2:28); but none of them has a place in the messianic kingdom. The prophets mention them only to point, in familiar terms, to the unknown realities that they foreshadowed: the sacrifice and priesthood of Christ. Thus, the promise of Jeremiah 33:18 that "the Levitical priests shall never lack a man in my presence to offer burnt offerings, to burn cereal offerings, and to make sacrifices for ever" has its fulfillment in the priesthood of Christ and his (once-for-all) self-sacrifice on the cross; but the prophet spoke of that reality in terms that his original hearers could grasp (*Com. Jer.,* on 33:18).

Moses' failure to mention Satan in his account of Eve's temptation may also be explained by the principle of accommodation: "Not only had [Moses] to instruct an untaught race of men, but the existing age of the Church was so puerile, that it was unable to receive any higher instruction. . . . They who have an aversion to this simplicity, must of necessity condemn the whole economy of God in governing the Church" (*Com. Gen.,* on 3:1).[20] Moreover, Calvin follows Chrysostom in believing that Christ at times spoke of his relationship to the Father in ways inadequate for expressing its true nature but accommodated to the capacity of his hearers (*Com. John,* on 7:16; on 8:17, 28). And as a final, rather more prosaic example of scriptural accommodation to the horizons of its first readers, we may note how Calvin explains why New Testament authors at times quote the Greek translation of the Old Testament even where this distorts the original Hebrew; it was, after all, the Greek form of the text with which their readers were familiar, and they saw no point in offending them by correcting their sacred texts (*Com. Gen.,* on 47:31; *Com. Ps.,* on 68:18; *Com. 1 Cor.,* on 2:9; *Com. Heb.,* on 10:6, 37; on 11:21).

In other cases, Scripture's statements are accommodated to the limited capacities of human beings in all ages. Calvin is no doubt best known for his belief in the predestination of saved and damned alike; from this belief, it follows that the elect can never fall short of their predestined salvation. If, then, the psalmist speaks of people being "blotted out" from the book of (those predestined for) life, then the expression must represent "an improper manner of speaking" — but one "adapted to our limited capacity." We can never understand "God's eternal purpose of election," but God accommodates its truth to our limited understanding by speaking of a book in which the names of the elect are written; correspondingly, the rejection of those who (though never appointed for salvation) appear for a time in the company of the faithful is spoken of as the "blotting out" of their names from that same book (*Com. Ps.,* on 69:28). Similarly, Jeremiah, indicating that God repudiates those among the physical descendants of Abraham who prove unworthy, speaks as though God had changed his mind about them; actually, of course, "God determined, before the creation of the world, what he pleased respecting each individual." But Jeremiah's way of speaking represents an accommodation of that doctrine to human beings from whom God's counsel is hidden and to whom it remains incomprehensible (*Com. Jer.,* on 18:7-10; cf. *Com. Ezek.,* on 18:32; *Com. Matt.,* on 23:37).

---

20. Here, however, Calvin does go on to note that, at least for some, the "secret illumination of the Spirit" supplied the information left unstated in the "outward expression; as appears plainly from the prophets, who saw Satan to be the real enemy of the human race" (*Com. Gen.,* on 3:1).

Old Testament and New, and the Law for All Ages

God himself does not change; nor, essentially, do his relationships with his people. Properly speaking, the "eternal and inviolable covenant" God made with Abraham is what governs those relationships in all ages: even today, the salvation enjoyed by Christians fulfills the promise given to Abraham of blessing to come through his "seed" (*Com. Exod.,* on 19:1; *Com. Jer.,* on 31:31; cf. Gal. 3:8, 29). What Israel entered at Mount Sinai was not a separate covenant but a renewal of the one given to Abraham. Salvation in Christ finds a place in this renewal of the covenant as well, in that Christ's salvific work is symbolically represented in the ceremonial law given to Moses.[21] If Scripture nonetheless speaks of an "old" covenant and a "new," it refers to differences in form, not substance, between God's dealings with his church before and after the coming of Christ (*Com. Jer.,* on 31:31; cf. *Inst.* 2.10.1; 2.11.1).[22]

Much that is different must simply be attributed to God's need to deal appropriately with people at different stages in their training and understanding: in the Old Testament, God dealt with his people as infants and children (cf. *Inst.* 2.11.5). We have already noted that temporal, material rewards were promised Israel and its patriarchs — so that God's people might one day fathom and appreciate eternal, spiritual blessings.[23] Similarly, God, whose desire for spiritual worship is ever the same, nonetheless accommodated himself to human weakness when he enjoined the external rites of Israel's worship: here, too, we see the kind of "preparatory training" needed by children (*Com. Isa.,* on 1:13; *Com. John,* on 4:23; *Inst.* 2.7.1), though Calvin is also careful to insist that the same

21. "The gospel did not so supplant the entire law as to bring forward a different way of salvation. Rather, it confirmed and satisfied whatever the law had promised, and gave substance to the shadows" (*Inst.* 2.9.4).

22. The boundaries of the church itself were altered by Christ's coming: "Until the advent of Christ, the Lord set apart one nation within which to confine the covenant of his grace. . . . 'But when the fullness of time came' [Gal. 4:4] . . . 'the wall' that for so long had confined God's mercy within the boundaries of Israel 'was broken down' [Eph. 2:14]. 'Peace was announced to those who were far off, and to those who were near' [Eph. 2:17] that together they might be reconciled to God and welded into one people [Eph. 2:16]" (*Inst.* 2.11.11).

23. From Heb. 11:13, however, Calvin concludes that the patriarchs themselves "were not so brutish in their minds, that they confined their thoughts to this world. . . . But the difference is, that God then set forth his grace under visible figures. . . . What is spiritual is conveyed under these figures, that the people might, by degrees, ascend to the spiritual kingdom of Christ, which was as yet involved in shadows and obscurity" (*Com. Jer.,* on 31:12).

blessings were conferred on the Old Testament faithful through these rites as New Testament believers enjoy (*Com. 1 Cor.,* on 10:3). The main difference, however, is that what God "shadowed forth under the law" was "accomplished through [God's] Son" (*Com. Jer.,* on 31:31). If the Old Testament faithful enjoyed the forgiveness of sins when they offered sacrifices, it was not because those sacrifices in themselves had the power to expiate sins; their efficacy was borrowed from the all-atoning sacrifice of Christ that they anticipated and foreshadowed (*Com. John,* on 1:29). With the coming of the reality to which Old Testament figures and types had pointed, the mode of teaching changed as well: now God could speak "openly" rather than "under a veil," as he had done through Moses (*Com. Jer.,* on 31:31; cf. on 31:33). But what is fulfilled and openly spoken of in the New Testament remains *in substance* the same as what was foreshadowed and obscurely presented in the Old: the form has changed, the substance remains the same.

> The ancient ceremonies . . . were like the rough outlines which are the foreshadowings of the living picture. Before they put on the true colours with paint artists usually draw an outline in pencil of the representation which they intend. . . . The apostle has established this difference between the Law and the Gospel, that the former has foreshadowed in elementary and sketchy outline what today has been expressed in living and graphically printed colour. . . . It is to be noticed that the things which were shown to [the Old Testament fathers] from a distance are the same as those which are now set before our eyes. Both are shown the same Christ, the same justice, sanctification, and salvation. Only in the manner of the painting is there difference. (*Com. Heb.,* on 10:1)

But what, then, of the Mosaic law? Does Paul not indicate that it has been "done away," and that believers have "died" to its statutes (e.g., Rom. 7:4-6; Gal. 2:19; 3:19-25)? Does this not represent a substantial difference between the old covenant and the new? Calvin can hardly think so, given his conviction that the Mosaic law and covenant represent merely a renewal of God's one and only "eternal and inviolable covenant" with his people. He maintains his point by suggesting that the term "law" is used in different ways, and by distinguishing between the use and abuse of God's eternal law.

Calvin sees the Mosaic law as consisting essentially of two parts: "a promise of salvation and eternal life, and a rule for a godly and holy living"

(*Com. Hos.,* argument).[24] The essence of the latter is found in the Ten Commandments: "Nothing can be wanted as the rule of a good and upright life beyond the Ten Commandments" (*Mosaic Harmony,* preface).[25] Here the difference between good and evil is set forth. That difference remains, whether or not human beings respect it; the content of a "good and upright life" is not subject to change. In fact, of course, human beings do not obey God's moral law, and the law condemns them. Therefore, Paul can speak of the "ministry" of the law as one of condemnation and death (2 Cor. 3:7, 9); but this *effect* of the law is "accidental" to its nature, determined rather by human response to its demands than by the nature of those demands themselves (*Com. Acts,* on 7:38). Like Luther, Calvin sees a divine purpose in the way the disobeyed law makes evident human corruption and liability to judgment, thus driving condemned human beings to seek grace in the Savior: this he calls the "proper office" of the law (*Com. John,* on 16:10; *Inst.* 2.5.6-8). But the same law that Paul calls a minister of death is said by David (in Ps. 19) to be "sweeter than honey and more to be desired than gold. . . . It cheers hearts, converts to the Lord and quickens." Paul is speaking of the law's effect on sinners; David, of how the same law affects those born again by God's Spirit (*Com. 1 John,* on 5:3). For Calvin, the moral law of the Ten Commandments remains the valid statement of God's will even for believers.[26] Indeed, he finds — in the direction and exhortation it gives them — the law's "third and principal use" (*Inst.* 2.7.12): in the "perfection to which it exhorts us, the law points out the goal toward which throughout life we are to strive" (*Inst.* 2.7.13).[27] It is only from the law's condemnation and curse that believers are delivered. And even these parts of the law are not simply done away; rather, believers are freed from their effects because Christ has borne them (*Inst.* 2.7.15).

But the law also contains "a promise of salvation and eternal life" in

24. Calvin goes on to add that the law has a third part, allowing a separate category for the "threatenings and reproofs" that are designed to restore transgressors to the fear of God (*Com. Hosea,* argument; cf. *Com. Isa.,* preface).

25. *Mosaic Harmony* refers to Calvin's commentary on Exodus through Deuteronomy (*Commentary on the Last Four Books of Moses, Arranged in the Form of a Harmony*). See Blacketer, "Commentator."

26. Calvin insists that Christ himself did not in any way alter the moral law given to Moses; in the Sermon on the Mount he showed himself rather "a faithful Interpreter, teaching us the nature of the Law, its object, and its scope" (*Com. Matt.,* on 5:21; cf. *Inst.* 2.8.7).

27. As we have seen, the law serves in the first place to drive sinners, convicted by its demands and sanctions, to seek the Savior's grace. Calvin finds a second use of the law in that, through its threats of punishment, it deters the unrighteous from committing at least some of the evil deeds they would otherwise be inclined to do (*Inst.* 2.7.10-11).

that its ceremonies foreshadowed the salvific work of Christ. The law's external rites were commanded, and meant to be observed, not for their own sake — on their own they are "vain and trifling" — but for their educational value (they set the faithful on the path to spiritual worship) and because of what they pointed to (*Mosaic Harmony,* preface). And, to be sure, they need no longer be observed now that their educational and foreshadowing work has been accomplished. But it is only their observance that has been done away; what they signified remains and is of lasting importance. "So Christ's coming did not take anything away, even from the ceremonies. . . . One does not do away with ceremonies, when their reality is kept, and their shadow omitted" (*Com. Matt.,* on 5:17-18; cf. *Inst.* 2.7.16).[28] In this way, the law — both in its moral and in its ceremonial aspects — is seen to be eternal, the gospel is seen to be contained in the law, and Christ is seen as the law's "goal" or fulfillment (Rom. 10:4).

That said, Calvin allows that the New Testament often distinguishes the law, its commands and condemnation, from Christ, the gospel, and the grace of salvation. When it is *contrasted* with the gospel, what the law *shares* with the gospel — the work and grace of Christ, foreshadowed in its ceremonies — must be left out of the picture, so that only what is *distinctive* about the law remains: its demands and the threats of judgment for transgressors (*Com. Rom.,* on 10:5; *Com. 2 Cor.,* on 3:7).[29] Paul found it important to speak in this way in responding to some who wished to make observance of the law's ceremonial demands binding even on believers (*Mosaic Harmony,* "Use of the Law"). But the "bare" law of which he speaks in these contexts is not the law in its fullness; it is the law *apart from Christ* (*Com. Gal.,* on 4:24); and apart from Christ, the law is like a dead body without a soul (*Com. John,* on 9:28). "If you separate the Law from Christ nothing remains in it save empty shapes" (*Com. John,* on 1:17; cf. *Com. 2 Cor.,* on 3:17). "Without Christ the whole ministry of Moses vanishes" (*Com. John,* on 5:46).

---

28. Thus, when Scripture says that statutes concerning the tabernacle's candlestick and lamps were to be observed "forever," the point is that they were to be observed until the day when the reality was revealed of which they were a type (*Com. Exod.,* on 27:20-21).

29. "Without Christ there is in the law nothing but inexorable rigour, which adjudges all mankind to the wrath and curse of God. And farther, without Christ, there remains within us a rebelliousness of the flesh, which kindles in our hearts a hatred of God and of his law, and from this proceed the distressing bondage and awful terror of which the Apostle speaks. . . . The design of Paul is to show what the law can do for us, taken by itself; that is to say, what it can do for us when, without the promise of grace, it strictly and rigorously exacts from us the duty which we owe to God" (*Com. Ps.,* on 19:8).

Interpreting Scripture: Keep It Simple

Calvin read, and commented on, the Bible in its original languages. He knew Hebrew well enough to explain in places how the Hebrew text had confused its Greek translators,[30] and even to propose emendations where he believed the existing manuscripts were in error (*Com. Ps.,* on 22:16; on 39:4). He was aware of variants in the manuscripts of the Greek New Testament and gave reasons for thinking one reading more original than another (*Com. John,* on 8:3, 59; on 10:6; on 19:31, etc.). He was also familiar with the work of other commentators, patristic as well as contemporary.[31] He was, in short, a learned reader of the Bible, one who prized and used the tools of biblical scholarship.

But Calvin was no fan of ingenious interpretations, however dogmatically sound and practically useful they might be. He was sure to reject any reading he found to be "subtle" or "refined" — in favor of a "simple" understanding of the words of a text (e.g., *Com. Ps.,* on 76:10; *Com. Hosea,* on 6:2). "Lofty mysteries" are not to be looked for beneath the text's surface, nor profound significance proposed for its every detail:[32] "The curiosity of the interpreters has done much harm, who by examining every single syllable [of a vision in Zechariah] have advanced many puerile things" (*Com. Zech.,* on 1:11).[33] Of course, divine accommodation to hu-

---

30. E.g., *Com. Gen.,* on 6:3. Calvin also knew, and found confirmation through mistranslations in the Septuagint, that the points indicating vowels in the Hebrew text were not original (*Com. Gen.,* on 4:7; *Com. Ps.,* on 15:4; *Com. Heb.,* on 11:21). In the century after Calvin, the authority of Scripture was thought by some to be undermined if the vowel points were not held to be an original part of the divinely revealed text. Muller, "Debate," traces the history of the ensuing debate.

31. Cf. Lane, *Student.*

32. Though the Mosaic law names many "unclean" land animals that the Israelites must not eat, the text is much less specific when it comes to fish. Some think this mysteriously indicates that the church, which is signified by the fish, seeks no mere earthly name. Calvin prefers a more straightforward explanation: since the Jews had no shores by the sea, and scarcely any river but the Jordan, they knew relatively few species of fish (*Com. Lev.,* on 11:9). He is similarly dismissive of attempts to find some "lofty mystery" in the number of fish miraculously caught by Jesus' disciples (*Com. John,* on 21:6). No profound truth is to be read into the reference to Lazarus's death as a "sleep"; the same way of speaking is found in secular writers (*Com. John,* on 11:12). As for the "philosophical and ingenious" meanings that Augustine attributed to the occurrence of a plural form of the word "life," they are "without foundation, as the plural of the word is quite commonly used in the singular significance" (*Com. Ps.,* on 63:3). Cf. *Com. Ps.* 22, introduction.

33. Other examples: "It was by no means the intention of God to include mysteries in every hook and loop" of the tabernacle; and even if some "mystical meaning" were attached

man weakness must be taken into account when we read Scripture, as we have seen. But as a general rule, Scripture means what any ordinary reader would take it to mean: "The Spirit of God would teach all men without exception"; the Bible is "the book of the unlearned" (*Com. Gen.,* on 1:6-8).

The problem with ingenious interpretations is that there is nothing sure, nothing "solid," about them: they please at first sight, then vanish (*Com. Hosea,* on 6:2). Like Luther, Calvin believed that, if divine revelation in Scripture is to provide the substance of our faith, its message must be clear and certain. For the same reason, he eschewed allegorical interpretations: they render "the doctrine of Scripture ambiguous and destitute of all certainty and firmness" (*Com. Gen.,* on 2:8; cf. *Com. Exod.,* on 17:10-12).[34] "Allegories, I know, delight many; but we ought reverently and soberly to interpret the prophetic writings, and not to fly in the clouds, but ever to fix our foot on solid ground" (*Com. Zech.,* on 6:1). At one point Calvin mocked the open-endedness of allegorical interpretation:

> The allegory will please many, that by the two bases [beneath each board of the tabernacle] are meant the Old and New Testament, or the two natures of Christ, because believers rest on these two supports. But with no less probability we might say, that two bases were placed beneath each of the boards; either because godliness hath the promise of this life and of that which is to come; or because we must resist on both sides the temptations which assail us from the right and from the left; or because faith must not limp nor turn to the right or left: thus there would be no bounds to trifling. (*Com. Exod.,* on 26:1-30)

"Trifling" captures well Calvin's sense of what allegorizers do with Scripture: "We should have more reverence for Scripture than to allow ourselves to transfigure its sense so freely" (*Com. Luke,* on 10:30-37).

---

to each part ("which no one in his sense will admit"), "it is better to confess our ignorance than to indulge ourselves in frivolous conjectures" (*Com. Exod.,* on 26:1; cf. on 25:8-15). No great benefit is to be found in protracted studies of the place names in Joshua (*Com. Josh.,* on 15:1). Cf. *Com. Heb.,* on 8:5.

34. See Puckett, *Exegesis,* 106-13. An obvious exception is to be made where an allegorical reading is found within Scripture itself; cf. *Com. Gen.,* on 6:14. Occasionally, Calvin confesses to finding other allegorical interpretations "pleasing," too — when they yield, without too much subtlety, gospel truth (e.g., *Com. Gen.,* on 27:27; *Com. Exod.,* on 28:31-35; *Com. Lev.,* on 11:3).

Many of the ancients without any restraint played all sorts of games with the sacred Word of God, as if they were tossing a ball to and fro. . . . Any mad idea, however absurd or monstrous, could be introduced under the pretext of an allegory. (*Com. 2 Cor.,* on 3:6)

Scripture, they say, is fertile and thus bears multiple meanings. I acknowledge that Scripture is the most rich and inexhaustible fount of all wisdom. But I deny that its fertility consists in the various meanings which anyone may fasten to it at his pleasure. Let us know, then, that the true meaning of Scripture is the natural and simple one, and let us embrace and hold it resolutely. Let us not merely neglect as doubtful, but boldly set aside as deadly corruptions, those pretended expositions which lead us away from the literal sense. (*Com. Gal.,* on 4:22)

But if "the true meaning of Scripture is the natural and simple one," then allegorizers are far from the only transgressors; many a well-meaning believer, bent on finding Christian truth in Old Testament texts, has, in Calvin's mind, crossed the line between natural and forced interpretation in order to do so.

Of course, Calvin himself read the Old Testament as a Christian theologian. He, too, was more than happy to find Christ[35] in passages where (what he took to be) a natural reading of the text allowed it; and there were many such. An obvious starting place was provided by the New Testament itself: where New Testament authors, inspired as they were by God's Spirit, interpreted Old Testament texts inspired by the same Spirit, then their interpretations must be accepted as true;[36] and, indeed, the New Testament finds Christ in a host of Old Testament passages, both by way of direct prophecies of the coming Messiah and through foreshadowings of Christ's work in the ceremonial laws of Moses.[37] Even so, Calvin is careful to add qualifications to the christological interpretation of certain Old

---

35. Or the Trinity. Calvin does think the plural forms in the divine speech of Gen. 1:26 ("let us make") point to "a plurality of Persons in the Godhead" (*Com. Gen.,* on 1:26). In Gen. 18, "the reason why Moses introduces, at one time, three speakers, while, at another, he ascribes speech to one only, is, that the three together represent the person of one God" (*Com. Gen.,* on 18:9).

36. "Who better than the Spirit of God will be a sure and faithful interpreter of this prophetic declaration, which He Himself dictated to Isaiah, seeing it was He who explained it by the mouth of Paul?" (*Com. 1 Cor.,* on 2:9; cf. *Com. Isa.,* on 28:16; *Com. 1 Cor.,* on 1:19).

37. For Calvin, the letter to the Hebrews and Stephen's speech in Acts 7 are our best guides to the interpretation of Old Testament "shadows and images" (*Com. Exod.,* on 25:8).

Testament texts, including some applied to Christ in the New Testament itself. He frequently notes, for example, that the initial referent of an Old Testament text[38] was someone who was contemporary with its composition — David,[39] Solomon,[40] Hezekiah,[41] Isaiah,[42] even Samson.[43] Since, however, that contemporary figure was a "type" of Christ, the application to Christ is legitimate.[44] Or he will observe that a passage meant generally in the Old Testament but applied specifically to Christ in the New is supremely, though not exclusively, true of him (*Com. Isa.,* on 61:1; *Com. Zech.,* on 13:7; *Com. Acts,* on 3:22; *Com. Eph.,* on 4:8). At times he suggests that a passage meant metaphorically in the Old Testament finds in Christ a particularly telling, literal application (*Com. Ps.,* on 22:18; on 69:21; *Com. Zech.,* on 9:9, on 11:14, on 12:10).[45]

On the other hand, the christological interpretation of many texts, though hallowed by centuries of repetition, was rejected by Calvin because it violated the natural sense of the text in its context.[46] Genesis 3:15 does

---

38. Calvin typically insists that the meaning ascribed to a text must be suited to its original historical context; this by no means prevents him from drawing out, by way of analogy, the text's significance for contemporary readers. Cf. Zachman, "Meaning," 14-15.

39. See *Com. Ps.,* on 2:1-2, 7; on 68:18; on 109, introduction.

40. See *Com. Ps.,* on 45, introduction.

41. See *Com. Isa.,* on 32:1, 3-4.

42. See *Com. Heb.,* on 2:13, referring to Isa. 8:18.

43. See *Com. Matt.,* on 2:23, referring to Judg. 13:5.

44. E.g., "David complains [in Ps. 22] that he is reduced to such circumstances of distress that he is like a man in despair. . . . At the same time, he sets before us, in his own person, a type of Christ, who he knew by the Spirit of prophecy behoved to be abased in marvellous and unusual ways previous to his exaltation by the Father" (*Com. Ps.* 22, introduction). "Although David speaks of himself [in Ps. 41], yet he speaks not as a common and private person, but as one who represented the person of Christ" (*Com. Ps.,* on 41:9). In such contexts, Calvin is wont to point out that the wording of the text goes far beyond anything that can be said of the psalmist himself or any of his contemporaries (e.g., *Com. Ps.,* on 2:8, 9; on 21:13; on 45:6).

45. See Pak, *Judaizing Calvin,* 77-101, for a discussion of the principles that determine for Calvin when a psalm can be applied to Christ.

46. Part of Calvin's concern in these cases is that overzealous Christians give nonbelievers (Jews are frequently specified) occasion to ridicule the faith when they advance unsupportable claims in its favor. Christians "with a pious diligence to set forth the glory of Christ, have, nevertheless, betrayed some excess of fervour. For while they lay too much stress on certain words, they produce no other effect than that of giving an occasion of ridicule to the Jews" (*Com. Gen.,* on 49:10; cf. *Com. Ps.* 72, introduction; *Com. Isa.,* on 4:2; on 6:3; *Com. Hosea,* on 11:1). For Calvin's understanding of the importance of context in determining what an author intended to say, see Zachman, "Meaning," 6-9. Chrysostom was "clearly Calvin's favorite patristic exegete" (Lane, "Calvin," 397), and in claiming that a

indeed indicate that the human race will one day be victorious over Satan, and that victory, to be sure, comes through Christ; but the expression "the seed of the woman" is "violently distorted" by those who believe it means Christ (*Com. Gen.,* on 3:15). Calvin has nothing but contempt for those who suggest that Psalm 72:10[47] or Isaiah 60:6-7[48] refers to the wise men of Matthew 2 (*Com. Ps.,* on 72:10; *Com. Isa.,* on 60:7); or that Isaiah 1:3[49] speaks of the manger in which Christ was laid (*Com. Isa.,* on 1:3); or that Isaiah 9:6[50] is a prophecy of Christ's cross (*Com. Isa.,* on 9:6). Nor is "the branch of the Lord" in Isaiah 4:2 a reference to Christ (*Com. Isa.,* on 4:2).

Forced readings supporting orthodox doctrine fare no better with Calvin. Those who use Isaiah 64:6[51] to prove that human works are "rotten and loathsome in the sight of God" distort the prophet's meaning (*Com. Isa.,* on 64:6); Jeremiah 13:23 is misused when thought to refute the notion that people have free will (*Com. Jer.,* on 13:23); John 8:46 cannot be used to prove Christ's sinlessness (*Com. John,* on 8:46). In none of these cases is Calvin disputing the doctrines themselves, since he believes that they are clearly taught elsewhere in Scripture. But shoddy arguments in their support only bring them into disrepute. At times, Calvin expresses sympathy for a doctrinal interpretation, but he feels the need nonetheless to caution that it is not solid enough to be used against heretics.

> The ancients quoted this passage [Isa 6:3, with its thrice-repeated "Holy"] when they wished to prove that there are three persons in one essence of the Godhead. I do not disagree with their opinion; but if I had to contend with heretics, I would rather choose to employ stronger proofs; for they become more obstinate, and assume an air of triumph, when inconclusive arguments are brought against them. (*Com. Isa.,* on 6:3; cf. *Com. 1 Cor.,* on 12:5)

---

consideration of context shows that the authors of numerous Old Testament texts did not intend the christological meanings attributed to them, Calvin resembles the Antiochene school of interpretation; see Chapter 5 above. That the author's meaning represents the proper object of the interpreter's endeavors is, for Calvin, self-evident: "It is almost [the interpreter's] only task to unfold the mind of the writer whom he has undertaken to expound" (*Com. Rom.,* dedication). For Calvin, the intention of Scripture's human authors is indistinguishable from that of the Spirit. Cf. Puckett, *Exegesis,* 32-37; cf. also Holder, *Grounding,* 58-68.

47. "The kings of Tarshish and of the isles shall bring presents."

48. "The multitude of camels shall cover thee . . . they shall bring gold and incense."

49. "The ox knoweth his owner, and the ass his master's crib."

50. "The government hath been laid upon his shoulder."

51. "But we are all as an unclean thing, and all our righteousnesses are as filthy rags."

The Truth of Scripture

The words of Scripture, though written by human beings, were spoken by God; within the broad limits allowed by divine accommodation to human weakness, what God says must be true.[52] Yet, by his insistence on the "natural and simple" meaning of a text and his rejection of allegory, Calvin has ruled out recourse to one of the standard ways in which earlier interpreters of Scripture had handled problematic texts.[53] How he deals with such texts says much both about the nature of Scripture's truth as he understands it, and about what he sees as the virtues of an interpreter.

As a general rule, for Calvin (and, indeed, for all but Origen, among the authors we have considered in this book), simple statements in Scripture are to be taken as factual. Calvin is at one with the tradition in insisting that apparent contradictions between the Gospels are not real; characteristic of Calvin is the declaration that their resolution is "easy" (e.g., *Com. Matt.*, on 26:71; *Com. Mark*, on 15:25; *Com. John*, on 20:1). That, as a rule, Scripture must be factual is the obvious presupposition underlying Calvin's rather creative explanations of certain problematic texts. Abimelech's surprising attraction to ninety-year-old Sarah (for example) is perhaps less to be explained "by the elegance of her form, than by the rare virtues with which he saw her, as a matron, to be endued" (*Com. Gen.*, on 20:2; one suspects that Calvin chose to see in Abimelech a man after his own heart).

Calvin's treatment of the final chapters of Exodus is telling. According to Exodus 33:7, Moses used to pitch the "tent of meeting" outside Israel's camp, where anyone could go who "sought the Lord." This has struck many readers as curious since construction of the "tent of meeting" is not said to begin for another two chapters (Exod. 35), nor is it finished for another six (Exod. 39); furthermore, once finished, it was to be situated at the center of the Israelite camp (Num. 2:2), not outside it. Honest workman that he is, Calvin will not accept the simple solution proposed by some, that the "tent of meeting" of Exodus 33:7 must be different from the "tent of meeting" in the rest of Exodus (*Com. Exod.*, on 25:2; on 40:2).[54] The only solution he can devise is that the instructions given for the making of the tent (begin-

---

52. Cf. Zachman, "Meaning," 22-24.

53. In this regard, too, Calvin and Chrysostom were in the same position (see Chapter 5 above).

54. On the other hand, Calvin does resolve the tension between the prohibition of a "staff" in Matt. 10:10 and Luke 9:3 and its allowance in Mark 6:8 by saying that the same Greek word means a heavy stick in Matthew and Luke, a light one in Mark (*Com. Matt.*, on 10:9).

ning in Exodus 25), as well as its actual construction, must have *preceded* Moses' ascent of Mount Sinai as told in Exodus 24. That way the "tent of meeting" could be in place, ready to be moved by Moses outside the camp (Exod. 33) as a punishment for Israel's idolatry (Exod. 32) (*Com. Exod.,* on 25:2). To be sure, Calvin was neither the first nor the last to defend the accuracy of the Bible by rewriting it, and the times when he does so are few; but on occasions at least, he certainly adds to their number.

It is also worth noting that Calvin does not think we should require of the biblical writers greater precision than their purpose in writing required. They must be permitted to use approximate figures,[55] hyperbole,[56] and some looseness of expression.[57] If Exodus 9:6 says that "all the [Egyptians'] cattle died" in one plague, though it is apparent from the subsequent narrative that "a considerable number of animals still remained," the point of the former statement must be that the pestilence "made havoc far and wide of a vast number of herds and flocks" (*Com. Exod.,* on 19:6). According to Joshua 11:23, Joshua took "the whole" of the Promised Land — "although it was far from being true that Joshua had actually acquired the whole land." But enough of the land had been taken for Israel to dwell in "for the present time"; and enough of the promise had been fulfilled to enable Joshua to divide the whole land by lot (*Com. Josh.,* on 11:23). As for the Gospel writers, "it is well-known that the Evangelists were not scrupulous in their time sequences, nor even in keeping to details of words and actions" (*Com. Luke,* on 8:19; cf. *Com. Matt.,* on 4:18). Where two or three evangelists tell much the same story, but differ in minor details, some insist that the differences mean that separate incidents must be described, since otherwise Scripture's truth would be impugned. Calvin dismisses their concern as "ridiculous," "making a fuss over nothing" (*Com. Matt.,* on 8:5; cf. on 9:18; on 20:29). Those who think that Matthew's Sermon on the Mount must have been delivered on an occasion other than Luke's

55. *Com. Exod.,* on 12:40; *Com. 1 Cor.,* on 10:8.

56. "When [prophets] adduce Sodom and Gomorrah as examples, they speak hyperbolically. . . . Now, someone may ask, Why does God thus exceed due limits in speaking? To this I answer, that it is not done without just reason and necessity. We indeed see that men are indifferent to God's judgments; for such is their sloth and insensibility, that they disregard as a light thing, or deem as nothing, what God threatens. As then men are so brutish, being unmoved by God's threatenings, it is necessary that such indifference should be roused and awakened" (*Com. Jer.,* on 49:18; cf. *Com. Jer.,* on 31:34; *Com. Joel,* on 2:28).

57. "It is certain that the Nile was not laid dry" — though Isaiah said it would be. The prophet meant, however, only to describe the coming calamity "in a lively manner" (*Com. Isa.,* on 19:6).

Sermon on the Plain because the location is said to be different make a "weak and trifling" argument. In fact, both evangelists have prepared "a short summary of the teaching of Christ, gathered from many and various discourses" (*Com. Matt.,* on 5:1).

Calvin's treatment of New Testament quotations of the Old is particularly illuminating of his sense of Scripture's truth. In no case will he allow that the New Testament writers distort the meaning of the text they cite;[58] yet he recognizes that they exercise great freedom in the wording of their citations.

> We know what freedoms the apostles took in quoting texts of Scripture; not, indeed, to wrest them to a meaning different from the true one. . . . They never had any hesitation in changing the words, provided the substance of the text remained unchanged. (*Com. Ps.,* on 8:5)

> We must always observe the rule, that as often as the Apostles quote a testimony from Scripture, although they do not render it word for word, in fact may move quite a way from it, they adapt it suitably and appropriately to the case in hand. (*Com. Matt.,* on 2:6)

The same insistence on the truth of Scripture while allowing for liberty with details is found in Calvin's interpretation of a number of Old Testament prophecies. We have already noted the healthy dose of accommodation he attributes to prophecies of the coming messianic kingdom.[59] Elsewhere, while finding it axiomatic that prophecies given by God cannot go unfulfilled,[60] Calvin grants that the foretelling of particular calamities in fact took effect in no single event, but only gradually, in a series of partial fulfillments lasting over centuries (*Com. Jer.,* on 50:39, 40; on 51:25, 44). So, too, the prophecies of Israel's return from exile to great blessing *began* to be fulfilled with the edicts of Cyrus, but the process continues with the spiritual redemption experienced by Christians and will only be

---

58. See *Com. Isa.,* on 28:16; on 64:4. Calvin does recognize that the apostles sometimes allude to Old Testament texts, taking over individual words to "embellish" their argument, but not intending to *interpret* the text to which they allude. In such cases, the apostles' point may well be different from that of the original. Cf. *Com. Ps.,* on 8:5; on 40:7-8; *Com. Hosea,* on 13:14; *Com. Eph.,* on 4:9; *Com. Heb.,* on 2:7.

59. Note, too, *Com. Hag.,* on 2:23: what Haggai prophesies of Zerubbabel "was never fulfilled in the person of Zerubbabel. It hence follows that it is to be applied to Christ" — granting that Zerubbabel was "a type of Christ."

60. "The prophet did not foretell what was not accomplished" (*Com. Isa.,* on 19:6).

completed at history's consummation with Christ's return (*Com. Isa.,* on 35:1; on 52:10; on 59:19; on 61:9).[61]

And, of course, everybody has limits. For Calvin — committed as he is to reading Scripture in its "natural" sense and to seeing its simple statements as factual — it is nonetheless self-evident that Scripture cannot mean *some* of the things it says.[62] He balks at no miracle stories: the "hand of God" is by no means "so restrained as to be unable to do anything which exceeds the bounds of human comprehension" (*Com. Exod.,* on 1:7; cf. *Com. Num.,* on 22:28). But what parent would really give his child the name Mahershalalhashbaz ("Ask me to build an ark, fine; just *don't* ask me to name my son 'the spoil speeds, the prey hastes'!"). Isaiah 8:1-4 presumably speaks of what Isaiah saw in a vision (which the text, to be sure, says nothing about) (*Com. Isa.,* on 8:3). It is "absurd" to think that Jeremiah journeyed all the way to the Euphrates River to hide a belt in a hole, then journeyed there again to examine it. Jeremiah 13:1-9 must likewise be speaking of an (unmentioned) vision (*Com. Jer.,* on 13:1-9). Only in a vision did Ezekiel lie on one side for 390 days (*Com. Ezek.,* on 4:4). And Calvin cannot believe, any more than Luther can, that Hosea married a prostitute: the prophet was only to relate this as a "parable" to his hearers (*Com. Hosea,* on 1:2; on 3:1).

Finally, Calvin's sense that the truth of Scripture need not mean precision in all its details expresses itself occasionally in a lack of concern for what he takes to be minor errors. "Jeremiah's name is put in error for Zechariah" in Matthew 27:9; but "how the name of Jeremiah crept in I

---

61. See Wilcox, "Prophets," 121-30.

62. At other times, sober Calvin allows that Scripture means what it says, but is quick to warn against drawing what he considers unwarranted inferences. Though Rebekah (after due consideration, and not without fault) accepted a golden earring from Abraham's servant, "we know how highly displeasing to God is not only pomp and ambition in adorning the body, but all kind of luxury" (*Com. Gen.,* on 24:22). Though Jacob loved Rachel because of her beauty, young men should not be misled: "This is a very culpable want of self-government, when any one chooses a wife only for the sake of her beauty, whereas excellence of disposition ought to be deemed of the first importance" (*Com. Gen.,* on 29:18). The "beating of timbrels" after Israel's deliverance at the Red Sea may be excused as "the custom of the nation"; we need to observe, however, "that musical instruments were among the legal ceremonies which Christ at His coming abolished; and therefore we, under the Gospel, must maintain a greater simplicity" (*Com. Exod.,* on 15:20). Christ may have eaten at the table of the wealthy, but "no doubt . . . He would have encouraged His guests to a frugal and restrained diet, and He would never have tolerated a wasteful profusion of expense" (*Com. Luke,* on 5:29). After all, the five thousand he fed "had to be satisfied with barley bread and dry fish" (*Com. John,* on 6:11).

cannot confess to know, nor do I make much of it" (*Com. Matt.,* on 27:9). The "seventy-five" of Acts 7:14 does not agree with the "seventy" of Genesis 46:27. But since readers of Acts would have been familiar with the larger number from the Greek version of Genesis, Calvin thinks Luke may not have regarded precision here as "such an important matter" to even bother correcting the number. In any case, "let us remember that it is not for nothing that Paul forbids us to be troubled and curious about genealogies" (*Com. Acts,* on 7:14; cf. Titus 3:9). There is an "obvious" error in Acts 7:16 (". . . in the tomb that Abraham bought for a price in silver from the sons of Hamor in Shechem"). Abraham bought a burial cave from Ephron the Hittite (Gen. 23); it was *Jacob* who purchased a field from the sons of Hamor in Shechem (Gen. 33:19). Calvin notes simply that "this verse must be amended accordingly" (*Com. Acts,* on 7:16).

Among problematic texts, we may include — as well as those raising questions of accuracy — narratives in which war is commanded and psalms in which enemies are cursed. Of the former, Calvin notes repeatedly that the judgments of God are just, though often beyond our comprehension.[63]

> That at which all would otherwise be justly horrified, it becomes them to embrace with reverence, as proceeding from God. . . . By this fact, then, not only are all mouths stopped, but all minds also are restrained from presuming to pass censure. . . . When it is added, that so God had commanded, there is no more ground for obloquy against [Joshua], than there is against those who pronounce sentence on criminals. . . . Let us remember that the judgment-seat of heaven is not subject to our laws. Nay, rather when we see how the green plants are thus burned, let us, who are dry wood, fear a heavier judgment for ourselves. . . . The potter will nevertheless have absolute power over his own vessels, or rather over his own clay. (*Com. Josh.,* on 10:40; cf. *Com. Deut.,* on 7:2; *Com. Josh.,* on 6:20)

As for the imprecations in the psalms (and Jeremiah), since the authors wrote under the direction of the Holy Spirit, we may be certain that they were not seeking personal revenge or, indeed, "influenced by any private personal considerations" (*Com. Ps.,* on 109:6; cf. *Com. Jer.,* on 11:20; on 15:15; on 18:21). If they spoke of hatred, it was directed toward the sins, not the persons, of the wicked (*Com. Ps.,* on 139:22); and the judgment they called for (again, since they were guided by the Spirit in what they said)

63. Cf. Blacketer, "Commentator," 47-48.

was only what God himself had determined to impose on those who were incurably reprobate (*Com. Ps.,* on 137:7; *Com. Jer.,* on 18:21, 23). In no way do these texts provide a model for others to follow: we are to wish for the "amendment and reformation" of "even our greatest enemies" (*Com. Ps.,* on 137:7) and, "so far as lies in us, to study peace with all men; we are to seek the good of all" (*Com. Ps.,* on 139:22).

Reading Scripture Aright

Since "it is God who speaks with us [in Scripture] and not mortal men," we must approach the text with "reverence, obedience, and willingness to learn" (*Com. 2 Pet.,* on 1:20). "It is only when men, divested of all self-confidence, submit themselves with humble and docile minds to God, that they are in a proper state for becoming proficient scholars in the study of the divine law" (*Com. Ps.,* on 119:130).

> If it be considered a sin to corrupt what has been dedicated to God, we assuredly cannot tolerate anyone who handles that most sacred of all things on earth with unclean or even ill-prepared hands. It is, therefore, presumptuous and almost blasphemous to turn the meaning of scripture around without due care, as though it were some kind of game that we were playing. (*Com. Rom.,* dedication)

> To revere God's Word is the only testimony that we fear [God]. (*Com. 1 John,* on 4:6)

But if "it is God who speaks with us" in Scripture, then we may be sure that none who approach the text aright will do so in vain. Even those deemed fools by the world will acquire from Scripture "wisdom sufficient to lead them to eternal salvation." They may not attain to "the highest degree in this wisdom," but they will certainly come to know the "unerring rule by which to regulate their life. Thus no man who surrenders himself to the teaching of God will lose his labour in his school, for from his first entrance he will reap inestimable fruit" (*Com. Ps.,* on 119:130).

Perseverance, to be sure, is called for.

> Nobody will be so raw and ignorant as not to get some benefit out of reading [Isaiah], yet perhaps he will hardly understand every tenth verse fully. . . . We ought to accept eagerly and with a ready mind those things

which are clear, and in which God reveals His mind; but it is proper to pass by those things which are still obscure to us, until a clearer light shines. But if we shall not be wearied by reading, the final result will be that constant use will make us familiar with Scripture. (*Com. Acts,* on 8:28)

So, too, is due diligence: "What hinders most men is that they look at [Scripture] only carelessly and as it were in passing" (*Com. John,* on 5:39). And though, without illumination from God's Spirit, God's word cannot be understood,[64] direct illumination should not be thought to replace the human help that God has ordained for our benefit.[65]

We must make use of all the aids which the Lord sets before us for the understanding of Scripture. Fanatics seek inspirations from heaven, and at the same time despise the minister of God, by whose hand they ought to have been ruled. Others, relying on their own penetrating insight, do not deign to hear anybody or to read any commentators. But God does not wish the aids, which He appoints for us, to be despised, and does not allow contempt of them to go unpunished. And we must keep in mind here, that not only is Scripture given to us, but interpreters and teachers are also added to help us. (*Com. Acts,* on 8:31)

The fact that the reading of the Scripture is recommended to all does not annul the ministry of pastors, so that believers should learn to profit both by reading and by hearing, since God has not ordained either in vain. (*Com. 2 Tim.,* on 4:1)[66]

If we are to derive benefit from Scripture, we must, of course, read it for the purpose for which it was given. We have already noted Calvin's

---

64. "The heavenly teaching is of no use or effect to us unless as far as the Spirit shapes our minds to understand it, and our hearts accept its yoke. . . . There is no worse screen to block out the light of the Spirit than confidence in our own intelligence" (*Com. Luke,* on 24:45). "So long as we use godly care, with humility and modesty, the Spirit of discernment will be with us and as a faithful interpreter will expound what He Himself speaks in Scripture" (*Com. 1 John,* on 4:6).

65. As we saw in Chapter 6, Augustine makes a similar point in the prologue to his *Teaching Christianity.*

66. It is assumed in these lines, and made explicit in their context, that the wisdom pastors impart is itself derived from Scripture; thus do they become its "living voice," while the text read privately is "silent Scripture" (*Com. 2 Tim.,* on 4:1).

insistence that "he who would learn astronomy, and other recondite arts, let him go elsewhere" (*Com. Gen.,* on 1:6-8). More generally, he condemns

> all who abandon concern for edification and agitate over ingenious but profitless questions. Whenever ingenious trifles of that kind are introduced, they should be warded off with this phrase as with a shield, "Scripture is profitable." . . . In giving us the Scriptures, the Lord did not intend either to gratify our curiosity or satisfy our desire for ostentation. . . . He intended rather to do us good. Thus the right use of Scripture must always lead to what is profitable. (*Com. 2 Tim.,* on 3:16)

> It is by the reading of the Scripture that we make progress in godliness and holiness of life. . . . All that we learn from Scripture is conducive to the advancement of godliness. (*Com. Rom.,* on 15:4)

And, like Luther, Calvin is convinced that we only read God's word aright when we read it as spoken to ourselves.

> We must always pay attention to this, that the will of God is made known to us in no other manner than by His Word. But it is not enough to have the Word in its general sense, unless we know that it is meant for ourselves. . . . It is a necessary requirement for a firm faith that everyone is fully convinced that he is included in the number of those God is addressing. (*Com. Acts,* on 2:39)

CHAPTER 10

The Pietists and Wesley

To the extent that evangelical Christians today are aware of their spiritual ancestry — and such awareness has not always been their forte — they acknowledge their indebtedness to the Protestant Reformation, with its affirmation of salvation by grace through faith and its insistence on the unique authority of Scripture. More distinctly evangelical emphases have their roots in the eighteenth-century revivals of John and Charles Wesley,[1] who themselves were indebted to the German Pietists. Included in these emphases were the personal and experiential aspects of faith (the "religion of the heart"), which in turn called for a personal and "spiritual"[2] reading of Scripture: the true Christian is thus a "Bible Christian," and true Christianity is "scriptural Christianity."[3] Yet, for all its attention to the religious "affections," the Pietist movement placed great importance on biblical learning as well. In Johann Albrecht Bengel, the Pietist movement produced one of the foremost biblical scholars of the eighteenth century, and John Wesley, for his part, may have been Bengel's greatest admirer.[4] The unique way in which the Pietists and Wesley combined concern for the *letter* of Scripture with zeal for its *spirit* merits a chapter in the story of Christian readings of the Bible.

---

1. And those of George Whitefield and Jonathan Edwards: for an introduction to the role played by each of these figures in the beginnings of modern evangelical Christianity, see Noll, *Rise.* Our focus in this chapter, however, is on John Wesley.

2. Here the term refers, not to the nonliteral reading of Scripture (as with Origen and his heirs), but to the personal application of the text, usually understood in its literal sense.

3. The expressions are common in John Wesley's writings.

4. "That great light of the Christian world (lately gone to his reward), Bengelius" (Wesley, *Notes NT* 4).

270

Philip Jacob Spener

Historians of Pietism routinely see the work of Johann Arndt (1555-1621) — a Lutheran pastor, theologian, and follower of Philipp Melanchthon — as a forerunner of the movement. In decrying the nominal Christianity of his day, where all were deemed Christians but few showed any inclination for godly living, Arndt's *True Christianity* effectively set the agenda that the Pietists would later pursue.[5]

The beginnings of Pietism proper are commonly traced to the publication of Philip Jacob Spener's *Pia Desideria* in 1675. In what was originally an extended preface to a collection of Arndt's sermons, Spener (1635-1705) elaborated on similar complaints about the state of Christendom in his day, but he went on to suggest "proposals to correct [these] conditions." The first of these proposals began as follows:

> Thought should be given to a *more extensive use of the Word of God among us*. We know that by nature we have no good in us. If there is to be any good in us, it must be brought about by God. To this end the Word of God is the powerful means, since faith must be enkindled through the gospel, and the law provides the rules for good works and many wonderful impulses to attain them. The more at home the Word of God is among us, the more we shall bring about faith and its fruits. (*Pia Desideria*, 87)

Spener then proceeded with practical suggestions as to how Scripture could be made "more at home . . . among us." The preaching of sermons based on particular biblical texts is good, but not enough: *all* scripture is "inspired" and "profitable" (2 Tim. 3:16), yet church congregations, even over many years, are exposed only to "a very small part of the Scriptures" through sermons (*Pia Desideria*, 88). "Solitary reading of the Bible at home is in itself a splendid and praiseworthy thing"; but it, too, is insufficient for most people in that it necessarily leaves them without explanation of things in Scripture they do not understand or would like to know (*Pia Desideria*, 88, 90).

"Diligent [family] reading of the Holy Scriptures" would certainly be a good thing; a further proposal sees times set aside in the public services

---

5. "In the history of Protestantism there is no book, apart from the Bible, that has had such a circulation as Johann Arndt's *Bücher vom wahren Christentum (True Christianity)*. It is the classic devotional book of Protestantism" (Wallmann, "Arndt," 21).

for the simple reading of books of the Bible — "one after another" and "without further comment" (*Pia Desideria,* 88-89). Still more promising would be "to reintroduce the ancient and apostolic kind of church meetings," where sermons were not preached but where, under the guidance of a minister (or ministers), passages of Scripture might be read and each verse discussed

> in order to discover its simple meaning and whatever may be useful for the edification of all. Anybody who is not satisfied with his understanding of a matter should be permitted to express his doubts and seek further explanation. On the other hand, those (including the ministers) who have made more progress should be allowed the freedom to state how they understand each passage. Then all that has been contributed, insofar as it accords with the sense of the Holy Spirit in the Scriptures, should be carefully considered by the rest, especially by the ordained ministers, and applied to the edification of the whole meeting. (*Pia Desideria,* 89-90)

Along these lines, "pious groups" ("collegia pietatis") — a precursor of the modern group Bible study — grew up, meeting biweekly in Frankfurt, where Spener was a Lutheran minister.

> This much is certain: the diligent use of the Word of God, which consists not only of listening to sermons but also of reading, meditating, and discussing (Ps. 1:2), must be the chief means for reforming something, whether this occurs in the proposed fashion or in some other appropriate way. The Word of God remains the seed from which all that is good in us must grow. If we succeed in getting the people to seek eagerly and diligently in the book of life for their joy, their spiritual life will be wonderfully strengthened and they will become altogether different people. (*Pia Desideria,* 91)

Here we see Pietism's characteristic emphasis on the importance of Scripture for the "spiritual life" of *every* believer. "All Christians" (Spener writes elsewhere) must "diligently" read the Scriptures since they are "the letter of the heavenly Father to *all* his children."[6] He dismisses any suggestion that the uneducated should simply believe what their preachers

---

6. Erb, *Pietists,* 54. Hereafter, page references to this work appear in parentheses within the text.

tell them: they, too, must search the Scriptures so that they can "test the teaching of their preacher" and so that their faith will rest solely on divine truth. After all, Christ's own teaching was not directed "to the wise and intelligent of this world, but to the simple"; the apostles, too, wrote their letters "for the most part to uneducated and plain people" (Erb, 55).

Nor should Scripture be deemed too obscure for the uneducated to understand. To be sure, Scripture's clarity is often obscured for us because our eyes have been darkened by sin; but such darkening afflicts the learned no less than the uneducated. And

> the principal points of doctrine and rules of life are given in the Scriptures so clearly and according to the letter that each uneducated person can learn and comprehend them as well as the learned. Thus when pious hearts have comprehended these and obediently used the first measure received, as they continue to read the Scriptures with meditation and prayer, God the Holy Spirit will open their understanding more and more, so that they may also learn and understand the higher and more difficult matters as far as is necessary for strengthening of their faith, instruction in life, and comfort. (Erb, 56)

"As far as is necessary for strengthening of their faith": for Spener, it is crucial that we remember the divine purpose served by Scripture. "The Scripture is given to us only to learn of God, and to understand from it his will and our blessedness" (Erb, 73). Of course, it would be "desirable" if all Christians read the Scriptures in their original languages; but translations are available, and even in translation "anyone can find enough for *the necessary knowledge of Christianity*" (Erb, 56; italics added). Nor are other scholarly aids "properly the means for the *saving knowledge* of the truth," though they "*explain further* the truth known through the Spirit" (Erb, 56; italics in original).

> Whence do simple pious Christians receive the understanding of the Scriptures? From the *enlightenment of the Holy Spirit,* by whose inspiration the Scriptures were first recorded, so that they cannot be understood without his light (2 Pet. 1:21; 1 Cor. 2:12). Now God has promised the Holy Spirit to all who call upon him in simplicity and, therefore, not only to the learned (Luke 11:13; James 1:5; 1 John 5:14, 15). By his anointing and illumination they, therefore, understand all in the Scriptures that they need *for their salvation and growth in the inner man.* (Erb, 56-57; latter italics added)

Thus, the study of Scripture is not to be confined to the learned. Nor is its message restricted to those to whom it was originally addressed: Scripture is "directed" to all, so that, "insofar as possible," readers should "direct" what it says to themselves. What God said in the past is what God says now: "God is an unchangeable God and his will always remains the same." Unless, then, a command in Scripture is expressly addressed to specific persons, it should be understood as meant for us all, "for we are all God's servants." And even where a command is specifically directed, we can still derive from it a more general duty at its root that we need to observe. Furthermore, since Scripture's promises of grace reflect God's unchanging love for all, "we can certainly at all times apply them to ourselves as if they were immediately and specially spoken to us if we on our side stand in the order required" (Erb, 75).

All Scripture must be read "as the Word of the great God"; as such, it commands not only our "deep reverence" but also our complete and immediate obedience. Any who read Scripture without a will to obey are not reading it as *God's* Word; they thereby deprive themselves both of a spiritual understanding of the text and of any experience of its power (Erb, 57-58). In Spener's insistence on the Spirit-illuminated, submissive reading of Scripture, understood as God's personal word to every believer, we see characteristically Pietist emphases. The importance of biblical *scholarship* is added to these themes in the work of August Hermann Francke and Johann Albrecht Bengel.

August Hermann Francke

It seems disproportionate to rank two men in one chapter among "the most remarkable people who have ever lived," but August Hermann Francke (1663-1727) and John Wesley both qualify. A disciple of Spener, Francke displayed a unique combination of gifts as a theologian, pedagogue, and entrepreneur.[7] In Halle, where he was both pastor and professor, he established Europe's largest and most progressive orphan house, a training school for teachers and pastors, other schools for various levels and classes of students (schools that were made agriculturally self-sufficient), a publishing house (making it possible for ordinary people to afford their own Bibles),[8] a science laboratory, and a pharmacy. He sent out the first

---

7. See Matthias, "Francke," 100.

8. "Through the copious production of New Testaments and the entire Bible in the

Protestant missionaries from Halle. In addition, he wrote books: "The bibliography of Francke's writings comprises about 850 texts," most of which — but by no means all — were sermons.[9]

Our concern here must be confined to his *Guide to the Reading and Study of the Holy Scriptures*. He first gives attention to the "letter" of Scripture. False meanings are easily attributed to the inspired authors when the text is read either in translation or with an imperfect grasp of the original languages; therefore, it is important that the "etymology, signification, syntax, and idiom" of Greek and Hebrew "be fully understood" (*Guide*, 3).[10] Francke outlines what he claims to be a tried-and-true method by which students can acquire these skills. Following his program, the student should have acquired *within three months* a good grasp of Greek grammar while reading through the Greek New Testament — *twice* (8). (Francke graciously concedes that such progress is possible only if students temporarily set other duties aside.) Learning Hebrew grammar and reading through the Hebrew Old Testament, he says, has been known to take another three months (20). Some will want to go on to read the church fathers in Greek as well as the Septuagint and the Apocrypha. Not that these latter writings possess the same authority as Scripture; but reading them undoubtedly assists in gaining mastery of the language. Students should also learn Aramaic ("Chaldee") for the sake of the few chapters in the Old Testament in that language. And they may also wish to read the Aramaic targum and make some acquaintance with rabbinic writings in Hebrew and Aramaic.

In addition to linguistic skills, appreciation of the "letter" of the text requires historical knowledge of the "sum and substance" of the Old and New Testaments as a whole, as well as of their individual writings; it also includes an awareness of the authorship and occasion of each part. Of course, students should also be aware of the different manuscripts and versions in which the sacred texts have been preserved. Like Origen and Augustine, Francke thinks some background knowledge of places, weights and measures, customs, natural history, and so on, is also relevant for grasping the historical sense of certain texts. Without retracting anything that he has

---

institute's own printing house and cheap prices, the pietistic goal was to place a Bible in every household" (Reventlow, *History*, 4.137).

9. Matthias, "Francke," 104.

10. In this and other quotations from Francke's work, the capitalization of many nouns and the frequent use of italics that were typical at the time when Franke's texts were published in English (1813) have been removed without comment. In this English publication, his name is given as Augustus Herman Franck.

said, Francke adds that one should nonetheless not be "immoderately anxious about things merely external," and one must be wary of the pride that readily accompanies such learning (46). And pride is not the only danger:

> There is also a necessity for the exercise of caution, lest a knowledge of external points render us less ardent and lively in reading the Word itself. How many are there who err in this respect, and feed contentedly on the husks, while those heavenly delights which flow from the volume of revelation remain untasted and unenjoyed. Inasmuch as the letter is examined only for the sake of the spirit of the sacred oracles, we should contemn whatever cannot be reduced to some useful purpose; and never give place to vain, unprofitable curiosity. (46-47)

Finally, attention to the letter of the biblical text demands that entire books and particular texts be subjected to "logical analysis" (50), noting their structure, train of thought, and order. Francke the pedagogue is ready with rules to follow and cautions to heed in making these analyses, beginning with the text as a whole, but gradually narrowing the focus to the point where individual words are carefully considered in the context of the whole. The student can thus avoid the danger of "mangl[ing] and dismember[ing] a text" because one has isolated a verse from what precedes and what follows it (60). In the process of logical analysis, too, however, there lurks great danger. Inasmuch as

> this species of reading is, properly speaking, confined to the letter of the Word, let us guard against supposing that we are "mighty in the Scriptures," if we be more solicitous to analyze a text, than concerned about understanding and applying it. In the exercise of refined subtleties, and the solution of difficult passages, we may lose sight of holy Christian simplicity, and sacrifice the edification of ourselves and others. (63)

When Francke then turns his attention to apprehension of the text's "spirit," he actually repeats much of what he has already said about the pursuit of its external sense, or "letter." However "empty and inconsistent" the "letter" may be apart from consideration of the "spirit" (2), the "spirit" for its part depends on the correct construction of the "letter." "Divinity" rests on "an uncertain foundation" if the "exposition" of Scripture is not solid (94). Francke defines the "expository reading" of Scripture as that concerned with "the literal sense *purposed by the Holy Spirit*" (65; italics added). This is distinguished from the (already discussed) "sense of the letter" in that the Spirit may intend to communicate more through a text than its words in themselves convey. Francke cites as an example the commandment "Thou shalt not kill": the Spirit's point in these words (as revealed in the Sermon on the Mount [Matt. 5:21-22]) includes, together with the forbidding of violent deeds, that of hurtful words and gestures (65-66). Proper "expository reading" thus presupposes a correct understanding of the literal sense of the text (of the latter, even "carnal and unregenerate" interpreters are capable), but goes beyond it to include "that sense which no one can apprehend, unless divinely illuminated by the Spirit who speaks in the Scriptures" (67). The fifth commandment is not understood in *this* sense (any more than it can be obeyed) without personal experience of the "genuine love to our neighbour" that flows from faith (68). Thus, "practical and spiritual" — not merely "theoretical and historical" — knowledge is the goal of "expository reading" (70).

Among the "internal helps" for proper expository reading, none is more important than the "analogy of faith." For Francke, the expression refers, not to the doctrine of any particular church, but to that which is consistent with the "universal agreement of the inspired writers": "It is by no means consonant with the principles of Divinity, to interpret Scripture by the hypotheses of a Church; because the sacred records are the proper mediums of ascertaining theological truth" (77-79). Particular texts of Scripture must thus be interpreted in a way consistent with the message of Scripture as a whole. Works of scholarship ("external helps") may be called on to assist in the interpretation of difficult texts, "though it is to be observed, that, in all things pertaining to eternal salvation, the Scriptures sufficiently explain themselves" (85). In general,

> we may safely assure those who read the word with devotion and simplicity, that they will derive more light and profit from such a practice, and from connecting meditation with it, . . . than can ever be acquired from drudging through an infinite variety of unimportant minutiae. (90-91)

Many commentaries attend at great length to matters "critical, controverted, and difficult," since discussion of such matters gives great scope to the "natural intellect"; but they offer little that will edify the spiritual reader (152-53). In the end, the student should avoid, on the one extreme, the error of those "who can admire nothing but their own meditations," while at the same time steering clear of the opposite extreme, that of relying solely on the authority of others (86). A spiritual understanding of the text comes only through *personal* (though Spirit-led) engagement with the text.

> Those persons are usually but indifferent examiners of the Scriptures, who, in searching into their meaning, depend, partially or entirely, on authority. It evidences, as Bernard has observed, that they do not read the Word, in the Spirit under whose influence it was written. (152)

Francke also gives guidance for the "doctrinal reading" of the text ("by which we so apprehend the truths contained in Scripture, as to derive thence a just and saving acquaintance with the nature and will of God" [94]); its "inferential reading" (by which truths both theoretical and practical are inferred from the text); and its "practical reading" (concerned with "the application of the Scriptures to faith and practice" [124]).

> Practical reading is of such a nature, that it may be prosecuted by an illiterate person; for the application of Scripture which it enjoins, is connected with salvation; and, therefore, if it were not within the ability of the unlearned, it would be vain to concede to them, the reading of the Scriptures. We do not, however, deny, but that, from an acquaintance with the Greek and Hebrew languages, several things of an edifying nature may arise, which would not be so obvious in a translation. It is, however, sufficient, that all things necessary to faith and practice may be acquired from versions. (124-25)

Francke reserves for an appendix "A Treatise on the Affections, as connected with the Study of the Holy Scriptures." The biblical writers themselves wrote "with affections": certainly "their minds were illuminated by the Spirit," but at the same time their wills were "inflamed with pious, holy, and ardent affections, so that they wrote as they *felt,* and as they were '*moved* by the Holy Ghost'" (149-50; see 2 Pet. 1:21). Inevitably, Spirit-led readings of texts so written will result in amending "our natural affections," and in the "overflow" of "gracious affections" from our hearts as well (143). Indeed, "the sacred records cannot be adequately expounded" by those who "never enter into the feelings of the inspired penmen" (145). Though "a carnal man can apprehend the terms of the proposition[s]" he encounters in Scripture, he cannot have any notion of what it means to be so "sanctified, and endued with heavenly knowledge and divine perception" that, in apprehending the divine truth of those propositions, one's affections are moved. "How is it possible for [an unrenewed person] to have any perception of the emotions of a holy soul?" (156-57); and without such emotions, how can any interpreter claim to know that of which the text is speaking? Conversely, "the more we 'put on' [the inspired writers'] affections, the more deeply shall we enter into their writings, and meditate on the truths which they reveal. . . . The meaning of Scripture, thus laid up in the heart, rather than the head, will transform our souls 'from glory into glory'" (175).

"Rather than the head": but Francke by no means discounts the importance of the intellectual labor involved in properly reading the text. He discounts only a reading that goes no further, while insisting (with all the Pietists) that the Spirit-led reading of Scripture "with devotion and simplicity" yields even to uneducated readers all that they need for "faith and practice."

Johann Albrecht Bengel

The characteristic emphases of Francke's writings on Scripture are all echoed in the work of Johann Albrecht Bengel (1687-1752),[11] a younger contemporary who met Francke on several occasions and revered him greatly.[12] Like Francke, Bengel both emphasized the importance of biblical scholarship and cautioned that such scholarship can become an end in itself, to the detriment of godly living. On the one hand, neither indolence nor a reliance on inner revelations should keep one from the serious study of Scripture.

> God teaches us by the written, as well as by the inward Word; and because his written Word was originally given in Hebrew and Greek, it is necessary[13] to learn these languages. He could sustain our animal life without agriculture; yet he has appointed that man should till the ground. He could increase in us mental and spiritual light without our seeking it; yet we are obliged to seek it, and to set our faculties to work for that purpose. . . . Nothing is more pernicious than indolence. (Burk, 61)

11. Bengel's professional life was largely spent teaching at a preparatory school for theology students in Denkendorf. He declined positions at the universities of Giessen and Tübingen. See Ehmer, "Bengel"; also Baird, *History,* 1.69-80.

12. See Burk, *Memoir,* 513-15. Hereafter, page references to this work appear in parentheses within the text.

13. Bengel is thinking of what is necessary for students of theology destined for ministry in the church.

We ought immediately to apply ourselves to learn whatever, by diligent research in the fear of God, and by calling upon Him, we may become enabled to learn; we ought to do this at once, rather than delay under the notion of waiting for extraordinary illumination or influence; lest by and by we should come to fancy that we want neither book nor human teacher. . . . [God] has moreover given the Bible. This also we are to make use of; and in so far as this may suffice, he bestows no additional revelation. (Burk, 260)

On the other hand, the study of Scripture *can* be pursued at the cost of one's spiritual health.

There is no bodily or mental labour which may not be made injurious to our secret and perpetual communion with God. Even scriptural researches may, without needful discretion, very easily occasion in learned men an indifference to true godliness, instead of nourishing any desire for it, or delight in it. As mere "knowledge" of every kind "puffeth up," so human ideas are apt to captivate human beings, and thus to check in the heart all easy and favourable germination, growth and influence of divine truth. . . . Such a fascinating ascendant does mere learning hold sometimes over men, that hereby they lose all relish for the salutary truths of the gospel. (Burk, 219)

To be sure, we cannot obey Scripture if we do not know it; but — Bengel, like Spener and Francke, insists — only if we obey Scripture is the knowledge we acquire put to proper use.[14] Those who study Scripture, not merely to increase knowledge, but so that they may conform their lives to the will of its divine Author, will find what they read "clear and intelligible enough" for the purpose; and in the process, they will derive "nurture" for their "inward man" (Burk, 262, 69). It is, indeed, a mark of the divine authority with which Scripture addresses us that it has power to convict, convert, instruct, and comfort the human heart (Burk, 262). The Scriptures

carry in themselves independent and convincing evidence of the truth, validity, and sufficiency of all the narratives, doctrines, promises, and threatenings they contain. Truth is its own witness, and exacts our as-

14. Bengel, *Gnomon,* 1.6. Hereafter, references to this work appear in parentheses within the text.

sent. I recognise the hand-writing of a friend, without needing to be told who has written to me. We want not the stars, much less a torch, to show us the sun; it is only the blind that cannot see it. . . . [The written word] possesses a supernatural efficacy. . . . It takes men captive, and kindles faith within them, before they have even thought what faith is, or considered whether they will believe, or why they should believe. This is a very different thing from conviction by moral, historical, or mathematical inference. (Burk, 253)

So different is Scripture's impact on the human heart from the effect of human argumentation that Scripture's power and authority are undermined, not strengthened, when we attempt to prove, "by our own mere reasonings," truths learned from the inspired texts. To Bengel's mind, "this looks like attempting by natural knowledge to supersede faith in the Divine testimony" — and the result is that falsehood is liable to proliferate; for "when we have done all that can be done in this way, the sneering infidel can quite as readily produce his rational arguments, contradictory to and equally valid with our own." Only divine power can bring "an unbelieving person to true and practical faith" (Burk, 257-58).[15]

That power, then, is found in the words of Scripture, where "the all-pure Spirit of God breathes" (Burk, 57). Scripture is "the LORD's own book" (Bengel, 1.5). As such, "it is *perfect,* as containing whatever is necessary to be known and believed in order to salvation" (Burk, 262). It is the standard by which "every controversy in matters of faith" is to be settled (Burk, 262). Bengel counsels us "to abide by that one dictum, 'It is written'; and leave, 'It appears to us,' to the philosophers" (Burk, 57). God knows best, and we should be content with what God has chosen to reveal:

> Considering God to be virtually addressing us in his word, we should concern ourselves first to understand him, and then how to communicate it to others. He is great, and past finding out; no wonder then that he does not teach us every thing in this life, which is but a pilgrimage; though he discloses enough for our direction and progress. More than this would not be useful just now; it is reserved for home. (Burk, 261-62)

---

15. Bengel was well aware of those in his day who were eager to replace the authority of Scripture with the pretensions of human reason: they "attribute too much to fallen nature's light, by adopting only such Scripture statements as we can explain and vindicate by human reason." Religion is then reduced to "decency and propriety of conduct"; it has no place for "an atoning Christ," "our righteousness in him," "the work of the Holy Spirit," or "any thing taught exclusively by revelation and above natural reason" (Burk, *Memoir,* 255).

We shall soon know, in the heavenly world, even as also we are known; and then the very Scriptures themselves will appear to have been worded to our comprehension after the manner of a little child's first book. (Burk, 370)

Clearly, Bengel's credentials as a Pietist are impeccable. Unlike Spener and Francke, however, Bengel also has an important place in the history of New Testament scholarship, based on his achievements as a textual critic and commentator. In both cases, his work was marked and inspired by his Pietist convictions.[16]

All the interpreters we have examined up to this point were aware of differences between the translations of Scripture in common use and the sacred text in its original languages; they also knew that the various manuscripts in which Scripture was preserved differed from each other at numerous points. Yet only Origen, of those we have studied, made the proper text of Scripture itself a central concern. Others at times suggested, on grounds that were rarely defensible, what the proper reading should be; at other times they offered an edifying interpretation of each of the variant readings without worrying about which was original.

Bengel worried. Living at a time when collecting the various readings in biblical manuscripts had become a scholarly preoccupation, and learning that there were some 30,000 variant readings in the manuscripts of the New Testament, Bengel wondered for a time how a text so uncertain could be trusted. Others, he knew, insisted simply on accepting the text of some printed edition, rejecting out of hand any alternative readings. Such an attitude he found "unworthy" of anyone who has "reached years of discretion. It encourages an obstinate and credulous attachment to the more received text, and a perverse and jealous distrust of ancient documents." Those who say that Scripture, or Christianity itself, is endangered if we do not simply accept a standard text are themselves a danger to Christianity; they "know not the meaning of faith." It is foolish to imagine that

---

16. Not all, however, was pure gold. Bengel is also known for his devotion to the study of biblical chronology (e.g., according to his calculations, Solomon's temple was completed 2933 years after the creation of the world [Burk, *Memoir,* 270]) and his intense preoccupation with discovering the secrets he believed hidden in the book of Revelation. In neither of these cases has his work stood the test of time: e.g., that 1836 came and went without the dawning of millennial blessings is sufficient to show that Bengel had not, after all, discovered the key to interpreting Revelation (see Burk, *Memoir,* 316). See also Sandys-Wunsch, *History,* 268-70.

Divine Providence, ever watchful over Holy Scripture, [has] bound itself down to the typography of the sixteenth century, the era, within whose narrow limits, the whole of the text defended by these zealots, was collected and defined. . . . We ought, indeed, laying aside all party feeling, to seek for an entire and unadulterated text; which many, however, disgraceful though it be, care less for than a patched glove. (Bengel, 1.17-18)[17]

The copyists of Scripture were, after all, fallible human beings. Had they all transcribed the text without error, such perfect preservation "would have been so great a miracle, that faith in the written word of God could be no longer faith" (Burk, 52). The actual results — predictably, and observably — were very different. To complain that those who study the variant readings are "putting weapons into the hands of infidels" is pointless: "infidels" are already well aware of the "many various readings" (Burk, 242). For Bengel, it was precisely an act of devotion to the Word of God to strive "laboriously . . . to obtain a pure text of the New Testament" (Bengel, 1.11).

Though much critical erudition as well as common reading has been applied to no better purpose than that of mere head knowledge, still there is no particle of God's word which does not deserve the most careful research, yes, which has not its appropriate and infallible use to those who will give it time and occasions for taking effect. (Burk, 427)

As a result of his study, Bengel became convinced that the manuscripts contain no readings "which in the least affect the foundation of our faith. You may therefore safely and securely have nothing to do with doubts, which at one time so distressingly perplexed myself" (Burk, 52). "By far the more numerous portions of the Sacred Text (thanks be to GOD) labour under no variety of reading deserving notice. These portions contain the whole scheme of salvation, and establish every particular of it by every test of truth" (Bengel, 1.13). Moreover, so extensive is the evidence for reconstructing the original New Testament text that we can be sure the genuine reading is always present in some manuscripts; we need never simply guess at what it might have been (Bengel, 1.14). Most importantly — and herein lies Bengel's signal contribution to the history of New Testament textual

17. Cf. Bengel, *Gnomon*, 1.28: "There are those who dare to limit the exercise of divine providence in preserving the integrity of the New Testament exclusively to the Stephanic Press [i.e., the 'Received Text'], and cease not to bring the charge of audacity against all, who endeavour to employ earnestly and reverently for the common edification all the helps which Divine Providence has vouchsafed to the age in which they live."

criticism — informed scholars are not helpless in the face of endless lists of variant readings. There are criteria by which the plausibility of readings can be assessed. (The criteria Bengel lists largely correspond to those in use among textual critics to this day.[18]) Putting such resources to use, Bengel produced a text of the New Testament in Greek, largely taken over from printed editions already in existence,[19] but accompanied by Bengel's own classification of variant readings, determined by what he deemed the likelihood with which each represented the original text.

A recent survey of the story of the New Testament text lists "three lasting contributions" that Bengel made to New Testament textual criticism.[20] (1) Where different manuscripts share a number of distinctive readings, Bengel realized that these manuscripts must be related to each other and come (broadly speaking) from the same geographical area. On this basis he distinguished "Asiatic" witnesses to the New Testament text from those of "African" origin. In so doing, "he was the first to group textual witnesses on the basis of their common readings." (2) "Since the *quality of readings* exhibited by witnesses was more important than the *number* of witnesses, he formulated the principle 'manuscripts must be weighed, rather than counted.'" (3) Realizing that those who copy texts would be tempted to make an obscure text clearer, or a difficult text more straightforward, Bengel "enunciated one of the most important principles, or 'canons,' for deciding between or among variant readings: 'The harder reading is to be preferred to the easier.'"

Finally, Bengel prepared and published the notes he used in teaching the New Testament in an extended commentary, *Gnomon of the New Testament*. He acknowledged that, when first published, the biblical writings were well suited to the needs of their readers and required no commentary. There is, however, a place now for "writings and commentaries" that aim to restore and defend "the purity of the *text*"; that clarify the full force of the words used (in Hebrew and Greek) by the sacred writers; that explain the circumstances under which any passage was originally uttered or written; and that "remove *errors* or abuses which have arisen in latter times."

The first hearers required none of these things. Now, however, it is the office of commentaries to effect and supply them in some measure, so

18. See Metzger and Ehrman, *Text,* 159.

19. The exception was the text of the book of Revelation, where the unsatisfactory nature of printed editions required Bengel to introduce readings found only in manuscripts (see Bengel, *Gnomon*, 1.19).

20. For what follows, see Hull, *Story,* 48.

that *the hearer of to-day, when furnished with their aid, may be in a condition similar to that of the hearer in primeval times who made use of no such assistance.* (Bengel, 1.6-7; italics in original)

Bengel saw no need to go beyond basic explanation by applying the message of the texts to his readers.

He who submits himself to the constraining influence of Divine Love in the search after Divine Truth, imbibes from the Divine Words, when he has once perceived their meaning, all things profitable for salvation, without labour, and without stimulus. (Bengel, 1.65)

The Pietist convictions that inspired Bengel's work are evident on its every page; so, too, is his careful attention to details of the Bible's vocabulary, grammar, style, and argumentation. In addition, Bengel had a gift for concise, memorable expression that, when coupled with his impressive learning, invites quotation even in modern commentaries. When John Wesley wanted to place in the hands of poor but devout readers notes on the New Testament,[21] which he himself lacked the opportunity to produce, he decided simply to summarize the work of Bengel.[22] The choice does credit to them both.

John Wesley

John Wesley (1703-1791) made it his goal to be "a man of one book."[23] The resolution fairly reflects his godly ambitions and wildly, almost comically, misrepresents his actual reading: the man's curiosity was simply insatiable.

21. "I write chiefly for plain, unlettered men, who understand only their mother tongue, and yet reverence and love the word of God, and have a desire to save their souls" (Wesley, *Notes NT* 3).

22. Wesley, *Notes NT* 4. Wesley based his *Notes* on the King James Version, though occasionally modifying its text where it could be brought "nearer to the original," or where (as guided by Bengel) he deemed a Greek reading other than that used by the KJV to be more correct. See Maddox, "Wesley," 4-6. At the same time, he appreciated the "solemn and venerable" language of the KJV, and thought it an "excusable infirmity, to be unwilling to part with what we have been long accustomed to; and to love the very words by which God has often conveyed strength or comfort to our souls" (*Notes NT* 3-4). Scholarly accuracy in the text was thus, for Wesley, an important, but not the only, consideration.

23. See *Serm.* 1.105; cf. *JD* 4.510 for the claim that in 1730 he began to be such a man, and *Serm.* 3.504 for a similar claim on behalf of the "early Methodists."

His *Journals* are filled with accounts of endless activity — ceaseless travel (over 250,000 miles in his lifetime, by nothing faster than a horse), constant preaching (some 800 sermons a year, for a half century), hair-raising encounters with mob violence (typically calmed, as far as the human eye could see, by sheer force of personality),[24] and remarkable conversions — but interspersed with all these accounts are Wesley's thoughts on whatever he happened to be reading, usually while riding on horseback from preaching in one field to another. That reading naturally included all manner of theological and devotional works, from the early church to contemporary writings[25] — but also such decidedly nontheological authors as Machiavelli, Voltaire, Rousseau, and Mandeville; add Swedenborg to the list, and classify *him* as you wish.[26] History was the subject of much reading,[27] of regions both large (e.g., Great Britain, Ireland, Scotland, America, China) and small (e.g., Palmyra, Cornwall, Norwich, "Whitby and Whitby Abbey," "the county and city of Waterford").[28] Historical biographies intrigued him, too (e.g., Alexander the Great, Charles V, Mary Queen of Scots, Nadir Kouli, Peter the Great, Richard III, Theodore King of Corsica),[29] as did accounts of significant events (e.g., the Irish rebellion and massacre of 1641, the London plague).[30] Whether people traveled around the world, to Barbary and the Levant, to Egypt and Abyssinia, to the North American interior, to Patagonia, Northern Europe, the continent, or Corsica, Wesley wanted to read about their discoveries.[31] He was also keen to learn about natural history, even that, specifically, of Norway — and, to be sure, the history of music.[32] Natural science proved fascinating (he prepared

24. To his own amazement, however, Wesley lived long enough to become a venerable figure throughout Great Britain: "I am become, I know not how, an honourable man. . . . All the kingdom, rich and poor, Papists and Protestants, behave with courtesy, nay, and seeming good-will! It seems as if I had well-nigh finished my course, and our Lord was giving me an honourable discharge" (*Works* 13.65).

25. Wesley also edited, abridged, and published, in inexpensive editions, a host of such works in his *Christian Library*.

26. On the former, see Wesley, *Journals and Diaries (JD)*, 1.175; 4.79 and 6.328; 5.214; 4.50; on Swedenborg, *JD* 5.216, 301; 6.126.

27. And also writing, for that matter. Wesley published his own *Concise History of England* (1776) and *Short Roman History* (1773), as well as a book entitled *Ecclesiastical History* (1781).

28. On large regions, *JD* 5.355; 3.220, 4.250, 5.11 and 380; 5.210 and 6.384; 5.358 and 6.213; 7.4. On small ones, *JD* 5.99; 4.124; 5.475; 6.137; 4.269.

29. *JD* 3.193; 5.319; 5.127; 4.83; 4.40; 5.188; 4.138.

30. *JD* 3.189, 4.142, and 5.196; 3.239.

31. *JD* 4.33, 5.394, and 7.148; 5.134; 5.99; 7.192; 5.176; 5.472; 5.306; 5.163.

32. *JD* 4.72; 4.344; 5.161-62.

and published his own *Survey of the Wisdom of God in the Creation; Or, a Compendium of Natural Philosophy* [1763]), as did works on astronomy, anatomy, and medicine;[33] his own (widely circulated) *Primitive Physick* was well ahead of its time in its concern for hygiene and preventive medicine. Elocution interested him,[34] but so did anything he could find about electricity.[35] He had a particular interest in questions of logic and epistemology,[36] and he published his own *Compendium of Logic*. He also published short grammars of English (1748), Latin (1748), Hebrew (1751), French (1751), and Greek (1765). His *Journals* contain countless allusions to, and quotations from, poetry, both ancient and modern. More could be said, of course, but this should suffice to prevent the drawing of false inferences from Wesley's claim — and aim — to be a "man of one book."

Yet the claim is not to be dismissed, either. For Wesley, true Christianity is "*scriptural* Christianity" (*Serm.* 1.174), and every true Christian is "a real Bible Christian" (*Works* 13.68). As Scripture is "of God," "we dare not turn aside from it to the right hand or to the left" (*Appeals* 49). "I allow no other rule, whether of faith or practice, than the Holy Scriptures" (*JD* 2.67; cf. *Works* 8.340). Few expressions can be more common in Wesley's writings than the admonition "To the law and to the testimony"; he understood those words, taken from Isaiah 8:20, as a command to consult and abide by Scripture (*JD* 1.132; 2.162; *Works* 9.466; 10.285; etc.). In the end, for all his interest in countless subjects, which led him to read hundreds of books, Wesley believed that only one thing really mattered — and for that one thing, only one book would do.

> I want to know one thing, the way to heaven — how to land on that happy shore. God himself has condescended to teach the way: for this very end he came from heaven. He hath written it down in a book. O give me that book! At any price give me the Book of God! I have it. Here is the knowledge enough for me. Let me be *homo unius libri* [a man of one book]. (*Serm.* 1.105)

Nor did Wesley have any patience with those who suggest that the unwashed masses should be kept from reading Scripture lest "more prejudice

---

33. *JD* 4.101 and 229; 4.159 and 5.418; 5.290, 343, and 6.387.

34. *JD* 5.458. Wesley published his own *Directions Concerning Pronunciation and Gesture* (1749).

35. *JD* 3.195, 446; 5.117. This, too, was a subject on which he published (*The Desideratum; Or, Electricity Made Plain and Useful* [1778]).

36. *JD* 4.83, 499.

than profit proceed from it." Of course there have been those, even in the days of the apostles, who have "wrested the Scriptures to their own destruction." The apostles responded, not by advising against reading Scripture, but with a warning not to be led astray; and they sought to prevent this by exhorting people to a "diligent perusal" of the Scriptures, which were, after all, "written for our learning" (*Works* 10.93, citing 2 Pet. 3:16; Rom. 15:4). "Every member of our Church, if he gives himself up to the guidance of God's Holy Spirit, may learn the foundation of his faith from the written word of God; may read and meditate therein day and night" (*Works* 10.139). In his letters and other writings, we find Wesley constantly advising people, whatever their station in life, to spend time, morning and evening, reading a portion of Scripture.

> You want to know God, in order to enjoy him in time and in eternity. All that you want to know of him is contained in one book, the Bible. Therefore your one point is, to understand this. And all you learn is to be referred to this, as either directly or remotely conducive to this. Might it not be well then to spend at least two hours every day, in reading and meditating upon the Bible? reading every morning (if not every evening too) a portion of the Old and then of the New Testament? (*Works* 12.260)

> All the knowledge you want is comprised in one book, — the Bible. When you understand this, you will know enough. I advise you, therefore, to begin every day (before or after private prayer) with reading a portion, more or less, of the Old or New Testament, or of both. (*Works* 12.440)

When Wesley speaks of the "means of grace," "searching the Scriptures (which implies reading, hearing, and meditating thereon)" is one — together with prayer and receiving the Lord's Supper: "These we believe to be ordained of God as the ordinary channels of conveying his grace to the souls of men" (*Serm.* 1.381; cf. *JD* 2.158). "Searching the Scriptures" communicates grace both to those still "in darkness, seeking him [God] whom they know not," and to those "men of God" who continually find Scripture "profitable for doctrine, for reproof, for correction, for instruction in righteousness." "This is a means whereby God not only gives, but also confirms and increases true wisdom" (*Serm.* 1.387-89, citing 2 Tim. 3:15-16).

Like the Reformers and Pietists, Wesley believed not only that "the Scriptures are a complete rule of faith and practice," but also that "they are clear in all necessary points" (*Works* 10.14). Not that everything in Scripture is equally or immediately clear; Wesley describes his own procedure with difficult passages as follows:

> Is there a doubt concerning the meaning of what I read? Does anything appear dark or intricate? I lift up my heart to the Father of lights: "Lord, is it not thy Word, 'If any man lack wisdom, let him ask of God'? Thou 'givest liberally and upbraidest not.' Thou hast said, 'If any man be willing to do thy will, he shall know.' I am willing to do, let me know, thy will." I then search after and consider parallel passages of Scripture, "comparing spiritual things with spiritual." I meditate thereon, with all the attention and earnestness of which my mind is capable. If any doubt still remains, I consult those who are experienced in the things of God, and then the writings whereby, being dead, they yet speak. (*Serm.* 1.106, citing James 1:5; John 7:17; 1 Cor. 2:13)[37]

Wesley goes into greater detail in advising others how to read Scripture profitably. Disciplined regularity is important: people should (as we have already seen) set aside time, morning and evening, to read a section, preferably from both the Old and the New Testaments. Furthermore, profitable reading is focused, *purposeful* reading: Scripture should be read with the sole purpose in mind of learning the will of God, and with "a fixt resolution to do it." Guidance in interpreting difficult texts is provided by "the analogy of faith": that is, the "connexion and harmony" between the fundamental doctrines of the faith determine the boundaries within which Scripture is to be interpreted. Prayer is essential, both before and after reading Scripture, because "scripture can only be understood thro[ugh] the same Spirit whereby it was given."[38] Since we read

---

37. For the illumination of Scripture, Wesley particularly commended the writings of church fathers of the first three centuries (*Works* 10.14). In these fathers he found "the most authentic commentators on Scripture, as being both nearest the fountain, and eminently endued with that Spirit by whom all Scripture was given. It will be easily perceived, I speak chiefly of those who wrote before the Council of Nice [Nicaea]. But who would not likewise desire to have some acquaintance with those that followed them? with St. Chrysostom, Basil, Jerome, Au[gu]stin; and, above all, the man of a broken heart, Ephraim Syrus?" (*Works* 10.484).

38. Elsewhere, Wesley writes: "I advise every one, before he reads the Scripture, to use this or the like prayer: — 'Blessed Lord, who hast caused all holy Scriptures to be written for our learning, grant that we may in such wise hear them, read, mark, learn, and inwardly digest them, that by patience and comfort of thy holy word, we may embrace, and ever hold fast, the blessed hope of everlasting life, which thou hast given us in our Saviour Jesus Christ'" (*Works* 14.307).

in order to nurture our own spiritual life, it is useful "frequently to pause, and examine ourselves by what we read, both with regard to our hearts, and lives." Finally,

> whatever light you then receive, should be used to the uttermost, and that immediately. Let there be no delay. Whatever you resolve, begin to execute the first moment you can. So shall you find this word to be indeed the *power of God unto* present and eternal *salvation*. (*Notes OT* ix, citing Rom. 1:16)

Scripture, then, is sufficient, and sufficiently clear, to meet the needs even of uneducated believers; but more is to be expected of ministers of the gospel.[39] "Whether it be true or not, that every good textuary [i.e., master of the biblical text] is a good Divine [i.e., clergyman], it is certain none can be a good Divine who is not a good textuary" (*Works* 10.482). Without a knowledge of Greek and Hebrew, will not a minister find himself frequently at a loss, unable to explain even practical texts — let alone those that are controversial? Wesley responds to the implied question:

> He will be ill able to rescue [controversial texts] out of the hands of any man of learning that would pervert them: For whenever an appeal is made to the original, his mouth is stopped at once. (*Works* 10.483)

39. Wesley was very sensitive to the charge that those he entrusted with the preaching of the gospel were often uneducated. He responded, in part, by noting that God is quite capable of using the uneducated for his purposes; in part also, however, by returning the charge:

> Men in general are under a great mistake with regard to what is called "the learned world." They do not know, they cannot easily imagine, how little learning there is among them. I do not speak of *abstruse* learning, but of what all divines, at least of any note, are supposed to have, viz., the knowledge of the tongues, at least Latin, Greek, and Hebrew, and of the common arts and sciences. How few men of learning, so called, understand Hebrew? Even so far as to read a plain chapter in Genesis? Nay, how few understand Greek? Make an easy experiment. Desire that grave man who is urging this objection only to tell you the English of the first paragraph that occurs in one of Plato's *Dialogues*. I am afraid we may go farther still. How few understand Latin? Give one of them an *Epistle* of Tully [Cicero], and see how readily he will explain it, without his dictionary.... And with regard to the arts and sciences: how few understand so much as the general principles of logic? Can one in ten of the clergy (O grief of heart!) or of the Masters of Arts in either university, when an argument is brought, tell you even the mood and figure wherein it is proposed? Or complete an enthymeme?... Can one in ten of them demonstrate a problem or theorem in Euclid's *Elements*? Or define the common terms used in metaphysics? (*Appeals* 294-95)

Wesley then picks up the refrain, originating with Origen, of how knowledge of such things as "profane history," geography, the sciences, logic, natural philosophy, and geometry is "a great help to the accurate understanding of several passages of Scripture" (*Works* 10.483-84). Never more at home than when searching his own or others' souls, Wesley then asks those who lack such knowledge to ask themselves, "How many years did I spend at school? How many at the University? And what was I doing all those years? Ought not shame to cover my face?" (*Works* 10.491). In any case,

> have I used all possible diligence to supply that grievous defect (so far as it can be supplied now,) by the most accurate knowledge of the English Scriptures? Do I meditate therein day and night? . . . Otherwise, how can I attempt to instruct others therein? Without this, I am a blind guide indeed! I am absolutely incapable of teaching my flock what I have never learned myself; no more fit to lead souls to God, than I am to govern the world. (*Works* 10.493)

Clearly, there is no depreciation of education or biblical learning with Wesley. At the same time, he is as critical as Francke and Bengel are of knowledge — even knowledge of sacred things — that remains merely intellectual.

> And what would it profit a man to "have all knowledge," even that which is infinitely preferable to all other, the knowledge of the Holy Scripture? I knew a young man about twenty years ago who was so thoroughly acquainted with the Bible that if he was questioned concerning any Hebrew word in the Old or any Greek word in the New Testament, he would tell, after a little pause, not only how often the one or the other occurred in the Bible, but also what it meant in every place. . . . Such a master of biblic knowledge I never saw before, and never expect to see again. Yet if with all his knowledge he had been void of love, if he had been proud, passionate, or impatient, he and all his knowledge would have perished together, as sure as ever he was born. (*Serm.* 3.303, citing 1 Cor. 13:2)

Scripture was written "not to gratify our curiosity, but to lead us to God" (*Notes OT* 6; cf. 284). Wesley expresses his impatience with those troubled to locate geographically the Garden of Eden: "Let it be our care to make sure a place in the heavenly paradise, and then we need not perplex ourselves with a search after the place of the earthly paradise" (*Notes OT* 12).

Linked with the notion that knowledge — even that derived from Scripture — must not remain merely intellectual is Wesley's insistence that faith means more than assent, even to "all that is contained in the Old and New Testament." After all, the devils themselves, Wesley is wont to note, have *that* kind of "faith." The faith that *saves* involves "a disposition of the heart" (*Serm.* 1.230; 1.119-20). And here, inevitably, our account of Wesley must turn biographical.

Wesley's resolution to be a "man of one book" preceded his own assurance of salvation by nearly a decade, though it originated at a time when his zeal for holiness and the love of God was already as strong as it would ever be (see *JD* 4.510; *Treatises* 2.137). In the spirit of William Law's *Serious Call to a Devout and Holy Life,* John Wesley, his brother Charles, and a few others (all mocked as "Methodists") gave themselves to the study of Scripture and other serious literature, prayer, attendance at Holy Communion, and deeds of charity. The quest for personal holiness through service then led the Wesley brothers on a mission to the North American Indians, an episode that ended in disaster for them both. John returned to England wondering whether he himself was even a believer.[40] The question was both provoked and pressed by Moravians (a group of German Pietists) whom he first encountered already on his voyage to America, and who clearly possessed a calm assurance of faith that he lacked.[41] When, after a prolonged period of inner anguish, he received in his spirit a *warm* assurance that Christ, as he famously put it, "had taken away *my* sins, even *mine,* and saved *me* from the law of sin and death" (*JD* 1.250), his faith had gained a dimension, and his message an emphasis, that would remain with him throughout his long career as an itinerant preacher. True religion is a "religion of the heart" (*Serm.* 2.46).

40. "I went to America to convert the Indians; but Oh! who shall convert me? Who, what is he that will deliver me from this evil heart of unbelief? I have a fair summer religion. I can talk well; nay, and believe myself, while no danger is near: but let death look me in the face, and my spirit is troubled. . . . It is now two years and almost four months since I left my native country in order to teach the Georgian Indians the nature of Christianity. But what have I learned myself in the meantime? Why (what I the least of all suspected), that I who went to America to convert others, was never myself converted to God" (*JD* 1.211, 214). It is worth noting, however, that Wesley in later years was less sure that his transition from an unconverted to a converted state was as clearly marked as it had seemed to him at that time (see *JD* 1.214, note "h").

41. Wesley would later part company with the Moravians, claiming (among other things) that they failed to give due attention to the means of grace and the active pursuit of holiness. It is nonetheless clear that he derived from these Pietists his lifelong insistence on the experiential dimensions of Christian faith.

Such religion, he noted, like that of the apostle Paul, is often deemed madness (cf. Acts 26:24), a charge unlikely to be provoked by those whose piety consists of outward duties decently performed, orthodox belief, and "some quantity of heathen morality." But as soon as you "talk of righteousness and peace and joy in the Holy Ghost," you are sure to hear that "much *religion* hath made you mad" (*Serm.* 2.46).

> They not only affirm but cordially believe that every man is beside himself who says the love of God is shed abroad in his heart by the Holy Ghost given unto him, and that God has enabled him to rejoice in Christ with joy unspeakable and full of glory. . . . It is easy to observe that the determinate thing which the world accounts madness is that utter contempt for all temporal things, and steady pursuit of things eternal; that divine conviction of things not seen; that rejoicing in the favour of God; that happy, holy love of God; and that testimony of his Spirit with our spirit that we are children of God. That is, in truth, the whole spirit and life and power of the religion of Jesus Christ. (*Serm.* 2.47, alluding to Rom. 5:5; 1 Pet. 1:8; 2 Cor. 4:18; Heb. 11:1; Rom. 8:16)

That Wesley's description of the "religion of the heart" is made up almost exclusively of phrases taken from Scripture is, of course, deliberate: this, he is insisting, is what "scriptural Christianity" is all about. A heart that knows nothing of the love of God or the testimony of the Spirit must lack the faith of which the Bible speaks. On the other hand, Wesley was as eager as the Reformers to declare that the movement of the Spirit is not to be detached from the word of God in Scripture.[42] We are taught by Christ, not by departing from the Bible, but by "keeping close to it. Both by the Bible and by experience we know, that his word and his Spirit act in connexion with each other" (*Works* 9.505).[43] Every purported revelation

---

42. In Luther and Calvin, the point is emphasized in opposition to those who subordinated Scripture to the direct revelations they claimed to have received. Wesley found himself opposing those making similar claims (e.g., *Works* 10.178; *JD* 2.78, etc.), but also defending himself against others who charged the Methodists themselves with taking their directions from inward "impulses" (*Appeals* 337) or "extraordinary revelations" (see Outler's introductory comments to Wesley's sermon "The Nature of Enthusiasm," *Serm.* 2.44-46).

43. See Wesley's respectful critique of Madame Guyon: "The grand source of all her mistakes was this, the not being guided by the written word. She did not take the Scripture for the rule of her actions; at most it was but the secondary rule. Inward impressions, which she called inspirations, were her primary rule. The written word was not a lantern to her feet, a light in all her paths" (*Works* 14.277).

must be tested by its conformity to Scripture.[44] If the Spirit is our guide, Scripture is the rule by which the Spirit guides us "into all truth" (*Works* 10.178).

Wesley was wary, too, of those who expected to receive "particular directions" from God for dealing with "the most trifling circumstances of life." He did not deny that God *could,* on occasion, work that way. "But how frequently do men mistake herein!" (*Serm.* 2.54).[45] Here, too, our normal starting point must be Scripture.

> How is a sober Christian . . . to know what is "the will of God"? Not by waiting for supernatural dreams. Not by expecting God to reveal it in visions. Not by looking for any "particular impressions," or sudden impulses on his mind. No, but by consulting the oracles of God. "To the law and to the testimony." (*Serm.* 2.54)

> Do not hastily ascribe things to God. Do not easily suppose dreams, voices, impressions, visions, or revelations to be from God. They may be from him. They may be from nature. They may be from the devil. Therefore "believe not every spirit, but try the spirits whether they be of God." Try all things by the written Word, and let all bow before it. (*Treatises* 2.112-13, citing 1 John 4:1)

Wesley gave the same counsel to one inclined to determine the right course of action by what he felt "freedom" to do.

> This is a word much liable to be abused. If I have plain Scripture, or plain reason, for doing a thing, well. These are my rules, and my only rules. I regard not whether I had freedom or no. This is an unscriptural expression, and a very fallacious rule. I wish to be, in every point, great and small, a scriptural, rational Christian. (*Works* 13.73)

If (as often happens) Scripture provides no specific direction, it none-theless states general rules that we can apply in determining what to do. From Scripture, it is clear, for example, that God's will for us is our "sanc-

---

44. In fact, Wesley repeatedly expressed great reserve when meeting those who claimed to be uttering direct revelations of the Spirit or to have experienced the Spirit in ways that he felt lacked scriptural warrant (e.g., *JD* 2.31-32, 33-34, 295-96; *Treatises* 2.179).

45. "Among them that despise and vilify reason you may always expect to find those enthusiasts who suppose the dreams of their own imagination to be revelations from God" (*Serm.* 2.587).

tification," "that we should *be good and do good* in every kind, and in the highest degree whereof we are capable" (*Serm.* 2.54-55). Confronted with the choice, say, whether a man should marry, or enter a new business, he need only apply Scripture's general directive to the options he is facing, posing for himself the question:

> "In which of these states can I be most holy, and do the most good?" And this is to be determined partly by reason and partly by experience. Experience tells him what advantages he has in his present state, either for being or doing good; and reason is to show what he certainly or probably will have in the state proposed. By comparing these he is to judge which of the two may most conduce to his being and doing good; and as far as he knows this, so far he is certain what is the will of God. (*Serm.* 2.55)

> Trust not in visions or dreams, in sudden impressions or strong impulses of any kind. Remember, it is not by these you are to know what is "the will of God" on any particular occasion, but by applying the plain Scripture rule, with the help of experience and reason, and the ordinary [i.e., not *extraordinary*] assistance of the Spirit of God. (*Serm.* 2.59)

This is, indeed, "*scriptural* Christianity" and "Bible religion" (*Serm.* 1.174; *Works* 13.344). In a way perhaps lacking a parallel in earlier centuries of Christian history, the Bible has become the veritable center of life for a vast movement of ordinary believers. That Wesley insisted on interpreting Scripture according to its "plain, literal sense, unless it implies an absurdity" (*Serm.* 3.49-50; cf. 3.215) is, of course, consistent with two centuries of Protestant tradition.[46] But it is also (as Origen himself knew) the way ordinary believers read the text. And though as convinced as any that true faith results from the work of God's Spirit, Wesley allows himself the kind of demonstration ("short, clear, and strong") of Scripture's inspiration that appeals to those sitting in the pews — or listening in a field. "The Bible," he writes, "must be the invention either of good men or angels, bad men or devils, or of God." But clearly neither good men nor angels would make a book claiming throughout to be the word of the Lord "when it was their own invention." Nor would "bad men or devils . . . make a book which

---

46. That descriptions of the bride and bridegroom in the Song of Songs, taken literally, would be indecent is for Wesley grounds for reading this particular book allegorically (*Notes OT* 1926).

commands all duty, forbids all sin, and condemns their souls to hell to all eternity." It follows, then, "that the Bible must be given by divine inspiration" (*Works* 11.484).

And from this conclusion follows the further conclusion that Scripture must be without error: "If there be one falsehood in that book, it did not come from the God of truth" (*JD* 6.25). "Will not the allowing there is *any error* in Scripture shake the authority of the whole?" (*Appeals* 504).

> This is what we now style the *Holy Scripture:* this is that *word of God which remaineth for ever:* of which, though *heaven and earth pass away, one jot or tittle shall not pass away.* The Scripture therefore of the *Old and New Testament,* is a most solid and precious system of Divine truth. Every part thereof is worthy of God; and all together are one entire body, wherein is no defect, no excess. (*Notes NT* 5, citing 1 Pet. 1:25; Matt. 5:18; italics in original)

Such convictions in place, Wesley typically settled on simple solutions for texts that others found problematic. Since Eve apparently was not surprised when a serpent addressed her, it is not at all improbable that snakes were then endued with the same gift of reason as humans (*Serm.* 2.401-2).[47] Calvin (as we have seen) reordered the scriptural account of the making of the tabernacle so that the "tent of meeting" of Exodus 33:7 can be the tent constructed in chapters 35–39; Wesley thinks the former reference may be to "a model of the tabernacle that was afterwards to be erected, a hasty draught from the pattern shewed him in the mount, designed for direction to the workman" (*Notes OT* 318). If the genealogy of Jesus in Matthew is not strictly accurate, no error should be attributed to the evangelist: he was simply reproducing Jewish sources, which he could not have corrected without provoking "endless disputes" with the Jews (*Notes NT* 10). The name of Jeremiah must have been mistakenly added to the text of Matthew 27:9 by later copyists (*Notes NT* 91). Whereas Calvin found a confusion of the stories of Abraham and Jacob in Acts 7:16, Wesley thinks Stephen has followed the practice ("common among the Hebrews") of contracting two incidents into one (*Notes NT* 292).

The assurance with which Wesley approached the truth and interpre-

---

47. To Calvin's suggestion about why particular species of fish are not identified as clean or unclean in Lev. 11 (the Israelites, living where they did, knew few species of fish), Wesley adds a further explanation: fish were not, after all, "brought to Adam and named by him as other creatures were" (*Notes OT* 379).

tation of the Bible is perhaps related to the age in which he lived, an age confident that the universe runs on reason, that its secrets can be solved by reason, and that human reason, rightly exercised, leads to truth. Indeed, rightly exercised, reason must lead *all* human beings to the *same* perception of truth. Wesley could not, of course, allow "reason" all its pretensions; but he certainly spoke of it in terms very different from those of Luther, for example, and even criticized the Reformer sharply for (what Wesley took to be) his cavalier dismissals of reason (*JD* 2.200-201). It is not clear that, in reality, the differences between them are quite as great as Wesley imagined. Wesley, we may say, thought of reason as the God-given capacity to think (see *Serm.* 2.590); Luther had in mind the way a world opposed to God *actually* thinks. Both can call on Paul for support (see 1 Cor. 14:20 *and* 1:20). Luther, no less than Wesley, allowed that in matters terrestrial, human reason rightly orders human affairs (Luther, *Works* 3.322-23; 24.214, 228; Wesley, *Serm.* 2.590-91). Wesley, no less than Luther, insisted that, in matters celestial, we are dependent on revelation (*Serm.* 4.29-34; *Appeals* 268-69).

Yet differences remain, even when variations in terminology and rhetorical excesses have been discounted. Wesley was confident that, whatever divine mysteries there may be, and however much they may lie beyond present human understanding, they are, and will one day show themselves to be, entirely *consistent* with reason — a power in which, though in different measure, God and human beings both share: "the whole of our religion is a 'reasonable service'" (*Serm.* 2.599; cf. 2.591-92); "faith must necessarily at length be resolved into reason" (*Letters* 1.175-76).[48]

Luther's thinking began and ended with a fear of the Lord bred by a perception of the chasm, broad beyond comprehension, between Creator and created beings, yet broadened still further by humanity's flight into sin; a chasm bridged only by points of revelation, wherein the otherwise hidden God disclosed ways for humans to approach and cling to him, believing in the face of contrary appearances. Kierkegaard is, in this regard, the true heir of Luther; other such heirs — God bless them! — are few. Both the Bible by which and the world in which Wesley lived were a good deal tidier than those of Luther; and Wesley's heirs — Lord bless them, too — are legion.

God bless us, every one!

---

48. Note also *Appeals* 55: "We join with you in desiring a religion founded on reason, and every way agreeable thereto. . . . This is the very religion *we* preach: a religion evidently founded on, and every way agreeable to, eternal reason, to the essential nature of things. Its foundation stands on the nature of God and the nature of man, together with their mutual relations."

CHAPTER 11

Schleiermacher

The life of Friedrich Schleiermacher (1768-1834) is a testimony to what could be accomplished before the invention of the television. In his day job he was professor of theology at the University of Berlin, which he helped to found after Napoleon shuttered a number of other Prussian institutions. Schleiermacher's accomplishments as a theologian are equal to any. His great work of systematic theology, *The Christian Faith,* stands with Thomas's *Summa,* Calvin's *Institutes,* and Barth's *Church Dogmatics* as the unquestioned masterpieces of the discipline. It presents an original understanding of religion and faith that set the agenda for a new tradition in Christian thought. Beyond his work in systematics, Schleiermacher lectured on every aspect of the theological curriculum at the University of Berlin except the Old Testament (an exception that was, as we shall see, not incidental). He ranks with the leading biblical scholars of his day, is credited with inventing the discipline that systematizes the inquiry into the interpretation of the biblical text, and reconceived the entire structure of theological education.

But, without easy distractions ready to hand, Schleiermacher managed to extend his interests beyond his day job. He was a leading philosopher during a seminal period in the development of Western thought.[1] He lectured on metaphysics, dialectics, logic, ethics, and political theory; served as the president of the philosophical section of the Berlin Academy of Sciences; and produced translations of Plato that remain standard today. He was politically engaged, acting at one point as a messenger to the Prussian

1. Schleiermacher was a contemporary of the figures associated with German Idealism. Philosophers themselves are giving increasing emphasis to Schleiermacher's importance within this movement.

court for a secret society that was planning an uprising against the French (failed attempts to communicate back to the group by way of an elaborate code seem to have limited the efficacy of his mission). He also spent most of his life in pastoral ministry. He was a chaplain at a hospital in Berlin for a number of years, and initially turned down a university position because it did not include preaching responsibilities. When he took up the professorship in Berlin, he also assumed a position as the minister of an influential church with a membership of 12,000. He preached more than a thousand sermons, and led weekly devotional studies that moved methodically through various books of the Bible. When he died, 20,000 people lined the streets to watch his funeral procession pass by. Contemporaries wrote of him that "what Goethe is to poetry, and Fichte is to philosophy, Schleiermacher is to humanity," and that, while "he was not the greatest man of his time, he was the greatest human being."[2]

Schleiermacher's legacy is, however, not uncomplicated. He is widely hailed as the father of modern theology; where the notions that cluster under that term are deemed problematic, the father is summarily dismissed. The innovations that followed from his attempt to mediate Christian faith to a world of ever-expanding scientific and historical understanding cause him to be omitted from some accounts of the contributions of the great thinkers of Christian history. But he should not be excluded from an inquiry into the nature of Scripture and what it means to read Scripture well. Few thought as long about these questions, or with as much influence. He was among the first generation of church leaders to wrestle with the demand that the Bible be read like any other book. On one hand, he granted the legitimacy of the demand within certain spheres of inquiry, and made seminal contributions to critical biblical scholarship. On the other hand, his understanding of the nature of religion and faith allowed him to reconcile this critical study with an account of the way Scripture furthers Christ's redemptive work. In effecting this reconciliation, he presents a new set of concepts regarding the reading of Scripture that is shaped by the concerns of the modern world, and that in turn has shaped a good deal of thought over the last two centuries.

Life and Theory of Religion

We cannot approach Schleiermacher's understanding of Scripture apart from some grasp of the account of religion that Schleiermacher developed

---

2. See Vial, *Schleiermacher,* 12.

in response to the challenges of his day. Schleiermacher was born in 1768 in Breslau, Prussia. His father, a chaplain in the Prussian army, had an intense religious experience in a Pietist community while Friedrich was a child. Friedrich's father sent him to a Pietist boarding school, and the richly experiential religion that was typical of the Pietists made a lasting impression on him. Throughout his mature work, he echoes the conviction of leading Pietists like Arndt and Spener that theology should grow from living Christian faith, and is in fact best done by those "who have experienced piety in their youth before they had any thought of vocation" (*OG,* 40-41). The primacy of youthful piety over vocational commitment was certainly true of Schleiermacher, who wrote that "religion was the maternal womb in whose holy darkness my young life was nourished and prepared for a world still closed to it" (*Speeches,* 84).

Schleiermacher's growth into that world was, however, not without friction. After four years at boarding school, he went on to a Pietist seminary, and began to fret under the teaching he received there. He formed a secret reading group that considered, among other things, the revolutionary new philosophy of Immanuel Kant, which students were otherwise forbidden to read. In face of advances in the understanding of philosophy, history, and natural science, aspects of the theology that he was taught began to seem implausible to him. In a moving exchange with his father, he asked his father to pray for him because he felt that he had lost elements of the faith required for salvation (*BW,* 49-52). His father responded that Schleiermacher's doubts were crucifying Christ again and disturbing his mother in her grave (*BW,* 53-56).

The exchange is famous, but it produces a misleading impression of both father and son. On the father's side, condemnation of an inquiring spirit was hardly the norm. Schleiermacher's father encouraged aspects of his questioning, and turned to him regularly for his thoughts on work by Kant, Fichte, and others (*BW,* 267-70, 288-90, 334-35). But before all else he sought always to counsel careful study of the Bible. In a rather more typical exchange, the elder Schleiermacher wrote: "Remember your calling, which is to seek truth and wisdom with unpresupposing character, sincere humility and a heart that trusts in God. Make wise use of your time, and, beside the Bible, which I ever commend you to take as your daily devotional book in the early hours and to read with careful precision in the original languages, let your other reading be guided by the advice of your dear uncle" (*BW,* 180).[3] Elsewhere, Schleiermacher's father encouraged his

---

3. Schleiermacher's uncle, Samuel Ernst Timotheus Stubenrauch, was professor of

son to "believe above all that the Bible is an inexhaustible source that can lavishly satisfy your thirst for understanding" (*BW,* 140).

On the son's side, seasoned readers suggest that Schleiermacher did not lose his faith so much as the understanding of faith in which he had been schooled.[4] The "dear uncle" to whom Schleiermacher's father referred wrote to his nephew some years later that what the latter insisted on calling his "unbelief" appeared as "a mere play of your fantasy" — and did not seem "in the least bit dangerous" (*BW,* 276). Schleiermacher's ongoing engagement with his faith is clear from the fact that, though he transferred from seminary to the University of Halle, he continued with his theological education, and passed — with a grade of merely "passable" in dogmatics — the qualifying exams for ministry in 1790.

Schleiermacher proceeded to work his way toward a new understanding of his faith — and, with it, to a new understanding of Scripture — over the course of the next decade as he moved between positions as a minister, private tutor, and hospital chaplain. The most significant milestone in this process was a reconsideration of the nature of religion itself that emerged in a set of essays presented as speeches on religion that Schleiermacher published in 1799. At the time, Schleiermacher was active in a group of intellectual and cultural elites in Berlin who were surprised by Schleiermacher's religious commitments. Schleiermacher sought to defend religion against its "cultured despisers" by offering a new account of its fundamental essence.

Schleiermacher's understanding of religion turns on the suggestion — indebted to his Pietist roots — that an elemental religious experience, spoken of in terms of "feeling," makes up the "essence" of religion (*Speeches,* 102). Human knowing and doing move exclusively within the sphere of the creaturely, but feeling is able to reach out beyond the creaturely to apprehend God as the limitless ground that makes the created sphere what it is. In knowing and doing, human beings are always caught up in a web of relationships with other created things in which they are both partially free and partially dependent. But, in feeling, human beings are aware of themselves as absolutely dependent because they are not the source of their own being and activity. Through feeling, human beings come to know God as the ground of their awareness of dependence. In his mature

---

theology in Halle through the 1780s and then retired and took up a position as the minister of a church in Drossen as Schleiermacher was finishing his schooling in 1790. The latter corresponded frequently with his uncle, who was an important influence in his life. Schleiermacher dedicated his first collection of sermons (published in 1801) to his uncle.

4. Gerrish, *Prince,* 26.

academic work, Schleiermacher identifies the "feeling of absolute dependence" as the essence of religion and piety. He suggests that pious living
is found wherever this feeling of dependence underwrites, accompanies,
and shapes all moments of knowing and doing (*CF,* 15-18). In a sermon
that is contemporaneous with his *Speeches,* Schleiermacher suggests that
his complex account of religion as a life-shaping feeling can be understood
simply in terms of prayer:

> To be a religious man and to pray are really one and the same thing.
> To join the thought of God with every thought of any importance that
> occurs to us; in all our admiration of external nature, to regard it as the
> work of His wisdom; to take counsel with God about all our plans, that
> we may be able to carry them out in His name; and even in our most
> mirthful hours to remember His all-seeing eye; this is the prayer without
> ceasing to which we are called, and which is really the essence of true
> religion. (*Sermons,* 31)

This account of religious feeling as the decisive center of piety represents a milestone in Christian thought. In the first place, it allows Schleiermacher to give what he takes to be a more faithful account of the essence
of Christian faith. We know, Schleiermacher says, that neither knowing
nor doing makes up the essence of faith, for neither knowledgeable professors nor efficient activists are necessarily pious (*CF,* 9-11). Secondly, it
also allows Schleiermacher to mediate Christianity to the modern world
by making peace with criticisms arising from advances in science, philosophy, history, and culture. Schleiermacher argues that the tension between
Christianity and modern understandings of history and of the world issue
from misconceptions in which the essence of piety is taken to lie in acceptance of certain claims about the world — e.g., that it was created in six
days — rather than in the religious feeling of dependence on God. Mistaken
understandings of the essence of religion threaten to bring the "tangle of
history" to the point that perpetual conflict exists between Christianity
and modern science, the latter appearing to be necessarily faithless and the
former identified with a primitive barbarism (*OG,* 61). One of his aims is
to ensure that Christian faith is understood in such a way that it may stand
in an "eternal covenant" — perhaps best understood as a mutual nonag-
gression pact — with scientific investigation in which each is permitted
the dignity that is proper to it (*OG,* 64). He claims that the office of the
theologian presupposes that "scientific orientation" and "Christian faith"
are compatible (*LJ,* 24).

The question for us is what place Scripture has in Schleiermacher's understanding of religion and of Christian faith. In his early speeches on religion, Schleiermacher speaks rather famously of holy writing everywhere as "merely a mausoleum of religion, a monument that a great spirit was there that no longer exists" (*Speeches,* 134). This claim presents a stark picture of Schleiermacher as impatient with Scripture; yet it needs to be approached with considerable care. In one sense it is useful in presenting a contrast between a living spirit and a dead letter that is foundational to Schleiermacher's thought. Throughout his work, Schleiermacher distinguishes between the living spirit of religious feeling that speaks through holy texts and is nourished by them, and an "ancient literalism" that separates the texts from pious Christian living and treats them as conveyors of claims to be accepted as true in abstraction from faith (*OG,* 61). This latter view is espoused by "paltry imitators" who "cling to a dead writing" and try to prove things from it (*Speeches,* 134); it is a key perpetuator of the disastrous conflict between religion and the modern world (*OG,* 61). Believers come closer to Christ "the more we eliminate this power of the dead letter" (*Sermons,* 208).

Elements in Schleiermacher's apparent impatience with Scripture thus present us with an important aspect of his work; yet his description of holy writing as a "mausoleum of religion" hardly reflects the full range even of his earlier thinking. At the same time that he directed a rhetorically loaded set of speeches to religion's "cultured despisers," he also preached regularly, and he treated Scripture as a living voice of Christian faith. The year 1800 was among the busiest in his career as a preacher. Each of his sermons is constructed around a passage of Scripture, not in order to "offer a proof" for some notion "from some particular passage of Scripture with appeal to its canonical authority," but rather so that the understanding of listeners might be "enlivened," a topic "illumined," and Christ made "increasingly glorious to us through our study of his words."[5] Schleiermacher's preaching presents a clear sense of the significance of Scripture. Even in his *Speeches,* encouragement to seek the living spirit that sets holy writings apart from others is not uncommon (*Speeches,* 210). These speeches are shot through with scriptural references — the Word made flesh (*Speeches,* 190), the servant form of this Word (*Speeches,* 208), a plentiful harvest that lacks workers (*Speeches,* 201) — references that aim to call his listeners to recognition of true religion beyond the "outer husks" toward which their criticisms are directed.

5. See the preface that Schleiermacher wrote to a collection of sermons published in 1801 (available in Tice, *Sermons,* 28-31).

It is these more positive conceptions that are most typical of Schleiermacher's mature teaching on Scripture. We may approach this teaching by way of a brief word about Schleiermacher's conception of the place of Scripture in theological training. One consequence of Schleiermacher's reconsideration of the essence of Christian faith was a new understanding of the proper form of a theological education. Since the Reformation, Protestant theological education had revolved around four areas of study: biblical exegesis, church history, Christian doctrine, and practical theology. Study of these disciplines was intended to equip ministers for service; but the four-pronged approach to theological education came under increased pressure during the seventeenth and eighteenth centuries as critical methods of study were applied to the Bible and to church history in particular. Within the confines of the university, critical inquiry into Scripture and ecclesiastical history had an uncomfortable relationship with study that was motivated by a concern for pastoral formation. A leading philosopher who, along with Schleiermacher, contributed to the founding of the University of Berlin, suggested that theology should be excluded from the university curriculum because it does not make up a unified discipline. Study of the Bible, of church history, of Christian doctrine, and of the practicalities of Christian life and ecclesiastical administration require different methods and work toward different ends.[6]

Schleiermacher sought to address this situation by restructuring theological education around three disciplines, each of which contributes to the formation of Christian ministers.[7] Philosophical theology addresses the essence of religion and the place of Christianity in relation to other religions. Historical theology gives an account of the faith of the Christian community from its earliest form to the present day. Practical theology completes theological education by concerning itself with church leadership. Crucially, within this tripartite structure, Schleiermacher holds that both exegesis and dogmatics belong under the rubric of historical theology. Exegesis, according to his account, is concerned with the New

6. These thoughts were expressed by J. G. Fichte, who was widely seen as the leading philosopher of the time, and who served as the first Rector of the University of Berlin. For an account of this situation, see Zachhuber, *Science,* 12-17.

7. Schleiermacher calls theology as a whole a "positive" science because its elements arise from and have their coherence in the requirements of a practical task: guiding the Christian church (*BO,* 1-3). He writes: "Christian theology, accordingly, is that assemblage of scientific information and practical instruction without the possession and application of which a united leadership of the Christian church, that is, a government of the church in the fullest sense, is not possible" (*BO,* 3).

Testament as the expression of the faith of the earliest Christians (*BO,* 35-36, 44-45). Dogmatics is concerned with doctrine as the expression of the faith of the contemporary church (*BO,* 36-37, 72-74). We can follow Schleiermacher's understanding of the nature of Scripture by attending, first, to the doctrine of Scripture that he develops in his dogmatic account of Christian faith as it exists in the present; and, second, to the account of biblical interpretation that he gives under the rubric of exegesis.

Schleiermacher's Dogmatic Account of Scripture

Schleiermacher's understanding of Christianity generally shapes his approach to the doctrine of Scripture. For him, Christianity has its origins in Christ, who brings salvation by awakening in those around him a consciousness of God and of sin and redemption (*CF,* 425-38). Christianity exists where the religious feeling of absolute dependence is awakened, shaped and continually accompanied by a feeling of sin and a consciousness of the redemption offered in Christ. The effect of Christ's work is transmitted through the church by way of the influence of successive generations of believers — a process that Schleiermacher takes to be coextensive with the work of the Holy Spirit (*CF,* 560-64). Faith in Christ in the church today is understood as entering into fellowship with Christ by sharing in the God-consciousness that Christ founded (*CF,* 427, 483). Within this sphere, doctrines are understood as expressions of the religious consciousness that marks a particular church at a particular time.[8]

This understanding of Christianity brings with it a heightened emphasis on the church as the community through which Christ's work is transmitted. Schleiermacher develops his doctrine of Scripture as an element within his broader doctrine of the church, identifying Scripture as one of the "immutable elements" in the church's life.[9] His identification of

---

8. Schleiermacher famously writes that "Christian doctrines are accounts of the Christian religious affections set forth in speech" (*CF,* 76). He thus holds that it is possible to "exhaust the whole compass of Christian doctrine" by considering "the facts of the religious self-consciousness" (*CF,* 123).

9. The treatment of the church is the longest section of Schleiermacher's systematics, in part because Schleiermacher's understanding of Christianity causes him to subsume a number of topics — e.g., theologies of election and of the Holy Spirit — that would conventionally be handled elsewhere within a treatment of the church. Scripture is presented alongside the ministry of the Word, baptism, the Lord's Supper, the power of the keys, and prayer, as "immutable elements" in the church's life.

teaching about Scripture as an element within teaching about the church represents a crucial feature of Schleiermacher's understanding of Scripture, and a departure from a Protestant tendency to place Scripture at the head of the theological enterprise as the source and guarantor of Christian teaching.

Schleiermacher begins his consideration of Scripture by inquiring into the authority of the scriptural texts. He is keen to suggest that Scripture should not be seen as a foundational authority that is itself the "source of the Christian faith"; instead, it should be recognized that the faith of the church is the basis of the authority of Scripture (*CF,* 591-92). The former view is, on his telling, caught up in difficulties resulting from the fact that the assertion of the authority of Scripture must in some way admit of being proved to reason if it is not to be wholly arbitrary. Some grounds must be given to reason for submitting to the authority of Scripture. Schleiermacher thus holds that the notion that Scripture is the basis of Christian faith leads, first, to a Roman Catholic understanding of church authority, for it requires the laity, who cannot themselves engage in the "critical and scientific use of the understanding" that is required to affirm the authority of Scripture, to believe on the authority of experts that the worth of Scripture can be established rationally (*CF,* 591-92). It also produces a troublesome situation in which even those who feel no need for redemption could potentially be brought to affirm the authority of Scripture, an arrangement that, instead of seeing faith as a "true living fellowship with Christ," would reduce it to intellectual assent to propositions proved from Scripture (*CF,* 591-92).

In place of this view, Schleiermacher argues that, just as the faith of the disciples and apostles was based on Christ's influence and was itself central to the "special condition of the apostolic mind" in which Scripture was written, so contemporary faith is based on Christ's ongoing influence as transmitted through the church, and is central to the "condition of mind" in which believers acknowledge the authority of Scripture (*CF,* 592-93). This view is demanded by the notion of equality in the church — why should some Christians have a different basis for faith than others? — and corresponds best to the fact that assertions of the authority of Scripture are intelligible only to those who believe. Schleiermacher points out that "the attempt to force unbelievers into faith" by way of "a special doctrine about these writings, as having had their origin in special divine revelation or inspiration . . . has had no success" (*CF,* 593). The authority of Scripture is recognized only by those who are members of the church by faith.

Two qualifications of the role of Scripture in the church's life follow from this view. The first is that Scripture is not properly seen as the *source* of Christian teaching. Schleiermacher holds that doctrines are proper to Christianity not because they are contained in Scripture but because they are true expressions of Christian faith. As he puts it, precautions should be taken "to avoid the impression that a doctrine must belong to Christianity because it is contained in Scripture, whereas in point of fact, it is contained in Scripture because it belongs to Christianity" (*CF,* 593). Scripture itself came into being as believers gave expression to the content of their faith. This priority of the faith of the believer over the reality of Scripture is paradigmatic of a proper relationship in which faith is seen as the broader whole within which Scripture fits as a part.

The second is that Scripture should not be seen as the *guarantor* of Christian teaching. The credibility of Christian claims is established by being vouched for, not by the authority of Scripture, but by believers' own consciousness of sin and of the pardon offered by Christ. Scripture is not needed as a guarantor of the credibility of this knowledge, for the believer's own feelings testify to this reality. Schleiermacher argues that, "where the need of redemption is really felt, the faith that makes alive may spring even from a message about Christ that is in no way bound up with the conviction that the books of Scripture possess a special character" (*CF,* 592). Conversely, where the need of redemption is not felt, no amount of conviction regarding the "special character" of the books of Scripture can produce living Christian faith (*CF,* 592).

If Scripture is neither the source nor the guarantor of faith, what function does it serve in the church? Schleiermacher suggests that Scripture is to be understood as an authoritative "norm" for presentations of the church's faith (*CF,* 594). This claim is crucial, for it is bound up with Schleiermacher's understanding of just what Scripture is. In the most straightforward sense, Schleiermacher argues that Scripture is a "presentation of the Christian faith" as it was held by the first generation of believers (*CF,* 594). It is a historical record of Christ's effect on his disciples in the faith that he called forth in them. It is because it is a historical record of this kind, "homogenous" in "form and content" with other presentations of Christian faith, that Schleiermacher presents the study of Scripture as a branch of historical theology (*CF,* 594; *BO,* 38).

The authority of this particular historical record as a norm for future presentations of Christian faith is a function of the fact that faith existed in its purest form in the first generation of believers. Religious feelings are always bound together with the influences of human knowing and doing and with wider human culture and concepts. These external realities detract from the purity of faith as awareness of dependence on God; yet they were prevented from tainting the faith of the apostles because of their proximity to Christ. With the disciples, "the danger of an unconsciously debasing influence" from other forms of thought and life "was averted in proportion as they stood near to Christ" (*CF,* 595). Christ's own faith exercised a "purifying influence" on the faith of those around him so that the disciples' "living memory of Christ" served to protect their faith from corruption (*CF,* 595-96). Christian faith existed in its purest form in those who stood closest to Christ.

It is the purity of the account of Christian faith given by the disciples that elevates their account of faith to canonical status for later presentations. Scripture presents a "regulative type for our religious thinking" because it is "unique" in its purity (*CF,* 606). Schleiermacher goes on to say that "the Church could never again reproduce the canonical, for the living intuition of Christ was never again able to ward off all debasing influences in the same direct fashion" (*CF,* 596). The canon is thus in an important sense closed. For all of history, the church finds in Scripture the norm of its presentation.

> Nothing can be regarded as a pure product of the Christian Spirit except so far as it can be shown to be in harmony with the original products; . . . no later product possesses equal authority with the original writings when it is a question of guaranteeing the Christian character of some particular presentation or of exposing its unchristian elements. (*CF* 596)

Appropriating a notion developed by the Protestant tradition, Schleiermacher argues that this affirmation is properly bolstered with an affirmation of the "sufficiency" of Scripture as the means through which the Holy Spirit leads believers "into all truth." To speak of the sufficiency of Scripture is to affirm that the Holy Spirit can lead believers "through our use of Scripture" just as "it led the apostles and others who enjoyed Christ's direct teaching." This means that "if one day there should exist in the Church a complete reflection of Christ's living knowledge of God, we may with perfect justice regard this as the fruit of Scripture" (*CF,* 606).

This account of the authority of Scripture as bound up with a purity of presentation grounded in the proximity of the writers to Christ reflects a christocentric understanding of Scripture that is typical of Schleiermacher's work. Having spoken of the purity of the canon, Schleiermacher considers the relationship between his account and conventional language regarding inspiration. He argues that the notion of inspiration risks producing considerable confusion, for it conveys the impression that the "sacred writers" were "informed of the content of what they wrote in a special divine manner." Schleiermacher argues that this notion has no basis in claims that Scripture makes about itself, undermines the unity of life of the scriptural writers, and feeds a "dead scholasticism" that removes "the whole subject from the domain of experiential insight" by losing itself in questions about the extent and mechanism of inspiration (*CF,* 598-600).

In place of this view, Schleiermacher suggests that the "inspiration" of Scripture is to be understood purely in terms of the activity of Christ. All that the sacred writers teach is a reflection of Christ's work in bringing their faith into being. All that they say "derives from Christ; hence in Christ himself must be the original divine bestowal of all that the Holy Scriptures contain" (*CF,* 598). The christocentrism of this understanding of inspiration does not exclude the notion that the writers of Scripture were "moved by the Holy Spirit," for this Spirit is the "common spirit of the Church" that stands as the source of "all spiritual gifts and good works"; but "the speaking and writing of the Apostles as moved by the Spirit was simply a communication drawn from the divine revelation in Christ" (*CF,* 598). Nothing that is not contained in the inspiration of Christ's own work is to be acknowledged as a proper part of the Christian faith.

Schleiermacher's christological concentration raises an important set of questions regarding the relationship of Christianity to Judaism. One consequence of Schleiermacher's understanding of religion quite generally is that Christianity is to be set apart from Judaism just as strongly as it is set apart from "heathenism," for Christianity is defined by a God-consciousness rooted in the work of Christ that is as absent from Judaism as it is from "Greek and Roman heathendom."[10] In turn, this notion dictates that, when Schleiermacher comes to the question of Scripture more particularly, he insists that strong distinctions are required between the writings of the Old Testament and those of the New. In his view, the former owe their place in the Christian Bible to the historical relationship between

---

10. Schleiermacher concedes that "Christianity has an historical connection with Judaism through the fact that Jesus was born among the Jewish people," but he insists that Judaism is no closer to Christianity than heathenism because, from either starting point, a conversion to Christianity "is a transition to another religion" (*CF,* 60-61). Jesus himself uses the Old Testament in his teaching, but "what is peculiar to Christ's teaching always appears at the same time as a polemic against the Old Testament tradition" (*LJ,* 236). It is by reflecting on the way that Christ "polemicizes" against the Old Testament that we first become convinced that Christianity is something "new and original" (*LJ,* 282).

Christianity and Judaism and the use that New Testament writers made of them, but they "do not on that account share the normative dignity and inspiration of the New" (*CF*, 608). They took on an air of significance in the early church because they were read in Christian services before the Christian canon itself was formed, but they reflect a fundamentally different religious consciousness and so their "gradual retirement into the background" was entirely appropriate (*CF*, 610). The deity displayed in the Old Testament bears a closer resemblance to the abstract omnipotent being of modern forms of rationalist philosophy than to the conceptions of living Christian piety (*OG*, 52).

> Even the noblest Psalms always contain something that Christian piety is unable to appropriate as a perfectly pure expression of itself, so that it is only after deluding ourselves by unconscious additions and subtractions that we can suppose we are able to gather a Christian doctrine of God out of the prophets and the Psalms. (*CF*, 609)

The attempt "to find our Christian faith in the Old Testament has injured our practice of the exegetical art" and given rise to "a flood of useless complications. Thus a thoroughgoing improvement is only to be looked for when we utterly discard Old Testament proofs for specifically Christian doctrines" (*CF*, 610).

This treatment of the Old Testament stands outside the bounds of traditional Christian teaching; it is an element in what Schleiermacher refers to as an "inspired heterodoxy" that he thinks will become orthodox "in due time" because it permits a unified presentation of Christian teaching that does not run into irresolvable conflict with modern understandings of the history of the Jewish people and the formation of Jewish Scripture (*OG*, 53). It has some further use for us as a point from which to enter into consideration of the way Scripture is actually used in Schleiermacher's dogmatics. Up to this point, we have encountered the concepts associated with Schleiermacher's explicit theology of Scripture; but there is a further set of questions to be asked regarding Schleiermacher's use of Scripture in the formulation and defense of his theology.

What we see in Schleiermacher's actual use of Scripture is perhaps more fluidity than his strict account of the New Testament as a dogmatic norm might suggest. Schleiermacher is happy, for instance, to appeal to Hebrew Scripture for support for theologies of creation (*CF*, 149-50), of the original perfection of creation (*CF*, 238-44), and of human creatures in particular (*CF*, 247-56). In the context of a theology of creation, he is pleased to find support in the Old Testament for a procedure through which he hands over questions regarding the "instrument or means" of creation to natural science and insists that a properly Christian doctrine confines itself to affirming that all things come into being through God, and that God stands apart from the sum total of the things that have come into being (*CF*, 149-50). This interpretive approach is, Schleiermacher thinks, contradicted by earlier writers — Luther comes up for censure here — who treat the scriptural record as a historical presentation that describes the means of the world's coming into being in terms that could be used in a "scientific" account (*CF*, 150-51). For Schleiermacher, this view is countered by the nature of the Mosaic narratives themselves, which, in their different creation accounts, show that they are not meant as a historical record, and by the way other writers in the Old Testament (particularly the psalmists and the writer of Job) handle the Genesis narratives "freely" as nonliteral accounts (*CF*, 151). Drawing straightforwardly from the Old Testament, Schleiermacher writes that "we have therefore no reason to maintain a stricter historical interpretation than the Hebrews themselves did in their best days" (*CF*, 151).

Schleiermacher's account of Christianity's relationship to the Old Testament is, moreover, an aspect of his thought in which we can see the effects of his view that the New Testament is a norm for Christian teaching. He strives to show that, however heterodox his account might appear, it does in fact conform to the faith of the first Christians. He finds support for the claim that Judaism reflects a fundamentally different spirit from the one that governs the Christian church in Paul's suggestions that the Old Testament law lacks the power of the Spirit, and that this law is proper to the time between reception of the promise and its fulfillment in Christ (*CF*, 608).[11]

A description of Schleiermacher's theology of Scripture can also be supplemented by the use he makes of Scripture in his sermons. In this context, Schleiermacher is able to wax as poetic as any Pietist regarding the benefits of Scripture. He speaks of the delightful freedom of the minister to draw from the "treasuries of the divine Word," which are "given by God" and "profitable for doctrine and instruction in righteousness" (*Sermons*, 242, alluding to 2 Tim. 3:16). He speaks of the "inspired unanimity" with

---

11. Schleiermacher cites here elements from Rom. 7 and 8, and Gal. 3. He writes elsewhere that Paul views the Mosaic laws as "a divine order designed for a state of immaturity, and thus a lower level of human development that could only have temporary validity" (*LJ*, 282).

which the Gospel writers appropriate the promises of Hebrew Scripture and apply them to Christ, and of the way Scripture testifies to Christ on every page (*Sermons*, 152). He speaks on Good Friday of the way that, whatever feelings and experiences are summoned up by the import of the day, believers will not have made "right use" of the day until they bring their "thoughts and feelings to the test of Scripture" (*Sermons*, 160).

Scripture retains a decisive place as a "treasury of the word" and a "test" for all thought and feeling because of the peculiar excellence that it possesses in its capacity to speak to contemporary circumstances:

> My friends, it is an important testimony to the excellence of holy scripture that we find such a similarity between the situation of those for whom these sacred books were initially written and our own situation that it must surely seem as though they were made for us. This is true not only in particular passages lifted out of their context but even in entire larger sections kept within the natural historical course of a particular book. This happens in that whatever still opens up the hidden depths of human life and with the selfsame power satisfies its innermost needs, after many, many centuries with the same simplicity and clarity as at its first appearance, must in its unchanging glory enable such similarity to arise for us.[12]

Yet, Scripture's importance is not reducible to its contemporary applicability. Preaching on the prayer of Stephen in Acts 7, Schleiermacher observes that the congregation might wonder what use this prayer is to them, given that they do not face persecution in the way that Stephen did. He responds that "all Scripture given by God is profitable for doctrine and instruction in righteousness; and there is no part of it, however slight its direct bearing on our circumstances may be, about which that statement does not always hold good" (*Sermons*, 242).

The irreducible usefulness of Scripture is, for Schleiermacher, finally a function of Christ's presence and activity in and through Scripture. In a sermon on Christ's promise of his presence "even to the end of the world [Matt. 28:20]," Schleiermacher presents Scripture as a central means of this presence:

> He is with us in the Scriptures. What He says Himself, even of the books of the Old Testament, "Ye search the Scriptures, because ye think that in

12. Tice, *Sermons*, 71.

them ye have eternal life, and it is they that testify of Me," — how much more gloriously, and in how much larger a sense, has this been true since we have had the Scriptures of the New Testament; since the narratives of His deeds and sufferings were recorded by His disciples, since the teachings and precepts collected in intercourse with Him, and presented and applied to the Christian Church by the apostles, have come down as a legacy to us! (*Sermons,* 268, citing John 5:39)

Schleiermacher goes on to say:

Whenever we search into those books, if we do it with a pure heart, everywhere He comes to meet us; everywhere He is pictured to us, everywhere we find a sacred bequest that He has left to us. And just as there are paintings in which all the light by which the rest of the objects become visible proceeds from Christ, so the Scriptures are such a painting, in which His image lights up everything else, that would otherwise be dark, with a heavenly radiance. (*Sermons,* 268)

He concludes by asking:

Who does not feel how important this holy possession is for our living relation to Him; how indispensable it was for all successive generations to have this compensation for His absence? Who does not feel what a held faith and love gain by this many-sided revelation of the Lord? And therefore this treasure will remain with us, according to His promise; He is with us in the Scriptures, even to the end of the world. And much as the spirit that is hostile to Christianity has sought to deface and depreciate these books, they will in the future, as they have done hitherto, surmount all opposition. (*Sermons,* 268-69)

The place of Scripture in the Christian life is thus finally a function of Christ's work. Scripture remains "indispensable . . . for all successive generations" and is able to "surmount all opposition" because when believers "search these books . . . with a pure heart, everywhere He comes to meet us." Warnings against a biblicism that separates the letter from the living presence of Christ to faith are never far from the surface, even in Schleiermacher's sermons. For example, he presents the Sadducees as "biblicists" who "did not want to accept anything as truth and revelation except what stood in the sacred books," quite apart from any consideration of living faith (*Sermons,* 248). But he balances critical suspicion of the deleterious influences of this kind of biblicism with a strong account of Scripture as a means of Christ's presence. By virtue of Christ's presence and the faith of the believer, Scripture stands as a "treasury of the divine Word" that edifies the church through all ages.[13]

Exegesis as Historical Theology

Up to this point, we have encountered Schleiermacher's dogmatic account of the nature of Scripture. On this account, Scripture is to be understood as a presentation of the faith of members of Jesus' inner circle, which, as an effect of the presence of Christ in their lives, serves to mediate Christ's work to future generations. This presentation functions as an authoritative norm for contemporary presentations of Christian faith by virtue of its purity; but, crucially, it is a historical presentation of faith that can be considered one historical presentation among others. It is this latter notion that grounds Schleiermacher's claim that, properly understood, scriptural exegesis is a subdiscipline of historical theology. Just as dogmatics is a historical discipline because it gives an account of the faith of contemporary believers, so exegesis is a historical discipline because it engages with an account of the faith of the first Christians. The question that this view raises is how a picture of the faith of the first believers is to be derived. How is the work of exegesis in particular to be carried out so that a picture that is capable of norming the faith of contemporary Christians may be formed?

The essential supposition of Schleiermacher's answer is that one is best assured of working with a reliable picture by ensuring that one works with reliable sources. Put differently, Schleiermacher supposes that a search for a reliable picture should aim at the establishment of a reliable source that vouches for the credibility of the picture. In thus emphasizing reliability of source, Schleiermacher stands in close proximity to the emphases of classical Protestant understanding of Scripture; yet, taken in conjunction with his other conceptions, this notion leads to a decisive shift in his account of the task of exegesis. We have seen that Schleiermacher rejects the view that the Bible is prior to faith as faith's authoritative source and guarantor, and suggests instead that faith itself is the basis of the authority of Scripture. On these terms, the reliability of a particular text is rooted not in the sheer fact that it is present in the Bible, but rather in the fact that it gives an accurate account of the essence of the faith of the first Chris-

---

13. For an account of this christological dynamic, see Nimmo, "On Scripture."

tians. Schleiermacher supposes that there is a continual critical question to be asked about how far a particular text succeeds in giving an account of this kind. He thus argues that exegesis must aim to establish just which texts ought to be taken as normative expressions of the faith of the early church. "The unique, essential task of exegetical theology" is the "correct understanding" of the parameters of the canon (*BO*, 44). Particular texts are proper to the canon, on his telling, neither because of their antiquity nor because of their authorship, but "only insofar as they are held capable of contributing to the original, consequently normative for all times presentation of Christianity" (*BO*, 44).[14]

> The New Testament canon has obtained its present form through the decision of the church, though this decision cannot be found expressed in any one particular act or declared with exactness. This is not a decision to which we attribute an authority exalted above all inquiry, and thus we are quite justified in starting fresh investigations in connection with earlier waverings of the boundary. (*BO*, 46)

The shift in the understanding of exegesis that we encounter here is foundational to the transition that Schleiermacher's work signals to more modern approaches to theology and scriptural interpretation. For many classical readers, every statement in Scripture is to be taken seriously (at least on some level!), and the interpreter is to find the principles that allow the apparent range of claims found in Scripture to be synthesized into a single coherent picture. For Schleiermacher, by contrast, the decisive center of Christian faith stands outside Scripture itself, and the task of the interpreter is to identify the biblical material that conveys this decisive center, and to employ this material as a critical standard for the church's use in separating the wheat from the chaff in the remainder of the text. The suggestion that anything in Scripture might qualify as chaff is, of course, anathema to many; yet Schleiermacher's proposal is perhaps not quite as dramatic a departure from traditional notions as it appears. Earlier decisions about which statements in Scripture were to be taken literally, and

---

14. This dismissal of authorship as a criterion for canonicity might appear strange given Schleiermacher's insistence on the need for proximity to Christ as a means of retaining purity in religious consciousness. Yet, as we shall see, Schleiermacher has an acute critical sense of the uncertainty surrounding the authorship of much biblical material, and so he makes it clear that his account of the authoritative character of Scripture is intended to permit what is identified as part of the canon to retain its authority regardless of the reliability of the authorship or date traditionally ascribed to it (*CF*, 604).

which ones taken spiritually or allegorically, presumed an understanding of the essence of Christian faith as a principle one could use to distinguish the literal from the nonliteral. That, for instance, a particular verse was to be taken allegorically was a reflection of the judgment that, based on an understanding of the true nature of God or of Christian faith, the biblical writer could not have meant it to be understood in any literal sense. Luther's antipathy toward James makes it clear that Schleiermacher was not the first to use an understanding of the true core of the Christian message as a critical standard against which other aspects of Scripture are to be measured.

The question, for Schleiermacher, is how this search for a more precise determination of the canon is to be carried out. On the face of it, Schleiermacher might appear to be caught in something of a circularity, for he supposes that the account of faith found in Scripture is to serve as the norm for contemporary understandings, but also that contemporaries are themselves responsible for determining what is and is not canonical. Scripture appears to be both norm and normed; but talk of circularity would be premature. Schleiermacher holds that the artful study of the texts themselves can produce a historical understanding capable of distinguishing between the true and the spurious on the text's own terms. It is in reflecting on questions regarding the proper, critical interpretation of texts that Schleiermacher makes a number of his most famous proposals for the study of the Bible. Schleiermacher identifies two undertakings that fall under the rubric of exegesis and are designed to permit the exegete to work toward the decisive core of the Christian canon. He calls one "hermeneutics," the other "criticism."

Exegesis as Historical Theology: Hermeneutics

Schleiermacher presents hermeneutics as "the art of understanding particularly the written discourse of another person correctly" (*HC*, 3). He is widely credited with founding the discipline that inquires into this art in a systematic way. Questions about principles for the interpretation of texts, of course, were not new (we encountered in Augustine's *Teaching Christianity* a handbook that was used to teach the interpretation of Scripture for centuries); but previous understandings tended to be occasional and unsystematic, and did not reflect the understanding of language and of the historically conditioned nature of consciousness that emerged in the modern period. Schleiermacher introduces his discussion of hermeneutics by claiming that this art *"does not yet exist* in a general manner; *there are instead only several forms* of specific hermeneutics," amounting to "collections of observations" that arbitrarily restrict themselves to "larger works or to difficult details" (*HC, 5-6, 21; BO, 53;* italics in original). Hermeneutics as an ordered discipline "exists only insofar as its prescriptions for interpretation form a system founded upon principles directly evident from the nature of thought and language" (*HC, 53*). Schleiermacher takes it as one of his tasks to work toward a system of this kind.

Hermeneutics seeks understanding by striving after "the inversion of the speech act"; that is, it aims to work backwards from words that are spoken or written to the thought that is the "basis of the speech" (*HC, 7*). Though Schleiermacher wishes to systematize this task so far as possible, he writes that this inversion is in fact "a kind of artistic achievement" because language and thought are both living, mobile realities, and thus an exhaustive set of principles for the disciplined execution of this task is impossible (*BO, 53*). General rules for the proper interpretation of a text may be established, but a further set of principles that determine which rules should be applied in a particular circumstance cannot be found (*BO, 53*). "Even where we think we can proceed in a manner that is free of art" through strict adherence to rules, "unexpected difficulties" arise that compel a turn away from rigid application of rules to "artistic" forms of judgment (*HC, 6*).

The artistic attempt to reconstruct the thought that stands behind speech involves attention to the grammatical, because all speech acts are shaped by the language that is available to the speaker, and to the psychological, because all acts of speech are also shaped by the thought and personality of the speaker. No merely passing acquaintance with these two fields will do. On the grammatical side, the ideal interpreter would possess "complete knowledge of language," understood not only as a mastery of grammar, syntax, and vocabulary, which is obviously essential, but also as a "living awareness of language, the sense of analogy and difference, etc." On the psychological side, the ideal interpreter would also possess "complete knowledge of the person," understood not only as an exhaustive comprehension of the "various relations important to the writers' lives," the lives of those for whom they wrote, and the "totality of their environments," but also as sufficient "knowledge of people" generally to be capable of "artistic presentation of a person." This requires the ability to present "the individual meaning of person[s] and of their particularities in relation to the concept of a human being" (*BO, 55-56; HC, 8-13*).

In practice, Schleiermacher is acutely aware of the impossibility of knowledge of this kind. He recognizes that we do not have exhaustive knowledge of our mother tongue, let alone of languages in which others write, and that we do not even know ourselves in the way that would be required to understand a piece of writing exhaustively. The attempt to understand the thought that lies behind a piece of writing thus appears to be doomed before it begins; yet Schleiermacher thinks that the difficulty can be eased if readers are sensitive to the peculiar interplay between the meaning of the text as a whole and the meaning of particular parts of the text. He holds that the whole of the text must be understood in terms of the organic unity of the parts, that the parts themselves must be understood in terms of the whole, and that the interplay between the two permits some advance in understanding. He writes:

> There is something which can reduce the trouble [with hermeneutics generally]. There is . . . an opposition between the unity of the whole and the individual parts of the work, so that the task [of hermeneutics] could be set in a twofold manner, namely, to understand the unity of the whole via the individual parts and the value of the individual parts via the unity of the whole. (*HC*, 109)

This procedure, which aims to "understand the whole via the particular and the particular via the whole," provides a "general canon" that permits hermeneutics to proceed (*HC*, 152). So long as readers work diligently to grasp the whole of a text in terms of its parts and its parts in light of its whole, there is some hope that the text will be understood in keeping with the author's thoughts. Schleiermacher thus suggests that, with any text, readers begin with "a cursory reading to get an overview of the whole," and then proceed to "more precise explication," moving ever in a "circle" between parts and whole (*HC*, 27).

On the basis of this "general canon," Schleiermacher goes on to construct a host of principles for grasping texts generally. Rather than following him through what is at times rather rugged conceptual terrain, we are best served at this point by turning to his consideration of New Testament hermeneutics in particular. This turn is significant because important elements in Schleiermacher's understanding of Scripture come to the fore through his consideration of the propriety of developing a special New Testament hermeneutics at all. Schleiermacher is keen in the first instance to resist the assumption that the New Testament requires a special hermeneutics, for this assumption undermines the integrity of hermeneutics as a unified discipline by reverting to the view that each text requires unique interpretive principles. It also rests on presumptions that compromise believers' understanding of the faith of the early Christians. The need for a special New Testament hermeneutics is often justified by suggesting that the Holy Spirit's work of inspiration determines that New Testament texts cannot be understood in terms of the language and lives of their authors; yet Schleiermacher insists that the apostles' acts of writing must be taken to be continuous with their thought and speaking more generally, for it was the apostles' verbal teaching that shaped the faith of the church before the canon had ever come into existence. To attribute special inspiration to the apostles' writings and to set the writings, as the basis of the faith of the contemporary church, apart from the apostles' spoken teaching is to suppose that the first churches had a rather less secure foundation for their faith than the later church (*HC,* 16-17). A proper understanding of the integrity of the faith of the first Christians is preserved only if the apostles' writings are not separated from their lives more generally. For Schleiermacher, then, it is proper to say that, "even if the writers were dead tools, the Holy Spirit could only have spoken through them in the way they themselves would have spoken" (*HC,* 17). The "general rules" that require texts to be understood in terms of the language and lives of their authors thus "remain" in relation to the New Testament (*HC,* 18).

Yet, once acknowledgment of the difficulties associated with positing a special New Testament hermeneutics is in place, Schleiermacher goes on to concede that a hermeneutics of this kind is in fact required because the New Testament is distinguishable from other texts even in the grammatical and psychological spheres. In the grammatical sphere, matters are complicated by the fact that the New Testament writers generally were not native Greek speakers, and so it is difficult to understand their Greek in terms of more general usage (*HC,* 19-20, 39-43).[15] Schleiermacher writes that Luke may have been a native Greek speaker; that Paul "constructs in the most Greek way" and John in the "least"; but that, throughout the New Testament, a tension between Hebrew thought and Greek language is present (*HC,* 39-48). New Testament Greek reflects a "hebrewising character" that introduces a good deal of complication into grammatical consideration. In the Sermon on the Mount, for example, the Greek term *dikaiosynē* is used in a sense that is continuous with Jewish understandings; in Paul's

---

15. Schleiermacher supposes that, in contrast to the writing of well-educated Jews like Philo and Josephus, the writers of the New Testament show plainly that they "do not know how to use the richness of Greek" (*HC,* 40).

letters, it is used in a sense that "cancels out" Jewish understandings; in both cases, a Greek term is used in a way that cannot be separated from a Jewish background (*HC,* 86). Standard hermeneutical consideration of the grammatical side of the text is thus rendered impossible in the case of the New Testament.

A further set of interpretive difficulties marks attempts to interpret the thought of the New Testament in the psychological sphere. Most basically, matters are complicated by the fact that, with a number of New Testament texts, the author is unknown, and so the text cannot be situated within the unity of a life (*HC,* 117-18). Additionally, the synoptic Gospels appear to Schleiermacher to consist of edited compilations of stories that lack obvious points of unity (*HC,* 80, 128). Most decisively, psychological interpretation is rendered difficult by the fact that Christianity brings with it a new "spiritual development" that cannot be reduced to existing notions (*HC,* 20). Psychological interpretation generally involves understanding an author in terms of the conceptions and conditions that are operative at a particular point in history, but to try to explain the New Testament "from what is already there" in the ancient world is to deny "the new concept-forming power of Christianity" (*HC,* 15). Because Christianity brings with it a new consciousness of God, it cannot be interpreted in terms of existing religious notions.

In view of the difficulties associated with the biblical text, Schleiermacher concedes that a special hermeneutics pertaining to scriptural material is required; but he holds that one further qualification is needed in order to clarify the functioning of this hermeneutics. As he understands it, the general procedure through which the reader considers the whole of the text in relation to the parts, and the parts in relation to the whole, appears to be rendered impossible by the fact that the New Testament does not represent an obvious whole. Schleiermacher writes that, considered philologically, the New Testament cannot be considered a unified whole, for it is written by different authors in different times and places using different vocabulary and concepts. General hermeneutical procedure thus appears to be jeopardized; yet Schleiermacher holds that the situation is ameliorated by the fact that the philological perspective is not decisive in considering the New Testament. As he understands it, the work of Christ would be reduced to "nothing" if it were supposed that the individuality of the authors' modes of expression wholly trumps the common spiritual direction that they received from Christ. Whatever their diversity, the writers of the New Testament were set in motion by an impetus received in common from Christ. In view of the unity of Christ's work, the New

Testament may be regarded as a unified "whole" that "forms a distinct individual world" (*HC,* 149).[16]

With this christological basis for hermeneutical procedure secured, Schleiermacher holds that New Testament exegesis may proceed by way of "more precise determinations of the general rules of hermeneutics, made with reference to the distinctive circumstances inherent in the canon" (*BO,* 54-55). New Testament hermeneutics may consider the part in relation to the whole and vice versa, and may then adapt other principles to suit the peculiar demands of the biblical text. The sense of a particular New Testament term, for instance, is to be derived from a holistic grasp of "the Greek meanings of a sign and the Hebrew meanings which correspond to them," as well as an exhaustive knowledge of Greek, Aramaic, and Hebrew more generally (*HC,* 47). Furthermore, "the rule must be established that in the exegetical process the particular theological use of language" that is current in the interpreter's own time "must be regarded as non-existent" in interpreting the language of the New Testament, for "artificial explications arise" when interpreters indulge the "disreputable habit" of taking the sense of a term from current debates rather than from its New Testament context (*HC,* 86, 130-31). In one sense, then, historical interpretation must be permitted because of "the connection of the N.T. writers to their age," and so the history of the Mediterranean world, the results of biblical archaeology, and the content of noncanonical Christian writings must be taken into account in understanding the text; but historical interpretation cannot be exhaustive because Christianity brings with it a new "concept-forming power" that is not reducible to its historical context (*HC,* 15). Equipped with these principles, readers should be positioned to make judicious judgments about the meaning of the New Testament as a unified whole.

Exegesis as Historical Theology: Criticism

The reader may recall that Schleiermacher claims that the task of exegesis is "more precise determination of the canon," which is to say that exegesis

16. Schleiermacher thus argues that Christianity is "destroyed" if the philological perspective triumphs over the dogmatic claim that the New Testament forms a unified whole. Yet he also argues that Christianity is destroyed if the dogmatic perspective wholly erases the philological recognition of the individuality of the writers from view, for then the differences between the language and style of different New Testament writers would have to be attributed to Christ and the Holy Spirit (*HC,* 52-53).

aims to distinguish between faithful and spurious expressions of the faith of the first Christians. He suggests that this enterprise centers around two disciplines: hermeneutics, which we have just encountered, is the art of understanding; criticism, to which we turn now, is, by contrast, the discipline that makes concrete judgments about the authentic and the inauthentic within a text.[17] Criticism is "the art of judging correctly and establishing the authenticity of texts and parts of texts from adequate evidence and data" (*HC,* 3-4). Hermeneutics and criticism go together, for criticism can only weigh the authenticity of parts of a text once the text as a whole is understood, and hermeneutics can only be sure of grasping the meaning of a text once it is assured that the material with which it is working is authentic (*HC,* 3-4). The two disciplines are thus related; but hermeneutics has a certain primacy, for in some cases criticism is not required at all (consideration of a recently published text, for instance), and, in all cases, the critical task of distinguishing the authentic from the inauthentic should in principle reach a point at which its work is done, while the hermeneutical task of understanding a text is sufficiently uncertain that one can never be assured of being finished (*HC,* 4).

The work of criticism involves a range of practices spanning a host of different fields. It involves careful manuscript work in seeking out and comparing different copies of a text, historical work in weighing the evidence for the veracity of particular claims, and linguistic and conceptual work in identifying and comparing terms, phrases, and concepts that mark the work of a particular writer. It also tends to rest on a measure of "divination," for definitive evidence regarding the authenticity of a text is rarely to be found, and so the critical task often turns on the judgment of artful readers who are able to distinguish the authentic from the inauthentic. Schleiermacher suggests that he himself has little difficulty distinguishing genuinely Platonic dialogues from "dialogues falsely attributed to Plato," which, "despite the dialogical form," are "dry, lack their own productivity and are merely directed at logical splitting, of which there is no trace in Plato's work" (*HC,* 143).

A great deal more could be said about the general principles of criticism, but we are best served by moving quickly into Schleiermacher's application of critical principles to biblical material in particular. Whereas, in the sphere of hermeneutics, Schleiermacher is best known for his theoretical account of the discipline, in the sphere of criticism he is best known

---

17. Authenticity is a matter of the degree to which a textual part fits within the whole, either because it is written by the author of the whole, or because it expresses the same spirit.

for the practical work that he carried out. Schleiermacher was the first to lecture publicly on the historical life of Jesus; he paved the way for deutero-Pauline scholarship by suggesting that Paul was not the author of 1 Timothy; his work on the structure of Colossians 1:15-20 set the parameters for interpretation of the text for more than a century.[18] A glance at his handling of the Gospels as historical sources for knowledge of the life of Jesus will best serve our purposes here. This material is of particular importance because Schleiermacher claims that "careful criticism" of the "so-called synoptic gospels" is "the most important task of our day" (*LJ,* 223). Advances in science and in the critical study of history had put aspects of Christian understandings of the person of Jesus in doubt. Schleiermacher held that the church itself had to engage in critical study of its sources in order to respond to these concerns and to train itself in a fruitful reading of Scripture.

> So far as we understand Christ in terms of a life that was subject to the general laws that govern all life, the Holy Scriptures can only be understood as a book subject to the law that governs human transmission and one that can only be comprehended when all the resources of the intelligence are brought into play. There must be a continuous application of all the skills of criticism and exegesis to the canonical books. In this way only can we gradually arrive at an artistic, that is, a complete understanding and use of Scripture. (*LJ,* 223-24)

Critical study of the New Testament Gospels leads Schleiermacher to a dramatic distinction between John and the other three Gospels. On one side, John presents an internally coherent text informed by "one and the same tendency from beginning to end" (*LJ,* 159). The narrative is not "full of gaps": John "specifies" the periods that he skips, "and he skips them because they contain nothing of interest to his special tendency" (*LJ,* 159). He speaks as an eyewitness to the matters he describes, narrating "what he himself has experienced" and giving an account of this material from his own perspective (*LJ,* 159). Schleiermacher concludes that "what John represents as the content of the discourses of Christ must have been what Christ really said, and there is no reason to believe that John introduced any of his own ideas into Christ's discourses" (*LJ,* 262).

On the other side, critical study reveals that Matthew, Mark, and Luke are edited compilations, or "aggregations," of stories that were circulat-

18. See Helmer, "Theology," 229-30.

ing among the early Christians (*LJ,* 37). No consistent narrative voice or viewpoint is visible in these Gospels, the stories do not occur in any logical order, and the sequence and locations in which events are presented differ between them. "The first three [Gospels] are so unmistakably accounts composed of originally separate narratives that, even if the composition were complete and without a gap . . . no account of the life of Christ as a unity could be discovered in them" (*LJ,* 158-59).

Within this disparate material, Schleiermacher holds that disciplined judgment is able to reach some conclusions about the character of the editors and the veracity of their material. Matthew and Luke contradict each other with sufficient frequency that they cannot have drawn from the same source (*LJ,* 47).[19] In contrast to Luke (who does not appear to have been a disciple, and who introduces "poetic elements" with sufficient frequency to throw the historical character of his narrative in doubt), Matthew shows little sign of having been reworked for dramatic effect, and is to be preferred as a broadly "historical" narrative (*LJ,* 52). Yet Matthew also takes considerable liberties in making connections between his story and material drawn from the Old Testament prophets. This, Schleiermacher thinks, is an impulse of his own that cannot be attributed to the sources from which he worked (*LJ,* 62-63). Differing sources and differing impulses led to differences in the presentation of the life of Christ, some of which are of substantial theological significance. The Lord's Prayer is understood very differently if, as in Matthew, Christ gives the prayer "unasked" in the context of "general polemical rules about prayer," as opposed to giving it, as Luke presents it, in response to a specific "request" and "need" of the disciples (*LJ,* 240).

How is the church to account for the relationship between John, on the one hand, and the three Synoptic evangelists, on the other? Schleiermacher holds that John "was the only one of the first circle of Christ's pupils who communicated his account directly in written form" (*LJ,* 260-61); yet he is aware that aspects of John's Gospel — particularly the first

---

19. Schleiermacher suggests, e.g., that Luke presents Mary and Joseph as living in Nazareth before the birth of Christ and returning to Nazareth after Christ is born, while Matthew gives good reason for thinking that, in going to Nazareth after their flight to Egypt, Mary and Joseph were going to a different place than they had lived before. Having considered the relationship among the stories relating to Christ's birth, and the sequence of them — the visitation of the magi, the flight to Egypt, and the presentation at the temple — Schleiermacher concludes that "we cannot avoid the conclusion that these two narrative sequences came from two different circles and are connected with each other in the gospels in such a way that both these contexts cannot at the same time be correct" (*LJ,* 71).

fourteen verses treating the eternal *Logos* — are widely taken to be artificial additions to the Gospel because no discussion of an eternal divine Word is found in the Synoptic Gospels. In face of this difficulty, Schleiermacher ventures the hypothesis that the other disciples were the sources of the oral tradition from which the other Gospels were drawn, but were themselves too busy to write down their accounts. As a "precautionary measure," they omitted claims about Christ's eternal personhood from this oral material for fear that they would be misunderstood (*LJ*, 260). "They suppressed what was difficult to understand and what could most easily be misrepresented as it passed from one mouth to another" (*LJ*, 262). Encountering this oral tradition, and recognizing that it lacked teaching about the eternal *Logos*, John took it upon himself to write a Gospel that gives a stronger account of Christ's divinity "as a supplement to the oral tradition" (*LJ*, 261). It follows that John "preferred to include in his written account teachings of Christ that had no place in the oral tradition" (*LJ*, 261).

Where, then, is the church left on the question of the authenticity and inauthenticity of various aspects of the Gospel narratives? Schleiermacher gives a host of conclusions culled from critical consideration of the Gospels. He thinks the "probability great" that narratives regarding the visit of the magi and the flight to Egypt are historically accurate, but he thinks the slaughter of young children in Bethlehem highly dubious. "In light of the character of Herod, the atrocity is by no means improbable," but "we have a historian of this period in Josephus . . . who could hardly have neglected to record such a fact as *the slaughter of all children* in a not unimportant center so near to Jerusalem" (*LJ*, 64-65; italics in original). The story of Christ's baptism is sufficiently attested that its reliability may be accepted; but the story of Christ's temptation, which is appended to the baptism story in the Synoptic Gospels, is spurious. It is entirely missing from John, and it is "scarcely possible" to find in John's Gospel a period of forty days after Christ's baptism during which it could have occurred (*LJ*, 144-45). Consideration of the improbability of the chronology, the differing nature and sequences of the temptations, and the magical character of the event more generally leads Schleiermacher to conclude that the story "contains absolutely nothing that makes it credible" (*LJ*, 149).

These claims give a representative sense of Schleiermacher's procedure in seeking to distinguish between the authentic and the inauthentic in the New Testament. The final point of significance for us in considering his conception of the task of criticism is to inquire into the relationship between the task of criticism and the life of faith. Schleiermacher's conclusions regarding the veracity of elements of the New Testament narratives appear destructive for an account that holds that faith is founded on Scripture as its source and guarantor. But, as we have seen, Schleiermacher wishes to reverse such a view by way of a reconsideration of the order of priority between Christ, church, faith, and Scripture. Whereas, according to some understandings, Scripture is the foundation of the life of faith because it alone gives witness to Christ, Schleiermacher points out that the early church came into being through the work of Christ and drew believers into its sphere before the New Testament was ever written and assembled. Schleiermacher sees this sequence as paradigmatic of the proper ordering of the life of faith. The communal faith of the church and the individual faith of the believer exist as effects of Christ's work. It is this work that is foundational for faith; it is, then, faith itself that invests Scripture with authority. Faith itself and the realities in which it is founded are not reducible to the content of Scripture; thus, critical inquiry may determine that aspects of the scriptural narrative are inauthentic without the faith that stands on the work of Christ coming into question. Because faith has its basis in Christ, it may make critical inquiry into Scripture using the resources of scientific and historical study without exposing itself to peril.

With Schleiermacher, we have crossed a barrier into decisively modern theology. He wishes to show how the life of faith may coexist with various forms of modern inquiry. The emphasis on experience that allows him to accomplish this brings with it a "paradigm shift" in theological inquiry.[20] In the words of one of Schleiermacher's successors, he did not found a new school but rather a new age in the history of theology.[21] This successor stands as one of Schleiermacher's most consistent critics; yet he also says that "anyone who has never noticed anything of the splendour this figure radiated and still does — I am almost tempted to say, [anyone] who has never succumbed to it — may honourably pass on to other and possibly better ways, but let him never raise so much as a finger against Schleiermacher."[22] This successor was Karl Barth. In Chapter 13 of this study we turn to a consideration of the revolution that Barth himself effected in his attempt to address the problems that he thought were created by Schleiermacher's project.

20. Pannenberg, *Systematic Theology*, 1.46.
21. Barth, *Protestant Theology*, 411.
22. Barth, *Protestant Theology*, 413.

CHAPTER 12

Kierkegaard

Søren Kierkegaard was born in Copenhagen in 1813 into an oppressively re-ligious household. Away from home, he proved to be a shiftless university student who counted on his father to pay his considerable debts. After his father died (1838), he settled down sufficiently to complete his degree, then lived on inherited wealth. Like Thoreau in Concord, Kierkegaard traveled a good deal in Copenhagen, but little elsewhere. Various possibilities for employment crossed his mind — university, church, government, the po-lice force — but he opted for walking the streets and writing strange books. His contemporaries concluded that he lacked seriousness and lamented his wasted talent. He never married. By breaking off his engagement with the young woman whom he continued to adore (1841), he enhanced his reputation for irresponsibility but gave himself more time to write strange books while retaining (in his mind, at least) an ideal reader to inspire them. And since, in his mind[1] (and, ultimately, in hers[2]), a prior commitment to

---

1. "After all, she does not have first priority in my life. No, no, yet humanly speaking yes, certainly, how much I would like to express the fact that she has, and shall have, the first and only priority in my life — but God has first priority. My engagement to her and breaking off the engagement are really my God-relationship — are, if I may be so bold, divinely speaking my engagement to God" (*PJ*, 553 [NB 27.21]; cf. *KJN* 5.369-70; 7.342).

Seven of a projected eleven volumes of *Kierkegaard's Journals and Notebooks* have been published. I cite these by volume and page number (e.g., *KJN* 5.369); where volumes are not yet available, I have cited existing translations (*JP* [with volume and entry number], *LY*, and *PJ*), but also included within parentheses the journal and entry number or the paper number (taken from *SKS*) to facilitate identification in forthcoming volumes of *KJN*. (For the abbreviations, see the bibliography.)

2. Many years later, an acquaintance recalled: "Kierkegaard's motivation for the break was his conception of his religious task; he dared not bind himself to anyone on earth in order not to be obstructed from his calling. He had to sacrifice the very best thing he owned

God compelled him to break the engagement, the experience contributed greatly to the fervor of his religious writings.

In 1846, Kierkegaard became the target of prolonged and juvenile caricaturing in the *Corsair,* a widely deplored, more widely read, gossip-and-scandal newspaper. After that publication drew attention to the (apparently) uneven length of his pant legs, he was mocked and gawked at wherever he went. He observed that, while his *Concluding Unscientific Postscript* — recognized today as one of the most important philosophical works of the nineteenth century — sold perhaps fifty copies, each edition of the *Corsair* sold 3,000 (*KJN* 6.165; cf. 6.311); at least his trousers, he noted, were understood.[3] The close of his life found him once again in the eye of an uncomprehending public as he published a series of religiously motivated attacks on the Danish church. He died in 1855, aged forty-two, little read[4] and less understood in Denmark — virtually unknown everywhere else.

That has changed, of course: now he is widely known, sometimes read, caricatured by Garrison Keillor, and understood by the odd "single individual."

Kierkegaard . . . and the Bible?

And it came to pass after these things, that God did tempt Abraham, and said unto him, Abraham: and he said, Behold, here I am. And he said, Take now thy son, thine only son Isaac, whom thou lovest, and get thee into the land of Moriah; and offer him there for a burnt offering upon one of the mountains which I will tell thee of. And Abraham rose up early in the morning . . . (Gen. 22:1-3; KJV)

The art of interpretation, Ben Meyer reminds us, has a "triangular structure," with three "indispensable" components: the interpreter, the

---

in order to work as God demanded of him: therefore he sacrificed his love for [his fiancée] for the sake of his writing" (Kirmmse, *Encounters,* 36-37).

3. "My contemporaries are especially sharp when it comes to sizing up the cut of my trouser legs — and in that my contemporaries are correct; it's more or less the only thing they understand about me" (*KJN* 4.141).

4. The obvious exception is *Either-Or,* the publication of which (in 1843) created a sensation. Though Kierkegaard's religious commitment was very much in place when he wrote the book (*PV,* 35-36; *KJN* 6.137), that commitment is not readily apparent in its pages (to say the least); but he hoped the popularity of the work would create an audience for his later, explicitly religious, publications (*PV,* 44). He is not otherwise known for erring on the side of optimism.

text to be interpreted *(Sprache),* and that to which the text refers *(Sache).*[5] Meyer goes on to note that interpretations may differ significantly, "even in kind, in accord with how the interpreter distributes his attention, co-nation, and care between text and referent, respectively." To illustrate the point, he discusses "two superior interpreters" of Genesis 22, Søren Kierkegaard and Gerhard von Rad: the latter's interpretation is "weighted towards the text"; the former's, "towards its referent." Whereas von Rad naturally and appropriately raises such topics as the stream of tradition (or "source") from which the narrative is taken, Kierkegaard's *Fear and Trembling* gives us "a subtle, powerful, and original panegyric on Abraham" as it examines what Genesis 22 tells us "of innocence and dread, of faith and hope against hope, of the reasonable and the absurd, ethics and divine madness." The question whether Kierkegaard "has truly caught the intention of the text" hardly occurs to the reader: "Beyond any doubt [Kierkegaard's] response to the text has, in a broad sense, richly registered the text's intended sense."[6]

The observation is astute, and can be said to apply not only to Kierkegaard's most famous work of biblical interpretation,[7] but to all the discourses[8]

---

5. Meyer quotes Luther (as cited by Gadamer): "One who does not understand *the things* is quite unable to draw the meaning from *the words*" ("Business," 743).

6. Meyer, "Business," 743-45.

7. Note, however, that Kierkegaard published *Fear and Trembling* (1843) under the pseudonym Johannes de Silentio. The pseudonymous works pose a problem for every interpreter of Kierkegaard, since they represent his attempts to articulate imaginatively the point of view of the pseudonymous author, not (in principle) his own. Yet no discussion of Kierkegaard and the Bible can afford to ignore such pseudonymous works as *Fear and Trembling* and *Concluding Unscientific Postscript.* We should, in any case, recognize that the pseudonymous works are not all of a piece. Those attributed to Anti-Climacus *(Sickness unto Death, Practice in Christianity),* for example, clearly express Kierkegaard's own under-standing of Christianity; at one point he even intended to publish them under his own name, though in the end he opted for a pseudonym lest readers attribute to him the presumption of thinking his life matched his ideals (cf. *KJN* 6.149). Among the earlier pseudonymous works, *Fear and Trembling* and *Concluding Unscientific Postscript* at least point toward positions Kierkegaard firmly embraced. Much of what follows in this chapter is based on Kierkegaard's journals and nonpseudonymous works; but I have not hesitated to draw on statements in the pseudonymous works as well when they help to fill out what appears to be a consistent approach to the reading of Scripture.

8. "Discourses," not sermons, Kierkegaard insisted, because they were "without au-thority" (i.e., he did not have the authority of an ordained minister to preach sermons; cf. *EUD,* 5; *CUP* 1.273; *WA,* 99 n. 52). On the distinctions Kierkegaard drew (but did not always maintain) between "upbuilding [or "edifying"] discourses," "occasional discourses," "devo-tional discourses," "Christian discourses," "Christian deliberations in the form of discourses," "Christian discourses and expositions for upbuilding, awakening, inward deepening, and

he devoted to scriptural texts — and there are many.[9] Today Kierkegaard's reputation may largely be that of the "father" of existential philosophy, "by far the greatest philosopher of the nineteenth century,"[10] a psychologist before Freud, an astute literary and cultural critic, and so on. But it is worth noting that in the overwhelming majority of works he published under his own name, Kierkegaard grappled with Scripture,[11] often exclusively, always profoundly, at times in passages whose "unearthly beauty"[12] matches that of *Fear and Trembling*.[13] His very mission in life — to introduce Christianity into Christendom (*PC*, 36; cf. *CD*, 214) — he derived from the discrepancy he noted (and undertook to expose) between religiosity in Denmark and the Christianity he read of in the New Testament. In all his treatments of Scripture, Kierkegaard's focus is firmly fixed on the subject matter *(Sache)* of the text. Though he read both Hebrew and Greek,[14] he never pauses to discuss issues of translation. Seldom does he raise other interpreters' bread-and-butter topics: the occasion that prompted the writing of a biblical text, its place in the larger context, and the like. Such discussions, he grants, have their place ("we do not disparage scholarship, no, far from it"); but he insists that they remain *preliminary* to — and not be confused with — the actual reading of God's word (*FSE,* 26-29). In a day when, at least among his edu-

---

self-examination," and "communion discourses," see Sylvia Walsh's introduction in Kierke-gaard, *Communion,* 7-17.

9. For a good introduction to the growing literature on Kierkegaard and the Bible, see Paul Martens, "Bible."

10. The words are those of Wittgenstein. See Malik, *Impact,* 380.

11. Not, to be sure, that probing Scripture is confined to works Kierkegaard published under his own name; in addition to *Fear and Trembling* (on Gen. 22), see *Practice in Christianity* (based on three Gospel texts). For nonpseudonymous works largely based on texts from Scripture, see *Eighteen Upbuilding Discourses* (a composite of six publications from 1843 to 1844), *Upbuilding Discourses in Various Spirits* (1847), *Works of Love* (1847), *Christian Discourses* (1848), *The Lily in the Field and the Bird of the Air* (1849), *Three Discourses at the Communion on Friday* (1849), *An Upbuilding Discourse* (1850), *Two Discourses at the Communion on Fridays* (1851), *For Self-Examination* (1851), and *The Changelessness of God* (1855). To these should be added the posthumously published *Judge for Yourself!* (1876).

12. Andrew Hamilton, a Scottish contemporary who lived for a time in Copenhagen, noted that Kierkegaard's writings have at times this character — adding that they are else-where marred by "an exaggerated display of logic" (a charge that can scarcely be brought against the "upbuilding" discourses). See Kirmmse, *Encounters,* 95.

13. See, e.g., a number of the *Christian Discourses* of 1848, and (perhaps particularly) *The Lily in the Field and the Bird of the Air* (1849). Such passages include parables as memorable as any since those of the Master Parabolist. See Oden, *Parables.*

14. He filled many pages of a notebook with his own (Latin!) translations of passages from the Greek New Testament (*KJN* 1.139-88).

cated peers, the art of reading Scripture *as Scripture* was largely forgotten, Kierkegaard showed how it is done. No one, I submit, has done it better.

And yet, to discuss Kierkegaard's understanding of Scripture and of how Scripture is to be read is to betray him.

Betraying Søren Kierkegaard

Kierkegaard knew well what awaited him. His legacy, he lamented, would be left to those he "deeply opposed": to professors, intent on summarizing what he had to say in digestible paragraphs, then assigning him a place within an all-encompassing system, remote from life (*LY,* 67 [NB 29.87]; *PJ,* 551 [NB 26.76]; cf. *FT,* 8).

The besetting sin of professors, Kierkegaard believed, was their propensity to distance themselves from their subject matter, to want to view it "objectively," in a "detached" way. Such a "disinterested" approach is innocent enough when dealing with "plants and animals and stars" (*KJN* 4.63) — though Kierkegaard cannot imagine why people would concern themselves with such things, other than as a hobby: "If one views the discovery of the microscope as a bit of an amusement, a bit of a pastime, that is all right, but as earnestness, it is infinitely stupid" (*KJN* 4.62). In any case, though such pursuits may be innocent in themselves, those who make natural science the object of their life's endeavors are likely to end up "enchant[ing] and amaz[ing] the whole world" with their "discoveries and ingenuity," while having no understanding of themselves (*KJN* 4.72).

But to treat that which pertains to our humanity — and, in particular, Christianity and the Bible — with objective detachment is the mark of an "inhuman curiosity" (*SUD,* 5). One's eternal happiness should be the pressing concern of every human being; but it goes unconsidered among those who choose to speak of Christianity objectively, arranging its tenets in tidy paragraphs (*CUP* 1.55-56). Christianity becomes for them a sum of doctrines to be lectured on, like ancient philosophy, the Hebrew language, or some other branch of knowledge — as though its relationship to the hearer were indifferent rather than decisive (*CD,* 214-15). While there is plenty of talk *about* Christianity, Christianity itself is left behind (*KJN* 6.237). And conveniently so, since the New Testament makes demands unwelcome to us all: a change of will, a dying to ourselves and the world in order to live before God. It is thus a "scoundrelly trick" of recalcitrant human beings to transfer "everything to intellectuality" (*LY,* 226 [NB 33.13]).

If it is really God's view that Christianity is only doctrine, a collection of doctrinal propositions, then the New Testament is a ridiculous book. . . . Mankind would surely have to say, "My heavens, if that is all you want, if that is what occupies you so much, we gladly accept whatever you want, we will do it as easily as if you asked us to wear a cocked hat instead of a round one." . . . But no: God who knows the scoundrel that man is aims at something else — at transforming character. (*LY*, 275 [NB 34.31])

None of this means that Kierkegaard dismissed the doctrinal aspect of Christianity, or regarded Christian faith as "empty of content" (*CUP* 1.380). On the contrary, he acknowledged that there was a time when the apostles were called on to preach unknown truth to the world, a time when it was crucial that doctrine be correctly defined (*CUP* 1.243; *PC*, 123; *KJN* 2.29-30; 4.312).[15] But different times call for different measures, and Kierkegaard saw the need of his day to lie in the insistence that Christianity must be personally appropriated and *lived*: "For a person to be a Christian, it certainly is required that what he believes is a *definite* something, but

15. "The essentially Christian exists before any Christian exists; it must exist in order for one to become a Christian. . . . Even if no one had become aware that God had revealed himself in human form in Christ, he still had revealed himself. . . . Christianly understood, [revelation] is an objective determinant, a qualitative paradox that must stand unshaken as such" (*BA*, 117-20; cf. Ziegler, "Criticisms," 438-42). No one has emphasized more pointedly than Kierkegaard the *revealed* nature of Christian truth (its central tenets, he claims, are such that no human being could have imagined them [*PF*, 35-36; *CUP* 1.579-81; *WL*, 24-25, 27; *CD*, 122]), or the imperative of believing in (rather than being offended by) these truths. That, in sum, is the purport of substantial sections of *Practice in Christianity,* where the incarnation (the God-man Jesus Christ) is the truth to which human beings respond either with faith or offense (cf. *PF,* 23-36; *SUD,* 83-87, 125-31). Like Luther, Kierkegaard believes that the doctrine becomes meaningful, however, only when personally applied: "When one thinks about what it means to dare to believe that God has come into the world, also for my sake . . . if it weren't God himself who said it . . . it would be the most awful of blasphemies" (*KJN* 4.361). Similarly, the atonement is fundamental to Kierkegaard's thinking, an essential counterpart (like "gospel" to "law," in Luther's understanding) to his insistence on the uncompromising demands of discipleship (*CD,* 298-99; *WA,* 123-24; *KJN* 6.395; cf. *PF,* 17). But he has no interest in "atonement theory," and he wonders how much the atonement really matters to those who speculate about it. The atonement becomes the object of meaningful faith only when grasped by an anguished conscience (*KJN* 4.68). Or take Christ's ascension: some give themselves importance by doubting it, others by "proving" it true (thereby fostering further doubt); for both, the subject is one of idle curiosity. But those who, venturing forth in faith, have forsaken all to follow Christ, who lack the idleness and luxury to doubt, find, in their faith in the ascension, strength to endure suffering; they also find, in their suffering, a strengthening of their faith (*FSE,* 67-69).

then with equal certainty it is also required that it be *entirely definite* that *he* believes" (*CD,* 244). The truth Kierkegaard was concerned with — that of a life truly lived in faith — cannot be imparted by lecturing; indeed, it is the kind of truth that lectures are likely to lose sight of. How, then, can we make one who emphasized the limits and distortions of academic discussion the subject of *our* academic discussion without, in effect, betraying him? Kierkegaard believed that the truth that matters is found, not in what we know, but in how we live. Thus we do him no honor when we make *him* a subject — of what we know.

We reach the same conclusion by a different route when we note that, for Kierkegaard (as we shall see), to be a human being in the fullest sense is to live before God. The summons to such a life cannot be directly communicated, nor faith given, by one human being to another; at most, one can be the occasion by which others come to recognize their own potential and responsibility.[16] Ultimately, then, the believer, as believer, owes nothing to any other human being, everything to God (*PF,* 101-2; cf. *FT,* 80-81). "Every human being is essentially taught solely by God" (*CUP* 1.101). Why, then, did Kierkegaard himself write edifying discourses? His answer, in part, is that he wrote for himself, as part of his own education.[17] If others nonetheless benefit from his writings, it is not, he insists, because of him. Repeatedly, he urges readers to read his discourses aloud, addressing to themselves — before God — the concerns so evoked. Whatever profit they gain from the discourse will then be due, not to the merits of its composition, but to their own appropriation of its content. No account need be taken of the writer.

---

16. Faith is the greatest gift one can wish for another, the only wish one can rightly entertain without reservation: however desirable earthly goods and goals may appear, they inevitably carry with them the peril of spiritual harm. (Conversely, the earthly adversity we would choose to avoid works for our eternal good — if we love God [*CD,* 195, on Rom. 8:28]; if we bear this in mind, we can see, even in adversity, a "good and perfect gift" from our heavenly Father [*EUD,* 32-48, on James 1:17].) Yet it is neither possible nor desirable that one human being should bestow faith on another; that, after all, would deprive the other of the experience of God on which true faith must rest (*EUD,* 8-16; *KJN* 4.300). But not to worry: "It is so vain of them to believe that some other human being needs one's assistance in his God-relationship, as if God were not able to help himself and the person involved" (*CUP* 1.78).

17. "I regard myself rather as a *reader* of the books, not as the *author.* 'Before God,' religiously, when I speak with myself, I call my whole work as an author my own upbringing and development" (*PV,* 12). "It is Governance that has brought me up, and the upbringing is reflected in the writing process. . . . Teacher I am not — only a fellow-pupil" (*PV,* 77-79; cf. *KJN* 6.366; *PC,* 7).

[My reader] will seek stillness, then he will read, not for my sake, not for the world's sake, but for his own sake; then he will read in such a way that he does not seek my acquaintance but avoids it — and then he is *my* reader. (*KJN* 4.53)

My dear reader, read aloud, if possible! If you do so, allow me to thank you for it; if you not only do it yourself, if you also influence others to do it, allow me to thank each one of them, and you again and again! By reading aloud you will gain the strongest impression that you have only yourself to consider, not me, who, after all, am "without authority," nor others, which would be a distraction. (*FSE*, 3)

The discourse does not address itself to you as a specific person, it does not even know who you are. But if you think about the occasion [that of the confession prior to receiving communion] very vividly, it will seem to you, whoever you are, as if it were speaking directly to you. This is not the merit of the discourse; it is the action of your self-activity that you on your own behalf assist the discourse and on your own initiative will to be the one intimately addressed as: you. (*UDVS*, 123; cf. *TDIO*, 5, 28)

How, then, are we to make Kierkegaard — and especially his edifying discourses — the focus of our attention without betraying the very vision that underlay their composition? Without further comment, Kierkegaard makes the point by concluding the preface to a series of edifying discourses with the following parable:[18]

When a woman works on a cloth for sacred use, she makes every flower as beautiful, if possible, as the lovely flowers of the field, every star as sparkling, if possible, as the twinkling stars of the night; she spares nothing but uses the most precious things in her possession; then she disposes of every other claim on her life in order to purchase the uninterrupted and opportune time of day and night for her sole, her beloved, work. But when the cloth is finished and placed in accordance with its sacred purpose — then she is deeply distressed if anyone were to make the mistake of seeing her artistry instead of the meaning of the cloth or

---

18. The parable is found at the conclusion of the preface to the first part of *Upbuilding Discourses in Various Spirits* (5-6). This part of the larger work was initially published separately in English under the title *Purity of Heart Is to Will One Thing* (New York: Harper and Row, 1938); it has become a devotional classic in its own right.

were to make the mistake of seeing a defect instead of seeing the meaning of the cloth. . . . It was permissible, it was fitting, it was a duty, it was a cherished duty, it was a supreme joy for the needlewoman to do everything in order to do her part, but it would be an offense against God, an insulting misunderstanding to the poor needlewoman, if someone were to make the mistake of seeing what is there but is to be disregarded, what is there — not to draw attention to itself but, on the contrary, only so that its absence would not disturbingly draw attention to itself.

I take no pleasure in betraying Søren Kierkegaard; at the same time, I believe that, on our subject, his voice should be heard. Perhaps the least unsatisfactory solution is simply to restate,[19] and to allow Kierkegaard, in his unique way, to state, (what he insists is) the right approach to Scripture, focusing on the subject matter — that to which the "cloth" directs attention — not on the "needlewoman" or "her work."

But, for Kierkegaard (indeed, for all who take the subject seriously), the right approach to Scripture is but one aspect of the more fundamental question: How are we to live? Before we take up the former, we must consider the latter, larger issue.

Living and Partly Living

Henry David Thoreau famously remarked that "the mass of men lead lives of quiet desperation."[20] Kierkegaard would have appreciated the observation, but qualified it: *All* human beings live (or have lived) in despair — and it is their distinctive *glory,* as human beings, that they are able to do so.[21]

Like the birds of the air and the lilies in the field, human beings are creatures of time. Unlike birds and lilies, however, human beings have a consciousness that enables them to transcend time, to inhabit more than

---

19. Alas, the restatement is inevitably in summary form — and in this case, to summarize is also to betray. Given that the point of Kierkegaard's writing was not to convey information but (often through "indirect communication") to evoke a response, it follows that conciseness and clarity are not the self-evident virtues for him that they were for John Calvin! The pace at which, and the manner in which, Kierkegaard proceeds are themselves integral to his purpose — though they cannot be reproduced here.

20. Thoreau, *Walden,* 111.

21. For the substance of the following paragraphs, see (in addition to the references given) "The Cares of the Pagans" (*CD,* 3-91) and *The Lily in the Field and the Bird of the Air: Three Devotional Discourses* (*WA,* 1-45).

the present in which they find themselves: they can, for example, worry about the morrow, as birds and lilies do not. Human beings can also overcome such worry through faith. Whether, in the end, they are worse or better off than birds and lilies thus depends on what they *do* with their unique capacity . . . to worry about the morrow.

Like the birds of the air and the lilies in the field, human beings owe their existence to God. The very sight of birds and lilies reminds us of the one who created them; yet birds and lilies lack the consciousness that would enable them to acknowledge, worship, and praise their Creator. As creatures of eternity as well as of time, human beings uniquely have the capacity to prostrate themselves in adoration and worship before God (*UDVS*, 192-93).

The bird is dependent on God to sustain its daily existence; but it does not pray — and "how poor not to be able to pray, how poor not to be able to give thanks, how poor to have to receive everything as if in ingratitude, how poor not to exist, as it were, for the benefactor to whom it owes its life!" (*CD*, 16). Human beings can pray, can receive with thanks their daily bread from God, treasuring it — like a gift from one's beloved — less for its own sake than for what it says of the giver. They thus live conscious of God, "awake to God" (*CD*, 64), in a way that birds and lilies cannot. Or, to be sure, human beings can live without God in anxiety.

Hard times come upon birds, lilies, and human beings alike. The birds and the lilies bear their suffering in silence. Human beings, conscious of what they undergo, but conscious, too, that it is God who rules and to whom alone wisdom and understanding belong, can bear suffering in silent reverence before God. Or, to be sure, they can forget God, fixate on the suffering, and even augment it with their unique capacity for speech (*WA*, 15-18).

And human beings have the capacity to *know* that they are loved by God. "Infinite, divine love" is lavished on all without distinction. Yet here again one human being differs from another.

> One person bears in mind that he is loved — keeps it in mind perhaps day in and day out, perhaps day in and day out for seventy years, perhaps with only one longing, for eternity, so that he can really grasp this thought and go forth, employed in this blessed occupation of keeping in mind that he — alas, not because of his virtue! — is loved.
>
> Another person perhaps does not think about his being loved, perhaps goes on year after year, day after day, without thinking about his being loved; or perhaps he is happy and grateful to be loved by his wife,

his children, by his friends and contemporaries, but he does not think about his being loved by God; or he may bemoan not being loved by anyone, and he does not think about his being loved by God. (*WA,* 165-66; cf. *WL,* 364)[22]

In short, human beings are truly themselves only when they realize their *human* potential by living in conscious relationship with God: "It is really the God-relationship that makes a human being a human being" (*CUP* 1.244; cf. *CD,* 44). "To be a [human] being is precisely to belong to the race that has the peculiar characteristic that every single individual is known qua single individual by God and is capable of knowing him" (*KJN* 5.109).[23] To fall short of knowing God is thus to cease to be a human being (*CD,* 35). It is to suffer the sickness of the spirit that is despair, properly so called, for in reality we "cannot avoid God" (*KJN* 2.180). "The possibility of this sickness is man's superiority over the animal, and this superiority distinguishes him in quite another way than does his erect walk, for it indicates infinite erectness or sublimity, that he is spirit" (*SUD,* 15).

Such despair is known by all human beings, since all are born with the potential to know God but need at some point to *choose* to do so (and so to set out on the path that leads *from* despair).

> The possibility of this sickness is man's superiority over the animal; to be aware of this sickness is the Christian's superiority over the natural man; to be cured of this sickness is the Christian's blessedness. (*SUD,* 15)

> The glorious thing [is] *that the human being is granted a choice.* What blessed happiness is promised hereby to the one who rightly chooses. . . . God, if language may be used this way, proposes [*frie*] to the human being. . . . A person *must* choose, for in this way God holds himself in honor while he also has fatherly solicitude for humankind. If God has

22. See *KJN* 4.216: "My view is not that God supposedly loves me more than anyone else, no matter who; rather, my view is simply that, quite a bit more than others, I think about the fact that God loves me. So let other people find it great objectively to consider the fact that God loves everyone; I find it blessed subjectively to consider the fact that God loves me and [I find it] blessed that this is something everyone is free to consider."

23. "Ethically understood, it is every individual's task to become a whole human being, just as it is the presupposition of ethics that everyone is born in the state of being able to become that" (*CUP* 1.346). The most miserable wretch no less than the fabulously rich king is able to grasp his utter dependence on God; and that is precisely "the beautiful and profound expression for the relationship with God" (*CUP* 1.383; cf. *UDVS,* 81; *CD,* 170).

lowered himself to being that which *can be chosen,* then a person indeed *must* choose — God is not mocked. (*UDVS*, 205-7; italics in original)

Despair, properly understood as a disease of the spirit, is thus not confined to those dejected because of the circumstances of their lives, nor even to those living in open defiance of God.[24] Indeed, the most common form of despair is found in those who never become conscious of their potential, as "spirit," to live "before God."[25] As long as circumstances are propitious, sickness of the spirit can very well be masked by apparent security and contentment (*SUD*, 26); in such cases, the despondency that follows an untoward change in circumstances is a mere symptom of the despair that was present all along (*SUD*, 51-54). The sorrows and anxieties of such people are worldly: their concern and comfort alike are found solely in "the necessities," in money, in a living, and the like (*KJN* 4.165). Typically, they ascribe infinite worth to the indifferent (*SUD*, 33; cf. *CD*, 124-25).[26] Whatever their distraction — "breathless busyness or worldly desire or abstract thinking or whatever" — they go through life "in a kind of absentmindedness and preoccupation," never discovering their need of God (*BA*, 103; *EUD*, 303).

> Only that person's life was wasted who went on living so deceived by life's joys or its sorrows that he never became decisively and eternally conscious as spirit, as self, or, what amounts to the same thing, never became aware and in the deepest sense never gained the impression that there is a God and that "he," he himself, his self, exists before this God. . . . I think that I could weep an eternity over the existence of such wretchedness! (*SUD*, 26-27)

> Think how impoverished a person would be if he could live through life, proud and self-satisfied, without ever having admired anything. But how horrible if a person could live through his life without ever having wondered over God, without ever, out of wonder over God, having lost himself in worship! (*CD*, 132)

24. Kierkegaard analyzes the various forms that despair takes in *SUD*.

25. "Most people do not experience becoming spirit at all: thus neither do they experience that qualitative encounter with the divine. For them, the divine is a simple, rhetorically nonsensical, vacuous superlative of the human" (*KJN* 6.225).

26. Or: They "relate" themselves "absolutely to the relative"; it is sheer madness when one created for eternity applies "all his power to grasp the perishable, to hold fast to the changeable, and to believe that he has won everything when he has won this nothing" (*CUP* 1.422).

And yet God is "always the nearest one to every human being" (*EUD*, 383; cf. *KJN* 2.164), infinitely closer to each than two lovers are to each other (*WA*, 23). "What is highest is what a [person] has closest at hand, which has walked alongside him all through life, though he has not appreciated it" (*KJN* 4.106). Within every human being there is a "wellspring" in which the deity resides, "that wellspring in the profound silence when all is quiet" (*CUP* 1.183). The problem, at one level, is that human beings have so filled their lives with noise and distractions that the presence of God goes unnoticed.[27]

> On the whole, the longing for solitude is a sign that there still is spirit in a person and is the measure of what spirit there is. [Bubbly subhumans who only know how to live in the company of others] feel such a meager need for solitude that, like lovebirds, they promptly die the moment they have to be alone. Just as a little child has to be lulled to sleep, so these people need the soothing lullaby of social life in order to be able to eat, drink, sleep, fall in love, etc. (*SUD*, 64)

For many, the "moment" when the presence of the Eternal could be sensed in time comes and goes unheeded.

> Only by being silent does one find the moment. . . . Because a person cannot keep silence, it rarely happens that he really comes to understand when the moment is and to use the moment properly. He cannot be silent and wait, which perhaps explains why the moment never comes for him at all. He cannot be silent, which perhaps explains why he was not aware of the moment when it did come for him. Although pregnant with its rich meaning, the moment does not have any message sent in advance to announce its coming; it comes too swiftly for that when it comes, and there is not a moment's time beforehand. Nor does the

---

27. Cf. *UDVS*, 310 (modified): "When the well-to-do person is riding comfortably in his carriage on a dark but starlit night and has the lanterns lit — well, then he feels safe and fears no difficulty; he himself is carrying along the light, and it is not dark right around him. But just because he has the lanterns lit and has a strong light close by, he cannot see the stars at all. His lanterns darken the stars, which the poor peasant, who drives without lanterns, can see gloriously in the dark but starlit night. The deceived live this way in temporality: busily engaged with the necessities of life, they are either too busy to gain the view, or in their prosperity and pleasant days they have, as it were, the lanterns lit, have everything around them and close to them so safe, so bright, so comfortable — but the view is lacking, the view, the view of the stars."

moment, no matter how significant it is in itself, come with noise or with shouting. No, it comes softly, with a lighter step than the lightest footfall of any creature, since it comes with the light step of the sudden; it comes stealthily — therefore one must be absolutely silent if one is to be aware that "now it is here." At the next moment it is gone, and for that reason one must have been absolutely silent if one is to succeed in making use of it. Yet everything depends on the moment. Indeed, the misfortune in the lives of the great majority of human beings is this, that they were never aware of the moment, that in their lives the eternal and the temporal are exclusively separated. And why? Because they could not be silent. (*WA*, 14)

God does not leave himself without a witness.[28] Longings for the eternal arise in every human heart. No responsible merchant would fail to take advantage of the opportune moment to do business; no responsible sailor would fail to make use of a favorable wind. Yet how often we waste God's gifts — the promptings of the Spirit, the pulling of the soul, the stirring of the heart — when God, in effect, offers to us his very self. And "what a terrible responsibility when at some time, if not sooner, then in eternity, a person's recollections rise up accusingly against him, recollections of the many times and the many ways God spoke to him, but futilely, in his inner being."

> A person can ignore [the inner] call [of longing]; he can change it into an impulse of the moment, into a whim that vanishes without a trace the next moment. He can resist it; he can prevent its deeper generation within him; he can let it die unused as a barren mood. But if you accept it with gratitude as a gift of God, it will indeed become a blessing to you. (*CD*, 253-54)

At one level, then, the problem with human beings is that noise and distractions allow them to pass their days unaware of God's nearness. At a deeper level, they are, with "the busyness of life," *diverting* their attention from that which, in their hearts, they fear: really "getting involved with God." "They wish to have that relationship at a distance" (*KJN* 4.109; cf. 4.113).

> It is heard again and again; it is regarded in the world as definitely settled that people would like to know the truth if only they had the capacity and the time for it and if it could be made clear to them. What a superflu-

---

28. See Acts 14:17, one of Kierkegaard's favorite texts.

ous concern, what an ingeniously fabricated evasion! Every human being truly has capacity enough to know the truth — would God in heaven be so inhuman as to have treated someone unfairly! . . . Truly, truly, this is not so. The one who has any knowledge of himself at all knows from his own experience that it is rather that one has in one's innermost being a secret anxiety about and wariness of the truth, a fear of getting to know too much. Or do you actually believe that it is everyone's honest desire to get to know very effectually what self-denial is . . . ! (*CD*, 170)

In a word, what, ultimately, keeps human beings in the less-than-human state of despair and prevents them from knowing God is rebellion, an unwillingness to obey (cf. *KJN* 4.87). In our day, insubordination likes to give itself importance by masquerading as doubt, pretending that the problem is intellectual rather than one of the will.[29] And in our day Christianity is commonly *betrayed*[30] by those who blithely accept insubordination's account of itself, responding to doubt — in the name of Christianity — with reasons for it to reflect on rather than the imperative to believe (cf. *KJN* 4.221).[31] What could be more blasphemous than abstractly to offer considerations that point in favor of God's existence, as one might for that of mermaids; as though the subject were open for debate among those who live every moment in God's presence, who bear his witness in themselves, and whose duty it is to fear him?[32] Would not a king be affronted if any in his realm should set about to "prove" his existence (*CUP* 1.545-46; cf. *TDIO*, 25)?

29. "Sin is not a matter of a person's not having understood what is right but of his being unwilling to understand it, of his not willing what is right. . . . Sin has its roots in willing, not in knowing, and this corruption of willing affects the individual's consciousness" (*SUD*, 95; cf. *EUD*, 23; *BA*, 5; *FSE*, 67-68).

30. "Theology seeks to establish the authority of Christianity by reasons, which is worse than any attack, since it confesses indirectly that there is no authority" (*LY*, 150 [NB 31.100]).

31. An unwarranted air of importance is assumed by those who combat doubt with reasons no less than by those who make themselves important by doubting. "The proper praise, hymn, and canticle of praise is namely this: by joyous and unconditional obedience to praise God when one cannot understand him. To praise him on the day everything goes against you, when everything goes black before your eyes, when others might readily want to demonstrate to you that there is no God — then, instead of becoming self-important by *demonstrating* that there is a God, humbly to demonstrate that you *believe* that there is a God, to demonstrate it by joyous and unconditional obedience — this is the hymn of praise" (*CD*, 86).

32. "God in heaven has to sit and wait for the decision on his fate, whether he exists, and finally he comes into existence with the help of a few demonstrations; human beings have to put up with waiting for the matter to be decided. Suppose that a person died before that time; suppose that when the matter was finally decided he was not in the practice of thinking about God as his Creator" (*EUD*, 242).

Equally misguided are attempts to argue recalcitrant human beings into faith in the God-man, Jesus Christ. What could be more absurd than to try to make "reasonable," or, indeed, "very probable," the inconceivable notion that God has appeared in the form of a particular human being?[33] Any who think otherwise have not begun to grasp the "infinite qualitative difference" between God and humankind[34] — as though it becomes plausible that a particular man is God once this or that condition is met (*PC*, 27-29)![35] Nor have they imagined themselves in the situation of contemporaneity with Christ, seeing *this* man, who looks like any other, yet hearing him speak as though he were God: in *that* situation, one can only believe — against all appearances[36] — or be offended (*PC*, 69-144).[37] Furthermore, if faith in the God-man is required for my eternal happiness, am I really to rest my eternal well-being on the strength of an argument for its plausibility?[38] Whatever the degree of likelihood we ascribe to our conclusions,

33. "To make Christianity probable is the same as to falsify it" (*BA*, 39; cf. *PC*, 26; *PF*, 94-95, note). As we have seen, Luther, too, was wont to emphasize that the Word of God "declare[s] things that are totally impossible to our mind and reason.... There is nothing less in agreement than His Word and our judgment." See Chapter 8 above.

34. "If God does exist, and consequently is separated from what it is to be human by an infinite qualitative difference — if I, then, or anyone starts with the assumption that [what appears to be a human existence] was [in fact] a human being, it can never in all eternity be shown that it was God" (*PC*, 28-29).

35. As the God-man, Christ is — and is meant to be — a paradox; and "it is impossible and impermissible to comprehend a paradox, for then it is not a paradox" (*KJN* 7.105).

36. "Someone who is condemned to death as a criminal, a blasphemer; abandoned by everyone, he is flogged, mocked, spat upon, and finally nailed to the cross — and he says: *Have faith* in me. Indeed, this is truly the place for faith, for all immediacy testifies against it — crying out to heaven, if you will — saying, Do not have faith in him" (*KJN* 7.75).

37. Miracles and the fulfillment of prophecy draw attention to Jesus and make unavoidable the choice between faith and offense; but they admit too much ambiguity and possibility of denial to compel faith. John the Baptist knew all about prophecy and was provided with evidence of the miracles; but offense remained a possibility, even for him (Matt. 11:2-6). "A theological professor who, with the help of everything that has been written earlier about it, has written a new book on the demonstrations of the truth of Christianity, would feel insulted if someone would not admit that it was now demonstrated; Christ himself, however, says no more than that the demonstrations are able to lead someone — not to faith, far from it (then it certainly would be superfluous to add: Blessed is he who is not offended), but to the point where faith can come into existence, are able to help someone to become aware and to that extent help him to come into the dialectical tension from which faith breaks forth: Will you believe or will you be offended?" (*PC*, 96).

38. Here Kierkegaard repeats a point made by Calvin: faith's own certainty that one has "a saving knowledge of God" cannot come from anything so *un*certain as a human argument. See Chapter 9 above.

we ask infinitely too much of our arguments if we think they can bear *that* weight (cf. *CUP* 1.23-34). And is not an argument-based faith bound in any case to remain insecure, knowing that a counterargument may be voiced tomorrow (cf. *CUP* 1.26-27)? Indeed, do not arguments for belief positively *invite* counterarguments,[39] in effect treating doubt as a monster to be fed rather than destroyed (*FSE*, 68), and preserving the illusion that human resistance to God is intellectual in its essence (*KJN* 4.87)? In fact, even were we to suppose that we could satisfactorily answer every objection to faith and resolve every doubt, we would merely have replaced a greater degree of knowledge for a lesser. The qualitative gap between knowledge and action would remain, only to be bridged by a leap of the will (*JFY*, 115-16; cf. *CUP* 1.21-22, 129-30).

> The more one impersonally struggles against all the objections of doubt and then, after having refuted all these objections, pretends that everything is now decided, the more one's attention is diverted from what is really decisive. Yes, people have often been busy in a strange way in the wrong place. They struggle and struggle, ponder and ponder, in order to demonstrate the truth of Christianity, and when it is demonstrated they reassure themselves and think that now everything is as it should be. This is settling down to rest at the beginning. . . . The person who has just a little understanding of the matter easily sees that everything else is only preliminary, an introduction to the main issue: Is this the way it is *for me*? But the matter has been all turned around, and therefore a work has been opened up that Christianity had least dreamed of. Christianity was proclaimed with divine authority; its intention was that not a single moment should be wasted on demonstrating that it is true, but

---

39. The point was already made by Bengel: When we use "our own mere reasonings" to promote faith in divine truth, the "sneering infidel" will no less readily produce opposing arguments. See Chapter 10 above.

It should also be noted that, when speaking of the true basis of faith, Kierkegaard is again at one with key figures in the tradition whom we have already considered: "There is only one proof of the truth of [Christianity]: the inner proof, *argumentum spiritus sancti*. This is already hinted at in 1 John 5:9: 'If we accept [human] witness' (this means all historical proofs and arguments) 'the witness of God is greater,' i.e., the inner proof is greater. And now, in v. 10, 'Whoever believes in the Son of God has this witness within.' . . . Everything prior to [conviction] is preparatory, a preliminary matter, something that will vanish as soon as conviction arrives and changes everything, transforming the relationship. If this weren't the case, there would be nothing comforting about a conviction, and having a conviction would then have to be a matter of constantly rehearsing one's arguments" (*KJN* 6.105). The possibility of faith is necessarily given by God himself (*PF*, 69, 99-105).

that each one individually should turn to himself and say: How do you relate yourself to Christianity? (*CD,* 189)

With demonstrations, one is not actually "dealing with God," but only "discussing something about God"; when God makes his presence known, demonstrations become superfluous (*TDIO,* 24-25). And it is in the fear and wonder evoked by God's presence that faith has its beginnings: in "the moment" when, alone and silent before God, one is "gripped by that which has gripped countless persons before him, but yet not in a less original way because of that" (*WL,* 27; cf. *WA,* 10-11; *PF,* 64-65). It is the needy, not the curious, who are so "gripped"; the needy, not those objectively persuaded of Christianity's plausibility, who venture all upon faith in Christ:

> This is how [Christianity] came into the world: it presupposed hardship, agony, the anguished conscience that suffered under the Law, the hunger that simply cries out for food — and then [Christianity] was the food. And nowadays, nowadays people think that an appetizer is needed in order to get people to go along with [Christianity]. What appetizers? . . . Proofs, reasons, probability, and the like. (*KJN* 7.87)

> If you aren't conscious of being a sinner to such a degree that, in the anxiety of the anguished conscience, you dare nothing other than commit yourself to [Christ] — then you will never be [Christian]. Only the agony of the consciousness of sin can explain the fact that a person will submit to this radical cure. (*KJN* 5.327; cf. 6.95)

Reading God's Word

To the word of God in Scripture,[40] as to other divine overtures, the stock human response is that of masked insubordination.

40. The overwhelming majority of Kierkegaard's scriptural discourses are based on NT texts. But there are important OT exceptions (e.g., *EUD,* 109-24, 233-51; *CD,* 163-75) — to say nothing of *Fear and Trembling* (see also *FSE,* 37-39)! For the OT as preparing for and anticipating the NT, see *EUD,* 207; cf. *KJN* 6.305. Note also the typological reflections at *KJN* 2.36-37; cf. *CD,* 9. That the OT (but not the NT) promises material blessings for the righteous has, Kierkegaard believes, caused a good deal of confusion in the church (we have seen that such OT texts, interpreted "spiritually" [allegorically], were commonly taken in the early church to refer to heavenly blessings). He understands these promises as "divinely sanctioned optimism," and sees them as an essential prerequisite for the radical renunciation

What the Bible says is "not something someone has thought up" (*KJN* 4.93). God "took possession" of ordinary human beings and commissioned them to convey, with divine authority, the message with which he entrusted them (*KJN* 6.308; *WA*, 100). That the apostles were "very simple [people] of the poorest class" accentuates the reality that "their *authority* was from God" (*KJN* 4.183). Nothing about them distinguished them from other human beings; in principle, no one person is better qualified to be an apostle than any other. But when an ordinary human being is "called and appointed by God and sent by him on a mission," he is "for all eternity made paradoxically different from all other human beings" (*WA*, 95). And yet he remains an ordinary human being, no more intelligent, or imaginative, or discerning than he was before his calling. All that separates him from other human beings, though it does so categorically, is the divine mission that makes him an apostle; similarly, the way in which the apostle's message came into the world sets it qualitatively apart from anything conceived by human beings (*WA*, 95-96). The word of God, once spoken, was later written down in Scripture (*PJ*, 527 [NB 24.66]).

By its very nature, the word of God commands our attention and obedience: where "the divine authority is the category . . . the matter is very simple: will you obey or will you not obey? will you in faith submit to his divine authority or will you take offense? or will you perhaps not take sides — be careful, that also is offense" (*BA*, 34). Moreover, the obedience God commands is absolute: it admits of no reservations.[41]

An honest and, indeed, very human response to God's demands would be for our race to collect every existing copy of the New Testament, "take them all out to an open place, or to the top of a mountain, and then, while we all kneel, let someone address God as follows: 'Take this book back again. We men, as we are now, are not fit to deal with this sort of thing. It only makes us unhappy'" — as the Gadarenes asked Christ to leave their shores (*LY*, 131 [NB 31.19]; cf. Luke 8:37; see also *FSE*, 31). Instead, how-

---

of earthly goods called for in the NT (*LY*, 67 [NB 29.90]; *JP* 2.2225 [NB 29.102]); i.e., were earthly goods not seen as good, and indeed as divine blessings, their renunciation would not be radical.

41. "The abominable era of bond service [i.e., the age of slavery] is past, and so there is the aim of going further — by means of the abomination of abolishing the person's bond service in relation to God, to whom every human being, not by birth but by creation from nothing, belongs as a bond servant, and in such a way as no bond servant has ever belonged to an earthly master, who at least admits that thoughts and feelings are free; but he belongs to God in every thought, the most hidden; in every feeling, the most secret; in every movement, the most inward" (*WL*, 115; cf. *KJN* 4.261).

ever, recalcitrant human beings have devised various means to mask their refusal to submit to God's word.[42]

One such means is to praise the writers of Scripture for all manner of irrelevant virtues while ignoring the authority with which, as commissioned by God, they wrote. We speak, for example, of their brilliance, their profundity, the beauty of their style, and so on, treating them as extraordinary people rather than ordinary people with a divine message: provided we say something good about them, piety is served and "everything is all right" (WA, 93-94).[43] In this way, we reduce texts divine in origin and authority to human categories, while concealing what we have done by giving them high marks as human achievements. In the process, Christianity is done away with. Works of genius, after all, have no authority; they command no obedience (WA, 93-108).

Alternatively, without obeying God's word, we devote extraordinary effort to its *interpretation*. Again, the appearance — but only the appearance — of piety is preserved: refusing to look at ourselves in the mirror of God's word, we energetically occupy ourselves with the *mirror*.[44] It raises — praise God! — all manner of questions: Which books were actually written by apostles? Were the writers themselves eyewitnesses of what they wrote? Should we not canvass the entire range of interpretive options before deciding what a text means?

> One could almost be tempted to assume that this is craftiness, that we really do not want to see ourselves in that mirror and therefore we have concocted all this that threatens to make the mirror impossible, all this that we then honor with the laudatory name of scholarly and profound and serious research and pondering. (FSE, 26)

> The person who can sit with ten open commentaries and read the Holy Scriptures — well, perhaps he will write the eleventh, but he is associating with the Holy Scriptures contra naturam. (KJN 7.154)[45]

---

42. In our day, "the divine authority of the Bible and everything pertaining to it has been abolished" (KJN 5.69).

43. One might as well admire Paul's skill as a tent maker (WA, 93-94).

44. For what follows, see FSE, 25-51, based on James 1:22-24.

45. Cf. FSE, 34: "All this interpreting and interpreting and scholarly research and new scholarly research that is produced on the solemn and serious principle that it is in order to understand God's Word properly — look more closely and you will see that it is in order to defend oneself against God's Word."

Not that erudition is to be despised. Certainly, scholars should read the sacred text in its original languages (*FSE,* 26).[46] But when we read God's word in a scholarly way, we are not reading God's word. We are not reading with a mind to obey. We expend great effort on interpreting obscure passages — while craftily ignoring commands that permit no misunderstanding.[47] And should the unwonted question ever arise in our minds whether we live by what we read, the remedy is close at hand. Are there not different readings in the manuscript tradition?

> And perhaps a new manuscript has just been found — good Lord! — and the prospect of new variations, and perhaps there are five interpreters with one opinion and seven with another and two with a strange opinion and three who are wavering or have no opinion, and "I myself am not absolutely sure about the meaning of this passage, or, to speak my mind, I agree with the three wavering interpreters who have no opinion etc." (*FSE,* 32; cf. *KJN* 7.247)

> Suppose that it was said in the New Testament — we can surely suppose it — that it is God's will that every man should have 100,000 dollars: do you think there would be any question of a commentary? . . . But what is found in the New Testament (about the narrow way, dying to the world, and so on) is not at all more difficult to understand than this matter of the 100,000 dollars. The difficulty lies elsewhere, in that it does not please us — and so we must have commentaries and professors and commentaries. . . . We really wish it to be doubtful, and we have a tiny hope that the commentaries may make it so. . . . We have invented learning in order to escape from doing God's will. (*LY,* 334-35 [Papers 490])

Of course, we assert that we would be willing to comply with God's word "as soon as the discrepancies are ironed out and the interpreters agree

---

46. Kierkegaard can, however, mock the pretension that knowledge of the original languages is needed to grasp what is essential about the Bible: "That man [who was lost in wonder over Abraham's readiness, at God's command, to sacrifice his son] was not an exegetical scholar. He did not know Hebrew; if he had known Hebrew, he perhaps would easily have understood the story and Abraham" (*FT,* 9).

47. Cf. *KJN* 5.338: "The matter is quite simple. Put the NT in front of you. Read it. Can you deny, dare you deny, that what you read in it about renouncing everything, giving up the world and being mocked and spat upon like your Lord and Master, can you deny, dare you deny, that it is so easy to understand, indescribably easy, that you do not need a lexicon or handbooks or anybody else's help in order to understand it?"

fairly well" — knowing full well that "that certainly will not be for a long time yet" (*FSE,* 32).

> How is God's Word read in Christendom? . . . The majority never read God's Word, a minority read it more or less learnedly, that is, nevertheless do not read God's Word but observe the mirror. To say it in other words, the majority regard God's Word as an obsolete ancient book one puts aside; a minority look upon God's Word as an extremely remarkable ancient book upon which one expends an amazing diligence, acumen, etc. — observing the mirror. (*FSE,* 33)

Again, an honest procedure would be to admit that we shrink from letting God's word gain power over us; or to simply pray for mercy, acknowledging that what God requires is beyond us. Instead, we mask our insubordination by making God's requirements a matter for interpretation rather than obedience, inserting one layer of interpretation after another between ourselves and God's word (much as a boy puts a cloth napkin inside his pants when about to receive a licking), all in "the name of earnestness and zeal for the truth" (*FSE,* 35).

Doubts about the reliability of the Bible provide yet another convenient camouflage for rebellion against God: as elsewhere, so with the Bible, humans prefer to represent the obstacles to faith and obedience as intellectual rather than moral in nature, demanding that their doubts be resolved before they commit themselves in faith.[48]

The proper starting place for dealing with Scripture is with Scripture's focal point, Jesus Christ (*KJN* 6.165), and with the fundamental question whether one will believe or be offended by the claim that he is God in human flesh. Where this, the crucial point, is at stake, the reliability of details in the New Testament narratives becomes a secondary matter; so, too, does the observation that historical study, which yields at best only prob-

---

48. The kind of divine revelation that humans would find unambiguous — a world so ruled that we could *directly* perceive that God is love; an inspired text whose reports show "the most perfect harmony . . . down to the most trivial detail"; an incarnate God whose deity shines through his humanity — is not what we have been given. Rather, God has revealed himself in paradoxical ways that call for faith, which we passionately cling to in the face of contrary appearances. In the case of the Bible, Kierkegaard suggests that its apparent discrepancies ("which will in any case be resolved into agreements in eternity") are divinely contrived "precisely because God wants Holy Scripture to be the object of faith and an offense to any other way of looking at it." Those who labor to remove the ambiguities (by proving, e.g., that Scripture shows "perfect harmony throughout") are people who "do not want to let [Christianity] be the paradox and be satisfied with that" (*KJN* 7.440-41, 150).

abilities and approximations, can provide no adequate basis for faith. The historical facts are not, in the end, the issue. Were we somehow to come into possession of complete and accurate reports of *everything* Jesus said and did, we would still be left with the dilemma faced by his contemporaries: the one they saw and heard, and the one we read about, was a lowly human being. History, as history, can at best tell us something about Jesus of Nazareth; it knows nothing of the God-man. That God was in Christ was in no way apparent to his contemporaries; and the most accurate report of what they saw and heard would not make it any more apparent to later generations. The condition for faith being given by God, we may believe — or we may be offended (*PF,* 92-93; *PC,* 23-26).

Should we believe "what, [humanly] speaking, is the most absurd of all absurdities, that an individual [human] being is God," it is utterly inconceivable that we would then allow ourselves to be troubled by particular details in the New Testament narratives (*KJN* 5.33).

> Lawyers say that a capital crime absorbs all the lesser crimes — so also with faith: its absurdity completely absorbs minor matters. Discrepancies, which usually are disturbing, do not disturb here and do not matter. (*PF,* 104)

If, acknowledging God in Christ, we then pray to him repeatedly every day, and find our joy in knowing him, it is, again, sheer nonsense to imagine that we will be greatly disturbed by reports that "one evangelist said one thing, a second another."

> When it is inwardly and infinitely more certain to you that [Christ] exists, more certain than any historical record, then the details of his historical existence will work themselves out for you — whether the wedding was in Cana or maybe some other place, whether there were two disciples or just one. (*KJN* 4.329-30)

To repeat, faith in Christ is not — and cannot be — arrived at through argument. The same is true of faith in the Bible as God's word (*KJN* 6.36). In view of the infinite chasm, the *qualitative* difference, that exists between God and humankind, we cannot spell out any conditions that could be met that would make it apparent that a particular human being is God. In the same way, no conditions can be spelled out that, if fulfilled, would prove a human book to be divinely inspired. The inspiration of Scripture, like the incarnation of the God-man, must remain a matter for faith. And here again, it needs to be said that human efforts to prove the Bible divine, however we assess their merits, fall far short of providing an adequate basis for faith where our eternal salvation is at stake. In reality, they serve only to invite counterarguments and further allegations of error in Scripture — and so the game continues. Were we to postpone the commitment of faith until these issues are resolved, we would live and die uncommitted (*CUP* 1.24-34).

And a further, more fundamental, danger lurks in the effort. All the while one is engaged in providing intellectual (objective!) support for the content of faith, the passion and commitment of faith are left to languish. "Freethinkers" attack Christianity, calling it mere mythology and poetry; "then come the defenders," who "protest, swear, and curse the despicableness of such a view; for them Christianity is anything but mythology, poetry." But in their insistence on Christianity's truth, the defenders say nothing of imitating Christ; and apart from such discipleship, Christianity — even as defended — becomes detached from life and thus, effectively, mythology and poetry.

> If a man stands there hacking wildly with an axe and protests by everything holy that he is a cabinet-maker, one counters quite confidently: No, anyone who handles an axe like that is certainly not a cabinet-maker, in spite of all protestations. (*PJ,* 550 [NB 26.74]; cf. *CA,* 142)

Those who truly believe Jesus Christ to be God can hardly allow questions about the minutiae of his life to trouble them. Similarly, those who truly believe the Bible to be God's word are not concerned by problems that others may discern in its pages. For example, the objection is raised that, on the one hand, the Bible tells us that God "created this world with all its delight and joy," while, on the other hand, God is said to require that we die from the world.

> To this, in a sense I have nothing to reply; such things do not concern me. As long as it is established as Christian teaching, such objections hold no interest for me.
>
> But in any case, is it not a contradiction on your part to accept a sacred text as God's word, accept Christianity as divine teaching — and then if you come across something that you cannot square with your thoughts or feelings to say that it is God rather than you who is contradicting himself, when either you must reject this divine teaching altogether or put up with it just as it is? (*PJ,* 526 [NB 24.20])

Confronted with learned claims that "Paul's epistles were not by Paul, or that Paul has simply never existed," the believer can simply turn to God in prayer and say:

> I'm no match for all this learning, but I abide by Paul's teaching — and you, my God, will not let me live in error no matter what the critic may prove about Paul's existence. I take what I read here about Paul and refer it to you, O God, and then you prevent what I read from leading me astray. (*PJ*, 533 [NB 25.11])[49]

Perhaps God has allowed skepticism to gain the upper hand in our day precisely to bring us back to "primitivity": to read Scripture "alone with God without others whom one can ape and refer to" — though that kind of reading, to be sure, is "something people would rather avoid" (*PJ*, 533 [NB 25.11]).[50]

> To be alone with Holy Scripture! I dare not! If I open it — any passage — it traps me at once; it asks me (indeed, it is as if it were God himself who asked me): Have you done what you read there? And, then, then — yes, then I am trapped. Then either straightway into action — or immediately a humbling admission.
>
> Oh, to be alone with Holy Scriptures — and if you are not, then you are not reading Holy Scripture. (*FSE*, 31)

To read aright, each individual must read the Bible as though it were a personal letter from God, to be read "before God, wholly as an individual" (*KJN* 7.450; cf. *WL*, 14); and one must then appropriate what one reads. There is something beautiful, something childlike, in learning the Holy

49. From passages like this, from his theological education in Copenhagen, and from the contents of his personal library, it is clear that Kierkegaard had encountered critical approaches to the Bible (see Müller, "Scholarship"). Nonetheless, in his own work he appears consistently to take what he reads in the Bible at face value as true (see, e.g., *PC*, 75-76), betrays no concern over passages others found problematic, and (as we have seen) refuses to engage those who raise questions about the Bible, insisting that human alienation from God, at its root, is moral rather than intellectual in nature. The temptation to label his approach to Scripture fundamentalist (so Müller) should, however, be resisted, for Kierkegaard betrays not a trace of fundamentalism's angst concerning the Bible's objective truth. The (objective) truth of the text before him is the assumed starting point of the Kierkegaardian discourse; its concerns lie elsewhere.

50. "It is frightful to fall into the hands of the living God — but it is even frightful to be alone with the N.T." (*KJN* 7.247).

Scriptures by heart, "but essentially the adult learns only by appropriating" (*TDIO,* 38). Scripture, for example, assures us that all things work for our good "when we love God" (Rom. 8:28). The text has been made the subject of countless expositions "for upbuilding, for comfort, for reassurance. . . . However different everything appears at the time or times of suffering, ordeal, and spiritual trial, yet finally everything must serve for good those who love God." About this, the expositions leave no room for doubt.

> But what then? Because it is eternally certain that all things serve for good those who love God, does it follow from this that *I* love God? And this indeed is precisely the decisive question. The more one impersonally struggles against all the objections of doubt and then, after having refuted all these objections, pretends that everything is now decided, the more one's attention is diverted from what is really decisive. (*CD,* 189)

Imagine a person gifted with extraordinary mental powers and clarity of expression, the author of a remarkable study proving that God is love and that, therefore, all things work together for good. The study is translated into every language, discussed approvingly in academic circles, and "from this book the pastors derive their demonstrations." Imagine, further, that the author then finds himself plunged into circumstances so difficult that he begins to doubt whether things *can,* after all, turn out for good, and whether God *is,* indeed, love. He seeks help from a pastor he does not know. The pastor finds himself out of his depth in conversation with so brilliant a thinker; unconcerned, he directs the seeking stranger to the definitive work on the subject. The stranger replies, "I wrote the book."

> What the thinker had understood about God was . . . true and profound. But the thinker had not understood himself; until now he had lived under the delusion that when it had been demonstrated that God is love, it followed as a matter of course that you and I believe it. As a thinker, he perhaps has taken a very dim view of faith, until — as a human being he learned to take a somewhat dimmer view of thought, especially of pure thought. . . . His train of thought became different. He did not say: God is love; ergo all things serve for one's good. But he said: *When* I believe that God is love, then all things serve *me* for good. (*CD,* 197-99)

Or again: the apostle Paul, on trial, speaks of his hope in the resurrection "of both the righteous and the unrighteous" (Acts 24:15). He does not use the occasion to prove the immortality of the soul. Had he done *that,* the "scholarly, cultured" Sadducees, though themselves denying immortality, would have been "broad-minded enough" to listen respectfully, perhaps granting the merits of several points in the argument. But God has "totally excused" us from the trouble of proving immortality. We *are* immortal, and we will give an account to God of how we have lived. So Paul's tack is in another direction: Immortality means judgment, "the separation between the righteous and the unrighteous." With that reminder, Paul abandons scholarly etiquette and presses on his listeners (and so, on the reader of Acts) the decisive, personal question: Is it the fate of the righteous or that of the unrighteous that awaits you (*CD*, 202-7)?

Or again: a familiar passage from 1 Timothy runs as follows:

And great beyond all question is the mystery of godliness: God was revealed in the flesh, justified in the Spirit, seen by angels, preached among the pagans, believed in the world, taken up in glory. (1 Tim. 3:16)

One line stands out from the other claims that are made. That "God was revealed in the flesh" tells us about Christ; so, too, that he was "justified in the Spirit," "seen by angels," "preached among the pagans," and "taken up in glory." But that he was "believed in the world" pertains not to the God-man, but to each reader of the text — "alone in the whole world!" And it asks of each the question, "Have *you* believed on him?"

Properly speaking, there is *no one* who puts to us such a question — distressingly enough, since another's questions can always be put off or evaded. Rather, the question arises, unsought, in our own minds as, alone before God, we read the text. Posed in that way, it permits no evasion. The historical question how many have believed is as irrelevant to personal concern as the question how many thousands died the day one lost one's beloved. Any who have truly loved will grieve their own loss: a personal sorrow on which the larger, purely factual question has no bearing. And faith, too, is essentially a personal concern, a question to be personally answered. It is mad, when asked about faith, to "talk about the whole world but not about oneself" (*CD*, 234-39).

And yet . . .

Imagine that a stranger enters a room full of people engaged in animated conversation. From the passion with which they speak and the loudness of their voices, the stranger assumes that the subject of discussion is of considerable importance. He inquires what it is, only to be met by an embarrassed silence. The heated talk, perhaps of an hour, has concerned matters too trite to bear repeating.

Yet an even more embarrassed silence greets any mention of the divine in human conversation. Of one man's conflict with his wife, of one scholar's conflict with another, of riots in the city, of the movement of troops — "this is what is talked about in the world, day in and day out, by thousands and thousands. If you have something to tell about conflict in that sense, you will easily find an audience; and if you wish to hear something, you will easily find talkers." But of the conflict in which we all must engage, of wrestling with God, nothing is spoken — as though this were the triviality not worth mentioning (*CD*, 124-25). Little wonder that the word of God finds no hearing.

*　　*　　*

What follows is an abridged form of the prayer that ends PC, *where it concludes Kierkegaard's seventh discourse on John 12:32. Selections from Kierkegaard's prayers, as well as from his parables, have been collected and published;*[51] *deservedly so, for they invite careful reflection. Frequently, as here, they are based on particular texts of Scripture. Given his understanding of a proper reading of the text — alone before God — such prayers form a natural, and necessary, part of what it means to read God's word aright.*

> And I, when I am lifted up from the earth, will draw all to myself.
> (John 12:32)

But you, Lord Jesus Christ, we pray that you will draw us, and draw us wholly, to yourself. Whether our lives are calm or embattled, whether spent in honor or in humiliation: draw us, and draw us wholly, to yourself. If you but draw us, all is won even if, humanly speaking, we win nothing; yes, all is won even if, humanly speaking, we lose everything.

We pray for all: for the tender baby, whom parents bring to you, that you will draw it to yourself. And when the parents later so influence the child that it is led to you, we pray that you will bless this, their labor; but should their influence on the child be disturbing, we pray that you will so work that the disturbance may not draw the child away from you, but that it, too, may serve to draw the child to you. We pray for those who renew their baptismal covenant with you, the covenant we all have entered and most of us have broken: we pray that you will draw them to yourself. And if that vow is broken, draw them again to yourself through the vow as it is

---

51. See LeFevre, *Prayers.*

renewed, again and yet again. We pray for those who, in an earthly sense, have experienced this earthly life at its most beautiful, for those who have found each other in love: we pray that they may not promise each other too much in love, so that their love becomes a hindrance to your drawing them to yourself; may it rather help them to that end. We pray for those in the evening of life, that now, when working days are over, the thought of you who draws them to yourself may entirely fill their souls. We pray for all: for those who just now greet the light of day, that they may find life's meaning in being drawn to you; and for the dying, that life for them may have meant that they were drawn to you.

We pray for those who are servants of the Word, whose task it is, in the measure granted human beings, to draw human beings to you. We pray that you will bless their work, but also that in this, their work, they themselves may be drawn to you, that in eagerness to draw others to you, they themselves may not be held back from you. And we pray for lay Christians, that they, themselves drawn to you, may not think poorly of themselves, as if it were not granted them, too, to draw others to you — in the measure we are able.

In the measure we are able: for you, who alone can draw to yourself, can use us all and every means — to draw all to yourself.

CHAPTER 13

Barth

Karl Barth (1886-1968) first gained theological notoriety by way of his new interpretation of Pauline theology, which he intended as a "corrective," " 'a pinch of spice' to the main meal" of Christian theology.[1] At the time, he was the minister of a small parish in Switzerland and had little more than a pastor's education; by the end of his life, he was the dominant theological figure in the Christian world, and had moved beyond seasoning the work of others to producing a theological feast in thirteen courses that subsequent generations continue to digest. His mature work is of a scope and originality that a contemporaneous pope identified as the greatest since Thomas Aquinas.[2]

Yet, just as Thomas's work was rejected by his immediate successors and saw its influence wax and wane for generations after his passing, so Barth's theological fortunes have been mixed in the half century since his death. One consistent area of concern has been his understanding and use of Scripture. Barth made it clear that he wished his work to be judged by its fidelity to Scripture, and scholars have suggested that "no theologian since John Calvin has been more committed to biblical exegesis than Karl Barth."[3] But for some of his critics, dating back even to Barth's early work, the result is a naive "reversion to biblicism" that is more extreme than anything found in Calvin and the other Reformers.[4] And for others, though Barth's commitment to Scripture is commendable, a contrast between his work and that of the Reformers is "painfully evident": unlike the "enduring

---

1. Barth, "Need," 104. He borrowed the phrase "a pinch of spice" from Kierkegaard.
2. The judgment comes from Pope Pius XII.
3. Burnett, *Exegesis,* 9.
4. Harnack, in exchange with Peterson, in Peterson, *Tractates,* 16.

biblical contribution" of the Reformers' work, Barth's exegesis consists in a "virtuoso performance" that has "left little lasting impact."[5] For still others, Barth's work contrasts painfully with the Reformers' in that it represents a continuation of the subjectivist interpretation of nineteenth-century liberal theology.[6]

If an initial claim is to be ventured, we could perhaps say that Barth stands among those who are most astonished by the Bible. Barth's early attempts to present what he called the "new world of the Bible" reflect a "joyful sense of discovery" that animated his work.[7] Much of his later work on Scripture was intended to preserve the Bible's capacity to astonish. Recognition of this capacity came as something of a surprise to Barth himself; in its wake, the form and intensity of his engagement with Scripture departed markedly from the theological conventions of his day. An account of what Barth himself called his "turn back to the Bible" will be useful as a point from which to approach his theology of Scripture.

Barth's Discovery of the Bible

Barth was born in 1886 in Basel, Switzerland. A month before his birth, his father took up a position in a college that sought to train "scriptural" preachers who would be able to teach something other than the dominant liberal theology of the day.[8] Three years later, his father moved to a chair at the University of Berne that was funded by a traditionally inclined branch of the Swiss Church. Despite his father's influence, Barth's sense of his own calling to theological study was bound up with convictions that could hardly be deemed conservative. He claims that his interest in theology came to life through confirmation classes that he received as a sixteen-year-old, which served to impress on him the dubious nature of the "later orthodox theory of the literal inspiration of the Bible" ("Theology," 225).

For his university training, Barth's father sent him to Berne, where he could be taught by more conservative figures. Yet he was unhappy there and pressed to be permitted to attend more liberal-leaning institutions. He first went to Berlin, as a sort of middle ground between his preferences and his father's, and was finally permitted to move to the University of Mar-

---

5. Childs, "Exegesis," 19 (quoting Paul McGlasson).
6. Muller, "Place," 142-43; Glomsrud, "Impulse."
7. Barth, "Preface 1," 2.
8. See Busch, *Barth*, 1.

burg, then a center of liberal theology, in 1908. Barth saw Marburg as his "zion."[9] He attached himself to the peculiar synthesis of Kant and Schleiermacher that he found in the work of Wilhelm Herrmann, the leading neo-Protestant theologian at Marburg. Kant and Schleiermacher were the "guiding stars" of Barth's student years ("Theology," 225), and he entered pastoral ministry in 1910 as a "convinced Marburger" ("Hermann," 238).

Barth wrote later in life that he began his work as a minister without a sense of the "worth" of the Bible (*Gespr. 1964-1968,* 432). According to his early understanding, faith and religion are matters of experiential encounter with God (*Konf.,* 13-16). The significance of the prophets of the Old Testament is rooted in the religious personalities that they developed on the basis of this experience. The Old Testament as a whole is significant only because it formed the religious consciousness out of which Jesus' own teaching grew (*Konf.,* 10-16). The New Testament consists of the apostles' accounts of their own experience of living faith; by reading it, believers share in these experiences, and God reveals himself anew. That Scripture is thus a vehicle for an encounter with God constitutes its "self-sufficiency." The Bible is holy not because its "letters" or "ideas" are holy, but because it speaks of the holy. The Protestant doctrine of "verbal inspiration," according to which God is the "author" of the Bible, is an aberration. It is not found in the best elements of the early church or in Luther. It leaves no space between human words and the divine word, and cannot account for the "variations, losses, mistakes" in Scripture (*Konf.,* 60-69).

Careful engagement with Scripture itself played a formative role in leading Barth away from these notions. This engagement came about, in the first instance, as a result of his work in ministry: "It was extremely fruitful for me, as I now entered upon twelve years in the pastorate, to be compelled to engage myself much more earnestly than ever before with the Bible as the root of all Christian thinking and teaching" ("Theology," 226). Barth's task was "above all to preach the Bible" (*Gespr. 1963,* 409); the problem of how to do that came increasingly to occupy his attention ("Sketches," 154-55). He was

> pushed by various and sundry circumstances more and more strongly toward the specific *pastoral* problem of the *sermon.* . . . As a pastor, I am supposed to speak to *individuals,* I am to speak into the egregious contradiction of their lives. But I must speak from the message of the *Bible,* which is no less outrageous, which stands over this contradiction of life

9. Busch, *Barth,* 44.

like a new riddle. Often enough these two greats, life and the Bible, have appeared to me (and still appear!) like Scylla and Charybdis: If *that* is the "Where from?" and "Where to?" of Christian proclamation, who should be a pastor? ("Need," 106)

The peculiar difficulty of the Bible for Barth, as well as his increasing engagement with it, were also a function of the social and political upheaval that marked his decade in ministry. Barth wrote that class struggles in the small industrial town in which he ministered first awoke him to the "real problems of real life"; for a time, he was far more engaged in reading trade manuals, union regulations, and safety laws than the Bible ("Sketches," 154-55). In the face of the difficulties faced by working-class members of his congregation, he found himself, to his own surprise, aligning with the religious socialists. But the beginning of World War I kept him from remaining content in their ranks. Barth expected socialists around Europe to stand together in opposing the war, but he found them to be as supportive of their countries' war efforts as anyone. Barth felt betrayed by the support for war given by both his fellow socialists and his theological teachers in Germany.[10] Disillusioned, he became convinced that a thorough rethinking of his convictions was required. Together with the minister in a neighboring village, he first examined the work of Kant and Schleiermacher, but then turned to consider the apostle Paul ("Sketches," 154-55).

Intensive study of Paul's letters during the tumultuous years of World War I proved decisive for Barth's thinking. It precipitated what he himself called a "turn back to the Bible" that would reshape twentieth-century theology (*FT*, 23). At the heart of the turn is a contrast between the world that Barth saw in Scripture and the world that had been presented to him during his schooling. Barth had been taught to understand the kingdom of God as a perfect moral kingdom in which the ideals of human morality find fulfillment; yet he found particularly in Paul's teaching a depiction of an absolute disjunction between human endeavors and the eschatological kingdom of God. Paul presents God's kingdom as a reality that rests on divine activity alone, and brings judgment on human speaking and doing. In the face of class struggles and war, this picture of disjunction between the divine and the human seemed rather more plausible than a presumption of continuity. Paul became, for Barth, a "special guide" to the gospel un-

---

10. On one popular relating of Barth's life, Barth made a decisive break with the liberal theology in which he was schooled after seeing that his liberal teachers had signed a declaration supporting the Kaiser's war efforts.

derstood in light of this disjunction ("Theology," 226). Kant had been the teacher of Barth's theological youth, but Barth's reading of the Bible caused Kant's God to move to second place (*Gespr. 1963,* 409). Barth claimed that a new "existence" began for him as he came to see that the Bible is a "good and worthwhile book," and that the God spoken of in Paul's letters is more interesting than the God of Kant (*Gespr. 1963,* 409; *Gespr. 1964-1968,* 432).

The task of presenting a new account of the Pauline gospel stood at the center of the new "existence" that began with Barth's turn to the Bible. Barth set about this task in sermons, in lectures, in speeches, and, most importantly, in commentaries on Scripture that formed the centerpiece of his work between 1915 and 1921.[11] A careful study of Romans was central to Barth's attempt to work out the basis of his own thought during World War I ("Need," 107); Barth found in Paul "one who *evidently sees and hears something that is above everything, which is absolutely beyond the range of my observation and the measure of my thought*" ("Questions," 61-63; italics in original). Training himself to grasp what Paul saw involved working slowly through Romans and taking careful notes. A commentary began to emerge. A first edition of the commentary was published in 1918. A revised second edition, completed in 1921, catapulted Barth to the center of theological debate. That commentary, *The Epistle to the Romans,* was widely seen as announcing the end of the theological project that marked nineteenth-century neo-Protestantism; it stands as a seminal work in twentieth-century theology.

Barth's Early Understanding of Scripture

The question for us here concerns the understanding of Scripture that underwrites the work that Barth undertook between 1915 and 1921. For reasons that we will examine in due course, explicit attention to a theology of Scripture was secondary during these years to considering the content of Scripture itself; but this work marks a turning point in theological history and reflects a set of instincts about the nature of Scripture that are foundational for Barth's later thought.

The focal point of Barth's thinking at this point was his account of just what the Bible presents. In 1917, Barth gave a lecture in which he asked: "What is in the Bible? What sort of house is it that the Bible is a door to?

---

11. On the basis of a first edition of a commentary on Romans, Barth was offered a position at the University of Göttingen in 1921.

What sort of land spreads out before our eyes when we open up the Bible?" ("New World," 16). His answer was that the Bible presents the activity of God as a sovereign reality that constitutes a new world. "'What is in the Bible?' ... In the Bible there is *a new world,* the world of God" ("New World," 18). The new world that is grounded in the activity of God stands in absolute opposition to an "old" world made up of morality, religion, culture, and all else that issues from human activity. Far from complementing and completing these human realities, divine activity represents "a blast of trumpets from another world" that "interrupts your reflections about yourself, and your life ... the nurturing of your religious thoughts and feelings" ("Righteousness," 4). It asserts the sovereignty of God over against all human speaking and doing. "A *new* world stands in the Bible. God! God's Lordship! God's honor! God's inconceivable love! Not the history of humanity but the history of God" ("New World," 26). "It is certain that the Bible, if we read it with careful attention, leads us exactly to the point at which we must decide to accept or disavow the royal sovereignty of God. This is precisely the *new* world of the Bible" ("New World," 23). The Bible is the place that human beings go to learn again to speak of the sovereignty of God, to recognize that "God is God" ("New World," 27; cf. "Society," 66; "Righteousness," 11).

The suggestion that the decisive content of the Bible is a new world that stands opposed to the "old world of war and money and death" presents a kind of scaffolding on which Barth's understanding of Scripture is constructed ("Righteousness," 13). The first point that issues from it is an account of the divine activity that is required if creatures are to grasp the true content of the Bible. Barth declares that, because human activity belongs to the "old, sick world" of human striving, the new world of divine activity may be apprehended only through the work of the divine Spirit ("New World," 29). "The Bible is 'understood' neither through this nor that 'mental or intellectual faculty,' but by the power of *the* Spirit, who is the *same* as its content, and that in *faith*" ("Answers," 167). The "hidden things" of the new world are "inaccessible to sensible perception"; they are "displayed" by the "Spirit of God" ("Preface 3," 20). They belong to a sphere of spirit that is inaccessible to the eyes of flesh, and must be understood "spirit through spirit" ("Questions," 86, alluding to 1 Cor. 2:13).

A particular understanding of biblical inspiration follows from this emphasis on the Spirit's work. In the preface to the first edition of his commentary on Romans, Barth writes that he would side with the "venerable doctrine of inspiration" if forced to choose between it and historical-critical study. This contrast might appear to reflect a kind of category mistake, for teaching about inspiration generally treats the way the text came into being, while the historical-critical method finds tools to under-stand the text today; but Barth supposes that these realities may, in fact, be placed side by side. On his terms, the doctrine of inspiration is concerned with the "labour of apprehending" rather than the formation of the text ("Preface 1," 1). It is a functional doctrine that establishes principles for understanding Scripture. At the heart of these principles is the stipulation that grasping the content of Scripture requires a "spiritual apprehension" grounded in the work of the divine Spirit. The doctrine of inspiration cod-ifies the notion that "penetrating the heart of a document" is a matter of presuming "that its spirit will speak to our spirit through the actual written words" ("Preface 3," 18). It secures a "correlation of 'Scripture' and 'Spirit'" that ensures that the latter is not displaced as the principle of the compre-hension of the former ("Letter," 177).

What does exegesis that is carried out in light of this principle look like? Barth's answer to this question revolves around a contrast between Calvin's work as a biblical commentator and the work of modern biblical scholars who follow in Schleiermacher's wake. In Chapter 11 we saw that Schleiermacher supposes that interpreting a text is a matter of reconstruct-ing the thought that underlies the written words via exhaustive grammati-cal and psychological study. Such study aims to overcome the historical gap between the writer and the reader. As Barth presents it, this understanding dominates modern exegesis, with the result that contemporary exegetes fixate on the historical, grammatical, and psychological aspects of the text:

> Recent commentaries contain no more than a reconstruction of the text, a rendering of the Greek words and phrases by their precise equivalents, a number of additional notes in which archaeological and philological material is gathered together, and a more or less plausible arrangement of the subject-matter in such a manner that it may be made historically and psychologically intelligible. ("Preface 2," 6)

Lost in this attention to the grammatical, psychological, and historical is the actual subject of the biblical text itself. "Real struggling with the raw material of the Epistle," "reconsideration of what is set out in the Epistle, until the actual meaning is disclosed," is given short shrift ("Preface 2," 6-7). Fixation on grammatical or historical elements means that the text as a whole "still remains largely unintelligible" ("Preface 2," 7).

By contrast, Barth proposes Calvin as a model of the "tenacious" exe-gete who grapples with the true subject matter of the gospel. Calvin begins with an attempt to establish "what stands in the text" in grammatical and historical terms, but he recognizes that this is nothing more than "prepara-tory" work and moves "energetically" beyond it in an attempt to "re-think the whole material and to wrestle with it." He engages in a "conversation" with Paul that "moves round the subject-matter" until the barriers of the grammatical, historical, and psychological disappear, "the walls which sep-arate the sixteenth century from the first become transparent," and the "actual meaning" of the text is disclosed. The subject matter of the text, rather than the thought of the one who wrote it, is the object of Calvin's interest. Concentration on the subject matter means that "the man of the sixteenth century" is able to hear when Paul speaks ("Preface 2," 7).

In attempting to engage Paul in conversation about his subject mat-ter, Calvin models biblical interpretation that derives its principles from the doctrine of inspiration. Modern critics dismiss Calvin's exegesis as a reflection of the "compulsion of inspiration," but Barth suggests that those who dismiss the hermeneutical force of the doctrine of inspiration in this way "betray" the fact that they have "never worked upon the interpretation of Scripture." They condemn themselves to a preoccupation with textual elements that does not permit a grasp of the text's subject matter as the reality that gives sense to the whole. Lacking a perception of the whole, they are quick "to dismiss this or that difficult passage as simply a peculiar doctrine or opinion of Paul," attributable to the idiosyncrasies of Paul's personality and historical location. By contrast, Calvin shows "tenacious determination to understand and to interpret" the subject matter in light of which Paul's letter as a whole has its sense ("Preface 2," 7-8).

Barth himself uses the exegetical principles that he associates with Calvin.[12] He writes that, in accordance with the hermeneutical direction contained in the doctrine of inspiration, "my whole energy of interpreting has been expended in an endeavour to see . . . into the spirit of the Bible, which is the Eternal Spirit" ("Preface 1," 1). This endeavor requires the kind of attempt to "rethink the whole material" through "conversation" between the first century and the present that Calvin exemplifies. It mandates that commentary on Scripture be understood not as matter of commentary *"on"* a text, as if the author and the text were ends in themselves, but rather commentary *"with"* Paul, "standing by Paul's side" in an effort to appre-hend the object of which Paul speaks ("Preface 3," 17-19).

---

12. Barth discusses Calvin in the preface to his commentary on Romans largely in order to elucidate his own approach. In lectures on Calvin delivered during 1922, Barth told his students that Calvin's exegesis "provided an external model for my own special study of Romans" (*TJC*, 393).

Proper concentration of exegesis presses behind the many questions to the one cardinal question by which all are embraced. . . . When an investigation is rightly conducted, boulders composed of fortuitous or incidental or merely historical conceptions ought to disappear almost entirely. The Word ought to be exposed in the words. Intelligent comment means that I am driven on till I stand with nothing before me but the enigma of the matter; till the document seems hardly to exist as a document; till I have almost forgotten that I am not its author; till I know the author so well that I allow him to speak in my name and am even able to speak in his name myself. ("Preface 2," 8)

"Paul knows of God what most of us do not know; and his Epistles enable us to know what he knew" ("Preface 2," 11). Through "creative straining of the sinews," "the matter contained in the text" can be "released" ("Preface 2," 8).

The challenge to the standards of modern biblical exegesis that accompanied Barth's commendations of Calvin occasioned no small amount of criticism. Barth was accused of imposing his own theological framework on Paul's text. His response points back to the contrast between old and new worlds as the structuring principle of his thinking about Scripture. He writes that his exegesis presumes no framework other than what Kierkegaard calls the "infinite qualitative distinction" between the divine and the creaturely ("Preface 2," 10). Echoing the comments in his early lecture on "The New World in the Bible," he asserts again that an absolute distinction of this kind is the decisive "theme" of the Bible, and suggests that this distinction is the only assumption that he brings to the text ("Preface 2," 10-11). It is his understanding of the Bible's essential content, and not general principles regarding textual interpretation or reflection on the task of reconstructing another's thinking, that supplies his interpretive framework. Barth concedes that this understanding may come into question in the course of actual exegesis; but he insists that, as a question of interpretive principle, his critics do more violence to the text by approaching it with hermeneutical precepts derived from various branches of modern study than he does in attempting to interpret it in light of its own subject matter ("Preface 2," 10-11).

Barth's conception of a contrast between old and new worlds permits him to respond to two other criticisms of his work. In the first place, it positions him to resist the charge that he is an "enemy of historical criticism" who wishes to return to a naive precritical biblicism ("Preface 2," 6). Barth claims that — "fortunately" — he need not choose between a doctrine of inspiration and the principles of historical-critical study ("Preface 1," 1). The latter concern the text as a quantity shaped by the old world of human activity. The critical scholar uses the results of historical, archaeological, and grammatical analysis to present a picture of the text as it reflects the elements of human language and activity. This endeavor is "both necessary and justified" as "preliminary work" that facilitates the reconstruction and comprehension of the text; but it is of strictly penultimate significance because it has no purchase on the new world of God ("Preface 2," 6-7). The tools used by the critical scholar can yield the conclusion that a human agent acted in a particular way, but they rest on assumptions about the causal continuity of all events in time in a way that precludes access to the activity of God. The standards used by historical scholarship permit it to speak to the old world of human being and doing but not the new world of God.

By contrast, the doctrine of inspiration calls the reader to understand the text in terms of the new world of the activity of God. Whereas historical-critical work seeks to understand Scripture "*apart from* the 'Spirit'" that is Scripture's proper object, the doctrine of inspiration secures the "correlation of 'Scripture' and 'Spirit'" and ensures that understanding Scripture is a matter of discerning "in spiritual fashion what is spiritually intended" ("Letter," 177; "Preface 3," 19). Crucially, restoring this "correlation" does not involve "repristination" of precritical modes of exegesis, but rather a call to scholars to take their critical work to its proper end ("Letter," 176-77). True criticism means "the measuring of words and phrases by the standard of that about which the documents are speaking"; thus, "the critical historian needs to be more critical" by moving beyond criticism of the text in light of historical inquiry to criticism in light of the text's subject matter ("Preface 2," 8). Barth thus supposes that, rather than opposing critical inquiry, his work shows a "meaningful way of incorporating it into theology" by permitting it to do its work, and then inviting it to complete itself in engaging in criticism in light of the subject matter of the text itself ("Letter," 176-77).

A similar radicalization of the position of his critics appears in Barth's response to a second concern that was raised regarding his exegesis. We saw in Chapter 11 that Schleiermacher supposes that exegesis involves a critical procedure through which the reader identifies the authentic core of a text and then applies this core as a standard according to which authentic and inauthentic elements may be distinguished within the text as a whole. Readers of Barth's commentaries faulted him for failing to make use of a similar procedure so that aspects of Paul's letters — for example,

his apparent reliance on Old Testament teaching about Adam and his attitude toward secular authority — could be shown to be incidental to his
true theme. But Barth claims that a grasp of the contrast between old and
new worlds makes this critical procedure inappropriate. On one level, all
the words of the Bible are human words that belong to the old world of
human speaking and doing. On another, all the words may point to the
new world of the activity of God and help readers to recognize its reality.
Barth's critic supposed that, through careful study, the words of the true
"Spirit of Christ" must be separated out from the words of "other spirits"
within Paul's letters. Barth responds:

> I must go farther than [my critic] does and say that there are in the
> Epistle no words at all which are not words of those 'other spirits.' . . .
> Is it really legitimate to extract a certain number of passages and claim
> that there the veritable spirit of Christ has spoken? . . . It seems to me
> impossible to set the Spirit of Christ — the veritable subject-matter of
> the Epistle — over against other spirits, in such a manner as to deal
> out praise to some passages and to depreciate others where Paul is not
> controlled by his true subject-matter. Rather, it is for us to perceive and
> to make clear that the whole is placed under the KRISIS of the Spirit
> of Christ. The whole is *litera,* that is, voices of those other spirits. The
> problem is whether the whole must not be understood in relation to the
> true subject-matter, which is — The Spirit of Christ. ("Preface 3," 16-17)

In effect, Barth's contrast between old and new worlds means that
there are two ways in which the Bible can be read. On one level, the realities associated with the old world of human activity — history, morality,
and religion — are to be found in the Bible.[13] On this level, it can be said
that "the Bible contains the literary monuments of an Ancient Near Eastern religion and of a religious cult of the Hellenistic epoch. As a human
document like any other, it can lay no *a priori* dogmatic claim for special
attention or consideration" ("Questions," 79). Historical-critical work
and moral, psychological, and religious inquiry have their justification
in the fact that the Bible may be read for its creaturely history, morality,
and religion. But, on another level, the fact that the true subject matter
of Scripture is the new world of the activity of God means that those who

---

13. Barth constructs his lecture on the new world in the Bible in part around the affirmations that history, morality, and religion are all to be found in the Bible, and then in calling
the importance of these affirmations into question. See "New World," 20, 21, 24.

approach the Bible on these terms miss its decisive element. Barth writes that ultimately the Bible confounds the historian, the moralist, and the religious thinker because it interrupts history, morality, and religion in the seminal events in which God acts. History "temporarily stops" because these events cannot be explained in terms of causes within the creaturely world; moral reflection is confounded because the Bible speaks of divine rather than human activity; and religion meets its end because the Bible presents God's thoughts about human beings rather than human thoughts about God ("New World," 22-25).

The final point to be made about Barth's early exegesis is that, while he is willing to grant legitimacy to historical, moral, and religious inquiry into Scripture, he is also insistent that the divine Spirit may unmask this inquiry as a strategy used by human readers to evade encounter with the new world of God. One of the consistent themes of Barth's work is that, through the divine Spirit, Scripture itself has an agency through which it turns human questions back onto the questioners and prods them beyond evasion to an acknowledgment of the reality of God. Barth writes that we might in fact do better not to ask, "What is in the Bible?" because that question "has a mortifying way of turning into the opposing question: 'Well, what do you want?'" ("New World," 18; cf. "Questions," 74). "We will find in it only as much as we are looking for: Great things and divine things if we look for great and divine things, or inane and 'historical' things if we look for inane and 'historical' things" ("New World," 18). The Bible "gives to each one what fits him"; but there is an agency at work in Scripture that does not leave readers free to rest with the penultimate versions of the content of Scripture that they construct:

> The Bible says quickly, very clearly, and in a very friendly manner about the certain "versions" we make of it: "So this is *you,* but not *me*! Now this is what perhaps in fact fits you very well, your emotional needs, and your views. . . . See, you wanted to mirror yourself in me, and sure enough, you have rediscovered your image in me! But now go and search for *me*! Look for what is there!" ("New World," 19)

The Development of a Theology of Scripture

The instincts regarding the theology of Scripture that are present in Barth's early work figure centrally in his mature work; but it is significant that these early notions resist summation into doctrinal formulation. Two reasons may be given for this. The first is that, in Barth's view, formulating a theology of Scripture risks appearing to be an evasion of an encounter with the object that Scripture wishes to present. Inquiry into the nature of Scripture as such may betray that one's commitment to the text is in fact limited, for a truly "loyal" reader does not make the text an object of interest for itself but seeks rather to understand all of its elements in terms of its "veritable subject-matter" ("Preface 3," 17). The second is that Barth's own understanding of Christology, the work of the Holy Spirit, and the way that creaturely realities such as the sacraments, Scripture, and preaching mediate the presence of God is underdeveloped. A strong opposition between divine and creaturely reality is central to his thinking. He has not yet worked through the ways that differing elements within the creaturely sphere mediate the presence of the divine.

Barth became painfully aware of the limitations of his theological background when, in 1921, he was invited (on the basis of his work on the book of Romans) to take up an honorary professorship at the University of Göttingen. He found himself required to teach subjects with which he had little familiarity, and he worked with extraordinary energy to fill gaps in his own understanding. During his first several years in Göttingen, the courses he taught were confined to scriptural exegesis and historical theology. Through his work in historical theology in particular, Barth began to develop the conceptual tools that shaped his mature theology of Scripture.

Two elements in this process are important for us.[14] The first is the theology of Scripture that Barth found in the Reformed tradition, and in Calvin's work in particular. As Barth lectured on Calvin's theology and the theology of the Reformed confessional statements, Calvin became for Barth a special guide to the theology of Scripture in the same way that Paul had been a guide to Scripture's meaning. This occurred in part because, as we have seen, Barth had already found in Calvin's exegesis an approach to Scripture that was companionable with his own concerns; but more systematic study of Calvin and the Reformed tradition also served to push Barth beyond his existing notions to a sharper understanding of the theology of Scripture.

This dynamic emerges first in the way engagement with Calvin filled out Barth's understanding of inspiration. In his early work, Barth tended to functionalize the notion of inspiration, treating it as a clue to the way Scripture is to be understood by the contemporary reader. This tendency

---

14. See Webster, *Earlier Theology*, 41-65; "John."

continues to be reflected at points in his lectures on Calvin,[15] but Calvin also presents Barth with an understanding of inspiration as a "twofold" divine act that is typical of Barth's own later work (*TJC*, 167). According to this understanding, there is a speaking of the Spirit among the writers of Scripture and a corresponding speaking of the Spirit among contemporary readers of Scripture. On the basis of the Spirit's movement "there and then," it may be said that "the Holy Spirit is in the letter" of the text; but the corresponding work of the Spirit "here and now" means that Scripture becomes "certain and authoritative," not merely by "an enforcing of the dictate of the letter" but also by the "voice of truth that makes itself heard . . . in the believing reader." This paired set of acts of divine speech means that inspiration appears in a "living sense" as "a conversation of the truth with itself" (*TJC*, 167). Elements in the later Reformed tradition go astray, according to Barth, by so emphasizing the speaking of the Spirit among the prophets and apostles that the biblical text is treated as identical with the speaking of God; but Calvin remains reliable in insisting that the Spirit must speak again through the text if the Word of God is to be found in Scripture.

On a related front, study of Calvin's work moved Barth toward a principled affirmation of the authority of Scripture as a decisive element within the church's life. In his earlier work, Barth had insisted on the authority of the subject matter of the text in order to resist those who emphasized the authority of a method of study ("Letter," 176); but he tended not to move from asserting the normative force of the subject to acknowledging the authority of the text itself. This changed as Barth began to absorb an insight that he took to be characteristic of Reformed theology generally. As he presented it, the Reformed tradition is distinguished by the development of a consistent "Scripture principle" that affirms "the Word of God in the Bible as the norm of faith and life" within the church (*TJC*, 386; *TRC*, 38-40). This affirmation rests on a threefold movement of thought. It declares that, by nature, only God is able to know God, progresses to the claim that God is therefore known by others only as he gives himself to be known, and concludes that Scripture is authoritative because it is in Scripture that God gives himself to be known (*TJC*, 386-88; *TRC*, 38-64). On these terms, an acknowledgment of the authority of Scripture rests on a prior confession of the sovereign uniqueness of God. "The Bible's *isolated* normativity" is understood as an "image" of the "isolated authority of God" (*TRC*, 49).

---

15. Barth asks about what, for Calvin, the doctrine of inspiration "amount[s] to in practice but the hypothesis that in some sense the text is trustworthy, the premise that there has to be a meaning in it, a meaning, indeed, in its wording" (*TJC*, 391).

This sequence of thought allowed Barth to move away from the worry that identification of an authoritative element in the creaturely sphere — the sphere in which Scripture is found — detracts from the sovereignty of God. By grounding the authority of Scripture in the sovereign uniqueness of God, the Reformed tradition equipped Barth to acknowledge the former without threatening the latter.

The final front on which the study of Calvin and the Reformers advanced Barth's theology of Scripture concerns the conceptual tools that allowed Barth to work through the relationship between the divine and the creaturely in Scripture. Barth's early work is marked by an opposition between the divine and the creaturely in which the former is present in the latter only in episodic moments of revelation; but Barth finds in Calvin a notion that helps him think through the perdurance of Scripture's authority without collapsing the distinction between the divine and the creaturely. This notion emerges from Reformation debates about the sacraments, in which the mode of divine presence in creaturely reality was precisely the issue. As Barth presents it, Calvin is able to see further than his contemporaries on this question because his work is shaped by a proper understanding of the difference between the Creator and the creature. "No Reformer was more strongly shaped than he was by the antithesis of time and eternity" (*TJC*, 125). Calvin rejects Lutheran notions of the real presence of the divine in the sacraments as a denial of this antithesis; he suggests, instead, that God is present in the sacraments in his *promise* to be present. God promises his presence; it is this promise that is present to the church. The promise is not a mere set of words but a positive form of the very presence that is promised. God is present in his promise in a form that is proper to life in time. Promise is, for Calvin, the "supreme and proper form in which God now draws near to us" (*TJC*, 175). "What we may be and have as Christians [is] promise and no more" (*TJC*, 125).

This understanding of promise as the proper mode of divine presence in time means that the uniqueness of Scripture is to be understood in terms of its connection with divine promise. The words of Scripture issue from the speaking of the divine Spirit "there and then." Though the words themselves are creaturely realities that are not to be identified with divine speech, they come with the promise that the Spirit's speaking "there and then" will be accompanied by a speaking "here and now."[16] This promise

---

16. Barth holds that Word and sacrament go together as the essential elements of the church's life because sacrament is the sign of the promise that accompanies the preaching of the Word.

is itself the proper mode of God's relationship to the words of Scripture. Equipped with this notion, Barth believes that he can affirm the authority of Scripture without weakening the distinction between the divine and the creaturely. Understanding promise as a positive mode of divine presence provides a conceptual anchor for the Reformed Scripture principle and grounds the hope that the "twofold" reality of the act of inspiration will be fulfilled. In its connection with Barth's understanding of the inspiration and authority of Scripture, it is a hinge point in the maturation of Barth's doctrine of Scripture that follows from Barth's encounter with the Reformed tradition in the early 1920s.

Barth's burgeoning theology of Scripture is further fleshed out in lectures on the Gospel of John that he delivered during the mid-1920s. These lectures position Barth to give a well-grounded account of a notion that is central to his theology of Scripture. We have begun to see that Barth's understanding of Scripture revolves around the notion that Scripture points beyond itself to the sovereign reality of God. The words of the Bible are not to be identified with divine speech; instead, the relationship between the two is to be understood in terms of promise. From the early 1920s onward, Barth adopted the language of "witness" to characterize this relationship (see, e.g., *GD*, 201-11). Though not the speech of God itself, Scripture is a witness to the reality and activity of God that is accompanied by the presence of God in promise. The notion of witness plays a central role in Barth's theology of Scripture from the early 1920s; but it is sharpened by Barth's study of the opening chapter of John's Gospel in particular. Two elements in this chapter are important. The first has to do with the presentation of John the Baptist. The second has to do with the theology of creation more generally.

In the first place, the description of John the Baptist that appears in John 1 captures Barth's attention as a "paradigm" of the work of witness that Scripture performs (*EJ*, 19). Barth supposes that the evangelist discusses John the Baptist, who came "to bear witness to the light" (John 1:6-8), in order to clarify the work of witness that he himself performs in writing a Gospel. "[The evangelist] instructs his readers regarding his own relation to his object insofar as he instructs them in the same relation with regards to John the Baptist. He wants to create clarity about what he, the evangelist, does and does not do as such, can and cannot do, is and is not" (*EJ*, 19). John 1 is thus, for Barth, the definitive statement of the terms on which Scripture itself wishes to be understood. "More clearly than anywhere else in the Bible . . . it is said to us here just what the Bible is: witness to revelation that is related to but also distinct from revelation itself" (*EJ*, 21). The two-sided "related to" but "distinct from" that appears here is foundational to Barth's understanding of Scripture. In Scripture's own account of its relationship to its object, there is on the one hand "the great 'Yes'" with which Scripture affirms its *relationship* to the speaking of God; but there is alongside it a "but" with which Scripture insists that it must be *distinguished* from the event of God's own speech (*EJ*, 21).

> Witness is truly and in the best sense speaking *about* a subject, describing it exactly and fully, pointing to it, confirming and repeating it, and all in such a way that the subject remains itself and can speak for itself. . . . Only where we have both supreme concern to speak with maximal proximity to the object and supreme concern to permit the object its distance so that it may speak for itself do we have witness. (*EJ*, 64)

Barth fleshes out this account of the work of witness by clarifying the dangers of confusing the witness with the reality to which it points. He suggests that the writer of the Fourth Gospel has a special reason for using John the Baptist to clarify the relationship of the witness to its object, for a "Baptist sect" had arisen in the first century that effaced the distinction and honored John the Baptist as the revealer (*EJ*, 19-21). In face of this situation, Barth suggests that the evangelist seeks, first, to ward off this misunderstanding by insisting that the Baptist "was not the light, but came to bear witness to the light"; second, to use Jesus' discussion of John's work as a "witness to the truth" to show the "danger" of the misunderstanding (*EJ*, 19-20, 65-66; cf. John 5:30-47). This latter discussion shows "what should not happen in the situation between the revealer, the witness, and the hearer" (*EJ*, 20). Jesus' hearers rejoiced "for a little while" in the light of John the Baptist, but they do not acknowledge Christ. That they rejoiced in John and ignore Christ shows that they have confused the witness with the reality. The hopelessness of their situation shows the danger of mistaking the witness to the light for the light itself. Driving the same point home in an exposition of 1 Corinthians, Barth writes that followers of Peter and Paul find themselves at odds in the church in Corinth because they have confused the witness of Peter and Paul with the word that may be spoken by God alone (*Resurrection*, 13-16). For Barth, religious turmoil and fractiousness in the church is what believers should expect when the witness to revelation is confused with revelation itself.

Engagement with John 1 permits Barth to go on to ground his account of the work of witness in the theology of creation. He interprets the emphasis in John 1 on the coming into being of all things through the Word as an attempt to provide the ontological framework within which the notion of witness may be understood. That "all that is" came into being through the Word indicates, first, that it is creaturely and not divine. It belongs within the "circle of becoming" and is thus wholly different from God (*EJ*, 41). A creaturely reality cannot be treated as a direct expression of the Word of God itself. The origin of creaturely reality through the Word means, second, that all creaturely being and activity is dependent on the Word. "Its existence cannot be understood in any other way than through the Word. Its own function is absolutely bestowed by the Word, by the Word that is God" (*EJ*, 41-42). Barth argues that John introduces this notion in order to establish a "criterion" in relation to which the Baptist's work of witness may be understood. The witness may not be taken to be identical with the Word; it also cannot be thought to possess a freestanding significance that is separable from the activity of the Word itself. Only by continual reference to the reality of the Word itself may the witness be understood. The witness thus functions within the parameters that are proper to it in its creatureliness only when it does not claim significance for itself but seeks instead to point beyond itself to the one through whom it came into being. Equipped with an understanding of the difference between the creature and the Creator and the dependence of the former on the latter, the evangelist, Barth thinks, is positioned to show that, in serving as a witness to the light, John fulfills the function that is proper to him as a creature.

Barth's Mature Theology of Scripture

Up to this point, we have encountered the fundamental building blocks of Barth's mature theology of Scripture. One further aspect of Barth's lectures on John is useful for us in making a turn to this theology. Barth reflects on what the notion that God is known through God alone means for the reading of Scripture.[17] It is this notion that he identified earlier as the basis of the Reformed Scripture principle. He suggests now that it has significant hermeneutical implications. It implies that Scripture is always encountered in "a concrete determined situation" that is shaped by divine rather than human activity, and that the factors that constitute this situation — the nature of the gospel message as good news that human beings cannot create for themselves, the presentation of this good news in the words of

---

17. This comes to the fore through Barth's invocation of 1 Cor. 2:14 ("the natural man cannot understand the things of the Spirit of God"), a verse that Barth sees as an expression of the principle that God alone knows God, and God alone gives himself to be known.

other human beings who are able to speak the truth only as illumined by God, the demand for faith that the Bible places on its readers — represent "the fundamental elements of a biblical hermeneutics" (*EJ*, 4-12). The affirmation that God is known through God alone means that the elements of biblical hermeneutics are not found in grammatical and psychological principles that facilitate apprehension of the human thinking that underlies the text, but rather in the divine activity that creates the "situation" in which the faithful reader encounters Scripture. The Reformed Scripture principle means that understanding Scripture requires consideration of the economy of divine activity (*EJ*, 4).

Barth's mature theology of Scripture is constructed in and around an account of the economy within which Scripture serves as witness. Scripture first appears in the *Church Dogmatics* as the basis for the possibility of theology at all. Barth opens his magnum opus with an inquiry into the "way of knowing" that is to be taken in theology. He writes that the theme of his treatment of the question will be the topic that "the older Protestant theology . . . treated under the title *De scriptura sacra [On Holy Scripture]*," and is "materially the same as the assertion of the authority and normativeness of Holy Scripture" (*CD* I.1, 43). Scripture is thus presented as the basis of the theological enterprise. All that is to be said about the possibility of theology is to be said in reference to the reality of Scripture; but Barth goes on to say that "what falls to be said about Holy Scripture . . . needs a comprehensive elucidation of context." It must be situated within an understanding of the theology of revelation generally, which in turn requires treatment of "the whole doctrine of the Trinity and the essentials of Christology" (*CD* I.1, 43-44). Understanding Scripture requires a comprehensive account of God's revealing activity that is rooted in an understanding of the triune being of God. The 1,400 pages of volume I of the *Church Dogmatics* are thus in one sense nothing more than a development of the claim that human speech about God finds its basis in the authority of Scripture; but the development of this claim involves a comprehensive account of the being and activity of the triune Revealer as the "context" in which the authority of Scripture may be understood.

Within Barth's account of this broader "context," Scripture appears as one "form" of revelation. Three forms are proper to revelation: the event of revelation itself, in which God fulfills the promise "Lo! I am with you always" (Matt. 28:20); the proclamation of the church, which involves presenting the promise of revelation in recollection of past revelation and expectation of future revelation; and Scripture, which consists in witness to past revelation and the promise of future revelation (*CD* I.1, 88-124).

Among these three forms, it is of revelation alone that Barth is willing to say that it is the Word of God, full stop. By contrast, proclamation and Scripture are to be understood as witnesses to the Word of God.[18] As witnesses, they are marked by the "distinction in unity" that we encountered as a central feature of Barth's earlier descriptions of Scripture:

> A real witness is not identical with that to which it witnesses, but it sets it before us. . . . We have to keep two things constantly before us and give them their due weight: . . . its distinctiveness from revelation, insofar as it is only a human word about it, and its unity with it, insofar as revelation is the basis, object and content of this word. (*CD* I.2, 463)

Barth's continued emphasis on the distinction in unity of the witness to revelation and revelation itself brings with it a reaffirmation of a series of claims that we have encountered in his earlier work. The speaking of the divine Spirit remains decisive for the witness of Scripture, for the Spirit "is indeed the power of the matter of Holy Scripture. By him it became Holy Scripture; by him and only by him it speaks as such."[19] Inspiration continues to be understood as a "twofold reality" that involves both the "engendering" of the text of Scripture through revelation in the past and the contemporary activity of God's Spirit through which "God Himself now says what the text says."[20] Scripture must ever *become* the Word of

18. As such, Barth is willing to say that church proclamation and Scripture belong to the same "genus." In the same way that Schleiermacher holds that Scripture belongs to the same genus as dogmatics because both are records of a presentation of Christian faith at a given time, so Barth holds that both Scripture and proclamation are "the commencement" and "the continuation" of "one and the same event, Jeremiah and Paul at the beginning and the modern preacher of the Gospel at the end of one and the same series" (*CD* I.1, 102). This series is made up of human witnesses to divine revelation. But Barth goes on to insist that while there is similarity in "genus," there is "dissimilarity in order" between Scripture and proclamation, for Scripture has "supremacy" and "absolutely constitutive significance" for preaching (*CD* I.1, 102).

19. Barth goes on to say that the Protestant principle of Scripture is that Scripture and Spirit are so related that "those who hear it, hear Him. Those who wish to hear Him must hear it" (*CD* I.2, 538).

20. Barth writes: "If God speaks to man, He really speaks the language of this concrete human word of man. That is the right and necessary truth in the concept of verbal inspiration" (*CD* I.2, 532). "To believe in the inspiration of the Bible" thus means finally "to believe in the God whose witness it is" (*CD* I.2, 534). To "regard the presence of God's Word in the Bible as an attribute inhering once for all in this book as such" would be to divinize the text in a way that violates the distinction between Creator and creature and the principle that God is known only through God (*CD* I.2, 530, 499).

God as God gives himself to be known in it.[21] The printed words on the page are not identical with the speech of God.[22] As witness, they "live" from the presence of divine promise (*CD* I.2, 541). In their humanity, it is entirely possible that they err.[23] In light of their humanity, the historical and critical study of the Bible is "obviously justified and can never be taken too seriously" (*CD* I.2, 464). Yet critical study remains of penultimate significance, for it criticizes the text in light of historical, psychological, and scientific study, but it does not attend to the object to which Scripture points. The faithful reader of Scripture may go beyond the critical scholar in taking up a criticism of the text in light of its proper subject matter while also enacting a new "naivety" in reading Scripture as witness to the Word of God.[24]

This set of claims presents us with the basic content of Barth's understanding of Scripture as witness to revelation; it involves rearticulations of elements in Barth's theology of Scripture that we encountered earlier.

---

21. "The Bible is God's Word to the extent that God causes it to be His Word, to the extent that He speaks through it. . . . The statement that the Bible is God's Word is a confession of faith, a statement of the faith which hears God Himself speak through the biblical word of man. . . . The Bible, then, becomes God's Word in this event, and in the statement that the Bible is God's Word the little word 'is' refers to its being in this becoming" (*CD* I.1, 109-10).

22. "It is quite impossible that there should be a direct identity between the human word of Holy Scripture and the Word of God, and therefore between the creaturely reality in itself and as such and the reality of God the Creator. It is impossible that there should have been a transmutation of the one into the other or an admixture of the one with the other. This is not the case even in the person of Christ where the identity between God and man, in all the originality and indissolubility in which it confronts us, is an assumed identity, one specially willed, created and effected by God, and to that extent indirect. . . . When we necessarily allow for inherent differences, it is exactly the same with the unity of the divine and human word in Holy Scripture" (*CD* I.2, 499). Barth writes later that a "divinisation" of creaturely realities is "unthinkable even in the case of the human word of the Bible, or the human nature of Jesus Christ Himself" (*CD* I.2, 683).

23. "As truly as Jesus died on the cross, as Lazarus died in John 11, as the lame were lame, as the blind were blind, as the hungry at the feeding of the five thousand were hungry, as the sea on which Jesus walked was a lake many fathoms deep: so, too, the prophets and apostles as such, even in their office, even in their function as witnesses, even in the act of writing down their witness, were real, historical men as we are, and therefore sinful in their action, and capable and actually guilty of error in their spoken and written word" (*CD* I.2, 528-29). But Barth will say that "even if the biblical witness is made in the realm of human systematics and therefore in the realm of human self-contradiction," the witness of the biblical writers "is valid . . . as witness to Him who does not contradict himself and who cannot allow them — else they would not be his witnesses — to contradict themselves in what they must say about him" (*CD* II.1, 106).

24. See Hunsinger, "Interpretation," 29-48.

The instincts that Barth developed as a minister in Switzerland and honed as a professor in Germany are everywhere echoed in his later work; yet Barth's more mature theology of Scripture does contain important elements that fill out his earlier insights. A number of these follow from his placement of the theology of Scripture within the context of an account of revelation. One consequence of this placement is that the notion of obedience comes to the fore as a key to the theology of Scripture. Barth claims that, in revelation generally, God appears irreducibly as Lord, and the human creature appears in a position of obedience through the work of the Holy Spirit. He goes on to suggest that the obedience that corresponds to revelation may be taken as a clue to the theology of Scripture. "A quite definite perception" of the nature of Scripture is presupposed in the fact that believers are obedient to the revelation that it presents; a theology of Scripture may derive its content from consideration of "the perception with regard to the character and basic significance of the witness which is contained in a genuine and necessary obedience to the biblical witness" (*CD* I.2, 459). "The doctrine of Holy Scripture as such involves therefore the confession in which the Church clarifies that perception which corresponds to a right and necessary attitude of obedience to the witness of revelation" (*CD* I.2, 460).

The consequences of Barth's emphasis on obedience as a clue to the theology of Scripture are most visible in his discussion of Scripture's authority and freedom. This discussion occupies the bulk of the theology of Scripture developed in *Church Dogmatics* I. Barth treats Scripture's authority and freedom as expositions of the two "definitions" of "true obedience to Scripture" (*CD* I.2, 462). If there is obedience in the church, it must come about as a result of the authority of Scripture, on the one hand, and the freedom of Scripture, understood as an element in the movement through which the Holy Spirit opens human beings for free response to God, on the other (*CD* I.2, 538-39, 661-62).

Barth turns first to authority as the "external determination" that makes possible obedience to God (*CD* I.2, 539). He suggests that the Bible has authority over other authorities within the church as the "source and norm" of the church's activity (*CD* I.2, 648-49). Development of this claim positions Barth to engage in critical dialogue with Schleiermacher. To begin with, Barth suggests that, as witness, Scripture is authoritative because it "stands in a closer relationship to the basis and nature of the Church" than any alternative authority (*CD* I.2, 540). "Fundamentally and in general, authority in the Church is an authority which has precedence because of its more primitive nature" (*CD* I.2, 540). This claim echoes

Schleiermacher's conception of the way Scripture's normativity is rooted in its writers' proximity to Christ; but Barth goes on to suggest that this point secures no more than a general, preliminary understanding of authority (*CD* I.2, 540-41). The question of a definite and final understanding of the authority of Scripture brings Barth to an "either-or" that marks out a significant departure from Schleiermacher. For Schleiermacher, the authority of Scripture can be affirmed in a deeper sense only as its relationship to Christian truth is "evaluated" by the church, using a standard external to Scripture itself. For Barth, this approach presumes that the church is itself a "direct, absolute, material authority" that is able to "give" authority to Scripture because it is itself in possession of the truth of revelation (*CD* I.2, 541-42).

In opposition to this approach, Barth argues that genuine comprehension of the authority of Scripture is derived from consideration of the *obedience* that is proper to the church. Obedience presumes "two partners" in an "antithesis in which there is an obvious and genuine above and below" (*CD* I.2, 542). An ordered relationship of this kind is exemplified in the apostles' obedience to Christ in serving as his witnesses. The apostles show no sign of having "control of their own over that which was revealed to them," and give no indication that a relationship of obedience would be "dissolved" so that later believers could claim lordship over revelation (*CD* I.2, 542-43). In their obedience to Christ, they establish the church as a sphere that is characterized by obedience to the Word of God. It is this obedience that makes the church what it is; thus, if the church exists at all, an ordered relationship of revelation and obedience must "continue to exist" (*CD* I.2, 543-44). Barth suggests that this relationship is found "indirectly" in a contemporary "copy" of the apostles' relationship to Christ. This copy consists in the obedience of the church to Scripture. Scripture is "the Word of God for the Church. . . . It is Jesus Christ for us, as He Himself was for the prophets and apostles" (*CD* I.2, 544). In submitting to its authority, the church repeats the obedience of the apostles and exists as the church.

According to this account, genuine understanding of the authority of Scripture is grounded not in Scripture's antiquity but in the recognition that this authority is the presupposition of the church's existence as the church. In order to be what it is, the church must acknowledge the authority of Scripture as the presupposition of the obedience in which it fulfills its own nature. It cannot presume that it possesses a measure by which the dignity of Scripture might be considered, for then the "copy" of the relationship to Christ in which the church is itself would be lost. If it is to exist as itself, "the Church cannot evade Scripture. It cannot try to appeal past it. . . . It cannot assess and adjudge Scripture from a view of revelation gained apart from Scripture. . . . Scripture confronts it commandingly as Holy Scripture. . . . [The church] obeys Holy Scripture" (*CD* I.2, 544).

One corollary of this account of the authority of Scripture is that faith in Christ is the presupposition of the recognition of Scripture's authority. Barth suggests that Schleiermacher is right to say that faith is the basis of Scripture's authority (*CD* I.2, 541), but Barth rejects the conclusion that Schleiermacher draws from this claim. Whereas Schleiermacher argued that the dependence of the authority of Scripture on the assent of faith means that the church has primacy over Scripture as the larger reality of which Scripture is a part, Barth claims that Scripture has priority over the church because it makes the church what it is. "Holy Scripture is the ground and limit of the Church, but for that very reason it constitutes it" (*CD* I.2, 539). This claim issues in a second inversion through which Barth rejects Schleiermacher's approach to questions of canonicity. Schleiermacher claims that exegesis must engage in continual critical consideration of the bounds of the canon; Barth suggests that to proceed in this way is again to act "as if we had in our hands a measure by which we could measure the Bible" (*CD* I.1, 107). He continues to reject any suggestion of this kind. "The fact that there exists a Canon of Holy Scripture . . . is posited in and with revelation itself. What this Canon is, of course, is also decided with revelation by God Himself. . . . It is marked off by God" (*CD* I.2, 597).

On one side, then, Barth affirms the authority of Scripture as a presupposition of the obedience that is proper to the church. He suggests that this authority is reflected in the way in which Scripture constitutes the church and remains Lord over it. This authority must be recognized because of its place as the "external," "objective" determination of human obedience to revelation; but it is improperly understood, on Barth's telling, unless it is paired with an inquiry into the freedom of Scripture as the correlate of Scripture's authority. On the other side, then, treatment of the freedom of Scripture is necessary because the authority of God "has nothing in common with tyranny . . . which annihilates all human response." It is rather an authority that shows that it truly "reaches" human beings by allowing itself to be recognized only in the "sphere of freedom" (*CD* I.2, 661-62). Freedom is the "internal determination" of obedience to revelation; but this freedom is to be understood in the first instance as the freedom of Scripture itself, for any freedom that is found in the church has its basis in the freedom that the divine Word exercises through Scripture (*CD* I.2, 669-71).

Barth's account of this freedom mirrors the structure of his account of Scripture's authority. It begins with the assertion that the freedom of

Scripture is rooted in the twofold freedom through which it is brought into being. The Word of God exercises freedom in calling forth witnesses to its activity; these witnesses exercise freedom in turn in assenting to this call. In this twofold exercise of freedom, a pattern is established that must be repeated if the church is to live as the church. "There cannot be a Church of Jesus Christ apart from a repetition of this freedom" (*CD* I.2, 670). The possibility of this repetition is grounded in the freedom that Scripture possesses as a living voice that speaks to the church in the power of the Holy Spirit. Through the work of the Spirit, Scripture is "even to-day . . . not mere writing but in its written character is Spirit and life" (*CD* I.2, 671). "Scripture itself is a really truly living, acting and speaking subject, which only as such can be truly heard and received by the Church" (*CD* I.2, 672). It possesses a freedom that is the proper form in which divine freedom operates in the church today. It demonstrates this freedom, first, in the "power" that it wields "in its opposition and relation to all other subjects," quietly and steadfastly realizing its superiority "in face of the totality of world principles" (*CD* I.2, 674, 677); second, in the way that it "chooses, defines, claims and conquers the Church as the special sphere of its effective power" (*CD* I.2, 686).

It is in the context of further discussion of the freedom of Scripture that Barth gives an account of scriptural exegesis. The decision to approach exegesis within this context is crucial. It means that exegesis is understood as an activity that is undertaken in the freedom that is given to the church through the freedom of the Scripture itself (*CD* I.2, 710-15). Rather than appearing as a scholarly discipline or personal practice that is rooted in a self-initiated and self-directed human freedom, exegesis appears as an act of the freedom through which believers respond in obedience to revelation. It is a freedom that has determinate shape and purpose. Readers are not free to choose the principles and norms by which their exegesis will be directed; they are rather called to exegesis that takes its shape from the obedience that is the proper response to revelation.

Based on this notion, Barth claims that responsible exegesis consists in "the freely performed act of subordinating all human concepts, ideas and convictions to the witness of revelation supplied to us in Scripture" (*CD* I.2, 715). This subordination occurs by way of a threefold movement. First, readers engage in a work of "observation," through which they strive to "follow the sense of the words of Scripture" in an attempt to "reproduce and copy the theme whose image is reflected in the picture of the prophetic-apostolic words and controls those words" (*CD* I.2, 722-24). The full set of tools available to the exegete — historical-critical, grammatical, and psychological — are to be used at this first stage. There is to be no shortchanging of the use of these tools; but, crucially, they facilitate no more than a first moment of well-rounded exegesis. Readers are to move from the work of observation to one of "reflection on what Scripture declares," a transitional step that will enable them to move from "sense" to use, explanation, and application (*CD* I.2, 727). At this "middle point," readers are concerned in particular to question the way in which their activity and forms of thought shape their understanding of the text, and to bring their thinking into conformity with the subject matter of the text (*CD* I.2, 727-36). This moment of accommodation to the text is then preparation for a third moment of "appropriation" through which the content of the text is permitted to "become the master of our thinking" by bringing the believer's "whole existence" into conformity with itself (*CD* I.2, 737). Appropriation means that the subject matter of Scripture stamps itself upon the believer's life because it is thought with a "necessity" in which "we cannot not think it, because it has become a fundamental orientation of our whole existence" (*CD* I.2, 736). It becomes the basis of all further thought, speech, and activity by becoming a "necessary and inward determination" of the believer's very "existence" (*CD* I.1, 188).

That scriptural exegesis has its end in a movement through which the subject matter of Scripture masters "our thinking and life generally, and our whole existence" (*CD* I.2, 737) is a reflection of the fact that Barth thinks through exegesis in terms of obedience to revelation. The final point to be made about Barth's account of obedience and of the freedom and authority of Scripture is that the appearance of this cluster of concepts in Barth's work is in no way incidental. The accounts of revelation and Scripture that occupied him in *Church Dogmatics* I were written between 1931 and 1938 at the same time that he was involved in the struggle of the Confessing Church in Germany against the co-option of the national church by the Nazi party. Barth was the lead author of the Barmen Declaration, a statement of faith issued in 1934 as the official creed of the Confessing Church. This declaration opens with an article affirming the sole authority of Scripture as the norm of the church and rejecting any attempt to redirect the church on the basis of other authorities. "The inviolable foundation of the German Evangelical Church is the gospel of Jesus Christ as it is attested for us in Holy Scripture and brought to light again in the Confessions of the Reformation. The full powers that the Church needs for its mission are hereby determined and limited." For Barth, the decision to open the creed with an affirmation of the authority of Scripture and the rejection of the need for any other "power" for the church was a matter of "neither accident nor caprice." It was the product of a conscious attempt to follow the great Reformation confessions that began in this way and that establish a standard for all later forms of Protestantism. The "attitude of obedience" that follows from this affirmation of the Scripture principle "is essential to Protestantism as such" (*CD* I.2, 460). Barth's own attempt to think through a theology of Scripture by considering the obedience that is demanded of the church is thus meant to secure the principles of Protestantism and to ward off forms of Christianity that are determined by other sources and norms.

Barth's Later Theology of Scripture

The theology of Scripture that Barth develops in *Church Dogmatics* I represents his most systematic treatment of the topic; but some readers hold that, in fact, later volumes of the *Church Dogmatics* present this theology in its most fruitful forms as Barth engages in concerted use of Scripture, and considers Scripture as a theme only in an ad hoc way, as engagement with the text itself demands.[25] The full sweep of the *Church Dogmatics* offers a treasure trove of concepts regarding the theology of Scripture; unfortunately, we must content ourselves with summary indications of a series of notions developed in the work as a whole.

Perhaps the most significant aspect of the *Church Dogmatics* in its entirety is its grounding in and saturation by Scripture. The work contains more than 2,000 exegetical discussions in an extraordinary range of forms: consideration of key biblical terms (*CD* IV.3, 8-9); typological discussions of the way Old Testament figures point to the christological shape of God's act of election (*CD* II.2, 343-409); discussions of the way in which apparent differences between the sources used in Genesis are in fact pointers to matters of theological significance (*CD* III.1, 229). In one sense, the *Church Dogmatics* appears as "nothing other than a sustained meditation on the texts of Holy Scripture."[26] At a number of points, its content is decisively shaped by submission to Scripture's authority. In his treatment of the theology of election, Barth writes that he would have liked to follow Calvin's doctrine quite closely, but that "as I let the Bible itself reach to me on these matters, as I meditated upon what I seemed to hear, I was driven irresistibly to reconstruction" (*CD* II.2, x). In his theology of

---

25. See, e.g., Frei, *Eclipse,* vii-viii.
26. Watson, "Bible," 57.

creation, he suggests that it is not self-evident that a theology of the Word of God, which has the relationship between God and human creatures as its essential concern, should include a discussion of angels, but that "the teacher and master to which we must keep in this matter can only be the Holy Scriptures of the Old and New Testament," and Scripture itself points to treatment of angelology as an element in a proper understanding of the relationship between God and creatures (*CD* III.3, 369-72).

The prevalence of Scripture in the *Church Dogmatics* reflects Barth's sense that the theologian has the task of inciting in readers "an interest and love" for Scripture as the "inexhaustible real ground and epistemological basis of the science of systematic theology" ("Theology," 226-27). Barth expressed growing concern about the neglect of Scripture in the life of the church and the individual believer. "Today theologians are always travelling. Instead of their staying at home, I fear that a great majority of them are out there sitting in cars, in waiting rooms, in trains or in airports. When do they ever find time to read the Bible?" (*Gespr. 1964-1968*, 390). "We need to take time again for Scripture. . . . Gather around the table to study Scripture together!" (*Gespr. 1964-1968*, 171). "Every believer needs to get used to reading continuous passages. . . . For me as a theology professor, it is a daily duty. . . . One needs to accustom oneself to reading the Bible" (*Gespr. 1964-1968*, 243).

Barth's later work emphasizes that the significance of Scripture is rooted in the irreducible significance of Christ himself. Barth is perhaps best known for a theological Christocentrism that mandates that all aspects of Christian teaching are to be rooted in Christology. In the sphere of the theology of Scripture, Barth's Christocentrism issued in an increased emphasis on Christ as the decisive center in relation to which all other aspects of Scripture are to be understood. Barth writes that, if we ask "concerning the one point upon which, according to Scripture, our attention and thoughts should and must be concentrated, then from first to last the Bible directs us to the name of Jesus Christ" (*CD* II.2, 53). "When Holy Scripture speaks of God it concentrates our attention and thoughts upon one single point and what is to be known at that point" (*CD* II.1, 52). Even in approaching scriptural teaching about creation, then, one must interpret the material christologically. The "impregnable basis" of a doctrine of creation "is indeed the *fact* that it is in the Bible"; yet a further step needs to be taken to the recognition that the Bible "gives us a reliable basis for our knowledge and confession" because "it gives us witness to Jesus Christ" (*CD* III.1, 23). "Its word in all words is this Word. . . . If, therefore, we are rightly to understand and estimate what it says about creation, we must first see that — like everything else it says — this refers and testifies first and last to Him. At this point, too, He is the primary and ultimate object of its witness" (*CD* III.1, 23).

Barth supposes that it is a Christocentrism of this kind that secures the uniqueness of Scripture in face of the demand that it be read "like any other book." He develops this notion by suggesting that, alongside "the right and necessary and central biblicism," there is a "scattered and peripheral" biblicism that "does not know that the Bible is a totality and that it is meant to be read in all its parts in the light of its unity, that is, of the one of whom it everywhere speaks" (*CD* III.1, 24). This latter biblicism takes the "verbal doctrine of inspiration" to mean that all elements of Scripture possess a freestanding significance that may be grasped apart from reference to Christ. "The question of Jesus Christ ceases to be the controlling and comprehensive question and simply becomes one amongst others" (*CD* IV.1, 368). Where this occurs, "secretly the book of revelation is being treated and read like other books," for it is "divorced from the living Word" and made "readily apprehensible as though it were an object of secular experience" (*CD* IV.1, 368). Scripture has its uniqueness in its witness to Christ; where it is read apart from this decisive center, it is reduced to a "repository of all sorts and degrees of pious knowledge" that might just as well be found elsewhere (*CD* III.1, 24; IV.1, 368).

Barth anchors his account of the christological shape of "the right and necessary and central biblicism" in a new christological emphasis in his theology of inspiration. From the early days of his lectures on Calvin, Barth understood inspiration as a "twofold" reality that consists in correspondence between an act of divine speaking among the prophets and apostles, and a further act of divine speaking among contemporary readers of the prophetic and apostolic witness. Through the opening volumes of the *Church Dogmatics,* Barth understands this divine speaking in terms of the work of the Holy Spirit; but the later volumes of the *Church Dogmatics* guard against a doctrine of inspiration that permits aspects of Scripture to float free of Christology by folding an account of inspiration into an understanding of the communicative quality of Christ's work. In the last part-volume of the *Church Dogmatics* that Barth completed, he develops the claim that Christ's work is marked by a prophetic character through which it is inherently communicative.[27] "As he lives, Jesus Christ

27. This affirmation belongs to Barth's use of the classical notion that Christ's work can be understood in terms of a "threefold office." As the anointed one of God, Christ performs the functions associated with the three offices in the Old Testament that required anointing:

speaks for Himself. . . . He is His own authentic witness. . . . Of Himself He grounds and summons and creates knowledge of Himself" (*CD* IV.3, 46). Christ's life is "eloquent and radiant" (*CD* IV.3, 79); the "twofold" reality of inspiration is a function of this radiance. On one side, "the word of the prophets and apostles" has its truth from the fact that they themselves "participated in the history of Jesus Christ" and had their word "formed and guided" by the one Word of God (*CD* IV.3, 113-14). On the other side, the contemporary reader of Scripture is enlightened by Christ's prophetic work, for the Christ whose life is light is the risen Christ who is not bound by history (*CD* IV.3, 46). This christological account of inspiration ensures that no part of Scripture might be taken to possess a significance that can be abstracted from Christ.

In contrast to the sequence of thought that we followed in Schleiermacher's work, a christocentric account of inspiration does not lead Barth to crowd the Old Testament out of the Christian canon. Barth makes clear that, while Christ "fulfils" and "transcends" the history of Israel (*CD* IV.3, 49-52), this history is not in any way "outmoded, replaced or dissolved" (*CD* IV.3, 70). Instead, it can be seen as "a type and prefiguration" of the revelation of Christ; but, crucially, it may be seen in this way only when it is grasped as an interconnected whole (*CD* IV.3, 53). Barth furthers his polemic against a "peripheral biblicism" by suggesting that dissimilarity outweighs similarity when we compare particular Old Testament figures or events to Christ; but we may see considerable structural similarity between the history of Israel and Christ's own history when we grasp the Old Testament "in its totality and interconnection as planned, initiated, controlled and determined by Yahweh" (*CD* IV.3, 52-69). In its totality, the history of Israel mirrors and anticipates Christ's history in that it "has its basis in an address, promise, command, order, and summons of Yahweh"; it has a universal significance for the lives of all nations; it is "overarched and stabilised and ordered by the grace of the covenant" in such a way that it is a history of reconciliation; and it presents a mediating reality between God and creation (*CD* IV.3, 53-63). In mirroring the structure of Christ's history in this way, the history of Israel is "co-ordinated" with Christ's history as a "definite pre-history" marked by expectation of the promised Messiah (*CD* I.2, 70).

One final aspect of Barth's theology of Scripture is connected to the emphasis on history that marks his handling of Israel and Christology. The

---

prophet, priest, and king. Volume IV of the *Church Dogmatics* has the division of Christ's work into prophetic, priestly, and kingly aspects as one of its structuring principles.

notion of history brings with it a host of questions that were formative of Barth's intellectual context. In what sense do the biblical texts present historical events? Is revelation identical with particular events in history? If so, is historical study best suited to discovering the truth about God? Influential voices in the generation that preceded Barth insisted that historical study is the proper means for understanding Christianity; this insistence was then taken by some to mean that Christianity cannot claim absolute significance, for realities that are known through historical study are made relative by the fact that they are understood with respect to and in analogy with other events. We have encountered elements of Barth's early response to these assertions in his claim that, while there is history in the Bible, history "stops" at the point where the new world of God breaks into the old world of flesh, for events rooted in divine activity are not conditioned by other causal forces and cannot be understood through analogy with other events. Further elements are found in Barth's later work as he engages with aspects of Scripture that raise the question of history in an acute form.

Four kinds of biblical texts are central in raising for Barth the question of revelation and history: discussions of creation, angels, miracles, and the resurrection. Barth is consistent in suggesting that these discussions present a form of " 'non-historical' history." They present history in one sense because they do not refer to abstract, timeless realities to which narrative form is an incidental pointer. They refer to events in space and time that have no meaning apart from their spatial-temporal occurrence; but they are to be understood as " 'non-historical' history" because divine activity is their essential "content," and they are thus inaccessible to historical study (*CD* III.1, 78-81; III.2, 446-47). They are not the work of one agent alongside others in continuous causal connection. They are not analogous to other events in time, and they cannot be understood through consideration of the set of possibilities that are known to human agents (*CD* III.3, 374-76). Because they have their basis in divine activity, they are "beyond the reach" of straightforward historical depiction and historical research (*CD* III.2, 452).[28] Barth writes that "the whole history of the Bible . . . intends to be and is real spatio-temporal history," but it has a "constant bias"

---

28. It is important to note that Barth's work is shaped quite heavily by a particular account of the principles used in proper historical research. In the generation prior to Barth, it was proposed that historical study is possible only where events exist in an interconnected network of causal forces and can be comprehended through analogy with known events in time (see Troeltsch, "Method"). In his own day, Barth responded critically to those who continued to suppose that only events that could be understood on these terms count as history (see *CD* III.2, 446-47).

toward a "non-historical" form of history because of its proximity to the activity of God (*CD* III.3, 375-76). "Every history is in fact 'non-historical'" where it stands "in immediacy to God" (*CD* III.1, 80).

Barth proposes that the term "saga" best corresponds to this kind of "'non-historical' history." Saga presents "imaginative," "poetic" descriptions of events that evade "historical depiction" (*CD* III.1, 81; III.2, 452; IV.1, 508). "Saga in general is the form which, using intuition and imagination, has to take up historical narration at the point where events are no longer susceptible as such of historical proof" (*CD* IV.1, 508). It is "an intuitive and poetic picture of a non-historical reality of history" (*CD* III.1, 81). How could anything other than a poetic picture be used, Barth asks, when Scripture deals with "the history of the work and revelation of God, which . . . is not confined to the sphere of ordinary earthly analogies?" (*CD* III.3, 376). It is entirely in order that, in seeking to deal with the singular activity of God, the biblical writers should reach for language, concepts, and images that are imaginative and poetic; but this does not mean that "we are in the sphere of Red Riding Hood and her grandmother and the wolf, or the stork that leaves babies, or the March Hare and Father Christmas" (*CD* III.3, 376). In the first place, the events themselves are not less real because they evade the categories of ordinary historical description. "Why should not imagination grasp real history, or the poetry which is its medium be a representation of real history, of the kind of history which escapes ordinary analogies?" (*CD* III.3, 374).[29] Second, the narratives themselves are not arbitrary and haphazard simply because they are imaginative. There is "meaningful as well as meaningless imagination . . . disciplined as well as undisciplined poetry . . . good saga and bad. . . . Both imagination and poetry can be ordered by orientation to the subject and its inner order" (*CD* III.3, 376). The reality to which the biblical writers attempt to give witness has a rationality of its own. Where this rationality forms the witness of the biblical writers, it gives coherence, meaning, and truth to their "divination . . . imagination and poetry" (*CD* III.3, 376).

How is the reader to approach events that are presented in the form of saga? Barth insists that these events "are not to be taken as 'history' in our sense of the word," which is to say that they are not to be thought capable of historical study or proof (*CD* III.2, 452). Attempts to harmonize differing

29. It is a "false conclusion" to assume that, because an event must be presented in the form of saga, the event itself "could not have occurred." "It is sheer superstition to suppose that only things which are open to 'historical' verification can have happened in time" (III.2, 446-47).

accounts of the resurrection, or to read 1 Corinthians 15:3-8 as an attempt to "prove" the resurrection, are "amusingly incongruous" (*CD* III.2, 452). Attempts to relate the Genesis narrative "either favorably or unfavorably to scientific paleontology, or to what we now know with some historical certainty concerning the oldest and most primitive forms of human life," miss "the unprecedented and incomparable thing" that Genesis seeks to relate (*CD* IV.1, 508). These attempts "do violence to the whole character of the event in question" by suggesting that it can be approached as a historical puzzle analogous to the questions raised regarding Hannibal's journey across the Alps (*CD* III.2, 452).

Barth suggests that, because the Bible speaks of events that stand outside of all continuity and analogy with other historical realities, "if we really want to know and understand the accounts . . . we too shall have to make that divinatory crossing of the frontier of historicism and enter the sphere of imagination and poetry" (*CD* III.3, 374-75). For readers, grasping the significance of the activity of God requires an imagination ordered by the inner logic and rationality of the activity of God. This, for Barth, involves taking the narratives literally, "not in a shallow but in a deep sense" (*CD* III.1, 84). The hasty reader supposes that taking the material literally means treating it as straightforward historical narrative, but Barth supposes that this view reduces the God presented in Scripture to an agent whose acts can be recounted and understood through the same categories used with respect to all other acts.

From the early days of his wrestling with Romans, Barth's reading of Scripture was shaped by the notion that God, in his sovereignty, stands in an infinite difference from all that is creaturely. The claim that grasping God's sovereign activity requires an imagination that is attuned to the rationality of this activity represents a working out of the consequences of this notion. It echoes Barth's earlier claim that understanding Scripture requires discerning "in spiritual fashion what is spiritually intended" ("Preface 3," 19). In both his early and late work, a mode of spiritual comprehension is required to grasp the work of an agent who stands in infinite difference from all that is creaturely. It requires the activity of the Holy Spirit, which speaks "now" in correspondence to its speaking "then" in a completion of the living circle of biblical inspiration.

CHAPTER 14

Bonhoeffer

In the 1950s, my father, a Baptist pastor in southern New Hampshire, was asked to conduct a Bible study in a town some twenty miles from his home. A friend from his church agreed to accompany him. On the day planned for the study, however, a winter storm arrived, leaving roads icy and my father wondering whether travel was wise. He phoned his friend, who harbored no doubts, cheerfully quoting what he had just read in the Psalms: "I have trusted also in the Lord; therefore I shall not *slide*" (Ps. 26:1, KJV). That, my father replied, was good enough for him. They drove to the Bible study and returned home safely that evening.

Whether with a condescending smile or a contemptuous snort, readers educated in the academic study of the Bible are likely to dismiss such a reading of the text as remote from what the "original author" intended or the "original audience" understood him to be saying. Yet Dietrich Bonhoeffer, one of the twentieth century's most brilliant theologians — and thoroughly trained in the historical-critical approach to the Bible — would no doubt have sided with my father and his friend. That, after all, was the way *he* read Scripture at a critical point in his own life.

In June 1939, Bonhoeffer left Germany for America, knowing that war was imminent and that his opposition to the Nazis exposed him to danger at home. Five weeks later, in a move that would cost him his life, he returned to Germany. On June 26, he had "happened to read" Paul's plea to Timothy: "Come before the winter" (2 Tim. 4:21). That verse had "haunted" him the whole day. More hermeneutically aware than my father and his friend, but reading the Bible, as they did, to hear what God would say to him that day, he wrote in his diary: "It is not a misuse of the Scripture if I allow this to be said *to me*" (15.232).[1]

Life

Dietrich Bonhoeffer (1906-1945) was born into a high-achieving, well-to-do family[2] noteworthy both for its profound sense of civic responsibility[3] and for its minimal religiosity.[4] Dietrich's decision to pursue a career in theology was apparently motivated, at least in part, by a desire to distinguish himself along a path different from the ones that his (very accomplished) older brothers had taken.[5] He managed to complete his doctoral dissertation in theology,[6] his *Habilitationsschrift*,[7] and a year of postgraduate studies at Union Theological Seminary in New York (1930-1931) without doing much praying or even attending church regularly.[8] Inevitably, given the nature of his academic studies and the circles within which he moved, Bonhoeffer was thoroughly familiar with the liberal the-

1. Quotations from Bonhoeffer are cited (with volume and page number) from the seventeen volumes of *Dietrich Bonhoeffer Works* (see bibliography).

2. After 1912, Karl Bonhoeffer, Dietrich's father, held "the leading professorship for psychiatry and neurology in Germany" (Bethge, *Bonhoeffer*, 21). That Karl had "heard from professional colleagues about [Hitler's] psychopathic symptoms" was only one of a number of reasons the whole family "disliked and mistrusted Hitler" from the start. The family was also certain from the start that Hitler's rise to power would lead to war (Bethge, *Bonhoeffer*, 257-58).

3. Dietrich, his brother Klaus, and his sisters' husbands, Rüdiger Schleicher and Hans von Dohnanyi, were all executed for their parts in conspiracies against Hitler.

4. The family did not attend church, and though Dietrich's mother, Paula, was a pious believer, his father and his brother Karl-Friedrich were agnostics. "The predominant atmosphere [in the home] was one of tolerant empiricism" (Bethge, *Bonhoeffer*, 18, 34-36).

5. Bethge, *Bonhoeffer*, 20, 37; cf. 44: "He was not yet driven by any love of the church or an articulated theological system of beliefs, and certainly not by a discovery of the Scriptures and their exegesis. His interest in the discipline of theology was still much more philosophical than religious. Bonhoeffer's path to theology began . . . in a 'secular' atmosphere." Dietrich's oldest brother, Karl-Friedrich, became a professor of physical chemistry. His brother Klaus completed a doctorate in jurisprudence before becoming a lawyer; he worked for a time in international law at the League of Nations in Geneva. Another brother, Walter, was killed in action in World War I.

6. *Sanctorum Communio*, 1927; published 1930.

7. *Act and Being*, written 1929-1930, published 1931. The *Habilitationsschrift* was required for Bonhoeffer to qualify as a university teacher.

8. For the infrequency of his praying, see 14.134; on his irregular church attendance, see Bethge, *Bonhoeffer*, 127, 203-4.

ology of his day[9] and the historical-critical approach to the Bible.[10] His credentials as an academic theologian notwithstanding, he was (in his own retrospective judgment) "not yet a Christian" (14.134).

In 1931, he began lecturing as a member of the theological faculty of the University of Berlin. It was at about this time — no precise date can be given — that he "came to the Bible" and everything "changed" (14.134). His new seriousness and fervent faith became apparent to all.[11] He began to ask of every passage in the Bible, "What is God saying to us here?" (14.168). In 1936, Bonhoeffer wrote:

> Since having learned to read the Bible in this way — and it has not been all that long — it becomes more miraculous to me each day. I read it each morning and evening, often during the day as well, and every day I focus on a text I have chosen for the entire week, trying to immerse myself in it entirely that I may truly hear it. I now know that I could no longer really live properly without this. . . . All that remains is the decision whether to trust the word of the Bible, whether to allow it to sustain us as does no other word in life or death. And I believe that we will genuinely become happy and at peace only after making this decision. (14.169-70)

Though never rejecting historical-critical methodology,[12] Bonhoeffer

---

9. Bonhoeffer's early attraction to the work of Karl Barth, however, put him at odds with the Berlin theologians.

10. He was a neighbor of Adolf van Harnack, attended his seminars, frequently walked with him to the streetcar station, and spoke at his memorial service (Bethge, *Bonhoeffer*, 29, 43, 67, 139). He and his family were on friendly terms with the eminent OT scholar Gerhard von Rad (47, 52, 701; *Works* 16.84). At one time he had a romantic interest in Elisabeth Zinn, a distant cousin who was herself an academic theologian (Bonhoeffer and von Wedemeyer, *Love Letters,* 246, 248 n. 4; cf. Bethge, *Bonhoeffer,* 468-69) and who later married the NT scholar Günther Bornkamm, whose books on Jesus and Paul were standard fare for a generation and more of NT scholars. With these names, the list of theologians and biblical scholars with whom Bonhoeffer routinely interacted has hardly begun.

11. Cf. 14.134; see also Bethge, *Bonhoeffer*, 202-6, where the transition is characterized as "from theologian to Christian."

12. Cf. 12.330-31. Indeed, throughout his life he presupposed what he regarded as assured results of historical-critical scholarship in his own (very differently oriented) work; see the discussion below. It is also worth noting that Bonhoeffer was sharply critical of those who would silence Rudolf Bultmann ("I would like to know if any of them has actually worked through [Bultmann's] commentary on John" [16.260]), at the same time as he emphasized his own disagreement with Bultmann's "liberal reductionism (the 'mythological' elements in Christianity are taken out, thus reducing Christianity to its 'essence')" (8.430);

sensed that "detached" scholarship of this kind had little to contribute to the church and the life of faith.[13] His own interpretive method he described as based on the presupposition that the Bible is "the book of the church" (3.22); for all practical purposes, he came to abandon historical-critical approaches in his private reflections as well as his public expositions of Scripture.[14] (Conversely, the guild of biblical scholarship was largely dismissive of his work.[15])

His opposition to Nazi policies left Bonhoeffer increasingly isolated and led to his withdrawal, for a time, to England (13.23); there he served as pastor of two German congregations and enlisted their support for the Nazi-resisting Confessing Church in Germany (1933-1935). When he returned to Germany in 1935, it was to head up an illegal seminary for prospective Confessing pastors in Finkenwalde. In a number of ways, life at the seminary resembled that of a monastery, as Bonhoeffer strove to introduce students to a communal life "under the Word" (5.27).[16] Students were taught that the day was lost in which they had not "deepened [their] knowledge of God's word in Holy Scripture"; that they could not interpret Scripture for others unless they had "allowed [Scripture] to speak to [them] each day"; that the goal in reading Scripture was "to encounter Christ in his own word. We come to the text anxious to hear what Christ wants to say and give to us today through his word" (14.931-32). Silent

---

cf. 8.372: "Bultmann's approach is still basically liberal (that is, it cuts the gospel short), whereas I'm trying to think theologically." On Bultmann, see also 16.347, 359.

13. Already a (Barth-influenced) student paper on the "Historical and Pneumatological Interpretation of Scripture" (1925) shows Bonhoeffer's awareness of the limitations of historical scholarship (9.285-300). His professor was not impressed (9.285 n. 1). Later, Bonhoeffer would tell candidates for the ministry that familiarity with "textual and literary criticism" was not "absolutely necessary"; otherwise, there would have been no genuine exposition of Scripture prior to the rise of these disciplines (14.391); and similarly: "Although it is good to read commentaries [in preparing a sermon], it is not absolutely necessary" (14.496). Though unobjectionable as far as it goes, critical scholarship proves incapable of disclosing "the essence of the Bible; it discloses merely its surface" (14.167).

14. According to Bethge, though Bonhoeffer had "mastered" the tools of historical-critical analysis, he "later chose not to use these means and methods" (*Bonhoeffer,* 78).

15. Of Bonhoeffer's work *Creation and Fall,* Bethge writes: "The exegetes regarded the work as systematics, and the systematicians viewed it as exegesis. One group was indignant, and the other took no notice" (*Bonhoeffer,* 217). For the very negative response of biblical scholars to Bonhoeffer's study of Ezra-Nehemiah — a study that, without explicitly addressing the current situation in Germany, highlighted what Bonhoeffer saw as parallels in the biblical story — see Bethge, *Bonhoeffer,* 526-29.

16. The experiment provided the background for what is perhaps Bonhoeffer's best-loved book, *Life Together* (5.1-140); cf. Bethge, *Bonhoeffer,* 469-72.

meditation on Scripture — a discipline Bonhoeffer required of his students and himself practiced the rest of his life[17] — drew particular attention (cf. 14.931-36).[18]

The seminary in Finkenwalde was closed by the Gestapo in 1937, but Bonhoeffer found less formal ways to train pastors until he deemed it prudent to retreat to America during the summer of 1939. Almost immediately, however, he regretted his decision and returned to share in (and, he hoped, to help shape) his country's fate.

He managed to avoid service in the German armed forces by taking on a position in the Military Intelligence Office. There he was made well aware of various plots to assassinate Hitler and, in his travels abroad, informed key figures and solicited support for the conspirators. Seeing parallels between his own situation and the calamitous times of the prophet Jeremiah, he took seriously Jeremiah's counsel to express his faith in a better future (8.50; cf. Jer. 32:15) and quietly became engaged to Maria von Wedemeyer, whom he had known in Finkenwalde when she was a very young girl. The engagement was made public immediately after Bonhoeffer's arrest on April 5, 1943. In prison he read the Bible voraciously and continued the daily discipline of scriptural meditation.[19] In letters to Eberhard Bethge, he began tentatively to explore new directions in theology, the nature of which remain controversial to this day. Suffice it to note here that the "religionless Christianity" he envisioned for the future was emphatically not one in which the importance of the Bible would be displaced. On the contrary, it was precisely a Christianity better in keeping with the witness of Scripture that he spent his last days attempting to articulate.[20] By then — and with the war all but over — the

17. "For me the daily silent reflection on the word of God as it applies to me — even if only for a few minutes — tends to become the crystallization of all that brings inner and outer order to my life" (16.254). Such meditation on Scripture remained a constant, though Bonhoeffer would later write of periods ("weeks," "days") when he actually "read very little of the Bible." After one such note, he added, "Then one day I pick it up again, and suddenly everything is so much more powerful, and I can't let it go at all" (16.133); after another, he wrote: "When I then open my Bible again, it is new and delightful to me as never before" (16.329; cf. 8.326).

18. Karl Barth, for one, was dubious about the practice, in part because of the suggested distinction "between theological work, on the one hand, and edifying reflection, on the other." Barth also confessed to being "bothered . . . by the smell — one rather difficult to articulate — of monastic eros and pathos, for which I now have neither the appropriate sensorium nor any real use" (14.268).

19. 8.62-63, 81, 179; Bethge, *Bonhoeffer*, 831, 843, 852, 882.

20. See 6.58; 8.367, 372-73, 479-80. Bonhoeffer was concerned that, where God is spo-

Nazi regime nonetheless found time to settle scores with its opponents. Dietrich Bonhoeffer was hanged on April 9, 1945. A mere three weeks later, Hitler committed suicide.

Revelation and Religion[21]

The characteristic feature that distinguishes human beings from animals (Bonhoeffer notes in one of his sermons) is "restlessness" (or "dread, anxiety, yearning, love"). "There is in the soul of human beings, as truly as they are human beings, something that makes them restless, something that points them towards the infinite, eternal." Such restlessness is "the power that creates history and culture": the soul, aware of its transitory nature, "wants to transcend itself, into permanence and stability. . . . The most grandiose and most gentle of all human attempts to attain the eternal from out of the anxiety and restlessness of the heart — is religion." Religion thus represents the attempts of human beings to discover and define the path that will lead them to God (10.481-83).

As such, religion is commonly seen as corresponding to, and satisfying, a deeply felt human need. It is something "beautiful," "valuable," "necessary," "the only thing that can make people most deeply happy." The crucial question often forgotten by those who speak this way is

> whether religion is also something true, whether it is the truth. For it might be that religion is beautiful but not true, and [that] this is all a beautiful, pious illusion, but an illusion nevertheless. . . . Whoever speaks that way sees religion only from the point of view of the human being and his needs and not from the point of view of God and what he demands. (11.433)

---

ken of at all in the modern age, it is as a "deus ex machina," brought in "to solve insoluble problems or to provide strength when human powers fail" (8.366). God is thus pushed to the "boundaries" of human knowledge and experience — and the boundaries keep receding, to the point where many people no longer see any need for God (8.425-26, 450). But such a deity is far from the God of the Bible (and particularly, Bonhoeffer noted, from the God of the Old Testament [8.367; cf. 8.213]). "God is the center of life and doesn't just 'turn up' when we have unsolved problems to be solved" (8.406-7). "Jesus claims all of human life, in all its manifestations, for himself and for the kingdom of God" (8.451). The church must learn to "confront [people] with God where they are strongest" (8.457).

21. The distinction Bonhoeffer draws between religion and revelation is clearly influenced by Barth, but too important to Bonhoeffer's own thought to be passed over here.

Indeed, the deity we "discover" on the basis of our own experiences and understanding — as though *we* could determine where God is to be found! — will inevitably be one we find suited and pleasing to ourselves (14.168). However "humbly and modestly" religion may speak, it is always in danger of thinking it has somehow grasped God, and even has God at its command (11.229).[22] It overlooks the "humanly unbridgeable gulf between God and human beings" (10.356). "Even in their most spiritual spirituality — in religion — human beings remain human beings, and that means sinners" (10.484).

After all, it is surely God alone who determines where God is to be found; the God-determined place is the cross of Jesus (14.168). Christianity stands or falls with its belief in a "real divine revelation" (9.285) in the person and story of Jesus Christ. To treat Jesus merely as a religious genius is to fail to take seriously "Christ's claim to speak and indeed to *be* the revelation of God." Plato and Kant were geniuses — and we can live well enough without them.

> But if there is something in Christ that makes claims upon my entire life, from top to bottom, and does so with the full seriousness of the realization that it is God who is speaking here, and if it is only in Christ that God's word once became a present reality, then Christ possesses for me . . . absolutely urgent significance. Although I am still free to say yes or no, it can no longer be an ultimately indifferent matter to me. (10.343)[23]

While religion talks (vainly) of the path of humans to God, Christianity tells of God coming to us (10.354, 483): "Man can find God only in Christ" (10.456-57). All our pious-sounding talk about searching for God takes place in a world where God has already spoken, and in which reality has been decisively shaped by that revelation (6.49).

22. Cf. 10.483: "The motives of our morality and our religion have been unmasked; we wanted to be masters of the eternal."

23. Throughout this latter discussion, Bonhoeffer echoes Kierkegaard's insistence on the difference between a genius and an apostle. The same essay of Kierkegaard presumably lies behind Bonhoeffer's insistence that preachers should never speak of Scripture as "profound" or "beautiful": such dubious praise distracts from the real reason Scripture must be heeded (14.343). Interestingly, Bonhoeffer even commended the reading of Kierkegaard to his fiancée (Bonhoeffer and Wedemeyer, *Letters,* 185-86) — a relationship where others might be hesitant to invoke the Dane.

The Word of God

It is in Holy Scripture, "God's revealed Word for all peoples, for all times" (5.59-60), that human beings today encounter God's revelation in Christ: "It pleased God to speak to us in the word of the Bible alone" (14.492); "God's speech in Jesus Christ meets us in the Holy Scriptures" (5.156). Scripture *in its entirety*[24] witnesses to Christ; it "is God's own word, in which, through the prophets and the apostles, he proclaims to me and to the church-community that Jesus Christ is God's Son and my sav[ior]" (14.785). As "the book in which God's word is preserved till the end of the world," the Bible is distinguished "from all other books" (14.517).

All of this is, of course, far from the presuppositions and practice of historical critics (who insist on reading the Bible "like any other book"). Yet Bonhoeffer never rejected the historical-critical scholarship in which he had been educated. On the contrary, that education left him prepared to concede far more to the human component in the writing of Scripture than theologians of the precritical period (and many since) could ever conceive of. As we have seen, people like Augustine and Calvin could, for example, allow inaccuracies in Scripture in matters of science, seeing them as divine accommodations to the limited understanding of those for whom the texts were written. Augustine suspected that Moses himself was aware of the whole truth even while he adapted what he wrote to the capacities of his readers. For his part, Bonhoeffer sees in such inaccuracies the limitations of the biblical authors' own understanding: "Here [he writes of Gen. 1:6-10] the ancient image of the world confronts us in all its scientific naiveté" (3.50).

> That the biblical author, to the extent that the author's word is a human word, was bound by the author's own time, knowledge, and limits is as little disputed as the fact that through this word God, and God alone, tells us about God's creation. (3.49)[25]

24. "The Scriptures are God's revealed Word as a whole. The full witness to Jesus Christ the Lord can be clearly heard only in its immeasurable inner relationships, in the connection of Old and New Testaments" (5.60). "Our faith rests on the unity of the scriptural testimony to Christ" (4.205).

25. Bonhoeffer's treatments of the opening chapters of Genesis are replete with claims of their scientific inadequacies accompanied by an insistence that God's word is nonetheless to be heard in what is written. See 11.261: "Every child knows that the earth did not come about simply in six days. Yet not everyone knows that God creates the world through his Spirit and human beings according to God's own image." The "pictures" that Genesis uses

We may cite other examples where what Bonhoeffer took to be the assured results of historical criticism are accepted without demurral. He agrees that the opening chapters of Genesis contain two creation accounts, derived from different sources (while insisting, it should be added, that the accounts represent "the same thing from two different sides," and that neither would be complete without the other [3.71-72]). He grants that the narratives of the Gospels do not provide us with material for a biography of Jesus, nor can historical research as such yield absolute certainty that he even existed. (Still, the risen Christ uses the Gospel stories to bear witness to himself, creating faith and making "possible our access to the historicity of Jesus" [12.328-31].) Critical scholars dispute the Mosaic or Davidic authorship of various psalms; Bonhoeffer sees no reason to disagree (14.392).[26] (What matters to him is that the voice of Christ is to be heard in *every* psalm.)

Other statements of agreement with historical-critical scholarship could be cited, but they, too, would represent statements made in passing in the context of discussions primarily focused on hearing what God is saying to us today through the very texts about whose *human* origins Bonhoeffer tends to agree with the critics.[27] It is, for Bonhoeffer, precisely

---

to speak of creation (and "who can speak of these things except in pictures?") "enable the underlying meaning to shine through" (3.81); see also 10.518.

26. For Bonhoeffer, "the dogmatic thesis of [Scripture's] verbal inspiration" represents a vain attempt to counter the claims of historical scholarship (cf. 3.50-51). As one example, he notes that, for proponents of that doctrine, "virtually everything depends on David and Moses really being the singers of the psalms ascribed to them" (14.390). But he also finds the doctrine *theologically* misleading, seeing it as a human attempt to secure a fixed place on earth (i.e., a verbally inspired, now canonized text) where, whenever *we* please, we can find God (14.389-90; cf. 12.331). In effect, *we* become the subject, and God the object, in the divine-human encounter, whereas in reality the reverse is always the case (cf. 9.290; 10.459; 11.232). The mistake Bonhoeffer sees as inherent in the doctrine of verbal inspiration is similar to that of Jews who "equated God and the law," thus reducing the living God (who is *Lord* of the law) to something they could master. We know God, not when we have mastered a God-inspired text, but only when we live in personal communion with him (4.117) — a communion that, to be sure, requires careful attentiveness to his word. Bonhoeffer himself can speak of the Bible's authors as "useful instruments" conveying a message they were directly commissioned to deliver, and of the prophetic word as "exclusively a word that God sends to a certain person" (14.387); but he worries that the language of "inspiration" carries with it the danger of "substantialization" (i.e., of identifying the living word of the living God with a mute earthly object — Scripture — at human disposal [14.493 n. 25]). When all emphasis is on God's *past* inspiration of the biblical authors, even a translation of their words moves the reader a step away from *God's* word (14.429).

27. He does, however, routinely speak of the Pastoral Epistles as Pauline (e.g., 5.29, 97; 15.427).

the "historic," "temporally bound and transient" word of Scripture that God owns as *his* word and through which he addresses human beings (14.421): "This word, spoken and heard as a human word, is the form of a servant in which from the beginning God encounters us and in which alone God wills to be found" (3.30). Bonhoeffer is adamant in rejecting the notion that interpreters of the Bible are somehow to "distinguish the word of God from the word of human beings and extract it," as though Scripture contains universal, timeless truths alongside much else that we must identify as merely human and time-bound, to be relegated to the past (14.420-21).[28]

> One and the same God is speaking throughout the entire Bible. . . . [The Bible] is not merely a collection of instructions and opinions; instead, it is the same God who is speaking in all those instructions and opinions. One cannot, for example, determine that God's word is *here* but *not there*. All of God can be found in every word of Scripture. (14.492; italics in original)[29]

> I am willing to grant that this or that passage in Scripture cannot yet be understood, though with the certainty that one day this passage will indeed be revealed as God's own word. . . . I would prefer to take this

28. The assumption behind such an approach, Bonhoeffer argues, is that we possess within ourselves — "in our reason, in our conscience, or in our ethnonational [*völkisch*] or other experiences" — the means of identifying what is properly God's word. In effect, we claim to possess the truth before we even begin our study of Scripture. The true situation, Bonhoeffer posits, is the reverse: the word of God itself is the norm, "and our own circumstances, reason, conscience, and ethnonational [*völkisch*] experience are the material to which this norm is to be applied" (14.418-21). Cf. 3.107-8: "Did God really say . . . ? [Gen. 3:1] — that is the utterly godless question. . . . Did God really claim to be a God of wrath toward those who do not keep God's commandments? Did God really demand the sacrifice of Christ — the God whom I know better, the God whom I know to be the infinitely good, all-loving Father? This is the question that appears so innocuous but through which evil wins its power in us and through which we become disobedient to God. . . . [The question proposes] that, on the basis of an idea, a principle, or some prior knowledge about God, humankind should now pass judgment on the concrete word of God. . . . At that point [human beings] have become God's master, they have left the path of obedience, they have withdrawn from being addressed by God."

29. Elsewhere, Bonhoeffer notes that the church has drawn knowledge of the truth from the Bible for two thousand years. "It is the book that has already comforted millions of hearts and led them to God; every word in it has a history in Christendom." The church is therefore entirely justified when it responds with "indignation and offense" at "every thoughtless dealing with its word" (14.517).

position rather than to say at my own discretion: This is divine, while that is human! (14.169)

What ties all of Scripture together is its witness, in its every part, to Christ; hence, the task of the interpreter is "to make the character of this word as a witness audible" (14.421) — in every passage.

Like Luther, Bonhoeffer also speaks of the word of God as something spoken by one believer to another[30] and, supremely, as the substance of the sermon that is faithful to Scripture.[31] In the sermon based on a biblical text, the "historical word of God in the Bible" becomes "God's word to the present — precisely because God remains God, yesterday as today." The sermon is thus "the locus at which past and present come together in God, but only because the God of Christ is our God, the God whom the Bible reveals" (10.382).

---

30. "God put this Word into the mouths of human beings so that it may be passed on to others. . . . God has willed that we should seek and find God's living Word in the testimony of other Christians, in the mouth of human beings. Therefore, Christians need other Christians who speak God's Word to them" (5.32). "How are we supposed to help rightly other Christians who are experiencing troubles and temptation [*Anfechtung*] if not with God's own Word? All our own words quickly fail. However, those who . . . can speak out of the abundance of God's Word the wealth of instructions, admonitions, and comforting words from the Scriptures will be able to drive out demons and help one another through God's Word" (5.63).

Bonhoeffer's indebtedness to Luther can be seen as well in his insistence that the word of God is an *external* word ("this alien word of God" [14.169]): "It can only come from the outside. In themselves [Christians] are destitute and dead. Help must come from the outside; and it has come and comes daily and anew in the Word of Jesus Christ, bringing us redemption, righteousness, innocence, and blessedness" (5.32). "The word that confronts us, seizes us, takes us captive, binds us fast, does not come from the depths of our souls. It is the foreign, the unfamiliar, unexpected, forceful, overpowering word of the Lord that calls into his service whomsoever and whenever God chooses" (13.350; cf. also 5.31).

31. The latter qualification is crucial, and Bonhoeffer repeatedly emphasizes it: "Because the sermon claims to be *God's word,* it is bound to Scripture. The promise that it is God who is speaking derives solely from the sermon itself being commensurate with Scripture. . . . *The best sign of a good pastor is that the congregation reads the Bible*" (14.497; italics in original; cf. 4.227). In the fragments of a novel Bonhoeffer wrote while in Tegel prison, he imagines a woman emerging enraptured from a Sunday morning worship service: "Didn't [the pastor] say it beautifully? Yes — uh, what did he say, anyway? It's so lovely one could never convey it. But it really doesn't matter at all, you can just feel it and it's so uplifting and you don't even know quite why, isn't that right? . . . [What the sermon was about] really doesn't matter at all, does it?" To this, her companion replies, "No, it really doesn't matter at all, because it wasn't about the Bible passage at all. . . . Did it escape you again that the pastor said what you wanted to hear, but didn't preach the word of God?" (7.78-79; cf. 13.322).

To the word of God in his sermon, the pastor must be careful to add "nothing of his own, confident that this word is capable of everything" (14.517). God's word needs no "ornamentation. It is clothed in its own glory. . . . Nothing foreign to it . . . should be used to adorn it" (13.355). Every sentence in a sermon should have its scriptural support (14.518). Nor is the pastor's job to justify the text as relevant for today — as though God's word must address our circumstances as *we* perceive them before it warrants our attention. The reverse is the case: it is from God's word that we learn what our true situation is — that of sinners before God — a dilemma to which God's word in the gospel provides the answer. The pastor who would make Scripture relevant for his hearers must simply "trust the text," clarify and proclaim its content, and allow the Holy Spirit to make its message real and contemporary for those who listen (14.413-31, 493-94). A miracle accompanies such preaching.

> The grace of God, who comes down from heaven into our midst and speaks to us, knocks on our door, asks questions, warns us, puts pressure on us, alarms us, threatens us, and makes us joyful again and free and sure. When the Holy Scriptures are brought to life in a church, the Holy Spirit comes down from the eternal throne, into our hearts, while the busy world outside sees nothing and knows nothing about it. (13.323)[32]

What we encounter in Scripture and the Scripture-based sermon is the voice of Jesus Christ offering us the grace of discipleship[33] — and compelling a response (4.202; 15.435). Rightly understood, the church is "a place

---

32. Bethge's biography contains a moving description of the seriousness with which Bonhoeffer treated the "voice of Christ" in sermons: "It initially seemed strange to his students that their sermons, however hesitant and inadequate, were treated in all seriousness as the expression of the true and living voice of Christ. Nothing, insisted Bonhoeffer, is more concrete than the real voice of Christ speaking in the sermon. He adhered strictly to this principle with regard to any sermon preached in the worship service. It was to be listened to in all humility, not analyzed. . . . Once, when Erich Klapproth read a sermon aloud during the class, he had no sooner finished than Bonhoeffer dismissed the class because he felt that at that moment a critical analysis would be inopportune. . . . Nothing was as chastening as Bonhoeffer's own method of listening to sermons" (*Bonhoeffer,* 441-42).

33. Thus expressed, the words capture a theme important to Bonhoeffer, though not, of course, one intended to exclude the grace of forgiveness. Bonhoeffer can say that, in its essence, every sermon is an interpretation of the sentence "We entreat you on behalf of Christ, be reconciled to God" (13.325, citing 2 Cor. 5:20); but in a phrase as famous as any he ever wrote, he repudiated the "cheap grace" that offers forgiveness apart from the obedience of discipleship (4.43-56).

where God's word is obediently received and believed" (13.323). Faith and obedience cannot be separated: there can be no obedience without faith, but neither is there faith without obedience (4.63-76).[34] To those desiring certainty of the truth of God's word before deciding whether or not they will obey, Jesus himself gives no assurance.

> But how can I recognize as truth that of which Christian proclamation speaks? And here the Bible gives a strange answer: "If you continue in my word, [you are truly my disciples; and you] will know [the truth]." Not through free research, not through disinterested thinking and searching for it, but solely through the free attempt to base one's life for once completely on the word of Christ. . . . Only in living does one know the truth. Only in battle can one test weapons. (11.434; cf. 15.421)[35]

Old Testament and New

In the Germany of the 1930s and early 1940s, statements regarding or assuming the importance of the Old Testament were far from platitudinous. At a large demonstration in the Berlin Sports Palace in November 1933, a prominent Nazi leader called for "liberation from the Old Testament with its Jewish money morality and from these stories of cattle dealers and pimps."[36] After Bonhoeffer published a paper on King David in a church journal in February 1936, a review appeared the following month in a Stuttgart newspaper under the heading "Praise of Judah in the Third Reich." Noting that David's conduct "clearly violates the moral and ethical sensibility of the Germanic race," the review lamented Bonhoeffer's glorification of "the adulterer, His Majesty David, King by the Grace of Yahweh!" It went on to condemn Bonhoeffer's "advocacy of an oriental doctrine of

---

34. "You complain that you cannot believe? No one should be surprised that they cannot come to believe so long as, in deliberate disobedience, they flee or reject some aspect of Jesus' commandment" (4.66).

35. We recognize and believe in God's word as *God's* only as God enables us to do so, not on the basis of human knowledge, experience, or argument. In this respect, too, God must come to us if we are to find him; sinful human beings do not possess within themselves the capacity to do so. God remains the subject in every God-human encounter (cf. 11.231-32).

36. Bethge, *Bonhoeffer*, 335. However crude the speech (it appalled even many "German Christians" who were otherwise supportive of the Nazis), this particular demand could find broad support in Harnack's claim that the church would be well advised to eliminate the OT from its canon (cited at 3.157).

faith that in the year 1936 still has the audacity to present the global enemy Judah as the 'eternal people,' as the 'true people of nobility,' as the 'people of God' " (14.893 n. 112). When, in such a climate, Bonhoeffer repeatedly emphasized the essential significance of the Old Testament for Christian faith, his statements were of a piece with his opposition to Nazi policies targeting "non-Aryans."

They were also, of course, consistent with his insistence that, as God's word, *all* of Scripture must be heard by believers. Four aspects of Bonhoeffer's understanding of the Old Testament call for attention here.

1. Interpreting the Bible as "the book of the church," Bonhoeffer read the Old Testament christologically.[37] In brief summary statements on the content of the Bible, he found the essence of the Old and New Testaments to be, respectively, that of promises of the Messiah and the witness to their fulfillment (9.297; 14.424, 785-86). The conviction that "Scripture as a whole and in all its parts is to be understood as a witness to Christ" raises the question whether Old Testament texts that, on the surface, appear to resist such a claim may not be read allegorically. Bonhoeffer replies that we must grant "the possibility that God does not allow his word to be exhausted in its [grammatical], logical, unequivocal meaning, but rather that this word has even other perspectives and can serve better understanding. . . . Why should the word not *also* have symbolic or allegorical meaning?"[38] Allegorical exegesis provides no *proof* of Christ's presence in the Old Testament; but when it discovers Christ in Scripture (and only when it does so is allegorical interpretation legitimate), it properly elicits "praise for the fullness of the scriptural witness to Christ" (14.428-29).

Bonhoeffer's paper on David (14.870-93) focuses on the king's significance as a "model and shadow" of Christ. It details remarkable parallels to the Jesus of the Gospels in the Old Testament books of Samuel.

37. The manuscript of Bonhoeffer's study of David is accompanied by a cover sheet whose reverse side contained the following note, in which he justified and defined the Christian reading of the Old Testament: "1. The God of the Old Testament is the father of Jesus Christ. The incarnate God in Jesus Christ is the God of the Old Testament. It is a triune God. 2. The Old Testament must be read from the perspective of the incarnation and cross, i.e., from the perspective of the revelation given to us. Otherwise our understanding of the Old Testament remains Jewish or pagan. 3. The people and stories of the Old Testament are not moral models but rather witnesses to the election and promise of God. The Old Testament testifies to God's free, gracious, and wrathful actions with regard to God's people, not to moral examples" (14.871 n. 2).

38. Indeed, given abundant New Testament precedents for such exegesis, "how might we then consider it impossible?" (14.429). In a paper he wrote while still a student, however, Bonhoeffer was himself dismissive of allegorical interpretations (9.288).

It is with the one spirit of God that both David *and Christ* were anointed. . . . The anointing immediately leads David into battle against the powers of the world. . . . The period before his accession to the throne is one of ongoing hostility toward him from every quarter. . . . David is a stranger in his own land and in the land of the Philistines; he does not even have a place to lay his head. . . . David becomes the companion of sinners, the friend and confidant of the tired and burdened, of those without hope, of those cast down. . . . The great *temptation* David experiences during these years of flight and persecution is to seize his kingship *by force,* to spill *blood,* to establish his reign prematurely before it pleases God. (14.875-78, italics in original; cf. 5.158-59)

The sarcastic Nazi reviewer of the piece failed to note Bonhoeffer's explicit distancing of David's dubious "moral qualities" from his role as model of Christ (14.891). But Bonhoeffer rightly observed that "any exposition of the stories of David must thus understand David in his person, his office, his words, and his stories as the one *in whom according to the witness of the New Testament Christ himself was present*" (14.874; italics in original).

Bonhoeffer's christological interpretation of the Old Testament is evident above all in his reading of the book of Psalms.[39] The paradox that the Psalms are both God's word and the prayers of human beings finds its resolution in the recognition of the Psalter as "the prayer book of Jesus Christ" (5.53-54).[40] Psalms in which the authors protest their innocence, call for vengeance, or speak of their extreme suffering find no resonance in the personal lives of most believers; yet, inasmuch as these psalms, too, are "words of the Holy Scriptures," Christians "cannot simply dismiss [them] as obsolete and antiquated, as a 'preliminary stage of religion'" (5.53).

The psalms that will not cross our lips as prayers, those that make us falter and offend us, make us suspect that here someone else is praying, not we — that the one who is here affirming his innocence, who is calling for God's judgment, who has come to such infinite depths of suffering,

39. "Jesus himself says of the Psalms in general that they announced his death and resurrection and the preaching of the gospel" (5.159, referring to Luke 24:44-47).

40. "If the Psalter is indeed God's word, then it is God who is doing the speaking in these prayers. God who is doing the praying. God as the one praying and God as the one answering the prayer; this problem is resolved only in Jesus Christ" (14.387-88). "In Jesus' mouth, the human word becomes God's Word. When we pray along with the prayer of Christ, God's Word becomes again a human word" (5.157).

is none other than Jesus Christ himself. It is he who is praying here, and not only here, but in the whole Psalter. The New Testament and the church have always recognized and testified to this truth. The *human* Jesus Christ to whom no affliction, no illness, no suffering is unknown, and who yet was the wholly innocent and righteous one, is praying in the Psalter. . . . His congregation prays too, and even the individual prays. But they pray only insofar as Christ prays within them; they pray here not in their own name, but in the name of Jesus Christ. (5.54-55)

Believers, in full knowledge of their hearts' perversity, can nonetheless (with the psalmists) call themselves "innocent, devout, and righteous" in that, by faith, they have a share in the innocence of the One who alone, of his own, can speak these words (5.56, 172). Christ experienced all the "unspeakable misery and suffering" reflected in the Psalms; believers may incorporate these words, too, in their prayers inasmuch as their "old self" (or "flesh") died with him on the cross (5.56-57). Believers may not pray psalms of vengeance while entertaining thoughts of evil; they can, however, repeat their words as the prayers of Christ, who took upon himself the wrath and vengeance of God therein invoked, and so forgave his enemies (5.56, 175).

2. The Old Testament is relevant for Christians of every age because "the church of God is One both then and today" (14.930).[41] The story of God's people Israel is the story of God's people in every age; hearing that story, and

> forgetting and losing ourselves, we too pass through the Red Sea, through the desert, across the Jordan into the promised land. With Israel we fall into doubt and unbelief and through punishment and repentance experience again God's help and faithfulness. All this is not mere reverie, but holy, divine reality. We are uprooted from our own existence and are taken back to the holy history of God on earth. There God has dealt with us, and there God still deals with us today, with our needs and our sins, by means of the divine wrath and grace. What is important is not that God is a spectator and participant in our life today, but that we are attentive listeners and participants in God's action in the sacred story. . . . What we call our life, our troubles, and our guilt is by no means the whole of reality; our life, our need, our guilt, and our deliverance

41. See 12.466: "The old story of Gideon is being played out in Christendom every day." See also 15.398: "Job's temptation is the prototype of all temptations."

are there in the Scriptures. Because it pleased God to act for us there, it is only there that we will be helped. Only in the Holy Scriptures do we get to know our own story. The God of Abraham, Isaac, and Jacob is the God and Father of Jesus Christ and our God. (5.62)

3. Bonhoeffer found in the Old Testament a crucial corrective to the otherworldliness that has often characterized the Christian church. He refused to follow the early church fathers in spiritualizing the Old Testament when it speaks of the "visible earthly blessings of God"; he also rejected the notion that prayers for such blessings in the Psalms represent "an early first stage of Old Testament piety that is overcome in the New Testament."[42] Those who so interpret the texts "want to be even more spiritual than God is." Bodily life is not to be disdained. Provided we remember that "life, health, peace, and earthly good" are all gracious gifts of God, whose "goodness is better than life," we need have no bad conscience in praying, with the Psalter, for earthly blessings (5.168-69; cf. 15.501).[43]

In the Old Testament, too, we see that loving God with our whole heart does not lead to a diminishing of earthly loves; rather, it gives them their necessary foundation: "Where the cantus firmus [i.e., our love for God] is clear and distinct, a counterpoint [of earthly loves] can develop as mightily as it wants" (8.394). (In this context, Bonhoeffer notes that "it's really good that [Song of Solomon] is in the Bible.")

4. In a number of respects, Bonhoeffer insists that the Old Testament provides the essential preconditions for the Christian faith of the New.

Only when one knows that the name of God may not be uttered [as in Jewish piety, in observance of Exod. 20:7] may one sometimes speak the name of Jesus Christ. Only when one loves life and the earth so much that with it everything seems to be lost and at its end may one believe in the resurrection of the dead and a new world. Only when one accepts the law of God as binding for oneself may one perhaps sometimes speak of grace. And only when the wrath and vengeance of God against God's enemies are allowed to stand can something of forgiveness and the love

---

42. Observing that the OT people of God suffered much, Bonhoeffer suggests that "the difference between OT and NT may consist solely in the fact that in the OT the blessing also includes the cross, and in the NT the cross also includes the blessing" (8.493).

43. Note also what Bonhoeffer, engaged to be married but imprisoned, and feeling at times that life was slipping away from him, wrote to Eberhard Bethge: "In such moments I am gripped with an incomparable longing to have a child and not to vanish without a trace — probably more of an Old Testament wish than a New Testament one" (8.222).

of enemies touch our hearts. Whoever wishes to be and perceive things too quickly and too directly in New Testament ways is to my mind no Christian. . . . One can and must not speak the ultimate word prior to the penultimate. We are living in the penultimate and believe the ultimate. (8.213)

Reading Scripture Aright

Though it is not like any other book, the Bible can, of course, be read as though it were. Its surface meaning can be grasped by simple reading; the discovery of its essence as the word of the living God requires much more (14.167).

1. Today people "hardly have time to catch their breath" after a day's work "before society — so-called entertainment — seizes them and sucks what energy is left over" (10.501). But God's word claims our time (15.517).[44] Reading by itself is never enough. We must give God's word the time to "enter us deeply, dwell in us like the Holiest of Holies in the sanctuary, so that we do not stray in thoughts, words, and deeds. Often it is better to read little and slowly in the Scriptures, and to wait until it has penetrated into us, than to know much about God's word but not to 'treasure' it" (15.514).

2. Hearing God's voice requires that we (who "are so accustomed to commotion and noise that we are uncomfortable amid silence") learn (by "work and practice") what it means to be silent — in submission — before God.[45]

> Being silent before God means yielding to God the right to have the first and last word concerning us, and means accepting that word whatever it may be, for all eternity. . . . The hour of silence is an hour of serious responsibility, of being genuinely serious with God and with ourselves, and yet is also always an hour of bliss since it is an hour lived in the calmness of God. My soul becomes silent before God. That means speak, Lord, for your servant is listening. (10.502, alluding to 1 Sam. 3:10)

44. And "every Christian will be granted the time that he needs if he truly seeks it" (15.517).

45. We are not to come to God only when we feel "in the mood" to do so. God is present whether or not we are in the mood to meet him. "Those who depend on their moods become impoverished. A painter who paints only when in the mood will not get very far. In religion, as in art and science, times of high tension alternate with times of sober work and practice" (10.503).

The day also needs certain times of silence under the Word and silence
that comes out of the Word. . . . The Word comes not to the noisemakers
but to those who are silent. The stillness of the temple is the sign of God's
holy presence in the Word. (5.84)

Such silence is devoted to meditating on God's word, "allow[ing]
ourselves to be seized and conquered" by what it says, "allow[ing] it to
bear us upward to eternal heights and expanses" (10.511). It does not mean
waiting with blank minds for the Spirit of God to descend upon us; the
Spirit comes to us through the word of Scripture (14.132; cf. 5.84-85). Nor
is time set aside for meditation to be used for biblical scholarship,[46] for
dealing with "incomprehensible passages," or even for sermon preparation.
Analysis of the text is no more called for here than with words spoken to
us by one we love.[47] Like the latter, the words of Scripture should follow
us around the entire day, constantly resonating in our ears and working
on us. And so they will, if we take time to ponder them in our hearts, as
Mary did (14.933-35; cf. 5.87).

To achieve its purpose, meditation necessarily occupies itself only
with a brief selected text. It should thus be added to (and not replace) time
given to reading longer portions, upon which our knowledge of Scripture
as a whole is dependent (5.87; 14.277).

3. God promises to speak to us through his word,[48] but his voice is
heard only when, with humility, we ask of every passage, "What is God
saying to us here? And [we] implore God to show us what he wants to say"
(14.167-68). "What we want is to encounter Christ in his own word. We
come to the text anxious to hear what Christ wants to say and give to us
today through his word" (14.932).[49]

4. What we seek is that God's word will come to us afresh each day.
God's guidance is not a one-time, good-for-the-rest-of-your-life communication. "God's word is new and free today and tomorrow, it is only applicable to the very moment in which we hear it. God wants us to go step by step
in order to drive us to Himself for help again and again" (13.399). "I tremble

---

46. A familiar translation serves meditation better than the Greek New Testament
(14.933).

47. Cf. 14. 933; 15.514. Again, the echo of Kierkegaard (*FSE,* 26-30) is unmistakable.

48. "Certainly, we can never seek God anywhere else but in his word, but this word is
alive and inexhaustible, for God himself lives in it" (15.513).

49. When we read the Bible in order to hear what God has to say to us personally, "we
are doing nothing but what the simplest, most unlearned Christian does every day. We are
reading the Word of God as God's Word for us" (5.87).

with each word that I receive from God's mouth and in anticipation of the next word and the continuation of grace. Thus I remain bound wholly to grace in all my ways and decisions, and no false security can beguile me out of the living community with God" (15.523).

5. Since it is God's voice we long to hear when we come to his word, we start with the prayer that God by his Spirit will reveal himself to us through his word, enlightening our minds (5.87). It is those who have "glimpsed the wondrous world of the law of God" who know how blind they still are and how great is their need for God to open their eyes.

> One whose eyes God has opened to his word will see into a world of wonders. What has appeared dead to me is full of life; contradictions resolve themselves into a higher unity; harsh demands become gracious commands. Within the human word I hear God's eternal word; in past history I recognize the present God and his working for my salvation. The merciful consolation becomes a new claim of God; the unbearable burden becomes an easy yoke. The great wonder in God's law is the revelation of the Lord Jesus Christ. Through him, the word receives life, contradictions receive unity, revealed things receive unfathomable depth. Lord, open my eyes. (15.520-21, citing Ps. 119:18)

CHAPTER 15

Beyond the Sacred Page

In Chapter 10, the claim of John Wesley — as widely read as anyone in his generation — to be a "man of one book" was admiringly mocked, then acknowledged, at another level, to be profoundly true. Something similar could be said of all the figures we have examined in this study. Their education was superior, their reading extensive. Several rank with the most brilliant minds in human history. Superficial observation would see them far removed from the millions of simple believers for whom the Bible has been, quite literally, the only literature they have read. The gap is reduced considerably, however, by the observation that the learned subjects of our study read the Bible as they read no other book. At critical points, the disparity vanishes entirely: the Bible has shaped the thinking and guided the lives of *all* who have approached it as sacred Scripture; and it has brought them into the presence of God.

Approaching Scripture

In Malory's retelling of the Arthurian legends, Sir Launcelot, the erstwhile "best knyght of the worlde," and still the best of any "synfull man," joined with other knights of Arthur's Round Table in a quest for the Holy Grail, from which Christ drank at the Last Supper. Lying one night by a wayside cross near a chapel, half asleep, half awake, he saw the holy vessel atop a silver table drawing near, then standing still. After a great while, the "Sangrail" disappeared into the chapel — and Launcelot, his quest notwithstanding, found himself unable to rise and follow. Sitting up, and overwhelmed by sorrow, Launcelot "wist" not what to do, and "so departed sore wepynge. . . . And than he called hymselff a verry wrecch and most unhappy of all knyghtes."

My synne and my wyckednes hath brought me unto grete dishonoure! For whan I sought worldly adventures for worldely desyres I ever encheved them and had the bettir in every place, and never was I discomfite in no quarell. . . . And now I take uppon me the adventures to seke of holy thynges, now I se and undirstonde that myne olde synne hyndryth me and shamyth me, that I had no power to stirre nother speke whan the holy bloode appered before me.[1]

Entrance into the felicity of God's presence is not granted everyone, nor was it taken for granted by the readers of Scripture we have considered. Like Launcelot, they knew that earthly achievements count for nothing here. Indeed, apart from divine intervention, the mystery clouding the infinite from finite minds, and the God-distancing attitudes and deeds of human beings, combine to prevent even a perception of divine presence.[2] God was present, uniquely and supremely, in the person of Jesus; yet Jesus was, for all the eye could see, and for all that many saw, a man like any other,

> . . . with a date, so tall, weighing
> So much, talking Aramaic, having learned a trade;
> . . . no beauty we could desire.[3]

His words commanded the obedience that only God is due. Yet words so unwelcome were the more easily dismissed in that they came from one so ordinary in his background and appearance; and he programmatically refused to do the spectacular that his underwhelmed contemporaries claimed would change their minds (Mark 8:11-13; cf. Matt. 4:5-7; 27:42). Kierkegaard noted that any argument brought to make it appear "reasonable" that this man was God must be advanced in opposition to the divine purpose by which God came hidden in the humblest human form;

---

1. Malory, *Works,* 520, 537-38. (He did not "know" what to do, and "so departed weeping sorely. . . . And then he called himself a very wretch and most unhappy of all knights. . . . 'My sin and my wickedness have brought me into great dishonor! For when I sought worldly adventures for worldly desires, I ever achieved them and had the better in every place, and never was I discomfited in any quarrel. . . . And now I take upon me the adventures to seek of holy things, now I see and understand that my old sin hinders me and shames me, so that I had no power to stir nor speak when the holy blood appeared before me.'")

2. Aquinas emphasized the inability of finite minds to grasp the infinite; Calvin, the spiritual blindness brought about by sin.

3. Lewis, *Poems,* 124.

in forgetfulness of the dilemma this posed for his contemporaries; and in defiance of the logical impossibility that the eternal, immutable God could be found in mortal, corruptible flesh, the infinite confined to the finite. The paradox, Kierkegaard concluded, must be left paradoxical: either one believes, or one is offended. The early church's most prolific apostle wrote from experience when he acknowledged that only the God who once said "Let there be light!" can so shine in human hearts that his glory is seen in the face of Jesus Christ (2 Cor. 4:6).

As Origen noted, much the same can be said of the Bible. He believed its writings were inspired by God's Spirit. He knew its power to transform lives. He heard in its words the sweet voice of the divine Bridegroom. Yet, just as the Word of God was once "clothed" in ordinary human flesh, so it is now "clothed" in the words of an ordinary-looking book; and the vision of many, then as now, is confined to what meets the eye. Only hearts open to God — only hearts opened *by* God — perceive the divinity within.

Augustine counted himself among those whose first encounters with Scripture brought only contempt. Accustomed to Cicero's "dignified prose," he deemed the style of Scripture not worth his attention — even apart from what seemed the texts' manifest contradictions and absurdi-ties. In time, he came to see that his early response was the product, not of honest inquiry and a willingness to learn, but of an arrogant sense of superiority that closed his mind to truth. Yet he added that even eagerness to learn does not bring a true understanding of Scripture if motivated by a desire to impress others: eyes focused on human opinion are blind to the divine. Nor should we be surprised when readers with no intention of obeying God fail to perceive him in his word. Only *as* God will God be found. God speaks, through his word, to those who make room for him.

Here, too, Kierkegaard summed up the futility of attempting to demonstrate, through human reason, the divine character of Scripture.[4] Like Luther, he insisted that nothing could be more contrary to human judgment than the content of divine revelation.[5] What is beyond human

---

4. On the other hand, John Wesley, a child of the "Age of Reason," thought he *could* prove the divine inspiration of Scripture with a simple syllogism. The demonstration may charitably be labeled optimistic. Schleiermacher, like Kierkegaard, saw no point in attempt-ing to prove Scripture's divine character, but he understood that character differently (see Chapter 11 above).

5. Aquinas, though allowing some value to external evidence for Christian truth, ac-knowledged that, inasmuch as matters of faith lie beyond natural human perception, we believe them only when inwardly moved by God to do so; and he, too, believed it a dan-gerous mistake to attempt to demonstrate, with human arguments, the mysteries of faith.

imagining must simply be proclaimed with authority. Like Calvin, he noted the folly of supposing that the faith on which one's eternal salvation depends could be built on a foundation so flimsy as human argument; belief inspired by argument one day will be vulnerable to counterargument the next.[6] Indeed, like Bengel, Kierkegaard observed that arguments for faith inevitably *provoke* counterarguments; and as long as the game continues — it can have no earthly ending — the commitment of faith is postponed. Like Augustine, Kierkegaard claimed that the true obstacles to faith are moral, not intellectual. Even were argumentation somehow to bring about an intellectual grasp of Christian truth, the commitment and passion of faith would not follow apart from a further act of a disinclined will. Like Bonhoeffer, Kierkegaard maintained that faith must begin with an openness toward God and a willingness to obey him (cf. John 7:17); it then grows in tandem with obedience. Faith's assurance comes from the inner testimony of the Spirit (Rom. 8:15-16; Gal. 4:6; cf. 1 John 2:20, 27; 3:24; 4:13; 5:6-9).

In the course of this study, we have nonetheless met with frequent claims that, in hearts that *are* open to God, or (as we may also say) in hearts that have been opened *by* God, the voice of God is heard through Scripture. For such readers, Calvin says, Scripture is "self-authenticating." Bengel speaks of how the text itself "exacts" readers' "assent" to its truth, an assent no more needing argumentative support than the presence of the sun needs pointing out by the stars. Our authors speak of knowing themselves confronted, in the words of Scripture, with their absolute duty toward God. They speak of how, through their reading of Scripture, God humbled their pride, induced their worship, nourished their spirits, roused them to virtue, inspired their love. They note that, as they meditate on Scripture, they enjoy communion with God.

> Delectable indeed are the meadow, and the garden, but far more delectable the study of the divine writings. For there indeed are flowers which fade, but here are thoughts which abide in full bloom; there is the breeze of the zephyr, but here the breath of the Spirit. . . . The garden is subject to the necessities of the seasons, but the Scriptures are rich in foliage, and laden with fruit alike in winter and in summer. Let us then give diligence to the study of the Scriptures; for if thou doest this the

---

6. Calvin did think that various arguments can be cited to *confirm an existing faith* in Scripture that originated with the "testimony of the Spirit." Apart from the latter, he insisted, such arguments are in vain.

Scripture will expel thy despondency, and engender pleasure, extirpate vice, and make virtue take root; and in the tumult of life it will save thee from suffering like those who are tossed by troubled waves. The sea rages but thou sailest on with calm weather; for thou hast the study of the Scriptures for thy pilot; for this is the cable which the trials of life do not break asunder. (Chrysostom, *Hom. Eutropius* 2.1)

Claims like these are common to Christian speech about Scripture in every age.

Bible Difficulties

As I am about to enter a library in Toronto, I meet my friend Alan, just returned from a year of study in Germany. We agree to get together later for dinner so that we can catch up on all that has happened since we last met. Inside the library, I meet another friend, Alex, who mentions Alan in passing, clearly assuming that Alan remains in Germany. I start to correct him, but Alex will hear none of it. For various reasons, more or less plausible in themselves, Alex is certain that Alan is still abroad.

Whether, or to what degree, I then argue with Alex will depend on my mood at the moment, the urgency of my other business, the importance I place on Alex knowing the truth, and so on. For my own part, nothing Alex says will cause me to doubt what I know to be true. Alan is back in Toronto: I just met him on the front steps.

No analogy is perfect, but perhaps an imagined incident such as this will serve to illustrate why readers convinced that the Bible is God's word seem little troubled by evidence suggesting the contrary. That such evidence exists is denied by none: even the most fervent defender of the Bible's harmony and truth concedes that it presents enough difficulties to fill an encyclopedia. Admittedly, most of the subjects of this study could know nothing of the particular challenges presented by archaeology, modern science, or historical-critical scholarship. But even the science of their own day raised questions for Augustine, Aquinas, and Calvin; and readers of Scripture in every age have found numerous examples of apparent contradictions and absurdities.

Clearly, the authors we have looked at did not believe Scripture to be divinely inspired *because* they deemed it obviously coherent and true; nor did they postpone belief until it could be shown to be so. They had met Alan on the steps. They knew God's voice in Scripture. In that assurance,

Luther, for one, could hardly be bothered to linger over the difficulties; he had more pressing business to attend to. On the other hand, Chrysostom and Aquinas, confident that any problem in Scripture is soluble, never missed an opportunity to illustrate the point in practice. That quite different ways of dealing with apparent difficulties were proposed by our various authors is due, in part at least, to different suppositions of what must be true of a text authored by human beings through which God speaks.

Among premodern interpreters, a conviction that God speaks through Scripture was generally combined with full awareness that its texts were written by human authors who brought to the task their own distinctive styles. At times, infelicities of style were pointed out, and judgments on authorship could be made on the basis of stylistic considerations. Furthermore, humans were allowed a role in the *content* of Scripture. Chrysostom noted Luke's dependence on eyewitnesses. Augustine repeatedly explained the different order of events in the Gospels as reflecting the order in which those events were recalled by the authors. Luther and Calvin suspected that Moses drew on oral traditions handed down from the patriarchs (or even from Adam) in writing his narrative. Luther noted how one Old Testament prophet borrowed words from another, and realized that neither Solomon nor certain prophets actually wrote the books attributed to them; their words were compiled by others. Calvin added that someone other than the psalmists must have been responsible for compiling the psalms into a book.

For these premodern interpreters, then, the authors of Scripture, all in their own styles, wrote material that they frequently (though not always) acquired by normal human means. Yet they insisted that Scripture's authors were so "moved" and "inspired" by God's Spirit as they wrote that their words were at the same time their own and those of God (cf. 2 Pet. 1:21; 2 Tim. 3:16). Therefore, when the living God addresses believers of subsequent ages with his living word, he does so through words he inspired long ago. The word of God so written rewards careful study: all these interpreters were serious students of Scripture. But their study operated within the framework of convictions that they believed followed from the divine role in its composition: what Scripture says throughout must be true, unified, and profitable.

Even within that framework, quite different procedures were adopted in dealing with the Bible's difficulties. Origen actually allowed for a good deal of *literal* falsehood in Scripture, though no *errors:* where the surface meaning of the text is untrue, the deliberate point being made by God's Spirit is that truth must be sought at a deeper level. Yet the allegorical interpretation of Scripture was, for Origen, much more than a way of dealing with difficult texts; that Scripture everywhere rewards such a reading, that it conveys truth at multiple levels, was for Origen precisely a mark of its divine inspiration.

Origen's pursuit of allegorical interpretations was largely taken up by Christian readers for a thousand years and more, though generally with less willingness to admit untruth at the literal level. (Error remained inconceivable.) On the one hand, even a reader as commonsensical in his approach to the text as John Wesley can claim, with Origen and his heirs, that any text whose plain sense yields an absurdity must be differently construed. On the other hand, even a reader as given to allegory as Augustine can write an extensive treatise harmonizing the accounts of the four Gospels.

Typically, harmonizing — at the literal level — texts that appear to contradict each other is a greater concern for those resistant to allegory (such as Chrysostom) than for those (such as Augustine) who, if all else failed, could always resort to "spiritual" interpretation. Even among harmonizers, however, there has always been diversity in the amount of variation deemed tolerable in a book inspired by God. Neither Augustine nor Calvin required wooden agreement between texts (though they wrote in clear awareness of others who did). Where the substance of different accounts is the same, variations in wording, chronology, or other details are generally dismissed as immaterial. If a centurion is said to address Jesus in person in one Gospel, through intermediaries in another, the former account merely abbreviates the latter. If the voice from heaven at Jesus' baptism is reported as saying "You are my beloved Son" in one account, "This is my beloved Son" in another, the latter version has been reworked to avoid a possible misunderstanding of the former. The basic harmony of the accounts can be assumed, but the point they are making does not require pedantic precision.

Elsewhere, too, we have seen abundant allowance being granted the divinely inspired text for rhetorical devices, hyperbole, approximation, and the like. In general, then, we are not to expect of the biblical writers greater precision than their purpose in writing required: the text may not be "concerned with minutiae" (so Aquinas).[7]

---

7. Calvin can even allow that there are errors in the texts of Matt. 27:9 and Acts 7:16 without making anything of the observation or feeling a need to account for how the errors got there. That Scripture's truth was not seriously contested in his day may have contributed to his indifference; more crucially, such was the strength of Calvin's conviction that Scripture is God's word that it required no explanation for apparent difficulties. No such messiness

Of greater significance because of its theological weight is the concept of divine accommodation. The principle is acknowledged by all: the God who is beyond our understanding must, in communicating with mortals, limit himself to ways of speaking that we can comprehend. Origen speaks of God's "pretending"; Calvin, of the divine "lisp." Scripture's anthropomorphic ways of speaking of God (his eyes, ears, and arm; his anger, inquiring, changing his mind, etc.) provide the most obvious examples. But some, particularly Chrysostom and Calvin, apply the principle much more broadly.

They see it at work, for example, in texts content to communicate a *measure* of truth to those who, because they lived at an early stage in the progressive history of revelation, were incapable of receiving a fuller statement.[8] God does not really desire worship confined to a physical temple, with animal sacrifices, rites of purification, and the like; such, nonetheless, was the worship God demanded of a people not yet ready for spiritual worship. The material blessings promised for obedience to God's commands in the Old Testament foreshadowed the spiritual blessings offered in the New; but God wisely began with what people would more readily understand.[9] The psalmists could be allowed, as believers now are not, to hate their enemies: the subtle distinction between an appropriate attitude toward *ungodliness* and an appropriate attitude toward the *ungodly* could wait until abhorrence of sin had taken root.[10] That God is *one* needed to be established (in the Old Testament) before the distinctive activity of each

---

could be left undisturbed in the world of Wesley's well-ordered, "reasonable" faith: "Will not the allowing there is *any error* in Scripture shake the authority of the whole?" (*Appeals*, 504).

8. At the time of Moses, "the existing age of the Church was so puerile, that it was unable to receive higher instruction.... They who have an aversion to this simplicity, must of necessity condemn the whole economy of God in governing the Church" (Calvin, *Com. Gen.*, on Gen. 3:1).

9. For the same reason, Calvin believes, the prophets frequently spoke of material blessings as marking the return of God's favor to his people. That such promises, understood literally, went (largely) unfulfilled is an indication that they must be interpreted spiritually. Calvin's understanding here has abundant precedent in patristic writings.

10. Thus Chrysostom. In the premodern period, these texts were more commonly treated allegorically, as were the stories of Israel's wars: the psalmists' and Israel's foes stand for the sins that believers must oppose "to the death." Dual constraints are at work in both Chrysostom's and the allegorical interpretations of these OT texts. As part of God's word, they cannot be dismissed; yet they cannot, in any straightforward way, provide a model for Christian behavior in the light of Jesus' words enjoining love for one's enemies (Matt. 5:43-48). It is safe to say that the last two thousand years would have looked very different if all those who name the name of Christ had read Scripture (and led their lives) under the same *dual* constraints.

"person" in the Trinity could be pointed out (in the New). Jesus could hardly speak openly of his divine nature to people who had no grasp of his divine mission.

Chrysostom and Calvin (among others) thus believed that God accommodated revealed truth to the capacities of its first hearers. Readers aware of this divine practice will avoid the error of taking each individual statement in Scripture as an expression of timeless truth, or each injunction in Scripture as applicable to anyone living anywhere at any time. To understand the nature, purposes, and will of God, we must take the whole testimony of Scripture into account.

Augustine applied the principle of accommodation when Scripture contradicted science as he understood it. To insist on the literal truth of such texts was to expose the Bible to the ridicule of informed nonbelievers (*Lit. Gen.* 1.39). It was not the purpose of the Spirit of God who inspired Scripture to teach people about things that "contribute nothing to their salvation" (*Lit. Gen.* 2.20). The concern of the creation account in Genesis is "to suggest sublime things to lowly people in a lowly manner" (*Unfin. Gen.* 3.8). Aquinas followed suit: Moses, in Genesis, "condescends to popular ignorance," describing the heavens as they appear to our senses rather than as they are in reality (*ST* 1.68.3; 1.70.1 ad 3). Luther, too, noted that Moses wrote for the uneducated, using language other than that of the astronomer (*Works* 1.19, 43, 47-49). Calvin is most emphatic: Scripture, "the book of the unlearned," speaks in a "popular" way "suited to the lowest apprehension." To insist on the scientific accuracy of what Moses writes is to mistake his point no less than if one were to dismiss Genesis as a product of ignorance. Those who would learn astronomy (and there is much to be gained by doing so) need to look elsewhere than Scripture. As teacher of "the unlearned and rude," Moses necessarily accommodates what he writes to their understanding.[11] Galileo would make the same point, though citing Calvin would not have suited his purpose.[12]

There is thus a good deal of diversity in the study of Scripture even when it is conducted within boundaries set by a conviction that its words are divine as well as human, and hence true, coherent, and profitable. Such study, pursued by all the premodern interpreters we have looked at, is carried on to this day by hosts of thoughtful believers and scholars. Though many of the questions they bring to Scripture and the answers they arrive at are identical with those of scholars who read the Bible as they would any

---

11. See the section entitled "The Divine Lisp" in Chapter 8 above.
12. Galileo, *Letter,* 181-93.

other book, others, necessarily, are not.[13] Most significantly, our premodern interpreters and their more recent and contemporary counterparts depart from purely historical students of the Bible in affirming its capacity to convey the living word of God to its attentive readers.

Among the interpreters we have investigated, Friedrich Schleiermacher marks the beginning of an approach to Scripture that makes a self-conscious effort to allow space for both the work of the historical critic and the reading of the believer who finds God's living word in Scripture. In identifying the essence of faith with religious feeling, Schleiermacher positions himself to suggest that the critical scholar might well find factual errors in Scripture without diminishing the irreducible significance of Scripture as the purest expression of Christian faith. As a historical record, the text may not be wholly accurate (perhaps there was not a mass slaughter of infants in Bethlehem shortly after Christ's birth); yet, as an expression of religious feeling, the text nonetheless mediates Christ's presence to the contemporary believer. It is "inspired" in the sense that it was written under the impulse that the apostles received from Christ's work, which served to purify the religious feelings that they express. It is sufficient because, in mediating the presence of Christ, it is able to lead believers "into all truth" (*CF,* 606). Its authority is confined to the church because it is derived from Scripture's place as a peerless expression of the church's faith, not from suppositions about its universal significance as a text that speaks all truth on all subjects. Still, within the church, the discovery that it might not present a completely factual account of ancient history does not detract from its place as the norm of the church's teaching.

Karl Barth follows Schleiermacher in presenting a theology of Scripture in which historical criticism and faithful reading may coexist without coming into conflict. He, too, supposes that the essential subject matter of the text stands at one remove from historical details; hence, historical criticism may carry out its work without threatening the reading of faith. Barth departs from Schleiermacher, however, in seeing Scripture's essential subject matter not as a peculiarly Christian form of religious experience, but as the sovereign activity of God. Since that activity is wholly discontinuous with all human speaking and doing, it evades historical description; as a result, at important points, details in the biblical narrative

---

13. The difference is, of course, most evident in the understanding of texts that speak of the miraculous: the believer sees no reason to discount, the critic no reason to allow, the claim that God has so intervened in history. Conversely, critics exploit the tensions in Scripture that believers are wont to harmonize.

are best understood as poetic and imaginative attempts to point toward a "non-historical history"; that is, to real events in time and space with no analogy in the nexus of events that make up human history. The writers of Scripture serve to *witness* to this divine activity.[14] Though their words issue from the speaking of God's Spirit "there and then," they remain creaturely realities that cannot simply be identified with the Word of God. Yet they are accompanied by the promise that the Spirit who spoke "there and then" to the prophets and apostles will, through their words, speak "here and now" as well: in this way Scripture *becomes* the Word of God. For Barth, the doctrine of Scripture's inspiration must be understood to include both moments of this divine speaking.

Finally, it is noteworthy how few of the authors we have examined betray the least concern over problems related to the biblical text itself. They knew well enough that the inspired text was written in Hebrew and Greek. Origen made the effort to learn Hebrew. Augustine gave token acknowledgment to the importance of doing so without taking his own advice. Luther, Calvin, and their heirs did, and they thought, as a general rule, that church leaders should know the biblical languages. Yet, even where it is granted that something is lost when the Bible is read in translation, the loss is seldom thought to be particularly harmful;[15] and most, even great theologians, were content with the translations before them. Moreover, in varying degrees, our authors were aware that different biblical manuscripts contained different readings. Only Origen and Bengel thought the subject worth much investigation; only Bengel found the issue troubling, and study quickly eased *his* concerns. The point, presumably, is similar to that proposed above: people who heard the voice of God through the texts that lay before them were little concerned with the intricacies of textual history.

Keys to Interpreting Scripture

If the Bible is like no other book, where, we may wonder, are we to look for guidance in interpreting it? The answer we are repeatedly given (even

---

14. John the Baptist was a "witness" to the light, but not himself the light (John 1:6-8); similarly, for Barth, Scripture is a witness to divine revelation though not itself that revelation. Revelation provides "the basis, object and content" of Scripture's witness (*CD* I.2, 463), and it is through Scripture's witness that God gives himself to be known.

15. Perhaps the most famous example to the contrary is Luther's insistence that the church's practice of penance was wrongly based on the Latin version of Matt. 4:17; what Matthew wrote cannot be so construed. See Bainton, *Life,* 67.

by those who wrote a book on the subject) is that the Bible itself reveals how it is to be interpreted.

In interpreting Scripture allegorically, Origen claimed that he was merely following the example of the apostle Paul (e.g., 1 Cor. 9:9-10; 10:4; Gal. 4:21-31; Eph. 5:31-32). But he also believed that he was heeding the message of the Holy Spirit conveyed through what he saw as an absence of truth, harmony, or edification at the literal level of many texts. In the eyes of critics, allegorical interpretation was purely arbitrary, the bright ideas of the interpreter being served up as the meaning of the text. What God has to say, he says plainly and simply, and we should be content with that. Origen, convinced that the Holy Spirit intended every text in Scripture to have allegorical significance, devoted all his resources and every effort to discovering what, in each case, that significance might be.

Augustine found the key to interpreting Scripture in the words of Jesus: If "all the Law and the Prophets depend on" the commandments to love God and our neighbor, then any interpretation of a passage in Scripture that does not promote such love is a misinterpretation (Matt. 22:37-38; cf. 1 Tim. 1:5, which Augustine quoted to similar effect).

Calvin is among the many who have cited 2 Timothy 3:16-17 as a guide in interpreting Scripture: since "all Scripture is . . . *profitable,*" it must be read for what is conducive to godliness. God did not give us the Bible to satisfy curiosity on matters indifferent to our salvation and edification. Nor did he mean for Scripture to serve as a basis for ostentatious displays of biblical knowledge or fanciful speculation on matters of no consequence. "Whenever ingenious trifles of that kind are introduced, they should be warded off with this phrase as with a shield, 'Scripture is profitable'" (*Com. 2 Tim.,* on 3:16).

Already Irenaeus insisted in his time that every *part* of Scripture must be interpreted in accordance with Scripture's "hypothesis," its message *as a whole.* Augustine conceded that, taken by itself, the wording of individual verses might yield a meaning inconsistent with that message; but any such interpretation is necessarily false. For a summary of Scripture's message as a whole, the early church fathers looked to the "rule of the truth," or "rule of faith," a primitive version of the Apostles' Creed. Later the Pietists, though suspicious of any formulation of faith not found in Scripture itself, affirmed the same principle: the "universal agreement of the inspired writers" provides the framework within which each part of Scripture must be read.

Luther found the key to interpreting Scripture in the distinction, derived from his reading of Paul, between "law" and "gospel": between what God asks of us and what God does for us or gives us. The demands of Scripture serve a divine function both in driving sinners to seek God's grace in Christ and in guiding the grateful lives of believers. But the reader of Scripture must carefully distinguish such *demands* from texts that speak of justification freely given to those who respond in faith to the gospel. There is a time for law and a time for gospel, but neither in life nor in the interpretation of Scripture are the two to be confused.

Perhaps the most important guideline for the Christian interpretation of Scripture is provided by the words of Christ himself: Scripture "bears witness" to him (John 5:39; cf. Luke 24:27, 44). That the New Testament does so is self-evident. Moreover, in its allusions and quotations, the New Testament offers christological readings of numerous Old Testament passages; these include both texts understood as messianic prophecies and those portraying aspects of Israel's cult that the New Testament (the letter to the Hebrews in particular) sees as foreshadowing Christ's salvific work (cf. 1 Cor. 5:7; Col. 2:16-17). Where the New Testament interprets particular Old Testament texts, its way of reading them naturally became the common starting point for later Christian exegetes. But when the latter came to the vast stretches of Old Testament Scripture not mentioned in the New, they pursued quite different paths.

In a broad sense, any follower of Christ who rejects divisions (like those of Marcion and the gnostics) between the Old Testament and the New will agree that the work of Christ, described in the New Testament, represents the intended climax of the divine plan and activity reflected in the Old.[16] The "big picture" is thus the same for all. Questions and disputes arise over particular texts. On the one hand, there are those — Irenaeus and Luther are good examples — who find Christ in the Old Testament wherever the wording of a text can be so construed, even where the construction does violence to the train of thought in the immediate context. On the other hand, there are those — the Antiochenes and Calvin are the obvious examples — whose insistence on reading Scripture historically and contextually, and whose awareness of the ridicule that outsiders heaped on the more venturesome christological interpretations, led them to considerably reduce the stock of Old Testament texts thought to prophesy Christ.

Genesis 3:15 is a good example of a text over which disputes among

16. For his own reasons (the "God-consciousness" found in Judaism and conveyed by the Old Testament differs from that of Christianity conveyed by the New), Schleiermacher, too, claims that the Old Testament books do not "share the normative dignity and inspiration of the New" (*CF*, 608). More traditionally, the Old Testament is distinguished from the New because it reveals the same content in a veiled form.

Christian interpreters have arisen. With a little good will and a conviction that the Old Testament everywhere bears witness to Christ, "the seed of the woman" has often been seen as referring to Christ. Calvin, however, denied the singular referent, noting that the collective noun "seed" speaks more naturally of the human race in general. Those looking everywhere for prophecies of Christ have found references to the crucifixion in Deuteronomy 28:66 (the Septuagint reads "Your life shall be *hanging* before your eyes"),[17] Isaiah 9:6 ("the government was *upon his shoulder*"),[18] and Isaiah 65:2 ("I *stretched out my hands* all day long to a disobedient and contrary people").[19] Such interpretations are typically rejected by those who read Scripture under historical[20] and contextual[21] constraints. In certain passages, Calvin (echoing the Antiochenes) adopted a mediating position: the initial and primary referent of a passage is to some other, but that other serves as a "type" of Christ. In this way, Calvin could allow that not everything said in the passage applied to Christ (naturally enough, since no type corresponds to that of which it is a type in *every* respect); at the same time, he noted that such passages often speak of their original referent in hyperbolic ways that apply more truly to Christ (thus, e.g., Ps. 2 and Ps. 45).

That Scripture — in *both* its Testaments — bears witness to Christ is fundamental to Barth's understanding of its nature and proper interpretation. As a result, he finds misguided any understanding of inspiration that permits parts of the text to be understood as freestanding elements that have significance in themselves apart from reference to Christ. A "peripheral biblicism" of this kind reduces "the question of Jesus" to "one amongst others," and Scripture as a whole to "a repository of all sorts and degrees of pious knowledge" that may be read as any other text is read (*CD* III.1, 24; IV.1, 368). Properly understood, the inspiration of Scripture itself is an expression of the prophetic character of Christ's work, bearing witness to himself. In writing Scripture, the prophets and apostles were "formed and guided" by Christ, God's Word; readers of Scripture, too, are enlightened by the risen Christ, whose life is light (*CD* IV.3, 113-14, 46).

Finally, Augustine and Bonhoeffer are perhaps the finest representa-

---

17. The verse in context speaks of the judgment that will befall disobedient Israel.

18. The passage speaks of the everlasting reign of a child to be born.

19. In the context, God is speaking of his readiness to show mercy to his rebellious people.

20. I.e., the text cannot mean something so remote from what its original hearers would have understood it to mean; it had to make sense to them.

21. I.e., the text cannot mean something that so drastically interrupts the surrounding train of thought.

tives of the venerable tradition that reads the Psalms as prayers of Christ. That Christ himself prayed the first-person words of Psalm 22:1 (Mark 15:34) and 31:5 (Luke 23:46) invites such an interpretation. Its appropriateness is underscored by the conviction that Christ alone can properly speak as the *righteous* sufferer whose voice is heard in a host of psalms. When the psalmists confess and lament their sins, Augustine detects the voice of Christ identifying with his people. Bonhoeffer notes that Christ alone can rightly call down God's judgment on sinners (as a number of psalms do), in that he took that judgment on himself. For Bonhoeffer, too, the mystery of the presence, in God's word, of the very human prayers of the Psalms is resolved when the latter are ascribed to the God-man, Jesus Christ.

The Interpreter of Scripture

When the eternal Word of God "became flesh," it was inevitable that the man Jesus would be encountered, observed, and known in varying degrees by many who would fail to perceive his divinity. Failure was assured among the ill-willed, some of whom made a point of attending to all he said and did; yet many a sympathizer fared no better. Imagine, for example, a kindly soul who, upon learning that Jesus would be charged with inciting rebellion, carefully noted every place he went, every contact he made, and every word he spoke in order to prove his innocence. Such observation, though thorough and well meant, would not uncover the mystery of Christ's person. We can be certain, moreover, that our sympathizer's detailed notebooks would have made no impact on those bent on destroying Jesus. Most importantly, Jesus was looking for disciples, not defenders.

It is a truism of Christian tradition that the word of God recorded in a book is read, studied, even learned by many who fail to hear its divine voice. As noted above, such failure is assured where there is a patent unwillingness to meet God. Barth claims that, for the historical critic, fixated on grammatical or historical questions, the text as a whole remains unintelligible, its essential subject matter foreign, its voice unheard. The results of historical-critical scholarship are of strictly penultimate significance: such scholarship can speak of the old world of human being and doing, but not of the new world of God. Because obedience is the proper response to the revelation of God, responsible exegesis of Scripture has its basis not in the norms of critical inquiry but in "the freely performed act of subordinating all human concepts, ideas and convictions to the witness of revelation supplied to us in Scripture" (*CD* I.2, 715). The interpretation of Scripture reaches its intended goal only when the text not merely "master[s] our thinking about it, but our thinking and life generally, and our whole existence" (*CD* I.2, 737).

The type of historical criticism to which Barth was responding was unknown to most of those we have looked at in this study.[22] But premodern interpreters, too, knew that there are ways of studying Scripture more likely to drown out than enhance the hearing of the Word within the words.

The Bible refers to many historical events and figures, to places on earth and stars in heaven, to plants, animals, and many types of precious stones. Origen commends learning all one can about all these things, from whatever source, in order to better understand the scriptural references. At the same time, he warns against becoming preoccupied with such study. Augustine repeated the point. But it is in the writings of the Pietists — who were by no means opposed to intellectual labor devoted to understanding the text — that the perils of a purely academic study of Scripture become a central theme. Repeatedly, they urge students of Scripture to recall the purpose for which Scripture was given: it is (in their frequently used metaphor) a personal letter from God, through which we are to learn of him and his will. For that end, scholarship is not essential, and from that end, scholarship is frequently a distraction — a "vain, unprofitable curiosity."

> There is no bodily or mental labour which may not be made injurious to our secret and perpetual communion with God. Even scriptural researches may, without needful discretion, very easily occasion in learned men an indifference to true godliness, instead of nourishing any desire for it, or delight in it.[23]

If the problem for some is that they fail to give the Bible the right *kind* of attention, others never pay the Bible much attention at all. Origen and Chrysostom frequently express their utter exasperation at the indifference shown God's word by churchgoers who (Chrysostom knows) can sit enthralled for hours at the theater, eagerly devour every tidbit of news

---

22. Such criticism was known to Kierkegaard, but largely ignored. For Kierkegaard, labored reading of Scripture in its original languages, concern over variants in the biblical manuscripts, troubling oneself over the historicity or authenticity of biblical writings: all *such* occupation with the word of God, however pious its appearance, readily lends itself to a cover for the natural human reluctance to encounter God himself. Bonhoeffer, like Barth, was open, in principle, to the results of historical-critical scholarship while emphasizing its inadequacy for the Christian reading of Scripture and abandoning it in practice.

23. Burk, *Memoir*, 219. The quotation is from Bengel.

about local charioteers, and devote endless concern to worldly affairs. Bonhoeffer laments that the lives of many are so consumed with work and entertainment that God's word is never allowed the time to penetrate and control their thoughts. Like Kierkegaard, he speaks of the importance of surrounding ourselves with silence so that we may, without distraction, attend to God's word. Luther notes that "Scripture is the stone of offense and rock of scandal for those who are in a hurry" (*Works,* 10.19).

Yet even sympathetic, careful attention to Scripture may fall short of the *engagement* with the text that our authors believe God's word requires. As readers of Scripture, we are to ask not simply what the text is saying, or even what God might be saying through the text; the crucial issue is what God is saying to *us*. The realization of *that* question's importance transformed Bonhoeffer's reading of the Bible. Fear of that question is what, according to Kierkegaard, keeps readers from wanting to be really "alone" with God's word. John Wesley, who had long believed in the death of Christ for sinners, found new life in the assurance (conveyed through Paul's letter to the Romans) that Christ "had taken away *my* sins, even *mine,* and saved *me* from the law of sin and death" (*JD* 1.250). Here, at least, he was at one with John Calvin: "It is not enough to have the Word in its general sense, unless we know it is meant for ourselves" (*Com. Acts,* on 2:39).

Augustine noted how personal experience of God's mercy made reading the Psalms more delightful. "It would be strange if anyone who had not personally learned the truth of what the psalm proclaims were able to perceive its sweetness" (*Exp. Ps.* 106.1). Above all, it was Luther who emphasized the importance of experience for understanding Scripture. Only those who themselves have cried to God "out of the depths" can know of what Psalm 130 is speaking. The simple words "Our Father, who art in heaven" become meaningful when one has suffered adversity at his hands. Indeed, "he who has had no experience of suffering or death cannot at all understand the comfort of the Bible" (*CS* 3.2.43-44).[24] As for the stories of Scripture, Luther lived them as he read them. With Noah, Abraham, Joseph, and others, he clung to God's promises when God himself seemed to have forgotten both them and him. With Noah, Abraham, Joseph, and others, he found that the God who kills is the God who makes alive.

At the heart of the Christian reading of Scripture, then, is the sense that God has spoken, and still speaks, through its texts and that no interest in the Bible *as such* should be allowed to replace the humble, engaged

---

24. Luther reminds us that words cannot be understood by those ignorant of the *subject* of which they speak (*Works* 4.13; cf. 1.264; 54.476).

reading that is attentive to God's voice. As noted in Chapter 1, the biblical texts themselves call for precisely this kind of reading. Not all who scan its pages attempt to measure up to its demands; in this book, we have looked at a few who did. At the same time, the Christian reading of Scripture has always been accompanied by an awareness that, apart from divine illumination, the words of the text remain, for the reader, mere words on a page. Hence, as we have invariably been reminded, a proper approach to Scripture must begin with prayer.

> Break Thou the bread of life, dear Lord, to me,
> As Thou didst break the loaves beside the sea;
> *Beyond the sacred page* I seek Thee, Lord;
> My spirit pants for Thee, O living Word.
>
> Oh, send Thy Spirit, Lord, now unto me,
> That He may touch my eyes and make me see;
> Show me the truth concealed within Thy Word,
> And in Thy Book revealed I see the Lord.[25]

25. Verses of a hymn by Mary A. Lathbury and Alexander Groves; italics added.

Bibliography

Allison, Dale C., Jr.

History　　　　*Constructing Jesus: Memory, Imagination, and History.* Grand
Rapids: Baker Academic, 2010.

Moses　　　　*The New Moses: A Matthean Typology.* Minneapolis: Fortress,
1993.

Althaus, Paul

Theology　　　*The Theology of Martin Luther.* Philadelphia: Fortress, 1966.

Anderson, Paul N., Felix Just, and Tom Thatcher, eds.

History　　　　*John, Jesus, and History.* Vols. 1 and 2. Atlanta: Society of Biblical
Literature, 2007-2009.

Aquinas, Thomas

Catena Aurea　*Catena Aurea.* Vols. 1-8. Translated by John Henry Newman. New
York: Cosimo, 2007.

Com. 1/2 Cor.　*Commentary on the Letters of Saint Paul to the Corinthians.* Translated by Fabian R. Larcher, Beth Mortensen, Daniel Keating.
Lander, WY: Aquinas Institute for the Study of Sacred Doctrine,
2012.

Com. Gal./Eph.　*Commentary on the Letters of Saint Paul to the Galatians and
Ephesians.* Translated by Fabian R. Larcher and Matthew Lamb.
Lander, WY: Aquinas Institute for the Study of Sacred Doctrine,
2012.

Com. Heb.　　*Commentary on the Letter of Saint Paul to the Hebrews.* Translated by Fabian R. Larcher. Lander, WY: Aquinas Institute for
the Study of Sacred Doctrine, 2012.

Com. Job　　*The Literal Exposition on Job: A Scriptural Commentary Concerning Providence.* Translated by Anthony Damico. Atlanta: Scholars
Press, 1989.

Com. John　　*Commentary on the Gospel of John.* Vols. 1-3. Translated by Fabian

Larcher and James A. Weisheipl. Washington, DC: Catholic University of America Press, 2010.

Com. Matt.   *Commentary on the Gospel of St. Matthew.* Translated by Paul M. Kimball. Dolorosa, 2012.

Com. Phil./Col./   *Commentary on the Letters of Saint Paul to the Philippians, Colos-*
1/2 Thess./1/2 Tim./   *sians, Thessalonians, Timothy, Titus, and Philemon.* Translated by
Titus/Philem.   Fabian R. Larcher. Lander, WY: Aquinas Institute for the Study of Sacred Doctrine, 2012.

Com. Psalms   *Commentary on the Psalms.* Posted at http://www.desales.edu/.

Com. Rom.   *Commentary on the Letter of Saint Paul to the Romans.* Translated by Fabian R. Larcher. Lander, WY: Aquinas Institute for the Study of Sacred Doctrine, 2012.

Creed   *The Apostles' Creed.* In *The Catechetical Instructions of St. Thomas Aquinas,* translated by Joseph B. Collins, 3-66. New York: Wagner, 1939.

"Inaug. Serm."   "The Inaugural Sermons (1256)." In *Thomas Aquinas: Selected Writings,* edited and translated by Ralph McInerny, 5-17. London: Penguin, 1998.

Power   *On the Power of God (Quaestiones Disputatae de Potentia Dei).* Vols. 1-3. Translated by the English Dominican Fathers. London: Burns, Oates and Washbourne, 1932-1934.

SCG   *On the Truth of the Catholic Faith: Summa Contra Gentiles.* Vols. 1-5. Garden City, NY: Doubleday, 1955-1957.

ST   *Summa Theologica.* Vols. 1-5. Translated by the Fathers of the English Dominican Province. New York: Benziger Brothers, 1948.

Truth   *The Disputed Questions on Truth.* Vols. 1-3. Chicago: Regnery, 1952-1954.

Augustine

Adimantus   *Answer to Adimantus, a Disciple of Mani.* In *The Manichean Debate.* Translated by Roland Teske. Works of Saint Augustine I.19. Hyde Park, NY: New City Press, 2006.

Advan. Believing   *The Advantage of Believing.* Translated by Ray Kearney. In *On Christian Belief.* Works of Saint Augustine I.8. Hyde Park, NY: New City Press, 2005.

Against Lying   *Against Lying.* In *Treatises on Various Subjects.* Translated by Harold B. Jaffee. Fathers of the Church 16. New York: Fathers of the Church, 1952.

Agreement   *Agreement among the Evangelists.* In *New Testament I and II.* Translated by Kim Paffenroth. Works of Saint Augustine I/15 and I/16. Hyde Park, NY: New City Press, 2014.

Answer to Enemy   *Answer to an Enemy of the Law and the Prophets.* In *Arianism and Other Heresies.* Translated by Roland J. Teske. Works of Saint Augustine I.18. Hyde Park, NY: New City Press, 2007.

City of God   *The City of God.* Translated by William Babcock. Works of Saint Augustine I.6-7. Hyde Park, NY: New City Press, 2012-2013.

Com. Gal.   *Commentary on Galatians.* In Eric Plumer, *Augustine's Commentary on Galatians: Introduction, Text, Translation, and Notes.* Oxford: Oxford University Press, 2003.

Conf.   *The Confessions.* Translated by Maria Boulding. Works of Saint Augustine I.1. Hyde Park, NY: New City Press, 2001 (1997).

Creed   *Faith and the Creed.* Translated by Michael G. Campbell. In *On Christian Belief.* Works of Saint Augustine I.8. Hyde Park, NY: New City Press, 2005.

Ench.   *Enchiridion.* Translated by Bruce Harbert. In *On Christian Belief.* Works of Saint Augustine I.8. Hyde Park, NY: New City Press, 2005.

Exp. Ps.   *Expositions on the Psalms.* Translated by Maria Boulding. Works of Saint Augustine III.15-20. Hyde Park, NY: New City Press, 2000-2004.

Faustus   *Answer to Faustus, a Manichean.* Translated by Roland Teske. Works of Saint Augustine I.20. Hyde Park, NY: New City Press, 2007.

Gen.   *On Genesis: A Refutation of the Manichees.* In *On Genesis.* Translated by Edmund Hill. Works of Saint Augustine I.13. Hyde Park, NY: New City Press, 2002.

Hom. 1 John   *Homilies on the First Epistle of John.* Translated by Boniface Ramsey. Works of Saint Augustine I.14. Hyde Park, NY: New City Press, 2008.

Instruct. Beg.   *Instructing Beginners in Faith.* Translated by Raymond Canning. Works of Saint Augustine. Hyde Park, NY: New City Press, 2006.

Letters   *Letters.* Translated by Roland Teske. Works of Saint Augustine II.1-4. Hyde Park, NY: New City Press, 2001-2005.

Lit. Gen.   *The Literal Meaning of Genesis.* In *On Genesis.* Translated by Edmund Hill. Works of Saint Augustine I.13. Hyde Park, NY: New City Press, 2002.

Lying   *Lying.* In *Treatises on Various Subjects.* Translated by Sister Mary Sarah Muldowney. Fathers of the Church 16. New York: Fathers of the Church, 1952.

Orosius   *To Orosius in Refutation of the Priscillianists and Origenists.* In *Arianism and Other Heresies.* Translated by Roland J. Teske. Works of Saint Augustine I.18. Hyde Park, NY: New City Press, 2007.

Questions   *Miscellany of Eighty-Three Questions.* In *Responses to Miscellaneous Questions.* Translated by Boniface Ramsey. Works of Saint Augustine I.12. Hyde Park, NY: New City Press, 2008.

Revisions   *Revisions.* Translated by Boniface Ramsey. Works of Saint Augustine I.2. Hyde Park, NY: New City Press, 2010.

Sermons   *Sermons.* Translated by Edmund Hill. Works of Saint Augustine III.1-11. Brooklyn/Hyde Park/New Rochelle, NY: New City Press, 1990-1997.

Simplician   *Miscellany of Questions in Response to Simplician.* In *Responses to Miscellaneous Questions.* Translated by Boniface Ramsey. Works of Saint Augustine I.12. Hyde Park, NY: New City Press, 2008.

Spirit and Letter *The Spirit and the Letter.* In *Answer to the Pelagians I.* Translated by Roland J. Teske. Works of Saint Augustine I.23. Hyde Park, NY: New City Press, 1997.

Teacher   *Concerning the Teacher.* In *Concerning the Teacher and On the Immortality of the Soul.* Translated by George G. Leckie. New York: Appleton-Century-Crofts, 1938.

Teaching Christianity *Teaching Christianity.* Translated by Edmund Hill. Works of Saint Augustine I.11. Hyde Park, NY: New City Press, 1996.

Tract. John   *Tractates on the Gospel of John.* Translated by John W. Rettig. Fathers of the Church 78, 79, 88, 90, 92. Washington, DC: Catholic University of America Press, 1988-1995.

Trin.   *The Trinity.* Translated by Edmund Hill. Works of Saint Augustine I.5. Brooklyn: New City Press, 1991.

Unfin. Gen.   *Unfinished Literal Commentary on Genesis.* In *On Genesis.* Translated by Edmund Hill. Works of Saint Augustine I.13. Hyde Park, NY: New City Press, 2002.

Aune, David E.
Environment   *The New Testament in Its Literary Environment.* Philadelphia: Westminster, 1987.

Babcock, William S.
"Interpretation" "Augustine's Interpretation of Romans (AD 394-396)." *Augustinian Studies* 10 (1979): 55-74.

Baglow, Christopher T.
Approach   *"Modus et Forma": A New Approach to the Exegesis of Saint Thomas Aquinas with an Application to the* Lectura super Epistolam ad Ephesios. Rome: Editrice Pontificio Istituto Biblico, 2002.

Bainton, Roland H.
Life   *Here I Stand: A Life of Martin Luther.* New York: New American Library, 1977.

Baird, William
History   *History of New Testament Research.* Vols. 1-3. Minneapolis: Fortress, 1992-2013.

Baldwin, Joyce C.
Daniel   *Daniel: An Introduction and Commentary.* Downers Grove, IL: InterVarsity, 1978.

Bibliography

Barr, James

"Chronology"　　　"Luther and Biblical Chronology." *Bulletin of the John Rylands University Library of Manchester* 72 (1990): 51-67.

Barrett, C. K.

"Review"　　　Review of James D. G. Dunn, *Christology in the Making: An Inquiry into the Origins of the Doctrine of the Incarnation. Journal for the Study of the New Testament* 15 (1982): 113-15.

Barth, Karl

"Answers"　　　"Fifteen Answers to Professor von Harnack." In *Beginnings of Dialectic Theology,* vol. 1, edited by James M. Robinson, 167-70. Richmond, VA: John Knox, 1968.

CD　　　*Church Dogmatics.* Vols. 1-13. Edited by G. W. Bromiley and T. F. Torrance. Translated by G. W. Bromiley et al. Edinburgh: T. & T. Clark, 1936-1975.

EJ　　　*Erklärung des Johannes-Evangelium (Kapitel 1-8).* Zürich: Theologischer Verlag, 1976.

FT　　　*Final Testimonies.* Grand Rapids: Eerdmans, 1977.

Gespr. 1963　　　*Gespräche, 1963.* Zürich: Theologischer Verlag, 2005.

Gespr. 1964-1968　　　*Gespräche, 1964-1968.* Zürich: Theologischer Verlag, 1996.

"Hermann"　　　"The Principles of Dogmatics according to Wilhelm Hermann." In Barth, *Theology and Church: Shorter Writings 1920-1928,* 238-71. New York: Harper and Row, 1962.

Konf.　　　*Konfirmandenunterricht, 1909-1921.* Zürich: Theologischer Verlag, 1987.

"Letter"　　　"An Answer to Professor von Harnack's Open Letter." In *Beginnings of Dialectic Theology,* vol. 1, edited by James M. Robinson, 175-85. Richmond: John Knox, 1968.

"Need"　　　"The Need and Promise of Christian Proclamation, 1922." In Barth, *The Word of God and Theology,* translated by Amy Marga, 101-29. London: T. & T. Clark International, 2011.

"New World"　　　"The New World in the Bible, 1917." In Barth, *The Word of God and Theology,* translated by Amy Marga, 15-29. London: T. & T. Clark International, 2011.

"Preface 1"　　　"The Preface to the First Edition." In Barth, *The Epistle to the Romans,* 1-2. London: Oxford University Press, 1933.

"Preface 2"　　　"The Preface to the Second Edition." In Barth, *The Epistle to the Romans,* 2-15. London: Oxford University Press, 1933.

"Preface 3"　　　"The Preface to the Third Edition." In Barth, *The Epistle to the Romans,* 15-20. London: Oxford University Press, 1933.

Protestant Theology　　　*Protestant Theology in the Nineteenth Century.* Grand Rapids: Eerdmans, 2002.

"Questions"　　　"Biblical Questions, Insights, and Vistas, 1920." In Barth, *The*

	Word of God and Theology, translated by Amy Marga, 71-100. London: T. & T. Clark International, 2011.
Resurrection	*The Resurrection of the Dead.* Translated by H. J. Stenning. Eugene, OR: Wipf and Stock, 2003 (reprint).
"Righteousness"	"The Righteousness of God, 1916." In Barth, *The Word of God and Theology,* translated by Amy Marga, 1-13. London: T. & T. Clark International, 2011.
Romans	*The Epistle to the Romans.* London: Oxford University Press, 1933.
"Sketches"	"Autobiographical Sketches of Karl Barth." In *Karl Barth–Rudolf Bultmann Letters, 1922-1966,* 150-57. Grand Rapids: Eerdmans, 1981.
"Society"	"The Christian in Society, 1919." In Barth, *The Word of God and Theology,* translated by Amy Marga, 31-69. London: T. & T. Clark International, 2011.
"Theology"	"Karl Barth and Oscar Cullmann on Their Theological Vocation: On Systematic Theology." *Scottish Journal of Theology* 14 (1961): 225-33.
TJC	*The Theology of John Calvin.* Grand Rapids: Eerdmans, 1995.
TRC	*The Theology of the Reformed Confessions.* Louisville: Westminster John Knox, 2002.

Barthélemy, Dominique

Devanciers	*Les Devanciers d'Aquila.* Leiden: Brill, 1963.

Barton, John

Writings	*Holy Writings, Sacred Text: The Canon in Early Christianity.* Louisville: Westminster John Knox, 1997.

Bauckham, Richard

Eyewitnesses	*Jesus and the Eyewitnesses: The Gospels as Eyewitness Testimony.* Grand Rapids: Eerdmans, 2006.
"Gospels"	"For Whom Were Gospels Written?" In *The Gospels for All Christians: Rethinking the Gospel Audiences,* edited by Richard Bauckham, 9-48. Grand Rapids: Eerdmans, 1998.

Baur, Chrysostomus

Chrysostom	*John Chrysostom and His Time.* Vols. 1-2. London: Sands, 1959-1960.

Beale, G. K., and D. A. Carson

Commentary	*Commentary on the New Testament Use of the Old Testament.* Edited by G. K. Beale and D. A. Carson. Grand Rapids: Baker Academic, 2007.

Bengel, John Albert

Gnomon	*Gnomon of the New Testament.* Vols. 1-5. Eugene, OR: Wipf and Stock, 2004 (1877).

Bernard of Clairvaux
Song   *On the Song of Songs.* Vols. 1-4. Translated by Kilian Walsh and Irene M. Edmonds. Kalamazoo, MI: Cistercian, 1971-1980.

Bethge, Eberhard
Bonhoeffer   *Dietrich Bonhoeffer: A Biography.* Rev. ed. Minneapolis: Fortress, 2000.

Bingham, D. Jeffrey
"Irenaeus"   "Irenaeus of Lyons." In *The Routledge Companion to Early Christian Thought,* edited by D. Jeffrey Bingham, 137-53. London: Routledge, 2010.

Blacketer, Raymond A.
"Commentator"   "Calvin as Commentator on the Mosaic Harmony and Joshua." In *Calvin and the Bible,* edited by Donald K. McKim, 30-52. Cambridge: Cambridge University Press, 2006.

Blomberg, Craig
Reliability   *The Historical Reliability of John's Gospel: Issues and Commentary.* Downers Grove, IL: InterVarsity, 2001.

Bonhoeffer, Dietrich
Works   *Dietrich Bonhoeffer Works.* Vols. 1-17. Edited by Victoria J. Barnett and Barbara Wojhoski. Minneapolis: Fortress, 1996-2014.

Bonhoeffer, Dietrich, and Maria von Wedemeyer
Letters   *Love Letters from Cell 92: The Correspondence between Dietrich Bonhoeffer and Maria von Wedemeyer 1943-45.* Edited by Ruth-Alice von Bismarck and Ulrich Kabitz. Nashville: Abingdon, 1995.

Bonner, Gerald
"Augustine"   "Augustine as Biblical Scholar." In *The Cambridge History of the Bible,* vol. 1: *From the Beginnings to Jerome,* edited by P. R. Ackroyd and C. F. Evans, 541-63. Cambridge: Cambridge University Press, 1970.

Bornkamm, Günther
"Stilling"   "The Stilling of the Storm in Matthew." In *Tradition and Interpretation in Matthew,* edited by Günther Bornkamm, Gerhard Barth, and Heinz Joachim Held, 52-57. London: SCM, 1963.

Bornkamm, Heinrich
Luther   *Luther and the Old Testament.* Philadelphia: Fortress, 1969.

Boyle, John F.
"Scripture"   "St. Thomas Aquinas and Sacred Scripture." *Pro Ecclesia* 4 (1996): 92-104.

Breck, John

Power   *The Power of the Word in the Worshiping Church.* Crestwood, NY: St. Vladimir's Seminary Press, 1986.

Bright, Pamela

"Augustine"   "Augustine." In *Reading Romans through the Centuries: From the Early Church to Karl Barth,* edited by Jeffrey P. Greenman and Timothy Larsen, 59-80. Grand Rapids: Brazos, 2005.

Brock, S. P.

"Translating"   "Translating the Old Testament." In *It Is Written: Scripture Citing Scripture; Essays in Honour of Barnabas Lindars, SSF,* edited by D. A. Carson and H. G. M. Williamson, 87-98. Cambridge: Cambridge University Press, 1988.

Brown, Raymond E.

Birth   *The Birth of the Messiah: A Commentary on the Infancy Narratives in Matthew and Luke.* Garden City, NY: Doubleday, 1977.

Bruce, F. F.

Thessalonians   *1 & 2 Thessalonians.* Waco, TX: Word, 1982.

Burk, John C. F.

Memoir   *A Memoir of the Life and Writings of John Albert Bengel, Prelate in Würtemberg.* Eugene, OR: Wipf and Stock, 2005 (1837).

Burnett, Richard E.

Exegesis   *Karl Barth's Theological Exegesis: The Hermeneutical Principles of the* Römerbrief *Period.* Grand Rapids: Eerdmans, 2004.

Busch, Eberhard

Barth   *Karl Barth: His Life from Letters and Autobiographical Texts.* London: SCM, 1976.

Byrskog, Samuel

Story   *Story as History — History as Story: The Gospel Tradition in the Context of Ancient Oral History.* Tübingen: Mohr Siebeck, 2000.

Teacher   *Jesus the Only Teacher.* Stockholm: Almqvist and Wiksell International, 1994.

Calvin, John

Com. N.T.   *Calvin's New Testament Commentaries.* Edited by David W. Torrance and Thomas F. Torrance. Grand Rapids: Eerdmans, 1959-1972.

Com. O.T.   *Calvin's Commentaries.* 45 volumes. Edinburgh: Calvin Translation Society, 1844-1856. Reprinted in 23 volumes. Grand Rapids: Baker, 2009.

Inst.   *Institutes of the Christian Religion.* Vols. 1-2. Edited by John T.

McNeill. Translated by Ford Lewis Battles. Philadelphia: Westminster, 1960.

Campenhausen, Hans von

Fathers   *The Fathers of the Greek Church.* New York: Pantheon, 1959.

Formation   *The Formation of the Christian Bible.* Philadelphia: Fortress, 1972.

Carson, D. A., and H. G. M. Williamson

Scripture   *It Is Written: Scripture Citing Scripture; Essays in Honour of Barnabas Lindars, SSF.* Edited by D. A. Carson and H. G. M. Williamson. Cambridge: Cambridge University Press, 1988.

Childs, Brevard S.

"Exegesis"   "Toward Recovering Theological Exegesis." *Pro Ecclesia* 6 (1997): 16-26.

Chilton, Bruce, and Craig A. Evans

"Scriptures"   "Jesus and Israel's Scriptures." In *Studying the Historical Jesus: Evaluations of the State of Current Research,* edited by Bruce Chilton and Craig A. Evans, 281-335. Leiden: Brill, 1994.

Chrysostom, John

Com. 1/2 Cor.   *Commentary on the Epistles of Paul to the Corinthians.* Oxford translation, revised by Talbot W. Chambers. Nicene and Post-Nicene Fathers, First Series 12. Grand Rapids: Eerdmans, 1997 (1889).

Com. Eccl.   *Commentary on Ecclesiastes.* In *Commentary on the Sages.* Vol. 2. Translated by Robert Charles Hill. Brookline, MA: Holy Cross Orthodox Press, 2006.

Com. Gal.   *Commentary on the Epistle to the Galatians.* Translated by Gross Alexander. Nicene and Post-Nicene Fathers, First Series 13. Grand Rapids: Eerdmans, 1979.

Com. Job   *Commentary on Job.* In *Commentary on the Sages.* Vol. 1. Translated by Robert Charles Hill. Brookline, MA: Holy Cross Orthodox Press, 2006.

Com. Prov.   *Commentary on Proverbs.* In *Commentary on the Sages.* Vol. 2. Translated by Robert Charles Hill. Brookline, MA: Holy Cross Orthodox Press, 2006.

Com. Ps.   *Commentary on the Psalms.* Vols. 1-2. Translated by Robert Charles Hill. Brookline, MA: Holy Cross Orthodox Press, 1998.

Com. Isa.   *Commentary on Isaiah 1–8.* See Garrett, *Analysis.*

Hom. 1 Thess.   *Homilies on 1 Thessalonians.* Oxford translation, revised by John A. Broadus. Nicene and Post-Nicene Fathers, First Series 13. Grand Rapids: Eerdmans, 1979.

Hom. Acts   *Homilies on the Acts of the Apostles.* Translated by J. Walker, J. Sheppard, and H. Browne; revised by George B. Stevens.

	Nicene and Post-Nicene Fathers, First Series 11. Grand Rapids: Eerdmans, 1975 (1889).
Hom. Col.	*Homilies on the Epistle to the Colossians.* Oxford translation; revised by John A. Broadus. Nicene and Post-Nicene Fathers, First Series 13. Grand Rapids: Eerdmans, 1979.
Hom. David/ O.T.H. 1	*Homilies on David and Saul.* In *Old Testament Homilies.* Vol. 1. Translated by Robert Charles Hill. Brookline, MA: Holy Cross Orthodox Press, 2003.
Hom. Eutropius	*Two Homilies on Eutropius.* Translated by W. R. W. Stephens. Nicene and Post-Nicene Fathers, First Series 9. Grand Rapids: Eerdmans, 1956 (1889).
Hom. Gen.	*Homilies on Genesis 1–17, 18–45, 46–68.* Translated by Robert C. Hill. Fathers of the Church 74, 82, 87. Washington, DC: Catholic University of America Press, 1986-1992.
Hom. Heb.	*Homilies on the Epistle to the Hebrews.* Oxford translation; revised by Frederic Gardiner. Nicene and Post-Nicene Fathers, New Series 14. Grand Rapids: Eerdmans, 1956 (1889).
Hom. Isa./O.T.H. 2	*Homilies on Isaiah.* In *Old Testament Homilies.* Vol. 2. Translated by Robert Charles Hill. Brookline, MA: Holy Cross Orthodox Press, 2003.
Hom. Jer. 10.23/ O.T.H. 2	*Homily on Jeremiah 10.23.* In *Old Testament Homilies.* Vol. 2. Translated by Robert Charles Hill. Brookline, MA: Holy Cross Orthodox Press, 2003.
Hom. John	*Commentary on Saint John the Apostle and Evangelist: Homilies 1-47, 48-88.* Translated by Sister Thomas Aquinas Goggin. Fathers of the Church 33, 41. Washington, DC: Catholic University of America Press, 1957-1959.
Hom. Matt.	*Homilies on the Gospel of Saint Matthew.* Translated by Sir George Prevost; revised by M. B. Riddle. Nicene and Post-Nicene Fathers, First Series 10. Grand Rapids: Eerdmans, 1995 (1888).
Hom. Obscurity/ O.T.H. 3	*Homilies on the Obscurity of the Old Testament.* In *Old Testament Homilies.* Vol. 3. Translated by Robert Charles Hill. Brookline, MA: Holy Cross Orthodox Press, 2003.
Hom. Ps./O.T.H. 3	*Homilies on the Psalms.* In *Old Testament Homilies.* Vol. 3. Translated by Robert Charles Hill. Brookline, MA: Holy Cross Orthodox Press, 2003.
Hom. Rom.	*Homilies on the Epistle to the Romans.* Translated by J. B. Morris and W. H. Simcox; revised by George B. Stevens. Nicene and Post-Nicene Fathers, New Series 11. Grand Rapids: Eerdmans, 1975 (1889).
Hom. Statues	*Homilies on the Statues.* Translated by W. R. W. Stephens. Nicene and Post-Nicene Fathers, First Series 9. Grand Rapids: Eerdmans, 1956 (1889).

Bibliography

Marcionists	*Homily against Marcionists and Manichaeans.* Translated by W. R. W. Stephens. Nicene and Post-Nicene Fathers, First Series 9. Grand Rapids: Eerdmans, 1956 (1889).
Priesthood	*On the Priesthood.* Translated by W. R. W. Stephens. Nicene and Post-Nicene Fathers, First Series 9. Grand Rapids: Eerdmans, 1956 (1889).

Collins, John J.

"Scriptures"	"Before the Canon: Scriptures in Second Temple Judaism." In *Old Testament Interpretation: Past, Present, and Future; Essays in Honor of Gene M. Tucker,* edited by James Luther Mays, David L. Petersen, and Kent Harold Richards, 225-41. Nashville: Abingdon, 1995.

Cross, F. L.

Dictionary	*The Oxford Dictionary of the Christian Church.* Edited by F. L. Cross. Third rev. ed., edited by E. A. Livingstone. Oxford: Oxford University Press, 2005.

Daniélou, Jean

Origen	*Origen.* London: Sheed and Ward, 1955.

Davies, W. D., and Dale C. Allison, Jr.

Matthew	*A Critical and Exegetical Commentary on the Gospel According to Saint Matthew.* Vols. 1-3. Edinburgh: T. & T. Clark, 1988-1997.

Dawson, John David

Reading	*Christian Figural Reading and the Fashioning of Identity.* Berkeley: University of California Press, 2002.
Readers	*Allegorical Readers and Cultural Revision in Ancient Alexandria.* Berkeley: University of California Press, 1992.

Deines, Roland

Gerechtigkeit	*Die Gerechtigkeit der Tora im Reich des Messias: Mt 5,13-20 als Schlüsseltext der matthäischen Theologie.* Tübingen: Mohr Siebeck, 2005.
"Righteousness"	"Not the Law but the Messiah: Law and Righteousness in the Gospel of Matthew — An Ongoing Debate." In *Built Upon the Rock: Studies in the Gospel of Matthew,* edited by Daniel M. Gurtner and John Nolland, 53-84. Grand Rapids: Eerdmans, 2008.

Dodd, C. H.

Tradition	*Historical Tradition in the Fourth Gospel.* Cambridge: Cambridge University Press, 1963.

Dunn, James D. G.

"Gospel"	"The Gospel According to St. Paul." In *The Blackwell Companion to Paul,* edited by Stephen Westerholm, 139-53. Chichester, UK: Wiley-Blackwell, 2011.

Edwards, Mark Julian
Origen   *Origen against Plato.* Aldershot: Ashgate, 2002.

Ehmer, Hermann
"Bengel"   "Johann Albrecht Bengel (1687-1752)." In *The Pietist Theologians: An Introduction to Theology in the Seventeenth and Eighteenth Centuries,* edited by Carter Lindberg, 139-53. Malden, MA: Blackwell, 2005.

Elliott, J. K.
"Codex"   "Manuscripts, the Codex and the Canon." *Journal for the Study of the New Testament* 63 (1997): 105-23.

Emery, Gilles
"Exegesis"   "Biblical Exegesis and the Speculative Doctrine of the Trinity in St. Thomas Aquinas's *Commentary on St. John.*" In *Reading John with St. Thomas Aquinas: Theological Exegesis and Speculative Theology,* edited by Michael Dauphinais and Matthew Levering, 23-61. Washington, DC: Catholic University of America Press, 2005.

Erb, Peter C., ed.
Pietists   *Pietists: Selected Writings.* New York: Paulist, 1983.

Eusebius
E.H.   *Ecclesiastical History.* Translated by Roy J. Deferrari. Fathers of the Church 19, 29. New York: Fathers of the Church, 1953-1955.

Evans, G. R.
Language   *The Language and Logic of the Bible.* Vol. 1: *The Earlier Middle Ages.* Vol. 2: *The Road to Reformation.* Cambridge: Cambridge University Press, 1984-1985.

Farkasfalvy, D.
"Theology"   "Theology of Scripture in St. Irenaeus." *Revue Benedictine* 78 (1968): 319-33.

Fee, Gordon D.
"Criticism"   "Textual Criticism of the New Testament." In *Studies in the Theory and Method of New Testament Textual Criticism,* edited by Eldon J. Epp and Gordon D. Fee, 3-16. Grand Rapids: Eerdmans, 1993.
"Myth"   "P75, P66, and Origen: The Myth of Early Textual Recension in Alexandria." In *Studies in the Theory and Method of New Testament Textual Criticism,* edited by Eldon J. Epp and Gordon D. Fee, 247-73. Grand Rapids: Eerdmans, 1993.
"Text"   "Origen's Text of the New Testament." *New Testament Studies* 28 (1982): 348-64.

Fernández Marcos, Natalio

Septuagint   *The Septuagint in Context: Introduction to the Greek Versions of the Bible.* Leiden: Brill, 2000.

Fitzmyer, Joseph A.

Luke   *The Gospel According to Luke.* Vols. 1-2. Garden City, NY: Double-day, 1981-1985.

"Use"   "The Use of Explicit Old Testament Quotations in Qumran Literature and in the New Testament." In Fitzmyer, *Essays on the Semitic Background of the New Testament,* 3-58. London: Geoffrey Chapman, 1971.

Franck, Augustus Herman

Guide   *A Guide to the Reading and Study of the Holy Scriptures.* London: D. Jaques, 1813.

Frei, Hans

Eclipse   *The Eclipse of Biblical Narrative.* New Haven: Yale University Press, 1974.

Froehlich, Karlfried

Interpretation   *Biblical Interpretation in the Early Church.* Philadelphia: Fortress, 1984.

Galileo

"Letter"   "Letter to the Grand Duchess Christina." In S. Drake, *Discoveries and Opinions of Galileo,* 181-93. New York: Doubleday, 1957.

Gamble, Harry Y.

Books   *Books and Readers in the Early Church: A History of Early Christian Texts.* New Haven: Yale University Press, 1995.

Canon   *The New Testament Canon: Its Making and Meaning.* Philadelphia: Fortress, 1985.

"Research"   "The New Testament Canon: Recent Research and the Status Quaestionis." In *The Canon Debate,* edited by Lee Martin McDonald and James A. Sanders, 267-94. Peabody, MA: Hendrickson, 2002.

Garrett, Duane A.

Analysis   *An Analysis of the Hermeneutics of John Chrysostom's Commentary on Isaiah 1–8 with an English Translation.* Lewiston, NY: Edwin Mellen, 1992.

Gerhardsson, Birger

Origins   *The Origins of the Gospel Tradition.* Philadelphia: Fortress, 1979.

"Secret"   "The Secret of the Transmission of the Unwritten Jesus Tradition." *New Testament Studies* 51 (2005): 1-18.

Testing   *The Testing of God's Son (Matt. 4:1-11 and par.): An Analysis of an Early Christian Midrash.* Eugene, OR: Wipf and Stock, 2009.

Gerrish, Brian

Prince   *A Prince of the Church: Schleiermacher and the Beginnings of Modern Theology.* Philadelphia: Fortress, 1984.

Gilson, Etienne

Elements   *Elements of Christian Philosophy.* New York: Doubleday, 1960.

Reason   *Reason and Revelation in the Middle Ages.* New York: Charles Scribner's Sons, 1938.

Glomsrud, Ryan

"Impulse"   "Karl Barth and Modern Protestantism: The Radical Impulse." In *Always Reformed: Essays in Honor of W. Robert Godfrey,* edited by R. Scott Clark and Joel E. Kim, 92-114. Escondido, CA: Westminster Seminary California, 2010.

Goppelt, Leonhard

Typos   *Typos: The Typological Interpretation of the Old Testament in the New.* Grand Rapids: Eerdmans, 1982.

Grant, Robert M.

Irenaeus   *Irenaeus of Lyons.* London: Routledge, 1997.

Gregory the Great

Gospel Homilies   *Forty Gospel Homilies.* Translated by David Hurst. Kalamazoo, MI: Cistercian, 1990.

Hom. Ezek.   *Homilies on the Book of the Prophet Ezekiel.* Translated by Theodosia Tomkinson. Etna, CA: Center for Traditionalist Orthodox Studies, 2008.

Job   *Morals on the Book of Job.* Vols. 1-3. Oxford: John Henry Parker, 1844-1847.

Halverson, John

"Gospel"   "Oral and Written Gospel: A Critique of Werner Kelber." *New Testament Studies* 40 (1994): 180-95.

Harl, Marguerite

Philocalie   *Origène: Philocalie, 1-20: Sur les écritures.* Paris: Cerf, 1983.

"Septante"   "La Septante aux abords de l'ère chrétienne. Sa place dans le Nouveau Testament." In *La Bible grecque des septante: Du judaïsme hellénistique au christianisme ancient,* edited by Marguerite Harl, Gilles Dorival, and Olivier Munnich, 269-88. Paris: Cerf, 1988.

Harnack, Adolf von

Marcion   *Marcion: The Gospel of the Alien God.* Durham, NC: Labyrinth, 1990.

Mission   *The Mission and Expansion of Christianity in the First Three Centuries.* New York: Harper, 1961.

Reading   *Bible Reading in the Early Church.* London: Williams and Norgate, 1912.

Bibliography

Hartman, Lars

"Gottesdienst"   "Das Markusevangelium, 'für die lectio sollemnis im Gottesdienst abgefasst'?" In *Geschichte — Tradition — Reflexion: Festschrift für Martin Hengel zum 70. Geburtstag,* vol. 3: *Frühes Christentum,* edited by Hermann Lichtenberger, 147-71. Tübingen: Mohr Siebeck, 1996.

"Letters"   "On Reading Others' Letters." In *Christians among Jews and Gentiles: Essays in Honor of Krister Stendahl on His Sixth-Fifth Birthday,* edited by George W. E. Nickelsburg and George W. MacRae, 137-46. Philadelphia: Fortress, 1986.

Hauser, Alan J., and Duane F. Watson

History   *A History of Biblical Interpretation,* vol. 2: *The Medieval through the Reformation Periods.* Grand Rapids: Eerdmans, 2009.

Healy, Nicholas M.

"Introduction."   "Introduction." In *Aquinas on Scripture: An Introduction to His Biblical Commentaries,* edited by Thomas G. Weinandy, Daniel A. Keating, and John P. Yocum, 1-20. London: T. & T. Clark, 2005.

Heath, Malcolm

"Rhetoric"   "John Chrysostom, Rhetoric and Galatians." *Biblical Interpretation* 12 (2004): 369-400.

Heil, John Paul

"Believers"   "Paul and the Believers of Western Asia." In *The Blackwell Companion to Paul,* edited by Stephen Westerholm, 79-92. Chichester, UK: Wiley-Blackwell, 2011.

Heine, Ronald E.

Origen   *Origen: Scholarship in the Service of the Church.* Oxford: Oxford University Press, 2010.

Helmer, Christine

"Theology"   "Schleiermacher's Exegetical Theology and the New Testament." In *The Cambridge Companion to Friedrich Schleiermacher,* edited by Jacqueline Mariña, 229-48. Cambridge: Cambridge University Press, 2005.

Hengel, Martin

Gospels   *The Four Gospels and the One Gospel of Jesus Christ: An Investigation of the Collection and Origin of the Canonical Gospels.* Harrisburg, PA: Trinity Press International, 2000.

Peter   *Saint Peter: The Underestimated Apostle.* Grand Rapids: Eerdmans, 2010.

Septuagint   *The Septuagint as Christian Scripture: Its Prehistory and the Problem of Its Canon.* Grand Rapids: Baker Academic, 2002.

Hill, Charles E.

Corpus   *The Johannine Corpus in the Early Church.* Oxford: Oxford University Press, 2004.

"Gospel"   "'The Orthodox Gospel': The Reception of John in the Great Church Prior to Irenaeus." In *The Legacy of John: Second-Century Reception of the Fourth Gospel,* edited by Tuomas Rasimus, 233-300. Leiden: Brill, 2010.

Gospels   *Who Chose the Gospels? Probing the Great Gospel Conspiracy.* Oxford: Oxford University Press, 2010.

Hill, Robert C.

"Introduction" "Introduction." In *St. John Chrysostom: Commentaries on the Sages,* vol. 1: *Commentary on Job,* edited by Robert C. Hill, 1-12. Brookline, MA: Holy Cross Orthodox Press, 2006.

Reading   *Reading the Old Testament in Antioch.* Atlanta: Society of Biblical Literature, 2005.

Holder, R. Ward

Grounding   *John Calvin and the Grounding of Interpretation: Calvin's First Commentaries.* Leiden: Brill, 2006.

Holmes, Jeremy

"Lectura"   "Aquinas' *Lectura in Matthaeum.*" In *Aquinas on Scripture: An Introduction to His Biblical Commentaries,* edited by Thomas G. Weinandy, Daniel A. Keating, and John P. Yocum, 73-97. London: T&T Clark, 2005.

Holmes, Michael W.

"Inerrancy"   "Origen and the Inerrancy of Scripture." *Journal of the Evangelical Theological Society* 24 (1981): 221-31.

Hull, Robert F., Jr.

Story   *The Story of the New Testament Text: Movers, Materials, Motives, Methods, and Models.* Atlanta: Society of Biblical Literature, 2010.

Hunsinger, George

"Interpretation" "Postcritical Scriptural Interpretation: Rudolf Smend on Karl Barth." In *Thy Word Is Truth: Barth on Scripture,* edited by George Hunsinger, 29-48. Grand Rapids: Eerdmans, 2012.

Hurtado, Larry W.

Artifacts   *The Earliest Christian Artifacts: Manuscripts and Christian Origins.* Grand Rapids: Eerdmans, 2006.

Irenaeus

A.H.   *Against Heresies.* Translated by Alexander Roberts and James Donaldson. Ante-Nicene Fathers 1. Repr. Grand Rapids: Eerdmans, 1979.

Dem.	*Demonstration of the Apostolic Preaching.* Translated by Joseph P. Smith. Ancient Christian Writers 16. New York: Newman, 1952.

Jobes, Karen H., and Moisés Silva

Introduction	*Introduction to the Septuagint.* Grand Rapids: Baker, 2000.

Jowett, Benjamin

"Interpretation"	"On the Interpretation of Scripture." In *Essays and Reviews,* edited by Frederick Temple et al., 330-433. London: John W. Parker and Son, 1860.

Kelber, Werner

Gospel	*The Oral and the Written Gospel: The Hermeneutics of Speaking and Writing in the Synoptic Tradition, Mark, Paul, and Q.* Philadelphia: Fortress, 1983.

Kelly, J. N. D.

Golden Mouth	*Golden Mouth: The Story of John Chrysostom: Ascetic, Preacher, Bishop.* Ithaca, NY: Cornell University Press, 1995.

Kierkegaard, Søren

BA	*The Book on Adler.* Translated by Howard V. Hong and Edna H. Hong. Princeton: Princeton University Press, 1998.
CA	*The Concept of Anxiety.* Translated by Reidar Thomte in collaboration with Albert B. Anderson. Princeton: Princeton University Press, 1980.
CD	*Christian Discourses.* In *Christian Discourses* and *The Crisis and a Crisis in the Life of an Actress.* Translated by Howard V. Hong and Edna H. Hong. Princeton: Princeton University Press, 1997.
Communion	*Discourses at the Communion on Fridays.* Translated by Sylvia Walsh. Bloomington: Indiana University Press, 2011.
CUP	*Concluding Unscientific Postscript to Philosophical Fragments.* Vols. 1-2. Translated by Howard V. Hong and Edna H. Hong. Princeton: Princeton University Press, 1992.
EUD	*Eighteen Upbuilding Discourses.* Translated by Howard V. Hong and Edna H. Hong. Princeton: Princeton University Press, 1990.
FSE	*For Self-Examination.* In *For Self-Examination* and *Judge for Yourself.* Translated by Howard V. Hong and Edna H. Hong. Princeton: Princeton University Press, 1990.
FT	*Fear and Trembling.* In *Fear and Trembling* and *Repetition.* Translated by Howard V. Hong and Edna H. Hong. Princeton: Princeton University Press, 1983.
JFY	*Judge for Yourself.* In *For Self-Examination* and *Judge for Yourself.* Translated by Howard V. Hong and Edna H. Hong. Princeton: Princeton University Press, 1990.
JP	*Søren Kierkegaard's Journals and Papers.* Vols. 1-7. Edited and

translated by Howard V. Hong and Edna H. Hong, assisted by Gregor Malantschuk. Bloomington: Indiana University Press, 1967-1978.

KJN — *Kierkegaard's Journals and Notebooks.* Vols. 1-7. Edited by Niels Jørgen Cappelørn et al. Princeton: Princeton University Press, 2007-2014.

LY — *The Last Years: Journals 1853-1855.* Edited and translated by Ronald Gregor Smith. New York: Harper and Row, 1965.

PC — *Practice in Christianity.* Translated by Howard V. Hong and Edna H. Hong. Princeton: Princeton University Press, 1991.

PF — *Philosophical Fragments.* In *Philosophical Fragments* and *Johannes Climacus.* Translated by Howard V. Hong and Edna H. Hong. Princeton: Princeton University Press, 1985.

PJ — *Papers and Journals: A Selection.* Translated by Alastair Hannay. London: Penguin, 1996.

PV — *The Point of View: On My Work as an Author; The Point of View for My Work as an Author; Armed Neutrality.* Translated by Howard V. Hong and Edna H. Hong. Princeton: Princeton University Press, 1998.

SKS — *Søren Kierkegaards Skrifter.* Text in vols. 1-28. Copenhagen: Gad, 1997-2012.

SUD — *The Sickness unto Death.* Translated by Howard V. Hong and Edna H. Hong. Princeton: Princeton University Press, 1980.

TDIO — *Three Discourses on Imagined Occasions.* Translated by Howard V. Hong and Edna H. Hong. Princeton: Princeton University Press, 1993.

UDVS — *Upbuilding Discourses in Various Spirits.* Translated by Howard V. Hong and Edna H. Hong. Princeton: Princeton University Press, 1993.

WA — *Without Authority: The Lily in the Field and the Bird of the Air; Two Ethical-Religious Essays; Three Discourses at the Communion on Fridays; An Upbuilding Discourse; Two Discourses at the Communion on Fridays.* Translated by Howard V. Hong and Edna H. Hong. Princeton: Princeton University Press, 1997.

WL — *Works of Love.* Translated by Howard V. Hong and Edna H. Hong. Princeton: Princeton University Press, 1995.

Kirmmse, Bruce H.

Encounters — *Encounters with Kierkegaard: A Life as Seen by His Contemporaries.* Collected, edited, and annotated by Bruce M. Kirmmse. Princeton: Princeton University Press, 1996.

Koch, Dieter-Alex

Schrift — *Die Schrift als Zeuge des Evangeliums: Untersuchungen zur Ver-*

wendung und zum Verständnis der Schrift bei Paulus. Tübingen: Mohr Siebeck, 1986.

Köhler, Wolf-Dietrich
Rezeption   *Die Rezeption des Mattäusevangeliums in der Zeit vor Irenäus.* Tübingen: Mohr Siebeck, 1987.

Kugel, James L.
As It Was   *The Bible as It Was.* Cambridge, MA: Harvard University Press, 1997.
Guide   *How to Read the Bible: A Guide to Scripture Then and Now.* New York: Free Press, 2007.

Kümmel, W. G.
History   *The New Testament: The History of the Investigation of Its Problems.* London: SCM, 1973.

Lamberton, Robert
Homer   *Homer the Theologian: Neoplatonist Allegorical Reading and the Growth of the Epic Tradition.* Berkeley: University of California Press, 1986.

Lane, Anthony N. S.
"Calvin"   "Calvin." In *Blackwell Companion to Paul,* edited by Stephen Westerholm, 391-405. Chichester, UK: Wiley-Blackwell, 2011.
Student   *John Calvin: Student of the Church Fathers.* Edinburgh: T. & T. Clark, 1999.

Lauro, Elizabeth Ann Dively
Soul   *The Soul and Spirit of Scripture within Origen's Exegesis.* Leiden: Brill, 2005.

LeFevre, Perry D.
Prayers   *The Prayers of Kierkegaard.* Chicago: University of Chicago Press, 1956.

Levenson, Jon D.
Criticism   *The Hebrew Bible, the Old Testament, and Historical Criticism: Jews and Christians in Biblical Studies.* Louisville: Westminster John Knox, 1993.

Lewis, C. S.
Poems   *Poems.* Edited by Walter Hooper. London: Geoffrey Bles, 1964.

Lim, Timothy H.
Formation   *The Formation of the Jewish Canon.* New Haven: Yale University Press, 2013.

Lubac, Henri de
History   *History and Spirit: The Understanding of Scripture according to Origen.* San Francisco: Ignatius, 2007.

Luther, Martin

C.S. *The Complete Sermons of Martin Luther.* Vols. 1-7. Edited by John Nicholas Lenker and Eugene F. A. Klug. Grand Rapids: Baker, 2000.

L.C. *The Large Catechism of Martin Luther.* Philadelphia: Fortress, 1959.

S.C. *The Small Catechism.* Minneapolis: Augsburg, 1979.

Works *Luther's Works.* Vols. 1-55. Edited by Jaroslav Pelikan and Helmut T. Lehmann. St. Louis: Concordia, and Philadelphia: Fortress, 1955-1986. Vols. 58-60, 69. Edited by Christopher Boyd Brown. St. Louis: Concordia, 2009-2012.

Luz, Ulrich

Matthew *Matthew 1–7: A Commentary.* Minneapolis: Fortress, 2007.

Studies *Studies in Matthew.* Grand Rapids: Eerdmans, 2005.

Maddox, Randy L.

"Wesley" "John Wesley — 'A Man of One Book.'" In *Wesley, Wesleyans, and Reading the Bible as Scripture,* edited by Joel B. Green and David F. Watso, 3-18. Waco: Baylor University Press, 2012.

Malik, Habib C.

Impact *Receiving Søren Kierkegaard: The Early Impact and Transmission of His Thought.* Washington, DC: Catholic University of America Press, 1997.

Malory, Sir Thomas

Works *Malory: Works.* Edited by Eugène Vinaver. 2nd ed. London: Oxford University Press, 1971.

Margerie, Bertrand de

Augustine *An Introduction to the History of Exegesis,* vol. 3: *Saint Augustine.* Petersham, MA: Saint Bede's Publications, 1991.

Martens, Paul

"Bible" "Kierkegaard and the Bible." In *The Oxford Handbook of Kierkegaard,* edited by John Lippitt and George Pattison, 150-65. Oxford: Oxford University Press, 2013.

Martens, Peter W.

Origen *Origen and Scripture: The Contours of the Exegetical Life.* Oxford: Oxford University Press, 2012.

"Revisiting" "Revisiting the Allegory/Typology Distinction: The Case of Origen." *Journal of Early Christian Studies* 16 (2008): 283-317.

Matthias, Markus

"Francke" "August Hermann Francke (1663-1727)." In *The Pietist Theologians: An Introduction to Theology in the Seventeenth and Eighteenth Cen-*

turies, edited by Carter Lindberg, 100-114. Malden, MA: Blackwell, 2005.

Mattox, Mickey L.
"Interpretation"   "Luther's Interpretation of Scripture: Biblical Understanding in Trinitarian Shape." In *The Substance of the Faith: Luther's Doctrinal Theology for Today,* edited by Dennis Bielfeldt, Mickey L. Mattox, and Paul R. Hinlicky, 11-57. Minneapolis: Fortress, 2008.

Mayer, Wendy
Homilies   *The Homilies of St John Chrysostom — Provenance: Reshaping the Foundations.* Rome: Pontifical Oriental Institute, 2005.

McGuckin, John Anthony
"Life"   "The Life of Origen." In *The Westminster Handbook to Origen,* edited by John Anthony McGuckin, 1-23. Louisville: Westminster John Knox, 2004.
"Works"   "The Scholarly Works of Origen." In *The Westminster Handbook to Origen,* edited by John Anthony McGuckin, 25-41. Louisville: Westminster John Knox, 2004.

McKim, Donald K., ed.
Dictionary   *Dictionary of Major Biblical Interpreters.* Downers Grove, IL: InterVarsity Academic, 2007.

Menken, Maarten J. J.
Bible   *Matthew's Bible: The Old Testament Text of the Evangelist.* Louvain: Leuven University Press, 2004.

Metzger, Bruce M.
Canon   *The Canon of the New Testament: Its Origin, Development, and Significance.* Oxford: Clarendon Press, 1987.

Metzger, Bruce M., and Bart D. Ehrman
Text   *The Text of the New Testament: Its Transmission, Corruption, and Restoration.* 4th ed. New York: Oxford University Press, 2005.

Meyer, Ben F.
Aims   *The Aims of Jesus.* London: SCM, 1979.
"Business"   "A Tricky Business: Ascribing New Meaning to Old Texts." *Gregorianum* 71 (1990): 743-61.

Minns, Dennis
Irenaeus   *Irenaeus: An Introduction.* London: T. & T. Clark, 2010.

Mitchell, Margaret M.
"Rhetoric"   "Reading Rhetoric with Patristic Exegesis: John Chrysostom on Galatians." In *Antiquity and Humanity: Essays on Ancient Religion and Philosophy Presented to Hans Dieter Betz on His 70th Birthday,*

| | edited by Adela Yarbro Collins and Margaret M. Mitchell, 333-55. Tübingen: Mohr Siebeck, 2001. |
| *Trumpet* | *The Heavenly Trumpet: John Chrysostom and the Art of Pauline Interpretation.* Louisville: Westminster John Knox, 2002. |

Moloney, Francis J.

| "Scripture" | "The Gospel of John as Scripture." *Catholic Biblical Quarterly* 67 (2005): 454-68. |

Momigliano, Arnaldo

| *Essays* | *Essays in Ancient and Modern Historiography.* Oxford: Blackwell, 1977. |

Moore, George Foot

| *Judaism* | *Judaism in the First Centuries of the Christian Era: The Age of the Tannaim.* Vol. 1. Cambridge, MA: Harvard University Press, 1927. |

Müller, Mogens

| *Bible* | *The First Bible of the Church: A Plea for the Septuagint.* Sheffield, UK: Sheffield Academic Press, 1996. |
| "Scholarship" | "Kierkegaard and Eighteenth- and Nineteenth-Century Biblical Scholarship: A Case of Incongruity." In *Kierkegaard and the Bible,* vol. 2: *The New Testament,* edited by Lee C. Barrett and Jon Stewart, 285-327. Farnham, Surrey: Ashgate, 2010. |

Muller, Richard A.

"Debate"	"The Debate over the Vowel Points and the Crisis in Orthodox Hermeneutics." In *After Calvin: Studies in the Development of a Theological Tradition,* edited by Richard A. Muller, 146-55. Oxford: Oxford University Press, 2003.
"Interpretation"	"Biblical Interpretation in the Era of the Reformation: The View from the Middle Ages." In *Biblical Interpretation in the Era of the Reformation: Essays Presented to David C. Steinmetz in Honor of His Sixtieth Birthday,* edited by Richard A. Muller and John L. Thompson, 3-22. Grand Rapids: Eerdmans, 1996.
"Place"	"The Place and Importance of Karl Barth in the Twentieth Century: A Review Essay." *Westminster Theological Journal* 50 (1988): 127-56.

Nardoni, Enrique

| "Concept" | "Origen's Concept of Biblical Inspiration." *Second Century* 4 (1984): 9-23. |

Nimmo, Paul T.

| "On Scripture" | "Schleiermacher on Scripture and the Work of Jesus Christ." *Modern Theology* 31 (2015): 60-90. |

448

Noll, Mark A.
Rise   *The Rise of Evangelicalism: The Age of Edwards, Whitefield and the
                    Wesleys.* Downers Grove, IL: InterVarsity, 2003.

Oberman, Heiko A.
Luther   *Luther: Man between God and the Devil.* New Haven: Yale Uni-
                    versity Press, 1989.

Oden, Thomas C., ed.
Parables   *The Parables of Kierkegaard.* Princeton: Princeton University
                    Press, 1978.

O'Keefe, John J., and R. R. Reno
Vision   *Sanctified Vision: An Introduction to Early Christian Interpretation
                    of the Bible.* Baltimore: Johns Hopkins University Press, 2005.

Origen
Cels.   *Contra Celsum.* Translated by Henry Chadwick. Cambridge: Cam-
                    bridge University Press, 1980 (1953).
Com. Cant.   *The Song of Songs: Commentary and Homilies.* Translated by R. P.
                    Lawson. Ancient Christian Writers 26. New York: Newman, 1957.
Com. Eph.   *The Commentaries of Origen and Jerome on St Paul's Epistle to the
                    Ephesians.* Translated by Ronald E. Heine. Oxford: Oxford Uni-
                    versity Press, 2002.
Com. John   *Commentary on the Gospel According to John, Books 1–10, 13–
                    32.* Translated by Ronald E. Heine. Fathers of the Church 80,
                    89. Washington, DC: Catholic University of America Press,
                    1989-1993.
Com. Matt.   *Commentary on Matthew.* Translated by J. Patrick. Ante-Nicene
                    Fathers 10. Grand Rapids: Eerdmans, 1974 (1897).
Com. Rom.   *Commentary on the Epistle to the Romans Books 1–5, 6–10.* Trans-
                    lated by Thomas P. Scheck. Fathers of the Church 103, 104. Wash-
                    ington, DC: Catholic University of America Press, 2001-2002.
Dial.   *Treatise on the Passover* and *Dialogue of Origen with Heraclides and
                    His Fellow Bishops on the Father, the Son, and the Soul.* Translated
                    by Robert J. Daly, SJ. Ancient Christian Writers 54. New York:
                    Paulist, 1992.
Ep. Afr.   *Epistle to Africanus.* Translated by Frederick Crombie. Ante-
                    Nicene Fathers 4, 386-92. Grand Rapids: Eerdmans, 1974 (1869).
F.P.   *On First Principles.* Translated by G. W. Butterworth. New York:
                    Harper and Row, 1966 (1936).
Hom. Cant.   *The Song of Songs: Commentary and Homilies.* Translated by R. P.
                    Lawson. Ancient Christian Writers 26. New York: Newman, 1957.
Hom. Exod.   *Homilies on Genesis and Exodus.* Translated by Ronald E. Heine.
                    Fathers of the Church 71. Washington, DC: Catholic University
                    of America Press, 1982.

Hom. Ezek.   *Homilies 1-14 on Ezekiel.* Translated by Thomas P. Scheck. Ancient Christian Writers 62. New York: Newman, 2010.

Hom. Gen.   *Homilies on Genesis and Exodus.* Translated by Ronald E. Heine. Fathers of the Church 71. Washington, DC: Catholic University of America Press, 1982.

Hom. Jer.   *Homilies on Jeremiah. Homily on 1 Kings 28.* Translated by John Clark Smith. Fathers of the Church 97. Washington, DC: Catholic University of America Press, 1998.

Hom. Josh.   *Homilies on Joshua.* Translated by Barbara J. Bruce. Fathers of the Church 105. Washington, DC: Catholic University of America Press, 2002.

Hom. Judg.   *Homilies on Judges.* Translated by Elizabeth Ann Dively Lauro. Fathers of the Church 119. Washington, DC: Catholic University of America Press, 2010.

Hom. Lev.   *Homilies on Leviticus 1–16.* Translated by Gary Wayne Barkley. Fathers of the Church 83. Washington, DC: Catholic University of America Press, 1990.

Hom. Luke   *Homilies on Luke. Fragments on Luke.* Translated by Joseph T. Lienhard, SJ. Fathers of the Church 94. Washington, DC: Catholic University of America Press, 1996.

Hom. Num.   *Homilies on Numbers.* Translated by Thomas P. Scheck. Downers Grove, IL: IVP Academic, 2009.

Pasch.   *Treatise on the Passover* and *Dialogue of Origen with Heraclides and His Fellow Bishops on the Father, the Son, and the Soul.* Translated by Robert J. Daly, SJ. Ancient Christian Writers 54. New York: Paulist, 1992.

Philoc.   *The Philocalia of Origen.* Translated by George Lewis. Edinburgh: T. & T. Clark, 1911.

Ottley, R. R.

Isaiah   *The Book of Isaiah according to the Septuagint (Codex Alexandrinus).* Vol. 1. London: C. J. Clay and Sons, 1904.

Pak, G. Sujin

Judaizing Calvin   *The Judaizing Calvin: Sixteenth-Century Debates over the Messianic Psalms.* Oxford: Oxford University Press, 2010.

Pannenberg, Wolfhart

Systematic Theology   *Systematic Theology,* vol. 1. Translated by Geoffrey W. Bromiley. Grand Rapids: Eerdmans, 1991.

Parker, T. H. L.

N. T. Commentaries   *Calvin's New Testament Commentaries.* London: SCM, 1971.

Pearson, Birger A.
Gnosticism   *Ancient Gnosticism: Traditions and Literature.* Minneapolis: Fortress, 2007.

Pelikan, Jaroslav
Expositor   *Luther the Expositor: Introduction to the Reformer's Exegetical Writings.* St. Louis: Concordia, 1959.

Perkins, Pheme
Introduction   *Introduction to the Synoptic Gospels.* Grand Rapids: Eerdmans, 2007.

Persson, Per Erik
Sacra Doctrina   *Sacra Doctrina: Reason and Revelation in Aquinas.* Oxford: Basil Blackwell, 1970.

Pesch, Otto Hermann
"Professor"   "Paul as Professor of Theology: The Image of the Apostle in St. Thomas's Thought." *Thomist* 38 (1974): 584-605.

Peterson, Erik
Tractates   *Theological Tractates.* Stanford: Stanford University Press, 2011.

Pietersma, Albert, and Benjamin G. Wright
Translation   *A New English Translation of the Septuagint and the Other Greek Translations Traditionally Included Under That Title.* Edited by Albert Pietersma and Benjamin G. Wright. New York: Oxford University Press, 2007.

Piper, Ronald A.
"Four"   "The One, the Four and the Many." In *The Written Gospel,* edited by Markus Bockmuehl and Donald A. Hagner, 254-73. Cambridge: Cambridge University Press, 2005.

Porter, Stanley E.
"Canon"   "When and How Was the Pauline Canon Compiled? An Assessment of Theories." In *The Pauline Canon,* edited by Stanley E. Porter, 95-127. Leiden: Brill, 2004.

Prügl, Thomas
"Interpreter"   "Thomas Aquinas as Interpreter of Scripture." In *The Theology of Thomas Aquinas,* edited by Rik van Nieuwenhove and Joseph Wawrykow, 386-415. Notre Dame, IN: University of Notre Dame Press, 2005.

Puckett, David L.
Exegesis   *John Calvin's Exegesis of the Old Testament.* Louisville: Westminster John Knox, 1995.

Quasten, Johannes
Patrology   *Patrology.* Vols. 1-4. Notre Dame, IN: Christian Classics, n.d.

Rendtorff, Rolf
Introduction *The Old Testament: An Introduction.* Philadelphia: Fortress, 1986.

Resch, Dustin G.
"Fittingness" "The Fittingness and Harmony of Scripture: Toward an Irenaean Hermeneutic." *Heythrop Journal* 50 (2009): 74-84.

Reventlow, Henning Graf
History *History of Biblical Interpretation.* Vols. 1-4. Atlanta: Society of Biblical Literature, 2009-2010.

Richards, E. Randolph
Secretary *The Secretary in the Letters of Paul.* Tübingen: Mohr Siebeck, 1991.

Rist, John
"Augustine" "Augustine of Hippo." In *The Medieval Theologians: An Introduction to Theology in the Medieval Period,* edited by G. R. Evans, 3-23. Malden, MA: Blackwell, 2001.

Sanders, E. P.
Jesus *The Historical Figure of Jesus.* London: Penguin, 1993.

Sandys-Wunsch, John
History *What Have They Done to the Bible? A History of Modern Biblical Interpretation.* Collegeville, MN: Liturgical Press, 2005.

Schleiermacher, Friedrich
BO *Brief Outline of Theology as a Field of Study.* Translated by Terrence N. Tice. 3rd ed. Louisville: Westminster John Knox, 2011.

BW *Friedrich Daniel Ernst Schleiermacher Briefwechsel 1774-1796.* Edited by Andreas Arndt and Wolfgang Virmond. Berlin: De Gruyter, 1985.

CF *The Christian Faith.* Edited by H. R. Mackintosh and J. S. Stewart. London: T. & T. Clark, 1999.

HC *Hermeneutics and Criticism and Other Writings.* Translated by Andrew Bowie. Cambridge: Cambridge University Press, 1998.

LJ *The Life of Jesus.* Translated by S. Maclean Gilmour. Philadelphia: Fortress, 1975.

OG *On the Glaubenslehre: Two Letters to Dr. Lücke.* Translated by James Duke and Francis Fiorenza. Chico, CA: Scholars, 1981.

Sermons *Selected Sermons of Schleiermacher.* Translated by Mary F. Wilson. New York: Funk and Wagnalls, 1890.

Speeches *On Religion: Speeches to Its Cultured Despisers.* Translated by Richard Crouter. Cambridge: Cambridge University Press, 1988.

Schneemelcher, Wilhelm
"Introduction" "General Introduction." In *New Testament Apocrypha,* vol. 1, edited by Wilhelm Schneemelcher, 9-75. Louisville: Westminster John Knox, 1991.

Scholtissek, Klaus

"Beobachtungen" " 'Geschrieben in diesem Buch' (Joh 20, 30) — Beobachtungen zum kanonischen Anspruch des Johannesevangeliums." In *Israel und seine Heilstraditionen im Johannesevangelium: Festgabe für Johannes Beutler SJ zum 70. Geburtstag,* edited by Michael Labahn, Klaus Scholtissek, and Angelika Strotmann, 207-26. Paderborn: Schöningh, 2004.

Schwartz, Barry

"Origins" "Christian Origins: Historical Truth and Social Memory." In *Memory, Tradition, and Text: Uses of the Past in Early Christianity,* edited by Alan Kirk and Tom Thatcher, 43-56. Atlanta: Society of Biblical Literature, 2005.

Seeligmann, I. L.

Version *The Septuagint Version of Isaiah: A Discussion of Its Problems.* Leiden: Brill, 1948.

Shuster, Marguerite

"Sin" "Sin and the Fall." In *The Blackwell Companion to Paul,* edited by Stephen Westerholm, 546-60. Chichester, UK: Wiley-Blackwell, 2011.

Simonetti, Manlio

Interpretation *Biblical Interpretation in the Early Church: An Historical Introduction to Patristic Exegesis.* Edinburgh: T. & T. Clark, 1994.

Skarsaune, Oskar

"Ebionites" "The Ebionites." In *Jewish Believers in Jesus: The Early Centuries,* edited by Oskar Skarsaune and Reidar Hvalvik, 419-62. Peabody, MA: Hendrickson, 2007.

Smalley, Beryl

"Bible" "The Bible in the Medieval Schools." In *The Cambridge History of the Bible,* vol. 2: *The West from the Fathers to the Reformation,* edited by G. W. H. Lampe, 197-220. Cambridge: Cambridge University Press, 1969.

Gospels *The Gospels in the Schools c. 1100–c. 1280.* London: Hambledon, 1985

Study *The Study of the Bible in the Middle Ages.* 3rd ed. Notre Dame, IN: University of Notre Dame Press, 1978.

Smith, D. Moody

"Gospels" "When Did the Gospels Become Scripture?" *Journal of Biblical Literature* 119 (2000): 3-20.

Spener, Philip Jacob

Pia Desideria *Pia Desideria.* Philadelphia: Fortress, 1964.

Stanton, Graham N.
Gospel　　　　　*Jesus and Gospel.* Cambridge: Cambridge University Press, 2004.

Steinmetz, David C.
Luther　　　　　*Luther in Context.* 2nd ed. Grand Rapids: Baker Academic, 2002.

Sternberg, Meir
Poetics　　　　　*The Poetics of Biblical Narrative: Ideological Literature and the Drama of Reading.* Bloomington: Indiana University Press, 1985.

Stuhlhofer, Franz
Gebrauch　　　　　*Der Gebrauch der Bibel von Jesus bis Euseb: Eine statistische Untersuchung zur Kanongeschichte.* Wuppertal: Brockhaus, 1988.

Stump, Eleonore
"Revelation"　　　　　"Revelation and Biblical Exegesis: Augustine, Aquinas, and Swinburne." In *Reason and the Christian Religion: Essays in Honour of Richard Swinburne,* edited by Alan G. Padgett, 161-97. Oxford: Clarendon, 1994.

Theodore of Mopsuestia
Com. John　　　　　*Commentary on the Gospel of John.* Translated by Marco Conti. Downers Grove, IL: IVP Academic, 2010.
Com. Twelve Prophets　　　　　*Commentary on the Twelve Prophets.* Translated by Robert C. Hill. Fathers of the Church 108. Washington, DC: Catholic University of America Press, 2004.

Thompson, Mark D.
Ground　　　　　*A Sure Ground on Which to Stand: The Relation of Authority and Interpretive Method in Luther's Approach to Scripture.* Milton Keynes: Paternoster, 2005.

Thoreau, Henry David
Walden　　　　　*Walden and Other Writings.* New York: Bantam, 1962.

Thurén, Lauri
"Critic"　　　　　"John Chrysostom as a Rhetorical Critic: The Hermeneutics of an Early Father." *Biblical Interpretation* 9 (2004): 180-218.

Tice, Terrence N.
Sermons　　　　　*Schleiermacher's Sermons: A Chronological Listing and Account.* Lewiston: Edwin Mellen, 1997.

Torjesen, Karen Jo
Procedure　　　　　*Hermeneutical Procedure and Theological Method in Origen's Exegesis.* Berlin: Walter de Gruyter, 1986.
"Theory"　　　　　"'Body,' 'Soul,' and 'Spirit' in Origen's Theory of Exegesis." *Anglican Theological Review* 67 (1985): 17-30.

Torrell, Jean-Pierre
Aquinas　　　　　*Saint Thomas Aquinas.* Vol. 1: *The Person and His Work.* Vol. 2:

Spiritual Master. Washington, DC: Catholic University of America Press, 1996-2003.

Tov, Emanuel

Criticism   *Textual Criticism of the Hebrew Bible.* 3rd ed. Minneapolis: Fortress, 2012.

"Synthesis"   "The Significance of the Texts from the Judean Desert for the History of the Text of the Hebrew Bible: A New Synthesis." In *Qumran between the Old and New Testaments,* edited by Frederick H. Cryer and Thomas L. Thompson, 277-309. Sheffield, UK: Sheffield Academic Press, 1998.

Trigg, Joseph Wilson

Origen   *Origen: The Bible and Philosophy in the Third-Century Church.* Atlanta: John Knox, 1983.

Troeltsch, Ernst

"Method"   "Historical and Dogmatic Method in Theology." In Troeltsch, *Religion in History,* 11-32. Edinburgh: T. & T. Clark, 1991.

Ulrich, Eugene

Origins   *The Dead Sea Scrolls and the Origins of the Bible.* Grand Rapids: Eerdmans, 1999.

"Text"   "Origen's Old Testament Text: The Transmission History of the Septuagint to the Third Century, c.e." In *Origen of Alexandria: His World and His Legacy,* edited by Charles Kannengiesser and William L. Petersen, 3-33. Notre Dame, IN: University of Notre Dame Press, 1988.

Valkenberg, Wilhelmus G. B. M.

Words   *Words of the Living God: Place and Function of Holy Scripture in the Theology of St. Thomas Aquinas.* Leuven: Peeters, 2000.

VanderKam, James C.

Scrolls   *The Dead Sea Scrolls Today.* Grand Rapids: Eerdmans, 1994.

van Seters, John

Abraham   *Abraham in History and Tradition.* New Haven: Yale University Press, 1975.

Verheyden, Joseph

"Dispute"   "The Canon Muratori: A Matter of Dispute." In *The Biblical Canons,* edited by J.-M. Aywers and H. J. De Jonge, 487-561. Louvain: Leuven University Press, 2003.

Vial, Theodore

Schleiermacher   *Schleiermacher: A Guide for the Perplexed.* London: Bloomsbury, 2013.

Wallmann, Johannes

"Arndt" "Johann Arndt (1555-1621)." In *The Pietist Theologians: An Introduction to Theology in the Seventeenth and Eighteenth Centuries,* edited by Carter Lindberg, 21-37. Malden, MA: Blackwell, 2005.

Watson, Francis

"Bible" "The Bible." In *The Cambridge Companion to Karl Barth,* edited by John Webster, 57-71. Cambridge: Cambridge University Press, 2000.

Webster, John

Earlier Theology *Barth's Earlier Theology.* London: T. & T. Clark International, 2005.

"John" "Barth's Lectures on the Gospel of John." In *Thy Word Is Truth: Barth on Scripture,* edited by George Hunsinger, 125-47. Grand Rapids: Eerdmans, 2012.

Wendel, Susan J.

Interpretation *Scriptural Interpretation and Community Self-Definition in Luke-Acts and the Writings of Justin Martyr.* Leiden: Brill, 2011.

Wesley, John

Appeals *The Appeals to Men of Reason and Religion and Certain Related Open Letters = The Works of John Wesley,* vol. 11. Edited by Gerald R. Cragg. Nashville: Abingdon, 1975.

JD *Journals and Diaries, vols. 1-7 = The Works of John Wesley,* vols. 18-24. Edited by W. Reginald Ward and Richard P. Heitzenrater. Nashville: Abingdon, 1988-1997.

Letters *Letters, vols. 1-2 = The Works of John Wesley,* vols. 25-26. Edited by Frank Baker. Nashville: Abingdon, 1980-1982.

Notes NT *Explanatory Notes upon the New Testament.* Salem, OH: Schmul, 1975.

Notes OT *Explanatory Notes upon the Old Testament.* Vol. 1-3. Salem, OH: Schmul, 1975.

Serm. *Sermons. Vols. 1-4 = The Works of John Wesley,* vols. 1-4. Edited by Albert C. Outler. Nashville: Abingdon, 1984-1987.

Treatises *Doctrinal and Controversial Treatises. Vols. 1-2 = The Works of John Wesley,* vol. 12, edited by Randy L. Maddox; and vol. 13, edited by Paul Wesley Chilcote and Kenneth J. Collins. Nashville: Abingdon, 2012-2013.

Works *The Works of John Wesley,* vols. 1-14. Edited by Thomas Jackson. London, 1872; repr. Grand Rapids: Zondervan, n.d.

Westerholm, Stephen

"Hearing" "Hearing the Gospels of Matthew and Mark." In *Mark and Matthew II: Comparative Readings; Reception History, Cultural*

	Hermeneutics, and Theology, edited by Eve-Marie Becker and Anders Runesson, 245-58. Tübingen: Mohr Siebeck, 2013.
"Law"	"Law in the New Testament." In *The New Interpreter's Dictionary of the Bible,* vol. 3, edited by Katherine Doob Sakenfeld, 594-602. Nashville: Abingdon, 2008.
"Meaning"	"*Torah, Nomos,* and Law: A Question of 'Meaning.'" *Studies in Religion* 15 (1986): 327-36.
Perspectives	*Perspectives Old and New on Paul: The "Lutheran" Paul and His Critics.* Grand Rapids: Eerdmans, 2004.
"Pessimism"	"Paul's Anthropological 'Pessimism' in Its Jewish Context." In *Divine and Human Agency in Paul and His Cultural Environment,* edited by John M. G. Barclay and Simon J. Gathercole, 71-98. London: T. & T. Clark, 2006.

Wevers, John Wm.

"Reflections"   "The Göttingen Septuagint: Some Post-Partum Reflections." In *VII Congress of the International Organization for Septuagint and Cognate Studies: Leuven 1989,* edited by Claude E. Cox, 51-60. Atlanta: Scholars, 1991.

Wilcox, Pete

"Prophets"   "Calvin as Commentator on the Prophets." In *Calvin and the Bible,* edited by Donald K. McKim, 107-30. Cambridge: Cambridge University Press, 2006.

Wiles, M. F.

"Theodore"   "Theodore of Mopsuestia as Representative of the Antiochene School." In *The Cambridge History of the Bible,* vol. 1: *From the Beginnings to Jerome,* edited by P. R. Ackroyd and C. F. Evans, 489-510. Cambridge: Cambridge University Press, 1970.

Wilken, Robert Louis

"Defense"   "In Defense of Allegory." *Modern Theology* 14 (1998): 197-212.

Williams, Rowan

"Origen"   "Origen." In *The First Christian Theologians: An Introduction to Theology in the Early Church,* edited by G. R. Evans, 132-42. Malden, MA: Blackwell, 2004.

"Orthodoxy"   "Does It Make Sense to Speak of Pre-Nicene Orthodoxy?" In *The Making of Orthodoxy: Essays in Honour of Henry Chadwick,* edited by Rowan Williams, 1-23. Cambridge: Cambridge University Press, 1989.

Williamson, H. G. M.

1 and 2 Chronicles   *1 and 2 Chronicles.* Grand Rapids: Eerdmans, 1982.

Yocum, John

"Exposition"   "Aquinas's Literal Exposition on Job." In *Aquinas on Scripture: An*

Introduction to His Biblical Commentaries, edited by Thomas G. Weinandy, Daniel A. Keating, and John P. Yocum, 21-42. London: T. & T. Clark, 2005.

Young, Frances
Exegesis   *Biblical Exegesis and the Formation of Christian Culture.* Peabody, MA: Hendrickson, 2002.

Zachhuber, Johannes
Science   *Theology as Science in Nineteenth-Century Germany: From F. C. Baur to Ernst Troeltsch.* Oxford: Oxford University Press, 2013.

Zachman, Randall C.
"Meaning"   "Gathering Meaning from the Context: Calvin's Exegetical Method." *Journal of Religion* 82 (2002): 1-26.

Ziegler, Philip G.
"Criticisms"   "Barth's Criticisms of Kierkegaard — A Striking out at Phantoms?" *International Journal of Systematic Theology* 9 (2007): 434-51.

Zuntz, Gunther
Text   *The Text of the Epistles: A Disquisition upon the Corpus Paulinum.* London: British Academy, 1953.

Index of Authors

Index of Authors

Index of Bible References

(Note: chapter and verse references are those of the standard English versions)